PROGRAMMING
WITH
DATA STRUCTURES

PROGRAMMING WITH DATA STRUCTURES

Pascal Version

Robert L. Kruse

Saint Mary's University
Halifax, Nova Scotia

Prentice Hall

Englewood Cliffs, New Jersey 07632

Library of Congress Cataloging-in-Publication Data

KRUSE, ROBERT LEROY
  Programming with data structures / Pascal version

  Bibliography: p. 614
  Includes index.
  ISBN 0-13-729238-4
  1. Electronic digital computers—Programming. 2. Data structures
  (Computer science) 3. Pascal (Computer program language) I. Title.
  QA76.6.K774 1989
  005.13′3—dc19   88–26015

Editorial production/supervision: *Debbie Young*
Interior design: *Dawn Stanley (Aurora Graphics)*
Cover design: *Christine Gehring-Wolf*
Page layout: *Kenny Beck*
Manufacturing buyer: *Mary Noonan*
Cover art: *Accent in Rose* (1926) by *Wassily Kandinsky* (1866–1944)
      Paris, Musée National d'Art Moderne
      RIRAUDON / Art Resource   CRL 28807

The typesetting and color separation were done by the author using PreTeX, a preprocessor and macro package for the TeX typesetting system and POSTSCRIPT page-description language. PreTeX is a trademark of Robert L. Kruse; TeX is a trademark of the American Mathematical Society; POSTSCRIPT is a registered trademark of Adobe Systems, Inc.

© 1989 by Prentice-Hall, Inc.
A Division of Simon & Schuster
Englewood Cliffs, New Jersey 07632

Printed in the United States of America

10 9 8 7 6 5 4 3 2 1

ISBN 0-13-729238-4

Prentice-Hall International (UK) Limited, *London*
Prentice-Hall of Australia Pty. Limited, *Sydney*
Prentice-Hall Canada Inc., *Toronto*
Prentice-Hall Hispanoamericana, S.A., *Mexico*
Pentice-Hall of India Private Limited, *New Delhi*
Prentice-Hall of Japan, Inc., *Tokyo*
Simon & Schuster Asia Pte. Ltd., *Singapore*
Editora Prentice-Hall do Brasil, Ltda., *Rio de Janeiro*

CONTENTS

PREFACE

An apprentice carpenter may want only a hammer and a saw, but a master craftsman employs many precision tools. Computer programming likewise requires reliable tools to cope with the complexity of real applications. This book treats structured problem solving, data abstraction, and the comparative study of algorithms as fundamental tools of program design. These tools are applied to develop both data structures and software engineering principles.

The goal of programming is the construction of programs that are clear, complete, and functional. Many students, however, find difficulty in translating abstract ideas into practice. This book, therefore, takes special care in the formulation of ideas into algorithms and in the refinement of algorithms into concrete programs that can be applied to practical problems. The process of data specification and abstraction, similarly, comes before the selection of data structures and their implementations.

I believe in progressing from the concrete to the abstract, in the careful development of motivating examples, followed by the presentation of ideas in a more general form. At an early stage of their careers most students need reinforcement from seeing the immediate application of the ideas that they study, and they require the practice of writing and running programs to illustrate each important concept that they learn. This book therefore contains many samples, both short procedures and complete programs of substantial length. The exercises and programming projects, moreover, constitute an indispensable part of this book. Many of these are immediate applications of the topic under study, often requesting that programs be written and run, so that algorithms may be tested and compared. Some are larger projects, and a few are suitable for use by a group of several students working together.

Synopsis

The reader of this book should have some experience in elementary Pascal programming, experience typical of a one-term introductory programming course.

Part I:
Programming
Principles

Part I summarizes many of the important principles of writing good programs and reviews some features of Pascal from an advanced point of view. Chapters 1 and 2 take, as an example, the problem of calculating and printing the calendar of any given year. In the context of this example, Chapter 1 reviews methods for problem solving and algorithm development, emphasizes the importance of exact specifications for subprograms, and illustrates the use of preconditions and postconditions to help ensure algorithm correctness. Chapter 2 continues the study of program development with questions of style, coding, debugging, and testing. Chapter 3 takes a fresh look at four structures provided by Pascal for data encapsulation: arrays, records, sets, and files. Its aim is not only to summarize and illustrate the syntax of these structures, but to exhibit their logical connections and plant the seeds of data abstraction.

Part II:
Linear Data
Structures

Part II develops the concepts of information hiding, data abstraction, and modular design. Chapter 4 studies stacks, Chapter 5 queues, and Chapter 6 lists and strings. Each of these data types is studied first as a simple concept, then in the precise specification of structure and operations as an abstract data type, then in its implementation in Pascal declarations and procedures, and finally as it is applied in complete programs.

Linked stacks, queues, and lists appear in Chapters 7 and 8. Many students will have had little or no previous experience with Pascal pointer types, so Chapter 7 carefully develops the ideas of dynamic memory allocation and linked structures, as it fully presents the necessary Pascal syntax. Linked stacks, queues, and lists are then developed as alternative implementations for abstract data types that are already familiar. The text emphasizes the importance of conforming with the specifications previously introduced for each abstract data type and maintaining the modularity of structure that allows the easy replacement of one implementation by another.

Part II develops several application programs that illustrate the methods of data abstraction and modular design. Chapter 4 presents a reverse Polish calculator that uses a stack; Chapter 5 applies queues to a program that simulates traffic patterns at a small airport; Chapter 6 develops a miniature text editor that does extensive list and string processing; and Chapter 8 outlines a group project for a program that performs calculations on polynomials represented as linked lists.

Part III:
Algorithms and
their Analysis

Part III broaches the comparative study and analysis of algorithms in the context of searching and sorting. With binary search as developed in Chapter 9, the student learns that vast improvements can be made over the naive methods of the introductory course. The translation of the idea of binary search into a precise algorithm, however, is fraught with danger, from which a simple algorithm verification, based on a loop invariant, provides release.

From the simple sorting methods developed in Chapter 10, the student learns that any one of several different methods can prove best in different applications.

Analysis of algorithms is therefore a worthy goal. This book, however, assumes very little mathematical preparation, and therefore takes a simple and intuitive approach to algorithm analysis. The principal tool is to draw comparison trees. The general shape and size of the tree demonstrate the differences between linear and logarithmic behavior. The big Oh notation is introduced in this part to express these differences. The study of comparison trees also leads naturally, in Chapter 11, to the introduction of binary trees as a new abstract data type.

Part IV:
Recursion

Recursion is a powerful tool, but one that is often misunderstood and sometimes used improperly. Some textbooks treat it as an afterthought, applying it only to trivial examples and apologizing for its alleged expense. Others give little regard to its pitfalls. I have therefore essayed to provide as balanced a treatment as possible. Whenever recursion is the natural approach it is used without hesitation, but it is neither introduced early and then ignored, nor is it applied first to problems (like linear lists or binary search) for which iterative methods are equally easy. Instead, in this text, its first use is in Chapter 11, where binary trees are developed as data structures based on ideas from linear lists, binary search, and comparison trees. Chapter 12 then provides a short, but extremely important discourse on the principles of recursion and its implementation. Chapter 13 further illustrates the importance of recursion by developing mergesort and quicksort and showing the great gains in efficiency that they provide. Chapter 14, finally, presents the examples of backtracking, lookahead in games, and compilation by recursive descent to illustrate some of the broad range of applications for recursion.

Part V:
Further
Structures and
Algorithms

The remaining chapters of the book collect further important topics from data structures and algorithms. Chapter 15 studies tables as structures accessed by key rather than by position. Chapter 16 further develops this idea by studying hash tables. Chapter 17 introduces graphs as mathematical models useful for problem solving and studies the ways in which they can be represented by the use of lists and of tables.

Just as Chapters 15–17 point to further study in data structures, Chapter 18 points to further study in software engineering, by introducing some of its major concerns, including problem specification and analysis, prototyping, algorithm design, refinement, verification, and analysis. These concerns are illustrated by working through an example project (CONWAY's game of Life). A simple prototype program is first developed and analyzed. This analysis leads to the development of a second program for the Life game, one based on an algorithm that is sufficiently subtle as to show the need for precise specifications and verification, and one that shows why care must be taken in the choice of data structures.

Appendices

The book concludes with three appendices. The first reviews important properties of logarithms and factorials used in algorithm analysis. The second summarizes the syntax of Pascal. The third is an annotated bibliography describing references appropriate to the topics studied in the book. Notes throughout the text urge the student to consult this bibliography for further information.

Course Structure

ACM course CS2

This book is intended primarily for a second course in computer science with one term of Pascal programming as prerequisite. The book is based on the ACM course CS2 and contains all the topics specified for this course. With the rapid development of computer science, however, this course is in continual change. This course usually includes some aspects of software engineering, some treatment of data structures and abstraction, and some survey of topics that will be studied further in more advanced courses. The degree of emphasis of each, however, differs from institution to institution. This book, therefore, contains significantly more material than can be reasonably studied in most one-term courses, so that an instructor can choose topics appropriate for any of the preceding emphases.

The core topics specified for ACM Course CS2 all appear in Chapters 1–12 of this book. A one-term course based closely on CS2 will normally include most of the content of these chapters, except for some of the algorithm analyses, verifications, and some of the example programs. The later chapters present advanced optional topics suggested for possible inclusion in CS2.

layered approach

In most of its chapters this book takes a layered approach that allows the instructor to decide easily the depth to which each topic will be studied. The fundamental topics of each chapter are developed early in the chapter. The later sections contain applications and more theoretical treatments that can be omitted with no loss of continuity. These more theoretical topics, included for the interested reader, are either not referred to again or are used only in the theoretical sections appearing at the end of later chapters.

Even if it is not covered in its entirety, this book will provide enough depth to enable interested students to continue using it as a reference in later work. It is important in any case to assign major programming projects and to allow adequate time for their completion.

Further Features

- *Chapter Previews.* Each chapter begins with an outline and a brief statement of goals and content to help the reader establish perspective.

- *Application Programs.* The text includes several large, complete programs that illustrate principles of good software design and application of the methods developed in the text. Code reading is an important skill for a programmer, but one that is often neglected in textbooks.

- *Software Diskette.* With each copy of the book is included a software diskette containing all the programs and program extracts appearing in the text. By starting from this software the student can learn many benefits of reusable programs while implementing new programming projects.

- *Programming Precepts.* Many principles of good programming are summarized with short, pithy statements that are well worth remembering.

- *Marginal Notes.* Keywords and other important concepts are highlighted in the left margin, thereby allowing the reader to locate the principal ideas of a section without delay.

- *Pointers and Pitfalls.* Each chapter of the book contains a section giving helpful hints concerning problems of program design.

- *Exercises.* Exercises appear not only at the ends of chapters but with almost every major section. These exercises help with the immediate reinforcement of the ideas of the section and develop further related ideas.

- *Projects.* Programming projects also appear in most major sections. These include simple variations of programs appearing in the text, completion of projects begun in the text, and major new projects investigating questions posed in the text.

- *Review Questions.* Each chapter concludes with simple review questions to help the student collect and summarize the principal concepts of the chapter.

- *Instructor's Supplements.* Instructors teaching from this book may obtain copies of all the following materials:

  - The *Instructor's Resource Manual* contains teaching notes on each chapter, together with complete, detailed solutions to every exercise and programming project in the text.

  - The *Transparency Masters* (several hundred in total) contain enlarged copies of almost all diagrams, specifications, program segments, and other important extracts from the text.

  - The package of *Software Diskettes* contains complete, running programs for every programming project in the text. These programs are supplied in two forms: one in standard Pascal, and one that employs Turbo Pascal units to accomplish data abstraction and information hiding as appropriate.

Acknowledgments

It is a pleasure to recognize the help of the people who have contributed in many ways to the writing and production of this book.

This book, first of all, derives part of its content from *Data Structures and Program Design*, published by Prentice Hall in 1984 and 1987. (The current book omits most of the advanced topics from that book, replacing them with additional examples and expanded explanation of more elementary topics.) My thanks, therefore, are due to the many people who have contributed to the continuing success that *Data Structures and Program Design* has enjoyed. These people—named in the preface to that book—include colleagues, students, and the editorial, marketing, and sales staff of Prentice Hall.

The writing, revision, and production of this book have been long and difficult but helped by the frequent encouragement I have received. My mother, first of all, gave me the patient understanding and love without which the work could not have been completed. Family and friends have cheered me on; colleagues have given valuable suggestions and advice; and students have shown the enthusiasm and joy of discovery that make the effort worthwhile.

ANDREW L. MEADE and J. DAVID BROWN have worked diligently and faithfully with me in producing solutions to all the exercises and programming projects, in preparing the solutions manual and the software diskettes, in testing all the programs from the book, in bringing the text files up to date, and in improving the consistency and clarity of exposition. STEVEN A. MATHESON has helped greatly with the design and programming of PreTEX, the preprocessor and macro package used to typeset this book in conjunction with DONALD KNUTH's typesetting system TEX and the page-description language POSTSCRIPT.

A good many reviewers have suggested ways to improve the organization and exposition of the book. Among these are ANDREW BERNAT (University of Texas), JOHN CUPAK (Pennsylvania State University), EILEEN ENTIN (Wentworth Institute of Technology), DAVID R. FALCONER (California State University at Fullerton), FRANK GERGELYI (New Jersey Institute of Technology), DAVID KROGER (Miami University), LAWRENCE M. LEVINE (Baruch College, City University of New York), IVAN LISS (Radford University), and EMIL C. NEU (Stevens Institute of Technology). Thanks are also due to other reviewers who did not wish to be named and to those whose contributions to *Data Structures and Program Design* have been carried into the present book.

The production of this book has given me the opportunity to meet and work with many members of the Prentice Hall staff, people who have been consistently pleasant and helpful in their dealings with me. ROB DEWEY, Marketing Manager for Computer Science and Engineering, has taken a keen interest in promoting this book. ALICE DWORKIN, Supplements Editor, has been unfailingly patient, understanding, and helpful in working to produce a comprehensive instructional package. The production editor, DEBBIE YOUNG, and the staff whose names appear on the copyright page have worked hard to expedite the publication of this book while maintaining standards of the highest quality.

But it is my editors who merit the greatest thanks: JAMES F. FEGEN, JR., who first encouraged me to undertake this project, and MARCIA J. HORTON, Editor-in-Chief for Computer Science and Engineering, who worked with me with cheerful patience and keen insight to bring it to fruition. I am proud to count Jim and Marcia not only as my respected colleagues in publishing, but even more as my friends.

ROBERT L. KRUSE

PROGRAMMING
WITH
DATA STRUCTURES

PROLOGUE

The greatest difficulties of writing large computer programs are not in deciding what the goals of the program should be, nor even in finding methods that can be used to reach these goals. The president of a business might say, "Let's get a computer to keep track of all our inventory information, accounting records, and personnel files, and let it tell us when inventories need to be reordered and budget lines are overspent, and let it handle the payroll." With enough time and effort, a staff of systems analysts and programmers might be able to determine how various staff members are now doing these tasks and write programs to do the work in the same way.

problems of large programs
This approach, however, is almost certain to be a disastrous failure. While interviewing employees, the systems analysts will find some tasks that can be put on the computer easily and will proceed to do so. Then, as they move other work to the computer, they will find that it depends on the first tasks. The output from these, unfortunately, will not be quite in the proper form. Hence they need more programming to convert the data from the form given for one task to the form needed for another. The software project begins to resemble a patchwork quilt. Some of the pieces are stronger, some weaker. Some of the pieces are carefully sewn onto the adjacent ones, some are barely tacked together. If the programmers are lucky, their creation may hold together well enough to do most of the routine work most of the time. But if any change must be made, it will have unpredictable consequences throughout the system. Later, a new request will come along, or an unexpected problem, perhaps even an emergency, and the programmers' efforts will prove as effective as using a patchwork quilt as a safety net to catch people jumping from a tall building.

purpose of book

The main purpose of this book is to describe programming methods and tools that will prove effective for projects of realistic size, programs much larger than those ordinarily used to illustrate features of elementary programming. Since a piecemeal approach to large problems is doomed to fail, we must first of all adopt a consistent, unified, and logical approach, and we must also be careful to observe important principles of program design, principles that are sometimes ignored in writing small programs, but whose neglect will prove disastrous for large projects.

problem specification

The first major hurdle in attacking a large problem is deciding exactly what the problem is. It is necessary to translate vague goals, contradictory requests, and perhaps unstated desires into a precisely formulated project that can be programmed. And the methods or divisions of work that people have previously used are not necessarily the best for use in a machine. Our approach must therefore be to determine overall goals, but precise ones, and then slowly divide the work into smaller problems until they become of manageable size.

program design

The maxim that many programmers observe, "First make your program work, then make it pretty," may be effective for small programs, but not for large ones. Each part of a large program must be well organized, clearly written, and thoroughly understood, or else its structure will have been forgotten, and it can no longer be tied to the other parts of the project at some much later time, perhaps by another programmer. Hence we do not separate style from other parts of program design, but, from the beginning, we must be careful to form good habits.

Even with very large projects, difficulties usually arise not from the inability to find a solution, but, rather, from the fact that there can be so many different methods and algorithms that might work that it can be hard to decide which is best, which may lead to programming difficulties, or which may be hopelessly inefficient. The greatest room for variability in algorithm design is generally in the way in which the data of the program are stored.

data structures

A second goal of this book, therefore, is to present elegant, yet fundamentally simple ideas for the organization of data, and to develop powerful algorithms for important tasks within data processing, such as sorting and information retrieval.

recursion

One of the most powerful tools for algorithm development is recursion, the ability of a subprogram to solve a problem by invoking itself for smaller cases of the same problem. We shall therefore devote considerable attention to the applications of recursion and to the principles that should govern its use.

analysis

When there are several different ways to organize data and devise algorithms, it becomes important to develop criteria to recommend a choice. Hence we develop methods to analyze the behavior of algorithms under various conditions.

program correctness

The difficulty of debugging a program increases much faster than its size. That is, if one program is twice the size of another, then it will likely not take twice as long to debug, but perhaps four times as long. Many very large programs (such as operating systems) are put into use still containing bugs that the programmers have despaired of finding, because the difficulties seem insurmountable. Sometimes projects that have consumed years of effort must be discarded because it is impossible to discover why they will not work. If we do not wish such a fate for our own projects, then we must use methods that will reduce the number of bugs, making it easier to spot those that remain. We shall also consider ways to verify in advance that our algorithms are correct.

maintenance

Informal surveys show that, once a large and important program is fully debugged and in use, then less than half of the programming effort that will be invested altogether in the project will have been completed. Maintenance of programs, that is, modifications needed to meet new requests and new operating environments, takes, on average, more than half of the programming investment. For this reason, it is essential that a large project be written to make it as easy to understand and modify as possible.

Pascal

The programming language Pascal has several features that make it an appropriate choice to express the algorithms we shall develop. Pascal has been carefully designed to facilitate the discipline of writing carefully structured programs, with requirements implementing principles of program design. It contains relatively few features, in comparison with most high-level languages, so that it can be mastered quickly, and yet it contains powerful features for handling data which ease the translation from general algorithms to specific programs. For the precise details of Pascal syntax (grammar), consult Appendix B.

PART I

PROGRAMMING PRINCIPLES

Good programming requires much more than knowing the rules of a programming language, and so this book begins with a study of the principles of careful programming. To solve a problem, we must first understand exactly what the problem is, then develop the method for its solution; only then can we start to develop a computer program. Chapter 1 describes this process of problem solving from the initial presentation of a problem through the precise formulation of an algorithm for its solution. Chapter 2 then considers the translation of the algorithm into a computer program. At the same time, Chapter 2 reviews several features of Pascal from an advanced point of view. Both chapters use the problem of printing a calendar for a given year as a case study to illustrate the ideas and methods that the book develops.

The greatest flexibility in program development and the greatest source of problems are in choosing the ways to store the data. Methods for this task are the major preoccupation of this book, and Chapter 3 begins this work by reviewing the four tools that Pascal provides for packaging many pieces of data together: arrays, records, sets, and files. The aim of the chapter is to show how these tools can be used to embody the logical structure of the data. The chapter also reviews some of Pascal's more difficult rules for these data types.

1

PROBLEM SOLVING

Before starting to write a program, we must understand both the problem and the method to be used in its solution. In this chapter we shall consider how to describe a problem precisely, use the method of top-down refinement to outline its solution, and show how the results can be formulated as a clear and precise algorithm, which we can then translate into a computer program. We shall use the problem of printing a calendar to illustrate the ideas that we develop.

1.1

THE CALENDAR PROBLEM: A FIRST EXAMPLE

case study

In this chapter we shall study one application which, while quite small by realistic standards, illustrates many of the methods of program design that we wish to develop. Sometimes the example motivates general principles; sometimes the general discussion comes first; always it is with the view of discovering general methods that will prove their value in a range of practical applications. In later chapters we shall employ similar methods for larger projects.

Our problem is:

> *Write a program that prints a calendar for a given year. That is, for each month of the year, print a table showing the days of the month arranged in weeks in the usual way.*

premature coding

There are two common approaches in tackling a problem like this, neither one of which is likely to be successful. The first approach is to start writing the program right away, setting up various loops for the days of the month and the days of the week and using variables to keep track of everything. The result is likely to be so disorganized that it is difficult to read, to understand, and to debug. Even if it works, the first approach to solving a problem is not necessarily the best; the resulting program may be more complicated than necessary.

premature specialization

The second approach is to start worrying right away about some of the more difficult problems and special cases that we must solve as part of the project, problems like calculating how many days are in each month, whether or not the year is a leap year, and on which day of the week the first of the month comes. If we concentrate on these problems too soon, they may make it more difficult to see the overall structure of the project and lead us into a view of the problem that is not best for the complete solution. Besides, difficult problems sometimes go away or become easier when attacked in the context of a more general approach.

Instead, we should approach a programming project by, first, *thinking* carefully about the problem, then *outlining* an overall approach to the solution, and, finally, *filling in* the details.

But what do we mean by thinking about the problem and outlining a solution? If we simply sit down with a blank sheet of paper, we may only become more and more frustrated. Instead, we must *organize* our thinking by following some definite patterns that we now explore.

1.2

FIRST STEP: SPECIFYING THE PROBLEM

If we are to solve any kind of a problem, then, before we start work, we must know *exactly* what we are supposed to do. Often a problem appears at first glance to be clearly stated, but, after additional consideration, it turns out to have many possible interpretations. Since a computer program will have to follow one of these interpretations, it is necessary that we determine which to use. Hence we should begin, not by trying to think of how to solve our problem, but by making sure we know what the problem is. Although this principle is obvious, it can require considerable work to put it into practice. We therefore highlight it as our first programming precept:

> ### Programming Precept
>
> Be sure you understand your problem completely.
> If you must make its terms more precise, explain exactly what you have done.

The more you think about a problem, the more information you may see that needs to be specified to make the problem complete and precise. Often much of this information is not included in the original statement of the problem. A problem that is stated very quickly may be so vague that it is not possible to see how to attack it, whereas several pages describing the same problem will present all the details that are required for the ensuing program. The information required before we can write a program includes, but may not be limited to, the following:

program specifications

- *Input Specifications*: What input will the program be given, and in what format will it appear?

- *Goal*: What is the program supposed to accomplish?

- *Output Specifications*: What output must the program produce, and how should it be arranged?

- *Requirements*: Are there special conditions on the way the program must proceed? For example, must it execute rapidly, or must it be portable from one computer to another?

- *Assumptions*: May the program assume that certain conditions occur and take advantage of them? For example, may it assume that there will be no errors in its input?

Note that not one of these topics specifies *how* the program will operate or the method it will use. Those questions we should postpone until we have considered the problem specification in much more detail.

Input Specifications

The first step is to decide what input data the program will require. Generally speaking, keep the input as short and simple as possible. A program that processes a list of items, for example, will usually need to know the number of items in the list, as well as the data for each item. One method is to ask the user first to give the number of items and then type in exactly that many data, one for each item. This method is prone to error, especially if the list is long. It is much better to let the program count the items as it receives data, and let the user terminate the list by entering some special symbol(s) such as an end-of-file mark.

test the input   Always check that the input data is valid, consistent, and reasonable. If a program asks for the number of children a person has, it should not accept an answer of -3 or 678. If it asks a person's salary and the reply is \$250,000, it might ask for confirmation via the question "Are you sure?" or something similar.

Goal

Sometimes the goal for a program can be stated immediately with precision and completeness. Often, however, the goal will be clarified only as the other aspects of the problem are considered. As we determine the output specifications we are at the same time determining the tasks that the program must accomplish.

Output Specifications

The output from a program must be well documented, that is, it must explain as necessary what the numbers are and what they mean. It is also necessary to decide how much output there should be. Sometimes the results can be stated succinctly, but sometimes important information is omitted. On the other hand, it is easy to make the program produce reams of output that will be of little use to anyone and can obscure the important results. Good general-purpose programs

flexibility   often provide flexibility to the user in deciding how much output and what kind will be provided. See Figure 1.1.

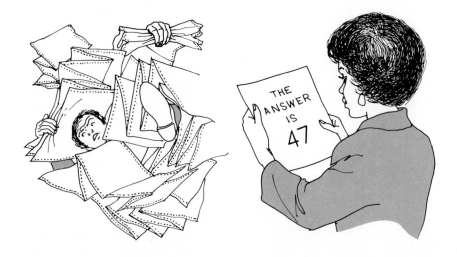

Figure 1.1. Poor forms of output

format   Sometimes the exact format of the output is specified as part of the problem; often it is left to the programmer to settle. When the output of one program becomes the input to another, or when the output appears on predetermined business forms, it is important that the form of the output meet precise specifications.

interpretation   A specification that seems clear to one person can easily be interpreted quite differently by someone else. Consider the calendar problem, for example. If you live in North America, then you likely think of the days of each month as appearing in horizontal rows, with each week in a different row and the days of the week in different columns. In other countries, however, the calendar is frequently printed with the days in vertical columns instead, so each week starts a new column and the rows correspond to days of the week. See Figure 1.2.

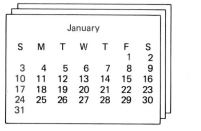

Figure 1.2. Two ways to make a calendar

Requirements

The same problem often arises in different applications, and the application may force special requirements on the solution to the problem. A program that controls industrial equipment may be required to react very quickly to keep the equipment on the right track. A game-playing program may need to be slowed down artificially to human speed. An accounting program for a bank needs to be made tamper proof. Later in this book we shall study several examples from the wide range of sorting methods in common use. We shall find that some are easy to write but run more slowly than others, that some are better for sorting short lists and others for long lists, some if the lists are nearly in order, others for lists in random order. Hence the choice of method and the writing of a program depend very much on the application and the specific requirements that it imposes.

Assumptions

Often the problem to be solved is not as general as it first appears. The input may satisfy special conditions that make it easier to process.

On the other side, sometimes the programmer is not able or does not have the time to solve the problem in the full generality in which it is stated, and, therefore, makes certain assumptions to simplify the program. Any such assumptions must always be fully stated.

1.3

THE CALENDAR PROBLEM: SPECIFICATIONS

Let us now apply this discussion of problem specifications by writing down detailed specifications for our calendar problem.

Input Specifications

The input, first of all, is simply the number of the year whose calendar we wish to create. We require this year to be typed in as an integer. What range of integers is valid? It might make sense to think of negative integers as corresponding to years B.C., but recall that the year before 1 A.D. is 1 B.C., not 0. Hence, for simplicity, we shall require that 1 be the smallest allowable integer, and we shall calculate the calendars only for years A.D. The largest year for which the program *restrictions* will work will depend on the computer on which it is run; it will depend on the size of maxint, the largest integer that can be represented. As it turns out, we shall need to calculate the total number of days over a large range of years. This calculation will require that the largest year number that we can allow is no more than about maxint **div** 365.

In the interest of making the program user friendly, we shall make one small change in the input specifications. After one calendar has been printed, the user may wish another, so we shall require the program to ask if the user so wishes, and then the program will repeat the calculation if desired.

Goal

The goal of our program is to calculate and print the calendar for a given year. *format* For the output, let us specify that each month is to contain a header line including the name of the month and the year. The days of the month are to be arranged in horizontal rows with columns corresponding to the days of the week. Certain columns may be blank before the first of the month and after the last day of the month. When a month occupies parts of six weeks, the calendar is often printed with some of the days in subdivided squares, so that the month takes only five rows, but we shall not do this. Hence the number of rows required for the month may be four (for February only), five, or six.

Requirements and Assumptions

There are no special requirements for our program, but we are making a very special assumption in our program that we have not yet discussed.

history: Julian The calendar we now use has not always been in effect. A calendar rather *and Gregorian* similar to the one we use was introduced by JULIUS CÆSAR in 45 B.C., but this ***Julian*** *calendars* calendar has simpler rules for leap years. By the time of POPE GREGORY XIII in the sixteenth century, it was obvious that the calendar year was moving out of synchronization with the seasons. He introduced certain changes in the rules for leap years in century years that bring the average length of the calendar year very close to the actual time needed for the earth to go around the sun. At the same time, he corrected the discrepancy that had developed over the centuries by decreeing that Thursday, October 4, 1582, would be followed by Friday, October 15. This change was accepted immediately in some countries, but only very slowly in others. The British empire did not adopt the new *Gregorian* calendar until 1752, and Russia, not until after the Soviet revolution in 1918.

Hence, to be complete, a calendar program should adapt to both calculations, but, for simplicity, we shall consider only the new-style Gregorian calendar and calculate Gregorian dates even for years before 1582. In this way, we are making a simplifying assumption for our program, but one that is contrary to history.

Summary

Finally, let us summarize these specifications in a form suitable for inclusion in the documentation for our program.

Specifications, calendar project

- *Input*: A positive integer corresponding to the year number, A.D.; after the program is complete, a request to allow the user to repeat the program.
- *Goal*: Calculate and print the calendar for the given year.
- *Output*: For each month, a header line naming the month and year, then four to six lines corresponding to the weeks of the month, with the days arranged in columns according to the day of the week, with blank entries as needed before the first of the month and after the last of the month.
- *Requirements*: No special requirements.
- *Assumptions*: Determines only the Gregorian calendar, no matter what the year.

1.4

OUTLINING THE METHOD: THE OVERALL STRUCTURE

problem solving

Once the requirements of a problem are fully and precisely stated, it is time to consider how the problem will be solved. Computers do not solve problems; people do. Usually the most important part of the process is dividing the problem into smaller problems that can be understood in more detail. If these are still too difficult, then they are subdivided again, and so on. In any large organization, the top management cannot worry about every detail of every activity; the top managers must concentrate on general goals and problems and delegate specific responsibilities to their subordinates. See Figure 1.3. Again, middle-level managers cannot do everything: They must subdivide the work and delegate it *subdivision*   to other people. So it is with computer programming. Even when a project is small enough that one person can take it from start to finish, it is most important to divide the work, starting with an overall understanding of the problem, dividing it into subproblems, and attacking each of these in turn without worrying about the others.

Figure 1.3. A hierarchy of managers

Let us restate this principle with a classic proverb:

Programming Precept

Don't lose sight of the forest for its trees.

top-down   This principle, called **top-down refinement**, is the real key to writing large pro-
refinement   grams that work. The principle implies the postponement of detailed consideration, but not the postponement of precision. It does not mean that the main
program becomes some vague entity whose task can hardly be described. On
the contrary, the main program will send almost all the work out to various
subprograms (procedures and functions). As we write the main program (which
specifications   we should do first), we decide *exactly* how the work will be divided among the

subprograms. Then, as we later work on a particular subprogram, we shall know before starting exactly what it is expected to do.

Notice the similarity between determining the specifications for subprograms and determining the specifications for the entire program that we have already discussed. In fact, when we turn to the subprograms, we wish to concentrate on each one of them separately, concerned only about its specifications. Once each subprogram meets all of its own specifications, we can then put them together and have a large and sophisticated program that works exactly as we intended. Hence this subdivision of the work is the real key to writing large programs that work.

1.5

THE CALENDAR PROGRAM: OVERALL STRUCTURE

As an application, let us see how this process works out for the calendar problem. The phrase "for each month of the year" in the statement of the problem, or the simple fact that we must do a similar task twelve times, makes it clear that we will need to use a loop through the months of the year. Hence we can write down an initial outline of the program:

```
program Calendar(input, output);                         {first outline}
   {prints a calendar for the year specified as input}
var
   y: year;                      {the year for which we wish the calendar}
   m: month;                     {used to loop through the months of the year}
begin
   repeat            {Use a loop to allow for printing more than one year.}
      FindYear(y);        {Ask the user for the number of the year to use.}
      for each month of the year do
         PrintMonth(m, y)                        {Print month m of year y.}
   until not UserSaysYes       {Find out if another year should be done.}
end.
```

Note that, even though this outline is far from a form that can be compiled and run, it is already starting to look like a program. We have assigned names (but not necessarily very good ones) to the month and year under consideration, and we have introduced two procedures to handle parts of the work. We have *postpone* also used two undefined data types, year and month. For right now, we have no *decisions* need to decide what these will be: integers, some subrange, enumerated types, or something else. Instead, by introducing but not defining year and month, we have made it logically clear what the variables y and m represent without committing ourselves prematurely to detailed declarations. Our next task is to concentrate on the specifications and workings of the two procedures whose goals are given as comments in the program outline.

1.6

REFINEMENT: SPECIFYING MORE DETAIL

One of the most important parts of the refinement process is deciding exactly what the task of each subprogram is. This includes specifying precisely what information it will need to have to do its task and what result it will produce. We also need to know what data and what other subprograms the given subprogram will use. Errors in these specifications are among the most frequent program bugs and are among the hardest to find. An excellent method to make the specifications of a subprogram precise is to state, first, exactly what conditions the subprogram expects to find when it is started and what input data it will use. These conditions are called the *preconditions* for the subprogram. The documentation, second, should indicate what changes the subprogram will make, and, therefore, what conditions will hold after the subprogram finishes and what will be its output data. These new conditions are called the *postconditions* for the subprogram. Thirdly, it is important to know which other subprograms will be used by the given subprogram; these are *imports* to the subprogram.

preconditions

postconditions

imports

Programming Precept

Know your problem.
Give precise preconditions and postconditions for each procedure.

We have already decided on the preconditions and postconditions for the calendar project. They are:

---
program Calendar (input, output):

precondition: None.

postcondition: The user has specified a positive integer corresponding to a year number. The program has printed the calendar for the year requested, consisting for each month of a header line naming the month and year, then four to six lines corresponding to the weeks of the month, with the days arranged in columns according to the day of the week, and with blank entries as needed before the first of the month and after the last of the month.

imports: FindYear, PrintMonth, UserSaysYes.

---

subprogram tasks

Once the preconditions and postconditions for a program have been decided, it is time to start dividing the program's task among subprograms. It is often not easy to decide exactly how to make this division, and sometimes a decision once made must later be modified. Formulating precise preconditions and postconditions for each subprogram can provide information helpful with such decisions, and two further guidelines can help as well.

Programming Precept

Each subprogram should do only one task, but do it well.

---

succinctness That is, we should be able to describe the purpose of a subprogram succinctly. If you find yourself writing a long paragraph to specify the preconditions, the postconditions, or the task of a subprogram, then either you are giving too much detail (that is, you are writing the subprogram before it is time to do so) or you should rethink the division of work. The subprogram itself will undoubtedly contain many details, but they should not appear until the next stage of refinement.

Programming Precept

Each subprogram should hide something.

---

information hiding A middle-level manager in a large company does not pass on everything he receives from his subordinates to higher management. The manager summarizes, collates, and weeds out the information, handles many requests himself, and sends on only what is needed at the upper levels. Similarly, the manager does not transmit everything he learns from higher management to his subordinates. He transmits to each person only what he needs to do his job; see Figure 1.4. The subprograms we write should do likewise.

Figure 1.4. Information hiding and transmission

While all these principles of top-down design may seem almost self-evident, the only way to learn them thoroughly is by practice. Hence, throughout this book, we shall be careful to apply them to the large programs that we write, and, in particular, to the calendar program that we are developing in this chapter.

1.7

REFINING THE CALENDAR ALGORITHM

So far, we have introduced two procedures for the calendar problem, FindYear and PrintMonth. The procedure FindYear(y) receives no input from the program—it has no preconditions—and asks the user for a year that it sends back as its output. More formally, we have decided on the following:

---

procedure FindYear(**var** y: year):

precondition: None.

postcondition: The variable y has been set to a year number entered by the user; this value has been checked to make sure that it is a number within the range of years whose calendars can be calculated.

imports: Not yet determined.

Writing the procedure involves no conceptual difficulties; hence we postpone its further consideration until it is time to write the program in a computer language.

Printing a Month

Procedure PrintMonth(m, y) has two inputs, the month and the year to be printed. The procedure will use a loop that runs through the days of the month and prints them out in a row. After we print a Saturday, however, we shall end one row and start the next. Constructing this loop will require two pieces of information.

First, we must know how many days are in the month, so that we can determine the upper limit for the loop. Finding the number of days is a subsidiary task that we shall postpone by introducing a function DaysinMonth that we shall consider later.

Second, we must know on which day of the week the first day of the month comes, so that we can determine in which column to begin printing the table. This calculation we postpone to a function that we call FirstDay. Later, we shall find that it is convenient to print the header line for each month separately from the table of days, and we shall introduce a procedure PrintHeader for this task.

With all of these decisions, we can now write down the specifications for procedure PrintMonth.

---

procedure PrintMonth(m: month; y: year):

precondition: m is a month in year y.

postcondition: The procedure has printed the calendar for month m of year y, consisting of a header line naming m and y, then four to six lines corresponding to the weeks of month m, with the days arranged in columns according to the day of the week, and with blank entries as needed before the first of the month and after the last of the month.

imports: DaysinMonth, FirstDay, PrintHeader.

Counting Days

Next, let us turn to the function DaysinMonth(m, y) that returns the number of days (its output) in month m of year y (its inputs). Since the lengths of the twelve months follow no regular pattern, this function must consider twelve cases. All are easy except for February, for which we must determine if y is a leap year. Again, let us introduce a new function Leap for this task. Hence we obtain the following specifications.

---

function DaysinMonth(m: month; y: year): integer:

precondition: The function is given month m of year y.

postcondition: The value of the function is the number of days in month m of year y.

imports: Function Leap(y).

Leap Years

Gregorian rules for leap years

The function Leap(y) returns *Boolean* values, the value true if y is a leap year and false if y is not a leap year. To determine how to write this function we must find out the rules for determining a leap year. These rules are: A year is a leap year if and only if its number is (evenly) divisible by 4, except that a century year is a leap year if and only if its number is divisible by 400. Hence, for example, the year 1900 is not a leap year, but the year 2000 is a leap year.

The rule, incidentally, for the old-style Julian calendar is simply that every fourth year is a leap year, with no special rules for century years. Hence the Julian calendar moves apart from the Gregorian calendar by three days (century years that are not leap years in the Gregorian calculation) in every four hundred years.

---

function Leap (y: year): Boolean:

precondition: y is a year.

postcondition: The function returns the value true if and only if year y is a leap year in the Gregorian calendar.

imports: None.

Day of the Week

Now let us turn to the question of finding the day of the week on which the first day of the given month comes. At first consideration, this problem may seem more difficult than those we have considered so far.

Let us therefore simplify the problem by noticing that we do not really need to find the weekday for the first of every month, since each month begins on the day of the week following that on which the previous month ends. If March, for example, ends on Wednesday, then April will begin on Thursday. By keeping *first of the year* track of the day of the week, we can then go through all twelve months after being given only the weekday on which January 1 comes. To do this, let us introduce a new variable startday that will be used to tell PrintMonth on which day of the week to start. When PrintMonth concludes, it will (as one of its outputs) update startday to give the correct starting day for the next month.

Our problem has now been reduced to finding the day of the week on which January 1 comes. We shall introduce still one more function, FirstDay(y), which will take the year as its input and return the day of the week on which January 1 comes in that year as its output.

---

function FirstDay (y: year): weekday:

precondition: y is a year.

postcondition: The function returns the day of the week on which January 1 falls in year y according to the Gregorian calendar.

imports: Not yet determined.

Updated Specifications

revisions The decisions we have just made modify the way that procedure PrintMonth will do its work. Whenever we revise any subprogram, it is essential that we bring its documentation up to date to prevent confusion when we later turn to filling in more of the details. In other words,

---

Programming Precept

Always keep your documentation up to date.
When you revise a subprogram, always revise its specifications accordingly.

Let us, therefore, now apply this general principle by writing down a revised version of the specifications for the procedure PrintMonth.

---

procedure PrintMonth (m: month; y: year; **var** startday: weekday) (*revised*):

precondition: m is a month in year y; startday gives the day of the week on which the first day of month m of year y falls in the Gregorian calendar.

postcondition: The procedure has printed the calendar for month m of year y, consisting of a header line naming m and y, then four to six lines corresponding to the weeks of month m, with the days arranged in columns according to the day of the week, and with blank entries as needed before the first of the month and after the last of the month. The variable startday has been updated to the day of the week on which the first of the month following m comes.

imports: DaysinMonth, PrintHeader.

Revision of the Main Program

With the changes we have made, we now obtain the following version of the program. Note that we have now written the specifications for the program as comments in the program itself. Doing so is normally a good practice, since it makes it easier to ensure that the program documentation is always consistent with the program itself.

main program

```
program Calendar(input, output);                    {second outline}
{Pre:  The user has specified a positive year number.
 Post: The program has printed the calendar for the year requested, con-
       sisting for each month of a header line naming the month and year,
       then four to six lines corresponding to the weeks of the month, with
       the days arranged in columns according to the day of the week, and
       with blank entries as needed before the first of the month and after
       the last of the month.
 Uses: FindYear, FirstDay, PrintMonth, UserSaysYes.}

{Declarations of data types will be inserted here.}

var
    startday: weekday;      {the day of the week on which a month starts}
    m:        month;                  {the month currently being printed}
    y:        year;            {the year for which the calendar is printed}

{Declarations of all procedures and functions will be inserted here.}

begin                                                {program Calendar}
    repeat                {Use a loop to allow for printing more than one year.}
        FindYear(y);         {Ask the user for the number of the year to use.}
        startday : = FirstDay(y);        {Determine weekday for January 1.}
        for each month of the year do
            PrintMonth(m, y, startday);
{Print month m of year y starting on day startday of the week. The procedure
 will update startday, so that, at the conclusion, it gives the weekday for the
 first day of the following month.}
    until not UserSaysYes        {Find out if another year should be done.}
end.                                                 {program Calendar}
```

Finding January 1

weekly cycle

Finally, we must determine how to find the weekday on which January 1 comes in a given year so that we can write the function FirstDay(y). To do so, we need an idea. One that works is to note that the cycle of the seven days of the week is independent of months and years. If we know, for example, that one date falls on a Thursday and another date comes exactly 56 days later, then the second date will also fall on a Thursday, regardless of the months or years involved, since $56 = 7 \times 8$ is an even number of weeks. Hence, to determine the weekday for a given date, we first calculate the absolute number of days from some fixed date. We shall use January 1, 1 A.D. by the Gregorian calendar. We must then divide by 7 and take the remainder (in Pascal we can use the **mod** operator) to determine how many days through the week to advance.

Absolute Days

To calculate the number of days from January 1, 1 A.D. to a given date, we need to add 365 days for each year preceding the given one, then one more day for each leap year, then the number of days in each month between (which we obtain by adding the values of DaysinMonth(m) for each month m preceding the given one), and finally the number of the date in the last month. If y is the year in which we are interested, then to find the number of leap years preceding year y, we first calculate the number of years with number divisible by 4; this number is (y − 1) **div** 4. From this number we subtract the century years, (y − 1) **div** 100, and finally add back the years divisible by 400, which are leap years, (y − 1) **div** 400.

This calculation of an absolute day number we can formalize with the following specifications.

---

function AbsoluteDay(d: monthday; m: month; y: year): integer):

precondition: The day d of month m of year y exists in the Gregorian calendar.

postcondition: The function value is the number of days from January 1, 1 A.D., to the given day using the rules of the Gregorian calendar.

imports: DaysinMonth.

---

days between two dates
The calculation of an absolute day number for a date allows us to find easily the number of days between *any* two dates by subtracting their absolute day numbers. This last calculation gives answers to some interesting questions, such as "How many days have you been alive?" or "How many days is it to summer vacation?" It also has important applications. Suppose, for example, that you take out a loan on March 4 and repay it on August 28. For how many days do you owe interest?

Algorithms

An ***algorithm*** consists of precise instructions which, if followed, will produce a solution to a problem in a finite number of steps. An algorithm may be written in a computer language or in a human language or even in mathematical notation. Although the instructions in an algorithm must be precise, the amount of detail specified may vary and will depend on how the algorithm will be used.

algorithms and pseudocode
We have now completed an algorithm for solving the calendar problem. We have described the main program in a form almost like a computer program. This way of presenting an algorithm is called ***pseudocode***, since it resembles computer programming code.

For the subprograms, we have presented the steps less formally, as paragraphs of English prose. Even so, you should now be able to see how each of these steps can be formulated, first, as pseudocode and then as a Pascal program.

In both cases, we have been careful to formulate precise specifications for each subprogram. Doing so not only helps to fix the ideas in our minds but also makes writing the actual computer code much easier and reduces the chance for bugs coming from specifications interpreted differently by different subprograms.

One more step remains before we can actually write down a complete program. We must settle the declaration of the data types used. We shall delay doing so until we have paused to consider some general principles for improving the style and quality of the programs we write. After we have done this, we shall apply these principles to the calendar program, and only at this time will we rewrite the algorithm as an actual Pascal program.

Structure Diagrams

large projects: librarian

As the number of different subprograms used in solving a problem increases, so does the difficulty of keeping track of all of them. For a large project, it becomes necessary for one member of the programming team to serve as a librarian who maintains the most up-to-date versions of each subprogram, its specifications and other documentation, and makes sure that all the programmers who need to use a particular subprogram have the most recent version.

Even for a small project, it is easy to lose track of the connections among the subprograms. An excellent way to see these connections is to draw a **structure diagram** such as that shown for the calendar project in Figure 1.5.

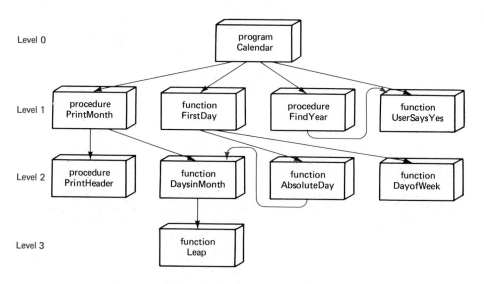

Figure 1.5. Structure diagram for the calendar project

levels of refinement

The main program is shown at the top of a structure diagram, and the subprograms that the main program itself invokes are shown on the next level down. Each of these subprograms may invoke others, which are in turn shown on the next level. Additional levels are added until all the subprograms are included.

multiple dependencies

It is, of course, possible that more than one subprogram will invoke a particular subprogram. In the calendar project, for example, both PrintMonth and Absolute-Day use the function DaysinMonth. Figure 1.5 shows it under PrintMonth, but it could equally as well be drawn under AbsoluteDay. To indicate this dependence, the diagram includes a line shown in color from AbsoluteDay to DaysinMonth. Similarly, the main program uses function UserSaysYes, and we shall find, when we code procedure FindYear in Chapter 2, that it is convenient again to use User-SaysYes. This use is shown by the second colored line in Figure 1.5.

1.8

DATA ABSTRACTION

refinement

When we think of the top-down design and refinement of a program, we generally think first of the design and refinement of algorithms, that is, of the action that the program performs. At the same time, we should also think of top-down design and refinement as applied to the way in which the data of the program are stored. That is, we should begin by considering the logical definitions of the kinds of data that we process and later determine the way in which these logical definitions translate into the type declarations of our programming language.

common abstractions

The term that is generally used for these logical definitions of data is **data abstraction**. The process of abstraction is to study many things together by recognizing their similarities, that is, by considering the properties that they all have in common. Abstraction is something we all do constantly, not just in mathematics. Color, for example, is an abstraction: We say that a sunset is red, an apple is red, or bricks are red, recognizing the abstract property *red*. So are emotions: If we say, "Bill is happy," it is not the same as "Ruth is happy," but we all know something about happiness. See Figure 1.6.

SHARP   SWEET

Figure 1.6. Common abstractions

data abstraction

So it is with data. Our first step will be to decide on the *properties* of the data that are important for our program. These properties lead us to what we call **abstract data types**. Later, we decide how the required properties can best be implemented in terms of the features allowed by our programming language.

Hence, in our outline of the calendar program, we were first able to use the abstract types year, month, and weekday without yet deciding how they will finally be declared. Later, we shall need to specify more detail, deciding exactly what numbers will be allowed as years, what months are, and so on. After we have translated these decisions into Pascal type declarations, we can write the lower-level subprograms that calculate with years, months, and days of the week.

example: accounting

Suppose, as a further example, that we are writing an accounting program that must make many calculations with sums of money. We should initially work with the abstract type money and deliberately refrain from thinking in terms of any computer declaration. Later, we may decide to make the Pascal type declaration money = real, so that we can calculate with dollars and fractions of a dollar.

first implementation: type real

second implementation: type integer

But an accountant, inspecting our work, may insist that the calculations be done in the way many accountants would, by rounding each calculation *separately* to the closest penny rather than by doing arithmetic with reals and rounding only the final answer. We may then decide to implement this requirement by using the declaration money = integer, performing all the calculations in an integer number of pennies, and finally dividing by 100 to get dollars.

third implementation: BCD arithmetic

Yet a third way to implement the abstract type money, available in some computer languages (but not Pascal) is to use BCD arithmetic, which stands for **Binary-Coded Decimal**. In BCD arithmetic, the computer is made to do all calculations with the ten decimal digits $0, 1, \ldots, 9$, imitating hand calculation, rather than converting the numbers to base 2, as is the usual way in which a computer's internal calculations are done.

abstract type weekday

first implementation: enumerated type

Finally, let us again consider the type declaration for the abstract type weekday that we have used for the seven days of the week. From the point of view of reading the program, the clearest translation into Pascal is to use the enumerated type

weekday = (Sun, Mon, Tue, Wed, Thu, Fri, Sat).

Pascal, however, does not allow us to do arithmetic with enumerated types. Hence, if our program requires many calculations with days of the week, calculations like finding the weekday w that comes four days after a given weekday d, then it may be better to think of the weekdays as numbered and declare the subrange type

second implementation: subrange

weekday = 1 .. 7.

This declaration allows easier arithmetic but has the disadvantage that, although Sunday is the first day of the week, the user may become confused in thinking of Monday as corresponding to 2 and so on. The experience of airlines is that their timetables are better understood if Monday is encoded as 1, Tuesday as 2, and so on. Hence, if we wish to keep Sunday at the beginning, we might use the subrange declaration

$$\text{weekday} = 0 \ldots 6$$

with Sunday encoded as 0, Monday as 1, and so on. This declaration also has the advantage that it allows us to use modular arithmetic more easily, since the result of Pascal's operation x **mod** y applied to positive integers x and y yields an integer between 0 and $y - 1$. Hence we can calculate the weekday w coming four days after d simply as w := (d + 4) **mod** 7.

conclusion   The point in looking at these examples so closely is to emphasize how important it is, first, to specify the data clearly and precisely on the abstract, logical level, then to refine our understanding of the ways the data will be used as we refine our algorithm by specifying more and more details, and only after the meaning and uses of the abstract data type are fully understood to make a decision as to how the abstract data type will be translated into the declarations of a programming language.

Programming Precept

First determine the properties of your data.
Refine your data types as you refine your algorithms.
Postpone specific declarations as long as you can.

1.9

NAMES

In the story of creation (Genesis 2:19), the LORD brought all the animals to ADAM to see what names he would give them. According to an old Jewish tradition, it was only when ADAM had named an animal that it sprang to life. This story brings an important moral to computer programming: Even if data and algorithms exist before, it is only when they are given meaningful names that their places in the program can be properly recognized and appreciated, that they first acquire a life of their own.

purpose of   For a program to work properly, it is of the utmost importance to know ex-
careful naming   actly what each variable represents, and to know exactly what each subprogram does. Documentation explaining the variables and subprograms should therefore always be included. The names of variables and subprograms should be chosen with care so as to identify their meanings clearly and succinctly. Finding good names is not always an easy task, but is important enough to be singled out as a programming precept:

> ### Programming Precept
> Always name your types, variables, and subprograms
> with the greatest care, and explain them thoroughly.

Pascal goes some distance toward enforcing this precept by requiring a section to declare variables and allows a more extensive use of names than most languages. Constants should be given names, and so should different data types, so that the compiler can catch errors that might otherwise be difficult to spot.

guidelines   The careful choice of names can go a long way in clarifying a program and in helping to avoid misprints and common errors. Some guidelines are:

subprograms

1. Give special care to the choice of names for procedures, functions, constants, and all global variables and types used in different parts of the program. These names should be meaningful and should suggest clearly the purpose of the subprogram, variable, and the like.

name length

2. Avoid names that are too short or cryptic. Someone reading your program should be able to tell immediately from each name what it stands for. If, for example, you were writing a program that processed the lines of some other program, then linecount might be a good name for a variable that counted the lines of the program being counted, but lc probably would not. It is, of course, possible to go overboard and use names that, while descriptive, are so long as to be cumbersome. The name

CountOfProgramLinesReadSoFar

is completely descriptive but so long that using it in a program would put off all but the most dedicated typist.

simplicity

3. Keep the names simple for variables used only briefly and locally. Even a single letter is sometimes a good choice for the variable controlling a short **for** loop, but a single letter would usually be a poor choice for a procedure or for a variable used three or four times in widely separated parts of the program.

prefixes and suffixes

4. Use common prefixes or suffixes to associate names of the same general category. The files used in a program, for example, might be called

InputFile   TransactionFile   TotalFile   OutFile   RejectFile.

misspellings

5. Avoid deliberate misspellings and meaningless suffixes to obtain different names. Of all the names

index   indx   ndex   indexx   index2   index3

only one (the first) should normally be used. When you are tempted to introduce multiple names of this sort, take it as a sign that you should think harder and devise names that better describe the intended use.

cuteness

6. Avoid choosing cute names whose meanings have little or nothing to do with the problem. The statements

> **while** TV **in** hock **do** study;
> **if not** sleepy **then** play **else** nap;

may be funny but they are bad programming!

similarity

7. Avoid choosing names that are close to each other in spelling or otherwise easy to confuse.

confusing letters

8. Be careful in the use of the letter "l" (lowercase ell), "O" (uppercase oh) and "0" (zero). Within words or numbers, these usually can be recognized from the context, and cause no problem, but "l" and "O" should never be used alone as names. Consider the examples

> l := 1;   x := 1;   x := l;   x := O;   O := 0.

DOCUMENTATION AND FORMAT

Most students initially regard documentation as a chore that must be endured, after a program is finished, to ensure that the marker and instructor can read it, so that no credit will be lost because of obscurity. The author of a small program indeed can remember all the details, and so needs documentation only to explain the program to someone else. With large programs (and with small ones after some months have elapsed), it becomes impossible to remember how every detail relates to every other. To write large programs, therefore, it is essential that appropriate documentation be prepared along with each small part of the program. A good habit is to prepare documentation as the program is being written, and an even better one, as we shall see later, is to prepare part of the documentation before starting to write the program.

the purpose of documentation

Not all documentation is appropriate. Almost as common as programs with little documentation or only cryptic comments are programs with verbose documentation that adds little to understanding the program.

> **Programming Precept**
>
> Keep your documentation concise but descriptive.

The style of documentation, as with all writing styles, is highly personal, and many different styles can prove effective. There are, nonetheless, some commonly accepted guidelines that should be respected:

guidelines

1. Place a prologue at the beginning of each subprogram including
   a. *Identification* (programmer's name, date, version number).
   b. Statement of the *purpose* of the subprogram and the *method* used.
   c. The *changes* the subprogram makes, what data it uses, what data it produces, and what data it changes (*preconditions* and *postconditions*).
   d. *Reference* to further documentation external to the program.

2. When each variable, constant, or type is declared, explain what it is and how it is used. Better still, make this information evident from the name.

3. Introduce each significant section (paragraph or subprogram) of the program with a comment stating briefly its purpose or action.

4. Indicate the end of each significant section if it is not otherwise obvious.

5. Avoid comments that parrot what the code does, such as

   count := count + 1;   {*Increase counter by 1.*}

   or that are meaningless jargon, such as

   {*horse string length into correctitude*}

   (This example was taken directly from a systems program.)

6. Explain any statement that employs a trick or whose meaning is unclear. Better still, avoid such statements.

7. The code itself should explain *how* the program works. The documentation should explain *why* it works and *what* it does.

8. Whenever a program is modified, be sure that the documentation is correspondingly modified.

format

Spaces, blank lines, and indentation in a program are important in producing good documentation. They make the program easy to read, allow you to tell at a glance which parts of the program relate to each other, where the major breaks occur, and precisely which statements are contained in each loop or each alternative of a conditional statement. There are many systems (some automated) for indentation and spacing, all with the goal of making it easier to determine the structure of the program.

prettyprinting

A **prettyprinter** is a system utility that reads a Pascal program, moving the text between lines and adjusting the indentation so as to improve the appearance of the program and make its structure more obvious. If a prettyprinter is available on your system, you might experiment with it to see if it helps the appearance of your programs.

consistency   Because of the importance of good format for programs, you should settle on some reasonable rules for spacing and indentation and use your rules consistently in all the programs you write. The rules used to format programs in this book are shown in Appendix B, but there are many other possible formats that are at least as good. Consistency, however, is essential if the system is to be useful in reading programs. Many professional programming groups decide on a uniform system and insist that all the programs they write conform. Some classes or student programming teams do likewise. In this way, it becomes much easier for one programmer to read and understand the work of another.

Even for short programs, the time spent debugging is usually more than the time first spent writing the program. For long programs, much more time is spent debugging and then modifying the program to meet new needs. Hence the advice:

Programming Precept

The reading time for programs is much more than the writing time.
Make reading easy to do.

1.11

CODING

In the next chapter, we shall consider some of the problems encountered in the actual coding of a computer program, and we shall continue to apply the ideas we discuss to the calendar project.

This note on coding comes at the end of the current chapter, however, to emphasize that it is important to settle the questions of problem specification, refinement, choice of data types, declaration of variables, and much of the documentation *before* starting to put the algorithms into an actual programming language like Pascal. Most programmers err by starting to code too soon. If coding is begun before the requirements are made precise, then unwarranted assumptions about the specifications will inevitably be made while coding, and these assumptions may render different subprograms incompatible with each other or make the programming task much more difficult than it need be.

Programming Precept

Never code until the specifications are precise and complete.

Sensible though this advice is, the natural human inclination is to plunge ahead with coding before the problems are fully understood. Almost every programmer learns this experience the hard way and can sympathize with the following:

Programming Precept

Act in haste and repent at leisure.
Code too soon and debug forever.

EXERCISES 1.11

E1. Read the following line of twelve letters and repeat it from memory:

$$s\ k\ e\ o\ c\ j\ y\ w\ l\ h\ q\ m.$$

memorization

Now do the same with the following four groups of three letters each:

$$k\ w\ e\qquad p\ x\ y\qquad i\ h\ r\qquad x\ k\ u.$$

Which of these tasks is easier? What does it say about programming?

E2. A *substitution cypher* encodes a message by replacing each letter by another letter according to a given *key*. The phrase mystery message becomes aqevxrq axeebwx when the key specifies that m is changed to a, y to q, and so on. Determine preconditions and postconditions for procedures doing each of the following tasks. (Do not write the procedures.)

substitution cypher

   a. Use a given key to encode a given message.
   b. Use a given key to decode a given message.
   c. Use a dictionary to find a possible decoding of a message without knowing the key in advance.

E3. A dairy farmer wishes to use a computer to keep track of some of his information. For each cow, the farmer needs to know the amount of milk produced each day, the amount of feed eaten each day, the age of the cow, a record of any calves she has had, a record of all inoculations she has had, and a record of any diseases she may have had. The dairy sells all its milk to one cooperative, but has several suppliers of goods and services. The dairy uses two different feed companies, three equipment companies, one drug supplier, one equipment repairman, and one veterinarian. For each of these, the farmer needs to keep track of the name, telephone number, and address, a record of the goods or services provided, the cost, and the amount currently owed to the supplier. Determine preconditions and

dairy farm

postconditions for procedures doing each of the following tasks. (Do not write the procedures.)

    a. For a particular cow, find the total cost (feed, drugs, and so on) and the total amount of milk produced in the last year.

    b. It is time for the regular quarterly maintenance of the milking machines. Update the file on the suppliers.

    c. A cow becomes sick and the veterinarian is called. Find the records the veterinarian will wish and then update the veterinarian's records in the file.

    d. Pay all the bills on the first of the month.

names

E4. If you were given a program containing some of the following variable and procedure names, what do you think they might stand for? Which have unclear meanings?

a. totalcost	**e.** interestrate	**i.** fln
b. flag	**f.** tmprslt	**j.** filename
c. x	**g.** tempres	**k.** fnl
d. amount4	**h.** temporaryresult	**l.** finalamount

calendars

E5. Find the lengths of the Julian, Gregorian, and solar (tropical) years. Determine how many years it will take for the Gregorian calendar to move one day from the solar (tropical) year. See the References in Appendix C for more information.

E6. Indicate exactly the changes needed in the algorithm devised in this chapter to calculate Julian calendars instead of Gregorian calendars. Pay special attention to the changes needed in the preconditions and postconditions for the various subprograms.

E7. Determine how to modify the calendar algorithm, and state the required changes in preconditions and postconditions, so it will calculate the Gregorian calendar for years after 1582 and the Julian calendar for years before 1582. The calendar for the year 1582, when the change was made, is more difficult: What special problems does it present?

E8. Devise an algorithm that will ask the user for a date (day, month, and year) and will return the day of the week on which that date falls according to the Gregorian calendar. State preconditions and postconditions for any new subprograms that are needed. Draw a structure diagram for the project.

E9. Devise an algorithm that will input any two dates and will calculate the number of days between them. State preconditions and postconditions for any new subprograms that are needed. Draw a structure diagram for the project.

algorithms

E10. Devise an algorithm for driving through an intersection controlled by a traffic signal. It may not be working, it may be blinking yellow or red, it may show a green arrow in some direction(s), or it may show green, yellow, or red. State preconditions and postconditions for any subprograms that are needed. Draw a structure diagram for the project.

E11. Devise an algorithm for trying to find a book in a library. It may or may not be owned by the library, it may be on reserve, or it may be checked out or lost. State preconditions and postconditions for any subprograms that are needed. Draw a structure diagram for the project.

E12. Devise an algorithm that reads a list of numbers and counts them according to their sign (that is, the number of negative numbers, positive numbers, and zeros). Be sure to make all specifications for the algorithm complete and precise. Draw a structure diagram.

tricky programs

E13. Rewrite the following procedure so that it accomplishes the same result in a less tricky way. Use meaningful names for the procedure and its variables.

```
procedure DoesSomething (var first, second: integer);
begin
    first := second − first;
    second := second − first;
    first := second + first
end;
```

E14. Given the **var** declarations

```
A:    array [1 .. n, 1 .. n] of integer;
i, j:  integer;
```

where n is a constant, determine what the following statement does. Rewrite the statement to accomplish the same effect in a less tricky way.

```
for i := 1 to n do
    for j := 1 to n do
        A [i, j] := (i div j) * (j div i);
```

E15. Determine what each of the following procedures does. Rewrite each procedure with meaningful variable names, with better format, and without unnecessary variables and statements.

mystery programs

a. function Calculate (apple, orange: integer): integer;
var peach, lemon: integer;
begin peach := 0; lemon := 0; **if** apple < orange **then begin**
peach := orange **end else if** orange <= apple **then begin**
peach := apple **end else begin** peach := maxint; lemon := maxint
end; if lemon <> maxint **then begin** Calculate := peach **end end;**

b. For this part, assume the declaration **type** vector = **array** [1 .. max] **of** real.

```
function Figure (var vector1: vector): real;
var loop1: integer; loop2: real; loop3: real; loop4: integer;
begin loop1 := 1; loop2 := vector1 [loop1]; loop3 := 0.0;
loop4 := loop1; for loop4 := 1 to max do begin loop1 := loop1 + 1;
loop2 := vector1 [loop1 − 1];
loop3 := loop2 + loop3 end; loop1 := loop1 − 1; loop2 := loop1;
loop2 := loop3/loop2; Figure := loop2 end;
```

c.
```
procedure question (var a17: integer; var stuff: integer);
var another, yetanother, stillonemore: integer;
begin another := yetanother; stillonemore := a17;
yetanother := stuff; another := stillonemore; a17 := yetanother;
stillonemore := yetanother;
stuff := another; another := yetanother; yetanother := stuff;
end;
```

d.
```
function mystery (apple, orange, peach: integer): integer;
begin if apple > orange then if apple > peach then if
peach > orange then mystery := peach else if apple < orange then
mystery := apple else mystery := orange else mystery := apple else
if peach > apple then if peach > orange then mystery := orange
else mystery := peach else mystery := apple end;
```

E16. The following statement is designed to check the relative sizes of three integers, which you may assume to be different from each other:

nested if statements

```
if x < z then if x < y then if y < z then c := 1 else c := 2 else
   if y < z then c := 3 else c := 4 else if x < y then
   if x < z then c := 5 else c := 6 else if y < z then c := 7 else
   if z < x then if z < y then c := 8 else c := 9 else c := 10;
```

a. Rewrite this statement in a form that is easier to read.
b. Since there are only six possible orderings for the three integers, only six of the ten cases can actually occur. Find those that can never occur, and eliminate the redundant checks.
c. Write a simpler, shorter statement that accomplishes the same result.

E17. The following Pascal function calculates the cube root of a real number (by the NEWTON approximation), using the fact that, if y is one approximation to the cube root of x, then

cube roots

$$z = \frac{2y + x/y^2}{3}$$

is a closer approximation. (You do not need to establish this fact.)

```
function Fcn(stuff: real): real;
var April, Tim, Tiny, Shadow, Tom, Tam, Square: real; flag: Boolean;
begin Tim := stuff; Tam := stuff; Tiny := 0.00001;
if stuff <> 0 then repeat Shadow := Tim + Tim;
Square := Tim * Tim;
Tom := (Shadow + stuff/Square);
April := Tom/3;
if April * April * April − Tam > −Tiny then if April * April * April − Tam
< Tiny then flag := true else flag := false else flag := false;
if flag = false then Tim := April else Tim := Tam until flag = true;
if stuff = 0 then Fcn := stuff else Fcn := April end;
```

    a. Determine what each variable represents, and change its name to something meaningful. Which of the variables are surplus to any significant need?

    b. Rewrite this function without the extra variables that contribute nothing to the understanding, with a better layout, and without the redundant and useless statements.

    c. Write a function for calculating the cube root of a parameter x directly from the mathematical formula. Start with the assignment y := x and then repeat

$$y := (2 * y + (x/sqr(y)))/3$$

until abs(y * y * y − x) < 0.00001.

    d. Is it easier to revise the program as given (and which already produces the correct result) or is it easier to write a new program directly from the formula?

E18. The *mean* of a sequence of real numbers is their sum divided by the count of numbers in the sequence. The (population) *variance* of the sequence is the mean of the squares of all numbers in the sequence, minus the square of the mean of the numbers in the sequence. The ***standard deviation*** is the square root of the variance. Write a well-structured Pascal function to calculate the standard deviation of a sequence of n numbers, where n is a constant and the numbers are in an array indexed from 1 to n, which is a parameter to the function. Use, then write, subsidiary functions to calculate the mean and variance. State preconditions and postconditions for each subprogram. Draw a structure diagram for the project.

statistics

E19. Design a program that will plot a given set of points on a graph. The input to the program will be a text file, each line of which contains two numbers that are the x and y coordinates of a point to be plotted. The program will use a procedure to plot one such pair of coordinates. The details of the procedure involve the specific method of plotting and cannot be written since they depend on the requirements of the plotting equipment, which we do not know. Before plotting the points, the program needs to know the maximum and minimum values of x and y that appear in its input file.

plotting

The program should therefore use another procedure Bounds that will read the whole file and determine these four maxima and minima. Afterward, another procedure is used to draw and label the axes; then the file can be reset and the individual points plotted. Be sure to include preconditions and postconditions in the documentation for each subprogram.

a. Write the main program, not including the procedures.

b. Write the procedure Bounds.

c. Write the header lines for the remaining procedures together with preconditions and postconditions showing their purposes and their requirements.

d. Draw a structure diagram for the project.

POINTERS AND PITFALLS

1. Be sure you understand your problem before you decide how to solve it.

2. Give precise specifications for the input to the program and to every subprogram.

3. Be sure the goals, specifications, requirements, and assumptions for the problem are fully and clearly stated.

4. Be sure you understand the algorithmic method before you start to program.

5. Solve your problem by dividing it into pieces and thinking of each part separately.

6. Make sure the division into subproblems is specified clearly and precisely, by giving preconditions and postconditions for each subprogram.

7. Strive for simplicity and generality. Avoid tricks in solving the problem, and try to minimize the number of special cases that must be considered.

8. Keep on subdividing the problem until each part is easy to solve.

9. Keep your subprograms short and simple; rarely should a single subprogram be more than a page long.

10. Decide on the logical data types you need by considering the properties of the data; postpone specific type declarations.

11. Work hard to choose the best possible names for all your subprograms, types, and variables.

12. Resist the temptation to code too soon.

13. Keep your documentation consistent with and complementary to your code. When reading a program, make sure that you debug the code and not just the comments.

14. Use good formatting to make your programs easy to read and understand.

15. Remember the Programming Precepts!

FOR FURTHER STUDY

Appendix C at the end of the book gives references for further study appropriate to each part and major topic in the book. You should turn to Appendix C to help locate supplementary sources or further information concerning both topics with which you may have difficulty or topics on which you would like more information.

In particular, Appendix C lists several books that give many helpful hints for problem solving, other books that provide guidelines for algorithm design and style, and for structured programming methods. Many variations and extensions are also possible for the calendar project, and the appendix gives several references that provide much additional information.

REVIEW QUESTIONS

Each chapter of this book concludes with a set of questions designed to help review the main ideas of the chapter. These questions can all be answered directly from the discussion in the book; if you are unsure of any answer, refer to the appropriate section.

1.2   **1.** What should be the first step in approaching a programming project?

      2. Name five kinds of information that need to be specified for a problem before it is programmed.

1.4   **3.** If you cannot immediately picture all the details needed for solving a problem, what should you do with the problem?

      4. What is *top-down refinement*?

1.6   **5.** What are *preconditions* and *postconditions* for a subprogram?

1.7   **6.** What is an *algorithm*? In what ways can one be formulated?

      7. What is *pseudocode*?

1.8   **8.** What is *data abstraction*?

      9. When should the details of data type declarations be decided?

      10. Name three different ways that amounts of money might be represented in a computer. Explain how *BCD* arithmetic works.

1.9   **11.** When may it be appropriate to use one-letter variable names?

      12. Why is it a bad idea to use short or cryptic names?

      13. Name some good and bad practices in choosing names.

1.10   14. Name four kinds of information that should be included in program documentation.

15. What does a *prettyprinter* do?

16. How does the time spent reading a program usually compare to the time first spent writing it?

1.11   17. When should coding be done?

2
PROGRAM DEVELOPMENT

After a problem has been formulated precisely and an algorithm for its solution has been constructed, it is time to translate the algorithm into a computer language. This chapter outlines this translation and summarizes important principles of good programming, especially as applied to large projects. We shall use stubs, drivers, and scaffolding to help construct programs, and we shall employ program testing methods to help assure ourselves of the correctness of the results. In the process, we shall review several features of Pascal from an advanced point of view.

DECLARATIONS

In the last chapter, we discussed the declaration of types and variables in terms of their logical meanings, that is, as *abstractions* used to solve problems. Now we consider the translation of these abstract types and variables into a program written in Pascal. To do this, we shall review the declaration of constants, simple types, and variables in Pascal. Our objective is not to repeat the details of Pascal features as found in introductory textbooks, nor to specify the rules or give examples of Pascal features. Instead, we wish to look at these features from the point of view of the logical specification of data. We shall thus try to assess the strong points and weak points of the various Pascal features as they are used to implement logical specifications.

2.1.1 Constants

From the point of view of the computer, constants are simply numbers, characters, or other pieces of data that do not change while the program is running. From the viewpoint of problem solving or that of understanding a program, however, constants have much more meaning, and that meaning should be made clear to the reader. Except for small integers like 0 and 1, every constant that appears in a program should be given a descriptive name and declared in the *naming* **const** declaration section of the program. There are two reasons for investing the effort required for doing this. The first is that a descriptive name explains the role of the constant and thereby clarifies the program. The second is that, after some time, the value of a constant may change. Consider, for example, a simple tax calculation:

example
```
function Tax(x: real): real;
begin
   if x <= 1900 then
      Tax := 0
   else if x <= 18000 then
      Tax := (x − 1900) * 0.15
   else
      Tax := 2415 + (x − 18000) * 0.28
end;
```

Now let us rewrite this function with descriptive names for the constants and for the data type. First come the declarations:

```
const
    exemption = 1900.00;          {amount of income exempt from tax}
    highbracket = 18000.00;       {income where high bracket starts}
    lowrate = 0.15;               {tax rate for low-income bracket}
    highrate = 0.28;              {tax rate for high-income bracket}
type
    money = real;
```

The function Tax now takes the form:

second version

```
function Tax(income: money): money;
begin                                           {function Tax}
  if income <= exemption then
      Tax := 0
  else if income <= highbracket then
      Tax := (income − exemption) * lowrate
  else
      Tax := (income − highbracket) * highrate +
             (highbracket − exemption) * lowrate
end;                                            {function Tax}
```

Notice how much easier the second version is to understand. It is also much easier to keep up to date when the tax rates or brackets are changed. Note also that the second version does not contain the constant 2415 that appeared in the first, but instead it contains the calculation

$$(\text{highbracket} - \text{exemption}) * \text{lowrate}$$

maintenance

that yields the number 2415. Hence the second version will actually run a little slower than the first, since it repeats this calculation each time a high-bracket tax is calculated. But this extra time is insignificant in comparison with the greater clarity of the program. If the income boundary between the two rates changes, moreover, the second version will automatically change correctly, whereas with the first version, a programmer who altered all occurrences of 18000 in the program might not realize that it is also necessary to change all occurrences of 2415, and therewith a new bug would appear.

Programming Precept

Name your constants, and choose the names carefully.

2.1.2 Data Types

Pascal, like most high-level languages, provides facilities for certain basic data types such as integer, real, and Boolean, and it provides ways to construct more complicated types such as arrays, records, and sets. Pascal, in fact, is superior to most programming languages in allowing the programmer to define new types, to use meaningful names to describe types, and in providing facilities for constructing more complicated types from simpler ones.

structured types

The major tools in Pascal for this construction are arrays, records, files, sets, and pointer types. We shall review all of these in the next chapter, except for pointer types, which are presented in Chapter 7. Even though these tools allow us to manipulate data efficiently, they are not by themselves adequate to describe the abstract, logical structure of the data. The major intent of this book is to present a wide variety of ways to abstract data, followed by methods to translate these abstractions into concrete implementations and algorithms.

simple types

For the current chapter, however, we need only the so-called *simple* types in Pascal: integers, reals, Boolean, subranges, and enumerated types. These types are called *simple* because a variable contains only one piece of data, whereas for a *structured* type, like an array or a record, one variable may contain many pieces of data. The simple types are the basic building blocks from which all other types are constructed.

Built-In Types

Boolean

Every Pascal compiler provides the four built-in types integer, real, char, and Boolean. The Boolean type provides only the two values false and true and is used primarily for decision making.

integer

When we come to the type integer, however, we find a difficulty for large programs that is generally ignored for short programs. This is the problem of *portability*: We wish a program in which we have invested a great deal of effort to run on as many different computers as possible. The largest value that a variable of type integer can assume is the constant maxint, and maxint differs

portability

from one computer to another. Hence a program that works correctly on one computer can cause an overflow error on another. But the problem is really more fundamental: it is a problem of data abstraction. If, while solving a problem, we decide that a variable is an integer, then we really mean it to be a mathematical integer, which could be as large as we wish. When we formulate our solution as a program, then we take the abstract mathematical integer and represent it as a variable of Pascal type integer, which, although it shares many properties of abstract integers, is not the same in that it allows only a certain range of integers.

real

The Pascal type real, similarly, has many pitfalls, since it is only a limited implementation of the abstract type of all real numbers. A variable of Pascal type real is stored as a floating-point number, that is, as a separate mantissa and exponent, each of which has only limited size and precision. Again, different computers will produce different results when calculating with variables of type real, and the arithmetic is done with only a limited amount of precision, so the answer will be subject to *round-off error*. And, in some calculations, a tiny round-off error can suddenly blow up into a very large error. Nor can variables of type real necessarily be assumed to be equal even when theoretically they should be. If x is a real variable, one should never write a statement like

if x = 0.0 **then** ... ,

but, instead, one should declare a very small but positive constant such as

tiny = 0.000001

and then write

if abs(x) < tiny **then** ....

char　　The built-in type char includes the characters that are ordinarily represented in a particular computer system and displayed or printed in that system. Just what characters these are, unfortunately, differs widely from system to system. Two common character sets are shown in Appendix B, but some systems use other character sets. The ordering of the characters also differs between systems. Whether the capital letters come before or after the small letters, for example, may determine that a list of words in alphabetical order for one system may not be in alphabetical order for another. With problems like these, it can be quite a challenge to make a program that processes character data completely portable between different computer systems.

Enumerated Types

Many times data processed by a program are neither numbers nor characters. Enumerated types may provide a good way to represent such data, one that often clarifies the structure of a program. In an enumerated type, every possible value that a variable can take on is given a name and listed by the programmer. These values are then constants as far as Pascal is concerned, and may be used like other constants, except that they are not numbers and so cannot appear in arithmetical expressions. In our calendar program, for example, the months of the year and the days of the week are not numbers, and so the abstract types weekday and month can conveniently be implemented as the enumerated types

```
type
    weekday = (Sun, Mon, Tue, Wed, Thu, Fri, Sat);
    month   = (Jan, Feb, Mar, Apr, May, Jun, Jul, Aug, Sep, Oct, Nov, Dec);
```

input and output　　One difficulty with enumerated data types is that standard Pascal provides no way to read or write variables of an enumerated type from the standard input or output, that is, from the user's terminal. Some compilers do provide such a facility, but using it will mean that the programs lose their portability to another system. Instead, reading or writing enumerated types is best done with a **case** statement, as we shall illustrate for the calendar program later in this chapter.

Subranges

translation of logical data types

Often a piece of data of some type can take on only a restricted set of values. An integer, for example, may be required to be nonnegative, or a character variable may be required to be one of the 26 lowercase letters. When we are considering the data on the logical, abstract level, we should specify as exactly as possible what values the data may take. When we translate the specifications into Pascal declarations, we wish to make the Pascal declaration fit as closely as possible to the set of possible values previously specified. Subranges provide a good tool for doing this. The nonnegative integers lead us to the subrange of type integer

$$0 .. maxint$$

and the 26 lowercase letters to the subrange of type char

$$'a' .. 'z'.$$

We can, moreover, construct subranges of enumerated types such as

$$summer = Jun .. Aug \quad or \quad workday = Mon .. Fri.$$

inaccurate translation

EBCDIC letters

It is important to notice that subranges may not correspond exactly to the desired values specified on the abstract level; they are imperfect reflections. There is no largest nonnegative integer, but maxint is the largest we can represent in the subrange given. If you check the table of EBCDIC characters in Appendix B, you will see that the characters {, }, and ~ appear in the midst of the lowercase letters; hence the subrange 'a' .. 'z' includes these characters as well as the letters.

On the logical level, moreover, there are specifications that do not correspond to any subrange. We may, for example, know that a variable must always be an even integer (divisible by 2), and there is no convenient way to specify this fact with subranges.

In spite of these drawbacks, subranges are a valuable tool in helping to make Pascal declarations come closer to the abstract specifications we desire. In particular, subranges are helpful for error checking during the debugging of a program; if a programming mistake causes a variable to take on an illegal value, the Pascal system may be able to detect an error more quickly by using subrange checking.

For the calendar program, for example, we would not wish a day of the month to be less than 1 or greater than 31, and we can enforce this restriction with the subrange declaration

$$\textbf{type } monthday = 1 .. 31.$$

This declaration will help with some error checking, but it is not perfect, since *error checking* it will not catch a nonsense date like February 30 or April 31. Similarly, the restriction of the calendar program to years A.D. can be enforced by the declaration

year = 1 .. maxint.

If a subrange error occurs, the system will respond with a message such as

Value out of bounds on line 372.

subrange checking Such a message may help the programmer with debugging, but it would be totally mystifying to anyone using the program except its author. Subrange checking should be used as a last line of defense against logic errors in the program, but subrange checking should *never* be the only guard against the input of faulty data. Instead, the input procedures should initially accept any data the user gives and then carefully check it for legality before sending it to the program for processing. In this way, the casual user should not be able to cause a subrange error in a program that is otherwise operating properly.

Programming Precept

Use subrange checking only as a last line of defense, not to detect user errors.

2.1.3 Variables

The data used in the program and in each subprogram must be precisely specified, with indication of what each variable is, where it is used, and how it is processed. Variables used for input and for output should be clearly indicated.

With regard to a subprogram, there are five kinds of variables:

parameters ■ *Input parameters* are used by the subprogram but are not changed by the subprogram. In Pascal, input parameters are usually value parameters. (Exceptions: Files must always be **var** parameters, even if used for input only; often large arrays are passed as **var** parameters to avoid the time and space needed to make a local copy.)

■ *Output parameters* contain the results of the calculations from the subprogram. In Pascal, output parameters must be **var** parameters.

■ *Inout parameters* are used for both input and output. The initial value of the parameter is used and then modified by the subprogram. In Pascal, inout parameters must be **var** parameters.

variables
■ *Local variables* are declared in the subprogram and exist only while the subprogram is being executed. They are not initialized before the subprogram begins and are discarded when the subprogram ends.

■ *Global variables* are used in the subprogram but not declared in the subprogram. It can be quite dangerous to use global variables in a subprogram, since, after the subprogram is written, its author may forget exactly what global variables were used and how. If the main program is later changed, then the subprogram may mysteriously begin to misbehave. If a subprogram alters the value of a global variable, it is said to cause a *side effect*.

side effects
Side effects are even more dangerous than using global variables as input to the subprogram because side effects may alter the performance of other subprograms, thereby misdirecting the programmer's debugging efforts to a part of the program that is already correct.

global variables
Some good programmers never use global variables. Others prefer to use global variables under carefully controlled circumstances. Certain variables may be used so often in a program that they appear in almost every subprogram; these variables really are global in nature, since they appear everywhere in the program. Readability (and efficiency, incidentally) may be improved if these variables are treated as global rather than listed as parameters for every subprogram.

Generally speaking, however, the best practice is to declare variables at the lowest possible level. This means that a variable used in several subprograms of a particular subprogram A should be declared in A but no higher in the structure diagram unless it is needed in subprograms not themselves included in A.

Programming Precept

Keep your connections simple. Avoid global variables whenever possible.

Programming Precept

Never cause side effects.
If you must use global variables as input, document them thoroughly.

---

functions
For functions the definition of a *side effect* is expanded to include changes made to parameters as well as global variables. A function should calculate just one result, returned as the value of the function. If a subprogram needs to produce more than one result, it should be written as a procedure, not as a function.

■■■■■■■ **EXERCISES 2.1**

E1. Rewrite each of the following program segments with named constants and with better names for the types and variables.

 a. The formula for the area of a circle:

```
function A(r: real): real;
begin
    A := 3.14159 * sqr(r)
end;
```

 b. The month's interest on a savings account, where a higher rate is paid if the balance is over $1000:

```
function i(x: real): real;
begin
    if x <= 1000 then
        i := 0.055 * x/12
    else
        i := 0.065 * x/12
end;
```

E2. Translate each of the following (abstract) data types into Pascal declarations. Indicate if and how the Pascal declaration fails to accurately reflect the logical type.

 a. A person's age.
 b. A person's height.
 c. The current weather conditions (sun, cloud, rain, snow, or wind).
 d. A color.
 e. The score on a test.
 f. The letter grade for a course.
 g. The room number in a building.
 h. The characters that can appear in Pascal identifiers (uppercase and lowercase letters and digits).

E3. In the calendar project, we have defined the *absolute day number* of a date as the number of days from January 1, 1 A.D. to the date. On most microcomputers, maxint has the value 32767. What may go wrong if we do not take this into account when implementing the calendar project on such a microcomputer? What method do you propose to solve this problem?

E4. Take a calculator with a square-root key, enter a positive number (not 1), and hit the square-root key until the display reads 1. Now square this result as many times as you took square roots. Do you recover the original number? Why not?

2.2

CODING

2.2.1 The Main Program

The specifications for the calendar problem are given in Section 1.3 and an algorithm for its solution appears in Section 1.7. We shall follow these sections in our work.

abstract data types

The algorithm for the main program in Section 1.7 mentions three abstract data types: weekday, month, and year. In addition, the program will calculate the absolute number of days from January 1, 1 A.D., to a given date, so we need another type that we call absday. Finally, we do calculations and printing with the days of the month, so we introduce the type monthday. Let us consider these types in reverse order as we decide on their Pascal declarations.

monthday

A day of the month is a number between 1 and 31, at the most, so we are clearly justified in declaring monthday to be the subrange type 1..31. The number of days from the fixed date could never be negative, but it could be any

absday

nonnegative integer; hence we can declare absday to be the subrange 0..maxint.

year

For the type year, since we must calculate the absolute number of days without exceeding maxint, the maximum year we can handle is approximately maxint **div** 365. Since this number depends on the computer, we shall introduce a new constant, maxyear, to stand for the largest year number the program will accept. If we wish, we can run experiments to find the largest year number for which the program works correctly; otherwise we can arbitrarily choose maxyear, subject to its not exceeding maxint **div** 365. We shall do the latter.

month

For the type month, we shall use an enumerated type, since it will help to clarify the program. For the type weekday, finally, we must make a decision

weekday

between using an enumerated type and a subrange type, as discussed in Section 2.1.2. There are advantages on both sides. An enumerated type produces a clearer program but makes the calculations more complicated than they would be with a subrange type. For the sake of clarity, and to illustrate these complications, however, we shall choose to declare weekday as an enumerated type. One of the programming projects requests rewriting the program with **weekday** declared as a subrange of the integers.

```
program Calendar (input, output);
{Pre:   None.
 Post:  The program prints the calendar for the year requested by the user.
        This consists, for each month, of a header line naming the month and
        year, then four to six lines corresponding to the weeks of the month,
        with the days arranged in columns according to the day of the week,
        and with blank entries as needed before the first of the month and
        after the last of the month.
 Uses:  FindYear, FirstDay, PrintMonth, UserSaysYes.}

const
    maxyear = 5000000;     {Maximum year allowed is about maxint div 365.}

type
    weekday = (Sun, Mon, Tue, Wed, Thu, Fri, Sat);
    month = (Jan, Feb, Mar, Apr, May, Jun, Jul, Aug, Sep, Oct, Nov, Dec);
    year = 1 .. maxyear;                          {Allow only years A.D.}
    monthday = 1 .. 31;                              {a day of the month}
    absday = 0 .. maxint;     {total number of days since 1 January, 1 A.D.}

var
    startday: weekday;      {the day of the week on which a month starts}
    m: month;                      {the month currently being printed}
    y: year;                {the year for which the calendar is printed}

{Declarations of all the procedures and functions must be inserted here.}


begin                                             {program Calendar}
   repeat          {Allow the user to repeat the program for another year.}
       FindYear (y);      {Ask the user for the number of the year to use.}
       startday := FirstDay (y);
                            {Determine on which weekday January 1 falls.}

      for m := Jan to Dec do
        PrintMonth (m, y, startday);

   {Print month m of year y starting on day startday of the week. The procedure
    will update startday so that, at the conclusion, it gives the weekday for the
    first day of the following month.}

        write ('Repeat for another year')
     until not UserSaysYes
   {The function returns a Boolean value according as the user wishes to repeat
    the computation for another year.}
   end.                                           {program Calendar}
```

2.2.2 Stubs

early debugging and testing

After coding the main program, most programmers will wish to complete the writing and coding of the subprograms as soon as possible, to see if the whole project will work. For a project as small as the calendar problem, this approach may work. For larger projects, however, writing and coding all the subprograms will be such a large job that, by the time it is complete, many of the details of the main program and subprograms that were written early will have been forgotten. In fact, different people may be writing different subprograms, and some of those who started the project may have left it before all subprograms are written. It is much easier to understand and debug a program when it is fresh in your mind. Hence, for larger projects, it is much more efficient to debug and test each subprogram as soon as it is written than it is to wait until the project has been completely coded.

Even for smaller projects, there are good reasons for debugging subprograms one at a time. We might, for example, be unsure of some point of Pascal syntax that will appear in several places through the program. If we can compile each subprogram separately, then we shall quickly learn to avoid errors in syntax in later subprograms. As a second example, suppose that we have decided that the major steps of the program should be done in a certain order. If we test the main program as soon as it is written, then we may find that sometimes the major steps are done in the wrong order. At this time, we can quickly correct the problem, doing so more easily than if we waited until the major steps were perhaps obscured by the many details contained in each of them.

stubs

To compile the program correctly, there must be something in the place of each subprogram that is used. Hence, we must put in short, dummy subprograms, called *stubs*. The simplest stubs are those that do nothing at all, for example:

```
procedure PrintMonth(m: month; y: year; var startday: weekday);
begin                                        {dummy stub only}
end;
```

or that produce only one answer, for example:

```
function UserSaysYes: Boolean;
begin                                        {dummy stub only}
   UserSaysYes := false
end;
```

Even with stubs like these, we can at least compile the program and make sure that the declarations of types and variables are syntactically correct. Normally, however, each stub should print a message stating that the subprogram was invoked or request the user to provide the information that the subprogram should calculate. As we slowly add code, replacing stubs by functioning subprograms and then testing and debugging the program at each stage, we can locate and correct errors much more quickly than if we did all the coding at once and attempted to do all the debugging only on the completed program.

2.2.3 Input and Output

Principles

In computer programs designed to be used by many people, the procedures performing input and output are often the longest. Input to the program must be fully checked to be certain that it is valid and consistent. Errors in input must be processed in ways to avoid catastrophic failure or production of ridiculous results. The goal, often unattainable, is *fail-safe* programs, that is, programs that will not fail no matter what input they receive. The procedures for input from the user should be designed to be as forgiving as possible, since people make many mistakes. For many applications, the input should be echoed back and the user given a chance to correct any errors before processing proceeds.

careful input and output

The output must be carefully organized and formatted, with considerable thought to what should or should not be printed, and with provision of various alternatives to suit differing circumstances. The programming tools needed to design comprehensive input and output procedures, unfortunately, still differ considerably from one computer system to another, and in any case are more concerned with the details of the language and the problem at hand than with general ideas. It is therefore impossible to include as much error checking as we would wish, working only within the provisions of standard Pascal. When the programs are implemented in a particular system, additional error checking can usually be included.

Programming Precept

Keep your input and output as separate modules,
so they can be changed easily
and can be custom-tailored to your computing system.

Programming Precept

Strive for fail-safe programming.

User Response

After printing the calendar, our program is supposed to determine from the user whether the whole calculation is to be repeated. Hence we need the function UserSaysYes that interactively asks the user to respond yes or no. To make the function easy to use, we ask not for the words *yes* or *no* but only for one of the letters *y* or *n*. To make the program forgiving, we let it accept either uppercase or lowercase, but if it receives a response other than the two allowed letters, it repeats the request with a fuller explanation. Note the use of Pascal sets to allow the program to handle several possibilities at once.

```
function UserSaysYes: Boolean;        {asks the user to respond yes or no}
{Pre:   None.
  Post:  The function has received a response beginning with either 'y' or 'n'
         (either upper or lower case), and returns the value true or false ac-
         cording as the response began with 'y' or 'n'.
  Uses: None.}
var
   response: char;                          {character typed in by the user}
   valid:     Boolean;               {Has the user responded appropriately?}
begin                                              {function UserSaysYes}
   repeat
      write(' (y,n)? ');
      readln(response);
      valid := (response in ['n', 'N', 'y', 'Y']);
      if not valid then
         write('Please respond by typing one of the letters y or n')
   until valid;
   UserSaysYes := (response in ['y', 'Y'])
end;                                               {function UserSaysYes}
```

utility function

There are many applications for a function asking a yes/no question; hence the effort required to write a flexible and forgiving function is justified, and the function should be regarded as a *utility* ready to be inserted into any program where it is needed.

finding the year number

Next we come to the procedure that asks the user for the year number. Again we embed the procedure in a loop that iterates until the response is valid. In this procedure, we receive the input in a variable of type integer, not year, so that Pascal's subrange checking will not abort the program if the user enters an incorrect response. Only after the response is valid is it assigned to the output variable y of type year.

This procedure contains an example where it is excusable to use an unusual constant in the body of the procedure, the year 1583. This number is an historical date that will not change, and its use is well explained in the accompanying message.

```
procedure FindYear(var y: year);
                                    {determines a year number from the user}
{Pre:   None.
  Post:  The parameter y has been set to a year number entered by the user;
         this value has been checked to make sure that it is a number within
         the range of years whose calendars can be calculated.
  Uses: None.}
var
   valid: Boolean;                              {Is the input a valid year?}
   x:     integer;              {number as input, not necessarily a valid year}
begin                                                     {procedure FindYear}
   repeat                                    {Keep trying until the input is valid.}
      write('Please give a year number: ');
      readln(x);
      valid := (x >= 1) and (x <= maxyear);   {Check range of type year.}
      if not valid then
         writeln('The year must be between 1 and ', maxyear);

      if valid and (x < 1583) then
                                  {Check for validity of Gregorian calendar.}
      begin
         writeln('This program will determine the Gregorian calendar, not');
         writeln('the Julian calendar that was in effect until October 1582.');
         write('Do you wish to continue');
         valid := UserSaysYes
      end
   until valid;
   y := x
end;                                                     {procedure FindYear}
```

Output Procedures

precise
specifications

Next let us consider the procedure that writes out one month of the calendar, with the days arranged in rows corresponding to weeks. Soon after we start work, we notice a gap in the specifications for the problem: The width of the calendar has not been specified. We shall want each date to take the same number of positions, but it would be a mistake to choose some size arbitrarily for the column width. Instead, we must allow some flexibility. There are two ways to solve this problem. One way is to introduce a variable columnwidth and ask the user to give it a value each time the program is used. The other way is to make a reasonable choice and specify it as a constant columnwidth, but make it easy to change, so that the width of the calendar can be altered if desired. We shall follow the latter course.

The procedure will use two local variables, one to loop through the days of the month and the other through the days of the week (corresponding to the columns of the calendar). Since we are using an enumerated type for the days of the week, we must use Pascal's successor function succ(d) to move from one day to the next. We also need a special, preliminary loop to start the first week, since we may need to leave some columns blank before starting to print the numbers. Finally, we postpone the problem of printing the header line for the month by making it a separate procedure.

```
procedure PrintMonth(m: month; y: year; var startday: weekday);
{Pre:   m is a month in year y; startday gives the day of the week on which
        the first day of month m of year y falls in the Gregorian calendar.
 Post:  The procedure has printed the calendar for month m of year y, con-
        sisting of a header line naming m and y, then four to six lines corre-
        sponding to the weeks of month m, with the days arranged in columns
        according to the day of the week, and with blank entries as needed
        before the first of the month and after the last of the month. The vari-
        able startday has been updated to the day of the week on which the
        first of the month following m comes.
 Uses: DaysinMonth, PrintHeader.}
const
    columnwidth = 8;         {How many spaces are reserved for each column?}
var
    d: weekday;                         {loops through the days of the week}
    n: monthday;                        {loops through the days of the month}

begin                                                      {procedure PrintMonth}
    PrintHeader(m, y);
    d := Sun;
    while d < startday do        {Print out the blanks as needed in first week.}
    begin
        write(' ': columnwidth);
        d := succ(d)
    end;

    for n := 1 to DaysinMonth(m, y) do    {loop through days of the month}
    begin
        write(n: columnwidth);
        if d = Sat then                                           {end of a week}
        begin                          {Finish one row and prepare to start the next.}
            writeln;
            d := Sun
        end
        else
            d := succ(d)
    end;
    writeln;
    startday := d                          {Update startday for the next month.}
end;                                                       {procedure PrintMonth}
```

header

We shall print a header line for each month consisting of a row of asterisks, followed on the next line by the name of the month on the left and the number of the year on the right. The following line will contain the names of the seven days of the week. There are some small complications because the width of the header lines depends on the value of columnwidth. It is also not possible, in standard Pascal, to print the values of an enumerated type directly; we must use a **case** statement.

```
procedure PrintHeader(m: month; y: year);
{Pre:  m is a month of year y.
  Post: The procedure prints a row of asterisks, then the name of month m
        on the left and the number of year y on the right, then a row of the
        names of the days of the week; the procedure automatically adjusts
        widths according to the constant columnwidth, which gives the width
        of one of the seven columns.
  Uses: Constant columnwidth.}
var i: integer;                                {general-purpose loop variable}
begin                                           {procedure PrintHeader}
  writeln;
  for i := 1 to 7 * columnwidth do
                         {Total width of calendar is 7 * columnwidth.}
     write('*': 1);
  writeln; writeln;
  case m of
          {Use case statement to print the values of an enumerated type.}
     Jan:  write('January     ');      Jul:  write('July        ');
     Feb:  write('February    ');      Aug:  write('August      ');
     Mar:  write('March       ');      Sep:  write('September   ');
     Apr:  write('April       ');      Oct:  write('October     ');
     May:  write('May         ');      Nov:  write('November    ');
     Jun:  write('June        ');      Dec:  write('December    ')
  end;
  for i := 1 to 7 * columnwidth − 13 do
                         {Save 9 spaces for month; 4 for year.}
     write(' ': 1);           {Fill in the blanks before the year number.}
  writeln(y: 4);
  writeln('Sun': columnwidth,  'Mon': columnwidth,  'Tue': columnwidth,
          'Wed': columnwidth,  'Thu': columnwidth,   'Fri': columnwidth,
          'Sat': columnwidth)
end;                                            {procedure PrintHeader}
```

2.2.4 Remaining Procedures

The remaining procedures for the calendar problem closely follow their algorithmic descriptions given in Section 1.7.

```
                       function Leap(y: year): Boolean;
leap years             {Pre:   y is a year.
                         Post: The function returns the value true if and only if year y is a leap year
                               in the Gregorian calendar.
                         Uses: None.}
                       begin
                         Leap := (y mod 4 = 0) and ((y mod 100 <> 0) or (y mod 400 = 0))
                       end;


                       function DaysinMonth(m: month; y: year): monthday;
days in a month        {Pre:   m is a month of year y.
                         Post: The value of the function is the number of days in month m of year y
                               according to the Gregorian calendar.
                         Uses: Function Leap(y).}
                       begin                                   {function DaysinMonth}
                         case m of
                           Apr, Jun, Sep, Nov:                 {Thirty days hath September,}
                             DaysinMonth := 30;                {April, June, and November;}
                           Jan, Mar, May, Jul, Aug, Oct, Dec:
                             DaysinMonth := 31;                {All the rest have thirty-one,}
                           Feb:     {Save February alone, which hath but twenty-eight in store}
                             if Leap(y) then                   {'Till leap year gives it one day more.}
                               DaysinMonth := 29
                             else
                               DaysinMonth := 28
                         end
                       end;                                    {function DaysinMonth}


                       function AbsoluteDay(d: monthday; m: month; y: year): absday;
count absolute         {Pre:   The day d of month m of year y exists in the Gregorian calendar.
       days             Post: The function value is the number of days from January 1, 1 A.D., to
                               the given day, inclusive, using the rules of the Gregorian calendar.
                         Uses: None.}
                       var
                         loopmonth: month;      {used to loop through the months preceding m}
                         total:     absday;          {the total number of days calculated so far}
                       begin                                   {function AbsoluteDay}
                         total := 365 * (y - 1)       {years before y, disregarding leap years}
                                  + (y - 1) div 4              {adds Julian leap years}
                                  - (y - 1) div 100            {subtracts century years}
                                  + (y - 1) div 400;       {except for those that are leap years}
                         if m <> Jan then            {adds on the days in the months preceding m}
                           for loopmonth := Jan to pred(m) do
                             total := total + DaysinMonth(loopmonth, y);
                         AbsoluteDay := total + d      {Finally, add the day of the current month.}
                       end;                                    {function AbsoluteDay}
```

finding a weekday

To convert an absolute day into a day of the week, we need to do some modular arithmetic: We divide by 7 and take the remainder by using the **mod** operator. The only problem is to determine how the seven possible remainders 0, ..., 6 correspond to the seven days of the week, and that depends on the day of the week on which January 1 fell in 1 A.D. (according to the Gregorian calendar). That turns out to be a Monday, but we don't have to know in advance. Instead, we can make the correspondence any way we wish, test the function on a known date, and then modify it to make the correspondence correct. The result follows.

```
function DayofWeek(a: absday): weekday;
{Pre:  a is a day specified absolutely from January 1, 1 A.D.
  Post: The function result is the day of the week on which a falls according
         to the Gregorian calendar.
  Uses: None.}
begin                                          {function DayofWeek}
  case (a mod 7) of

      0: DayofWeek := Sun;              4: DayofWeek := Thu;
      1: DayofWeek := Mon;              5: DayofWeek := Fri;
      2: DayofWeek := Tue;              6: DayofWeek := Sat
      3: DayofWeek := Wed;
    end
end;                                            {function DayofWeek}
```

first day of the year

```
function FirstDay(y: year): weekday;
{Pre:  y is a year number.
  Post: The function returns the day of the week on which January 1 falls in
         year y according to the Gregorian calendar.
  Uses: AbsoluteDay, DayofWeek.}
begin
  FirstDay := DayofWeek(AbsoluteDay(1, Jan, y))
end;
```

2.2.5 Drivers

separate debugging

For small projects, each subprogram is usually inserted in its proper place as soon as it is written. The resulting program can then be debugged and tested as far as possible. For large projects, however, compilation of the entire project can overwhelm that of a new subprogram being debugged. It can be difficult to tell, looking only at the way the whole program runs, whether a particular subprogram is working correctly or not. Even in small projects, the output of one subprogram may be used by another in ways that do not immediately reveal whether the information transmitted is correct.

driver program

One way to debug and test a single subprogram is to write a short auxiliary program whose purpose is to provide the necessary input for the subprogram, call it, and evaluate the result. Such an auxiliary program is called a ***driver*** for the subprogram. By using drivers, each subprogram can be isolated and studied by itself, and thereby bugs can often be spotted quickly.

Drivers are especially useful for subprograms whose results are used by other subprograms but are not directly given to the user. An error in such a subprogram may not be obvious, and, instead, the subprogram that uses the result may appear to be malfunctioning. The function AbsoluteDay is such a subprogram in the calendar project. Another application of drivers is to help design subprograms whose details are not immediately obvious, such as the function DayofWeek, which needed to be adjusted according to the weekday for January 1, 1 A.D. As an example, therefore, let us write a driver program for these two subprograms.

```
program DriveWeekday(input, output);
   {driver program to test the subprograms AbsoluteDay and DayofWeek}
   {declarations of constants and types to be copied from program Calendar}
var
   d : monthday;
   m : month;
   y : year;
   n : integer;                        {for input; will be converted to month}
   {Insert functions AbsoluteDay, DayofWeek, and UserSaysYes here.}
begin                                   {main program DriveWeekday}
   repeat                   {Insert a loop so calculations can be repeated.}
      write('Day of month?');
      readln(d);
      write('Month (1 - 12)?';
      readln(n);
      case n of                      {Use to change an integer to a month.}
         1: m := Jan;          5: m := May;           9: m := Sep;
         2: m := Feb;          6: m := Jun;          10: m := Oct;
         3: m := Mar;          7: m := Jul;          11: m := Nov;
         4: m := Apr;          8: m := Aug;          12: m := Dec
      end;
      write('Year?');
      readln(y);
      n := AbsoluteDay(d, m, y);
      writeln('Absolute day number is ', n);
      write('Day of week is ');
      case DayofWeek(n) of
         Sun:  writeln('Sun');          Thu:  writeln('Thu');
         Mon:  writeln('Mon');          Fri:  writeln('Fri');
         Tue:  writeln('Tue');          Sat:  writeln('Sat')
         Wed:  writeln('Wed');
      end;
      write('Repeat ');
   until not UserSaysYes
end.                                    {main program DriveWeekday}
```

As you can see, the logic of this program is very simple, even though it is made rather long because Pascal cannot handle enumerated types directly for input or output. Note that no error checking is done in the input; the program is not written for users other than its author, nor will it be kept permanently.

The driver program should first be run for several dates with small year numbers (100 or less) to verify that it calculates absolute dates correctly, since these can be checked by hand for early dates. Then it should be run for dates for which the weekday is known (perhaps from the current year), so that its calculation of days of the week can be checked and corrected as necessary.

PROJECTS 2.2

P1. Write and run driver programs for the remaining subprograms of the calendar project:

a. UserSaysYes
b. FindYear
c. PrintHeader
d. Leap
e. DaysinMonth
f. PrintMonth

P2. On short-word machines, such as most microcomputers, where maxint is typically 32767, the calculation of absolute day numbers will be incorrect. Modify the procedures as required to correct this defect, and test the modifications by writing appropriate driver programs.

2.3

DEBUGGING

Structured Walkthroughs

After all the subprograms have been assembled into a complete program, it is time to check out the completed whole. One of the most effective ways to uncover hidden defects is called a *structured walkthrough*. In this activity, the programmer shows the completed program to another programmer, or a small

group discussion

group of programmers, and explains exactly what happens, beginning with an explanation of the main program followed by the subprograms, one by one. Structured walkthroughs are helpful for three reasons. First, programmers who are not familiar with the actual code can often spot bugs or conceptual errors that the original programmer overlooked. Second, the questions that other people ask can help you to clarify your own thinking and discover your own mistakes. Third, the structured walkthrough often suggests tests that prove useful in later stages of software production.

Scaffolding

It is unusual for a large program to run correctly the first time it is executed as a whole. If it does not, it may not be easy to determine exactly where the errors are. On many systems, sophisticated *trace tools* are available to keep track of subprogram calls, changes of variables, and so on. A simple and effective debugging tool, however, is to take *snapshots* of program execution by inserting write statements at key points in the main program. For large projects, it may be appropriate to write a separate procedure to print the data and call the procedure at key points in the program. A message can also be printed each time a subprogram is called, and the values of important variables can be printed before and after each subprogram is called. Such snapshots can help the programmer converge quickly on the particular location where an error is occurring.

scaffolding **Scaffolding** is another term frequently used to describe code inserted into a program to help with debugging. Never hesitate to put scaffolding into your programs as you write them; it will be easy to delete once it is no longer needed, and it may save you much grief during debugging. Some Pascal compilers, in fact, treat the two comment constructions { ... } and (* ... *) as different, allowing one to be nested inside the other. If your compiler does this, then it is often helpful to leave the scaffolding permanently in the program by using one kind of brackets for ordinary comments and the other kind for scaffolding that is no longer needed.

Static Analyzers

For very large programs yet another tool is sometimes used. This is a *static analyzer*, a program that examines the source program (as written in Pascal, for example) looking for uninitialized or unused variables, sections of the code that can never be reached, and other occurrences that are probably incorrect.

Fail-Safe Programming

A good attitude to maintain while writing programs is to make all the code as fail safe as possible; that is, to design the code so that, if something goes wrong, it will be detected very quickly and can then be corrected easily. In this connection, we have already discussed the detection of errors in the input as well as the use of subranges as a means of catching illegal values. As you write each statement of a program you should mentally ask yourself, "How could this statement fail?" Perhaps a variable might take on an illegal value; the termination

guarding against condition for a loop might be incorrect; an array index might be off. Next you
errors should convince yourself that none of these erroneous conditions can occur. Perhaps subrange checking will ensure that the variables are in range; perhaps you have carefully checked the extreme cases for loop termination; perhaps you have inserted scaffolding to make sure the array entries and indices are correct. If you are not absolutely sure that no illegal condition might arise, then ask yourself how much trouble it would be to include code checking that the values are legal before proceeding. It takes very little time to write one **if** statement, even less time to execute it, and the error message it may provide can save much time and grief spent in debugging.

Some kinds of logic errors in programs are much more common than others. Subrange errors, incompletely checked input, and off-by-one counts occur

compound conditionals frequently. Another error is exceedingly common in Pascal programs, and that is the incorrect use of conditionals in **while** or **repeat** loops. It is tempting to write a construction such as

      while (i is within range) **and** (i satisfies condition) **do** ...

The error is that Pascal will check whether i satisfies the condition whether or not it is in range, and, when it is not in range, checking the condition will probably cause an error. In Pascal, instead, it is often necessary to introduce a Boolean variable, set it true or false according as i is in range, and only if it is true check the other condition. The Boolean variable is then used by itself to control the loop. The preceding example then takes the form

      continue := (i is within range);   {*Use the Boolean variable* continue.}
      if continue **then**
         continue := (i satisfies the condition);
      while continue **do** ...

    {*The value of* continue *must be set again at the conclusion of the loop.*}

This error of incorrect compound conditionals is so common that we highlight it with a programming precept:

Programming Precept

Be wary of using **and** or **or** in the conditions
for **while** and **repeat** loops.

---

multiple bugs Finally, let us note that program bugs tend to come in swarms; where there is one bug, there are likely several others nearby. Therefore, take your time in debugging. Don't swat one bug and then take all the time needed to exit the text editor, recompile your program, and run it to the point of difficulty. Instead,:

- Look carefully at the surrounding code.

- See if you have made the same mistake other places in the program.

- See if your correction has modified something else that will cause another error.

- Read the affected subprogram again, rechecking its logic to see how it works and if it is correct as changed.

In this way you can speed your debugging by exterminating whole colonies at once.

EXERCISES 2.3

E1. The following function calculates the *geometrical mean* of two numbers:

```
function Mean(x, y: real): real;
begin
    Mean := sqrt(x * y)
end;
```

What can go wrong with this function? How should we detect it?

E2. What can fail in the following function that calculates the tangent of a number? How can we detect it?

```
function tan(x: real): real;
begin
    tan := sin(x)/cos(x)
end;
```

E3. The following short program contains at least three errors, each of which is enough to put the program into an infinite loop. Erroneous input from the user could also cause an infinite loop. Debug the program, if possible, without entering it into a computer.

```
program InfiniteLoop(input, output);
{Pre:   None.
  Post: The user is asked for a number and the program prints out all the
        integers from that number down to 0.}
var sinking: integer;                    {number that is slowly reduced to 0}

procedure ReducebyOne(sinking: integer);
{Pre:   sinking contains an integer value.
  Post: The value of sinking is reduced by 1.}
begin
    sinking := sinking − 1
end;

begin                                    {main program InfiniteLoop}
    write('Please enter a number.');
    readln(sinking);
    while (sinking <> 0) do
        writeln('The next number is ', sinking, '.');   {Write out number and}
        ReducebyOne(sinking)                            {go on to the next.}
    writeln('Program has finished.')
end.                                     {main program InfiniteLoop}
```

2.4

PROGRAM TESTING

choosing test data

So far we have said nothing about the choice of data to be used to test programs and subprograms. This choice, of course, depends intimately on the project under development, so we can make only some general remarks. First we should note:

Programming Precept

The quality of test data is more important than its quantity.

Many sample runs that do the same calculations in the same cases provide no more effective a test than one run.

Programming Precept

Program testing can be used to show the presence of bugs,
but never their absence.

It is possible that other cases remain that have never been tested even after many sample runs. For any program of substantial complexity, it is impossible to perform exhaustive tests, yet the careful choice of test data can provide substantial confidence in the program. Everyone, for example, has great confidence that the typical computer can add two floating-point numbers correctly. This confidence, however, is certainly not based on testing the computer by having it add all possible floating-point numbers and checking the results. If a double-precision floating-point number takes 64 bits, then there are 2^{128} distinct pairs of numbers that could be added. This number is astronomically large: all computers manufactured to date have performed altogether but a tiny fraction of this number of additions. Our confidence that computers add correctly is based on tests of each component separately, that is, by checking that each of the 64 digits is added correctly, and that carrying from one place to another is done correctly.

testing methods

There are at least three general philosophies that are used in the choice of test data.

The Black-Box Method

Most users of a large program are not interested in the details of its functioning; they only wish to obtain answers. That is, they wish to treat the program as a black box; hence the name of this method. Similarly, test data should be chosen according to the specifications of the problem, without regard to the internal details of the program, to check that the program operates correctly. At a minimum, the test data should be selected in the following ways:

data selection

■ *Easy values.* The program should be debugged with data that are easy to check. More than one student who tried a program only for complicated data, and thought it worked properly, has been embarrassed when the instructor tried a trivial example.

■ *Typical, realistic values.* Always try a program on data chosen to represent how the program will be used. These data should be sufficiently simple so that the results can be checked by hand.

■ *Extreme values.* Many programs err at the limits of their range of applications. It is very easy for counters or array bounds to be off by one.

■ *Illegal values.* "Garbage in, garbage out" is an old saying in computer circles that should not be respected. When a good program has garbage coming in, then its output should at least be a sensible error message. It is preferable that the program should provide some indication of the likely errors in input and perform any calculations that remain possible after disregarding the erroneous input.

The Glass-Box Method

The second approach to choosing test data begins with the observation that a program can hardly be regarded as thoroughly tested if there are some parts of its code that, in fact, have never been executed. In the *glass-box* method of testing, the logical structure of the program is examined, and for each alternative that may occur, test data are devised that will lead to that alternative. Thus care

path testing

is taken to choose data to check each possibility in every **case** statement, each clause of every **if** statement, and the termination condition of each loop. If the program has several selection or iteration statements, then it will require different combinations of test data to check all the paths that are possible. Figure 2.1 shows a short program segment with its possible execution paths.

For a large program the glass-box approach is clearly not practical, but for a single small module, it is an excellent debugging and testing method. In a well-designed program, each module will involve few loops and alternatives. Hence only a few well-chosen test cases will suffice to test each module on its own.

modular testing

In glass-box testing, the advantages of modular program design become evident. Let us consider a typical example of a project involving 50 subprograms, each of which can involve 5 different cases or alternatives. If we were to test the whole program as one, we would need $5^{50} \approx 10^{35}$ test cases to be sure that each alternative was tested. This number is far greater than the total number of calculations done by all computers ever built. Each module, on the other hand, separately requires only 5 (easier) test cases, for a total of $5 \times 50 = 250$. Hence

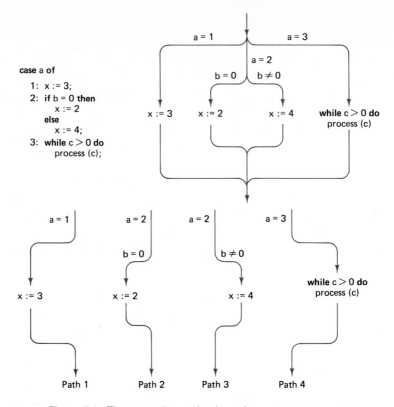

Figure 2.1. The execution paths through a program segment

a problem of impossible size has been reduced to one that, for a large program, is of quite modest size.

comparison   Before you conclude that glass-box testing is always the preferable method, we should comment that, in practice, black-box testing is usually more effective in uncovering errors. Perhaps one reason is that the most subtle programming errors often occur not within a subprogram, but in the interface between subprograms, in misunderstanding of the exact conditions and standards of information interchange between subprograms. It would therefore appear that a reasonable testing philosophy for a large project would be to apply glass-box methods to each small module as it is written and use black-box test data to test larger sections of the program when they are complete.

interface errors

The Ticking-Box Method

To conclude this section, let us mention one further philosophy of program testing, a philosophy that is, unfortunately, quite widely used. This might be called the *ticking-box* method. It consists of doing no testing at all after the project is fairly well debugged, but, instead, turning it over to the customer for trial and acceptance. The result, of course, is a time bomb.

EXERCISES 2.4

E1. Find suitable black-box test data for each of the following:

    a. A function that returns the largest of its three parameters, which are real numbers.

    b. A function that returns the square root of a real number.

    c. A function that returns the least common multiple of its two parameters, which must be positive integers. (The *least common multiple* is the smallest integer that is a multiple of both parameters. *Examples*: The least common multiple of 4 and 6 is 12, of 3 and 9 is 9, and of 5 and 7 is 35.)

    d. A procedure that sorts three integers, given as its parameters, into ascending order.

    e. A procedure that sorts an array A of integers indexed from 1 to a variable n into ascending order, where A and n are both parameters.

E2. Find suitable glass-box test data for the following statement:

> **if** a < b **then if** c > d **then** x := 1 **else if** c = d **then** x := 2
> **else** x := 3 **else if** a = b **then** x := 4 **else if** c = d **then** x := 5
> **else** x := 6;

PROJECTS 2.4

P1. Eliminate the parameter startday from the calendar program by using DayofWeek to find the first of every month. Which version is easier to understand? Which will run faster? Run both and see if the time difference is noticeable.

P2. Modify the calendar program to convert type weekday to be the subrange 0..6. Which version is easier?

P3. Write and test (with a driver program) a procedure FindDate that will ask the user for the day, month, and year constituting a date. Make sure your procedure accepts all valid dates and only valid dates.

P4. Traditional forms of output are not always the most useful on a computer screen. Rather than seeing a full calendar for a given year, a user might often wish to give only a specific date and then obtain the day of the week on which it falls. Modify the calendar project to produce such a program.

P5. Write a program DaysBetween that will take two dates and calculate the number of days between them.

P6. Write a program DaysAway that requests a date (usually the current date) and a number of days, and responds with the date (day, month, and year) that comes the given number of days after the given date.

P7. Modify the original calendar program to print the weeks in columns, not rows. See Figure 1.2.

P8. Modify the original calendar program to limit its output to five rows for each month by combining the last two weeks if necessary.

P9. Rewrite the project to calculate the Julian calendar instead of the Gregorian for dates preceding October 15, 1582.

P10. In the Julian calendar, the extra day in leap years was called *bisexto*. It did not have a number, and it was added between February 24 and 25, not after February 28. Modify the program for printing Julian calendars in the last project to take this fact into account.

POINTERS AND PITFALLS

1. Take special care to make sure your declarations and the names you choose for constants, types, and variables accurately reflect the logical structure of your data.

2. Remember that Pascal data types may not correspond exactly to your logical types. You will have to guard against the differences in your program.

3. For each parameter and variable, decide the scope of its validity (input, output, inout, local, or global) and treat it accordingly.

4. Declare variables as locally as possible, that is, in only the subprograms in which they are needed. Constants and types may be declared in the main program if you wish.

5. Use stubs and drivers to debug small parts of the program before they are all put together.

6. Be especially careful of input, and validate all the input before using it.

7. Use both black-box and glass-box testing to simplify debugging.

8. Use plenty of scaffolding to help localize errors.

9. Keep your programs well-formatted as you write them—it will make debugging much easier.

10. Keep your documentation consistent with your code, and when reading a program make sure that you debug the code and not just the comments.

11. Explain your program to somebody else: Doing so will help you understand it better yourself.

12. Remember the Programming Precepts!

REVIEW QUESTIONS

2.1   1. Give two reasons why constants should be named in the declarations rather than written as numbers into the program.

2. What is the difference between a *simple* and a *structured* type?

3. Why are programs that calculate with integers or real numbers sometimes not portable from one computer to another?

4. Could words considered in alphabetical order on one computer be considered not in order on another? Why?

5. Give one advantage and one drawback of enumerated types in Pascal.

6. Why should subrange checking not be used to detect input errors?

7. Name five kinds of parameters and variables.

8. Why should side effects of subprograms be avoided?

2.2   9. What is a program stub?

10. What is a *fail-safe* program?

11. Why should extensive input or output be done in a separate procedure?

12. What is the difference between stubs and drivers, and when should each be used?

2.3   13. What is a *structured walkthrough*?

14. What are *snapshots* in a program?

15. What is program *scaffolding*?

16. Name at least three practices helping to achieve *fail-safe programming*.

2.4   17. Name two methods for testing a program, and discuss when each should be used.

18. What kinds of data should be used in black-box testing?

3

DATA PACKAGING

In this chapter, we review the tools provided in Pascal for packaging data: arrays, records, sets, and files. We will not be primarily concerned with the details of Pascal syntax (grammar), but rather with ways to specify the logical structure of data and to translate these logical specifications into Pascal declarations and procedures.

The previous chapters have emphasized the importance of understanding the logical nature of the data used in a program, first specifying it in abstract terms *simple and* and then translating these specifications into Pascal declarations. So far, we have *structured types* needed only *simple* data types, where each variable holds a single piece of data. For most applications, however, we shall need *structured* types, in which each variable collects more than one piece of data. The structured types that Pascal provides are arrays, records, sets, and files. We shall study each one of these in turn, again emphasizing data abstraction as our main concern.

For structured types, it is even more important than for simple types that we first consider the data on the logical level and then decide how it will be han- *top-down design* dled via programming language declarations, since structured types can become very complicated: We can have arrays of records, records of arrays, records containing other records, arrays of files, and so on. It is impossible for anyone to comprehend all these complications at once, so we shall see that we must refine our data specifications at the same time as we refine the algorithms that process the data.

In this chapter, therefore, we will not be primarily concerned with the details of Pascal syntax (grammar), but rather with ways to specify the logical structure of data and to translate these logical specifications into Pascal declarations and *logical* *specifications* procedures. You should consult a textbook on Pascal with any questions you have on the rules for arrays, records, sets, and files, as well as to see examples of their application.

3.1

ARRAYS

Arrays provide the most familiar way to group many pieces of data together. *entries and* An **array** consists of **entries**, one entry corresponding to each possible different *indices* value of an **index**. The entries are all required to have the same type. Most programming languages restrict the values that are allowed for indices; in Pascal, the indices are required to come from an enumerated type or a subrange of the integers (for one-dimensional arrays) or are required to be made up of several such values (for multidimensional arrays). An individual entry of an array in Pascal is accessed by giving the name of the array followed by the value of the index in square brackets [...].

For these reasons, we use arrays when we have several pieces of data. The data are not necessarily related to each other in a logical sense, but the data in an array must all share the same type. Suppose, for example, that we are keeping *example:* the personnel records for a business. The records for one employee have no *personnel data* necessary logical connection with those of another—they may have different job categories, different earnings, different names and addresses—but all the records share the same basic kinds of information: a job category, a wage rate, a name, an address. Therefore we can process all the records by defining a new type personnelrecord that contains all the information on one employee and then using an array to hold the records for all the employees.

Note that we have not said how to combine the job category, wage rate, name, and address as part of the type personnelrecord. In accordance with the principles of top-down design, we postpone this task to the next section, where we shall study records in detail. For now, we shall look only at the outer level, where we have records for many different employees, and where we can process them by using an array.

3.1.1 One-Dimensional Arrays

The simplest kind of arrays consists of those with only one index, called *one-dimensional*. The index for a one-dimensional array can be an enumerated type, as in an array declared as

array [month] **of** integer

that holds the number of days in each month, or it can be a subrange, as in the type declaration

type vector = **array** [1 .. 3] **of** real.

The number of entries that exist in an array is fixed when the program is written, but the number of and exactly which entries are actually used need not be fixed. The number of months in the year is fixed at 12; for an array indexed by type month, we expect to use all the entries in the array, as we would while studying vectors in three-dimensional space. For the personnel records, if we knew that the business has exactly 23 employees and will never have any more or fewer, then we could set up the array of personnel records to have size 23 and use all its entries. This assumption, however, is entirely unrealistic. We should instead set up the array of personnel records to be as large as the business is likely to grow in the foreseeable future, use a counter to keep track of the current number of employees, and leave part of the array unused if the actual number of employees is less than the maximum.

vector   Hence there are really two quite different uses of an array. The first we can call that of a *vector*, where the size is fixed in advance and is known never to change. For a vector, all entries of the array are occupied and may be used in the computations. All arrays, of course, commonly require loops for their processing. Since the number of entries in a vector is known in advance, **for** loops are most commonly used for vectors:

Programming Precept

Use **for** loops for processing arrays used as fixed-size vectors.

---

workspace   The second use of an array is that of a *workspace*, where we do not know beforehand how many entries of the array will actually be used, but we set aside a maximum amount of space and then use counters to keep track of the amount of space actually used.

Programming Precept

In programming with arrays, distinguish carefully between vectors and workspaces.

In fact, this distinction between the two ways to use an array can be a cause of much difficulty for beginners. Soon after the introduction of loops and arrays, every elementary programming class attempts some programming exercise like the following:

Read an integer n, which will be at most 25, then read a list of n numbers, and print the list in reverse order.

This exercise will probably cause problems for some students. Most will realize that they need to use an array, but some will attempt to set up the array to have *n* entries and will be confused by the error message resulting from attempting to use a variable rather than a constant to declare the size of the array. Other students will say, "I could solve the problem if I knew that there were 25 numbers, but I don't see how to handle fewer." Or, "Tell me before I write the program how large *n* is, and then I can do it."

lists and arrays

The difficulties of these students come from thinking logically. In a beginning course, there is sometimes not enough distinction drawn between two quite different concepts. First is the concept of a *list* of *n* numbers, a list whose size is variable, that is, a list for which numbers can be inserted or deleted, so that, if $n = 3$, then the list contains only 3 numbers, and if $n = 19$, then it contains 19 numbers. Second is the programming feature called an *array*, which contains a constant number of positions, that is, whose size is fixed when the program is compiled. The two concepts are, of course, related in that a list of variable size

implementation

can be implemented in a computer as occupying part of a workspace array of fixed size, with some of the entries in the array remaining unused.

When we use an array as a workspace, we must always maintain a counter to keep track of the number of entries in use. Failure to maintain or use the counter properly is a common source of bugs in programs.

Programming Precept

When using an array as a workspace,
always be sure that the counters are maintained correctly.
Be wary of off-by-one errors.
Always check the extreme cases, a full workspace and an empty workspace.

3.1.2 *Multidimensional Arrays and Arrays of Arrays*

In many applications, the entries of an array depend on two or more indices, as we generally indicate by writing the indices separated by commas. If city is an enumerated or subrange type, then we can declare an array distance with type

$$\textbf{array}\,[\text{city, city}]\ \textbf{of}\ \text{integer}$$

two-dimensional array

that will hold the distances between all pairs of cities; the distance from city i to city j is then given by distance [i, j]. Or, if type

$$\text{monthday} = 1\,..\,31$$

enumerates the days of the month and hour = 0..23 the hours of the day, then array temperature of type

$$\textbf{array}\,[\text{monthday, hour}]\ \textbf{of}\ \text{real}$$

can be used to keep a table of hourly temperatures for a full month. The average temperature at noon throughout the month can then be calculated by adding the entries temperature (d, 12) for all the days d of the month and dividing by the number of days. This calculation adds the entries in each *column* of the array. Similarly, the average temperature for a single day d can be found by fixing d and adding over the hours, taking the sum of temperature [d, h] for h := 0 to 23. This calculation adds the temperatures in each *row* of the array.

rows and columns

In general, we say that the index in the first position refers to the **row** of a multidimensional array, and the second position refers to the **column**. If there are more than two dimensions, then there is no standard way to name the indices in the remaining positions.

Multidimensional arrays are the most appropriate way to store data whenever some calculations require fixing one index and having a loop that runs over another index, while other calculations do the reverse, looping over the index that was previously fixed. That is, multidimensional arrays should be used for tables of data for which it makes sense to look at the data arranged either by rows or by columns.

application of multidimensional arrays

For some applications, however, such a view does not make sense. Suppose, for example, that we wish to keep an array of exactly wordcount words, where wordcount is a constant, and suppose that each word is to be stored as a string of exactly maxword characters. We can then keep the words in a two-dimensional array with type

$$\text{wordlist} = \textbf{array}\,[1\,..\,\text{wordcount, }1\,..\,\text{maxword}]\ \textbf{of}\ \text{char.}$$

It makes good sense to think of looking at one row of the array (which holds one word) and processing all the entries (characters) in that row (a word). It does not make sense, however, to think of fixing one column and processing all the entries in that column. Why would we wish to do something with the third letter, say, in each word?

hierarchical
arrays
  For this example, it is much better to think of the table in a *hierarchical* way, as made up first of words, and then each word as made up of letters. That is, we should introduce *two* data types, first considering the structure of the list without worrying about the composition of a word:

wordlist = **array** [1 .. wordcount] **of** word.

Afterward, we define a word to be made up of characters by declaring the type

word = **array** [1 .. maxword] **of** char.

In this two-step process, we exhibit the logical structure of the word list much more clearly than is done by the two-dimensional array. See Figure 3.1.

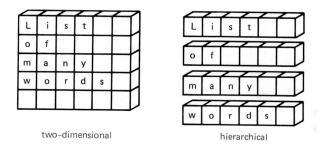

two-dimensional   hierarchical

Figure 3.1. Two-dimensional and hierarchical arrays

What we have done, of course, is to define wordlist as an array of arrays. We could, in fact, have equivalently declared it as

wordlist = **array** [1 .. wordcount] **of array** [1 .. maxword] **of** char.

Character j of word i is then referred to as wordlist [i] [j]. Note how much more difficult this is to understand than the declaration in two stages. Although a Pascal compiler has no trouble with declarations nested to great depth, such as arrays of arrays of arrays, or records containing arrays containing other records containing other arrays, the human mind quickly loses touch with such complications. Indeed, the human mind needs a *name* attached to each concept. Type declarations, therefore, should be written out one level at a time. Each level should then be named so that the programmer can easily keep track of the level of declarations.

Programming Precept

Name every level of a hierarchical data declaration,
and declare each level separately.

Pascal rules

Notice also, in our example, that we declared the type wordlist first and then declared the lower-level type word. Since type word is used in the declaration of wordlist, Pascal will, of course, require that the declarations be given in the reverse order. But that does not mean that we should have thought of them in the reverse order. Top-down design means that we should consider the overall structure first, postponing the more detailed declarations until later. In the final Pascal program, the lowest-level declarations must come first, but they should, in fact, be the last ones we actually determine.

Programming Precept

The top-down design of a program should proceed in an order
almost exactly the reverse of its final appearance in Pascal.

The same phenomenon occurs in the processing of hierarchical data structures. Even if we have an array of arrays, we should *never* write expressions like wordlist[i] [j]. Instead, we should use several levels of subprograms to process several levels of data structures. On the outer level, we refer to a particular word in the word list with expressions like wordlist[i], but, on this level, we think of a word as indivisible. Then, on a lower level, we write subprograms that process the individual letters of a word. But on this level we call the word by some other name, such as wd, and then refer to its characters with expressions like wd[j]. On this lower level, we do not need to consider or even remember that the word wd actually comes from an array of words.

Programming Precept

Match the levels of subprograms to the levels of type declarations.
Declare hierarchical data structures by different levels of type declarations,
and make the levels of subprograms match up to the levels of declarations.

EXERCISE 3.1

E1. Determine whether a two-dimensional array or a hierarchical array of arrays is better for each of the following kinds of data. Give your reason for each decision.

a. You have a portfolio of stocks and bonds, and you wish to keep track of the price of each stock or bond at the end of each week for the past year.

b. You are running for political office and wish to know the votes, by precinct, for each candidate in the last election.

c. You are conducting a survey of consumer preferences, and, for each of the consumers in your survey, you need to keep note of all the items purchased in a grocery store last week.

d. You are helping a school put its records on a computer, and you wish to store the attendance records (absences by various students on various days).

e. You are helping a dairy farmer keep track of milk production by day for each cow.

f. You are writing a program that will play card games, and, for each player, you need to keep track of a hand of cards.

g. You are writing a program that draws graphs, and you need to keep track of the values of various functions at different points.

∎ PROJECTS 3.1

P1. A *magic square* is a square array of integers such that the sum of every row, the sum of every column, and the sum of each of the two diagonals are all equal. Two magic squares are shown in Figure 3.2.[1]

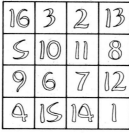

sum = 34   sum = 65

Figure 3.2. Two magic squares

a. Write a program that reads a square array of integers and determines whether or not it is a magic square.

b. Write a program that generates a magic square by the following method. This method works only when the size of the square is an odd number. Start by placing 1 in the middle of the top row. Write down successive

---

[1] The magic square on the left appears as shown here in the etching *Melancolia* by Albrecht Dürer. Note the inclusion of the date of the etching, 1514.

integers 2, 3, ... along a diagonal going upward and to the right. When you reach the top row (as you do immediately since 1 is in the top row), continue to the bottom row as though the bottom row were immediately above the top row. When you reach the rightmost column, continue to the leftmost column as though it were immediately to the right of the rightmost one. When you reach a position that is already occupied, instead drop straight down one position from the previous number to insert the new one. The 5×5 magic square constructed by this method is shown in Figure 3.2.

P2.   a. Write a program that reads in a table of distances between cities, so that the entry in position $[i, j]$ is the distance from city i to city j.
      b. Check that the distance from any city to itself is 0.
      c. Check that the table is *symmetric*, that is, the distance from city i to city j is the same as the distance from city j to city i.
      d. Check the *triangle rule*: The distance from city i to city j is never more than the distance from city i to a third city k plus the distance from city k to city j.

P3. Write a program that reads a text file and counts the number of times each letter appears in the text.

P4.   a. Write a program that reads a text file and makes a list of all the words in the text, where a word consists of a sequence of letters and is terminated by the first non-letter that appears.
      b. Write out the list of all the words.
      c. Remove all the duplicates from the list of words and print the resulting list of distinct words. One way to remove the duplicates is first to sort the words into alphabetical order.

3.2

RECORDS

3.2.1 Definition and Examples

In an array, all the entries have the same type. Often, however, we have several pieces of data which may have different types but are logically related to each other. A personnel record, for example, may consist of a job classification (perhaps an enumerated type), a pay rate (a number), a name (a string of characters), and an address (another string of characters). The **record** structure allows us to collect all of these pieces of data together as a single package, a record, that we can regard as a single package for the outer levels of a program and still subdivide into its pieces for processing on the inner levels.

The type declaration

record ... **end**

fields   in Pascal establishes a type consisting of several **fields** (also called **components**), each of which is itself of some (arbitrarily defined) type.

The personnel records, for example, may take the form

```
type
    personnelrecord = record
        classification: jobtype;
        payrate: money;
        name,
        address: stringtype
    end;
```

As a second example, let us consider the logical structure of a list. It really has two parts. First is a variable that gives the number of items in the list. Second is a workspace array that contains the items on the list. In most languages, the programmer must carry the counter variable and the array separately (and doing so is a frequent source of trouble for beginners). In our case, we may define a type called list with declarations such as the following:

declaration of list

```
const
    maxlist = 200;                          {maximum size of lists}
type
    list = record
        count: 0 .. maxlist;
        entry: array [1 .. maxlist] of entrytype
    end;                        {The type entrytype is defined elsewhere.}
```

field access

Individual parts of a Pascal record variable are referenced by giving first the name of the variable, then a period (.), then the name of the part as declared in the type statement for the record. Thus if L is a list, that is, a record variable of type list, then its counter is accessed as L.count. If P is a personnel record, then the corresponding job classification is P.classification, the wage rate is P.payrate, the name is P.name, and the address is P.address.

3.2.2 Hierarchical Records: Data Abstraction

Next let us suppose that we wish to set up a workspace array holding a list of all personnel records. We can do so simply by defining the array A to have type

```
array [1 .. maxemployee] of personnelrecord.
```

This gives us an example of records contained as entries within an array. But we can go much farther. The list of employees should not be regarded simply as a workspace array, but as a list in the sense previously declared, that is, as a record consisting of a count field and a workspace array called entry. Similarly, at the other end of the refinement, each personnel record contains a field called address which is a string of characters. A string of characters can itself be stored as a list, with separate counter and entry fields:

```
stringtype = record
      count: 0 .. maxstring;
      entry: array [1 .. maxstring] of char
end;
```

hierarchical records and arrays

Note that we now have an example of a record (list), with a field that is an array (entry) whose entries are records (personnelrecord), one of whose fields is another record (address), which in turn has a field that is another array, an array of characters. Such records and arrays are called *hierarchical*. By putting records within records, records in arrays, and arrays in records, we can build up exceedingly complicated data structures that precisely describe the relationships in the data processed by a program.

top-down design of data structures

Although compilers and computer systems have no trouble working with such complicated data structures, programmers working with records and arrays, however, should never think of them as having such a complicated structure. The human mind is simply not equipped to handle more than two or three levels of nesting without becoming confused. Instead, we should always use top-down design for our data structures as well as for our algorithms. When we process the large, outer records, we need not be concerned about the exact structure of each component within the record. When we write algorithms to manipulate the innermost components, we should treat them only in terms of their simple structure and not be concerned as to whether they may later be embedded in larger records or arrays. We can thus use records to accomplish *information hiding*, whereby we can design the upper levels both of algorithms and data structures without worrying about the details that will be specified later on lower levels of refinement.

3.2.3 The with *Statement*

To access the individual fields within a hierarchical record, we must work our way from the top level down, using a period (.) each time we take a field within a record, and brackets ([ ]) each time we take an entry of an array. To obtain, for example, character k in the address of employee i, we could write

employeelist.entry [i] .address.entry [k] .

Such notation may cause the computer no problem, but it is very hard for people to trace through and understand such a complicated expression. A good programmer should regard such notation as abominable. There are two ways to avoid such complication. One is to use nested procedures for processing hierarchical data structures, and the other, related, way is to use the special Pascal statement

with recordvariable **do begin** ... **end**.

field access

The block of statements **begin** ... **end** under control of the **with** statement is called the *range* of the **with** statement. In this range, the specified record variable has a special status, so that its various fields can be accessed by giving only their names, without having to repeat the name of the record variable each time.

Let us continue with our example of personnel records by seeing how their processing can be expedited by nested subprograms and **with** statements. On the outermost level we might wish a loop to run through all entries in the employee list. Such a loop takes the form

top level
```
with employeelist do   {We can now refer directly to the count and entries.}
   for i := 1 to count do                {This count is now the list counter.}
      Process (entry [i] );        {Use a subprogram to process one record.}
```

On the next level of refinement, we process a single personnel record, and, on this level, we no longer need be concerned that the record actually came from a list:

second level
```
procedure Process (var employee: personnelrecord);
begin
   with employee do
   begin        {We can now refer directly to the various fields in the record.}
      Reassess (classification);        {Use procedures to process the fields.}
      Raise (payrate);
      Edit (name);
      Edit (address)
   end
end;
```

Finally, we wish to edit the name or address with a procedure of the following form:

bottom level
```
procedure Edit (var s: stringtype);                {edits any string of characters}
begin
   with s do
   begin
   {Editing instructions now can access the individual characters in the array
      entry [  ]  and can use or change the variable count keeping track of the
      number of characters in the string.}
   end
end;
```

Programming Precept

Avoid more than one field reference (.) or array reference ([ ])
in accessing a variable:
Use nested subprograms and **with** statements instead.

There is considerable danger when the range of a **with** statement is large: It becomes easy to forget the record variable to which the fields refer. Keep procedures short if they include a **with** statement. Similarly, it is dangerous to have more than one **with** statement in any single subprogram, since it becomes very easy to confuse references to the fields of one record with references to the field of the other.

Programming Precept

Keep the range of each **with** statement short.
Avoid nested **with** statements in one procedure;
instead, use nested procedures with at most one **with** statement in each.

3.2.4 Variant Records

Depending on the particular information stored in a record, some of the fields may sometimes not be used. If the data are of one kind, then one field may be required, but if they are of another kind, a second field will be needed. Suppose,

example for example, that records represent geometrical figures. If the figure is a circle, then we wish a field giving the *radius* of the circle. If it is a rectangle, then we wish the *height* and the *width* of the rectangle and whether or not it is a *square*. If it is a triangle, we wish the three *sides* and whether it is *equilateral, isosceles,* or *scalene*. For any of the figures, we wish to have the *area* and the *circumference*. One way to set up the record type for all these geometrical figures would be to have separate fields for each of the desired attributes, but then, if the figure is a rectangle, the fields giving the radius, sides of a square, and kind of triangle would all be meaningless. Similarly, if the figure is a circle or a triangle, several of the fields would be undefined.

To avoid this difficulty, Pascal provides *variant records* in which certain fields are defined only when the information in the record is of a particular kind.

fixed and variant Variant records have two parts: in the *fixed* part, all the fields remain the same
parts no matter what kind of information is in the record, but in the *variant* part, the fields differ according to the kind of information. What kind of information is in the record (and therefore which variant is used) depends on the value of a special

tag field field called the *tag field*. The type of the tag field can be any ordinal type, and the variant part, introduced by the word **case**, is superficially similar to a **case** statement with the tag field in place of the case selector. The different variants are selected by constants of the ordinal type, and the fields in each variant are enclosed in parentheses (...).

All this will be clarified by returning to our geometrical example. The ordinal type specifying the kind of information in the record is the enumerated type

type figuretype = (circle, rectangle, triangle) ;

and the record can then be declared as follows:

geometry example

```
type
  figure = record
             area,                              {This is the fixed part of the record.}
             circumference: real;
           case shape: figuretype of            {This is the tag field.}
             circle:                                                {first variant}
               (radius: real);
             rectangle:                                            {second variant}
               (height,
                 width: real;
                 square: Boolean);
             triangle:                                              {third variant}
               (side1,
                 side2,
                 side3: real;
                 kind: (equilateral, isosceles, scalene))
           end;                                      {end of record declaration}
```

advantages of variant records

The first advantage of variant records is that they clarify the logic of the program by showing exactly what information is required in each case. A second advantage is that they allow the system to save space when the program is compiled. Since the fields in only one of the variants are usable for a particular record, the fields in different variants can be assigned to the same space by the compiler. Hence the total amount of space that needs to be set aside for the record is just the amount needed if the largest variant is the one that occurs. This situation is illustrated in Figure 3.3 for the example of records describing geometrical shapes.

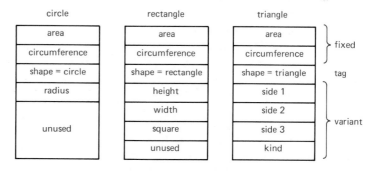

Figure 3.3. Storage of variant records

Here are some rules and guidelines concerning the use of variant records in Pascal:

rules and guidelines for records

1. The fixed part of the record must come first, then the tag field and the variant part, if any.

2. A record may contain only one variant part, although any fields within a record may be other records with their own variant parts.

3. All the field identifiers used in a record must be different, even when they appear in different variants.

4. The tag field identifier may be omitted, but it is not recommended to omit it, and the tag *type* must be included if there is a variant part.

5. The variants are selected by constants from the tag type. Several constants, separated by commas, can specify the same variant.

6. The list of fields in a variant is enclosed in parentheses (...). A field list for a variant can be empty; this is denoted by ( ).

7. The variant to be used in a particular record is determined at run time by assigning a value to the tag field and the fields of the corresponding variant. The variant can be changed at any time by changing the tag field and the variant fields. If the variant is changed, the variant fields belonging to the previous variant are lost.

EXERCISES 3.2

E1. Define record types (no variant records needed) for each of the following applications:

    a. A *complex number* consisting of a *real* part and an *imaginary* part, both of which are real numbers.

    b. A *string* of characters consisting of an integer *counter* together with an array of characters.

    c. An *address* consisting of a *street*, a *city*, and a *state* or country, each of which is a string (defined in part (b)).

    d. The type personaldata consisting of a *name*, which is a string (defined in part (b)), an *address* (defined in part (c)), a *sex* (one of *male* or *female*), a marital status (one of *single*, *married*, *widowed*, or *divorced*), and a number of *dependants* between 0 and 20.

E2. Write procedures that will copy one list to another list (as the record type defined in the text). Use the following methods:

    a. Copy the entire records.

    b. Use a loop to copy only the entries.

    c. Which version is easier to write? Which version will usually run faster, and why?

E3. Define a record type using variant records for the following simplified kind of bank account. The record includes a *name*, which is a string (as defined in Exercise E1(b)), an *address* (as defined in E1(c)), an integer account *number*, the date the account was *opened* (a string), and an account *balance* (real number). There are three kinds of accounts: *savings*, *checking*, and *term*. For a savings account, there is a *deposit* list, a *withdrawal* list, and a current interest *credit* (a real number). For a checking account, there is a *transaction* list (including deposits, credits, cheques, and debits as positive or negative numbers) and a current *service charge* (a real number). All these lists are set up similarly to the lists in the text, but their entries are real numbers. For a term account, there is an *initial* balance (real number), an interest *rate* (real number), an *accumulated* interest amount (real number), and a *maturity* date (string).

E4. Develop a package of declarations for keeping track of student records for a registrar. For each student, there is a name, an address, a date of entry, a date of leaving (that will not be present for currently enrolled students), name of the school from which the student came, an indication of the student's current status (full time, part time, withdrawn, graduated), the degree being sought (if any), and a list of courses. For each course, the transcript gives the department, number, and name, the grade or the status of the course, such as audited or withdrawn. The transcript also contains the total number of courses passed and the grade-point average for the student.

■ PROJECTS 3.2

P1. **a.** Write a program that does simple arithmetic on fractions (addition, subtraction, multiplication, and division, as well as reading and writing), where the fractions are stored as records consisting of a numerator and a denominator, both integers.

   b. Include a procedure that reduces the fractions to lowest terms, by finding any factors that divide (evenly) into both the numerator and denominator and dividing them out.

P2. A *complex number* has the form $z = a + bi$, where a and b are real numbers and $i^2 = -1$. The number real number a is called the *real part* of z, and real number b is called the *imaginary part* of z. Represent a complex number as a record consisting of its real and imaginary parts (both of which are real numbers), and write a program that reads, writes, adds, subtracts, multiplies, and divides complex numbers. You will first need to find formulas for the real and imaginary parts of the sum, difference, product, and quotient of two complex numbers. The most difficult one of these operations is the quotient, for which the answer is

$$\frac{a + bi}{c + di} = \left(\frac{ac + bd}{c^2 + d^2} \right) + \left(\frac{bc - ad}{c^2 + d^2} \right) i.$$

Verify this equation by multiplying both sides by $c + di$.

3.3

SETS

Sets form one of the basic building blocks of mathematics, one of the tools most commonly used to present mathematical information. Sets also form one of the basic tools for describing the logical structure of data and can often be used to improve the clarity and precision of programs.

Sets in Mathematics

In mathematics, a *set* is made up of objects called its ***elements*** or ***members***, and there are several important rules that these objects satisfy:

requirements

- All the objects come from some ***universe***.

- For each object in the universe, there are only two possibilities: It is either in the set or not. The set says nothing more about the objects.

- No object appears in the set more than once; a set has no duplicate objects.

- The objects in a set have no particular order; if the objects are put into the set in a different order, it does not matter or change the set.

set-builder notation

Sets with only a few members are often given by the ***set-builder*** notation of listing the elements inside of curly braces. An example of this mathematical notation is the set of integers

$$\{1, 2, 3, 4\}.$$

Since order or repetitions make no difference, this same set could be denoted in any of the following ways:

$$\{4, 1, 3, 2\} \quad \text{or} \quad \{2, 3, 4, 3, 1\} \quad \text{or} \quad \{1, 1, 1, 3, 2, 4, 4\}.$$

Sets as Abstract Data Types

For describing the logical structure of data, we can use sets in a similar way, considering sets as new abstract data types. The universe becomes all the possible values of some data type. Hence we can speak of a set of integers, or a set of reals, or a set of months, or a set of personnel records. This universe is called

base type for sets

the ***base type*** for the set. The conditions for mathematical sets translate directly into conditions for sets as abstract data types. Let us formulate these conditions as questions, all of which must be answered *no* if the abstract data type is to be a set.

- Do any of the objects have different types?

- Is any more information needed about the objects other than whether or not the objects are in the collection?

- Can the same object appear more than once in the collection?

- Does the order in which the objects appear in the collection make any difference?

applications

Sets appear in many different applications. With personnel records, we might speak of the set of all employees who belong to the group life insurance plan or the set of employees who have worked at least five years. A doctor might be interested in the set of diseases that might induce certain given symptoms or in the set of medicines useful for treating a disease. A merchant might think of the set of products temporarily out of stock and back ordered. A magazine might use the set of all its subscribers.

In some of these examples, however, other data structures (particularly *lists*) may prove more appropriate than sets. Perhaps different employees subscribe to different amounts of group life insurance, and so the additional data of the insurance amount should be kept. The merchant might prefer a list of back-ordered merchandise with the date of expected delivery with each item. The magazine might find that it has some subscribers who take multiple subscriptions. A teacher may be interested in the *set* of all students in a class, but more likely in a *list* of the students sorted alphabetically.

Implementation of Sets

Although sets appear frequently in the logical specification of data as abstract types, most computer languages do not provide for their implementation directly. Pascal is exceptional in providing the built-in type constructor **set**, but Pascal sets are very limited compared to the use of sets as abstract data types. First of all, the base type (universe) used for Pascal sets must be an ordinal type that is an enumerated type or a subrange. Second, the base type must have only a limited number of possible values, and what the limit is depends on the computer. Hence we can speak of a set of month, a set of weekday, a set of digits 0..9, but not a set

set of char

of integer, a set of real, or a set of personnelrecord. This book occasionally uses **set of** char, a declaration that will be accepted by most, but not all compilers, since the type char may take on as many as 256 different values, and some compilers limit the base types for sets to as few as 16 different values.

Whether or not a set can be implemented directly in our computer language should not stop us from using sets on the logical level to help describe our data, and then, if necessary, we can use other methods in the implementation phase to represent the abstract sets concretely. Two such methods that we shall study later in this book are to use *lists* or *tables* to represent abstract sets.

> **Programming Precept**
>
> Use sets whenever appropriate as abstract data types,
> but rely on other structures for their implementation.

Operations on Sets in Pascal

Some of the standard operations on sets in mathematics are to build sets by the *set builder* notation of putting a list of elements between braces, such as the set of six integers $\{1, 2, 3, 5, 8, 13\}$, to take set unions $\cup$, set intersections $\cap$, set difference $-$ or $\backslash$, and the empty set $\emptyset$. There are also relational operators that return a Boolean (true/false) result. Among these are set equality $=$, set inequality $\neq$, set containment $\subseteq$, set contains $\supseteq$, and set membership $\in$.

All of these operations can also be done on Pascal sets, but because the various symbols are not available on computer keyboards, alternative symbols are used. A list of elements to be in a set is enclosed in square brackets instead of curly braces, as in the sets

Fibonacci := [1, 2, 3, 5, 8, 13]   and   summer := [Jun, Jul, Aug].

Subranges can be used to build sets, as in

letters := ['a' .. 'z']   and   allyear := [Jan .. Dec].

Union of Pascal sets is denoted by + , intersection by *, set difference by − , and the empty set by []. Set equality is denoted by = , inequality by <> , containment by <= , contains by >= , and membership by **in**. These operations are summarized in the following table.

Mathematics	Pascal	Mathematics	Pascal
{ }	[ ]	=	=
∅	[]	≠	<>
∪	+	⊆	<=
∩	*	⊇	>=
− or \	−	∈	**in**

Consider the following illustrations of some of these operations.

```
empty := [];
schoolyear := allyear − summer;
vacation := summer + [Dec];
longdays := [May .. Jul];
longandhot := longdays * summer;
```

EXERCISES 3.3

E1. Consider the following three Pascal sets:

A = [1, 3, 5, 7, 9, 11]; B = [0, 2, 4, 6, 8, 10]; C = [1 .. 10].

Determine the numbers that are in each of the following set expressions.

a. A + B.
b. A * B.
c. A * C.
d. B + C.
e. A + (B * C).
f. A * (B + C).

g. C − A.
h. A − C.
i. B + [1 .. 5].
j. B − [1 .. 5].
k. B * [1 .. 5].
l. C * [].

m. C + [].
n. C − [].
o. [] − C.
p. (A + B) − C.
q. A + (B − C).
r. ((A * A) + A) − A.

E2. For each of the following, give a type declaration for an appropriate type of Pascal set, and give assignment statements to put the indicated elements in the given sets.

a. Within the set of integers between 0 and 10, inclusive, assign even to be the set of even integers, odd to be the set of odd integers, and prime to consist of 2, 3, 5, and 7.

b. Within the set of lowercase letters, assign vowel to be the set of vowels (*a, e, i, o, u*) and consonant to be the set of remaining letters.

c. Within the set of months of the year (the enumerated type introduced in Section 2.1.2), assign summer to contain June through August, spring to contain March through May, autumn to contain September through November, and winter to contain December through February.

E3. For this exercise, suppose that all sets have type

$$settype = \textbf{set of } 0 \,..\, maxset.$$

Write Pascal procedures for each of the following tasks.

a. Write the numbers in a set.
b. Read integers and put them in a set.
c. Calculate the complement of a set (within the universe $0 \,..\, maxset$).

3.4

FILES

3.4.1 Files and Arrays

Files are much like one-dimensional arrays. Both are arranged sequentially, with a first component (or entry), a second component, and so on. In both, all the entries or components have the same type, a type that can be simple or a large structured type made up of many smaller parts. On an abstract level, the similarities between files and one-dimensional arrays outweigh the differences, but, on a programming level, there are several important differences that make it important for us to choose carefully which to use.

external data structure

■ Most files are permanent, although Pascal does permit temporary files that are created during program execution and disappear when the program terminates. Usually, however, input files exist before the program starts, and both input and output files remain after the program terminates to keep the results for future use by other programs or by people. Hence files provide the only *external* data type that outlives the program's execution; all other data types are *internal*.

dynamic size

■ Files are *dynamic*; arrays are *static*. The size of an array is fixed when the program is written and cannot be changed while the program is running.

There is no predetermined limit to the size of a file; the program may put as much information as desired into a file. Some languages (not Pascal), by the way, allow dynamic arrays whose size can change while the program is running. In such languages this distinction between arrays and files is blurred.

■ Standard Pascal files allow only sequential access; arrays allow direct access to all their entries. Standard Pascal files should be regarded as a sequence of entries to be read or written one at a time. There is no way to skip entries except by going past the intermediate ones one at a time. There is no way to move backward through a file except by starting over again at the beginning. Again, many systems blur this distinction between arrays and files by providing ***direct-access files*** which allow the program to refer directly to any entry in the file. Most languages designed for data processing, and even many Pascal compilers, provide direct-access files, but there is no standard way of doing so, so we cannot say more here.

sequential access

direct access

There are two ways to process Pascal files. One is to use the standard procedures read and write, while the other is to use file windows and the procedures get and put. There are, moreover, special features for text files such as input and output and special problems for interactive input. We shall consider each of these topics in turn.

3.4.2 Pascal Processing with read and write

All files in Pascal are treated as generalizations of a magnetic tape. This means that file operations always start at the beginning of the file and go only one way. It also means that it is not allowed to mix input and output operations for the same file without starting over again at the beginning. Since the amount of space on a tape needed for a write operation could not be determined in advance, it might erase tape that had not yet been read. But the analogy with magnetic tapes does make it easy to picture one way of doing Pascal file operations. Let us think of the file as consisting of a sequence of components that we can regard like squares on the tape. Each component holds one value of the type for which the file is declared. If the file is declared as "**file of** integer" then each component holds one integer; if it is declared as "**file of** char" then each component holds only one character; if it is declared as "**file of** personnelrecord" then each component holds an entire personnel record, which might be quite a large record containing other records and arrays. See Figure 3.4.

magnetic tape

Like all variables, files must be declared in the **var** declaration section of the program. External (permanent) files, however, require more attention, since they must have names that will be known to the system, not just the Pascal program. The standard Pascal way to indicate that a file is external is to give its name as a parameter in the **program** header line. This method, however, is not entirely satisfactory, since often the same program is to be run on different external files, and the name of the file may change from one run to the next. Hence different Pascal systems use different, nonstandard methods to connect an internal name

declarations

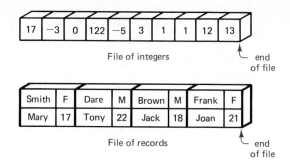

Figure 3.4. Files of integers and records

for a file with an external name. Some modify the reset and rewrite procedures; some use nonstandard system procedures called, for example, assign or open.

input files
To read a file F, the first step is to position it at its beginning, which we do with the statement reset(F). Then we can read the entries from the file one at a time with a statement such as read(F, x), where x is a variable of the same type as the components of the file. After we have read the last entry of the file, the function eof(F) becomes true, and it is then an error to continue trying to read from the file. Hence this simple form of file input is illustrated by the following program extracts:

```
var
   F: file of sometype;    {Declare the file and give the type of its entries.}
   x: sometype;                   {Declare a variable of the file's base type.}
begin
   reset(F);
   while not eof(F) do
   begin
      read(F, x);
      Process(x)
   end
end
```

output files
Output to a file is even easier, since there is no bound on the number of components we can write to the file, and we therefore are not concerned about the end of the file. First we use the procedure rewrite(F) to position the file at its beginning and prepare to write into it; then we use the procedure write(F, x) whenever we wish to write the value of a variable x (of the proper type) to F.

guidelines
Here are some guidelines concerning the general use of files:

1. The components of a file can be of any type, except that they cannot be files or contain files. Some systems put further restrictions on files; arrays of files, for example, are often not allowed.

2. A file is either in input condition (use procedures reset and read) or in output condition (use procedures rewrite and write), but never both at once.

3. A file can be processed by reset or rewrite as often as desired, but (except for the standard input and output) it must be reset or rewritten before being used the first time.

4. A file can first be written and later read by invoking reset before starting to read.

5. A file can also be read and then rewritten with new information by first invoking rewrite. For an external input file, however, doing so is a poor practice because rewrite destroys the previous contents of the file. A program failure or a power failure after the rewrite but before the new information is completely written to the file may therefore cause irrecoverable loss of data. It is better to write the output to a new file and regard the old file as backup.

6. A file of arbitrary type is a sequence of components of that type. It is *not* divided into lines or pages. The procedures readln, writeln, page, and the function eoln are *not* available for arbitrary files. (They are for text files only.)

7. The information in files of arbitrary type is usually written in the same form that the machine uses to keep it internally. A file of integers may be written as binary integers, completely unreadable to a person. Hence files of arbitrary type should be written by programs to be read by other programs. The type declarations for the components *must* be identical in both the writing program and the reading program. For files that are to be read by people, always use type text.

8. As variables, files can appear as **var** parameters in subprogram calls, but not as value parameters. Files cannot be used in assignments or any other kind of statements.

3.4.3 File Windows

Next let us take a closer look at the process of reading or writing a component in a file, and we begin by reconsidering the analogy with magnetic tapes. A tape drive has a read/write head that, at any moment, is located above some position on the tape, and that is the position that can be read or written at the moment. But because of the mechanical and electrical problems of communication between the computer and the tape drive, there must be a location in the computer memory, *buffers* called a ***buffer***, where the information to be read or written is stored. When the tape is read, the contents of its component under the head are copied to the buffer. When the tape is written, the contents of the buffer are copied to the component of the tape under the head.

Pascal files operate in exactly this way. The buffer is called the ***window*** *file window* into the file, and the window for file F is denoted F↑ in Pascal. The upward arrow (↑) may be thought of as pointing to a particular location in the file. The symbol ↑ prints as ∧ or as ^ on many terminals. In some character sets it is not available, in which case the symbol @ is used instead. Note that F↑ is *not* a position in the file; it is a *variable* in the computer memory that has the same type as a component of the file and is used to copy information to or from the file. This situation is illustrated in Figure 3.5.

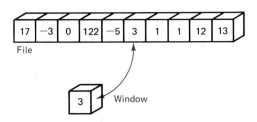

Figure 3.5. The window into a file

starting file input

Let us look at the steps that occur while reading a file. When the file is reset, its window is positioned to the first entry of the file, and the component at that position is copied into the window variable. Hence, to read the first entry of file F into variable x, we could write x := F↑ instead of read(F, x). We could also use the variable F↑ in many other ways; it could appear in arithmetic expressions, and we can assign a new value to it. Changing the value of F↑ changes only the copy in the computer memory; it has no effect at all on the file F.

advancing in a file

Now suppose that we wish to read the next component of F. To do so, we must advance the window to the next position in the file. This task is done by the standard procedure get(F). More specifically, get(F) advances one component through the file and copies the value of this next component into the file window F↑. Hence the steps needed to read values from F into a variable x are, first, the assignment x := F↑ and, second, a call get(F) to advance to the next position in the file. In fact, standard Pascal *defines* the meaning of read(F, x) to be precisely the pair of statements x := F↑; get(F). The steps required to read a short file are shown in Figure 3.6.

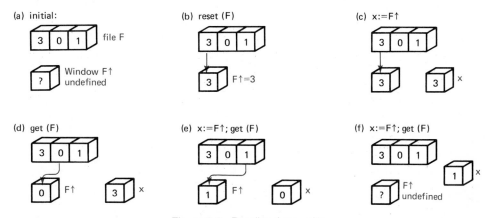

Figure 3.6. Reading from a file

end of file

Finally, we get to the end of the file. Just before the end, the file window will hold a copy of the last component of the file. A subsequent get reveals that the end of the file has been reached, so the function eof(F) becomes true, and there is no value to copy into the file window, so the value in the file window becomes undefined. At this point no error has occurred. It is an error, however, to attempt another get when the previous get reached the end of file, and it is also an error to attempt to use the file window when the end of file has been reached.

file output The process of writing to a file is quite similar in form. When the file is rewritten, its window is positioned to the beginning and the value in the window variable is undefined. To write the value of x to the file F we therefore first assign F↑ := x. Then we use the standard procedure put(F), which copies F↑ into the file and advances the window one position. The value in F↑ then again becomes undefined. While writing a file, the window position always remains just beyond the information previously written, and eof(F) always remains true. In standard Pascal, the statement write(F, x) is defined to mean F↑ := x; put(F). The steps of writing a file are illustrated in Figure 3.7.

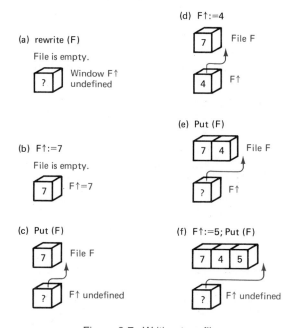

Figure 3.7. Writing to a file

If you wish, you may do all of your input and output to arbitrary files by using file windows and the procedures get and put (in fact, some early Pascal compilers required doing so by allowing read and write only for text files). Generally speaking, however, it is much more convenient to use read and write.

lookahead Why, then, should we refer to file windows at all? For input, file windows have one important property: lookahead. While reading a file F, the value in F↑ is *not* the value that has just been returned by read(F, x); it is instead the value that *will be* returned by the *next* read. In some applications, it is very convenient to look ahead in this way. The processing of one item may depend on the item that follows it in the file, and the file window provides a way of looking at that item before it is time to read and process it officially.[2]

3.4.4 Text Files

Text files are intended as the communication medium between the program and its user. They are therefore arranged so that they can be read by people and so that a file created by a person (using a text editor, say) can be read by the program. For this reason, text files provide several additional features and several additional complications not found in processing other files.

Files of type text are made up of characters; in fact, the first version of Pascal defined

text = file of char.

Hence characters may be used for input and output with text files, and, if a file window is used, it will hold one character at a time.

Standard Files

input *and* output

The first important difference between text files and others is that there are two predefined standard files of type text, the files input and output. In all the standard procedures and functions that use files, the name of the file can be omitted from the parameters and it will be assumed to be the appropriate one of input and output. When the program begins there is an implicit call to reset(input) and rewrite(output), so these statements need not be included in the program. The only time when it is appropriate to reset the file input is when the end-of-file condition has been used to terminate the input from the terminal, and the program later needs additional input from the terminal. In this case, a call to reset(input) will clear the end-of-file condition from the standard input, allowing additional reading to take place.

Input and Output

type coercion

The next important difference between files of type text and others is that, with text files, we can read or write not only characters, but also integers and real numbers. We can, moreover, also write out Boolean values and strings, which are either strings of characters enclosed in single quotes ' ... ' or packed arrays of characters. Yet another extension to the write procedure is to allow the programmer to specify the number of positions to be occupied by each output value by using a colon (:) after the quantity being written and then specifying the number of positions to be used. For quantities of type real, two colons may be used, specifying the total number of positions and the number after the decimal point.

---

[2] Turbo Pascal does not provide file windows or the get and put procedures. The lookahead features are therefore not available in Turbo Pascal.

The ability of processing data of one type as if they had another type, as the procedures read and write do, is called *coercion* of the data types.

reading characters

Since the procedure read can process either characters or numbers, we should be careful to understand how it works. For a character, it is quite simple: If ch has type char, then read(ch) takes the next character from the input and places it in ch. The character could be a letter, a digit, a blank, or any other symbol. Note that a character digit is not at all the same as an integer.

When the variable to be processed by read on a text file F is of type integer or real, the procedure has the following effect:

Skip to the next nonblank character of F; that is, do:

while F↑ = ' ' **do** get(F);

reading numbers

if this nonblank character is not one of '+', '−', '0', . . . , '9' **then** an error occurs

else construct a string of characters beginning with this first nonblank character and continuing as long as the characters can legitimately appear in the number; the legitimate characters are digits and, for real numbers, one decimal point '.' and the letter 'E' or 'e';

Convert this string to an integer or real as required and assign it to the parameter;

Advance the file window F↑ to the first character that is not part of the number.

If, for example, the next four characters of input are ' x17' (beginning with a blank, but not including the quotes), then an attempt to read an integer first skips the blank, then encounters the x, and an error occurs because x cannot appear within a number. If, on the other hand, the next characters are ' 17x', then no error occurs, the number 17 is returned, and the file window is positioned over the character x.[3] Hence a subsequent attempt to read an integer will produce an error, but if the next read specifies a character, then it will return the x without error. See Figure 3.8.

Lines

The final important difference between text files and others is the concept of *lines* in files of type text. The output can be arranged in lines by use of the writeln procedure. Input can be read in lines by use of the readln procedure, and the end of lines can be detected by the eoln function.

pages

There is also a standard procedure page for output files of type text. On a printer, it should start a new page. On a video terminal, its effect (if any) depends on the system and the terminal; often it clears the screen.

---

[3] Turbo Pascal uses different rules, with which ' 17x' will produce an error when an integer is read.

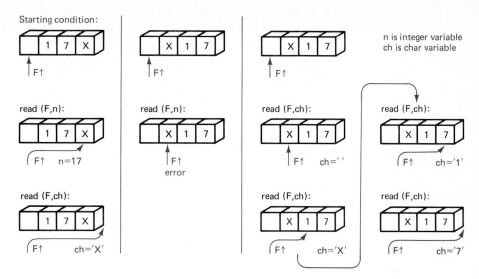

Figure 3.8. Reading integers and characters

The presence of lines can complicate the input procedures. Consider the following program segment:

```
while not eof do
begin
    read(i);                    {i has been declared as an integer.}
    Process(i)          {This procedure does not do any input or output.}
end;
```

This code is guaranteed to misbehave, no matter what the input. Here is the reason. After the last integer has been read, the input is not at the end of file, because it is at the end of the last line instead. Hence the loop attempts to iterate once more, the read statement encounters the end of file, and an error occurs.

ends of lines   To understand the exact effect of ends of lines on input, it is helpful to think of the text file as containing one special character at each point where an end of line occurs, and another special character at the end of the file. This may or may not reflect what actually happens. On many systems, a carriage-return character is placed at the end of each line; on others, a line-feed character is used; on some, both carriage return and line feed occur at the end of each line; on some systems, there is no special character at the end of lines, each line being stored as an integer length followed by the characters. With standard Pascal, it does not matter which of these actually occurs, since the end of a line is detected by the function eoln becoming true. When eoln is true, moreover, the file window will contain a blank. Hence, for purposes of reading data, ends of lines act very much like blanks. Finally, standard Pascal places an end of line immediately before the end of the file. This situation is pictured in the short text file shown in Figure 3.9.

Figure 3.9. A text file divided into lines

reading characters   A series of reads into a character variable would first return the character '3', then a series of five blanks corresponding to both blanks and ends of lines in the file, then the character '1', another blank, the character '7', then the character '2', then a blank, the character '8', a blank, and then the end of file appears, and an error occurs if an attempt is made to read further.

reading integers   Now suppose the same file is read, but each read is to an integer variable. The first one will return the value 3, and the file window will be left over the first end of line. The next read considers ends of lines as blanks and will skip over the next five characters of the file and return the integer 1, leaving the file window over the following blank. The next read skips this blank and returns the integer 72, leaving the file at the end of line following. The next read returns the integer 8 and leaves the file at the final end of line. At this point, eof is not true, but a subsequent read would encounter the end of file and cause an error.

readln   Pascal also provides the procedure readln, which functions exactly like read except that, after the variables specified are read, the procedure skips to the next end of line that appears and then moves past the end of the line to the next character. Procedure readln (unlike read) can also be called with no parameters, in which case it simply skips past the next end of line.

reading lines   If the file shown in Figure 3.9 is processed by a series of readln(ch) statements, where ch is a character variable, then the first character returned is '3' and the window is positioned on the blank after the end of the first line. The next character returned is that blank, and the window is moved after the second end of line, so it is now above the (immediately following) third end of line. Since the window contains a blank at the end of a line, the next character returned is also blank. The following readln(ch) again returns a blank, and skips past '1 72' and the end of line. The next readln returns the character '8' and eof becomes true.

If, finally, this file is processed by a series of statements readln(i), where i is an integer variable, then the first call returns the integer 3. The second call continues to skip over blanks and ends of lines until it reaches the integer 1, which it returns, and then it skips to the beginning of the next line (losing the integer 72). The third call returns the value 8 and eof becomes true.

correcting the code   Let us conclude this section by returning to the misbehaving segment of code at its beginning. There are two ways to resolve the problem. The simple way is to replace the read statement by readln and require the user to enter only one integer per line. This method will lose numbers if the user enters more than one per line, and, more seriously, it will cause an error if the end of file mark is not entered immediately after the line containing the last integer; that is, it will misbehave if the user enters an extra line before the end of file or some blanks before the end of file.

skip blanks

The better method to resolve the problem of an undetected end of file is to introduce a short procedure that will skip over blanks and ends of lines in the file. This procedure should then be called immediately before the end of file is checked. It is tempting to write the procedure as consisting simply of the statement "**while** F↑ = ' ' **do** get(F)" in order to move the window to the first nonblank character. This version will fail to detect the end of the file. Adding "**and not** eof(F)" to the **while** condition will not help, since Pascal may attempt to evaluate the undefined F↑ even when eof(F) is true. Instead, we need to introduce a Boolean variable, and we then obtain the following version. This procedure should be considered as a basic utility to be copied into application programs whenever it is needed.

utility procedure

```
procedure SkipBlanks(var F: text);
   {Pre:   The file F has been reset at some time.
    Post:  The current position in the file F has been advanced past any blanks
           and is now the next nonblank character if there is one, or is at the
           end of the file otherwise.}
   var
      finished: Boolean;                      {Are we finished skipping blanks?}
   begin                                              {procedure SkipBlanks}
      finished := false;
      repeat
         if eof(F) then
            finished := true                          {at the end of the file}
         else if F↑ <> ' ' then
            finished := true                          {at a nonblank character}
         else
            get(F)                                    {skip a blank}
      until finished
   end;                                               {procedure SkipBlanks}
```

Interactive Input

the problem

Recall that, when a program begins execution, the call reset(input) is implicitly made, and reset obtains the first piece of input to put in the file window input↑. Hence, when the Pascal language was first devised, it was required that the system would immediately (before executing any statements in the program) obtain the first datum from the input file and place the datum in the file window. In the old days of batch processing, with the input on punched cards or magnetic tape, this caused no problem. But when Pascal was run on interactive terminals, it meant that it was impossible to write a prompting message to an interactive terminal before the program requested the first input from the terminal. Since this situation is clearly unacceptable, various solutions to this problem have been implemented in different systems, and there is, unfortunately, no universal method to accomplish interactive input in Pascal.

lazy input

There is one convention that is more common among compilers than any other and has now been adopted as the standard method. It will work properly on many systems, but by no means on all. This convention is called *lazy input*. The reference manuals for your Pascal system should discuss input-output conventions, and from these manuals you can determine what changes, if any, will be required for your computer.

sample input procedure

With lazy input, the system does not try to fill its file window when it is reset, but waits until it is necessary. The reset operation prepares the file (actually, for our purposes, the input terminal) for input, but does not actually look in the file (or at the terminal's keyboard). Only when one of the other file operations (get, read, eof, or eoln) appears does the system actually look in the file (or at the keyboard) the first time. Hence there is no difficulty in writing a prompt (or doing other instructions) before the first read from the terminal. When we check for the end of file, however, using the function eof forces the system to fill its file window. Hence we must write a prompt *before* checking eof. Reading input will therefore take the following general form.

```
write ('First prompt');
while not eof do
begin
    read (data);
    Process (data);
    write ('Continuing prompt')
end;
```

■ PROJECTS 3.4

P1. a. Write a Pascal program that reads integers from the terminal and stores them in a file of integers (not a text file). Use the end-of-file condition on the terminal to stop reading.

b. Write a Pascal program that reads integers from a file of integers (not a text file) and prints them on the terminal. The program should also print on the terminal the sum of all the integers that are in the file. Use the two programs written in this project to test each other.

P2. Write and test a Pascal procedure FindDigit that reads a text file and stops reading when the next character is a digit or at the end of file, whichever comes first. (This procedure can be used like SkipBlanks to find the beginning of a number but will skip all characters except digits.)

P3. Write and test a Pascal procedure SkiptoNumber that reads a text file and stops reading when the next character is the legitimate first character of a number according to the rules of Pascal, or the reading goes all the way to the end of file, whichever comes first. The legitimate first characters in a number in Pascal are the digits, the plus sign '+', and the minus sign '−'. (The procedure to be written in this project is similar to that in the preceding project but allows certain further possibilities.)

P4. Write and test a Pascal program that reads a text file and writes all the words in the input file into another file with one word per line. For this project, a word is considered to be a sequence made entirely of uppercase and lowercase letters, with no other characters. The program should delete all characters that are not part of a word.

P5. Modify the preceding project to allow the following more general definition of a word. To allow contractions and possessives, one apostrophe (') but no more may appear within a word. Hyphens (-) may also appear in words, but not adjacent to each other or at the beginning or end.

P6. Write a Pascal program that will read a text file containing a Pascal program and will print out the number of assignment statements in the program. (The program need only count the number of occurrences of the symbols := that are not in comments or character strings. You may assume that the program satisfies the rules of Pascal, that is, that it would compile without error.)

P7. Write a Pascal program that will read a text file containing a Pascal program and will print out the number of **if** statements in the program. (The program need only count the number of occurrences of the word **if** that are not in comments or character strings. You may assume that the program satisfies the rules of Pascal, that is, that it would compile without error.)

3.5

CHOOSING DATA STRUCTURES

In this chapter, we have studied four facilities that Pascal provides for packaging many pieces of data together as a single structure: arrays, records, sets, and files. For each application, the programmer should carefully decide which of these structures is appropriate.

homogeneity

A data structure is called **homogeneous** if all of its entries or components have the same type. Arrays, sets, and files are all homogeneous, but records are not. Records are therefore the appropriate structure to use whenever there are several pieces of data that are logically related to each other but have different types. Even when the data have the same type, it is frequently appropriate to group logically related data together as a record. Such groupings appear very frequently, and records are therefore the basic building blocks from which all data structures are constructed.

> ### Programming Precept
>
> Use records to group logically related data;
> doing this is the basic step for structuring data.

After groups of logically related data have been collected as records, then the groups *do* have the same type (the record type), and so it may be appropriate to *choosing structures* use one of the homogeneous structures to store the records. It is now time to ask how many data there are and how they will be used. Sets are very restrictive in their use (and, in Pascal, in their size); their only use is to answer whether or not a particular value is in the set. If more information is needed, then another data structure is needed. Files are unique in being external, permanent structures, and in being unlimited in size. Arrays, on the other hand, allow direct access to arbitrary entries, but (in Pascal) their size is determined when the program is written, not when it runs.

naming and anonymity The distinction among the four structures may be clarified by considering some further properties. The data in the structure are *named* if they have names or indices by which they can be obtained directly; otherwise, they are *anonymous*. The data within a record are named by their field names; the data in an array are named by the indices with which they are accessed. On the other hand, the data in a set or a file are anonymous; they cannot be addressed directly by name.

ordering A second property of the data in a structure is ordering; are the data arranged in a sequential order? The data in one-dimensional arrays and in files are so ordered. The data in sets are not ordered at all, and the fields of a record are in no particular order—nothing significant changes if the fields are listed in a different order in the declarations.

Note that the two questions "named?" and "ordered?" both have two possible answers, giving four altogether, and these four possibilities correspond exactly to the four structures we have studied. For arrays, the answers are both *yes*; for sets, the answers are both *no*. The data in files are ordered but not named; the data in records are named but not ordered.

packing We should, finally, mention one other feature of Pascal's built-in structures: packing. When it is introduced, a structure can be declared to be **packed**, which instructs the compiler to save as much space as possible by packing the entries of the structure as closely together as possible. The extent to which packing is done, however, depends on the compiler. Some compilers simply ignore the keyword **packed**. Others automatically pack certain types, such as arrays of characters or Boolean values. Packing has the disadvantages that processing may become slower and that individual entries or components of packed structures cannot be used as **var** parameters. The best advice concerning packing is perhaps not to do it unless lack of memory space becomes a problem.

POINTERS AND PITFALLS

1. Does the number of positions actually used in a one-dimensional array stay the same throughout a program? If so, the array is being used as a vector; if not, it is being used as a workspace. Use **for** loops to process vectors. With workspaces, be careful of the extreme cases of an empty or a full array.

2. In applications where the entries of an array depend on two or more indices, decide carefully whether the indices can be varied independently of each

other or there is a precedence order. In the first case, use a multidimensional array; in the second case, set up a hierarchical declaration of one-dimensional arrays.

3. Design your data structures from the top down, and let the levels of declaration of data structures correspond to the levels of declaration of subprograms. The top-down design of a program should proceed in almost the reverse of its final appearance in Pascal.

4. Records are the fundamental tool for grouping logically related data and are the most common building block in constructing hierarchical structures.

5. Nest your **with** statements as you nest your procedures: Use one level of **with** statement for each procedure.

6. Sets, as an abstract type, are useful for applications where only a yes/no question needs to be asked about each possible data value. On the implementation level, sets are usually quite restricted.

7. File processing has many peculiarities, depending on the computer system and compiler. Try to localize file processing to specific subprograms so that it can be adapted as necessary.

8. When read and write produce unexpected results, trace their action by thinking in terms of file windows, get, and put.

9. Always use files of type text for data that needs to be examined by people or by programs written in languages other than Pascal. For other kinds of files, be certain that the file declarations in the program writing the file and in the program reading the file are identical.

REVIEW QUESTIONS

3.1   1. What is a *vector*? What kind of Pascal loops should be used to process vectors?

2. What is a *workspace*? How does it differ from a vector?

3. Name three common bugs that arise in processing workspaces.

4. What is the criterion for deciding between multidimensional arrays and hierarchical arrays of arrays?

3.2   5. What is the main reason for using records rather than separate variables in Pascal?

6. What are *hierarchical* records? How should they be processed?

7. Give two reasons why *variant* records are useful.

3.3   8. Name three levels of problem solving and program design on which the idea of a *set* may appear. Give an example of using a set on each of these levels.

3.4   **9.** How are files similar to one-dimensional arrays?

      10. How do files differ from one-dimensional arrays?

      11. When should file windows together with the operations get and put be considered or used?

      12. When should files of type text be used? When should other files be used?

      13. Name three features of text files not shared by others.

      14. Why do blanks and ends of lines sometimes cause trouble in reading text files?

      15. What is *lazy* input? How does it work?

3.5   **16.** What are *homogeneity*, *anonymity*, and *ordering* for data structures? How do they relate to arrays, records, sets, and files?

PART II

LINEAR DATA STRUCTURES

In the last chapters, we have seen how careful application of the principles of good programming helps us build software that is reliable, effective, easy to understand and to maintain. In this work, however, we have used only the methods and tools that appear as part of an introductory course in Pascal programming. It is now time for us to begin developing more sophisticated methods and tools by introducing new ways for structuring data.

In the coming chapters, we shall see that there are many different ways to keep a list within computer memory, and therefore the careful programmer needs to make a conscious decision about which of these to choose. The need for careful decision making about how to store data, in fact, extends back even further in the process of program design. We shall soon see that there are many kinds of lists (stacks and queues are the first two kinds we study), and, therefore, the programmer must first decide what kind of list (or what other conceptual structure) is needed for the data and then must decide how the conceptual structure will be implemented in computer memory. Starting in Chapter 5, we shall find that there are often many different ways to implement the same conceptual structure, and so, by keeping decisions about conceptual structures separate from implementation decisions, we shall be able both to simplify the programming process and avoid some of the pitfalls that attend premature commitment.

In the data structures with which we work, we shall always emphasize the *operations* that can be done on the structure, and we shall be careful to separate the study of a data structure and its operations from the application programs in which it may be used.

Through Chapter 6, records and workspace arrays are the main tools used from the programming language Pascal. Chapter 7 introduces Pascal pointer types and linked lists, which provide a great deal of flexibility that is important in many applications.

In this part, we shall develop several programs that illustrate the methods and the application of the data structures under consideration. Chapter 4 presents a reverse Polish calculator using a stack; Chapter 5 uses queues in a program that simulates traffic patterns at a small airport; Chapter 6 develops a miniature text editor which does extensive list and string processing; and Chapter 8 outlines a group project for a program that performs many calculations on polynomials.

4

STACKS

This chapter introduces the study of data structures, methods for organizing and accessing data in computer storage. The data structures we shall study in this chapter are called *stacks*. We shall look at them both from the point of view of their general properties and from the perspective of their implementation in computer storage and Pascal procedures. We shall always emphasize the separation between the use of data structures and their implementation. In this chapter we shall develop several examples, including a program that simulates a reverse Polish calculator and a procedure for translating an expression into postfix (reverse Polish) form.

DEFINITION AND OPERATIONS

stacks The easiest kind of list to use is called a *stack*. It is defined formally as a list in which all insertions and deletions are made at one end, called the *top* of the stack. A helpful analogy (see Figure 4.1) is to think of a stack of trays or of plates sitting on the counter in a busy cafeteria. Throughout the lunch hour, customers take trays off the top of the stack, and employees place returned trays back on top of the stack. The tray most recently put on the stack is the first one taken off. The bottom tray is the first one put on, and the last one to be used.

Figure 4.1. Stacks

Sometimes this picture is described with plates or trays on a spring-loaded device, so that the top of the stack stays near the same height. This imagery is poor and should be avoided. If we were to implement a computer stack in this way, it would mean moving every entry in the stack whenever one entry was inserted or deleted. This would be costly. It is far better to think of the stack as resting on a firm counter or floor, so that only the top entry is moved when it is added or deleted. The spring-loaded imagery, however, has contributed a

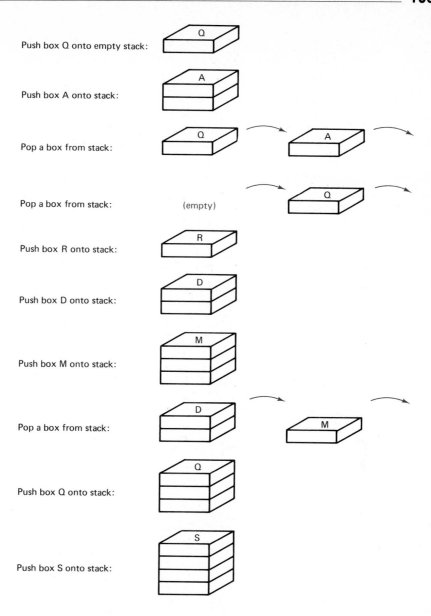

Push box Q onto empty stack:

Push box A onto stack:

Pop a box from stack:

Pop a box from stack: (empty)

Push box R onto stack:

Push box D onto stack:

Push box M onto stack:

Pop a box from stack:

Push box Q onto stack:

Push box S onto stack:

Figure 4.2. Pushing and popping a stack

push and pop pair of colorful words that are firmly embedded in computer jargon, and that we shall use. When we add an entry to a stack, we' say that we **push** it onto the stack, and when we remove an entry, we say that we **pop** it from the stack. From the same analogy, the term **push-down list** is used synonymously with stack, but we shall not employ this term. See Figure 4.2.

4.1.1 Examples

Stack Frames for Subprograms

As one important application of stacks, consider what happens within the computer system when subprograms are called. The system (or the program) must remember the place where the call was made, so that it can return there after the subprogram is complete. It must also remember all the local variables, CPU registers, and the like, so that information will not be lost while the subprogram is working. We can think of all this information as one large record, a temporary storage area for each subprogram.

subprogram data storage

Suppose now that we have three subprograms called A, B, and C, and suppose that A invokes B and B invokes C. Then B will not have finished its work until C has finished and returned. Similarly, A is the first to start work, but it is the last to be finished, not until sometime after B has finished and returned. Thus the sequence by which subprogram activity proceeds is summed up as the property *last in, first out*. If we consider the machine's task of assigning temporary storage areas for use by subprograms, then these areas would be allocated in a list with this same property, that is, in a stack (see Figure 4.3). Hence yet one more name sometimes used for stacks is **LIFO lists**, based on the acronym for this property.

LIFO list

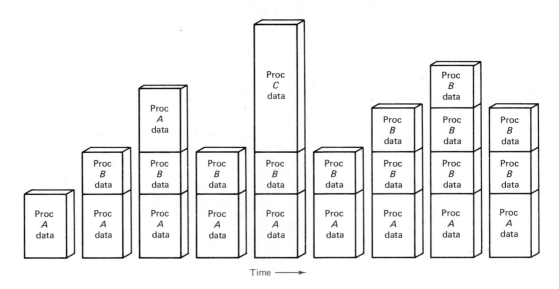

Figure 4.3. Stack frames for subprogram calls

Reversing a Line

Let us see how the operations on stacks work for a simple example. Suppose that we wish to make a procedure that will read a line of input and will then write it out backward. We can accomplish this task by pushing each character onto a stack as it is read. When the line is finished, we then pop characters off the stack, and they will come off in the reverse order. Hence our procedure takes the following form:

```
procedure ReverseRead;
{Pre:   The user supplies one line of input.
 Post:  The procedure writes out the line backward.
 Uses: Stack-processing operations.}
var
   S: stacktype;
   ch: char;
begin                                    {procedure ReverseRead}
   CreateStack(S);                  {First make the stack ready to use.}
   while (not eoln) and (not StackFull(S)) do
   begin               {Push each character in the line onto the stack.}
      read(ch);
      Push(ch, S)
   end;
   readln;
   while not StackEmpty(S) do
   begin               {Pop each character from the stack and write it.}
      Pop(ch, S);
      write(ch)
   end;
   writeln
end;                                     {procedure ReverseRead}
```

In this procedure, we have used not only Push and Pop, but also a procedure CreateStack that initializes a stack to be empty. There are also two Boolean-valued functions used to check the current status of a stack: StackEmpty checks whether a stack is empty or not, and StackFull checks if it is completely full.

stack size

top of stack

There are, finally, two more operations that are sometimes useful for stacks. One is the function StackSize, which returns the number of entries in the stack. The other is the procedure StackTop, which returns the entry on the top of the stack but does not change it. We could, of course, construct this procedure from Push and Pop by first popping the entry from the stack, retaining its value as the output, and then pushing it back onto the stack. Usually, however, it is better to think of StackTop as a fundamental operation on a stack.

4.1.2 Information Hiding

use of procedures

Notice that we have been able to write our procedure for reversing a line of input before we consider how the stack will actually be implemented in storage and before we write the details of the various procedures and functions. In this way, we have an example of *information hiding*: If someone else had already written the procedures and functions for handling stacks, then we could use them without needing to know the details of how stacks are kept in memory or of how the stack operations are actually done.

*information
hiding*

*built-in
structures*

*alternative
implementations*

*change of
implementation*

*clarity of
program*

top-down design

As a matter of fact, we have already practiced information hiding in our previous programs without thinking about it. Whenever we have written a program using an array or a record, we have been content to use the operations on these structures without considering how the Pascal compiler actually represents them in terms of bits or bytes in the computer memory or the machine-language steps it follows to look up an index or select a field. The only real difference between practicing information hiding with regard to arrays and records and practicing information hiding with regard to stacks is that Pascal provides built-in operations for arrays and records but not for stacks.

Some computer languages do provide stacks as a built-in data type. If we were using one of these languages, we would be performing operations on stacks as readily as we do on arrays or records. There is a good reason, however, why Pascal does not provide stacks as a built-in data type. In the coming chapters, we shall see that for stacks (as for almost all the data types we shall study) there are several different ways to represent the data in the computer memory, and there are several different ways to do the operations. In some applications, one method is better, while in other applications another method proves superior. In Pascal we can choose whichever method is best for our application and then include the appropriate procedures and functions that implement our choice.

Even in a single large program, we may first decide to represent stacks one way and then, as we gain experience with the program, we may decide that another way is better. If the instructions for manipulating a stack have been written out every time a stack is used, then every occurrence of these instructions will need to be changed. If we have practiced information hiding by using separate procedures and functions for manipulating stacks, then only the declarations will need to be changed.

One more advantage of information hiding for stacks is that the very appearance of the words *Push* and *Pop* will immediately alert a person reading the program to what is being done, whereas the instructions themselves might be more obscure.

A final advantage we shall find is that separating the use of data structures from their implementation will help us improve the top-down design of both our data structures and our programs.

4.1.3 Specifications for a Stack

To conclude this section, let us consider the precise specifications for a stack in terms of the preconditions and postconditions for each procedure and function that we have introduced. In these declarations, we shall use the type stacktype for the stack. In accordance with the principles of information hiding and top-down design, we shall leave this type unspecified until we consider the implementation of stacks in the next section. The entries that are stored in a stack will have a type that we call stackentry, which will change according to the application. For reversing the line of input, we need the declaration

stackentry = char.

For other applications, we shall assign the type stackentry in different ways.

The first step we must perform in working with any stack is to use the procedure CreateStack to initialize it for further use:

---

procedure CreateStack(**var** S: stacktype)

precondition: None.

postcondition: The stack S has been created and is initialized to be empty.

Next come the operations for checking the status of a stack.

---

function StackEmpty(S: stacktype): Boolean

precondition: The stack S has been created.

postcondition: The function returns true or false according as stack S is empty or not.

---

function StackFull(S: stacktype): Boolean

precondition: The stack S has been created.

postcondition: The function returns true or false according as stack S is full or not.

The declarations for the fundamental operations on a stack come next.

---

procedure Push(x: stackentry; **var** S: stacktype)

precondition: The stack S has been created and is not full.

postcondition: The item x has been stored in the stack as its top entry.

---

procedure Pop(**var** x: stackentry; **var** S: stacktype)

precondition: The stack S has been created and is not empty.

postcondition: The entry on the top of the stack has been removed and returned as the value of x.

Note from the preconditions that it is an error to attempt to push an item onto a full stack or to pop an entry from an empty stack. If we write the procedures Push and Pop carefully, then they should return error messages if they are used incorrectly. From the declarations, however, there is no guarantee that the procedures will catch the errors, and, if they do not, then they may produce spurious and unpredictable results. Hence the careful programmer should always make sure, whenever invoking a subprogram, that its preconditions are guaranteed to be satisfied.

There remain two more stack operations that are sometimes useful.

---

function StackSize(S: stacktype): integer

precondition: The stack S has been created.

postcondition: The function returns the number of entries in the stack S.

---

procedure StackTop(**var** x: stackentry; S: stacktype)

precondition: The stack S has been created and is not empty.

postcondition: The variable x is a copy of the top entry in S; the stack S remains unchanged.

Note that, in all these specifications, some of the parameters are shown as **var** parameters and others as value parameters. In giving specifications for the operations on any data type, we shall generally be careful to use **var** parameters exactly when a subprogram may change the parameter. When we come to the implementation details of actually writing the subprograms, however, we shall usually take a different point of view, in order to avoid a very wasteful inefficiency: When a value parameter appears in Pascal, a new copy of the parameter is made whenever the subprogram is started. If we are working with a very large stack or other data structure, then it takes a great deal of time and space to make a new copy, time and space much greater than required to evaluate simple functions like StackSize, StackEmpty, or StackFull. Hence, when we implement subprograms to process stacks or other data structures, we shall often make the list a **var** parameter, whether or not it is changed by the subprogram.

■ EXERCISES 4.1

E1. Draw a sequence of stack frames like Figure 4.2 showing the progress of each of the following segments of code. (S is a stack of characters, and x, y, z are character variables.)

a. CreateStack(S);
  Push('a', S);
  Push('b', S);
  Push('c', S);
  Pop(x, S);
  Pop(y, S);
  Pop(z, S);

b. CreateStack(S);
  Push('a', S);
  Push('b', S);
  Push('c', S);
  Pop(x, S);
  Pop(y, S);
  Push(x, S);
  Push(y, S);
  Pop(z, S);

c. CreateStack(S);
  Push('a', S);
  Push('b', S);
  CreateStack(S);
  Push('c', S);
  Pop(x, S);
  Push('a', S);
  Pop(y, S);
  Push('b', S);
  Pop(z, S);

d. CreateStack(S);
  Push('a', S);
  Push('b', S);
  Push('c', S);
  while not StackEmpty(S) **do**
    Pop(x, S);

E2. Let S be a stack of integers and x be an integer variable. Use the procedures Push, Pop, and CreateStack, and the functions StackEmpty and StackFull to write procedures doing each of the following tasks. [You may declare additional variables in your procedures if needed.]

  a. Set x to the top element of the stack S and leave the top element of S unchanged. If S is empty, set x to maxint.
  b. Set x to the third element from the top in S, provided that S contains at least three integers. If not, set x to maxint. Leave S unchanged.
  c. Set x to the bottom element of S (or to maxint if S is empty), and leave S unchanged. [*Hint*: Use a second stack.]
  d. Delete all occurrences of x from S, leaving the other elements of S in the same order.

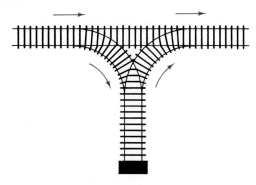

Figure 4.4. Switching network for stack permutations

E3. A stack may be regarded as a railway switching network like the one in Figure 4.4. Cars numbered 1, 2, ..., n are on the line at the left, and it *stack permutations*

is desired to rearrange (permute) the cars as they leave on the right-hand track. A car that is on the spur (stack) can be left there or sent on its way down the right track, but it can never be sent back to the incoming track. For example, if $n = 3$, and we have the cars 1, 2, 3 on the left track, then 3 first goes to the spur. We could then send 2 to the spur, then on its way to the right, then send 3 on the way, then 1, obtaining the new order 1, 3, 2.

a. For $n = 3$, find all possible permutations that can be obtained.
b. For $n = 4$, find all possible permutations that can be obtained.

4.2

ARRAY IMPLEMENTATION OF STACKS

In the previous section, we studied all the operations on stacks and considered some simple examples of their application, but we have not yet considered how to write the details of the subprograms that do the various operations. This task we now address.

Declarations

To implement a stack in a computer, we shall set up an array that will hold the entries in the stack and a counter that will indicate how many entries there are. In Pascal we shall make the following declarations, where maxstack is a constant giving the maximum size allowed for stacks, and stackentry is the type describing the data that will be put into the stack. Type stackentry depends on the application and can range from a single number or character to a large record with many fields.

stack type

```
type stacktype = record
         top:   0 .. maxstack;
         entry: array [1 .. maxstack] of stackentry
     end;
```

Pushing and Popping

Pushing and popping the stack are then implemented as follows. We must be careful of the extreme cases: We might attempt to pop an entry from an empty stack or to push an entry onto a full stack. These conditions are errors.

There are two different ways that we could handle errors. In production programs that have been thoroughly debugged, the occurrence of an error usually indicates that something serious has gone wrong, and so errors are usually fatal to the execution of the program. That is, the program would print an error message and terminate. While we are developing and debugging a program, however, errors are quite likely to occur. We shall therefore adopt a different philosophy of error handling. Instead of terminating the program, an error will make the program write an informative message indicating what went wrong. The program will then skip the affected operation and continue. In this way we can continue to study the program and learn more of what went wrong. The programmer is responsible, of course, to correct the program so that, eventually, it will run without any of the error messages. After this, the implementation subprograms can be changed to production versions in which the occurrence of an error will terminate the program.

push

```
procedure Push(x: stackentry;  var S: stacktype);
begin                                          {procedure Push}
  with S do
    if top = maxstack then
      writeln('Error: Attempt to push an entry onto a full stack')
    else begin
      top := top + 1;
      entry[top] := x
    end
end;                                           {procedure Push}
```

pop

```
procedure Pop(var x: stackentry;  var S: stacktype);
begin                                          {procedure Pop}
  with S do
    if top = 0 then
      writeln('Error: Attempt to pop an entry from an empty stack')
    else begin
      x := entry[top];
      top := top - 1
    end
end;                                           {procedure Pop}
```

Other Operations

empty

```
function StackEmpty(var S: stacktype): Boolean;
begin
  StackEmpty := (S.top = 0)
end;
```

full

```
function StackFull(var S: stacktype): Boolean;
begin
  StackFull := (S.top = maxstack)
end;
```

Note that we have declared S to be a **var** parameter in these two functions, even though it is used only as an input parameter. The reason is that of efficiency: If S were declared as a value parameter, the system would make a complete copy of S every time the function was used.

One more procedure is needed to initialize a stack before it is first used in a program:

initialize

```
procedure CreateStack(var S: stacktype);
begin
    S.top := 0
end;
```

We shall leave the procedure StackTop that returns the top of the stack without changing the stack and the function StackSize that returns the number of entries in the stack as exercises.

Advantages of the Operational Approach

As you can see from the Pascal code in this section, the implementation of stacks in Pascal turned out to be easy. It would be natural to conclude that we have been belaboring the obvious, making the easy difficult by introducing many procedures and functions whose substance is so simple that they could easily be written out wherever they are needed in a program.

For large and complicated programs, however, there are several important advantages to information hiding, as we can recall from the last section:

- *Separation* of our problems between the application and the implementation of data structures;

- *Variety* of implementations that can prove best for different applications;

- *Change* of the data structures in a program to meet changing requirements;

- *Clarity* of style;

- *Top-down* design of the program.

Keeping the different tasks needed for writing a large program separate from each other is one of the most important ways to manage complexity. It is as though we were building a wall between the implementation details of our data structures and their applications, as shown in Figure 4.5. While we are working on the right-hand side of the wall, we are concerned only about how the data structures are used and what operations are available. When we work on the other side, we are constructing tools, and our job is to make the tools sturdy and reliable, but it is not to consider the applications for which they may be used.

Figure 4.5. Implementations and applications of data structures

EXERCISES 4.2

E1. Write the function StackSize that returns the number of entries in a stack. Use the declarations developed in this section.

E2. Write the procedure StackTop(**var** x: stackentry; **var** S: stacktype).

    a. Use the procedures Push and Pop to construct StackTop. Your procedure should use only the basic subprograms that manipulate stacks; it should not rely on the method of implementation developed in this section.

    b. Write the procedure StackTop on the lower level of looking directly inside the array, using the declarations developed in this section.

    c. What are the advantages and disadvantages of each of these ways to construct StackTop?

E3. A *traversable stack* is defined in the same way as a stack, except that it is permissible to move through all the entries of the stack, looking at each entry but not changing any entries. (The only way to change the traversable stack is by using Push and Pop, whereby all changes are made at its top.) With the implementation in this section, write a procedure that will move through a traversable stack and write out the value of all the entries in the stack from its top to its bottom. You may assume that the type stackentry is a type such as integer, real, or char whose values can be written out by using the write instruction. Is it possible to solve this problem using only the basic operations on a stack, without either using the details of implementation or some auxiliary storage (such as a separate array or another stack)?

two coexisting stacks

E4. Sometimes a program requires two stacks containing the same type of entries. If the two stacks are stored in separate arrays, then one stack might overflow while there was considerable unused space in the other. A neat way to avoid this problem is to put all the space in one array and let one stack grow from one end of the array and the other stack start at the other end and grow in the opposite direction, toward the first stack. In this way, if one stack turns out to be large and the other small, then they will still both fit, and there will be no overflow until all the space is actually used. Declare a new record type doublestack that includes the array and the two indices topA and topB, and write procedures CreateDoubleStack, PushA, PushB, PopA, and PopB to handle the two stacks within one doublestack.

■ PROJECTS 4.2

P1. Write a demonstration program that can be used to check the procedures and functions written in this section for manipulating stacks. The entries in your stack should be characters. Your program should write a one-line menu from which the user can select any of the stack operations. After your program does the requested operation, it should inform the user of the result and ask for the next request. When the user wishes to push a character onto the stack, your program will need to ask what character to push.

Be careful to maintain the principles of information hiding. You should not make any changes in the subprograms for the stack operations, so that, when we later develop a different implementation of stacks, you can replace the subprograms for the stack operations with the new versions and compile and run the program correctly with no further changes.

P2. Write a program that uses a stack to read an integer and print all its prime divisors in descending order. For example, with the integer 2100 the output should be

prime divisors

$$7 \quad 5 \quad 5 \quad 3 \quad 2 \quad 2.$$

[*Hint*: The smallest divisor greater than 1 of any integer is guaranteed to be a prime.]

P3. Write a program using stack operations that will read a text file and check to see that all brackets found in the file are properly paired; that is, for each opening bracket of the form (, [, or { there is a closing bracket of the same type, properly nested. If a construct such as (... [...) ...] is encountered, or if a bracket does not have a mate, the program should generate an error message to that effect, along with the line number where the error was located.

4.3

APPLICATION: REVERSE POLISH CALCULATOR

Purpose of the Project

As an application of stacks, this section develops a program that will imitate the behavior of a simple calculator that does addition, subtraction, multiplication, division, and perhaps some other operations for real numbers.

reverse Polish calculations

There are many kinds of calculators available, and we could model our program after any of them. To provide a further illustration of the use of stacks, however, let us choose to model what is often called a *reverse Polish* calculator. In such a calculator, the operands are entered *before* the operation is specified. The operands are pushed onto a stack. When an operation is performed, it pops its operands from the stack and pushes its result back onto the stack.

If ? denotes pushing an operand onto the stack, $+$, $-$, $*$, and / represent arithmetic operations, and $=$ means printing the top of the stack (but not popping it off), then ? ? $+$ $=$ means reading two operands, then calculating and printing their sum. The instruction ? ? $+$? ? $+$ $*$ $=$ requests four operands. If these operands are a, b, c, d, then the result printed is $(a + b) * (c + d)$. Similarly, ? ? ? $-$ $=$ $*$? $+$ $=$ pushes a, b, c onto the stack, replaces b, c by $b - c$ and prints its value, calculates $a * (b - c)$, pushes d on the stack, and finally calculates and prints $(a * (b - c)) + d$.

The advantage of a reverse Polish calculator is that any expression, no matter how complicated, can be specified without the use of parentheses. A few minutes of practice with a reverse Polish calculator will make you quite comfortable with its use.

As a matter of fact, our customary way to write arithmetic or logical expressions with the operator between its operands is slightly illogical. The instruction

> *"Take the number 12 and multiply by ...."*

is incomplete until the second factor is given. In the meantime, it is necessary to remember both a number and an operation. From the viewpoint of establishing uniform rules, it makes more sense either to write

> *"Take the numbers 12 and 3; then multiply."*

or to write

> *"Do a multiplication. The numbers are 12 and 3."*

Polish Notation

This method of writing all operators either before their operands or after them is called *Polish notation*, in honor of its discoverer, the Polish mathematician

JAN ŁUKASIEWICZ. When the operators are written before their operands, it is called the **prefix form**. When the operators come after their operands, it is called the **postfix form**, or, sometimes, the **reverse Polish form** or **suffix form**. Finally, in this context, it is customary to use the coined phrase **infix form** to denote the usual custom of writing binary operators between their operands.

The expression $a \times b$ becomes $\times ab$ in prefix form and $ab\times$ in postfix form. In the expression $a + b \times c$, the multiplication is done first, so we convert it first, obtaining first $a + (bc\times)$ and then $abc \times +$ in postfix form. The prefix form of this expression is $+a \times bc$. Note that prefix and postfix forms are not related by taking mirror images or other such simple transformation. The major advantage of both Polish forms is that no parentheses are needed to prevent ambiguities in the expression.

stacks   To evaluate an expression in postfix form, it is necessary to remember the operands until their operator is eventually found some time later. The natural way to remember them is to put them on a stack. Then, when the first operator to be done is encountered, it will find its operands on the top of the stack. If it puts its result back on the stack, then its result will be in the right place to be an operand for a later operator. When the evaluation is complete, the final result will be the only value on the stack. In this way, we have the method that will lead to a procedure to evaluate a postfix expression.

First Outline

The task of the calculator program is to accept new commands and perform them as long as desired. In preliminary outline, the main program takes the form

first outline

```
program Calculator (input, output);            {preliminary outline}
begin
   CreateStack(S);           {Let S be the stack; initialize it to be empty.}
   while there are more commands do
   begin
      ReadCommand(com);
                       {Let com denote the command ready to be done.}
      DoCommand(com, S)
   end
end.
```

Performing Commands

To turn this outline into Pascal, we must specify what it means to obtain commands and how this will be done. Before doing so, let us make the decision to represent the commands by the characters ? , = , + , − , * , /. Given this decision, we can immediately write the procedure DoCommand in Pascal, thereby specifying exactly what each command does:

procedure DoCommand(com: char; **var** S: stacktype);

stack operations {**Pre:** *The stack S has been created, and* com *is one of the operations allowed in the calculator. If* com = ${}'?'$ *then S is not full. If* com = ${}'='$ *then S is not empty. Otherwise, S must contain at least two entries.*

{**Post:** *The specified operation* com *has been performed and the top entries of S have been changed accordingly.*}

var
    p, q: operand;   *{names for the operands in use}*
begin   *{procedure DoCommand}*
  case com **of**

input
    ${}'?'$: **begin**   *{Input an operand and push it onto the stack.}*
          ReadOperand(p);
          Push(p, S)
       end;

output
    ${}'='$: **begin**   *{Print the operand on top of the stack.}*
          StackTop(p, S);
          WriteOperand(p)
       end;

addition
    ${}'+'$: **begin**
           {Pop the top two operands, add them, and push the answer.}
          Pop(p, S);
          Pop(q, S);
          Push(p + q, S)
       end;

subtraction
    ${}'-'$: **begin**
           {Pop the top two operands, subtract them, and push the answer.}
          Pop(p, S);
          Pop(q, S);
          Push(q − p, S)
       end;

multiplication
    ${}'*'$: **begin**
           {Pop the top two operands, multiply them, and push the answer.}
          Pop(p, S);
          Pop(q, S);
          Push(p ∗ q, S)
       end;

division
    ${}'/'$: **begin**
           {Pop the top two operands, divide them, and push the answer.}
          Pop(p, S);
          Pop(q, S);
          Push(q/p, S)
       end
  end
end;   *{procedure DoCommand}*

Stack Processing

packages

The next requirement for our program is to include the procedures and functions needed for processing the stack. Doing this does not mean that we should type the various subprograms directly into the calculator program. Instead, we should collect all the procedures and functions for processing a general stack from Section 4.3 into a single *package* for stack processing, a package that we can then use in any program requiring a stack.

separate compilation

The best way to have such a package for stack processing would be to put all the declarations and subprograms together and compile them separately. We would then provide only enough information to the application program to allow it to use the declarations and subprograms from the stack package, but not enough information to rely on the details of the implementation. Standard Pascal, unfortunately, provides no way to do this. Certain newer languages, including Modula-2 and Ada, are designed specifically to include this capability.

units in Turbo Pascal

For microcomputers, the Turbo Pascal[1] compiler, starting with Version 4.0, provides a feature called a *unit* in which declarations, initialization code, and various subprograms can be combined and compiled separately from the program that uses the unit. The part of the unit introduced by the keyword **interface** contains the parts that are to be shared with the application program. Then comes the keyword **implementation**, which introduces the code that is hidden from the application program. The use of units in Turbo Pascal makes it easy to enforce the principles of information hiding.

included files

With standard Pascal, we can still achieve most of the advantages of information hiding, but we cannot use the compiler to enforce these principles. Many Pascal compilers provide a feature called an **include** directive that instructs the compiler to read the code in another file as part of the program being compiled. By using this feature, we need not be concerned about the details of processing stacks while we write the remainder of the program, nor need we fear that we might introduce new errors into the program by making typographical errors while copying the stack-processing subprograms. In general, whenever we write a package of declarations and subprograms that will be used in a variety of different programs, we should keep the package in a separate file that we can then include in an application program whenever necessary.

If your Pascal compiler does not provide the include directive or a similar feature, then you should still collect the stack-processing subprograms as a single package and use your text editor to copy the package into your application programs whenever required.

Finally, we should note that the stack-processing subprograms in Section 4.3 all refer to the type stackentry, whereas we need the type operand for our calculator program. To adapt the general stack-processing subprograms to our application, we need only place the declaration

---

[1] Turbo Pascal is a trademark of Borland International.

type stackentry = operand

before we include the stack-processing package in the calculator program.

Reading Commands: The Main Program

Now that we have decided that the commands are to be denoted as single characters, we could easily program procedure GetCommand to read one command at a time from the terminal. It is often convenient, however, to read a string of several commands at once, such as ? ? + ? ? + * = , and then perform them all before reading more. To allow for this possibility, let us read a whole line of commands at once and set up an array to hold them. With this decision, we can now write the main program in its final form. We shall use a procedure Read-Command to read the string of commands; this procedure will also be responsible for error checking.

main program

```
program Calculator(input, output);
{Pre:    None.
  Post:  The program accepts commands from the user and performs them on
         a stack containing real numbers.
  Uses:  Procedures Prompt, ReadCommand, and DoCommand, utility func-
         tion UserSaysYes, and package of stack declarations and operations}
const
  max = 80;       {maximum number of commands to be done at one time}
type
  index = 0 .. max;
  commandstring = array [1 .. max] of char;
                            {holds the list of commands to be done}
  operand = real;
var
  command: commandstring;
  i,                                  {index of current command}
  count: index;           {total number of commands in current string}
  S: stacktype;
{Declarations of procedures and functions are to be inserted later.}
begin                                    {main program Calculator}
  CreateStack(S);
  repeat
    Prompt;
    ReadCommand(command, count);
    for i := 1 to count do
      DoCommand(command[i], S);
    write('Continue?')
  until not UserSaysYes
end.                                      {main program Calculator}
```

Input and Output Procedures

To complete the project, we must still give the details for the input and output procedures. The procedures for reading and writing operands are simply:

```
procedure ReadOperand(var x: operand);
{Pre:   None.
   Post:  Parameter x has been set to an operand (real number) received from
          the user.}
begin
   write('Value of operand?');
   readln(x)
end;
```

```
procedure WriteOperand(x: operand);
{Pre:   Parameter x is the value of an operand.
   Post:  The value of x has been written out for the user.}
const
   space = 10;          {number of columns reserved to write operand}
   decimal = 4;         {number of spaces reserved after decimal point}
begin
   writeln('Result is ', x: space: decimal)
end;
```

Next comes the prompting procedure, which need only write one line, but note that this line gives the user the opportunity to request further instructions if desired.

prompting user

```
procedure Prompt;
{Pre:   None.
   Post:  A one-line prompt has been written for the user.}
begin
   writeln('Enter a string of commands or ! for instructions.')
end;
```

Procedure ReadCommand must check that the symbols typed in represent legitimate operations and must provide instructions, if desired, along with doing its main task. If there is an error or the user requests instructions, then the command string must be re-entered from the start.

read commands

```
procedure ReadCommand(var command: commandstring; var count: index);
{Pre:   None.
   Post:  The parameter command has been set to a string of legitimate com-
          mands ready to be performed by the calculator. The parameter count
          is the number of commands in this string.
   Uses: Procedure Prompt.}
var
   legal: Boolean;      {Have all characters read so far been acceptable?}
```

```
              begin                                      {procedure ReadCommand}
                 repeat                    {Main loop will repeat until the whole line is legal.}
                    count := 0;
                    legal := true;
                    while legal and (not eoln) do
                    begin
                       count := count + 1;
                       read(command[count]);
                       if command[count] in [' ',','] then
                          count := count − 1
                                    {Skip blanks and commas in the command stream.}
                       else if command[count] = '!' then    {User requests instructions.}
                       begin
                          legal := false;
                          writeln('Enter a string of instructions in reverse Polish form.');
                          writeln('The allowable instructions are:');
                          writeln('? Read an operand onto stack.  =  Print top of stack.');
                          writeln('+ Add top two on the stack.    −  Subtract top two.');
                          writeln('* Multiply top two on stack.   /  Divide top two.')
                       end
                       else
                          legal := (command[count] in ['?','=','+',' −','*','/'])
                                  and (count < max)
                    end;        {end of while loop considering one character per iteration}
                    readln;
                    if not legal then                {Request repetition of the entire line.}
                       Prompt
                 until legal;
              end;                                         {procedure ReadCommand}
```

instructions is noted in the left margin beside the writeln block.
error checking is noted in the left margin beside the legal assignment.

A structure diagram showing the relationships among the subprograms of the calculator project and the stack package is shown in Figure 4.6.

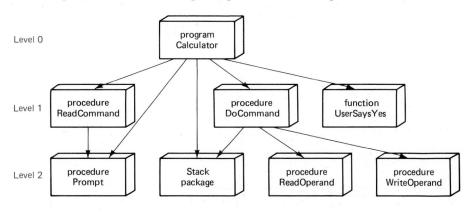

Figure 4.6. Structure diagram for the calculator project

EXERCISES 4.3

E1. Evaluate each of the following postfix expressions.

    a. 2 3 5 × +.
    b. 2 3 5 + ×.
    c. 2 3 + 5 ×.
    d. 2 3 × 4 1 + −.
    e. 1 2 3 + 2 − 3 × +.
    f. 7 3 + 2 × 3 5 × 1 + −.

E2. Translate each of the following postfix expressions into infix. Use parentheses as necessary to avoid ambiguities.

    a. a b + c ×.
    b. a b c +   ×.
    c. a ! b !   / c d − a !   −   ×.
    d. a b <   **not** c d × e <   **or**.

E3. Try to convert each of the following from postfix form into infix form, and thereby determine which of these expressions are correct postfix expressions. Show the error in each incorrect expression. Translate each correct expression into infix form, using parentheses as necessary to avoid ambiguities.

    a. a × b +
    b. a 3   × b −
    c. a 3   × b − c
    d. a b ×   −
    e. a b −   ×
    f. a b c +   × a / c b + d /   −
    g. a b + c a × b c / d −
    h. a b + c a ×   − c ×   + b c −

PROJECTS 4.3

P1. Supply the missing procedures, combine them all, then test and exercise the reverse Polish calculator. If you are using the Turbo Pascal compiler, make the stack-processing package into a unit. Otherwise, use the include directive (or equivalent feature) for the stack-processing package if it is available for your compiler.

P2. Add the following capabilities to the reverse Polish calculator by writing appropriate subprograms and modifying the other procedures as required. Be sure to include error checking as appropriate for each of these calculations.

    a. Square root $\sqrt{x}$.
    b. Natural logarithm $\ln x$.
    c. Exponential e^x.
    d. Exponentiation x^y.

4.4

TRANSLATION INTO POSTFIX FORM

Very few programmers habitually write algebraic expressions in postfix form, and so to make the postfix form more usable, we need algorithms to translate an expression from ordinary infix notation into postfix form.

Historical Introduction

One of the most important accomplishments of the early designers of computer languages was allowing a programmer to write arithmetic expressions in something close to their usual (infix) mathematical form. It was a real triumph to design a compiler that understood expressions such as

$$(x + y) * \exp(x - z) - 4.0$$
$$a * b + c/d - c * (x + y)$$
$$\textbf{not } (p \textbf{ and } q) \textbf{ or } (x <= 7.0)$$

etymology:
FORTRAN

and produced machine-language output. In fact, the name FORTRAN stands for

FORMULA TRANSLATOR

in recognition of this very accomplishment. It often takes only one simple idea that, when fully understood, will provide the key to an elegant solution of a difficult problem, in this case the application of the postfix form to the translation of expressions into sequences of machine-language instructions.

The triumph of the method to be developed in this section is that, in contrast to the first approach a person might take, it is not necessary to make repeated scans through the expression to decipher it, and, after a preliminary translation, neither parentheses nor priorities of operators need be taken into account, so that evaluation of the expression can be achieved with great efficiency.

Problems and Specifications

Before we discuss this idea, let us briefly imagine the problems an early compiler designer might have faced when confronted with a fairly complicated expression. Even the quadratic formula produces problems:

$$x := (-b + (b \uparrow 2 - (4 \times a) \times c) \uparrow \tfrac{1}{2})/(2 \times a)$$

(Here, and throughout this section, we denote exponentiation by $\uparrow$. We limit our attention to one of the two roots.) Which operations must be done before others? What are the effects of parentheses? When can they be omitted? As you answer these questions for this example, you will probably look back and forth through the expression several times.

In considering how to translate such expressions, the compiler designers soon settled on the conventions that are familiar now: operations are ordinarily done left to right, subject to the priorities assigned to operators, with exponentiation highest, then multiplication and division, then addition and subtraction. This order can be altered by parentheses. For the quadratic formula, the order of operations is

$$x := (\dot{-}b + (b \uparrow 2 - (4 \times a) \times c) \uparrow \tfrac{1}{2}) / (2 \times a)$$

$$\begin{array}{cccccccccc} \uparrow & \uparrow & \uparrow & \uparrow & \uparrow & \uparrow & \uparrow & \uparrow & \uparrow & \uparrow \\ 10 & 1 & 7 & 2 & 5 & 3 & 4 & 6 & 9 & 8 \end{array}$$

Note that assignment := really is an operator that takes the value of its right operand and assigns it to the left operand. The priority of := will be the lowest of any operator, since it cannot be done until the expression is fully evaluated.

Unary Operators and Priorities

With one exception, all the operators in the quadratic equation are **binary**, that is, they have two operands. The one exception is the leading minus sign in $-b$. This is a **unary** operator, and unary operators provide a slight complication in determining priorities. Normally we interpret -2^2 as -4, which means that negation is done after exponentiation, but we interpret 2^{-2} as $1/4$ and not as -4, so that here negation is done first. It is reasonable to assign unary operators the same priority as exponentiation and, in order to preserve the usual algebraic conventions, to evaluate operators of this priority from right to left. Doing this, moreover, also gives the ordinary interpretation of $2 \uparrow 3 \uparrow 2$ as

$$2^{(3^2)} = 512 \quad \text{and not as} \quad (2^3)^2 = 64.$$

The unary minus also causes an ambiguity that will haunt us later if we do not correct it. The first $-$ (minus) in the expression is unary negation, and the second is binary subtraction. In Polish form, it is not obvious which is which. When we go to evaluate the postfix string we will not know whether to take *special symbol* one operand for $-$ or two, and the results will be quite different. To avoid this ambiguity, we shall reserve $-$ to denote binary subtraction, and use the special symbol $\dot{-}$ for unary negation. (This terminology is certainly not standard. There are other ways to resolve the problem.)

There are unary operators other than negation. These include such operations as taking the factorial of x, denoted $x!$, the derivative of a function f, denoted f', as well as all functions of a single variable, such as the exponential, logarithmic, and trigonometric functions. There is also the Boolean operator **not**, which negates a Boolean variable.

Several binary operators also have Boolean results: the operators **and** and **or** as well as the comparison operators $=$, $\neq$, $<$, $>$, $\leq$, and $\geq$. These comparisons are normally done after the arithmetic operators, but before **and**, **not**, and assignment.

priority list   We thus obtain the following list of priorities to reflect our usual customs in evaluating operators:

Operators	Priority
$\uparrow$, all unary operators	6
$\times$ / **div mod**	5
$+$ $-$ (binary)	4
$=$ $\neq$ $<$ $>$ $\leq$ $\geq$	3
not	2
and **or**	1
:=	0

Pascal priorities for operators

Note that the priorities shown in this table are not the same as those used in Pascal. Under the syntax rules of Pascal, **and** has priority 5 and **or** has priority 4. This means that parentheses must often be used in Pascal expressions, even though, by assigning **and** and **or** a lower priority, the expression reads unambiguously to a person. For example, the expression

$$x < 10 \textbf{ and } y < 12$$

will be incorrectly interpreted by Pascal as meaning

$$x < (10 \textbf{ and } y) < 12,$$

which is obviously nonsense. As long as we are designing our own system, however, we are free to set our own conventions in any way we wish. By using the priorities shown in the table, we interpret expressions in a way that most people find more natural than the way that Pascal uses.

The Method for Translation

To simplify our problem, we shall exclude unary operators that are placed to the right of their operands. Such operators cause no conceptual difficulty, but would make the algorithms more complicated.

Since, in postfix form, all operators come after their operands, the task of translation from infix to postfix form is simply

delaying
operators

> Delay each operator until its right-hand operand has been translated.
> Pass each simple operand through without delay.

This action is illustrated for some simple expressions and for the quadratic formula in Figure 4.7.

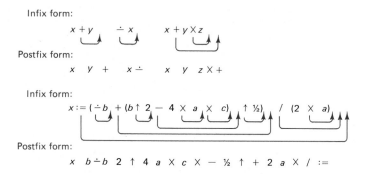

Figure 4.7. Delaying operators in postfix form

The major problem we must resolve is to find what token will terminate the right-hand operand of a given operator. We must take both parentheses and priorities of operators into account. The first problem is easy. If a left parenthesis is in the operand, then everything through the matching right parenthesis must also be. For the second problem, that of priorities of operators, we consider binary operators separately from those of priority 6, namely, unary operators and exponentiation.

finding the end of
the right operand

Most binary operators are evaluated from left to right. Let op_1 be such a binary operator, and let op_2 be the first nonbracketed operator to the right of op_1. If the priority of op_2 is less than or equal to that of op_1, then op_2 will not be part of the right operand of op_1, and its appearance will terminate the right operand of op_1. If the priority of op_2 is greater than that of op_1, then op_2 is part of the right operand of op_1, and we can continue through the expression until we find an operator of priority less than or equal to that of op_1; this operator will then terminate the right operand of op_1.

right-to-left
evaluation

Next, suppose that op_1 has priority 6 (it is unary or exponentiation), and recall that operators of this priority are to be evaluated from right to left. If the first operand op_2 to the right of op_1 has equal priority, it therefore will be part of the right operand of op_1, and the right operand is terminated only by an operator of strictly smaller priority.

There are two more ways in which the right operand can terminate: the expression can end, or the given operator may itself be within a bracketed subexpression, in which case its right operand will end when an unmatched right parenthesis ')' is encountered. In summary, we have the rules:

> *If op is an operator in an infix expression, then its right-hand operand contains all tokens on its right until one of the following is encountered:*
>
> *1. the end of the expression;*
>
> *2. an unmatched right parenthesis ')';*
>
> *3. an operator of priority less than or equal to that of op, and not within a bracketed sub-expression, if op has priority less than 6;*
>
> *4. an operator of priority strictly less than that of op, and not within a bracketed subexpression, if op has priority 6.*

stack of operators

From these rules, we can see that the appropriate way to remember the operators being delayed is to keep them on a stack. If operator op_2 comes on the right of operator op_1 but has higher priority, then op_2 will be output before op_1 is. Thus the operators are output in the order last in, first out.

The key to writing an algorithm for the translation is to make a slight change in our point of view by asking, as each token appears in the input, which of the operators previously delayed (that is, on the stack) now have their right operands terminated because of the new token, so that it is time to move them into the output. The preceding conditions then become

> *1. At the end of the expression, all operators are output.*
>
> *2. A right parenthesis causes all operators found since the corresponding left parenthesis to be output.*
>
> *3. An operator of priority not 6 causes all other operators of greater or equal priority to be output.*
>
> *4. An operator of priority 6 causes all other operators of strictly greater priority to be output, if such operators exist.*

To implement the second rule, we shall put each left parenthesis on the stack when it is encountered. Then, when the matching right parenthesis appears and the operators have been popped from the stack, the pair can both be discarded.

The Translation Procedure

We can now incorporate these rules into a procedure. To do so, we shall use several auxiliary data types and procedures, which we shall leave undefined because they depend on the form of input and output and other considerations that have not been specified. First, we shall use a type called token, where a token is any one of an operand, an operator, a parenthesis, or a special symbol indicating the end of the expression. Next, we use a function Kind(t: token): tokenkind, where the result is a value in the enumerated type

the result is a value in the enumerated type

tokenkind = (operand, unaryop, binaryop, leftparen, rightparen, endexpression).

We also use a stack S for holding the tokens (operators) being delayed. The input expression will be called infix and the output postfix, both of a type called expression.

We shall need two procedures,

GetToken(**var** t: token; **var** infix: expression)

that obtains the next token from the input (infix expression), and

PutToken(t: token; **var** postfix: expression)

that puts the given token into the postfix expression. Thus these two procedures might read and write with files or might only refer to arrays already set up, depending on the desired application. Finally, we shall use a function Priority(op) that will return the priority of an operator op.

With these conventions, we can write the procedure.

translation into postfix

procedure Translate(**var** infix, postfix: expression);
{**Pre:** infix *is an expression in infix (ordinary) notation that is correctly formed with no syntax errors.*
  Post: postfix *is the same expression rearranged into postfix form.*
  Uses: *Types* token *that represents a single token of the expression and expression that represents a list of tokens in either infix or postfix form; procedures* GetToken *and* PutToken *that take tokens from the infix expression and put them into the postfix expression; function* Kind *that determines whether a token is an operand, a binary or unary operator, or an opening or closing parenthesis; the package for processing stacks.*}

var
  S: stacktype;   {*holds the operators being delayed*}
  t,   {*token currently being processed*}
  x: token;   {*operator popped from or on top of stack*}
  endright: Boolean;   {*End of right operand reached?*}

begin   {*procedure Translate*}
  CreateStack(S);   {*Initialize stack to be empty.*}
  repeat
    GetToken(t, infix);
    case Kind(t) **of**
      operand:
        PutToken(t, postfix);

```
        leftparen:
            Push(t, S);

        rightparen:
            begin
                Pop(t, S);
                while Kind(t) <> leftparen do
                begin
                    PutToken(t, postfix);
                    Pop(t, S)                        {Discard the left parenthesis.}
                end
            end;

        unaryop,                            {Treat both kinds of operators together.}
        binaryop:
            begin
                repeat
                    if StackEmpty(S) then
                        endright := true
                    else begin
                        StackTop(x, S);
                        if Kind(x) = leftparen then
                            endright := true
                        else if Priority(x) < Priority(t) then
                            endright := true
                        else if (Priority(x) = Priority(t))
                                        and (Priority(t) = 6) then
                            endright := true
                        else begin
                            endright := false;
                            Pop(x, S);
                            PutToken(x, postfix)
                        end
                    end
                until endright;
                Push(t, S)
            end;                                        {processing operator}

        endexpression:
            while not StackEmpty(S) > 0 do            {Empty the stack.}
            begin
                Pop(x, S);
                PutToken(x, postfix)
            end
    end                                                {case statement}
    until Kind(t) = endexpression;
    PutToken(t, postfix);                      {Put endexpression into postfix.}
end;                                                {procedure Translate}
```

As an illustration, Figure 4.8 shows the steps that this procedure will perform while translating the quadratic formula

$$x := (\dot{-} b + (b^2 - 4 \times a \times c)^{\frac{1}{2}})/(2 \times a)$$

into postfix form. Recall that we are using $\dot{-}$ to denote unary negation, so that there will be no confusion between the unary and binary operators.

Input Token	Contents of Stack (rightmost token is on top)	Output Token(s)
x		x
:=	:=	
(	:= (	
$\dot{-}$	:= ($\dot{-}$	
b	:= ($\dot{-}$	b
+	:= (+	$\dot{-}$
(	:= (+ (	
b	:= (+ (	b
↑	:= (+ (↑	
2	:= (+ (↑	2
−	:= (+ (−	↑
4	:= (+ (−	4
×	:= (+ (− ×	
a	:= (+ (− ×	a
×	:= (+ (− ×	×
c	:= (+ (− ×	c
)	:= (+	× −
↑	:= (+ ↑	
½	:= (+ ↑	½
)	:=	↑ +
/	:= /	
(	:= / (	
2	:= / (	2
×	:= / (×	
a	:= / (×	a
)	:= /	×
endexpression		/ :=

Figure 4.8. Translation of the quadratic formula into postfix form

EXERCISES 4.4

E1. Convert each of the following expressions into postfix form. Use the table of operator priorities displayed earlier in this section as your guide, and not the rules of Pascal.

    a. $a < b + c$.

    b. $a - b < c - d$ **or** $e < f$.

    c. $n!$ **div** $(k! \times (n - k)!)$ (Formula for binomial coefficients).

    d. $s := (n/2) \times (2 \times a + (n - 1) \times d)$ (Sum of the first n terms of an arithmetic progression).

    e. $g := a \times (1 - r^n)/(1 - r)$ (Sum of the first n terms of a geometric progression).

    f. $a = 1$ **or** $b \times c = 2$ **or** $(a > 1$ **and not** $b < 3)$.

E2. Note that in procedure Translate the action taken at the end of the input is much the same as when a right parenthesis is encountered. Suppose that the entire expression is enclosed in a pair of parentheses to serve as sentinels for the beginning and end. Write a simplified version of procedure Translate that no longer needs to check explicitly for the end of input.

E3. Modify procedure Translate so that it will accommodate unary operators that are written to the right of their operands. You should assume that the function Kind(...) returns the answer rightunary when such an operator appears.

POINTERS AND PITFALLS

1. Practice information hiding: First think in terms of the properties and operations of a data structure. In writing an application program, use a package of procedures and functions to access your data structures.

2. Choose your data structures as you design your algorithms, and avoid making premature decisions.

3. Always keep the implementation details separate from the applications.

4. Stacks are the simplest kind of lists; use stacks when possible.

5. Avoid tricky ways of storing your data; tricks usually will not generalize to new situations.

6. Be sure to initialize your data structures.

7. Check to be sure that your preconditions are satisfied before you invoke any subprogram.

8. Always be careful about the extreme cases and handle them gracefully. Trace through your algorithm to determine what happens when a data structure is empty or full.

REVIEW QUESTIONS

4.1   1. Define the term *stack*.

2. List all the operations that can be done on a stack.

3. Why are stacks often called *last-in-first-out* lists?

4. What are *stack frames* for subprograms? What do they show?

5. What is *information hiding*?

6. Why may it be advantageous for a data type like stacks not to be built into a programming language?

4.2   7. Give five reasons for practicing information hiding.

8. In twenty words or less, describe how we have implemented stacks in Pascal in this chapter.

4.3   9. What are the *prefix* and *postfix* forms of an expression? What advantage do they have over the ordinary (infix) way to write expressions?

4.4   10. What are *priorities* of operators, and what are they used for?

11. In twenty words or less, present the basic idea used to translate expressions from infix to postfix notation.

5

QUEUES

A queue is a data structure modeled after a line of people waiting to be served. After stacks, queues are the simplest form of restricted list. This chapter studies queues together with their implementations in computer storage and Pascal procedures, and applies them to the simulation of an airport.

DEFINITIONS

In ordinary English, a queue is defined as a waiting line, like a line of people waiting to purchase tickets, where the first person in line is the first person served. For computer applications, we similarly define a *queue* to be a list in which all additions to the list are made at one end, and all deletions from the list are made at the other end. Queues are also called *first-in, first-out lists*, or *FIFO* for short. See Figure 5.1.

Figure 5.1. A queue

applications   Applications of queues are, if anything, even more common than are applications of stacks, since in performing tasks by computer, as in all parts of life, it is so often necessary to wait one's turn before having access to something. Within a computer system there may be queues of tasks waiting for the line printer, for access to disk storage, or even, in a time-sharing system, for use of the CPU. Within a single program, there may be multiple requests to be kept in a queue, or one task may create other tasks, which must be done in turn by keeping them in a queue.

front and rear   The entry in a queue ready to be served, that is, the first entry that will be removed from the queue, we call the *front* of the queue (or, sometimes, the *head* of the queue). Similarly, the last entry in the queue, that is, the one most recently added, we call the *rear* (or the *tail*) of the queue.

operations   To complete the definition of a queue, we must specify the operations that it permits. We shall do so by listing the procedure or function name for each operation, together with the preconditions and postconditions that complete its specifications. As you read these specifications, you should note the similarity with the corresponding operations for a stack.

The first step we must perform in working with any queue is to use the procedure CreateQueue to initialize it for further use:

---

procedure CreateQueue (**var** Q: queuetype)

precondition: None.

postcondition: The queue Q has been created and is initialized to be empty.

Next come the operations for checking the status of a queue.

---

function QueueEmpty (Q: queuetype) : Boolean

precondition: The queue Q has been created.

postcondition: The function returns true or false according as queue Q is empty or not.

---

function QueueFull (Q: queuetype) : Boolean

precondition: The queue Q has been created.

postcondition: The function returns true or false according as queue Q is full or not.

The declarations for the fundamental operations on a queue come next.

---

procedure Append (x: queueentry; **var** Q: queuetype)

precondition: The queue Q has been created and is not full.

postcondition: The entry x has been stored in the queue as its last entry.

---

procedure Serve (**var** x: queueentry; **var** Q: queuetype)

precondition: The queue Q has been created and is not empty.

postcondition: The first entry in the queue has been removed and returned as the value of x.

*alternative
names*

The names *Append* and *Serve* are used for the fundamental operations on a queue to indicate clearly what actions are performed and to avoid confusion with the terms we shall use for other data types. Other names, however, are also often used for these operations, terms such as *Insert* and *Delete* or the coined words *Enqueue* and *Dequeue*.

Note from the preconditions that it is an error to attempt to append an entry onto a full queue or to serve (remove) an entry from an empty queue. If we write the procedures Append and Serve carefully, then they should return error messages when they are used incorrectly. The declarations, however, do not guarantee that the procedures will catch the errors, and, if they do not, then they may produce spurious and unpredictable results. Hence the careful programmer should always make sure, whenever invoking a subprogram, that its preconditions are guaranteed to be satisfied.

There remain two more queue operations that are sometimes useful.

---

function QueueSize(Q: queuetype): integer

precondition: The queue Q has been created.

postcondition: The function returns the number of entries in the queue Q.

---

procedure QueueFront(**var** x: queueentry; Q: queuetype)

precondition: The queue Q has been created and is not empty.

postcondition: The variable x is a copy of the first entry in Q; the queue Q remains unchanged.

Some parameters in these specifications are shown as **var** parameters and others as value parameters, depending on whether they are used for input or for output by the subprogram. When we implement these subprograms, however, we shall sometimes use **var** parameters when only input is needed, in order to save the time that would otherwise be required to make a local copy of the entire queue.

EXERCISES 5.1

E1. Suppose that Q is a queue that holds characters and that x, y, z are character variables. Show the contents of the queue Q at each step of the following code segments.

a. CreateQueue(Q);	b. CreateQueue(Q);	c. CreateQueue(Q);
Append('a', Q);	Append('a', Q);	Append('a', Q);
Serve(x, Q);	Append('b', Q);	x := 'b';
Append('b', Q);	Serve(x, Q);	Append('x', Q);
Serve(y, Q);	Append('c', Q);	Serve(y, Q);
Append('c', Q);	Append(x, Q);	Append(x, Q);
Append('d', Q);	Serve(y, Q);	Serve(z, Q);
Serve(z, Q);	Serve(z, Q);	Append(y, Q);

accounting

E2. Suppose that you are a financier and purchase 100 shares of stock in Company X in each of January, April, and September and sell 100 shares in each of June and November. The prices per share in these months were

Jan	Apr	Jun	Sep	Nov
$10	$30	$20	$50	$30

Determine the total amount of your capital gain or loss using **(a)** FIFO (first-in, first-out) accounting and **(b)** LIFO (last-in, first-out) accounting (that is, assuming that you keep your stock certificates in **(a)** a queue or **(b)** a stack). The 100 shares you still own at the end of the year do not enter the calculation.

E3. Use the procedures developed in the text to write other procedures that will do the following tasks. In writing each procedure be sure to check for empty and full structures as appropriate.

a. Move all the entries from a stack into a queue.

b. Move all the entries from a queue onto a stack.

c. Empty one stack onto the top of another stack in such a way that the entries that were in the first stack keep the same relative order.

d. Empty one stack onto the top of another stack in such a way that the entries that were in the first stack are in the reverse of their original order.

e. Start with a queue and an empty stack, and use the stack to reverse the order of all the entries in the queue.

f. Start with a stack and an empty queue, and use the queue to reverse the order of all the entries in the stack.

5.2

IMPLEMENTATIONS OF QUEUES

Now that we have considered how queues are defined and the operations they admit, let us change our point of view and consider how queues can be implemented in computer storage and Pascal procedures.

The Physical Model

As we did for stacks, we can create a queue in computer storage easily by setting up an ordinary array to hold the entries. Now, however, we must keep track of both the front and the rear of the queue. One method would be to keep the front of the queue always in the first location of the array. Then an entry could be appended to the queue simply by increasing the counter showing the rear, in exactly the same way as we added an entry to a stack. To delete an entry from the queue, however, would be very expensive indeed, since after the first entry was served, all the remaining entries would need to be moved one position up the queue to fill in the vacancy. With a long queue, this process would be prohibitively slow. Although this method of storage closely models a queue of people waiting to be served, it is a poor choice for use in computers.

Linear Implementation

For efficient processing of queues, we shall therefore need two indices so that we can keep track of both the front and the rear of the queue without moving any entries. To append an entry to the queue, we simply increase the rear by one and put the entry in that position. To serve an entry, we take it from the position at the front and then increase the front by one. This method, however, still has a major defect. Both the front and rear indices are increased but never decreased. Even *defect* if there are never more than two entries in the queue, an unbounded amount of storage will be needed for the queue if the sequence of operations is

Append, Append, Serve, Append, Serve, Append, ...

The problem, of course, is that, as the queue moves down the array, the storage space at the beginning of the array is discarded and never used again. Perhaps the queue can be likened to a snake crawling through storage. Sometimes the snake is longer, sometimes shorter, but if it always keeps crawling in a straight line, then it will soon reach the end of the storage space.

advantage   Note, however, that for applications where the queue is regularly emptied (such as when a series of requests is allowed to build up to a certain point, and then a task is initiated that clears all the requests before returning), at a time when the queue is empty, the front and rear can both be reset to the beginning of the array, and the simple scheme of using two indices and straight-line storage becomes a very efficient implementation.

Circular Arrays

In concept, we can overcome the inefficient use of space simply by thinking of the array as a circle rather than a straight line. See Figure 5.2. In this way, as entries are added and removed from the queue, the head will continually chase the tail around the array, so that the snake can keep crawling indefinitely but stay in a confined circuit. At different times, the queue will occupy different parts of the array, but we never need worry about running out of space unless the array is fully occupied, in which case we truly have overflow.

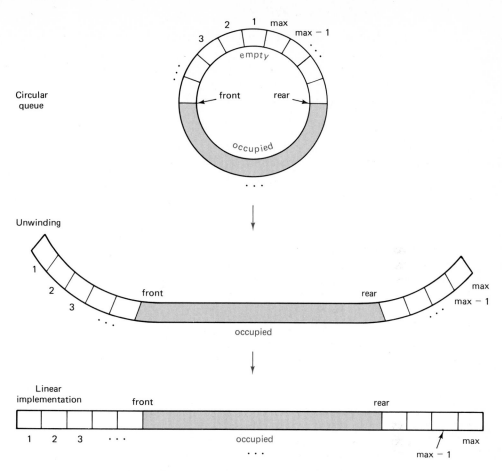

Figure 5.2. Queue in a circular array

Implementation of Circular Arrays

Our next problem is to implement a circular array as an ordinary linear (that is, straight-line) array. To do so, we think of the positions around the circle as numbered from 1 to max, where max is the total number of entries in the circular array, and to implement the circular array, we use the same-numbered entries of a linear array. Then moving the indices is just the same as doing modular *modular* arithmetic: When we increase an index past max, we start over again at 1. This *arithmetic* is like doing arithmetic on a circular clock face; the hours are numbered from 1 to 12, and if we add four hours to ten o'clock, we obtain two o'clock.

Perhaps a good human analogy of this linear representation is that of a priest serving communion to people kneeling at the front of a church. The communicants do not move until the priest comes by and serves them. When the priest reaches the end of the row, he returns to the beginning and starts again, since by this time a new row of people have come forward.

Circular Arrays in Pascal

In Pascal, we can increase an index i by 1 in a circular array by writing

$$\textbf{if } i = max \textbf{ then } i := 1 \textbf{ else } i := i + 1;$$

or even more easily (but perhaps less efficiently at run time) by using the **mod** operator:

$$i := (i \textbf{ mod } max) + 1.$$

A more natural way to express this latter form is to index the array from 0 to max − 1, so that the addition comes before the **mod**:

$$i := (i + 1) \textbf{ mod } max.$$

(You should check to verify that the result of the latter expression is always between 0 and max − 1, whereas the previous expression is always between 1 and max.) Starting the indices at 0 proves even more natural when it is necessary to increase the index i by an arbitrary amount k > 0. If we index the array from 0 to max − 1, we need only write

$$i := (i + k) \textbf{ mod } max$$

whereas if we index the array from 1 to max, we must write

$$i := (i + k - 1) \textbf{ mod } max + 1.$$

In Pascal, unfortunately, starting the indices at 0 means that we must declare two constants, both max and another equal to max − 1, and doing so sometimes causes confusion. For simplicity, we therefore retain the traditional indexing starting at 1 whenever we implement a queue in a circular array.

Boundary Conditions

empty or full?

Before writing formal algorithms to add to and delete from a queue, let us consider the boundary conditions, that is, the indicators that a queue is empty or full. If there is exactly one entry in the queue, then the front index will equal the rear index. When this one entry is removed, then the front will be increased by 1, so that an empty queue is indicated when the rear is one position before the front. Now suppose that the queue is nearly full. Then the rear will have moved well away from the front, all the way around the circle, and when the array is full the rear will be exactly one position behind the front. Thus we have another difficulty: The front and rear indices are in exactly the same relative positions for an empty queue and for a full queue! There is no way, by looking at the indices alone, to tell a full queue from an empty one. This situation is illustrated in Figure 5.3.

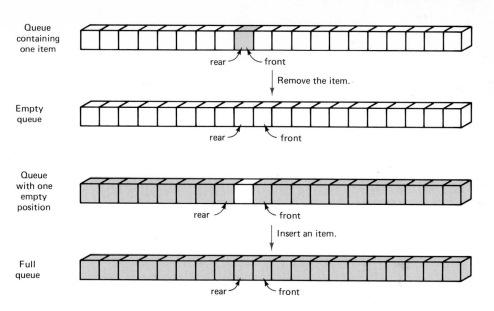

Figure 5.3. Empty and full queues

Possible Solutions

1. empty position

There are at least three essentially different ways to resolve this problem. One is to insist on leaving one empty position in the array, so that the queue is considered full when the rear index has moved within two positions of the front. A second method is to introduce a new variable. This can be a Boolean variable that will be used when the rear comes just before the front to indicate whether the queue is full or not (a Boolean variable to check emptiness would be just as good) or an integer variable that counts the number of entries in the queue. The third method is to set one or both of the indices to some value(s) that would otherwise never occur in order to indicate an empty (or full) queue. If, for example, the array entries are indexed from 1 to max, then an empty queue could be indicated by setting the rear index to 0.

2. flag

3. special values

Summary of Implementations

To summarize the discussion of queues, let us list all the methods we have discussed for implementing queues.

- The physical model: a linear array with the front always in the first position and all entries moved up the array whenever the front is deleted. This is generally a poor method for use in computers.

- A linear array with two indices always increasing. This is a good method if the queue can be emptied all at once.

- A circular array with front and rear indices and one position left vacant.

- A circular array with front and rear indices and a Boolean variable to indicate fullness (or emptiness).

- A circular array with front and rear indices and an integer variable counting entries.
- A circular array with front and rear indices taking special values to indicate emptiness.

postpone implementation · decisions

In Chapter 7, we shall find still other ways to implement queues. The most important thing to remember from this list is that, with so many variations in implementation, we should always keep questions concerning the use of data structures like queues separate from questions concerning their implementation; and, in programming we should always consider only one of these categories of questions at a time. After we have considered how queues will be used in our application, and after we have written the procedures employing queues, we will have more information to help us choose the best implementation of queues suited to our application.

Programming Precept

Practice information hiding:
Separate the application of data structures from their implementation.

This division between applications of data structures and their implementation details can be pictured as in Figure 5.4, which shows a shop full of various data structures implemented in many different ways, all available for incorporation into various applications as appropriate.

Figure 5.4. A data structures shop

5.3

CIRCULAR QUEUES IN PASCAL

Next let us write formal Pascal procedures for some of the possible implementations of a queue. We wish to illustrate some of the variety that is possible, so we shall choose the last two implementations described in the previous section and leave the others as exercises. In all cases, however, we take the queue as stored in an array indexed with the range

$$1 .. \, \text{maxqueue}$$

and containing entries of a type called queueentry. The variables front and rear will point to appropriate positions in the array.

5.3.1 Implementation with a Counter

type queue

First, we take the method in which a variable count is used to keep track of the number of entries in the queue. The record declaration for a queue takes the form

```
queuetype = record
    count,
    front,
    rear: 0 .. maxqueue;
    entry: array [1 .. maxqueue] of queueentry;
end;
```

The first procedure we need will initialize the queue to be empty.

initialize

```
procedure CreateQueue (var Q: queuetype);
{Pre:   None.
  Post:  The queue Q has been initialized to be empty.}
begin                                     {procedure CreateQueue}
  with Q do begin
    count := 0;
    front := 1;
    rear := 0
  end
end;                                      {procedure CreateQueue}
```

The procedures for adding to and deleting from a queue follow our preceding discussion closely. As in our error processing for stacks, we shall only write out an informative message when an error occurs, and then continue processing, rather than terminating the program as would often be done in a production version.

insertion

```
procedure Append(x: queueentry; var Q: queuetype);
{Pre:   The queue Q has been created and is not full.
  Post: The entry x has been stored in the queue as its last entry.}
begin                                              {procedure Append}
  with Q do
    if count = maxqueue then
      writeln('Error: Attempt to append an entry to a full queue')
    else begin
      count := count + 1;
      rear := (rear mod maxqueue) + 1;
      entry[rear] := x
    end
end;                                               {procedure Append}
```

deletion

```
procedure Serve(var x: queueentry; var Q: queuetype);
{Pre:   The queue Q has been created and is not empty.
  Post: The first entry in the queue has been removed and returned as the
        value of x.}
begin                                              {procedure Serve}
  with Q do
    if count = 0 then
      writeln('Error: Attempt to remove an entry from an empty queue')
    else begin
      count := count - 1;
      x := entry[front];
      front := (front mod maxqueue) + 1
    end
end;                                               {procedure Serve}
```

We shall also find use for three functions concerning the size of the queue, all of which are easy to write in this implementation.

size

```
function QueueSize(var Q: queuetype): integer;
{Pre:   The queue Q has been created.
  Post: The function returns the number of entries in the queue Q.}
begin
  QueueSize := Q.count
end;
```

empty?

```
function QueueEmpty(var Q: queuetype): Boolean;
{Pre:   The queue Q has been created.
  Post: The function returns true or false according as queue Q is empty or
        not.}
begin
  QueueEmpty := (Q.count = 0)
end;
```

```
        function QueueFull(var Q: queuetype): Boolean;
full?      {Pre:   The queue Q has been created.
            Post:  The function returns true or false according as queue Q is full or not.}
        begin
            QueueFull := (Q.count = maxqueue)
        end;
```

Note that the queue is specified as a **var** parameter in each of these functions, even though it is not modified by any of them. This is a concession to efficiency that saves the time required to make a new local copy of the entire queue each time one of the functions is evaluated.

There remains one more operation on queues, the procedure QueueFront. This procedure will be left as an exercise.

5.3.2 Implementation with Special Index Values

type declaration

Next, let us turn to the method that relies on special values for the indices. Most of the necessary changes in declarations are clear. We have

```
            queuetype = record
                front,
                rear: 0 .. maxqueue;
                entry: array [1 .. maxqueue] of queueentry;
            end;
```

We shall use the conditions

$$\text{rear} = 0 \quad \text{and} \quad \text{front} = 1$$

to indicate an empty queue. The initialization procedure is

```
            procedure CreateQueue(var Q: queuetype);
initialization  {Pre:   None.
                Post:  The queue Q has been initialized to be empty.}
            begin
                Q.front := 1;
                Q.rear := 0
            end;
```

To write the procedure for adding to the queue, we must first (for error checking) find a condition indicating whether the queue is full or not. Fullness is typically indicated by rear = front − 1 together with rear > 0, but it is also possible that front = 1 and rear = maxqueue. Building these conditions into the procedure, we obtain

insertion

```
procedure Append(x: queueentry; var Q: queuetype);
{Pre:   The queue Q has been created and is not full.
 Post:  The specified item x has been appended to the end of the queue Q.}
begin                                          {procedure Append}
   with Q do
      if ((rear = front − 1) and (rear > 0)) or
         ((rear = maxqueue) and (front = 1)) then
            writeln('Error: Attempt to append an entry to a full queue')
      else begin
         rear := (rear mod maxqueue) + 1;
         entry[rear] := x;
      end
end;                                           {procedure Append}
```

Since emptiness is indicated by rear = 0, the deletion procedure closely resembles the previous version.

deletion

```
procedure Serve(var x: queueentry; var Q: queuetype);
{Pre:   The queue Q has been created and is not empty.
 Post:  The first entry in the queue has been removed and returned as the
        value of x.}
begin                                          {procedure Serve}
   with Q do
      if rear = 0 then
         writeln('Error: Attempt to remove an entry from an empty queue')
      else begin
         x := entry[front];
         if front = rear then                  {The queue is now empty.}
         begin
            front := 1;
            rear := 0
         end
         else
            front := (front mod maxqueue) + 1
      end
end;                                           {procedure Serve}
```

The functions QueueSize, QueueEmpty, QueueFull, and the procedure QueueFront will be left as exercises.

EXERCISES 5.3

E1. Write the procedure QueueFront that returns the entry at the front of the queue but does not change the queue itself. It is an error if the procedure is called for an empty queue. Do you need to write separate versions for the two implementation methods, or will the same version work correctly with either implementation?

E2. Write the procedures and functions needed for the implementation of queues in a linear array when it can be assumed that the queue can be emptied when necessary. Write a procedure Append that will add an entry if there is room and, if not, will call another procedure (ServeAll) that will empty the queue. While writing this second procedure, you may assume the existence of an auxiliary procedure Service(x: queueentry) that will process a single entry that you have just removed from the queue.

E3. Write Pascal procedures and functions to implement queues by the simple but slow method of keeping the front of the queue always in the first position of a linear array.

E4. Write Pascal procedures and functions to implement queues in a linear array with two indices front and rear, such that, when rear reaches the end of the array, all the entries are moved to the front of the array.

E5. Write the three functions QueueSize, QueueEmpty, and QueueFull for the implementation of a queue in a circular array with special index values to indicate emptiness.

E6. Rewrite the first set of Pascal procedures for queue processing from the text, using a Boolean variable full instead of a counter of entries in the queue.

E7. Write Pascal procedures and functions to implement queues in a circular array with one unused entry in the array. That is, we consider that the array is full when the rear is two positions before the front; when the rear is one position before, it will always indicate an empty queue.

PROJECTS 5.3

P1. Write a demonstration program for manipulating queues. This program should have a form similar to that written to demonstrate stacks in Project P1 of Section 4.2. The entries in your queue should be characters. Your program should write a one-line menu from which the user can select any of the queue operations. After your program does the requested operation, it should inform the user of the result and ask for the next request. When the user wishes to append a character onto the queue, your program will need to ask what character to use.

P2. Write a procedure that will read one line of input from the terminal. The input is supposed to consist of two parts separated by a colon ':'. As its result, your procedure should produce a single character as follows:

N   No colon on the line.
L   The left part (before the colon) is longer than the right.
R   The right part (after the colon) is longer than the left.
D   The left and right parts have the same length but are different.
S   The left and right parts are exactly the same.

Examples:	Input	Output
	Sample Sample	N
	Short:Long	L
	Sample:Sample	S

Use a queue to keep track of the left part of the line while reading the right part.

5.4

APPLICATION OF QUEUES: SIMULATION

5.4.1 Introduction

Simulation is the use of one system to imitate the behavior of another system. Simulations are often used when it would be too expensive or dangerous to experiment with the real system. There are physical simulations, such as wind tunnels used to experiment with designs for car bodies and flight simulators used to train airline pilots. Mathematical simulations are systems of equations used to describe some system, and computer simulations use the steps of a program to imitate the behavior of the system under study.

computer simulation In a computer simulation, the objects being studied are usually represented as data, often as data structures like records or arrays whose entries describe the properties of the objects. Actions in the system being studied are represented as operations on the data, and the rules describing these actions are translated into computer algorithms. By changing the values of the data or by modifying these algorithms, we can observe the changes in the computer simulation, and then, we hope, we can draw worthwhile inferences concerning the behavior of the actual system in which we are interested.

While one object in a system is involved in some action, other objects and actions will often need to be kept waiting. Hence queues are important data structures for use in computer simulations. We shall study one of the most common and useful kinds of computer simulations, one that concentrates on queues as its basic data structure. These simulations imitate the behavior of systems (often, in fact, called *queueing systems*) in which there are queues of objects waiting to be served by various processes.

5.4.2 Simulation of an Airport

As a specific example, let us consider a small but busy airport with only one runway (see Figure 5.5). In each unit of time, one plane can land or one plane can take off, but not both. Planes arrive ready to land or to take off at random

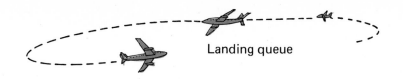

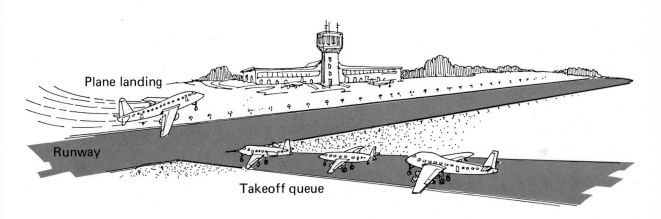

Figure 5.5. An airport

times, so at any given unit of time, the runway may be idle or a plane may be landing or taking off, and there may be several planes waiting either to land or take off. We therefore need two queues, called landing and takeoff, to hold these planes. It is better to keep a plane waiting on the ground than in the air, so a small airport allows a plane to take off only if there are no planes waiting to land. Hence, after receiving requests from new planes to land or take off, our simulation will first service the head of the queue of planes waiting to land, and only if the landing queue is empty will it allow a plane to take off. We shall wish to run the simulation through many units of time, and, therefore, we embed the main action of the program in a loop that runs for curtime (denoting *current time*) from 1 to a variable endtime. With this notation, we can write an outline of the main program.

rules

first outline

```
program Airport(input, output);
var
    curplane: plane;                    {plane currently being processed}
    landing,
    takeoff: queuetype;                 {lines of planes waiting}
    curtime,                            {current time unit}
    endtime,                            {time when simulation ends}
    counter: integer;                   {loop control variable}
```

```
            begin                                   {main program Airport}
              CreateQueue(landing);        {Set the queues to be empty at the start.}
              CreateQueue(takeoff);
              for curtime := 1 to endtime do
              begin                      {Commence the main loop on units of time.}
                for counter := 1 to RandomNumber do
                begin                        {Add new planes to the landing queue.}
                  NewPlane(curplane);         {Get information on the new plane.}
                  if QueueFull(landing) then
                    Refuse(curplane)     {Include error processing for a full queue.}
                  else
                    Append(curplane, landing)    {Put each new plane into queue.}
                end;
                for counter := 1 to RandomNumber do
                begin                        {Add new planes to the takeoff queue.}
                  NewPlane(curplane);
                  if QueueFull(takeoff) then
                    Refuse(curplane)
                  else
                    Append(curplane, takeoff)
                end;
                if not QueueEmpty(landing) then
                begin                         {If a plane is waiting to land, let it.}
                  Serve(curplane, landing);
                  Land(curplane)                      {Process a landing plane.}
                end
                else if not QueueEmpty(takeoff) then
                begin                     {Only if none landing can one take off.}
                  Serve(curplane, takeoff);
                  Fly(curplane)                     {Process a departing plane.}
                end
                else
                  Idle                   {Runway is idle; there is nothing to do.}
              end;
              Conclude                              {Finish up the simulation.}
            end.                                     {main program Airport}
```

new plane ready to land

new plane ready to take off

plane landing

plane taking off

idle runway

5.4.3 The Main Program

Although this outline clearly shows the use of queues in this simulation, more detail is needed to keep track of all the interesting statistics concerning the problem, such as the number of planes processed, the average time spent waiting, and the number of planes (if any) refused service. These details are reflected in the declarations of constants, types, and variables to be inserted into the main program. We shall then need to write the subprograms to specify how this information is processed. The declaration of type **queuetype** is deliberately omitted from the following list, in order that we can postpone until later the decision concerning which method will be used to implement the queues. Most of the remaining declarations are self-explanatory, except for the last three variables, which are concerned with generating random numbers, and will be explained when we consider the use of random numbers.

declarations

```
const maxqueue = 5;                    {Use a small value for testing.}
type
   action = (arrive, depart);          {What is the plane wishing to do?}
   plane = record
      id,                              {identification number of plane}
      tm: integer;                     {time of arrival in queue}
   end;
   queueentry = plane;
{Insert declaration of type queuetype here.}
var
   landing,
   takeoff: queuetype;
   curplane: plane;
   curtime,    {current time; one unit = time needed for takeoff or landing}
   nplanes,                        {number of planes processed so far}
   endtime,                        {total number of time units to run}
   idletime,                       {number of units when runway is idle}
   nland,                              {number of planes landed}
   ntakeoff,                        {number of planes taken off}
   nrefuse,                   {number of planes refused use of airport}
   landwait,                   {total waiting time for planes landed}
   takeoffwait,              {total waiting time for planes taking off}
   counter: integer;                       {loop control variable}
   expectarrive,    {expected number of planes arriving to land in one unit}
   expectdepart: real;   {expected number of planes newly ready to leave}
   seed: integer;                  {used for generating random numbers}
```

simulation statistics

The version of the main program in runnable Pascal differs little from the preceding outline except for the inclusion of the many parameters used to update all the variables just declared.

```
program Airport(input, output);
{Pre:   The user must supply the number of time intervals the simulation is to
        run, the expected number of planes arriving, and the expected number
        of planes departing per time interval.
 Post:  The program performs a random simulation of the airport, showing the
        status of the runway at each time interval, and prints out a summary
        at the conclusion.
 Uses:  Queue package, random-number package, procedures Start, New-
        Plane, Refuse, Land, Fly, Idle, and Conclude.}
{Declarations of constants, types, and variables are to be inserted here.}
```

```
                              begin                              {main program Airport}
                                CreateQueue(landing);
    initialize                  CreateQueue(takeoff);
                                Start(endtime, nplanes, nland, ntakeoff, nrefuse, landwait, takeoffwait,
                                      idletime, expectarrive, expectdepart);

                                for curtime := 1 to endtime do
                                begin
                                  for counter := 1 to RandomNumber(expectarrive) do
  new plane(s)                    begin                          {Add a new plane to the landing queue.}
  ready to land                     NewPlane(curplane, nplanes, curtime, arrive);
                                    if QueueFull(landing) then
                                      Refuse(curplane, arrive, nrefuse)
                                    else
                                      Append(curplane, landing)
                                  end;

                                  for counter := 1 to RandomNumber(expectdepart) do
  new plane(s)                    begin                          {Add a new plane to the takeoff queue.}
  ready to take off                 NewPlane(curplane, nplanes, curtime, depart);
                                    if QueueFull(takeoff) then
                                      Refuse(curplane, depart, nrefuse)
                                    else
                                      Append(curplane, takeoff)
                                  end;

                                  if not QueueEmpty(landing) then
  plane landing                   begin                          {Bring a plane in to land.}
                                    Serve(curplane, landing);
                                    Land(curplane, curtime, nland, landwait)
                                  end
                                  else if not QueueEmpty(takeoff) then
  plane taking off                begin                          {Allow a plane to take off.}
                                    Serve(curplane, takeoff);
                                    Fly(curplane, curtime, ntakeoff, takeoffwait)
                                  end
                                  else
                                    Idle(curtime, idletime);
  runway idle                   end;
                                Conclude(nplanes, nland, ntakeoff, nrefuse, landwait, takeoffwait,
  finish simulation                   idletime, takeoff, landing)
                              end.                               {main program Airport}
```

5.4.4 Steps of the Simulation

The actions of the procedures for doing the steps of the simulation are generally straightforward, so we proceed to write each in turn, with comments only as needed for clarity.

Initialization

```
        procedure Start (var endtime, nplanes, nland, ntakeoff, nrefuse, landwait,
                takeoffwait, idletime: integer; var expectarrive, expectdepart: real);
        {Pre:   None.
          Post: Asks user for responses and initializes all variables specified as pa-
                rameters.}
        var
            acceptable: Boolean;                    {Are the input numbers acceptable?}
            response: char;                                          {answer from user}
        begin                                                      {procedure Start}
```
initialize
```
            nplanes := 0;
```
counters
```
            nland := 0;
            ntakeoff := 0;
            nrefuse := 0;
            landwait := 0;
            takeoffwait := 0;
            idletime := 0;
```
instruct user
```
            writeln ('This program simulates an airport with only one runway.');
            writeln ('One plane can land or depart in each unit of time.');
            writeln ('Up to ', maxqueue: 3, ' planes can');
            writeln ('be waiting to land or take off at any time.');
```
input parameters
```
            write ('How many units of time will the simulation run? ');
            readln (endtime);
            Randomize (seed);                    {required for random-number generation}
            repeat
                write ('Expected number of arrivals per unit time (real number)?');
                readln (expectarrive);
                write ('Expected number of departures per unit time?');
                readln (expectdepart);
```
error checking
```
                if (expectarrive < 0.0) or (expectdepart < 0.0) then
                begin
                    writeln ('These numbers must be nonnegative.');
                    acceptable := false
                end
                else if expectarrive + expectdepart > 1.0 then
                begin
                    write ('The airport will become saturated. Read new numbers?');
                    readln (response);
                    acceptable := response in ['N', 'n']
                end
                else
                    acceptable := true
            until acceptable
        end;                                                       {procedure Start}
```

Accepting a New Plane

```
procedure NewPlane(var curplane: plane; var nplanes: integer;
                            curtime: integer; kind: action);
{Pre:   None.
  Post: Makes a new record for a plane and updates nplanes.}
begin                                          {procedure NewPlane}
   nplanes := nplanes + 1;
   curplane.id := nplanes;
   curplane.tm := curtime;
   case kind of
      depart: writeln('    Plane ', nplanes: 3, ' ready to take off.');
      arrive: writeln('    Plane ', nplanes: 3, ' ready to land.')
   end
end;                                            {procedure NewPlane}
```

Handling a Full Queue

```
procedure Refuse(curplane: plane; kind: action; var nrefuse: integer);
{Pre:   None.
  Post: Processes a plane wanting to use runway, but the queue is full.}
begin                                           {procedure Refuse}
   case kind of
      depart: writeln('    Plane ', curplane.id: 3, ' told to try later.');
      arrive: writeln('    Plane ', curplane.id: 3, ' directed to another airport.')
   end;
   nrefuse := nrefuse + 1
end;                                            {procedure Refuse}
```

Processing an Arriving Plane

```
procedure Land(curplane: plane; curtime: integer; var nland, landwait: integer);
{Pre:   None.
  Post: Processes a plane curplane that is actually landing.}
var
   wait: integer;
begin                                           {procedure Land}
   wait := curtime − curplane.tm;
   writeln(curtime: 4, ': Plane', curplane.id: 3, ' landed; in queue', wait: 2, ' units.');
   nland := nland + 1;
   landwait := landwait + wait
end;                                            {procedure Land}
```

Processing a Departing Plane

```
procedure Fly(curplane: plane; curtime: integer; var ntakeoff, takeoffwait: integer);
{Pre:  None.
  Post:  Process a plane curplane that is actually taking off.}
var
   wait: integer;
begin                                               {procedure Fly}
   wait := curtime − curplane.tm;
   writeln(curtime: 4, ': Plane', curplane.id: 3, ' took off; in queue ', wait: 2, ' units.');
   ntakeoff := ntakeoff + 1;
   takeoffwait := takeoffwait + wait
end;                                                {procedure Fly}
```

Marking an Idle Time Unit

```
procedure Idle(curtime: integer; var idletime: integer);
{Pre:  None.
  Post:  Updates variables for a time unit when the runway is idle.}
begin
   writeln(curtime: 4, ': Runway is idle.');
   idletime := idletime + 1
end;
```

Finishing the Simulation

```
procedure Conclude(nplanes, nland, ntakeoff, nrefuse, landwait, takeoffwait,
                   idletime: integer; var takeoff, landing: queuetype);
{Pre:  None.
  Post:  Writes out all the statistics and concludes the simulation.}
begin                                               {procedure Conclude}
   writeln('Simulation has concluded after     ', endtime: 4, ' units.');
   writeln('Total number of planes processed: ', nplanes: 4);
   writeln('     Number of planes landed:      ', nland: 4);
   writeln('     Number of planes taken off:   ', ntakeoff: 4);
   writeln('     Number of planes refused use: ', nrefuse: 4);
   writeln('     Number left ready to land:    ', QueueSize(landing): 4);
   writeln('     Number left ready to take off: ', QueueSize(takeoff): 4);
   if endtime > 0 then
      writeln('Percentage of time runway idle: ', (idletime/endtime) ∗ 100: 7: 2);
   if nland > 0 then
      writeln('Average wait time to land:       ', (landwait/nland): 7: 2);
   if ntakeoff > 0 then
      writeln('Average wait time to take off:   ', (takeoffwait/ntakeoff): 7: 2)
end;                                                {procedure Conclude}
```

Queue Processing

Still missing from our simulation program are the subprograms for processing queues. All of these subprograms should be collected as a single package and kept in one file. With Turbo Pascal, the subprograms should be compiled separately as a *unit*. With other compilers, the directive include (if it is available) should be used to instruct the compiler to use the queue-processing package. If the compiler does not allow this directive or a similar feature, then we can still use the text editor to copy the queue-processing package into our application program.

By following these steps, we shall find it much easier to change from one implementation of queues to another if we so desire.

5.4.5 Random Numbers

A key step in our simulation is to decide, at each time unit, how many new planes become ready to land or take off. Although there are many ways in which these decisions can be made, one of the most interesting and useful is to make a random decision. When the program is run repeatedly with random decisions, the results will differ from run to run, and with sufficient experimentation, the simulation may display a range of behavior not unlike that of the actual system being studied.

system random-number generator

Many computer systems include random-number generators, and if one is available on your system, it can be used in place of the one developed here. Since standard Pascal, however, does not include random-number generation, we discuss it briefly here.

In any case, we should regard the random-number generator and all the subprograms in this section as a *package* for producing random numbers. Once we have developed the package, we should be able to use it in our simulation program or any other application we wish, but we should not need to look inside it to see how it functions. Hence all the details in this section (which are rather mathematical) should be considered part of the implementation with which we need not be concerned when we use random numbers in an application.

seed for pseudorandom numbers

The idea we shall use to generate random numbers is to start with one number and apply a series of arithmetic operations that will produce another number with no obvious connection to the first. Hence the numbers we produce are not truly random at all, as each one depends in a definite way on its predecessor, and we should more properly speak of **pseudorandom** numbers. The number we use (and simultaneously change) is called the *seed*.

If the seed begins with the same value each time the program is run, then the whole sequence of pseudorandom numbers will be exactly the same, so we normally begin by setting the seed to some random value, for example, the time of day:

```
procedure Randomize(var seed: integer);
{Pre:   None.
  Post: The seed becomes a random value so that different runs of the ap-
        plication program will produce different results.
  Uses: Function clock (not part of standard Pascal).}
begin
    seed := clock;
end;
```

A sample function for producing one pseudorandom number from its predecessor is

sample generator

```
function Random(var seed: integer): real;
{Pre:   None.
  Post: Produces a pseudo-random number x in the range 0 ≤ x < 1.
  Uses: Depends on and changes the value of seed (side effect).}
const
    m = maxint;
    a = 2743;
    c = 5923;
begin
    seed := (seed * a + c) mod m;
    if seed < 0 then seed := seed + m;
    Random := seed/m
end;
```

The constants m, a, and c in this function should not be chosen at random, but
should be carefully chosen to make sure that the results pass various tests for
randomness. The given constants seem to work fairly well on 16-bit computers,
but other choices should be made for other machines.

uniform distribution

The function Random, like most pseudorandom generators, produces as its
result a real number between 0.00 and 1.00. We must take numbers produced
this way and convert them to the form we need.

For our simulation, we wish to obtain an integer giving the number of planes
arriving ready to land (or take off) in a given time unit. We can assume that the
time when one plane enters the system is independent of that of any other plane.
The number of planes arriving in one unit of time then follows what is called a
Poisson distribution in statistics. To calculate the numbers, we need to know
the ***expected value***, that is, the average number of planes arriving in one unit of
time. If, for example, on average one plane arrives in each of four time units,
then the expected value is 0.25. In one time unit, it is possible that several planes
may arrive together, but in many other time units, no plane at all may arrive.
Although there is no upper bound on the number of planes that might arrive at
once, it is very unlikely to be a large number. In fact, there will be enough time
units when no plane arrives so that, when we calculate the average by adding

Poisson distribution

up the total number of planes that arrive and dividing by the number of time units, we obtain only the expected value of 0.25.

The following function determines the number of planes by generating pseudorandom integers according to a Poisson distribution. The derivation of this method and the proof that it works correctly require techniques from calculus and advanced mathematical statistics that are far outside the scope of this book, but that doesn't mean that we cannot apply the theory to calculate the numbers that we want. The result is:

Poisson generator

```
function RandomNumber (expectedvalue: real): integer;
{Pre:   None.
  Post: Generates a random nonnegative integer according to a Poisson dis-
        tribution with the expected value given as the parameter.
  Uses: Random, a function generating uniformly distributed random numbers
        on the interval from 0 to 1.}
var
   limit: real;                    {$e^{-v}$, where $v$ is the expected value}
   count: integer;                                      {count of iterations}
   product: real;             {pseudorandom number, $0 <$ product $< 1$}
begin                                              {function RandomNumber}
   limit := exp (−expectedvalue);
   product := Random (seed);
   count := 0;
   while product > limit do
   begin
      count := count + 1;
      product := product ∗ Random (seed)
   end;
   RandomNumber := count
end;                                               {function RandomNumber}
```

5.4.6 Sample Results

We conclude this section with the output from a sample run of the airport simulation. You should note that there are some periods when the runway is idle and others when one or both of the queues are completely full, and in which some planes must be turned away. If you run this simulation again, you will obtain different results from those given here, but, if the expected values given to the program are the same, then there will be some correspondence between the numbers given in the summaries of the two runs.

This program simulates an airport with only one runway.
One plane can land or depart in each unit of time.
Up to 5 planes can
be waiting to land or take off at any time.

How many units of time will the simulation run ? 30
Expected number of arrivals per unit time (real number) ? 0.47
Expected number of departures per unit time ? 0.47
Plane 1 ready to land.
1: Plane 1 landed; in queue 0 units.

both queues are   2: Runway is idle.
empty
Plane 2 ready to land.
Plane 3 ready to land.
3: Plane 2 landed; in queue 0 units.

4: Plane 3 landed; in queue 1 units.
Plane 4 ready to land.
Plane 5 ready to land.
Plane 6 ready to take off.
Plane 7 ready to take off.
5: Plane 4 landed; in queue 0 units.
Plane 8 ready to take off.
6: Plane 5 landed; in queue 1 units.
Plane 9 ready to take off.
Plane 10 ready to take off.
7: Plane 6 took off; in queue 2 units.

8: Plane 7 took off; in queue 3 units.

9: Plane 8 took off; in queue 3 units.
Plane 11 ready to land.

landing queue is   10: Plane 11 landed; in queue 0 units.
empty
Plane 12 ready to take off.
11: Plane 9 took off; in queue 4 units.
Plane 13 ready to land.
Plane 14 ready to land.
12: Plane 13 landed; in queue 0 units.

13: Plane 14 landed; in queue 1 units.

14: Plane 10 took off; in queue 7 units.
Plane 15 ready to land.
Plane 16 ready to take off.
Plane 17 ready to take off.
15: Plane 15 landed; in queue 0 units.
Plane 18 ready to land.
Plane 19 ready to land.
Plane 20 ready to take off.
Plane 21 ready to take off.
16: Plane 18 landed; in queue 0 units.
Plane 22 ready to land.

17: Plane 19 landed; in queue 1 units.
takeoff queue is   Plane 23 ready to take off.
full
Plane 23 told to try later.

18: Plane 22 landed; in queue 1 units.
    Plane 24 ready to land.
    Plane 25 ready to land.
    Plane 26 ready to land.
    Plane 27 ready to take off.
    Plane 27 told to try later.
19: Plane 24 landed; in queue 0 units.
    Plane 28 ready to land.
    Plane 29 ready to land.
    Plane 30 ready to land.

landing queue is
full

    Plane 31 ready to land.
    Plane 31 directed to another airport.
20: Plane 25 landed; in queue 1 units.
    Plane 32 ready to land.
    Plane 33 ready to take off.
    Plane 33 told to try later.
21: Plane 26 landed; in queue 2 units.
22: Plane 28 landed; in queue 2 units.
23: Plane 29 landed; in queue 3 units.
    Plane 34 ready to take off.
    Plane 34 told to try later.
24: Plane 30 landed; in queue 4 units.
    Plane 35 ready to take off.
    Plane 35 told to try later.
    Plane 36 ready to take off.
    Plane 36 told to try later.
25: Plane 32 landed; in queue 4 units.
    Plane 37 ready to take off.
    Plane 37 told to try later.
26: Plane 12 took off; in queue 15 units.
27: Plane 16 took off; in queue 12 units.
28: Plane 17 took off; in queue 13 units.
29: Plane 20 took off; in queue 13 units.
    Plane 38 ready to take off.
30: Plane 21 took off; in queue 14 units.

summary

Simulation has concluded after 30 units.
Total number of planes processed: 38
  Number of planes landed: 19
  Number of planes taken off: 10
  Number of planes refused use: 8
  Number left ready to land: 0
  Number left ready to take off: 1
  Percentage of time runway idle: 3.33
  Average wait time to land: 1.11
  Average wait time to take off: 8.60

EXERCISES 5.4

E1. In the airport simulation, we did not specify which implementation of queues to use. Which of the implementations would be best to use, and why? If the choice of implementation does not make much difference, explain why.

E2. The function Random has the side effect of changing the value of its parameter seed. Side effects in functions are normally very dangerous. By considering the use of the variable seed, explain why this side effect is not as dangerous as most, and may actually help to indicate what the function does.

PROJECTS 5.4

P1. Combine all the subprograms for the airport simulation into a complete program. Use units, the include directive, or a similar feature, if one of these is available for your compiler, both for the package of queue-processing subprograms and for the package for generating random numbers. Experiment with several sample runs of the airport simulation, adjusting the values for the expected numbers of planes ready to land and take off. Find approximate values for these expected numbers that are as large as possible subject to the condition that it is very unlikely that a plane must be refused service. What happens to these values if the maximum size of the queues is increased or decreased?

P2. Modify the simulation to give the airport two runways, one always used for landings and one always used for takeoffs. Compare the total number of planes that can be served with the number for the one-runway airport. Does it more than double?

P3. Modify the simulation to give the airport two runways, one usually used for landings and one usually used for takeoffs. If one of the queues is empty, then both runways can be used for the other queue. Also, if the landing queue is full and another plane arrives to land, then takeoffs will be stopped and both runways used to clear the backlog of landing planes.

P4. Modify the simulation to have three runways, one always reserved for each of landing and takeoff and the third used for landings unless the landing queue is empty, in which case it can be used for takeoffs.

P5. Modify the original (one-runway) simulation so that when each plane arrives to land, it will (as part of its record) have a (randomly generated) fuel level, measured in units of time remaining. If the plane does not have enough fuel to wait in the queue, it is allowed to land immediately. Hence the planes in the landing queue may be kept waiting additional units, and so may run out of fuel themselves. Check this out as part of the landing procedure, and find about how busy the airport can become before planes start to crash from running out of fuel.

P6. Write a stub to take the place of the random-number function. The stub can be used both to debug the program and to allow the user to control exactly the number of planes arriving for each queue at each time unit.

P7. Write a driver program for function RandomNumber; use it to check that the function produces random integers whose average over the number of iterations performed is the specified expected value.

scissors-paper-stone

P8. In a certain children's game, each of two players simultaneously puts out a hand held in a fashion to denote one of scissors, paper, or rock. The rules are that scissors beats paper (since scissors cut paper), paper beats rock (since paper covers rock), and rock beats scissors (since rock breaks scissors). Write a program to simulate playing this game with a person who types in S, P, or R at each turn.

P9. After leaving a pub, a drunk tries to walk home, as shown in Figure 5.6. The streets between the pub and the home form a rectangular grid. Each time the drunk reaches a corner, he decides at random what direction to walk next. He never, however, wanders outside the grid.

random walk

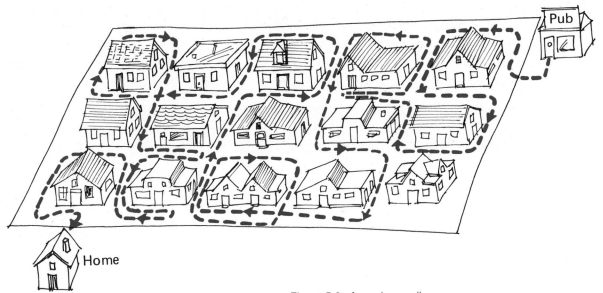

Figure 5.6. A random walk

a. Write a program to simulate this random walk. The number of rows and columns in the grid should be variable. Your program should calculate, over many random walks on the same grid, how long it takes the drunk to get home on average. Investigate how this number depends on the shape and size of the grid.

b. To improve his chances, the drunk moves closer to the pub—to a room on the upper left corner of the grid. Modify the simulation to see how much faster he can now get home.

c. Modify the original simulation so that, if the drunk happens to arrive back at the pub, then he goes in and the walk ends. Find out (depending on the size and shape of the grid) what percentage of the time the drunk makes it home successfully.

d. Modify the original simulation so as to give the drunk some memory to help him, as follows. Each time he arrives at a corner, if he has been there before on the current walk, he remembers what streets he has already taken and tries a new one. If he has already tried all the streets from the corner, he decides at random which to take now. How much more quickly does he get home?

POINTERS AND PITFALLS

1. Write your application programs in a way that does not depend on how your data structures will be implemented.

2. Postpone decisions on the details of implementing your data structures as long as you can. Consider which operations are done more frequently in your application to help in choosing an implementation.

3. Remember to check the preconditions before a subprogram is invoked. Always be careful about the extreme cases and handle them gracefully.

4. Don't optimize your code until it works perfectly, and then only optimize it if improvement in efficiency is definitely required. First, try a simple implementation of your data structures. Change to a more sophisticated implementation only if the simple one proves too inefficient.

REVIEW QUESTIONS

5.1   1. Define the term *queue*. What operations can be done on a queue?

5.2   2. List at least four different implementations of queues.

3. Is there one implementation of a queue that is almost always better than any other in a computer? If so, which?

4. Is there one implementation of a queue that is almost always worse than any other in a computer? If so, which?

5. How is a circular array implemented in a linear array?

6. What problem occurs for the extreme cases in a circular array?

5.3   **7.** Which Pascal implementation of queues do you find easier to understand, the one using a counter or the one using special index values? Why? Which one takes more space for the record holding the queue? Is this difference in space worth investing extra programming effort or time?

5.4   **8.** Define the term *simulation*.

9. Why are random numbers used in computer programs usually not really random?

10. What is the *seed* for a random-number generator?

6

LISTS AND STRINGS

This chapter turns from the restricted lists, stacks and queues, in which operations occur only at the ends of the list, to more general lists in which insertions, deletions, and retrieval may occur at any point of the list. We shall consider first the definition and then the implementation of lists in computer storage and Pascal procedures, reinforce the ideas by developing a package of procedures for processing character strings, and conclude the chapter with an application of its methods to the construction of a simple text-editing program. The separation among the specification, the application, and the implementation of data structures is emphasized throughout.

6.1

OPERATIONS ON LISTS

Stacks are the easiest kind of list to use because all additions and deletions are made at one end of the list. In queues, changes are made at both ends, but only at the ends, so queues are still relatively easy to use. For many applications, however, it is necessary to access all the elements of the list and to be able to make insertions or deletions at any point in the list. It might be necessary, for example, to insert a new name into the middle of a list that is kept in alphabetical order, delete an entry from the middle of a list, or exchange two entries in different parts of a list.

operations,
information
hiding, and
implementations

When we first studied stacks, we practiced *information hiding* by separating our uses for stacks from the actual programming of these operations. In studying queues, we continued these methods and soon saw that many variations in *implementation* are possible. With general lists, we have much more flexibility and freedom in accessing and changing entries in any part of the list, and, therefore, the principles of information hiding are even more important for general lists than for restricted lists. Let us therefore begin by enumerating preconditions and postconditions for all the operations that we may wish to perform with lists, even though for many applications not all of these operations are required.

6.1.1 Simple Operations

First, there are some simple operations analogous to similar operations for stacks and queues.

initialization

> **procedure** CreateList(**var** L: listtype)
>
> *precondition*:   None.
>
> *postcondition*: The list L has been created and is initialized to be empty.

Next come the operations for checking the status of a list.

status operations

> **function** ListEmpty(L: listtype): Boolean
>
> *precondition*:   The list L has been created.
>
> *postcondition*: The function returns true or false according as list L is empty or not.

172

---

function ListFull(L: listtype): Boolean

precondition: The list L has been created.

postcondition: The function returns true or false according as list L is full
                  or not.

---

function ListSize(L: listtype): integer

precondition: The list L has been created.

postcondition: The function returns the number of entries in the list L.

---

parameters and efficiency

Note that in procedure CreateList, the list L is a **var** parameter, but in the functions, it is a value parameter. The reason is that CreateList changes the list, but the functions do not. For the specifications of all the subprograms in this section, we shall be careful to use **var** parameters exactly when a subprogram may change the parameter. When we come to the implementation details, however, we shall always make the list a **var** parameter, whether it is changed or not. In this way, we avoid the wasteful inefficiency of making a new copy of a value parameter whenever the subprogram is started.

6.1.2 Windows

window into a list

With stacks and queues, we look only at the ends of the list, but with general lists, we usually want to look at arbitrary entries, and we generally wish to move back and forth through the list, looking at different entries at different times. For this reason, we introduce the concept of a movable *window* into the list. The window will be located at the place in the list where we are currently working, and we will have operations that will access the list at the window, and other operations that will move the window wherever we wish in the list. Sometimes, moreover, we shall want more than one window into the same list. We may, for example, need to compare or to interchange two entries in a list. See Figure 6.1.

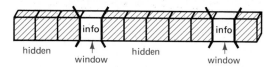

Figure 6.1. A list with two windows

file windows

Notice that a window into a list is rather similar to the window into a file except that the file window is a copy of the entry in the file, whereas a list window provides a way to access the entries but is not itself an entry or a copy of an entry. We speak instead of "the entry at the window." We have, moreover, more flexibility in moving a list window than is provided for file windows. A list, finally, may have more than one window into it, whereas a file has only a single window.

As the window moves, it is necessary to check whether it reaches an end of the list, which can be done with the following functions.

check window
position

---

function IsFirst(w: window; L: listtype): Boolean

precondition: The list L has been created.

postcondition: The function indicates whether the entry at w is first in L.

---

function IsLast(w: window; L: listtype): Boolean

precondition: The list L has been created.

postcondition: The function indicates whether the entry at w is last in L.

---

function OnList(w: window; L: listtype): Boolean

precondition: The list L has been created.

postcondition: The function indicates whether the window w is pointing to an entry of L.

The function OnList may require further explanation. All the procedures and functions we write will treat the window separately from the list, rather than integrating the window as a part of the list structure itself and dropping it as a separate parameter. By keeping the window separate from the list, we have the flexibility of using more than one window if we wish or of introducing a local window that can move through the list without changing the value of any other window. Keeping the window separate from the list means, however, that either the window or the list might be changed without updating the other, and there is therefore the possibility that, at some time, the window might be pointing to a position that is not in the list. Or the programmer might inadvertently use the window for one list to refer to another. The function OnList helps to guard against such errors by checking that the window references a current entry of the list.

Here are some operations useful for positioning a window for a list. If an attempt is made to position a window in an empty list, then the window is initialized to a position that does not exist in any list.

window positioning

---

procedure StartList(**var** w: window; L: listtype)

precondition: The list L has been created.

postcondition: If L is not empty, the window w points to the first entry of L. If L is empty, w points to a position that does not exist in any list.

---

procedure FinishList(**var** w: window; L: listtype)

precondition: The list L has been created.

postcondition: If L is not empty, the window w points to the last entry of L. If L is empty, w points to a position that does not exist in any list.

---

procedure NextList(**var** w: window; L: listtype)

precondition: The list L has been created, is not empty, and w points to an entry of L (which means OnList(w, L) = true).

postcondition: If w is not already the last entry of L, then w moves to the next entry of L. If w is the last entry, then w moves to a position that is not on the list.

---

procedure PrecedingList(**var** w: window; L: listtype)

precondition: The list L has been created, is not empty, and w points to an entry of L (which means OnList(w, L) = true).

postcondition: If w is not already the first entry of L, then w moves to the entry of L immediately preceding its former position. If w is the first entry, then w moves to a position that is not on the list.

These operations provide only the basic facilities needed to start at either end of the list and move in either direction.

One more operation is frequently useful, one that positions a window to an arbitrary position in a list, and hence we give specifications for such a procedure.

---

procedure PositionList(**var** w: window; target: integer; **var** L: listtype);

precondition: The list L has been created, and target is a positive integer.

postcondition: The window w points to the entry in position target of the list, or is not on the list if the list does not contain target entries.

6.1.3 List Changes

Now we come to the operations that actually change entries of the list L. All of these use the window to specify where the change is to be made. The procedures should all check that the window refers to a valid position in the list; it is an error if it does not. With this requirement, however, we cannot insert an entry into an empty list, since there is no entry to which the window can refer. Let us therefore, by convention, allow procedures InsertAfter and InsertBefore to insert an entry into an empty list and set the window, whatever its previous value, to the new entry. When inserting or deleting from other lists, we must specify where the window goes after the change, as indicated for each of the following procedures.

deletion

---

procedure DeleteList(**var** w: window; **var** L: listtype)

precondition: The list L has been created and w points to an entry of L.

postcondition: Deletes the entry at window w of L and moves w to the next entry of L if it exists, otherwise off the list.

---

insertion

---

procedure InsertAfter(**var** w: window; x: listentry; **var** L: listtype)

precondition: The list L has been created and is not full. If L is not empty, then w points to an entry of L.

postcondition: Inserts item x into L in a new position. If L was previously empty, then w points to the new entry. If L was not empty, then the location of the window w remains unchanged and the new entry is inserted immediately after window w.

---

procedure InsertBefore(**var** w: window; x: listentry; **var** L: listtype)

precondition: The list L has been created and is not full. If L is not empty, then w points to an entry of L.

postcondition: Inserts item x into L in a new position. If L was previously empty, then w points to the new entry. If L was not empty, then the location of the window w remains unchanged and the new entry is inserted immediately before window w.

access

procedure ReplaceList(w: window; x: listentry; **var** L: listtype)

precondition: The list L has been created and w points to an entry of L.

postcondition: Replaces the entry in the window position w with x.

procedure RetrieveList(w: window; **var** x: listentry; **var** L: listtype)

precondition: The list L has been created and w points to an entry of L.

postcondition: Sets x to be the entry in the window position w.

Although the list of operations that we have now specified is rather long, it indicates some of the flexibility available to us in processing lists. For many applications, however, only a few of these many operations are actually needed. Some operations are easier with one implementation of a list; others are easier with another implementation. In deciding, therefore, on implementation methods, we should always keep in mind the requirements of the particular application.

6.1.4 Other Operations

For some applications, there are even further operations that are needed. Sometimes it is necessary to program such operations on the same level as those already specified, but often a new operation can be programmed by using operations already developed as building blocks. Suppose, for example, we wish to be able to interchange two entries in a list. Then we can use the following procedure.

swap

```
procedure Interchange (v, w: window; var L: listtype);
{Pre:   The list L has been created, and both windows v and w refer to entries
        of L.
 Post:  Interchanges the entries in the two windows v and w of L.
 Uses:  Procedures OnList, RetrieveList, and ReplaceList.}
var
  x, y: listentry;
begin                                          {procedure Interchange}
  if (not OnList(v, L)) or (not OnList(w, L)) then
    writeln('Error: Attempt to interchange windows not on the list')
  else begin
    RetrieveList(v, x, L);
    RetrieveList(w, y, L);
    ReplaceList(v, y, L);
    ReplaceList(w, x, L)
  end
end;                                            {procedure Interchange}
```

One more action is commonly done with lists, called *traversal* of the list. *Traversal* means to start at the beginning of the list and do some action for each entry in the list in turn, finishing with the last entry in the list. What action is done for each entry depends on the application. For generality, we say that we *visit* each entry in the list. Hence we have the final procedure for list processing:

traverse and visit

---

procedure TraverseList(**var** L: listtype; **procedure** Visit(**var** x: listentry))

precondition: The list L has been created.

postcondition: The action specified by procedure Visit has been performed on every entry of the list L, beginning at the first entry and doing each in turn.

---

procedural parameters

(Yes, this procedure declaration is standard Pascal; procedures are allowed as formal parameters for other procedures, although this feature is not often used in elementary programming and is not implemented in all compilers.) To be sure that TraverseList functions properly, it is necessary to assume that procedure Visit makes no insertions or deletions in the list L.

Here is a version of procedure TraverseList that is built from the procedures and functions previously specified.

traversal

```
procedure TraverseList(var L: listtype; procedure Visit(var x: listentry));
var
  current: window;          {local window giving the current position in the list}
  currententry: listentry;                      {the entry at the window current}
```

```
begin                                          {procedure TraverseList}
   StartList(current, L);
   while OnList(current, L) do      {Loop through all positions of the list.}
   begin
      RetrieveList(current, currententry, L);
      Visit(currententry);
      NextList(current, L)
   end
end;                                           {procedure TraverseList}
```

EXERCISES 6.1

E1. Given the functions and procedures for operating with lists developed in this section, write procedures to do the following tasks. Be sure to specify the preconditions and postconditions for each procedure.

- a. Insert an item at the beginning of a list.
- b. Insert an item at the end of a list.
- c. Delete the last entry of a list.
- d. Delete the first entry of a list.
- e. Position the window to the central entry of a list if it has an odd number of entries or to the left-central element if it has an even number of entries.
- f. Copy all the entries in one list into a second list, so that the second list contains entries the same as those in the first list.
- g. Copy all the entries in one list onto the end of a second list, so that the second list is increased in size.
- h. Copy all the entries in one list onto the beginning of a second list, so that the new entries are in the same order as in the first list and precede all the old entries of the second list.
- i. Reverse the order of the entries in a list.
- j. Split a list into two other lists, so that the entries that were in odd-numbered positions are now in one list (in the same relative order as before) and those from even-numbered positions are in the other new list.

E2. A file declared as **file of** listentry in Pascal is a list whose entries have type listentry. If F is a file, then the file window F↑ is analogous to the list window discussed in this section. The operations that can be done conveniently with a file, however, are more restricted than are those given in the text. Determine which list operations or combinations of list operations (if any) correspond to each of the following standard file operations (where x is a variable of type entrytype). In the cases where the correspondence is not exact, explain the differences between the list and file operations.

file operations

- a. rewrite(F)
- b. reset(F)
- c. get(F)
- d. put(F)
- e. x := F↑
- f. F↑ := x
- g. eof(F)
- h. eoln(F)

6.2

IMPLEMENTATION OF LISTS

At this point, we have specified how we wish lists to behave under all the operations we have discussed. It is now time to turn to the details of implementing lists in Pascal.

6.2.1 Type Declarations

For both stacks and queues, our implementations used a workspace array and a counter (or counters) to keep track of the entries in the array in use. The simplest implementation of general lists proceeds in the same way and provides our first method. In later chapters, we shall study other implementations.

To set up a workspace array, we must first decide how much space to allocate, which we do by introducing the constant maxlist that will be set to an appropriate value determined by the application. Next, we set up two subrange types, one to index the array and the other extended to include 0, so that it can serve as a count of the number of entries in the list. We thus arrive at the following declarations.

```
const
    maxlist = 100;      {Change to suit the requirements of the application.}
type
    listindex = 1 .. maxlist;
    listcount = 0 .. maxlist;
    listtype = record
        entry: array [listindex] of listentry;
        count: listcount
    end;
```

The final type declaration needed is that of a window. We shall make a window an index referring to a position in the workspace array entry, and shall represent the possibility that a window refers to no position of the list by setting the window to the value 0. These decisions are implemented with the type declaration

window = listcount.

6.2.2 Simple Operations

The first operations specified for a list now take on the following simple forms.

initialization
```
procedure CreateList (var L: listtype);
{Pre:   None.
   Post: The list L has been created and is initialized to be empty.}
begin
    L.count := 0
end;
```

```
function ListEmpty (var L: listtype): Boolean;
{Pre:    The list L has been created.
  Post:  The function returns true or false according as the list L is empty or
         not.}
begin
   ListEmpty := (L.count = 0)
end;



function ListFull (var L: listtype): Boolean;
{Pre:    The list L has been created.
  Post:  The function returns true or false according as the list L is full or not.}
begin
   ListFull := (L.count = maxlist)
end;



function ListSize (var L: listtype): listcount;
{Pre:    The list L has been created.
  Post:  The function returns the number of entries in the list L.}
begin
   ListSize := L.count
end;
```

These subprograms all require only a single reference to L.count. You might thus ask why we should bother to write them as separate subprograms rather than include the appropriate use of L.count in the application program. After all, procedure and function calls do require some time, so it would be more efficient simply to refer to L.count.

information hiding   Doing this, however, violates the principles of *information hiding*. When we write an application program, we should not need to think at all about how our data structures are implemented, and, if another implementation proves better than the one previously used, we should be able to change implementations without altering anything else in the application program. Similarly, while we are writing the implementation subprograms, as in this section, we should not have to worry about how the subprogram will be used in an application. By separating our concerns in this way, we divide the work into parts, each of which is much easier than the whole. We can thus write larger and more interesting programs than we could if we fail to separate writing the application program from writing the subprograms required to implement our data structures.

efficiency   In writing these subprograms, we have made one concession to efficiency, by giving the list L as a **var** parameter whether or not it is changed by the subprogram. Doing so eliminates the considerable time and space that would be required to make a local copy of a large array every time one of the subprograms is invoked.

6.2.3 Window Operations

The subprograms for checking and changing a window variable are also quite simple, and most of them will be left as exercises, but the following show what they are like.

```
function IsFirst(w: window; var L: listtype): Boolean;
{Pre:    The list L has been created.
  Post:  The function indicates whether the entry at w is first in L.}
begin
   IsFirst := (w = 1) and (L.count <> 0)
end;
```

```
procedure StartList(var w: window; var L: listtype);
{Pre:    The list L has been created.
  Post:  If L is not empty, the window w points to the first entry of L. If L is
         empty, w points to a position that does not exist in any list.}
begin
   if ListEmpty(L) then
      w := 0
   else
      w := 1
end;
```

```
procedure NextList(var w: window; var L: listtype);
{Pre:    The list L has been created, is not empty, and w points to an entry of
         L (which means OnList(w, L) = true).
  Post:  If w is not already the last entry of L, then w moves to the next entry
         of L. If w is the last entry, then w moves to a position that is not on
         the list.}
begin
   if not OnList(w, L) then
      writeln('Error: Attempt to advance a window not on the list')
   else if IsLast(w, L) then
      w := 0
   else
      w := w + 1
end;
```

The procedures StartList and NextList illustrate the common practice of using subprograms previously written to help simplify and clarify later subprograms.

If we can write a procedure by using only previously written procedures, we can obtain independence from the choice of implementation, and this is often a worthy goal. Sometimes, however, a version written for a specific implementation proves better. Here, for example, is a version of the procedure PositionList that moves to the target position by starting at the beginning of the list and moving one position at a time.

```
procedure PositionList(var w: window; target: integer; var L: listtype);
{implementation-independent version}
{Pre:    The list L has been created, and target is a positive integer.
 Post:  The window w points to the entry in position target of the list, or is not
         on the list if the list does not contain target entries.}
var
    count: integer;              {used to count from 1 up to the target position}
begin                                              {procedure PositionList}
  if target <= 0 then
      writeln('Error: Attempt to move a window to a nonexistent position')
  else begin
      StartList(w, L);
      count := 1;
      while OnList(w, L) and (count < target) do
      begin
          NextList(w, L);
          count := count + 1
      end
end;                                               {procedure PositionList}
```

Here is the same procedure written specifically for the implementation of the current section.

```
procedure PositionList(var w: window; target: integer; var L: listtype);
{implementation-dependent version}
{Pre:    The list L has been created, and target is a positive integer.
 Post:  The window W points to the entry in position target of the list.}
begin                                              {procedure PositionList}
  if target <= 0 then
      writeln('Error: Attempt to move a window to a nonexistent position')
  else if target > L.count then
      w := 0                                       {Set w off the list.}
  else
      w := target
end;                                               {procedure PositionList}
```

As you can see, the second version is not only shorter than the first, but it will run much quicker, since it goes immediately to the desired target, whereas the first works it way one position at a time from the beginning of the list.

6.2.4 List Changes

In making changes to the list, it is usually necessary to move entries. When an entry is deleted, for example, all later entries (if any) must be moved forward one position to fill in the hole. Similarly, insertion requires moving all later entries one position down the list to make room for the new item, as shown in the following procedure.

```
procedure InsertBefore(var w: window; x: listentry; var L: listtype);
{Pre:    The list L has been created and is not full. If L is not empty, then w
         points to an entry of L.
 Post:   Inserts item x into L in a new position. If L was previously empty,
         then w points to the new entry. If L was not empty, then the location
         of the window w remains unchanged and the new entry is inserted
         immediately before window w.}
var
    i: listindex;                    {local index used in for loop to move entries}
begin                                            {procedure InsertBefore}
    if ListFull(L) then
        writeln('Error: Attempt to insert before entry of a full list')
    else if ListEmpty(L) then
        begin                        {Put the new item as the unique entry of L.}
        L.count := 1;
        w := 1;
        L.entry[1] := x
    end
    else if not OnList(w, L) then
        writeln('Error: Attempt to insert before a nonexistent entry of a list')
    else with L do
    begin
        count := count + 1;
        for i := count downto w + 1 do
                                {Move entries to make room for new one.}
            entry[i] := entry[i − 1];
        entry[w] := x;
        w := w + 1
    end
end;                                              {procedure InsertBefore}
```

The procedures InsertAfter and DeleteList are similar in form, and the procedures ReplaceList and RetrieveList are quite simple, so these are all left as exercises.

■ EXERCISES 6.2

E1. Write Pascal functions and procedures to implement the remaining operations on a list, as follows.

    a. **function** IsLast(w: window; **var** L: listtype): Boolean;
    b. **function** OnList(w: window; **var** L: listtype): Boolean;
    c. **procedure** FinishList(**var** w: window; **var** L: listtype);
    d. **procedure** PrecedingList(**var** w: window; **var** L: listtype);
    e. **procedure** DeleteList(**var** w: window; **var** L: listtype);
    f. **procedure** InsertAfter(**var** w: window; x: listentry; **var** L: listtype);
    g. **procedure** ReplaceList(w: window; x: listentry; **var** L: listtype);
    h. **procedure** RetrieveList(w: window; **var** x: listentry; **var** L: listtype);

deque The word **deque** (pronounced either "deck" or "DQ") is a shortened form of **double-ended queue** and denotes a list in which entries can be added or deleted from either the first or the last position of the list, but no changes can be made elsewhere in the list. Thus a deque is a generalization of both a stack and a queue.

E2. Which of the general list operations are allowed for deques? If not, write implementation-independent procedures for the remaining deque operations (by using the list operations within your procedures).

E3. Write the four procedures needed to add an entry to each end of a deque and to delete an entry from each end of a deque, implemented in a linear array. These procedures will be similar to the list procedures developed in this section.

E4. Write the four procedures needed to add an entry to each end of a deque and to delete an entry from each end of a deque, implemented in a circular array. These procedures will be similar to the queue procedures developed in the last chapter.

E5. Is it more appropriate to implement a deque in a linear array or in a circular array? Why?

E6. Note from Figure 4.5 that a stack can be represented pictorially as a spur track on a straight railway line. A queue can, of course, be represented simply as a straight track. Devise and draw a railway switching network that will represent a deque. The network should have only one entrance and one exit.

E7. Suppose that data items numbered 1, 2, 3, 4, 5, 6 come in the input stream in this order. That is, 1 comes first, then 2, and so on. By using (1) a queue and (2) a deque, which of the following rearrangements can be obtained in the output order? The entries also leave the deque in left-to-right order.

(a) 1 2 3 4 5 6   (b) 2 4 3 6 5 1   (c) 1 5 2 4 3 6
(d) 4 2 1 3 5 6   (e) 1 2 6 4 5 3   (f) 5 2 6 3 4 1

E8. A *scroll* is a data structure intermediate to a deque and a queue. In a scroll, all additions to the list are at its end, but deletions can be made either at the end or at the beginning. Answer Exercises E2 to E7 for the case of a scroll rather than a deque.

scroll

E9. Suppose that we think of dividing a deque in half by fixing some position in the middle of it. Then the left and right halves of the deque are each a stack. Thus a deque can be implemented with two stacks. Write procedures that will add to and delete from each end of the deque considered in this way. When one of the two stacks is empty and the other one not, and an attempt is made to pop the empty stack, you will need to move entries (equivalent to changing the place where the deque was broken in half) before the request can be satisfied. Compare your procedures with those of Exercise E4 in regard to the following:

a. clarity;
b. ease of composition;
c. storage use;

d. time used for typical accesses;
e. time used when items must be moved.

unordered list

E10. In this section, we have assumed that all operations on a list were required to preserve the order of the entries in the list. In some applications, however, the order of the entries is of no importance. For such applications, when we need to delete an entry from the list, we can fill its hole simply by moving the last entry from the list into the vacant position and reducing the count of entries on the list by 1. Procedure DeleteList thus takes the form

procedure DeleteList(**var** w: window; **var** L: listtype);

{for unordered lists}

{**Pre:**   *List L has been created and is not empty.*
   Post: *The entry at w has been removed.*
   Uses: *OnList.*}
begin   *{procedure DeleteList}*
  if not OnList(w, L) **then**
    writeln('Error: Attempt to delete an entry not in the list')
  else begin
    entry[w] := entry[count];
    count := count − 1
  end
end;   *{procedure DeleteList}*

Determine which other operations on lists from this section will be simplified if the order of entries in the lists can be changed as desired. Rewrite the associated procedures for these operations.

■ PROJECTS 6.2

P1. Prepare a package containing the declarations for a list and all the procedures and functions for list processing. This package should be suitable for inclusion (either as a unit in Turbo Pascal or via the include directive if it is available for your compiler) in any application program that uses lists.

P2. Write a menu-driven demonstration program that will manipulate a list of characters (that is, declare the type listentry to be char). By typing a letter denoting a command, the user should be able to select any of the list-processing functions and procedures developed in this section.

P3. Write a menu-driven demonstration program for manipulating a deque of characters, similar to the demonstration program for lists specified in the preceding project.

6.3

STRINGS

definition

In this section, we further illustrate operations on lists by studying strings of characters, where a **string** is defined as a list whose entries are characters.

Examples of strings are 'This is a string' or 'Name?', where the quotes (' ')
are not part of the string. There is an *empty* string, denoted ''.

Many Pascal compilers include capabilities for manipulating strings similar
to the operations described in this section, but string operations are not part of
standard Pascal, and therefore the names used for the operations and the implementation details differ from one system to another. The package of functions
and procedures developed here may be regarded as giving some string capabilities to Pascal systems that do not already have them.

6.3.1 String Operations

Since strings are lists, we can, of course, use all the list operations we have
already developed for strings as well. Other operations are usually required
for strings, however, since we much more often wish to manipulate strings as
single entities rather than work with their individual characters as entries. Since
strings are used quite commonly, we make special type declarations for strings
and name their operations differently, so that other lists can appear in the same
program without causing a conflict of doubly defined names in Pascal.

specifications
Here is a list of the operations that we shall develop for strings. As for lists,
we use two types stringindex (to refer to positions in a string) and stringlength (to
keep track of the length of a string).

initialize

> **procedure** CreateString(**var** s: stringtype)
>
> *precondition*:   None.
>
> *postcondition*: The string s has been created and set to an empty string.

length

> **function** LengthOfString(**var** s: stringtype): stringlength
>
> *precondition*:   The string s has been created.
>
> *postcondition*: The function returns the length of (number of characters in)
>   string s.

input

> **procedure** ReadString(**var** F: text; **var** s: stringtype)
>
> *precondition*:   The text file F has been reset (and so can be read).
>
> *postcondition*: The string s has been created and contains characters read
>   from the file F until the end of a line of F is reached or the
>   string s is full, whichever occurs first.

output

procedure WriteString (**var** F: text; **var** s: stringtype)

precondition: The text file F has been rewritten (and so can be written to); the string s has been created.

postcondition: The string s is written to (part of) one line of the text file F.

copy

procedure CopyString (instring: stringtype; **var** outstring: stringtype)

precondition: The string instring has been created.

postcondition: The string outstring has been created and is a copy of instring.

combine

procedure Concatenate (first, second: stringtype; **var** out: stringtype)

precondition: The strings first and second have been created.

postcondition: The string out has been created and contains all the characters in string first followed by all the characters in string second.

extract

procedure Substring (instring: stringtype; start: stringindex; substringlength: stringlength; **var** outstring: stringtype)

precondition: The string instring has been created and contains at least substringlength characters beginning at position start.

postcondition: The string outstring has been created and contains substringlength characters copied from instring starting at start.

search

function PositionString (**var** target, source: stringtype): stringlength

precondition: The strings target and source have been created.

postcondition: The function returns the first position in source starting a substring equal to target; it returns 0 if no such position exists.

6.3.2 Implementation of Strings

The type declarations for strings are essentially the same as those given for lists, except that we do not give a type window, since we are primarily concerned with operations on entire strings rather than on single components of a string. Hence we do not consider windows into a string. The constant maxstring depends on the application and should be chosen large enough to accommodate all strings that may occur.

declarations

```
type
    stringindex = 1 .. maxstring;              {a position within a string}
    stringlength = 0 .. maxstring;             {the possible length of a string}
    stringtype = record
        character: packed array [stringindex] of char;
        length: stringlength
    end;
```

We begin the operations with the easiest ones:

initialization

```
procedure CreateString (var s: stringtype);
{Pre:   None.
  Post:  The string s has been created and set to an empty string.}
begin
    s.length := 0
end;
```

length

```
function LengthOfString (var s: stringtype): stringlength;
{Pre:   The string s has been created.
  Post:  The function returns the length of (number of characters in) string s.}
begin
    LengthOfString := s.length
end;
```

As we saw for lists, it would be a mistake to replace a call to this function by a use of s.length in the calling program, since this would confuse the application programming with the implementation programming and would violate the principles of information hiding and separation of programming concerns.

Input and output of strings are accomplished by the following procedures. Since a string can contain any characters, we must, while reading a string, have some way to determine when to stop reading characters into the string. We shall use the criterion of reading until either we reach the end of a line or the string is full. Neither of these conditions will be an error.

input

procedure ReadString (**var** F: text; **var** s: stringtype);
{**Pre:** *The text file* F *has been reset (and so can be read).*
 Post: *The string* s *has been created and contains characters read from the file* F *until the end of a line of* F *is reached or the string* s *is full, whichever occurs first.*}
begin {*procedure ReadString*}
  with s **do**
  begin
    length := 0;
    while (**not** eoln(F)) **and** (length < maxstring) **do**
    begin
      length := length + 1;
      read(F, character[length])
    end
  end
end; {*procedure ReadString*}

Next comes the procedure that writes out a string.

output

procedure WriteString (**var** F: text; **var** s: stringtype);
{**Pre:** *The text file* F *has been rewritten (and so can be written to); the string* s *has been created.*
 Post: *The string* s *is written to (part of) one line of the text file* F.}
var
  i: stringindex; {*loop control variable*}
begin {*procedure WriteString*}
  with s **do**
    for i := 1 **to** length **do**
      write(F, character[i])
end; {*procedure WriteString*}

These procedures can be used for input and output at the terminal by invoking them with input or output as the actual parameter corresponding to the file F.

There are two possible versions of a procedure to copy one string to another. The first is:

copying

procedure CopyString (**var** instring, outstring: stringtype);
{**Pre:** *The string* instring *has been created.*
 Post: *The string* outstring *has been created and is a copy of* instring.}
begin
  outstring := instring
end;

The second is:

```
procedure CopyString (var instring, outstring: stringtype);
{Pre:   The string instring has been created.
  Post:  The string outstring has been created and is a copy of instring.}
var
   i: stringindex;                            {loop control variable}
begin                                         {procedure CopyString}
   for i := 1 to instring.length do
      outstring.character [i] := instring.character [i];
   outstring.length := instring.length
end;                                          {procedure CopyString}
```

comparisons   Notice the differences in these two versions. The first is certainly easier to write and will run efficiently if instring is nearly full. If the strings are very short, however, but the space reserved for each is large, then the second version will run more quickly than the first.

concatenation   Next we turn to the problem of concatenating two strings, that is, of attaching one string onto the end of another, putting the output into a third string. The only possible difficulty is in the loop copying the second string onto the end of the output string, where different values of an index must be used to refer to the two strings. To increase our confidence in the correctness of this loop, we should first check that it iterates the correct number of times (the length of the second string), that it begins at the right place (the first character of the second string, which goes after the last character of the first string in the output), that it ends at the right place (when i = second.length, the last character put in the output string is in the position corresponding to the sum of the two lengths, as it should be), and then we should check the extreme cases where either the first or the second string is empty.

```
procedure Concatenate (first, second: stringtype; var out: stringtype);
{Pre:   The strings first and second have been created.
  Post:  The string out has been created and contains all the characters in
         string first followed by all the characters in string second.}
var
   i: stringindex;                            {loop control variable}
begin                                         {procedure Concatenate}
   if first.length + second.length > maxstring then
      writeln ('Error: Concatenated string is too long.')
   else begin
      CopyString (first, out);     {First, move the first string to the output.}
      for i := 1 to second.length do          {Then copy the second string.}
         out.character [first.length + i] := second.character [i];
      out.length := first.length + second.length
   end
end;                                          {procedure Concatenate}
```

The checks on the correct values of indices in the loop are even more important for the Substring procedure that extracts a substring of given length from a given string.

extracting a substring

procedure Substring (instring: stringtype; start: stringindex;
                 substringlength: stringlength; **var** outstring: stringtype);
{**Pre:** *The string* instring *has been created and contains at least* substring-
      length *characters beginning at position* start.
  Post: *The string* outstring *has been created and contains* substringlength
      characters copied from instring *starting at* start.}

var
  i: stringindex;   {*loop control variable*}

begin   {*procedure Substring*}
  if start + substringlength − 1 > instring.length **then**
    writeln ('Error: Substring extends beyond end of source string')
  else begin
    for i := start **to** start + substringlength − 1 **do**
      outstring.character [i − start + 1] := instring.character [i];
    outstring.length := substringlength
  end
end;   {*procedure Substring*}

searching for a target

The final string operation that we shall develop is also the most complicated. It begins with a *source* string and a *target* string. It then searches the source to see whether or not the target appears as a substring anywhere within the source. If so, the function PositionString returns the location in the source where the target first begins. The target might appear in the source more than once, but our function will determine only the place where it first appears.

To illustrate the approach we shall take to devising this function, let us consider a simple example. Suppose we wish to find the target string 'ant' in the source string 'an ant and an anteater'. We begin with both the source and the target in position 1 and begin matching characters:

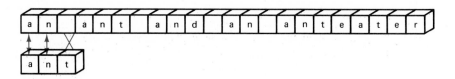

The first two positions match, but the source and target differ in position 3. We then back up to the beginning of the target, move over one position in the source, and try again:

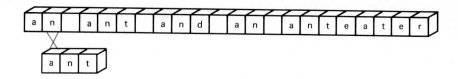

This time, we find a mismatch immediately in position 1, so again we start over, now at position 3 of the source:

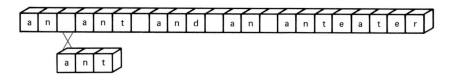

Again, there is an immediate mismatch, so we go to position 4 of the source:

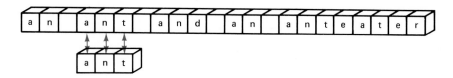

This time, the complete target matches with the source, and so the algorithm terminates successfully. We do not continue searching to find the match that appears later in the string between the target 'ant' and the first three letters of 'anteater'.

The algorithm will terminate unsuccessfully if we move the target all the way to the end of the source without finding a match; the last position of the source that could start a match is the one for which the number of remaining characters in the source is the same as the length of the target.

backtracking   This method of repeatedly backing up, undoing previous work to try a new possibility, is called **backtracking**.

Translating this algorithm into Pascal gives the following function.

searching
```
function PositionString (var target, source: stringtype): stringlength;
   {Pre:   The strings target and source have been created.
    Post:  The function returns the first position in source starting a substring
           equal to target; it returns 0 if no such position exists.}
var
   tryposition: stringindex;          {position in source currently being tried}
   lastposition: integer;              {last position that might start a match}
   match: stringlength;               {number of positions in target matched}
```

```
begin                                        {procedure PositionString}
    lastposition := source.length − target.length + 1;
    tryposition := 1;              {Start trying for match at start of source.}
    match := 0;                    {Initially, no characters are known to match.}
    while (tryposition <= lastposition) and (match < target.length) do
        if target.character [match + 1] =
            source.character [tryposition + match] then
            match := match + 1        {One more character is known to match.}
        else begin
            match := 0;                          {Start matching over again,}
            tryposition := tryposition + 1       {one position later in source.}
        end;
    if match = target.length then
        PositionString := tryposition
    else
        PositionString := 0
end;                                         {procedure PositionString}
```

EXERCISES 6.3

E1. Trace the comparisons of characters the function PositionString will make in searching for each of the following targets in the source strings shown.

> a. Target 'ant' in source 'anteater'. c. Target 'anteater' in source 'ant'.
> b. Target 'and' in source 'anteater'. d. Target 'tear' in source 'anteater'.

E2. Which of the string operations in this section are really list operations with different names?

E3. Write Pascal functions and procedures to perform each of the following tasks with strings. Use the subprograms already written as far as possible, rather than write out the code again.

> a. Delete characters from a string. The first parameter specifies the string, the second parameter the position of the first character to delete, and the third parameter gives the number of characters to delete.
> b. Insert one string (the first parameter) into a second string (the second parameter) immediately before the position specified as the third parameter.
> c. Write a function that checks whether or not two strings are equal, that is, whether they have the same number of characters, and, if so, if all characters in corresponding positions are equal.
> d. Write a function that checks whether one string comes (strictly) before another in *lexicographic* order. This means that in the first position where the two strings differ, the character in the first precedes the character in the second (and the strings are not equal).

e. Read letters from a text file into a string, stopping before the first non-letter is read.

f. Skip over blanks and ends of lines in a text file, then read characters into a string, stopping just before the next blank.

g. Read an integer from a text file into a string. Follow the Pascal rules for the syntax of an integer. It is an error if the first character read from the file cannot legitimately begin an integer. Stop just before reading the first character that cannot appear as part of the integer.

palindromes

E4. A ***palindrome*** is a string which reads the same forward as backward, that is, a string in which the first character equals the last, the second equals the next to last, and so on. Examples of palindromes include 'radar' and 'ABLE WAS I ERE I SAW ELBA'. Write a function that checks whether or not a string is a palindrome.

alternative implementation

E5. Devise an implementation of strings that does not use a counter for the length of a string, but instead puts a special character (guaranteed not to appear elsewhere in a string) at the end of each string. Rewrite the procedures and functions for string processing with this new implementation.

■ PROJECTS 6.3

P1. Prepare a package containing the declarations and all the procedures and functions for string processing. This package should be suitable for inclusion (as a unit under Turbo Pascal or via the include directive if it is available for your compiler) in any application program that uses strings.

P2. Write a menu-driven demonstration program that will manipulate a string of characters. By typing a letter denoting a command, the user should be able to select any of the string-processing functions and procedures developed in this section.

P3. Different authors tend to employ different vocabularies, sentences of different lengths, and paragraphs of different lengths. This project is intended to analyze a text file for some of these properties.

text analysis

a. Write a program that reads a text file and counts the number of words of each length that occurs, as well as the total number of words. The program should then print the mean (average) length of a word and the percentage of words of each length that occurs. For this project, assume that a word consists entirely of (uppercase and lowercase) letters and is terminated by the first non-letter that appears.

b. Modify the program so that it also counts sentences and prints the total number of sentences and the mean number of words per sentence. Assume that a sentence terminates as soon as one of the characters period (.), question mark (?), or exclamation point (!) appears.

c. Modify the program so that it counts paragraphs and prints the total number of paragraphs and the mean number of words per paragraph. Assume that a paragraph terminates when a blank line or a line beginning with a blank character appears.

6.4

APPLICATION: A TEXT EDITOR

We shall conclude this chapter with an application showing the use of both lists and strings. Our project is the development of a miniature text-editing program. This program will allow only a few simple commands and is, therefore, quite primitive in comparison with a modern text editor or word processor. Even so, it illustrates some of the basic ideas involved in the construction of much larger and more sophisticated text editors.

6.4.1 Specifications

Our text editor will allow us to read a file into memory, where we shall say that it is stored in a *buffer*. We shall consider each line of text to be a *string*, and the buffer will be a *list* of these lines. We shall then devise editing commands that will do list operations on the lines in the buffer and will do string operations on the characters in a single line.

Since, at any moment, the user either may be typing characters to be inserted into a line or may be giving commands, a text editor should always be written to be as forgiving of invalid input as possible, recognizing illegal commands, and asking for confirmation before taking any drastic action like deleting the entire buffer.

Here is the list of commands to be included in the text editor. Each command is given by typing the letter shown in response to the prompt ′?′. The command letter may be typed in either uppercase or lowercase.

commands

′R′ Read the text file called intext into the buffer. Any previous contents of the buffer are lost. At the conclusion, the current line will be the first line of the file.

′W′ Write the contents of the buffer to the text file called outtext. Neither the current line nor the buffer is changed.

′I′ Insert a single new line typed in by the user before the current line (if any). The prompt ′I:′ requests the new line.

′A′ Append a single new line typed in by the user after the current line (if any). The prompt ′I:′ requests the new line.

′D′ Delete the current line and move to the next line.

′F′ Find the first line, starting with the current line, that contains a target string that will be requested from the user.

′L′ Show the length in characters of the current line and the length in lines of the buffer.

′C′ Change the string requested from the user to a replacement text, also requested from the user, working within the current line only.

'Q' Quit the editor; terminates immediately.

'H' Print out help messages explaining all the commands. The program will also accept '?' as an alternative to 'H'.

'N' Next line: advance one line through the buffer. Since this command is very common, it can also be entered by typing a space or simply a carriage return.

'P' Previous line: back up one line in the buffer.

'B' Beginning: go to the first line of the buffer.

'E' End: go to the last line of the buffer.

'S' Substitute a line typed in by the user for the current line. The procedure should ask for the line number to be changed, print out the line for verification, and then request the new line.

6.4.2 Implementation

The Main Program

The tasks of the main program are to set up all the constants and data types needed for the program, declare the global variables required to hold the buffer and the current line, and then to coordinate execution of commands. We shall do this with a loop that first prints the contents of the current line to show the user where it is and what changes it has made, then requests a command, and then does the command. The resulting program follows.

```
program Editor(input, output, intext, outtext);
{reads the text file intext into a list of strings, performs simple editing opera-
    tions on the strings, and writes the edited version to outtext}
const
    maxlist = 200;                        {maximum number of lines allowed}
    maxstring = 80;                          {maximum length of any line}
type
{Insert the type declarations for strings here.}
    listentry = stringtype;
{Insert the type declarations for a list here.}
var
    buffer: listtype;                        {the list of lines being edited}
    curline: window;                         {the current line (its location)}
    curlinecontents: stringtype;            {the contents of the current line}
    command: char;                          {the command currently being done}
    intext,                                                  {the input file}
    outtext: text;                                          {the output file}
{Include the packages of list-processing subprograms and string-processing
    subprograms here.}
```

```
begin                                          {main program Editor}
   CreateList(buffer);
   StartList(curline, buffer);
   writeln('Welcome to the text editor.');
   writeln('At each ''?'' type one of the following commands:');
   writeln('R, W, I, A, D, F, L, C, Q, N, P, B, E, S, H(elp)');
   repeat                                      {start of the main loop}
      if not OnList(curline, buffer) then    {Print current line or message.}
         writeln('[not on a line of buffer]')
      else begin
         RetrieveList(curline, curlinecontents, buffer);
         WriteString(output, curlinecontents);
         writeln
      end;
      GetCommand(command);          {Request a command from the user.}
      DoCommand(command, buffer, curline)    {Do command specified.}
   until command = 'Q'        {The loop terminates with the Quit command.}
end.                                           {main program Editor}
```

Receiving a Command

Since a text editor must be tolerant of invalid input, we must carefully check the commands typed in by the user and make sure that they are legal. The first step is to translate lowercase letters into uppercase, as is done by the following utility procedure. This procedure is worth keeping available as a standard utility, since its task is one required by many different programs. Different computer systems, however, encode the letters of the alphabet into binary numbers in different ways; hence this procedure works properly on many, but not all systems.

```
procedure Uppercase(var ch: char);
{Pre:  ch is any character; assumes that there is a constant difference be-
       tween the binary codes for an uppercase letter and the binary code
       for the corresponding lowercase letter.
 Post: If ch is a lowercase letter, then ch is changed to the corresponding
       uppercase letter. If ch is not a lowercase letter, then it remains un-
       changed.}
var
   changecase: integer;
{This difference in codes for lowercase and uppercase letters is system de-
 pendent. For ASCII, the difference is 32; for EBCDIC, it is −64.}
begin
   changecase := ord('a') − ord('A');
   if ch in ['a'..'z'] then
      ch := chr(ord(ch) − changecase)
end;
```

The procedure GetCommand needs to obtain a response from the user, translate a letter to uppercase, take care of the special responses allowed for commands Next and Help, and check that the response is valid.

```
procedure GetCommand(var command: char);
{Pre:    None.
  Post:  Returns a character ch corresponding to a legal command as input
         from the user; continues to request response until the character re-
         ceived is a legal command; ignores case distinction for letters.
  Uses: procedure Uppercase}
var
  valid: Boolean;                    {Is the user's response a valid command?}
begin                                             {procedure GetCommand}
  repeat                           {Main loop iterates until the input is valid.}
    write('?');       {Use a very short prompt, since it appears frequently.}
    readln(command);
    Uppercase(command);

    if command = ' ' then
      command := 'N';
    if command = '?' then
      command := 'H';
    valid := (command in ['R', 'W', 'I', 'A', 'D', 'F', 'L', 'C', 'Q', 'H',
                          'N', 'P', 'B', 'E', 'S']);
    if not valid then
        write('Respond R, W, I, A, D, F, L, C, Q, N, P, B, E, S, H(elp)')
  until valid
end;                                              {procedure GetCommand}
```

Performing Commands

The procedure DoCommand that does the commands as specified consists essentially of one large **case** statement that sends the work out to a different procedure for each command. Some of these procedures (StartList and FinishList) come directly from the list-processing package; some we must write later; and some (like NextLine and DeleteLine) are closely based on corresponding list-processing procedures, but have additional processing to handle erroneous cases.

The version of DoCommand included here is not quite in final form. Writing the procedures for several of the commands is left to the exercises, and, rather than writing separate stubs for these missing procedures, we can insert short code segments into DoCommand indicating that the appropriate procedure is not yet available. For others of the missing procedures, the name is specified in DoCommand, and a short stub will be needed until the procedure is written.

```
       procedure DoCommand (command: char;  var buffer: listtype;
                            var curline: window);
{Pre:   command is a valid command for the editor program.
  Post: The command designated by command has been performed on the
        lines in buffer or the line curline (depending on the command).
  Uses: All the procedures that perform editor commands}

begin                                        {procedure DoCommand}
  case command of
    'R' : ReadFile (intext, curline, buffer);
    'W' : WriteFile (outtext, buffer);   {not in the text; left as an exercise}
    'I'  : InsertLineBefore (curline, buffer);
    'A' : InsertLineAfter (curline, buffer);            {left as an exercise}
    'D' : DeleteLine (curline, buffer);
    'F' : FindString (curline, buffer);
    'L' : writeln ('[length of current line and buffer not implemented]');
    'C' : ChangeString (curline, buffer);
    'Q' : writeln ('[Editor program terminates]');
    'H' : writeln ('[Help procedure not yet written]');        {exercise}
    'N' : NextLine (curline, buffer);
    'P' : writeln ('[preceding line move not implemented]');   {exercise}
    'B' : StartList (curline, buffer);
    'E' : FinishList (curline, buffer);
    'S' : writeln ('[substitute line not implemented]');       {exercise}
  end
end;                                         {procedure DoCommand}
```

To complete the project, we must, in turn, write each of the procedures invoked by DoCommand.

Reading and Writing Files

This version of the input procedure is written in standard Pascal, which associates an internal name for a file with the external file only by putting the name of the file as a parameter in the **program** statement. Many Pascal systems, however, provide mechanisms by which the user can select the name of a file while the program is running. When such mechanisms are available, they should be included in this procedure, which should thus be modified to request the name of the file from the user, then open and reset it before reading.

Since this procedure destroys any previous contents of the buffer, it requests confirmation before proceeding unless the buffer is empty when it begins.

reading a file

procedure ReadFile (**var** intext: text; **var** w: window; **var** buffer: listtype) ;
{**Pre:** *None.*

Post: *Reads the file* intext *into* buffer, *stopping at the end of file or when the list is full; any contents of the buffer before the read are discarded after approval from the user; leaves* w *at the first line of the buffer.*

Uses: *Procedures from the list and string packages, utility procedure User-SaysYes}*

var
    s: stringtype;
    proceed: Boolean;   {*Is it OK to discard the previous buffer?}*
begin   {*procedure ReadFile}*
    if ListEmpty (buffer) **then**
        proceed := true
    else begin
        write ('Buffer is not empty; the read will destroy it. OK to proceed') ;
        proceed := UserSaysYes
    end;
    if proceed **then**
    begin
        CreateList (buffer) ;
        reset (intext) ;
        while (**not** eof (intext)) **and** (**not** ListFull (buffer)) **do**
        begin
            FinishList (w, buffer) ;   {*Keep the window at the end of the buffer.}*
            ReadString (intext, s) ;
            readln (intext) ;
            InsertAfter (w, s, buffer)
        end;
        if not eof (intext) **then**
            writeln ('[Buffer is full; file was not completely read.]') ;
        StartList (w, buffer) {*At conclusion, set current line to first line of file.}*
    end
end;   {*procedure ReadFile}*

writing a file   The procedure WriteFile is somewhat simpler than ReadFile, and it is left as an exercise. To design WriteFile, you will need to set up a local window variable and *traverse* the list. See Section 6.1 for a traversal procedure. When the traversal visits each list entry it will use procedure WriteString to write out each line to the file specified as a parameter to WriteFile.

Insertion of a Line

For insertion of a new line before the current line, we must first check that the buffer is not full, else there is no room for insertion. Then we use the string procedure ReadString and the list procedure InsertBefore to complete the task.

```
     procedure InsertLineBefore (var curline: window; var buffer: listtype) ;
     {Pre:   None.
       Post:   Reads one line from input (the terminal) and inserts it before curline
               unless buffer is full, in which case the user is informed and no change
               is made.}
     var
        s: stringtype;
     begin                                        {procedure InsertLineBefore}
        if ListFull (buffer) then
           writeln ('[Buffer is full; no insertion is possible.]')
        else begin
           write ('I:') ;                          {prompt for input string}
           ReadString (input, s) ;
           readln (input) ;
           InsertBefore (curline, s, buffer)
        end
     end;                                         {procedure InsertLineBefore}
```

Insertion of a line after the current line is similar and is left as an exercise.

Deletion

An error occurs in deletion if the window is not a current entry of the list. Rather than leaving the error checking to the list-processing procedure DeleteList, which in some versions might terminate the program if this error occurred, we check for it in DeleteLine and inform the user that no deletion is possible.

```
     procedure DeleteLine (var curline: window; var buffer: listtype) ;
     {Pre:   None.
       Post:   If curline is a line in buffer, then it is deleted and curline moves to the
               next entry of buffer, if any.  If curline is not a line in buffer, then the
               user is informed and no change is made.}
     begin                                        {procedure DeleteLine}
        if not OnList (curline, buffer) then
           writeln ('[no line here to delete]')
        else
           DeleteList (curline, buffer)
     end;                                         {procedure DeleteLine}
```

Moving to the Next Line

The procedure NextLine also requires some error checking to inform the user of erroneous use of the command.

```
procedure NextLine(var curline: window; var buffer: listtype);
{Pre:   None.
 Post:  If curline is a line in buffer, then it is advanced to the next line, if any.
        If curline is the last line, it is not changed and the user is informed.
        If curline is not in buffer, then it is set to the first line (if any) and the
        user is informed.}
begin                                               {procedure NextLine}
    if not OnList(curline, buffer) then
        StartList(curline, buffer)
    else if IsLast(curline, buffer) then
        writeln('[at last line of buffer]')
    else
        NextList(curline, buffer)
end;                                                {procedure NextLine}
```

Searching for a String

Now we come to a more difficult task, that of searching for a line that contains a target string that the user will provide. The heart of the procedure is a call to the string function PositionString, but we embed this call in list-processing code that will traverse the buffer from the current line to the end. If the current line is not in the buffer, then we search the entire buffer. If and when the target is found, then we highlight it by printing out the line where it was found, which now becomes the current line, together with a series of upward arrows (↑) showing where in the line the target appears.

```
procedure FindString(var curline: window; var buffer: listtype);
{Pre:   None.
 Post:  Obtains a target string from the user and moves curline to the first
        line on or after its previous position that contains the target string
        (or to the first line of buffer containing the target if curline is not a
        line in buffer); prints line where target is found, with the target high-
        lighted. If the target is not found, no change is made, and the user is
        informed.
 Uses:  procedure PositionString and the list-processing package}
var
    finished: Boolean;                    {Is the search complete?}
    targetposition: stringlength;   {Where in the line does the string start?}
    count: stringindex;                      {loop variable for printing}
    searchline: window;
                {local variable; curline is changed only if target is found}
    searchlinecontents,
            {the contents of the line being searched, considered as a string}
    target: stringtype;                          {string to search for}
```

```
                        begin                              {procedure FindString}
                          if ListEmpty(buffer) then
                            writeln('[empty buffer; cannot search]')
initialize search       else begin
                          if not OnList(curline, buffer) then
                            StartList(searchline, buffer)
                          else
                            searchline := curline;
obtain target           write('String to search for? ');
                        ReadString(input, target);
                        readln;
begin search            finished := false;
                        repeat          {Loop from curline until the end or the target is found.}
                          RetrieveList(searchline, searchlinecontents, buffer);
                          targetposition := PositionString(target, searchlinecontents);
                          if (targetposition > 0) or IsLast(searchline, buffer) then
                            finished := true
                          else
                            NextList(searchline, buffer)          {Advance the current line.}
                        until finished;
unsuccessful            if targetposition = 0 then
                          writeln('[String was not found]')
                        else begin
successful              curline := searchline;          {Change current to target line.}
                     {Write the line where target was found; highlight it with upward arrows.}
                        WriteString(output, searchlinecontents);
                        writeln;
                        for count := 1 to targetposition − 1 do
                          write(' ');    {Space over to the place where target was found.}
                        for count := targetposition to
                                        targetposition + LengthOfString(target) − 1 do
                          write('^');
                        writeln
                          end
                        end
                      end;                                {procedure FindString}
```

Changing One String to Another

In accordance with the practice of several text editors, we allow the searches instituted by the Find command to be global, continuing to the end of the buffer, but we restrict the Change command to make changes only in the current line. It is very easy to make a mistake while typing a target or its replacement text. The Find command changes nothing, so such a mistake is not too serious. If the Change command were to work globally, a spelling error might cause changes in far different parts of the buffer from the previous location of the current line.

The procedure ChangeString first obtains the target from the user, then locates it in the current string. If it is not found, the user is informed; otherwise, the user is requested to give the replacement text, after which a series of substring and concatenation operations remove the target from the current line and replace it with the replacement text.

```
procedure ChangeString(var curline: window; var buffer: listtype);
  {Pre:   None.
   Post:  If curline is not in buffer, then the user is informed. Otherwise, a target
          is obtained from the user and located in curline. If it is not found, the
          user is informed. Otherwise, a replacement string is obtained from
          the user and substituted for the target string.
   Uses:  String-processing package and list-processing package}
  var
    targetposition: stringlength;   {Where in the line does the target start?}
    curlinecontents,                          {the current line  as a string}
    firstpart,                      {part of current line before the target}
    lastpart,                        {part of current line after the target}
    temporary,                          {temporary string being built}
    replacement,                              {the replacement text}
    target: stringtype;                        {string to search for}
  begin                                     {procedure ChangeString}
    if not OnList(curline, buffer) then
      writeln('[no line to process]')
    else begin
      write('Text to replace? ');
      ReadString(input, target);                     {Input the target.}
      readln;
      RetrieveList(curline, curlinecontents, buffer);
      targetposition := PositionString(target, curlinecontents);
      if targetposition = 0 then
        writeln('[string not found]')
      else begin
        write('Replacement text? ');              {Input the replacement.}
        ReadString(input, replacement);
        readln;
        Substring(curlinecontents, 1, targetposition − 1, firstpart);
        Substring(curlinecontents, targetposition + LengthOfString(target),
                LengthOfString(curlinecontents) − targetposition −
                LengthOfString(target) + 1, lastpart);
        Concatenate(firstpart, replacement, temporary);
        Concatenate(temporary, lastpart, curlinecontents);
        ReplaceList(curline, curlinecontents, buffer)
      end
    end
  end;                                      {procedure ChangeString}
```

■ PROJECTS 6.4

P1. Supply the following procedures; test and exercise the text editor. If you are using Turbo Pascal, import both the string-processing and list-processing procedures from separate units. Otherwise, if it is available with your compiler, use the include directive (or similar feature) for both the list-processing and string-processing packages.

    a. WriteFile.

    b. InsertLineAfter.

    c. Print the length of the current line and the number of lines in the buffer.

    d. Provide help to the user on the commands.

    e. Move to the preceding line of the buffer.

    f. Substitute another line from the buffer for the current line.

P2. Add a feature to the text editor to put text into two columns, as follows. The user will select a range of line numbers, and the corresponding lines from the buffer will be placed into two queues, the first half of the lines in one, and the second half in the other. The lines will then be removed from the queues, one at a time from each, and combined with a predetermined number of blanks between to form a line of the final result. (The white space between the columns is called the *gutter*.)

P3. Add a new feature to the text editor so that it will format a paragraph when requested, as follows. It will use a given maximum desired line length (which may be less than maxstring). If a line in the paragraph (except the last) is shorter than the desired length, then it will move words from the next line(s) to fill the line until the next word would take the length beyond the desired maximum. If a line is longer than the desired maximum, then it will move words to the next line so as to shorten the line to the desired maximum or less. For this project, a word consists of any sequence of characters not including any blanks. The paragraph continues until an empty line or a line beginning with a blank is found.

POINTERS AND PITFALLS

1. Don't confuse lists with arrays.

2. Lists are flexible and powerful data structures. Before using general lists, make sure that none of the restricted lists (stacks, queues, deques) satisfy your requirements.

3. In deciding on your data structures, consider carefully which operations will be required for your application, and choose the simplest data structure possible that provides those operations.

4. In selecting the implementation of your data structures, consider which operations will be more frequent or critical for your application, and choose an implementation that makes those operations easier.

5. Don't optimize your code until it works perfectly, and then only optimize it if improvement in efficiency is definitely required. First try a simple implementation of your data structures. Change to a more sophisticated implementation only if the simple one proves too inefficient.

REVIEW QUESTIONS

6.1
1. What is the difference between an *array* and a *list*?

2. What are the advantages of writing the operations on a data structure as procedures and functions?

3. What is a *window* into a list?

4. Why is the window kept separate from the list? Why might we need multiple windows for one list?

5. Which of the operations specified for general lists can also be done for queues? For stacks?

6. List three operations possible for general lists that are not allowed for either stacks or queues.

7. What is *list traversal*?

6.2
8. Many of the list-processing procedures and functions are only one line long. Why should these be written as separate subprograms rather than be written into the application program when needed?

9. With the implementation of lists presented in this chapter, why is it generally slower to insert a new entry at the beginning of a list than at its end?

10. With the implementation of lists presented in this chapter, is it faster to delete an entry from the beginning or the end?

11. What is a *deque*? A *scroll*?

6.3
12. What is a *string*?

13. Which of the string operations are actually list operations with new names?

14. Describe in forty words or less how the string-searching procedure Position-String works.

7

LINKED STACKS AND QUEUES

This chapter introduces a new technique for implementing lists in a computer, that of dynamic memory allocation and pointers. We shall find that this method provides many advantages of flexibility over arrays. We shall then apply this method to obtain new and powerful implementations for stacks and queues.

DYNAMIC MEMORY ALLOCATION AND POINTERS

7.1.1 The Problem of Overflow

In the examples and implementations of data structures we have studied in the previous chapters, we have assumed that all pieces of data are kept within arrays, arrays that must be declared to have some size that is fixed when the program is written, and that therefore cannot be changed while the program is running. When writing a program, we have had to decide on the maximum amount of memory that would be needed for our arrays and set this aside in the declarations. If we run the program on a small sample, then much of this space will never be used. If we decide to run the program on a large set of data, then we may exhaust the space set aside and encounter overflow, even when the computer memory itself is not fully used, simply because our original bounds on the array were too small.

misallocation of space

Even if we are careful to declare our arrays large enough to use up all the available memory, we can still encounter overflow, since one array may reach its limit while a great deal of unused space remains in others. Since different runs of the same program may cause different lists to grow or shrink, it may be impossible to tell before the program actually executes which lists will overflow.

We now exhibit a way to keep lists and other data structures in memory without using arrays, whereby we can avoid these difficulties.

7.1.2 Pointers

The idea we use is that of a pointer. A *pointer*, also called a *link* or a *reference*, is defined to be a variable that gives the location of some other variable, typically of a record containing data that we wish to use. If we use pointers to locate all the records in which we are interested, then we need not be concerned about where the records themselves are actually stored, since by using a pointer, we can let the computer system itself locate the record when required.

pointers referring nowhere

Figure 7.1 shows pointers to several records. Pointers are generally depicted as arrows and records as rectangular boxes. In the diagrams throughout this book, variables containing pointers are generally shown as colored boxes. Hence, in the diagram, r is a pointer to the record "Lynn" and v is a pointer to the record "Jack." As you can see, the use of pointers is quite flexible: two pointers can refer to the same record, as t and u do in Figure 7.1, or a pointer can refer to no record at all. We denote this latter situation within diagrams by the electrical *ground symbol*, as shown for pointer s. Care must be exercised when using pointers, moreover, to be sure that, when they are moved, no record is lost. In the diagram, the record "Dave" is lost, with no pointer referring to it, and therefore there is no way to find it.

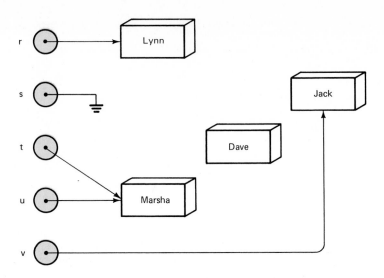

Figure 7.1. Pointers to records

linked list   The idea of a **linked list** is, for every record in the list, to put a pointer into the record giving the location of the next record in the list. This idea is illustrated in Figure 7.2.

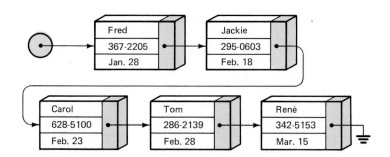

Figure 7.2. A linked list

As you can see from the illustration, a linked list is simple in concept. It uses the same idea as a children's treasure hunt, where each clue that is found tells where to find the next one. Or consider friends passing a popular cassette around. Fred has it, and has promised to give it to Jackie. Carol asks Jackie if she can borrow it, and then will next share it with Tom. And so it goes. A linked list may be considered analogous to following instructions where each instruction is given out only upon completion of the previous task. There is then no inherent limit on the number of tasks to be done, since each task may specify

analogies

a new instruction, and there is no way to tell in advance how many instructions there are. The list implementations studied in Chapters 4–6, on the other hand, are analogous to a list of instructions written on a single sheet of paper. It is then possible to see all the instructions in advance, but there is a limit to the number of instructions that can be written on the single sheet of paper.

With some practice in their use, you will find that linked lists are as easy to work with as lists implemented within arrays. The methods differ substantially, however, so we must spend some time developing new programming skills. Before we turn to this work, let us consider a few more general observations.

7.1.3 Further Remarks

Contiguous and Linked Lists

definitions The word **contiguous** means *in contact, touching, adjoining*. The entries in an array are contiguous, and, from now on, we shall speak of a list kept in an array as a **contiguous list**. We can then distinguish as desired between contiguous lists and linked lists, and we shall use the unqualified word *list* only to include both.

Pointers for Contiguous Lists

A pointer is simply a variable giving the location of some item, and, for contiguous lists, we have in fact been using pointers informally throughout the last chapters. The variable *top* is a pointer giving the location of the entry on the top of a stack, and the variables *front* and *rear* give the locations of the front and rear of a queue. To avoid possible confusion between linked lists and contiguous lists, however, we shall generally reserve the word *pointer* for use with linked lists and continue to use the word *index* (and, at the end of the next chapter only, the word *cursor*) to refer to a location within an array.

Dynamic Memory Allocation

As well as preventing unnecessary overflow problems caused by running out of space in arrays, the use of pointers has advantages in a multiprogramming or time-sharing environment. If we use arrays to reserve in advance the maximum *time sharing* amount of memory that our task might need, then this memory is assigned to it and will be unavailable for other tasks. If it is necessary to page our task out of memory, then there may be time lost as unused memory is copied to and from a disk. Instead of using arrays to hold all our data, we can begin very small, with space only for the program instructions and simple variables, and whenever we need space for more data, we can request the system for the needed memory. Similarly, when an item is no longer needed, its space can be returned to the *advantages of* system, which can then assign it to another task. In this way, a program can *dynamic memory* start small and grow only as necessary, so that when it is small, it can run more *allocation* efficiently, and, when necessary, it can grow to the limits of the computer system.

Even with only one task executing at a time, this dynamic control of memory can prove useful. During one part of a task, a large amount of memory may be needed for some purpose, which can later be released and then allocated again for another purpose, perhaps now containing data of a completely different type than before.

7.2

POINTERS AND DYNAMIC MEMORY IN PASCAL

Most newer programming languages, including Pascal, provide powerful facilities for processing pointers and standard procedures for requesting additional memory and for releasing memory during program execution.

Static and Dynamic Variables

Variables that can be used during execution of a Pascal program come in two varieties. *Static variables* are those that are declared and named, as usual, while writing the program. Space for them exists as long as the program in which they are declared is running. *Dynamic variables* are created (and perhaps destroyed) during program execution. Since dynamic variables do not exist while the program is compiled, but only when it is run, they cannot be assigned names while it is being written.

The only way to access dynamic variables is by using pointers. Once it is created, however, a dynamic variable does contain data and must have a type like any other variable. Thus we can talk about creating a new dynamic variable of type x and setting a pointer to point to it, or of moving a pointer from one dynamic variable of type x to another, or of returning a dynamic variable of type x to the system.

Static variables, on the other hand, cannot be created or destroyed during execution of the program in which they are declared, and pointer variables cannot be used to point to static variables. Static variables are referenced only by using their names—just as we have always done—and if we wish to refer to positions within arrays, then, as before, we do so with variables (*indices*) of the same type that indexes the array.

Pascal Notation

Pascal uses an upward arrow ↑, caret ∧, or circumflex ^ to denote pointers. (These three symbols are usually different ways that the same computer character may be printed.) When this character is not available, the symbol @ is used instead. If node denotes the type of items in which we are interested, then we declare a pointer type that is bound to type node with the declaration

$$\textbf{type } \text{pointer} = \uparrow \text{node}.$$

The type node to which a pointer refers can be arbitrary, but in most applications it will be a record. Note that the word pointer is not a reserved word in Pascal; we have declared it like any other identifier denoting a newly defined type. The words link and reference are also frequently used to designate pointer types. As we can with any other type, we can now declare variables that have type pointer, and these variables point to dynamic variables of type node.

When more than one type of dynamic variable is in use, we can name the pointer type to reflect the type of dynamic variables, with declarations such as

type pointitem = ↑item;
      pointnode = ↑node;

A pointer to dynamic variables of type item is then declared as a variable of type pointitem, and a pointer to a variable of type node is a variable of type pointnode.

Type Binding

Pascal sets stringent rules for the use of pointer variables. Each pointer is **bound** to the type of variable to which it points, and the same pointer can never be used to point (at different times) to variables of different types. Variables of two different pointer types cannot be mixed with each other; Pascal will allow assignments between two pointer variables of the same type, but not between pointer variables of different types. If we have declarations

var a, b: pointitem;
    x, y: pointnode;

then the assignments x := y and a := b are legal, but the assignment x := a is illegal.

Creating and Destroying Dynamic Variables

The creation and destruction of dynamic variables are done with standard procedures in Pascal. If p has been declared as a pointer to type node, then the procedure

new(p)

creates a new dynamic variable of type node and assigns its location to the pointer p. Similarly, the procedure

dispose(p)

returns the space used by the variable of type node to the system (*Warning*: Some Pascal systems will lose the space and never reuse it.) After the procedure dispose(p) is called, the pointer variable p is undefined, and so cannot legally be used until it is assigned a new value. These actions are illustrated in Figure 7.3.

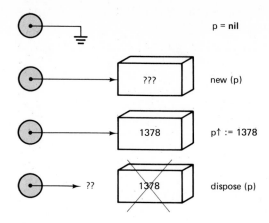

Figure 7.3. Creating and disposing of dynamic variables.

Nil Pointers

Sometimes a pointer variable p has no dynamic variable to which it currently refers. This situation can be established by the assignment

$$p := \textbf{nil}$$

and subsequently checked by a condition such as

if p <> nil then . . . .

In diagrams we use the electrical ground symbol

for **nil** pointers. The word **nil** is a reserved word in Pascal, not an identifier whose meaning can be changed if desired. It is used in the same way as a constant for pointer types and is generic in that the same value **nil** can be assigned to a variable of any pointer type.

undefined pointers versus nil pointers Note carefully the distinction between a pointer variable whose value is undefined and a pointer variable whose value is **nil**. The assertion p = **nil** means that p currently points to no dynamic variable. If the value of p is undefined, then p might point to any random location in memory. As with all variables, when the program begins execution, the values of pointer variables are undefined. Either a call new(p) or an assignment such as p := q or p := **nil** is required before p can be used. After a call dispose(p), the value of p is undefined, so it is wise to set p := **nil** immediately, to be sure that p is not used with an undefined value.

Following the Arrows

Upward arrows (↑) to denote *pointer* appear not only in the declarations of a Pascal program, but also in the action part. But here the arrow appears not to the left of a type, but to the right of a pointer variable. Thus p↑ denotes the variable to which p points. At first, this notation may appear slightly confusing, but its logic will become clear if you remember that ↑ means *points*. Thus the declaration

$$\text{p: } \uparrow \text{item}$$

dereferencing pointers

file window

is read "p points to an item" and p↑ is read "what p points to." Again, the words *link* and *reference* are often used in this connection. The action of taking p↑ is sometimes called "dereferencing the pointer p."

Notice the similarity between this notation and that used in Pascal for a **file window**. If F is a file, then F↑ denotes the one entry of the file that is currently accessible to the program. In other words, F↑ is the position within the file to which the program currently points, just as p↑ is the position within memory to which the pointer p currently points.

Restrictions on Pointer Variables

pointer operations

The only use of variables of type ↑item is to find the location of variables of type item. Thus pointer variables can participate in assignment statements, can be checked for equality, and (as parameters) can appear in calls to subprograms, but they can appear nowhere else. The programmer is not allowed to do arithmetic with pointers, since they are addresses, not numbers with intrinsic meaning. Reading or writing the values of pointers is also not allowed, since they are addresses assigned while the program is running, since they may differ from one run of the program to the next, and since their values (as addresses in the computer memory) are implementation features with which the programmer should not be directly concerned. (Some Pascal systems do allow pointer values to be written out, for debugging purposes, so that the programmer can check that appropriate equalities hold and that appropriate pointer assignments have been made.)

Note that these restrictions on using pointers do not apply to the dynamic variables to which the pointers refer. If p is a pointer, then p↑ is not usually a pointer (although it is legal for pointers to point to pointers), but a variable of some other type node, and therefore p↑ can be used in any legitimate way for type node.

assignment

With regard to assignment statements, it is important to remember the difference between p := q and p↑ := q↑, both of which are legal (provided that p and q are bound to the same type), but which have quite different effects. The first statement makes p point to the same object to which q points, but does not change the value of either that object or of the other object that was formerly p↑. The latter object will be lost unless there is some other pointer variable that still refers to it. The second statement, p↑ := q↑, on the contrary, copies the value of the object q↑ into the object p↑, so that we now have two objects with the same value, with p and q pointing to the two separate copies. Finally, the two assignment statements p := q↑ and p↑ := q have mixed types and are illegal (except in the rare case that both p and q point to pointers of their same type!). Figure 7.4 illustrates these assignments.

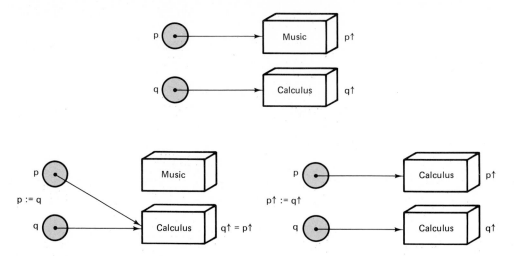

Figure 7.4. Assignment of pointer variables

EXERCISES 7.2

These exercises are based on the following declarations, where we assume that the type node has been previously declared in the program.

> **type** pointer = ↑node;
> **var** p, q, r: pointer;
>   x, y, z: node;

E1. For each of the following statements, either describe its effect, or state why it is illegal.

a. new(p)	f. r := **nil**	k. dispose(r)
b. new(q↑)	g. z := p↑	l. x := new(p)
c. new(x)	h. p := ↑x	m. q↑ := **nil**
d. p := r	i. dispose(y)	n. p↑ := x↑
e. q := y	j. dispose(p↑)	o. z := **nil**

E2. Write a Pascal procedure to interchange pointers p and q, so that after the *swap* procedure is performed, p will point to the node to which q formerly pointed, and vice versa.

E3. Write a Pascal procedure to interchange the values in the dynamic variables to which p and q point, so that, after the procedure is performed, p↑ will have the value formerly in q↑ and vice versa.

E4. Write a Pascal procedure that makes p point to the same node to which q points, and disposes of the node to which p formerly pointed.

E5. Write a Pascal procedure that creates a new variable with p pointing to it, and with contents the same as those of the node to which q points.

7.3

THE BASICS OF LINKED LISTS

With these tools of pointers and pointer types, we can now begin to consider the implementation of linked lists into Pascal. The place to begin is the declarations we shall need to set up a linked list.

Nodes and Type Declarations

Recall from Figure 7.2 that a linked list is made up of records, each containing both the information which is to be stored as an entry of the list and a pointer telling where to find the next record in the list. We shall refer to these records *nodes and links* making up a linked list as the **nodes** of the list, and the pointers we shall call **links**. Since the link in each node tells where to find the next node of the list, we shall use the name nextnode to designate the link. Translating these definitions into Pascal yields

```
type
    link = ↑node;
    node = record
        entry:      entrytype;      {the information fields being put in the list}
        nextnode: link              {link to the next node in the list}
    end;
```

use before declaration Note that we have a problem of circularity in this declaration. The field nextnode of type link is part of the record of type node, so Pascal requires that type link be declared before node, as we have done. On the other hand, type link is declared as ↑node and thus uses type node within its declaration. Hence it would appear that type node would have to be declared before link. To avoid this problem of circular declarations, for pointer types (and only for pointer types) Pascal relaxes the rule that every identifier must be declared before being used. Instead, the construction

↑sometype

is valid anytime in the type declarations, even if sometype has not yet been declared. (Before the program ends, however, sometype must be defined or it is an error.)

space for pointers: word of storage

The reason why Pascal can relax its rule in this way and still compile efficiently is that all pointers take the same amount of space in memory, usually the same amount as an integer requires (often called one *word*), no matter to what type they refer. Hence when encountering the declaration of a pointer type, the compiler can set aside the right amount of storage and postpone the problems of checking that all declarations and use of variables are consistent with the rules.

Beginning of the List

In our linked list, we shall use the pointer field nextnode to move from any one node in the linked list to the next one, and thereby we can work our way through the list, once we have started. We must now, however, address a small problem that never arises with contiguous lists or other static variables and arrays: How do we find the beginning of the list?

Perhaps an analogy with reading a magazine article will help. If we are in the middle of reading an article, then upon reaching the bottom of a page we often find the instruction *"Continued on page . . ."*. By following such instructions, we can continue reading until we reach the end of the article. But how do we find the beginning? We look in the table of contents, which we expect to find in a fixed location near the beginning of the magazine.

static head

For linked lists also, we must refer to some fixed location to find the beginning; that is, we shall use a static variable to locate the first node of the list. One method of doing this is to make the first node in the list a static variable, even though all the remaining nodes are dynamically allocated. In this way, the first node will have a unique name to which we can refer. Although we shall sometimes use this method, it has the disadvantage that the first node of the list is treated differently from all the others, a fact that can sometimes complicate the algorithms.

Headers

For linked stacks and queues, and sometimes for other kinds of linked lists, we shall employ another method that avoids these problems. The **header** for a linked list is a pointer variable that locates the beginning of the list. The header will usually be a static variable, and, by using its value, we can arrive at the first (dynamic) node of the list. The header is also sometimes called the **base** or the **anchor** of the list. These terms are quite descriptive of providing a variable that ties down the beginning of the list, but since they are not so widely used, we shall generally employ the term *header*.

A short linked list with a header attached is shown in the first part of Figure 7.5. This diagram also illustrates the division of each node of the list into an entry part and a link part that points to the next node. In this diagram and throughout this book color shading is used to distinguish all links and other pointer variables.

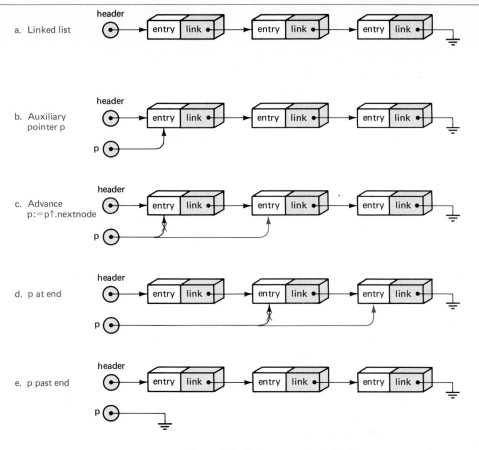

a. Linked list

b. Auxiliary
   pointer p

c. Advance
   p:=p↑.nextnode

d. p at end

e. p past end

Figure 7.5. Pointers and a linked list

initialization   When execution of the program starts, we shall wish to initialize the linked list to be empty; with a header pointer, this is now easy. The header is a static variable; so it exists when the program begins. That is, the variable header is declared and named like any other (static) variable. To set its value to indicate that its list is empty, we need only the assignment

header := **nil**;

The End of the List

Finding the end of a linked list is a much easier task than is finding its beginning. Since each node contains a link to the next, the link field of the last node of the list has nowhere to point, so we give it the special value **nil**. This situation is also illustrated in Figure 7.5. In this way, we know that we are at the end of the list if and only if the node we are using has a **nil** link to the next. Here we have one small advantage of linked lists over a contiguous implementation: We do not have to keep an explicit counter of the number of nodes in the list.

Moving through the List

In most of the work we do with linked lists, we need to process nodes other than the one at the beginning of the list, to which header points. For this work, we shall need additional pointer variables. Figure 7.5 shows one such variable, called p (for *pointer*). Note that, although p is a pointer, it is a static variable; that is, it has a name and must appear in the declarations like any other static variable.

To start p at the beginning of the list, we use the assignment p := header. This statement, in copying the value in header to that in p, makes p point to the same node to which header points, that is, the first node of the list.

Next, we wish to move the pointer p one position through the list, as shown in the third part of Figure 7.5. If p is pointing to one node of the list, then that node is denoted p↑, and the nextnode field of p↑ points to the next node of the list. Hence this is the value that we wish to assign to p in order to move it one position through the list. In other words:

> *The assignment* p := p↑.nextnode *advances the pointer variable* p *one position through a linked list.*

This operation is one of the most fundamental ones in working with linked lists.

Note the close analogy between the pointer assignment p := p↑.nextnode and the index assignment i := i + 1, which advances the index i one position through an array or a contiguous list.

By repeating the assignment p := p↑.nextnode, we can advance p one position at a time through the list until it reaches the last node, as shown in the fourth part of Figure 7.5. If we advance p one more time, it moves off the end of the list. When this happens, p is assigned to the nextnode field of the last node, and this field has the value **nil**. Hence the situation when p has moved off the end of the list can be recognized by the condition p = **nil**, as shown in the final part of Figure 7.5.

When we work with linked lists, therefore, we frequently need checks such as "**if** p <> **nil then** ..." or "**while** p <> **nil do** ..." to ensure that we are working with an actual node of the list. A loop, for example, that goes through each node of the list often takes the form

```
p := header;                    {Start p at the head of the list.}
while p <> nil do               {Keep going until we pass the end.}
begin

{Statements here process node p↑.}

    p := p↑.nextnode            {Advance p one position through the list.}
end;
```

Finally, we should note that, while it is easy to move forward through a linked list, there is no simple way to back up, since the links (as we have shown them) give only one-way directions through the list. The only obvious way to move back one node is to start again at the head of the list and trace down until arriving at the node that points to the original one.

For this reason, also, we should never change the value in the header once it is attached to the first node of the list. We could, of course, perform the assignment header := header↑.nextnode, but, if we do so, the first node of the list will be irretrievably lost (unless, of course, we still have some other variable that points to it). Although the data will still remain in the first node, and its space remains unavailable for any other use, there will be no way for us to find or access this data, or even to dispose of the node.

EXERCISES 7.3

These exercises all use the declarations of pointers, nodes, and linked lists given in this section.

E1. Suppose that there are two pointer variables and two nodes whose nextnode fields are arranged as shown in the following diagram. The entry field in each node is an integer.

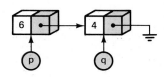

State whether each of the following expressions is true, false, or nonsense. If it is nonsense, state why.

a. p↑.nextnode = q.　　e. p↑.entry < q↑.entry.　　i. q↑.entry = 4.
b. q↑.nextnode = **nil**.　　f. p↑ < q↑.　　j. p↑.nextnode = 4.
c. q↑ = 4.　　g. p↑ = 6.　　k. q↑ = **nil**.
d. p < q.　　h. q = 4.　　l. p↑ = 6.

E2. For each of the following statements, draw a diagram showing the results of the statement on the (original) diagram shown in Exercise E1. Some of the statements will produce errors; explain why.

a. p := p↑.nextnode.　　g. p := q.
b. q↑.nextnode := p.　　h. p↑.nextnode := p.
c. p↑.entry := 5.　　i. p := **nil**.
d. p↑.entry := q↑.entry.　　j. p↑.nextnode := **nil**.
e. p↑.nextnode := q↑.nextnode.　　k. p↑.nextnode↑.nextnode := p.
f. p↑ := q↑.　　l. q↑.nextnode↑.nextnode := q.

E3. Write one Pascal statement to produce the change shown by the dashed line in each of the following diagrams.

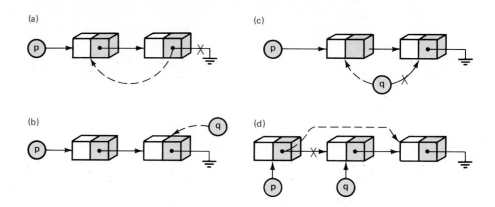

7.4

LINKED STACKS

With these tools of pointers and linked lists, we can now begin to consider linked implementations in Pascal of the various data types that we have already studied. Since stacks and queues are among the easiest lists to process, we shall study them in the next two sections. The following chapter then turns to more general linked lists.

7.4.1 Declarations

To set up the declarations we need for a linked stack, we shall begin with the declarations of nodes and links from the last section. For stacks, we have previously defined stackentry to be the type designating the items in the stack. For linked stacks, the structure of a node can then be declared as follows.

```
type
    stackpointer = ↑stacknode;
    stacknode = record
        entry:      stackentry;
        nextnode: stackpointer        {link to the next node in the list}
    end;
```

7.4.2 Pushing and Popping Entries

Let us now turn to writing procedures for processing linked stacks. As with the entries of contiguous stacks, we shall *push* and *pop* nodes from one end of a linked stack, called its *top*. We now face a problem of inconsistency with the

entries and nodes

declaration and implementation of stacks in Chapter 4: The entries of contiguous stacks were declared to have type stackentry, whereas the entries of linked stacks will have type stacknode, which we have already declared to consist of a stackentry together with a stackpointer. For some applications of linked stacks, we wish to process nodes, but, for other applications, we wish to be able to process entries directly, so that we can substitute a linked implementation of stacks for a contiguous implementation without having to make any changes in the rest of the program.

*PushNode and
PopNode
operations*

For this reason, we introduce two new operations, PushNode and PopNode, which will process nodes in a linked stack. We can then use these procedures to write linked versions of the procedures Push and Pop, which, as in previous chapters, will process entries directly. If we have an item x that we wish to push onto a linked stack, we must first make a new node and put x into the node, and then push the node onto the stack. Hence we obtain:

*stackentry
processing*

```
procedure Push(x: stackentry; var S: stacktype);          {linked version}
{Pre:   The stack S has been created.
  Post: The item x has been stored in the stack as its top entry.}
var p: stackpointer;                              {used to make a new node}
begin                                                      {procedure Push}
   new(p);
   p↑.entry := x;
   PushNode(p, S)
end;                                                       {procedure Push}
```

The connection between the two procedures for popping the stack is just as close.

```
procedure Pop(var x: stackentry; var S: stacktype);       {linked version}
{Pre:   The stack S has been created and is not empty.
  Post: The entry on the top of the stack has been removed and returned as
         the value of x.}
var p: stackpointer;                              {used for a temporary node}
begin                                                       {procedure Pop}
   if StackEmpty(S) then
      writeln('Attempt to pop an empty stack')
   else begin
      PopNode(p, S);
      x := p↑.entry;
      dispose(p)
   end
end;                                                        {procedure Pop}
```

7.4.3 Processing Nodes

Before we turn to the procedures PushNode and PopNode, which process nodes in a linked stack, we must consider some more details of how a linked stack will be implemented.

The Top of the Stack

node *processing* The first question to settle is to determine whether the beginning or the end of the linked list will be the top of the stack. At first glance, it may appear that (as for contiguous lists) it might be easier to add a node at the end of the list, but this method makes popping the stack difficult: There is no quick way to find the node immediately before a given one in a linked list, since the pointers stored in the list give only one-way directions. Thus, after we remove the last element, finding the new element at the end of the list might require tracing all the way from the head of the list. To pop our linked stack, it is much better to make all additions and deletions at the beginning of the list. Hence the top of the stack will always be the first node of the linked list.

The Stack Declaration

Each linked list has a header variable that points to its first node; for a linked stack this header variable will always point to the top of the stack. Since each node of a linked list points to the next one, the only information needed to keep track of a linked stack is the location of its top. We shall therefore declare a linked stack by setting up a record giving the top of the stack and nothing else:

type stacktype = **record** top: stackpointer **end**.

Since this record contains only one field, we could, if we wish, dispense with the record structure and refer to the top of the stack by the same name that we assign to the stack itself.

There are three reasons, however, for using the record structure we have introduced. The most important is to maintain the logical distinction between the stack itself, which is made up of all of its entries, and the top of the stack, which is a single entry. The fact that, in this linked implementation, we need only keep track of the top of the stack to find all its entries is irrelevant to this logical structure. The second reason is to maintain consistency with other data structures and other implementations, where records are needed to collect several pieces of information. Thirdly, keeping a stack and a pointer to its top as incompatible data types helps with debugging by allowing the compiler to perform better type checking.

Pushing a Node

Let us start with an empty stack, which now means

S.top = **nil**,

and add the first node. We shall assume that this node has already been made somewhere in dynamic memory, and we shall locate this node by using a pointer variable p. The node itself is then referred to as p↑. Pushing p↑ onto the stack consists of the instructions

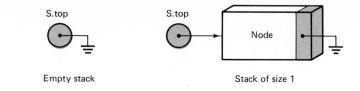

Empty stack   Stack of size 1

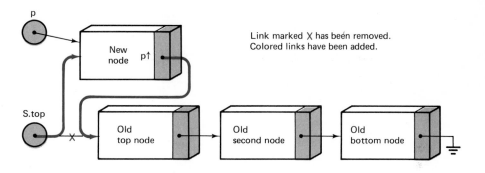

Link marked X has been removed.
Colored links have been added.

Figure 7.6. Pushing a node onto a linked stack

$$S.top := p; \quad p\uparrow.nextnode := \textbf{nil}.$$

As we continue, let us suppose that we already have a nonempty stack and that we wish to push a node $p\uparrow$ onto it. The required adjustments of pointers are shown in Figure 7.6. First, we must set the pointer coming from the new node $p\uparrow$ to the old top of the stack, and then we must change the top to become the new node. The order of these two assignments is important: If we attempted to do them in the reverse order, the change of the top from its previous value would mean that we would lose track of the old part of the list. We thus obtain the following procedure.

push node

```
procedure PushNode(p: stackpointer; var S: stacktype);
  {Pre:   The stack S has been created, and p points to a node that is not
          already in S.
   Post:  The node p↑ has been pushed onto the linked stack S.}
begin                                              {procedure PushNode}
  if p = nil then
    writeln('Error: Attempt to push a nonexistent node onto the stack')
  else begin
    p↑.nextnode := S.top;
                    {The new node points to the former top of the stack.}
    S.top := p                              {Set the top to the new node.}
  end
end;                                               {procedure PushNode}
```

In all our procedures, it is important to include error checking and to consider extreme cases. Hence it is an error to attempt to push a nonexistent node onto the stack.

One extreme case for the procedure is that of an empty stack, which means S.top = **nil**. Note that, in this case, the procedure works just as well to add the first node to an empty stack as to add another node to a nonempty stack.

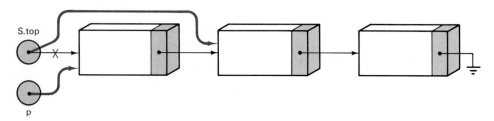

Figure 7.7. Popping a node from a linked stack

Popping a Node

It is equally simple to pop a node from a linked stack. This process is illustrated in Figure 7.7 and is implemented in the following procedure.

pop node
```
procedure PopNode(var p: stackpointer; var S: stacktype);
   {Pre:   The stack S has been created and is not empty.
    Post:  The node on the top of the stack has been removed and the output
           parameter p points to this node.}
begin                                              {procedure PopNode}
   if S.top = nil then
      writeln('Error: Attempt to pop an empty stack')
   else begin
      p := S.top;                                  {Pop the top node.}
      S.top := p↑.nextnode
                        {The stack now begins with the former second node.}
   end
end;                                               {procedure PopNode}
```

Note that the principal instructions for popping the linked stack are exactly the reverse of those for pushing a node onto the stack. In popping the stack, it is necessary to check the stack for emptiness, but in pushing it, there is no need to check for overflow, since the procedure itself does not call for any additional memory. The extra memory for the new node is already assigned to p↑.

Finally, you should note that both parameters in the procedure that pops the stack are called by reference, that is, they are **var** parameters. In pushing

value and
variable
parameters

p↑ onto the stack, on the other hand, only the stack itself need be called by reference. The formal reason, of course, is that in procedure PopNode, both the variables S.top and p are changed, while in procedure PushNode, the variable p is not changed. The point of possible confusion, however, is that, even though parameter p is only a local copy of some actual parameter, the local copy p and the actual parameter both point to the same node p↑, and so procedure PushNode is quite capable of making changes in the actual node p↑, whether its parameter p is called by value or by reference.

7.4.4 Other Operations

The remaining operations that were defined for stacks in Chapter 4 are Create-Stack, StackEmpty, StackFull, StackTop, and StackSize. All of these are quite simple, and most will be left as exercises. CreateStack, for example, takes the following form.

```
procedure CreateStack(var S: stacktype);
{Pre:   None.
  Post:  The stack S has been created and is initialized to be empty.}
begin
   S.top := nil
end;
```

There are two new operations that are appropriate for linked stacks that we have not used for contiguous stacks. The first of these is a procedure

```
procedure StackTopNode(var p: stackpointer; var S: stacktype);
```

that returns a pointer to the top node of the stack but does not change the stack. Implementation of this procedure will be left as an exercise.

The other new operation is that of clearing a stack, that is, of deleting all the entries that it contains. This operation is as appropriate for contiguous stacks as for linked stacks, but, in the contiguous case, it would be accomplished by setting the counter (called top) of stack entries to 0. Hence its action is identical to the way that CreateStack is implemented for a contiguous stack. There was therefore no need for a separate procedure (and it seems very strange that the creation and destruction of a data structure amount to exactly the same thing).

To clear a linked stack, however, we wish not only to set the header variable to **nil**, but we wish to dispose of all the nodes in the stack so that the system may reclaim their space. This action, therefore, is quite different from that of CreateStack. To program this operation, we shall need a loop that runs through all the nodes in the stack, disposing of each one in turn. The simplest way to do this is to pop each node off and dispose it before going on to the next. Here is the resulting procedure.

```
procedure ClearStack(var S: stacktype);
{Pre:   The stack S has been created.
  Post: All nodes in S have been disposed and S is empty.}
var
  p: stackpointer;                    {pointer to the node being processed}
begin
  while not StackEmpty(S) do
  begin
    PopNode(p, S);
    dispose(p)
  end
end;
```

EXERCISES 7.4

E1. **a.** When deleting an item from a linked stack, we checked for emptiness, but when adding an item, we did not check if the stack is full. Why?

b. Write the function StackFull for a linked stack.

c. Since the function StackFull is so trivial, why is it still important that it remain available as a separate function in the package of operations for linked stacks?

E2. Write the following Pascal procedures and functions for linked stacks. (*Note*: StackTopNode is to return a pointer to the top *node* on the stack, whereas StackTop returns the top *entry*).

a. procedure CreateStack.   **c.** procedure StackTop.
b. function StackEmpty.   **d.** procedure StackTopNode.

E3. For a linked stack, the function StackSize requires a loop that moves through the entire stack to count the entries, since the number of entries in the stack is not kept as a separate field in the stack record.

a. Write the Pascal function StackSize for a linked stack by using a loop that moves a pointer variable from node to node through the stack.

b. Consider modifying the declaration of a linked stack to make a stack into a record with two fields, the top of the stack and a counter giving its size. What changes will need to be made to all the procedures and functions for linked stacks? Discuss the advantages and disadvantages of this modification compared to the original implementation of linked stacks.

PROJECTS 7.4

P1. Assemble a package of declarations, procedures, and functions for processing linked stacks, suitable for use by an application program (either as a unit in Turbo Pascal or by means of an include directive or similar feature).

The package should contain both procedures for processing nodes and for processing entries directly.

P2. In the calculator project developed in Section 4.4, replace the package for processing contiguous stacks with the package for linked stacks. If you have designed the packages carefully, the program should run in exactly the same way with no further change required.

7.5

LINKED QUEUES

For queues, we have previously defined queueentry to be the type designating the items in the queue. For linked queues, the structure of a node can then be declared as follows, in close analogy to what we have already done for stacks.

```
type
    queuepointer = ↑queuenode;
    queuenode    = record
                       entry:      queueentry;
                       nextnode:   queuepointer    {link to next node in list}
                   end;
```

In contiguous storage, queues were significantly harder to manipulate than were stacks, because it was necessary to treat straight-line storage as though it were arranged in a circle, and the extreme cases of full queues and empty queues caused difficulties. It is for queues that linked storage really comes into its own. Linked queues are just as easy to handle as are linked stacks. We need only keep two pointers, front and rear, that will point, respectively, to the beginning and the end of the queue. The operations of insertion and deletion are both illustrated in Figure 7.8.

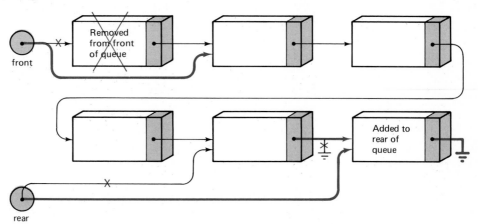

Figure 7.8. Operations on a linked queue

type queuetype To exhibit the logical connection between the two pointers of a linked queue, we shall introduce a record type:

```
queuetype = record
                front,
                rear: queuepointer
            end;
```

initialize A queue should be initialized to be empty with the procedure:

```
procedure CreateQueue(var Q: queuetype);
{Pre:   None.
   Post:  The queue Q has been created and is initialized to be empty.}
begin
   Q.front  := nil;
   Q.rear   := nil
end;
```

The procedures Append and Serve that process *entries* of a linked queue are similar to the analogous procedures for linked stacks, and we shall leave them as exercises.

Let us then turn to the procedures that process *nodes*. To add a node p↑ to the rear of a queue, we write:

insert node

```
procedure AppendNode(p: queuepointer; var Q: queuetype);
{Pre:   The queue Q has been created and p points to a node not already in
         Q.
   Post:  The node to which p points has been placed in the queue as its last
          entry.}
begin                                    {procedure AppendNode}
   if p = nil then
      writeln('Error: Attempt to add a nonexistent node to the queue')
   else begin
      with Q do
         if front = nil then          {Q is empty; set both front and rear to p.}
         begin
            front := p;
            rear := p
         end
         else begin
            rear↑.nextnode := p;      {Place p↑ after previous rear of queue.}
            rear := p                 {Update the rear to be the new node.}
         end;
         p↑.nextnode := nil           {Indicate that new node is at the end of list.}
   end
end;                                     {procedure AppendNode}
```

Note that this procedure includes error checking to prevent the insertion of a nonexistent node into the queue. The cases when the queue is empty or not must be treated separately, since the addition of a node to an empty queue requires setting both the front and the rear to the new node, whereas addition to a nonempty queue requires changing only the rear.

To remove a node from the front of a queue, we use the following procedure:

```
procedure ServeNode (var p: queuepointer; var Q: queuetype);
{Pre:   The queue Q has been created and is not empty.
  Post: The first node in the queue has been removed and the output param-
        eter p points to this node.}
begin                                              {procedure ServeNode}
  with Q do
    if front = nil then
      writeln ('Error: Attempt to delete a node from an empty queue')
    else begin
      p := front;          {Pull off the front entry as the procedure's result.}
      front := front↑.nextnode;   {Advance front of queue to next node.}
      if front = nil then                    {Is the queue now empty?}
        rear := nil
    end
end;                                               {procedure ServeNode}
```

Again the possibility of an empty queue must be considered separately. It is an error to attempt deletion from an empty queue. It is, however, not an error for the queue to become empty after a deletion, but then the rear and front should both become **nil** to indicate clearly that the queue is empty.

simplicity   If you compare these algorithms for linked queues with those needed for contiguous queues, you will see that the linked versions are both conceptually easier and easier to program.

implementations   The procedures we have developed process nodes; to enable us to change easily between contiguous and linked implementations of queues, we also need versions of procedures Append and Serve that will process entries directly for linked queues. We leave writing these procedures as exercises, along with the remaining procedures and functions for processing queues: CreateQueue, QueueEmpty, QueueFull, QueueSize, QueueFront, and two new procedures. The first is QueueFrontNode, which returns a pointer to the front node in the queue but does not change anything. The second is ClearQueue, which disposes of all the nodes in a queue and sets the queue to be empty.

EXERCISES 7.5

E1. a. When deleting an entry from a linked queue, we checked for emptiness, but when adding an entry, we did not check for overflow. Why?

  b. Write a linked version of the function QueueFull.

c. In light of the simplicity of the function QueueFull in the linked implementation, why is it still important to include it in the package of linked
queue operations?

E2. By creating nodes and disposing of nodes, write procedures **(a)** Append and
(b) Serve that will process entries for linked queues and that can be substi-
tuted directly for their contiguous counterparts.

E3. Write the following Pascal procedures and functions for linked queues:

a. Function QueueEmpty.

b. Procedure QueueFront.

c. Procedure QueueFrontNode.

Procedure QueueFrontNode is to return a pointer to the *node* at the front of
the queue, whereas procedure QueueFront returns the front *entry*.

E4. For a linked queue, the function QueueSize requires a loop that moves
through the entire queue to count the entries, since the number of entries in
the queue is not kept as a separate field in the queue record.

a. Write the Pascal function QueueSize for a linked queue by using a loop
that moves a pointer variable from node to node through the queue.

b. Consider modifying the declaration of a linked queue to add a count
field to the record. What changes will need to be made to all the procedures and functions for linked queues? Discuss the advantages and
disadvantages of this modification compared to the original implementation of linked queues.

E5. Write the procedure ClearQueue that disposes of all the nodes in a queue
and sets the queue to be empty. See the corresponding procedure for linked
stacks as a model.

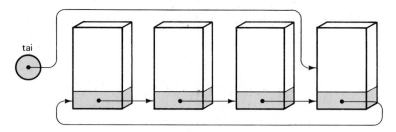

Figure 7.9. A circularly linked list with tail pointer

A *circularly linked list*, illustrated in Figure 7.9, is a linked list in which the
node at the tail of the list, instead of having a **nil** pointer, points back to the node
at the head of the list. We then need only one pointer tail to access both ends of
the list, since we know that tail↑.nextnode points back to the head of the list.

E6. If we implement a queue as a circularly linked list, then we need only one pointer tail (or rear) to locate both the front and the rear. Write Pascal procedures to process a queue stored in this way:

a. Procedure CreateQueue.   d. Function QueueSize.
b. Procedure AppendNode.   e. Procedure QueueFrontNode.
c. Procedure ServeNode.   f. Procedure ClearQueue.

What are the disadvantages of implementing this structure, as opposed to using the version requiring two pointers?

E7. Recall (Section 6.2, Exercise E2) that a **deque** is a list in which additions or deletions can be made at either the first or the last position, but not elsewhere in the list. With a deque stored as a circularly linked list, three of the four procedures to add a node to either end of the deque and to delete a node from either end become easy to implement, but the fourth does not.

a. Which one of the four operations is the most difficult? Why?
b. Write a Pascal procedure to create an empty circularly linked deque.
c. Write Pascal procedures for the three easy operations on a linked deque.
d. Write a Pascal procedure for the fourth operation.

■ PROJECTS 7.5

P1. Assemble a package of declarations, procedures, and functions for processing linked queues, suitable for use by an application program (by means of a Turbo Pascal unit, an include directive, or a similar feature). The package should contain both the subprograms for processing nodes and for processing entries directly.

P2. Take the menu-driven demonstration program for a queue of characters (Section 5.3, Project P2) and substitute the package of linked queue subprograms for the package of contiguous queue subprograms. If you have designed the program and the packages carefully, then the program should work correctly with no further change.

P3. In the airport simulation developed in Section 5.4, replace the package for processing contiguous queues with the package for linked queues. If you have designed the packages carefully, the program should run in exactly the same way with no further change required.

7.6
ABSTRACT DATA TYPES AND THEIR IMPLEMENTATIONS

7.6.1 Introduction

Suppose that in deciphering a long and poorly documented program you found the following pieces of code. The first is:

$$\text{xxt}\uparrow.\text{xlnk} := \text{w}; \qquad \text{w}\uparrow.\text{xlnk} := \textbf{nil}; \qquad \text{xxt} := \text{w};$$

reading programs   The second is:

```
if ((xxh = xxt + 1) and (xxt > 0)) or ((xxt = mxx) and (xxh = 1))
    then tryagain
    else begin
        xxt := xxt + 1;
        if xxt > mxx then xxt := 1;
        xx [xxt] := wi
    end;
```

In isolation, it may not be clear what either of these sections of code is intended to do, and without further explanation, it would probably take some minutes to realize that in fact they have essentially the same function! Both segments are intended to add an entry to the end of a queue, the first queue in a linked implementation and the second queue in contiguous storage.

analogies   Researchers working in different subjects frequently have ideas that are fundamentally ·similar but are developed for different purposes and expressed in different language. Often years will pass before anyone realizes the similarity of the work, but when the observation is made, insight from one subject can help with the other. In computer science, even so, the same basic idea often appears in quite different disguises that obscure the similarity. But if we can discover and emphasize the similarities, then we may be able to generalize the ideas and obtain easier ways to meet the requirements of many applications.

similarity   When we first introduced stacks and queues in Chapters 4 and 5, we considered them only as they are implemented in contiguous storage, and yet, upon introduction of linked stacks and queues in this chapter, we had no difficulty in recognizing the same underlying logical structure. The obscurity of the code at the beginning of this section reflects the programmer's failure to recognize the general concept of a queue and to distinguish between this general concept and the particular implementation needed for each application.

implementation   The way in which an underlying structure is implemented can have substantial effects on program development, and on the capabilities and usefulness of the result. Sometimes these effects can be subtle. The underlying mathematical concept of a real number, for example, is usually (but not always) implemented by computer as a floating-point number with a certain degree of precision, and the inherent limitations in this implementation often produce difficulties with round-off error. Drawing a clear separation between the logical structure of our data and its implementation in computer memory will help us in designing programs. Our first step is to recognize the logical connections among the data and embody these connections in a logical data structure. Later, we can consider our data structures and decide what is the best way to implement them for efficiency of programming and execution. By separating these decisions, they both become easier, and we avoid pitfalls that attend premature commitment.

To help us clarify this distinction and achieve greater generality, let us now reconsider some of the data structures we have studied from as general a perspective as we can.

7.6.2 General Definitions

Mathematical Concepts

Mathematics is the quintessence of generalization and therefore provides the language we need for our definitions. The place to start is the definition of a type:

> A *type* is a set, and the elements of the set are called the *values* of the type.

We may therefore speak of the type *integer*, meaning the set of all integers, the type *real*, meaning the set of all real numbers, or the type *character*, meaning the set of symbols that we wish to manipulate in our algorithms.

Notice that we can already draw a distinction between an abstract type and its implementation: The Pascal type integer, for example, is not the set of all integers; it consists only of the set of those integers directly represented in a particular computer, the largest of which is maxint. Similarly, the Pascal type real generally means a certain set of floating-point numbers (separate mantissa and exponent) that is only a small subset of the set of all real numbers. The Pascal type char also varies from computer to computer; sometimes it is the ASCII character set given in Appendix B; sometimes it is the EBCDIC character set; sometimes it is some other set of symbols. Even so, all these types, both abstract types and implementations, are sets and hence fit the definition of a type.

Atomic and Structured Types

Types such as integer, real, and character are called *atomic* types because we think of their values as single entities only, not something we wish to subdivide. Computer languages like Pascal, however, provide tools such as records, arrays, files, sets, and pointers with which we can build new types, called *structured* types. A single value of a structured type (that is, a single element of its set) may be an array or file or linked list. A value of a structured type has two ingredients: It is made up of *component* elements, and there is a *structure*, a set of rules for putting the components together.

building types   For our general point of view, we shall use mathematical tools to provide the rules for building up structured types. Among these tools are sets, sequences, and functions. For the study of lists, the one that we need is the *finite sequence*, and, for its definition, we use mathematical induction. A definition by induction (like a proof by induction) has two parts: First is an initial case, and second is the definition of the general case in terms of preceding cases.

DEFINITION

> A *sequence of length* 0 is empty. A *sequence of length* $n \geq 1$ of elements from a set T is an ordered pair (S_{n-1}, t), where S_{n-1} is a sequence of length $n - 1$ of elements from T, and t is an element of T.

From this definition, we can build up longer and longer sequences, starting with the empty sequence and adding on new elements from T, one at a time.

sequential versus contiguous

From now on, we shall draw a careful distinction between the word *sequential*, meaning that the elements form a sequence, and the word *contiguous*, which we take to mean that the elements have adjacent addresses in memory. Hence we shall be able to speak of a *sequential* list in either a *linked* or *contiguous* implementation.

Abstract Data Types

The definition of a finite sequence immediately makes it possible for us to attempt a definition of a list: A *list* of entries of a type T is simply a finite sequence of elements from the set T. Next we would like to define stacks and queues, but if you consider the definitions, you will realize that there will be nothing regarding the sequence of items to distinguish these structures from a list. The only difference among stacks, queues, and more general lists is in the *operations* by which changes or accesses can be made to the list. Hence, before turning to these other structures, we should complete the definition of a list by specifying what operations can be done with a list. Including a statement of these operations with the structural rules defining a finite sequence, we obtain

DEFINITION

> A *list* of elements of type T is a finite sequence of elements of T together with the following operations:
>
> 1. Create the list, and make it empty.
> 2. Determine whether the list is empty or not.
> 3. Determine whether the list is full or not.
> 4. Find the size of the list.
> 5. Retrieve any entry from the list, provided that the list is not empty.
> 6. Store a new entry replacing the entry at any position in the list, provided that the list is not empty.
> 7. Insert a new entry into the list at any position, provided that the list is not full.
> 8. Delete any entry from the list, provided that the list is not empty.
> 9. Clear the list to make it empty.

Windows into a list provide a way to locate arbitrary entries in the list and thereby supply a way to represent these operations as algorithms.

It is now easy to see what changes are needed to define stacks and queues.

DEFINITION

A *stack* of elements of type T is a finite sequence of elements of T together with the following operations:

1. Create the stack, and make it empty.
2. Determine if the stack is empty or not.
3. Determine if the stack is full or not.
4. Determine the number of entries in the stack.
5. If the stack is not full, then insert a new entry at one end of the stack, called its *top*.
6. If the stack is not empty, then retrieve the entry at its top.
7. If the stack is not empty, then delete the entry at its top.
8. Clear the stack to make it empty.

DEFINITION

A *queue* of elements of type T is a finite sequence of elements of T together with the following operations:

1. Create the queue, and make it empty.
2. Determine if the queue is empty or not.
3. Determine if the queue is full or not.
4. Determine the number of entries in the queue.
5. Insert a new entry after the last entry in the queue, if it is not full.
6. Retrieve the first entry in the queue, if it is not empty.
7. Serve (delete) the first entry in the queue, if it is not empty.
8. Clear the queue to make it empty.

abstract data type

Note that these definitions make no mention of the way in which the abstract data type (list, stack, or queue) is to be implemented. In the past several chapters, we have studied different implementations of each of these types, and these new definitions fit any of these implementations equally well. These definitions produce what is called an *abstract data type*, often abbreviated as *ADT*. The important principle is that the definition of any abstract data type involves two parts: First is a description of the way in which the components are related to each other, and second is a statement of the operations that can be performed on elements of the abstract data type.

7.6.3 Refinement of Data Specification

top-down specification

Now that we have obtained such general definitions of abstract data types, it is time to begin specifying more detail, since the objective of all this work is to find general principles that will help with designing programs, and we need more detail to accomplish this objective. There is, in fact, a close analogy between the process of top-down refinement of algorithms and the process of top-down specification of data structures that we have now begun. In algorithm design, we begin with a general but precise statement of the problem and slowly specify more detail until we have developed a complete program. In data specification, we begin with the selection of the mathematical concepts and abstract data types required for our problem and slowly specify more detail until finally we can describe our data structures in terms of a programming language.

stages of refinement

The number of stages required in this specification process depends on the application. The design of a large software system will require many more decisions than will the design of a single small program, and these decisions should be taken in several stages of refinement. Although different problems will require different numbers of stages of refinement, and the boundaries between these stages sometimes blur, we can pick out four levels of the refinement process.

conceptual

1. On the **abstract** level, we decide how the data are related to each other and what operations are needed, but we decide nothing concerning how the data will actually be stored or how the operations will actually be done.

algorithmic

2. On the **data structures** level, we specify enough detail so that we can analyze the behavior of the operations and make appropriate choices as dictated by our problem. This is the level, for example, at which we choose between contiguous lists and linked lists. In the next chapter, we shall see that some operations are easier for contiguous lists and others for linked lists: finding the length of the list and retrieving the kth element are easier for contiguous lists; inserting and deleting are easier for linked lists. Some applications require many insertions or deletions at arbitrary positions in a list, so we prefer linked lists. For other problems, contiguous lists prove better.

programming

3. On the **implementation** level, we determine the details of how the data structures will be represented in computer memory. Here, for example, we decide whether a contiguous queue will be implemented with a counter or with special index values to indicate emptiness.

4. On the **application** level, we settle all details required for our particular application, such as names for variables or special requirements for the operations imposed by the application.

The first two levels are often called **conceptual** because, at these levels, we are more concerned with problem solving than with programming. The middle two levels can be called **algorithmic** because they concern precise methods for representing data and operating with it. The last two levels are specifically concerned with **programming**.

Figure 7.10 illustrates these stages of refinement in the case of a queue. We begin with the mathematical concept of a sequence and then the queue considered as an abstract data type. At the next level, we choose from the various data structures shown in the diagram, ranging from the physical model (in which all entries move forward as each one leaves the head of the queue) to the linear model (in which the queue is emptied all at once) to circular arrays and finally linked lists. Some of these data structures allow further variation in their implementation, as shown on the next level. At the final stage, the queue is coded for a specific application.

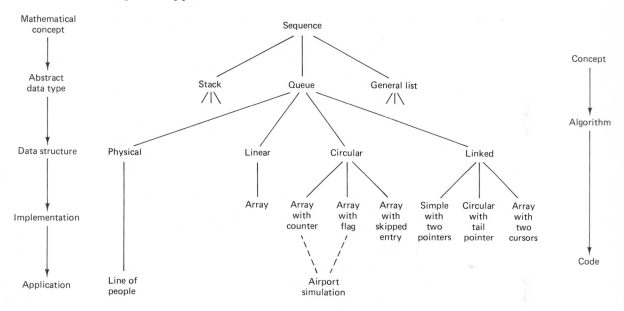

Figure 7.10. Refinement of a queue

Let us conclude this section by restating its most important principles:

Programming Precept

Let your data structure your program.
Refine your algorithms and data structures at the same time.

Programming Precept

Once your data are fully structured,
your algorithms should almost write themselves.

EXERCISES 7.6

E1. Draw a diagram similar to that of Figure 7.10 showing levels of refinement for a stack.

E2. Give formal definitions of the terms **(a)** *deque* and **(b)** *scroll*, using the definitions given for stack and queue as models.

E3. In mathematics, the ***Cartesian product*** of sets $T_1, T_2, \ldots, T_n$ is defined as the set of all n-tuples $(t_1, t_2, \ldots, t_n)$, where t_i is a member of T_i for all $i, 1 \leq i \leq n$. Use the Cartesian product to give a precise definition of a *record* that has no variant part.

POINTERS AND PITFALLS

1. For general advice on the use of stacks, queues, and other lists, see the Pointers and Pitfalls at the ends of previous chapters.

2. Before choosing implementations, be sure that all the data structures and their associated operations are fully specified on the abstract level.

3. Design your packages of subprograms for processing data structures to be as modular as possible, so that the implementation can be changed without changing the application program.

4. Always be sure to use CreateStack, CreateQueue, or (for other data structures) a similar such procedure to initialize your data structures before you use them.

5. Remember that you cannot read, write, or calculate pointer values; they are used only to locate other variables. Be careful not to confuse pointers with the variables to which they point.

6. Remember to dispose, and thereby return to memory, all the nodes that you no longer need. If a previously created structure is to be rebuilt completely, be sure to clear it first.

7. For safety's sake, set each pointer variable to **nil** when its value is no longer meaningful.

8. The use of the **and** condition in a loop is especially dangerous with pointer variables. Constructions like

while (p <> nil) **and** (condition using p↑) **do** ...

will cause an error in standard Pascal when p = **nil**, since the condition using p↑ will still be evaluated.

REVIEW QUESTIONS

7.1

1. Give two reasons why dynamic memory allocation is a valuable device.

2. Define the terms *linked* and *contiguous*.

3. What is a *pointer*?

4. Besides preventing overflow problems, why is dynamic memory allocation valuable in a time-sharing system?

7.2

5. Define the terms *static variable* and *dynamic variable*.

6. Do dynamic variables have names that are permanently attached to them? If not, how are they referenced in a program?

7. What is the difference between "p = **nil**" and "p is undefined"?

8. What operations are permissible for pointer variables in Pascal?

7.3

9. Why does Pascal allow pointer types to refer to (be bound to) types that are not yet defined?

10. Is the header for a linked list usually a static variable or a dynamic variable?

11. What is the basic step required to advance a pointer p one step through a linked list?

12. What condition is checked to determine if p has moved past the end of a list?

13. Why is it more difficult to move backward than forward in a linked list?

7.4

14. In popping a linked stack, we first checked that the stack was not empty, but, in pushing it, we did not first check that it was not full. Why not?

15. For linked stacks, why are there separate operations Push and PushNode for processing entries and nodes, respectively?

16. Why should we bother to make a function StackFull for a linked stack, even though it is trivial and always returns the same result?

17. Why is it more important to have a procedure ClearStack for the linked implementation than for the contiguous implementation?

7.5

18. Are the procedures for processing queues simpler for contiguous queues or for linked queues? Why?

19. What extreme case requires special treatment in writing the subprograms that process linked queues? Why?

7.6

20. What is the (mathematical) definition of a general *type*?

21. What are *atomic* and *structured* types?

22. What is a *sequence*?

23. What two parts must be in the definition of any abstract data type?

24. In an abstract data type, how much is specified about implementation?

25. Name (in order from abstract to concrete) four levels of refinement of data specification.

8

LINKED LISTS

This chapter continues the study of the implementation of lists by the use of pointers and dynamic memory. We shall take the methods developed for the implementation of stacks and queues in the last chapter and apply them to more general lists. We shall find that there are several variations in implementation that we can use, depending on which list operations are the most important. As an application of these methods, we shall develop a large program for performing arithmetic on polynomials. Finally, we shall introduce a way to implement linked lists within workspace arrays without using pointers or dynamic memory. This method proves useful when it is necessary to program in a language that does not provide pointers.

In the last chapter, we studied linked stacks and queues, where the operations are performed by manipulating pointers only at one of the ends of the list. In Chapter 6, we studied more general lists in which changes, insertions, or deletions may be made at any point. It is now time to put these ideas together by considering the implementation of general lists by means of pointers and dynamic memory.

8.1

SIMPLY LINKED IMPLEMENTATION OF LISTS

Declarations

For the linked implementation of a general list, we can begin with declarations of pointers and nodes similar to those we used for linked stacks and queues:

```
type
    listpointer = ↑listnode;
    listnode    = record
                      entry: listentry;
                          {This part may contain several fields of information.}
                      nextnode: listpointer     {link to the next node in the list}
                  end;
```

For contiguous lists, the window into the list is an index; for linked lists, analogously, we shall take the window into the list to be a pointer:

type window = listpointer.

The only remaining information that we need in order to keep track of a linked list is a pointer to the first node of the list. Hence we could define listtype to be the same as listpointer. It is better, however, to emphasize the logical distinction between a linked list and a pointer to its first node. Therefore, just as we declared a linked stack to be a record consisting of one **top** field, we shall declare a linked list to be a record containing only one field:

type listtype = record head: listpointer end.

Examples

To illustrate the kind of actions we can perform with linked lists, let us consider for a moment the problem of editing text, and suppose that each node holds one word as well as the link to the next node. The sentence "Stacks are lists" appears as in (a) of Figure 8.1. If we *insert* the word "simple" before the word "lists" we obtain the list in (b). Next we decide to *replace* "lists" by "structures" and *insert* the three nodes "but important data" to obtain (c). Afterward, we decide to *delete* "simple but" and so arrive at list (d). Finally, we *traverse* the list to print its contents.

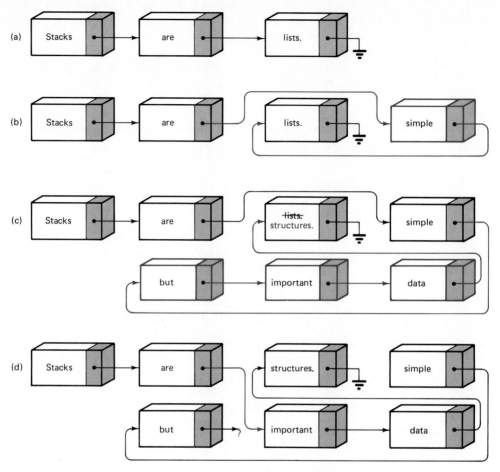

Figure 8.1. Actions on a linked list

Simple Operations

Some of the operations for linked lists can be implemented in the same way as for linked stacks and queues. To initialize a linked list to be empty, for example, we need only set the variable pointing to the head of the list to **nil**, as follows.

```
procedure CreateList(var L: listtype);
                                    {initializes linked list L to be empty}
{Pre:   None.
 Post:  The list L has been created and is initialized to be empty.}
begin
    L.head := nil
end;
```

The functions ListEmpty, ListFull, and ListSize, similarly, are analogous to the corresponding functions for linked stacks and queues. We shall leave all of these as exercises.

Just as for linked stacks and queues, we shall sometimes need to reset a list to be empty after it has been created. The specifications for this operation are:

---

procedure ClearList(**var** L: listtype);

precondition: The list L has been created.

postcondition: All nodes in L have been disposed and L is empty.

Window Operations

Since we have implemented windows as pointers to positions in the list, we can, for example, set a window w to the first entry of a list L by assigning w := L.head, or we can initialize w to a value not on any list by setting w := **nil**.

For most of the remaining operations, we need to move through the list, and to do so we must employ the nextnode field that appears in each node. The basic step is that of advancing one node through the list, as illustrated in Figure 8.2 and implemented in the following procedure.

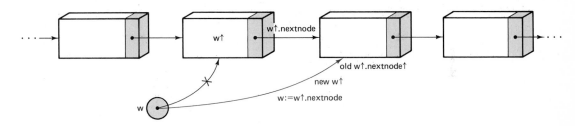

Figure 8.2. Advancing one node

procedure NextList(**var** w: window; **var** L: listtype);

advancing one node

{**Pre:** *The list* L *has been created, is not empty, and* w *points to an entry of* L *(which means* OnList(w, L) = true*).*

Post: *If* w *is not already the last entry of* L, *then* w *moves to the next entry of* L. *If* w *is the last entry, then* w *moves to a position that is not on the list.*}

begin {*procedure NextList*}
  if not OnList(w, L) **then**
    writeln('Error: Attempt to move a window not on the list')
  else
    w := w↑.nextnode
end; {*procedure NextList*}

There are two different versions of the function OnList. The first is the one usually used; it is simple and runs quickly:

fast version

```
function OnList(w: window; L: listtype): Boolean;
  {checks that w may point to some entry of some linked list}
  begin                                          {function OnList}
    OnList := (w <> nil)
  end;                                           {function OnList}
```

If we know that the window w has been set to an entry of L and then, perhaps, advanced through L by the procedure NextList, then this version will properly check that w has not moved past the end of the list. It is possible, however, that the programmer made a mistake and w points to an entry in some other list, not L. Since this version of OnList does not refer to the list L itself, it cannot tell whether a non-nil node to which w refers is in fact in the list L. To be certain that w refers to an entry of L, we must start at the first node and *traverse* L until we either find the node to which w points or we reach the end of the list. This method leads to the following procedure.

slow version

```
function OnList(w: window; L: listtype): Boolean;
  {Pre:  The list L has been created.
   Post: The function indicates whether the window w is pointing to an entry
         of L.}
var
  current: window;                      {local window used to traverse list L}

begin                                              {function OnList}
  if w = nil then
    OnList := false
  else begin
    current := L.head;      {Initialize current to the first entry (if any) of L.}
    while (current <> w) and (current <> nil) do
                                              {Advance current until}
      current := current↑.nextnode;
                                  {it hits w or moves past the end of L.}
    OnList := (current = w)
  end
end;                                               {function OnList}
```

Although this version of OnList is more secure than the first if there is any danger that w might refer to an entry of the wrong list, it will take considerably longer to run, on average, because it must traverse part of the list L each time it is used. If the list contains n entries, then the second version of OnList will require an average of about $\frac{1}{2}n$ steps, whereas the first version requires only 1 step.

For this reason, the second version of the function should generally be used only while debugging and testing a program, or if there is obvious danger that the window might be referring to the wrong list. In most applications, however, the only question is whether the window has moved past the end of a list, not whether it is on the correct list. In these applications, we should use the first version throughout our development of the program.

List Traversal

With a contiguous list, it is possible, by changing an index, to refer immediately to any entry of the list. With a linked list, however, we cannot usually go directly to any entry but instead we must begin at a known entry (usually the first) and move through the list one node at a time until we find the desired entry. Hence traversal is an important operation for linked lists. To achieve greater efficiency, moreover, linked list traversal is usually written in a way that depends on the implementation, as we shall now do.

List traversal means to move through the list, visiting the entry in each node in turn. What we mean by *visiting* an entry depends entirely on the application; it might mean printing out some information or doing some task that depends on the data. Thus we leave the task unspecified and, as in Section 6.1.4, use a call to a procedure named Visit(x), where x is an entry.

To traverse the list, we shall need a local pointer p that will start at the first node on the list and move from node to node. We need a loop to accomplish this movement, and since we wish to allow the possibility of an empty list (for which the loop will not iterate at all), the correct form will be a **while** loop. Termination occurs when p points off the end of the list, whereupon we have p = **nil**. The procedure then becomes

linked traversal

```
procedure TraverseList(L: listtype; procedure Visit(var x: listentry));
{Pre:   The list L has been created.
  Post: The action specified by procedure Visit has been performed on ev-
        ery entry of the list L, beginning at the first entry and doing each in
        turn.}

var
   current: window;                    {local window that moves through the list}

begin                                               {procedure TraverseList}
   current := L.head;                         {current starts at the first node.}
   while current <> nil do
   begin
      Visit(current↑.entry);
      current := current↑.nextnode   {Move current one entry down the list.}
   end
end;                                                {procedure TraverseList}
```

Compare this procedure with the general procedure for list traversal given in Section 6.1.4. The general procedure given there could, of course, be used for linked lists as easily as for contiguous lists. You will see that, in place of the general list operations used in the procedure in Section 6.1.4, the procedure now contains manipulations of pointers. In fact, for contiguous lists, we can make a similar translation from the general operations to manipulations of array indices. When we do so, we obtain the following procedure, which is very similar in form as well as identical in function to the one we have developed for linked lists. The following procedure is based on the implementation of contiguous lists given in Section 6.2.

contiguous
traversal

```
procedure TraverseList(var L: listtype; procedure Visit(var x: listentry));
  {Pre:   The list L has been created.
   Post:  The action specified by procedure Visit has been performed on ev-
          ery entry of the list L, beginning at the first entry and doing each in
          turn.}

var
  current: window;                    {local window that moves through the list}

begin                                              {procedure TraverseList}
  current := 1;                                {current starts at the first node.}
  while current <= L.count do
  begin
    Visit(L.entry[current]);
    current := current + 1           {Move current one entry down the list.}
  end
end;                                               {procedure TraverseList}
```

Comparing the three versions of traversal that we have developed shows clearly the similarities and the differences among the contiguous and linked implementations of lists and their general counterparts.

Insertion After a Node

Next let us consider the problem of inserting a new entry into a linked list. As with stacks and queues, we shall need two sets of procedures for making changes to a linked list, one set that processes *nodes* and another set that processes *entries*, so that we shall be able to substitute linked lists for contiguous lists without making any changes in other parts of the application program.

If we wish to insert a new node *after* a given node of a linked list, then the method we used for appending a new node at the rear of a queue works with little change. We shall let newnode point to the new node to be inserted and current point to the node after which newnode↑ is to go. The action of the main part of this procedure is illustrated in Figure 8.3.

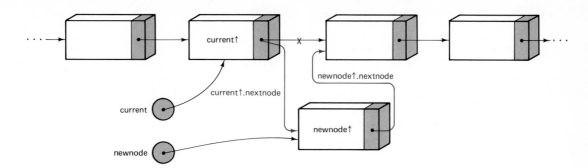

Figure 8.3. Insertion after a node

procedure InsertNodeAfter (current, newnode: listpointer; **var** L: listtype) ;
{**Pre:**   current *points to a node in a linked list, and* newnode *points to a node*
            that is not already in the linked list.
  Post: *The node* newnode↑ *has been inserted after* current↑ *in the linked*
            list.}
begin   {*procedure InsertNodeAfter*}
   if (current = **nil**) **or** (newnode = **nil**) **then**
      writeln ('Error: Attempt to make an incorrect insertion after a node')
   else begin
      newnode↑.nextnode := current↑.nextnode;
      current↑.nextnode := newnode
   end
end;   {*procedure InsertNodeAfter*}

Note the order in which the two assignments of pointers are made. The nextnode
field of the new node newnode↑ was previously undefined; hence we first assign
it to its new value, current↑.nextnode. This pointer variable then becomes free
to receive its new value. If we attempted the assignment statements in the
reverse order, then the previous value of current↑.nextnode would be lost before
it was used, and there would be no way to attach the new node newnode↑ to the
remainder of the list.

   Note also that (in order to concentrate on the pointer manipulations) we have
written this procedure under entirely different conventions than the standard
declarations for list processing in Chapter 6. We did not use any direct reference
to the list L itself, and we considered the case current = **nil**, which would occur if
the list were empty, to be an error. In our standard list-processing procedures, on
the other hand, the procedure InsertAfter is required to make an insertion into an
empty list without error. Since we have written a procedure with a new name,
these changes are permissible, but, to ensure compatibility with other similar
procedures, we have included L as a parameter. Let us now write a version of

procedure InsertAfter for processing *entries* in a linked list that will conform to the specifications given in Section 6.1.

insertion of entry

```
procedure InsertAfter(var w: window; x: listentry; var L: listtype);
   {Pre:   The list L has been created. If L is not empty, then w points to an
           entry of L.
    Post:  Inserts item x into L in a new position. If L was previously empty,
           then w points to the new entry. If L was not empty, then the location
           of the window w remains unchanged and the new entry is inserted
           immediately after window w.}
var
   newnode: listpointer;                  {used to reference the new node}
begin                                              {procedure InsertAfter}
   new(newnode);                  {Make a new node to hold the given entry.}
   newnode↑.entry := x;
   if L.head = nil then
   begin                                  {Process a previously empty list.}
      L.head := newnode;
      w := newnode;
      newnode↑.nextnode := nil
   end
   else if not OnList(w, L) then
      writeln('Error: Attempt to insert after a node not on the list')
   else
      InsertNodeAfter(w, newnode, L)
end;                                               {procedure InsertAfter}
```

Insertion Before a Node

Suppose now that current points to some node in the list, and we wish to insert a new node newnode↑ *before* current↑. We now have a difficulty, since the link that must be changed is the one coming into current↑, and there is no way to find this link directly from current and newnode, since we have no way to move backward through the list. Given the implementation of linked lists that we have been studying, the only way that we can find the link entering current↑ is to start *tracing the list* at the beginning of the list and traverse it until the node trailing↑ before current↑ is found. We can then insert the new node newnode↑ after trailing↑, as follows.

```
procedure InsertNodeBefore(current, newnode: listpointer; var L: listtype);
   {Pre:   current points to a node in the linked list L, and newnode points to a
           node that is not already in L.
    Post:  The node newnode↑ has been inserted before current↑ in L.}
var
   trailing: listpointer;          {will point to the node preceding current↑ in L}
```

```
begin                                    {procedure InsertNodeBefore}
    if newnode = nil then
        writeln('Error: Attempt to insert a nonexistent node before a node')
    else if current = L.head then
    begin                      {Insert the new node at the beginning of the list.}
        newnode↑.nextnode := L.head;
        L.head := newnode
    end
    else begin
        trailing := L.head;          {Look for the predecessor of current↑.}
        while (trailing↑.nextnode <> current) and (trailing↑.nextnode <> nil) do
            trailing := trailing↑.nextnode;
        if trailing↑.nextnode = nil then
            writeln('Error: Attempt to insert before a node not on the list.')
        else
            InsertNodeAfter(trailing, newnode, L)
    end
end;                                      {procedure InsertNodeBefore}
```

As you can see, this procedure is considerably more complicated than the procedure InsertNodeAfter or, indeed, than any of the other insertion procedures. Its performance, moreover, is likely to be poor, since its running time is proportional to the length of the list up to current↑, a length that we do not know in advance and that might be prohibitively large. In the next section, we shall study variations in the implementation of linked lists that overcome these problems.

EXERCISES 8.1

E1. Write the following procedures and functions for linked lists as implemented in this section. Be sure that each conforms to the specifications given in Section 6.1. Some of these operations can be done efficiently (with only a small, constant number of steps), but others require traversing part or all of the list and will be much slower. Determine into which category each goes. For some of these operations, it is necessary to traverse part of the list to find the node preceding w↑.

a. **function** ListEmpty(L: listtype): Boolean.
b. **function** ListFull(L: listtype): Boolean.
c. **function** ListSize(L: listtype): integer.
d. **procedure** ClearList(**var** L: listtype).
e. **function** IsFirst(w: window; L: listtype): Boolean.
f. **procedure** StartList(**var** w: window; L: listtype).
g. **procedure** FinishList(**var** w: window; L: listtype).
h. **procedure** PrecedingList(**var** w: window; L: listtype).

     i. **procedure** PositionList(**var** w: window; target: integer; **var** L: listtype);

     j. **procedure** DeleteList(**var** w: window; **var** L: listtype).

     k. **procedure** InsertBefore(**var** w: window; x: listentry; **var** L: listtype).

     l. **procedure** ReplaceList(w: window; x: listentry; **var** L: listtype).

     m. **procedure** RetrieveList(w: window; **var** x: listentry; L: listtype).

E2. The function ListFull is trivial for a linked list, since its value is always false. Why is it included in the preceding list anyway?

E3. The function IsLast(w: window; L: listtype): Boolean is similar to the function OnList.

    a. Write a simple version of IsLast using the assumption that w either points to an entry of L or is **nil**.

    b. Write a version of IsLast that makes no assumption about w.

E4. For the contiguous implementation of lists, we specified L to be a **var** parameter even when it was only an input parameter and not changed by the subprogram. Why did we do this? Why is it much less important to do the same thing when L is a linked list?

E5. The procedure ReplaceList changes the entry in a node but does not need to change the links in the list. Write a procedure

$$\text{ReplaceNode}(p, q: \text{window}; \textbf{var } L: \text{listtype})$$

that replaces the node p↑ by q↑. Be sure to include preconditions and postconditions in your procedure. You will need to find the node preceding p↑ in L in order to change the links properly.

E6. This exercise shows that, even with care, changing the implementation of a list can change the way an application program works.

    a. Suppose that K and L are two variables declared to have type list. What does the assignment statement K := L do when the type list is the contiguous list presented in Section 6.2? What does the same assignment statement do when the type list is the linked list presented in this section?

    b. Write a procedure CopyList(L: listtype; **var** K: listtype) that makes a new copy K of a linked list L.

E7. Write a procedure that will concatenate two linked lists. The procedure should have two parameters, pointers to the beginning of the lists, and the procedure should link the end of the first list to the beginning of the second.

E8. Write a procedure that will split a list in two. The procedure will use two pointers as parameters; p will point to the beginning of the list, and q to the node at which it should be split, so that all nodes before q↑ are in the first list and all nodes after q↑ are in the second list. You may decide whether the node q↑ itself will go into the first list or the second. State a reason for your decision.

E9. Write a version of procedure InsertBefore (w, x, L) that uses the following method. First, create a new node and insert it *after* w↑. Next, copy the entry (information) field of w↑ into the new node. Finally, put the new entry field into w↑. [This method, while it often runs faster than the one presented in the text, may become very slow if the entry field is large and will be dangerous if not fatal if there are other variables elsewhere in the program that point to w↑ and that may expect it to contain the same information as before.]

E10. Write a procedure that will reverse a linked list while traversing it only once. At the conclusion, each node should point to the node that was previously its predecessor; the head should point to the node that was formerly at the end, and the node that was formerly first should have a **nil** link.

E11. Write a procedure that will split a linked list into two linked lists, so that successive nodes go to different lists. (The first, third, and all odd-numbered nodes go to the first list, and the second, fourth, and all even-numbered nodes go to the second.)

■ PROJECTS 8.1

P1. Assemble a package of declarations, procedures, and functions for processing linked lists as implemented in this section, suitable for use by an application program (by means of a Turbo Pascal unit, an include directive, or a similar feature). The package should contain both procedures for processing nodes and for processing entries directly.

P2. Substitute the package of linked list subprograms for the package of contiguous list subprograms in the menu-driven demonstration program specified in Section 6.2, Project P2. If you have designed the packages carefully, the program should operate correctly with no further change required.

8.2

DOUBLY LINKED LISTS AND OTHER VARIATIONS

Insertion before a given node of a linked list requires finding the node preceding the given node; several of the other operations require the same. In the last section we solved this problem by traversing the list from its beginning until the desired node was found, but this solution is generally unsatisfactory. Its programming is more difficult, and the running time of the program will depend on the length of the list, which may be quite long.

There are several methods that can be used to overcome this problem of finding the node preceding the given one. In this section, we shall study the simplest and, in many ways, the most flexible and satisfying method.

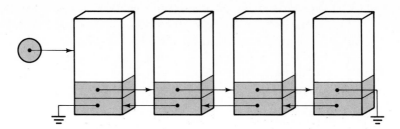

Figure 8.4. Doubly linked list with header

8.2.1 Declarations for a Doubly Linked List

doubly linked list

The idea, as shown in Figure 8.4, is simply to keep two links in each node, pointing in opposite directions. Hence, by following the appropriate link, we can move either direction through the linked list with equal ease. We call such a list a ***doubly linked list***.

In a doubly linked list, the declaration of a node becomes

```
type
    listnode = record
                   entry: listentry;
                   nextnode,
                   previousnode: listpointer
               end;
```

It is thus possible to move in either direction through the list while keeping only one pointer as the window into the list.

8.2.2 Operations on Doubly Linked Lists

With a doubly linked list, traversals in either direction, insertions, and deletions from arbitrary positions in the list can be accomplished without difficulty. Some of the procedures that make changes in the list are longer than those for simply linked lists, because it is necessary to update both kinds of pointers when a node is inserted or deleted from the list. These procedures, however, are conceptually no more difficult than those for simply linked lists, and often they are much easier because there is no need to make a partial traversal of the list to find a node.

The cost of a doubly linked list, of course, is the extra space required in each node for a second link. For most applications, however, the amount of space needed for the information field entry in each node is much larger than the space needed for a link, so the second link field in each node does not significantly increase the total amount of storage space required for the list.

Here, as an example of the list-processing procedures for doubly linked lists, is a procedure to insert one node before a given node of a doubly linked list. You should compare this procedure with both of the procedures InsertNodeBefore and InsertNodeAfter for simply linked lists.

procedure InsertNodeBefore (current, newnode: listpointer; **var** L: listtype) ;
{**Pre:** current *points to a node in a linked list, and* newnode *points to a node that is not already in the linked list.*
   Post: *The node* newnode↑ *has been inserted before* current↑ *in the linked list.*}
var
   previous: listpointer;   {*pointer to the node before* current↑}
begin
   if (current = **nil**) **or** (newnode = **nil**) **then**
      writeln ('Error: Attempt to make an incorrect insertion before a node')
   else begin
      previous := current↑.previousnode;   {*Keep node before* current↑.}
      current↑.previousnode := newnode;
      if previous = **nil then**   {*Insert at head of* L.}
         L.head := newnode
      else
         previous↑.nextnode := newnode;
      newnode↑.nextnode := current;   {*links previously undefined*}
      newnode↑.previousnode := previous
   end
end;

The action of this procedure is shown in Figure 8.5. You should note how much simpler this procedure is than the corresponding one for simply linked lists, which required traversing the list to find the node preceding the given one. Note that, for consistency with versions of this procedure for other implementations, we have included the list L as a parameter, even though it is not explicitly used.

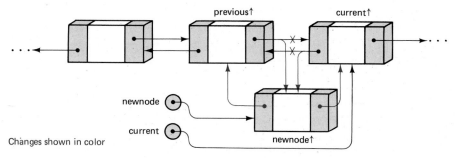

Figure 8.5. Insertion before a node of a doubly linked list

8.2.3 Other Variations

There are several other ways in which linked lists can be constructed, some of which are useful for different purposes.

Trailing Pointers

two pointers

Insertion before a node of a simply linked list, for example, can be simplified if we keep a trailing pointer throughout all our processing of the list. This second pointer will move in lock step with the first, always kept exactly one node closer to the head of the list. Inserting a new node before the current pointer is now easy, since it is only inserting it after the trailing pointer, and then moving the trailing pointer to the new node. Inserting the new node before the first node of the list (in which case the trailing pointer is not yet defined) is a special case, but an easy one, similar to adding a node to a linked stack. This action is illustrated in Figure 8.6. The details of the resulting procedure are left as an Exercise.

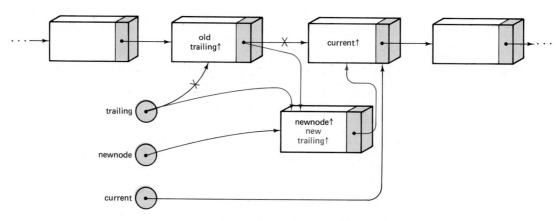

Figure 8.6. Insertion into a linked list with a trailing pointer

Two-Pointer Windows

new data structure

Keeping a trailing pointer at all times really means that we are making a change in our definition of a linked list. Instead of defining a window to be a single pointer into the list, we can define it to consist of a pair of pointers, as follows.

```
type
  window = record
              current,
              trailing: listpointer
           end;
```

When current points to the first node in the list, trailing is undefined, and we shall then generally set trailing to be **nil**.

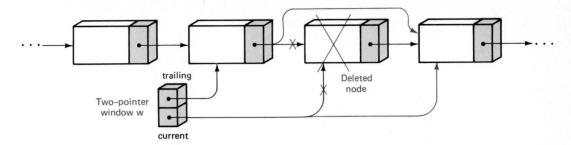

Figure 8.7. Deletions from a two-pointer linked list

Deletion of a node from a linked list is another operation in which the two-pointer window simplifies the work. If we wish to delete a node that is not the first one on the list, then to adjust the links, we must locate the link coming into the node. In a simply linked list with only one pointer, this task is difficult, but with a trailing pointer it is easy. After including appropriate error checking, we obtain the following procedure, which is illustrated in Figure 8.7.

two-pointer
deletion

procedure DeleteList(**var** w: window; **var** L: listtype);
{**Pre:** *The two-pointer linked list L has been created and* w *points to a node of* L.
  Post: *Deletes the entry at window* w *of* L *and moves* w *to the next node of L if it exists, otherwise off the list.*}
begin   {*procedure DeleteList*}
  if not OnList(w, L) **then**
    writeln('Error: Attempt to delete a node not on the list')
  else with w **do**
    if current = L.head **then**
    begin   {*Delete the first node of the list.*}
      current := current↑.nextnode;   {*Advance past the deleted node.*}
      L.head := current;   {*Change the beginning of the list.*}
      trailing := **nil**   {*The first node has no trailing pointer.*}
    end
    else begin
      current := current↑.nextnode;   {*Advance past the deleted node.*}
      dispose(trailing↑.nextnode);   {*Delete the node.*}
      trailing↑.nextnode := current;   {*Skip the deleted node.*}
    end
end;   {*procedure DeleteList*}

Dummy Node

Yet one more variation of linked lists is to include a ***dummy node*** at the beginning (or, less commonly, at the end) of a linked list. This dummy node contains no information and is used only to provide a link to the first true node of the list. It is never deleted and, if desired, can even be a static variable (that is, one declared as the program is written). Use of a dummy node at the head of the list simplifies the form of some procedures. Since the list is never empty, the special case of an empty list need not be considered, and neither does the special case of inserting or deleting at the head of the list.

8.2.4 Comparison of Implementations

Now that we have seen several algorithms for manipulating linked lists and several variations in their structure and implementation, let us pause to assess some relative advantages of linked and of contiguous implementation of lists.

advantages

overflow

The foremost advantage of dynamic storage for linked lists is flexibility. Overflow is no problem until the computer memory is actually exhausted. Especially when the individual records are quite large, it may be difficult to determine the amount of contiguous static storage that might be needed for the required arrays, while keeping enough free for other needs. With dynamic allocation, there is no need to attempt to make such decisions in advance.

changes

Changes, especially insertions and deletions, can be made in the middle of a linked list more quickly than in the middle of a contiguous list. Even queues are easier to handle in linked storage. If the records are large, then it is much quicker to change the values of a few pointers than to copy the records themselves from one location to another.

disadvantages

The first drawback of linked lists is that the links themselves take space, space that might otherwise be needed for additional data. In most systems, a pointer requires the same amount of storage (one word) as does an integer. Thus a list of integers will require double the space in linked storage that it would require in contiguous storage. On the other hand, in many practical applications, the nodes in the list are quite large, with data fields taking hundreds of words altogether. If each node contains 100 words of data, then using linked storage will

space use

increase the memory requirement by only one percent, an insignificant amount. In fact, if extra space is allocated to arrays holding contiguous lists to allow for additional insertions, then linked storage will probably require less space altogether. If each entry takes 100 words, then contiguous storage will save space only if all the arrays can be filled to more than 99 percent of capacity.

random access

The major drawback of linked lists is that they are not suited to random access. With contiguous storage, the program can refer to any position within a list as quickly as to any other position. With a linked list, it may be necessary to traverse a long path to reach the desired node. Access to a node in linked storage may take slightly more computer time, since it is necessary, first, to obtain the pointer and then go to the address. This last consideration, however, is usually

programming

of no importance. Similarly, you may find at first that writing procedures to manipulate linked lists takes a bit more programming effort, but, with practice, this discrepancy will decrease.

In summary, therefore, we can conclude that contiguous storage is generally preferable when the records are individually very small, when few insertions or deletions need to be made in the middle of a list, and when random access is important. Linked storage proves superior when the records are large and flexibility is needed in inserting, deleting, and rearranging the nodes.

To help choose one of the many possible variations in structure and implementation, finally, the programmer should consider which of the many operations will actually be performed on the list, and which of these are the most important. To help with this decision, the table in Figure 8.8 indicates the relative ease of doing each of the operations in each variation we have studied. In this table, + indicates a relative advantage and − a relative disadvantage. For the operations, + indicates that the operation can be done in time that does not depend on the length of the list. The plus-or-minus sign shown for the space used by a contiguous list indicates that the relative advantages depend on the application: If a contiguous list is full or nearly full, then it has a relative advantage in space used over a linked list; but if it is far from full, then it is at a relative disadvantage.

	Contig-uous	Simply linked	Two pointer	Doubly linked
CreateList	+	+	+	+
ListEmpty	+	+	+	+
ListFull	+	+	+	+
ListSize	+	−	−	−
IsFirst	+	+	+	+
IsLast	+	−	−	−
OnList	+	−	−	−
StartList	+	+	+	+
FinishList	+	−	−	−
NextList	+	+	+	+
PrecedingList	+	−	−	+
PositionList	+	−	−	−
DeleteList	−	−	+	+
InsertAfter	−	+	+	+
InsertBefore	−	−	+	+
ReplaceList	+	+	+	+
RetrieveList	+	+	+	+
space used	±	+	+	−

Figure 8.8. Relative ease of performing list operations

8.2.5 Programming Hints

To close this section, we include several suggestions for programming with linked lists, as well as some pitfalls to avoid.

pointers and pitfalls
1. Draw "before" and "after" diagrams of the appropriate part of the linked list, showing the relevant pointers and the way in which they should be changed.

If they might help, also draw diagrams showing intermediate stages of the process.

2. To determine in what order values should be placed in the pointer fields to carry out the various changes, it is usually better first to assign the values to previously undefined pointers, then to those with value **nil**, and finally to the remaining pointers. After one pointer variable has been copied to another, the first is free to be reassigned to its new location.

undefined links

3. Be sure that no links are left undefined at the conclusion of your procedure, either as links in new nodes that have never been assigned or links in old nodes that have become dangling, that is, that point to nodes that no longer are used. Such links should either be reassigned to nodes still in use or set to the value **nil**.

extreme cases

4. Always verify that your procedure works correctly for an empty list and for a list with only one node.

multiple dereferencing

5. Never use constructions such as p↑.nextnode↑.nextnode, even though they are syntactically correct. A single variable should involve only a single pointer reference. Constructions with repeated references usually indicate that the procedure can be improved by rethinking what pointer variables should be declared in the algorithm, introducing new ones if necessary, so that no variable includes more than one pointer reference (↑).

alias variable

6. It is possible that two (or more) different pointer variables can point to the same node. Since this node can thereby be accessed under two different names, it is called an ***alias variable***. The node can be changed using one name and later used with the other name, perhaps without the realization that it has been changed. One pointer can be changed to another node, and the second left dangling. Alias variables are therefore dangerous and should be avoided as much as possible. Be sure you clearly understand whenever you must have two pointers that refer to the same node, and remember that changing one reference requires changing the other.

■■■■■ EXERCISES 8.2

E1. Indicate which of the following procedures and functions are the same for doubly linked lists as described in this section, and for simply linked lists. For those that are different, write new versions for doubly linked lists. Be sure that each subprogram conforms to the specifications given in Section 6.1.

a. **function** ListSize (L: listtype): integer.
b. **function** IsFirst (w: window; L: listtype): Boolean.
c. **function** IsLast (w: window; L: listtype): Boolean.
d. **procedure** ClearList (**var** L: listtype).
e. **procedure** StartList (**var** w: window; L: listtype).
f. **procedure** FinishList (**var** w: window; L: listtype).
g. **procedure** NextList (**var** w: window; L: listtype).

    h. **procedure** PrecedingList(**var** w: window; L: listtype).
    i. **procedure** PositionList(**var** w: window; target: integer; **var** L: listtype);
    j. **procedure** DeleteList(**var** w: window; **var** L: listtype).
    k. **procedure** InsertNodeAfter(current, newnode: listpointer; **var** L: listtype).
    l. **procedure** InsertAfter(**var** w: window; x: listentry; **var** L: listtype).

E2. The procedure ReplaceList changes the entry in a node but need not change the links in the list. Write a procedure

ReplaceNode(w: window; p: listpointer; **var** L: listtype)

for doubly linked lists that replaces the node w↑ by p↑. Compare your procedure with the similar one for simply linked lists.

E3. **(1)** Indicate if each of the following procedures and functions is the same for linked lists with two-pointer windows as presented in this section as for simply linked lists. **(2)** Write those that are different in the two pointer version. Be sure that each conforms to the specifications given in Section 6.1. Some of these operations can be done efficiently (with only a small, constant number of steps), but others require traversing part or all of the list and will be much slower. Determine into which category each goes.

    a. **procedure** CreateList(**var** L: listtype)
    b. **procedure** ClearList(**var** L: listtype).
    c. **function** ListEmpty(L: listtype): Boolean.
    d. **function** ListFull(L: listtype): Boolean.
    e. **function** ListSize(L: listtype): integer.
    f. **function** IsFirst(w: window; L: listtype): Boolean.
    g. **function** IsLast(w: window; L: listtype): Boolean.
    h. **function** OnList(w: window; L: listtype): Boolean.
    i. **procedure** StartList(**var** w: window; L: listtype).
    j. **procedure** FinishList(**var** w: window; L: listtype).
    k. **procedure** NextList(**var** w: window; L: listtype).
    l. **procedure** PrecedingList(**var** w: window; L: listtype).
    m. **procedure** PositionList(**var** w: window; target: integer; **var** L: listtype);
    n. **procedure** InsertBefore(**var** w: window; x: listentry; **var** L: listtype).
    o. **procedure** InsertAfter(**var** w: window; x: listentry; **var** L: listtype).
    p. **procedure** ReplaceList(w: window; x: listentry; **var** L: listtype).
    q. **procedure** RetrieveList(w: window; **var** x: listentry; **var** L: listtype).

E4. In a circularly linked list, as illustrated in Figure 7.9, the tail of the list, instead of having a **nil** pointer, points back to the head of the list. The pointer specified as the name of the list points to the last node of the list, not the first. Take windows for the list to be single pointers. Write the following subprograms for circularly linked lists.

    a. **function** IsFirst(w: window; L: listtype): Boolean.
    b. **function** IsLast(w: window; L: listtype): Boolean.
    c. **procedure** ClearList(**var** L: listtype).
    d. **procedure** StartList(**var** w: window; L: listtype).

e. **procedure** FinishList (**var** w: window; L: listtype).

f. **procedure** NextList (**var** w: window; L: listtype).

Make a new column for the table in Figure 8.8 for circularly linked lists.

E5. Write a procedure that will concatenate two circularly linked lists, producing a circularly linked list.

E6. A doubly linked list can be made circular by setting the values of links in the first and last nodes appropriately. Discuss the advantages and disadvantages of a circular doubly linked list in doing the various list operations.

■ PROJECTS 8.2

P1. Take the text-editing program f om Chapter 6 and replace the contiguous list-processing package by an equivalent package using doubly linked lists. No matter how carefully the contiguous version was written, some changes will have to be made in order for the linked version to run correctly. What are these changes? (*Hint*: when using two windows to a list, what happens to the second window when an entry is deleted or inserted in the contiguous case, and in the linked case?)

P2. Write a program that will do addition, subtraction, multiplication, and division for arbitrarily large integers. Each integer should be represented as a list of its digits. Since the integers are allowed to be as large as you like, linked lists will be needed to prevent the possibility of overflow. For some operations, it is useful to move backwards through the list; hence, doubly-linked lists are appropriate. Multiplication and division can be done simply as repeated addition and subtraction.

a. Write the complete program, using this simple method for multiplication and division.

b. Write a more efficient algorithm for the multiplication procedure.

8.3

APPLICATION: POLYNOMIAL ARITHMETIC

8.3.1 Purpose of the Project

In this section, we shall outline a program for manipulating polynomials. This program will use lists extensively, and, because of the ways the lists are manipulated, provides a good application for linked lists.

calculator for polynomials

Our program will imitate the behavior of a simple calculator that does addition, subtraction, multiplication, division, and perhaps some other operations, but one that performs these operations for polynomials rather than for numbers.

There are many kinds of calculators available, and we could model our program after any of them. In Chapter 4, however, we have already developed a calculator (for real numbers) that uses the *reverse Polish* (postfix) technique.

Let us therefore simplify our current project by building on the work that has already been done.

reverse Polish calculations In our calculator, then, the operands (which will be polynomials for us) are entered *before* a command is specified. The operands are pushed onto a stack. When a command is performed, it pops its operands from the stack and pushes its result back onto the stack.

If we review the calculator project in Section 4.3, we see that almost all of it can be adapted to calculate with polynomials with very little, if any, change. In fact, the main program needs only to change the type declaration for operand from real to polynomial, and we shall then need to add type declarations and procedures to process polynomials. These concerns we shall consider later.

The procedure DoCommand processes operands from the stack and will remain almost the same as in Section 4.3. The major change is that arithmetic operations on reals were done directly in the procedure in Section 4.3 (such as the expressions p + q and p/q that were pushed onto the stack), and, for polynomials, the arithmetic will be more complicated. Hence let us introduce four new procedures that will be invoked from DoCommand. We shall consider the details of these procedures later:

Add(p, q: polynomial; **var** r: polynomial);	{*sets* r := p + q}
Subtract(p, q: polynomial; **var** r: polynomial);	{*sets* r := p − q}
Multiply(p, q: polynomial; **var** r: polynomial);	{*sets* r := p ∗ q}
Divide(p, q: polynomial; **var** r: polynomial);	{*sets* r := q ÷ p}

The procedure ReadCommand from Section 4.3 needs no modification at all.

8.3.2 Data Structures and Their Implementation

Let us now turn to our principal task by deciding how to represent polynomials and writing procedures to manipulate them. If we carefully consider a polynomial such as

$$3x^5 - 2x^3 + x^2 + 4$$

essence of a polynomial we see that the important information about the polynomial is contained in the coefficients and exponents of x; the variable x itself is really just a place holder (a dummy variable). Hence, for purposes of calculation, we may think of a polynomial as made up of terms, each of which consists of a coefficient and an exponent. In a computer, we can similarly represent a polynomial as a *list* of pairs of coefficients and exponents. Each of these pairs will constitute a record, so a polynomial will be represented as a list of records. We must then build into our procedures rules for performing arithmetic on two such lists.

implementation of a polynomial Should we use contiguous or linked lists? If, in advance, we know a bound on the degree of the polynomials that can occur and if the polynomials that occur have nonzero coefficients in almost all their possible terms, then we should probably do better with contiguous lists. But if we do not know a bound on the degree, or if polynomials with only a few nonzero terms are likely to appear, then we shall find linked storage preferable. Since we need to go through the terms of a polynomial in only one direction, simply linked lists will prove adequate. To illustrate the use of linked lists, we adopt this implementation, as illustrated in Figure 8.9. We shall write all the procedures, however, using only our standard operations specified for general lists, and hence we can, if we wish, change to any other implementation of lists without needing to rewrite any part of the project.

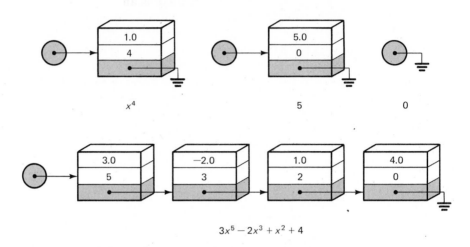

$$x^4 \qquad\qquad 5 \qquad\qquad 0$$

$$3x^5 - 2x^3 + x^2 + 4$$

Figure 8.9. Polynomials as linked lists

Kruse 4.14

assumptions   We shall consider that each node contains one term of a polynomial, and we shall keep only nonzero terms in the list. The polynomial that is always 0 (that is, it consists of only a 0 term) will be represented by an empty list. We call this the *zero polynomial* or say that it is *identically 0*.

As usual for linked lists, each node consists of an entry of type listentry and a pointer to the next term of the polynomial. We shall declare type listentry to be the same as term, and each term will be a record containing a nonzero coefficient (a real number) and an exponent a (nonnegative integer, which we shall call a *cardinal*).

type polynomial   As Pascal declarations to insert in the main program, we thus obtain

```
type
    cardinal = 0 .. maxint;
    term = record
        coef: real;
        exp: cardinal
    end;
    listentry = term;
    polynomial = listtype;
```

We have not yet indicated the order of storing the terms of the polynomial. If we allow them to be stored in any order, then it might be difficult to recognize that

$$x^5 + x^2 - 3 \quad \text{and} \quad -3 + x^5 + x^2 \quad \text{and} \quad x^2 - 3 + x^5$$

restriction
all represent the same polynomial. Hence we adopt the usual convention that the terms of every polynomial are stored in the order of decreasing exponent within the linked list, and we further assume that no two terms have the same exponent and that no term has a zero coefficient. (Recall that the polynomial that is identically 0 is represented as an empty list.)

8.3.3 Reading and Writing Polynomials

With polynomials implemented as lists, writing out a polynomial becomes simply a traversal of the list, as follows. We shall use a separate procedure WriteTerm to write out one term of the polynomial during the traversal.

writing

```
procedure WritePolynomial(P: polynomial);
{Pre:   The polynomial P has been created.
  Post: The coefficients and exponents in P have been written out for the
        user.}
var
    firstterm: Boolean;                {Is this the first term of the polynomial?}
{The preceding variable is used by WriteTerm to determine whether or not to
 put a plus sign in front of a term. It is set to false by WriteTerm as a side
 effect after the first term is written.}
begin                                  {procedure WritePolynomial}
    if ListEmpty(P) then
        writeln('zero polynomial')
    else begin
        firstterm := true;
        TraverseList(P, WriteTerm);
        writeln
    end                                {case of nonempty polynomial}
end;                                   {procedure WritePolynomial}


procedure WriteTerm(currentterm: term);
begin
    if (not firstterm) and (currentterm.coef > 0) then
        write(' + ');
    write(currentterm.coef: 5: 2, 'x^', currentterm.exp: 1);
    firstterm := false
end                                    {printing one term}
```

As we read in a new polynomial, we shall be constructing a new list, adding an entry to the list for each term (coefficient-exponent pair) that we read. The process of creating a new term, appending it to the end of a list, and updating the window to point to the new term will reappear in almost every procedure for manipulating polynomials. We therefore write it as a separate utility that we shall use whenever convenient to help construct a new polynomial.

making one term

procedure AppendTerm (coefficient: real; exponent: cardinal;
                       var last: window; **var** result: polynomial);
  {**Pre:** *Either the polynomial* result *is empty or the window* last *points to the last term of* result.
     Post: *A new term with the coefficient and exponent supplied as parameters has been added to the end of polynomial* result, *and* last *has been moved to point to this last term.*}
var newterm: term;
begin   {*procedure AppendTerm*}
   newterm.coef := coefficient;
   newterm.exp := exponent;
   if ListEmpty (result) **then**
     InsertAfter (last, newterm, result)
   else if not IsLast (last, result) **then**
     writeln ('Error: Window last is not at the last term.')
   else begin
     InsertAfter (last, newterm, result);
     NextList (last, result)
   end
end;   {*procedure AppendTerm*}

We can now use this procedure to make and insert new terms as we read coefficient-exponent pairs. Note that it was necessary to treat the case when the list is previously empty separately from other cases. The reason is that the window current, which normally points to the last entry of the list, has no entry to which to point for an empty list. One method that can be used to avoid this special case is to insist that the list always be nonempty. This can be done either by changing the specifications in order to represent the zero polynomial by a list containing one term with coefficient and exponent 0, or by introducing a *dummy node* into the list, that is, a node that will always be present at the beginning of the list but which will contain no term. Both of these methods, however, induce additional problems, so we shall remain with the specifications we have already introduced.

reading

procedure ReadPolynomial (**var** result: polynomial);
  {**Pre:** *The list* result *has been created.*
     Post: *The user has supplied coefficients and exponents that have been assembled into the polynomial* result *in order of decreasing exponents.*}
var
   finished: Boolean;   {*Has reading the polynomial been finished?*}
   coefficient: real;
   exponent,
   lastexponent: cardinal;   {*used to check that exponents descend in size*}
   current: window;   {*window to the term currently being constructed*}

```
                    begin                                  {procedure ReadPolynomial}
instructions          writeln('Enter coefficients and exponents for the polynomial, one per line.');
                      writeln('Exponents must be in descending order.');
                      writeln('Enter coefficient or exponent of 0 to terminate.');
initialize            lastexponent := maxint;      {sentinel to check that exponents descend}
                      if not ListEmpty(result) then
                        ClearList(result);       {assumes result has previously been created}
                      repeat
read one term           write('coefficient?');
                        readln(coefficient);
                        finished := (coefficient = 0.0);
                        if not finished then
                        begin
                          write('exponent?');
                          readln(exponent);
                          if (exponent >= lastexponent) or (exponent < 0) then
error checking          begin
                            finished := true;
                            writeln('Bad exponent. Polynomial terminates without its last term.')
                          end
                          else begin
make one term             AppendTerm(coefficient, exponent, current, result);
                            lastexponent := exponent;
                            finished := (exponent = 0)
                          end
                        end
                      until finished
                    end;                                   {procedure ReadPolynomial}
```

In this procedure, we see one problem of space management, the use of the procedure ClearList. It is quite possible that ReadPolynomial is called to read a polynomial more than once. When a second polynomial is read into result, the former one should be discarded. But we do not wish the space occupied by the former polynomial to be lost, and therefore we use the procedure ClearList to return the unused space to the system so that it can be reallocated. ClearList, however, requires that its list be previously created. Hence, to protect ClearList and other procedures from error, the main program will need additional code to invoke procedure CreateList for every polynomial list that it uses.

8.3.4 Addition of Polynomials

The requirement that the terms of a polynomial appear with descending exponents in the list simplifies their addition. To add two polynomials, we need only scan through them once each. If we find terms with the same exponent in the two polynomials, then we add the coefficients; otherwise, we copy the term of larger exponent into the sum and go on. When we reach the end of one of the polynomials, then any remaining part of the other is copied to the sum. We must also be careful not to include terms with zero coefficient in the sum.

```
procedure Add (summand1, summand2: polynomial; var result: polynomial);
{Pre:   Polynomials summand1, summand2, and result have been created.
 Post: result becomes the sum of the two summands.}
var
    first,                          {window to traverse first summand}
    second,                         {window to traverse second summand}
    last: window;                           {window to traverse result}
    firstterm,
    secondterm: term;         {terms at the windows first and second}
    sum: real;                       {coefficient of a tentative term}
begin                                                {procedure Add}
```

initialize
```
    ClearList (result);        {Make sure the result polynomial is empty.}
    if ListEmpty (summand1) then
        ListCopy (summand2, result)
    else if ListEmpty (summand2) then
        ListCopy (summand1, result)
    else begin
        StartList (first, summand1);
        StartList (second, summand2);

        while OnList (first, summand1) and OnList (second, summand2) do
        begin
            RetrieveList (first, firstterm, summand1);
            RetrieveList (second, secondterm, summand2);
            if firstterm.exp = secondterm.exp then
```

equal-exponent terms
```
            begin                        {Add terms with equal exponents.}
                sum := firstterm.coef + secondterm.coef;
                if sum <> 0.0 then        {Exclude terms with 0.0 coefficient.}
                    AppendTerm (sum, firstterm.exp, last, result);
                NextList (first, summand1);             {Advance both windows.}
                NextList (second, summand2)
            end
```

unequal exponents
```
            else if firstterm.exp > secondterm.exp then
            begin        {Copy from first, since first has the larger exponent.}
                RetrieveList (first, firstterm, result);
                AppendTerm (firstterm.coef, firstterm.exp, last, result);
                NextList (first, summand1)
            end
            else begin   {Copy from second, since it has the larger exponent.}
                RetrieveList (second, secondterm, result);
                AppendTerm (secondterm.coef, secondterm.exp, last, result);
                NextList (second, summand2)
            end
        end;                                   {loop processing both summands}
```

remaining terms   {*At this point one of the two summands has been exhausted. At most one of
                             the following copying loops will be executed.*}

```
            while OnList(first, summand1) do
            begin
                AppendTerm(firstterm.coef, firstterm.exp, last, result);
                NextList(first, summand1)
            end;
            while OnList(second, summand2) do
            begin
                AppendTerm(secondterm.coef, secondterm.exp, last, result);
                NextList(second, summand2)
            end
        end                              {case when both summands are not empty}
    end;                                                        {procedure Add}
```

8.3.5 Completing the Project

The Missing Procedures

At this point, the remaining procedures for the calculator project are sufficiently
similar to those already written that they can be left as exercises. Procedures
for the remaining arithmetical operations have the same general form as our
procedure for addition. Some of these are easy: Subtraction is almost identical
with addition. For multiplication, we can first write (a simple) procedure that
multiplies a polynomial by a monomial, where **monomial** means a polynomial
with only one term. Then we combine use of this procedure with the addition
procedure to do a general multiplication. Division is more complicated.

Group Project

Production of a coherent package of subprograms for manipulating polynomials
makes an interesting group project. Different members of the group can write
functions or procedures for different operations. Some of these are indicated
as projects at the end of this section, but you may wish to include additional
features as well. Any additional features should be planned carefully to be sure
that they can be completed in a reasonable time, without disrupting other parts
of the program.

specifications   After deciding on the division of work among its members, the most important decisions of the group relate to the exact ways in which the procedures and
functions should communicate with each other, and especially with the calling
program. If you wish to make any changes in the organization of the program,
be certain that the precise details are spelled out clearly and completely for all
members of the group.

Next, you will find that it is too much to hope that all members of the group
will complete their work at the same time, or that all parts of the project can be

cooperation　combined and debugged together. You will therefore need to use program stubs and drivers (see Sections 2.2.2 and 2.2.5) to debug and test the various parts of the project. One member of the group might take special responsibility for this testing. In any case, you will find it very effective for different members to read, help debug, and test each other's subprograms.

coordination　Finally, there are the responsibilities of making sure that all members of the group complete their work on time, of keeping track of the progress of various aspects of the project, of making sure that no subprograms are integrated into the project before they are thoroughly debugged and tested, and then of combining all the work into the finished product.

EXERCISES 8.3

E1. Decide whether the stack for the calculator should be contiguous or linked, and indicate why.

E2. If the polynomial that is identically 0 is represented as one term with coefficient and exponent of 0, rather than an empty list, then the procedure AppendTerm need not consider the case of an empty list separately. What other problems would this change in representation cause?

E3. A function in Pascal can return a pointer as its result. Since a linked list can be described by a single pointer to its head, we could define

polynomial = listpointer.

Then we could write the arithmetic operations as functions, for example

function Subtract(p, q: polynomial): polynomial;

We could also write Pop(S) as a function that returns the top polynomial on the stack as its result. Then procedure DoCommand could then be shortened considerably by writing such statements as

Push(Subtract(Pop(S), Pop(S)), S);

a. Assuming that this statement works correctly, explain why it would still be bad programming style.

b. It is possible that two different Pascal compilers, both adhering strictly to standard Pascal, would translate this statement in ways that would give different answers when the program runs. Explain how this could happen.

E4. Discuss the possible generalization of the project of this section to polynomials in several variables.

PROJECTS 8.3

P1. Assemble the procedures developed in this section, together with those from Section 4.3, and make the necessary changes in the code so as to produce a working skeleton for the calculator program, one that will read, write, and add polynomials.

P2. Write procedure Subtract.

P3. Write a procedure that will multiply a polynomial by a monomial (that is, by a polynomial consisting of a single term).

P4. Use the procedure of the preceding problem, together with the procedure that adds polynomials, to write the procedure Multiply.

P5. Write procedure Divide.

P6. The procedure ReadCommand, as written, will accept any sequence of commands, but some sequences are illegal. If the stack begins empty, for example, then the sequence + ? ? is illegal, because it is impossible to add two polynomials before reading them in. Modify procedure ReadCommand as follows so that it will accept only legal sequences of commands. The procedure should set up a counter and initialize it to the number of polynomials on the stack. Whenever the command ? appears in the stream, the counter is increased by one (since the read command ? will push an additional polynomial onto the stack), and whenever one of + , − , * , or / appears, it is decreased by one (since these commands will pop two polynomials and push one onto the stack). If the counter ever becomes zero or negative, then the sequence is illegal.

P7. Many reverse Polish calculators use not only a stack but also provide memory locations where operands can be stored. Extend the project to provide for memory locations for polynomials, and provide additional commands to store the top of the stack into a memory location and to push the polynomial in a memory location onto the stack.

P8. Write a procedure that will discard the top polynomial on the stack, and include this capability as a new command.

P9. Write a procedure that will interchange the top two polynomials on the stack, and include this capability as a new command.

P10. Write a procedure that will add all the polynomials on the stack together, and include this capability as a new command.

P11. Write a procedure that will compute the derivative of a polynomial, and include this capability as a new command.

P12. Write a procedure that, given a polynomial and a real number, evaluates the polynomial at that number, and include this capability as a new command.

P13. Modify the procedure Divide so that the result of the procedure will be two new polynomials, the quotient and the remainder, where the remainder, if not 0, has degree strictly less than that of the divisor. First push the quotient onto the stack, then the remainder.

8.4

LINKED LISTS IN ARRAYS

old languages

Several of the older but widely used computer languages, such as FORTRAN, COBOL, and BASIC, do not provide facilities for dynamic storage allocation or pointers. Even when implemented in these languages, however, there are many problems where the methods of linked lists are preferable to those of contiguous lists, where, for example, the ease of changing a pointer rather than copying a large record proves advantageous. This section shows how to implement linked lists using only integer variables and arrays.

The Method

The idea is to begin with a large workspace array (or several arrays to hold different parts of a logical record, in the case when the programming language does not support records) and regard the array as our allocation of unused space. We then set up our own procedures to keep track of which parts of the array are unused and to link entries of the array together in the desired order.

dynamic memory

The one feature of linked lists that we must invariably lose in this implementation method is the dynamic allocation of storage, since we must decide in advance how much space to allocate to each array. All the remaining advantages of linked lists, such as flexibility in rearranging large records or ease in making insertions or deletions anywhere in the list, will still apply, and linked lists still prove a valuable method.

advantages

The implementation of linked lists within arrays even proves valuable in languages like Pascal that do provide pointer types and dynamic memory allocation. The applications where arrays may prove preferable are those where the number of entries in a list is known in advance, where the links are frequently rearranged, but relatively few additions or deletions are made, or applications where the same data are sometimes best treated as a linked list and other times as a contiguous list.

multiple linkages

An example of such an application is illustrated in Figure 8.10, which shows a small part of a student record system. Identification numbers are assigned to students first-come, first-served, so neither the names nor the marks in any particular course are in any special order. Given an identification number, a student's records may be found immediately by using the identification number as an index to look in the arrays. Sometimes, however, it is desired to print out the student records alphabetically by name, and this can be done by following the links stored in the array nextname. Similarly, student records can be ordered by marks in any course by following the links in the appropriate array.

To show how this implementation of linked lists works, let us trace through (traverse) the linked list nextname shown in the first part of Figure 8.10. The list header (shown below the table) contains the value 9, which means that the entry in position 9, Arthur, E., is the first entry on the list. Position 9 of nextname then contains the the value 1, which means that the name in position 1, Clark, F., comes

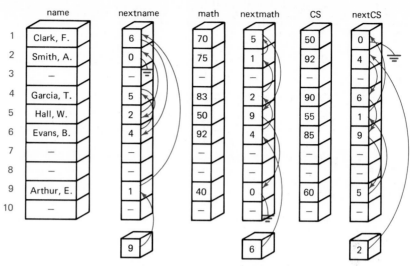

Figure 8.10. Linked lists in arrays

next. In position 1, nextname contains 6, so Evans, B. comes next. Position 6 points to position 4 (Garcia, T.), which points to position 5 (Hall, W.), and position 5 points to position 2 (Smith, A.). In position 2, nextname contains a 0, which means that position 2 is the last entry on the linked list.

The array nextmath, similarly, describes a linked list giving the scores in the array math in descending order. The first entry is 6, which points to 4, and the following nodes in the order of the linked list are 2, 1, 5, and 9. The order in which the nodes appear in the linked list described by nextCS is 2, 4, 6, 9, 5, and 1.

shared lists and random access

As the example in Figure 8.10 shows, implementation of linked lists in arrays can achieve the flexibility of linked lists for making changes, the ability to share the same information fields (such as the names in Figure 8.10) among several linked lists, and, by using indices to access entries directly, the advantage of *random access* otherwise available only for contiguous lists.

cursors

In the implementation of linked lists in arrays, pointers become indices relative to the start of arrays, and the links of a list are stored in an array, each entry of which gives the index where, within the array, the next entry of the list is stored. To distinguish these indices from the pointers of a linked list in dynamic storage, we shall refer to links within arrays as **cursors** and reserve the word *pointer* for links in dynamic storage.

nil cursors

For the sake of writing programs, we shall declare two arrays for each linked list, entry[ ] to hold the information in the nodes and nextnode[ ] to give the cursor to the next node. For most applications, entry is an array of records, or it is split into several arrays if the programming language does not provide for records. Both the arrays entry and nextnode will be indexed from 1 to max, where max is a constant. Since we begin the indices with 1, we can make another arbitrary choice, and use the cursor value 0 to indicate the end of the list, just as the pointer value **nil** is used in dynamic storage. This choice is also illustrated in Figure 8.10.

You should take a moment to trace through Figure 8.10, checking that the cursor values as shown correspond to the colored arrows shown from each entry to its successor.

Operations: Space Management

To obtain the flavor of implementing linked lists in arrays, let us rewrite several of the subprograms of this chapter with this implementation.

stack of
available space

Our first task is to set up a list of available space and write procedures to obtain a new node and to return a node to available space. All the space that we are using comes from the workspace array nextnode, but this space comes in two varieties. First, there are nodes that have never been allocated, and, second, there are nodes that have previously been used but have now been released.

We shall initially allocate space starting at the beginning of the array; hence we can keep track of how much space has been used at some time by an index lastused that indicates the position of the last node that has been used at some time. Locations with indices greater than lastused have never been allocated.

For the nodes that have been used and then returned to available space, we need to use some kind of linked structure to allow us to go from one to the next. Since linked stacks are the simplest kind of such structure, we shall use a linked stack to keep track of the nodes that have been previously used and then returned to available space.

This stack will be linked by means of cursors in the array nextnode. Since, moreover, the cursors not only for the available space but for all the linked lists will coexist in the same array nextnode, this array is intrinsically global, and we

global array
with side effects

shall treat it as a global variable. All procedures that change cursors in lists, therefore, will cause side effects by modifying the array nextnode.

To keep track of the stack of available space, we need an integer variable avail that will give the index of its top. If this stack is empty (which will be represented by avail = 0), then we will need to obtain a new node, that is, a position within the array that has not yet been used for any node. We do so by increasing the index variable lastused that will count the total number of positions within our array that have been used to hold list entries. When lastused exceeds max (the bound we have assumed for array size), we will have overflow and the program can proceed no further. When the main program starts, both variables avail and lastused should be initialized to 0, avail to indicate that the stack of space previously used but now available is empty, and lastused to indicate that no space from the array has yet been assigned.

To emphasize the use of avail and lastused, we shall list them as parameters in the procedures that process the stack of available space. For the procedures (those processing entries in a list, for example) that must create and dispose of space, we have a problem. The specifications of the list operations in Section 6.1 never mention these variables for space management. Hence, to preserve compatibility with these specifications, we cannot list avail and lastused as parameters, but must

more side effects allow the list-processing procedures to treat them as global variables and cause side effects. Hence our desire to maintain conformity with previously given specifications and the restrictions of Pascal force us to adopt what we would normally consider poor programming style.

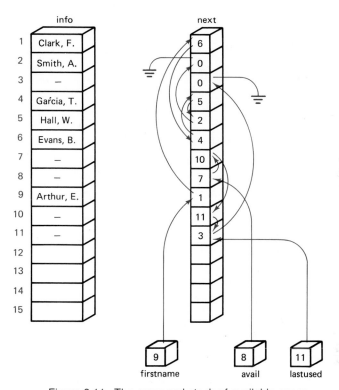

Figure 8.11. The array and stack of available space

The available-space list is illustrated in Figure 8.11. This figure, by the way, also illustrates how two linked lists can coexist in the same array. The arrows shown on the left of the array nextnode describe a linked list that produces the names in the array info in alphabetical order. The arrows on the right side of array nextnode, with header variable avail, show the nodes in the stack of (previously used but now) available space. Notice that the indices that appear in the available-space list are precisely the indices in positions 11 or earlier that are not assigned to names in the array info. Finally, none of the entries in positions 12 or later has been assigned. This fact is indicated by the value lastused = 11. If we were to insert additional names into the list headed by firstname, we would first pop nodes from the stack with top avail, and only when the stack is empty would we increase lastused to insert a name in previously unused space.

The decisions we have made translate into the following declarations to be placed in the main program:

declarations

```
type
    cursor = 0 .. max;
    table = array [1 .. max] of cursor;
    listtype = cursor;
    window = cursor;
var
    avail,                              {top of the stack of unused space}
    lastused,                           {last location in the array used for a node}
    L.head: cursor;                     {start of a linked list in the array}
    nextnode: table;                    {used to store the links in the list(s)}
    entry: array [1 .. max] of listentry;   {used for the entries in the list(s)}
```

With these declarations, we can now rewrite the procedures for keeping track of unused space. At the start of the program, the lists should be initialized by invoking the following:

initialization

```
procedure InitializeSpace (var avail, lastused: cursor);
{Pre:   None.
  Post:  An array nextnode of cursors has been initialized to be empty.}
begin
    avail := 0;      {The stack of previously used available nodes is empty.}
    lastused := 0;   {None of the positions in the array has been used yet.}
end;
```

The procedures NewNode and DisposeNode now take the form:

new

```
procedure NewNode (var c, avail, lastused: cursor, var nextnode: table);
{Pre:   The procedure InitializeSpace has been invoked, and the cursors de-
          scribing the list of available space in nextnode and the variables avail
          and lastused have been used or modified only by NewNode and by
          DisposeNode. Available space remains in nextnode.
  Post:  The cursor c has been set to the first available location in nextnode,
          and the cursors in avail, lastused, and nextnode have been updated
          as necessary.}
begin                                              {procedure NewNode}
    if avail <> 0 then
    begin
        c := avail;
        avail := nextnode [avail]
    end
    else if lastused < max then
    begin
        lastused := lastused + 1;
        c := lastused
    end
    else
        writeln ('Error: Overflow, the array is completely full.')
end;                                               {procedure NewNode}
```

dispose

procedure DisposeNode(c: cursor; **var** avail: cursor; **var** nextnode: table);
{**Pre:** *The procedure* InitializeSpace *has been invoked, and the cursors describing the list of available space in* nextnode *and the variables* avail *and* lastused *have been used or modified only by* NewNode *and by* DisposeNode. *The cursor* c *refers to a node that has been used (is not in the list of available space).*
 Post: *The node to which cursor* c *points has been pushed onto the stack of available space, and the cursors in* avail, lastused, *and* nextnode *have been updated as necessary.*}

```
begin                                    {procedure DisposeNode}
  if c = 0 then
    writeln('Error: Attempt to dispose of a nonexistent node.')
  else begin
    nextnode[c] := avail;
    avail := c
  end
end;                                     {procedure DisposeNode}
```

Other Operations

The translation of other procedures so as to manipulate linked lists implemented within arrays proceeds in much the same way, and most of these will be left as exercises. To provide further models, however, let us write translations of the procedures to traverse a list and to add a node after a given one in a list.

traversal

procedure TraverseList(**var** L: listtype; **procedure** Visit(**var** x: listentry));
{**Pre:** *The linked list* L *has been created, with links as cursors in global table* nextnode; *the entries in* L *are stored in the global array* entry.
 Post: *The action specified by procedure* Visit *has been performed on every entry of the list* L, *beginning at the first entry and doing each in turn.*}

```
var current: cursor;          {starts at head of L and moves through list}
begin                                    {procedure TraverseList}
  current := L.head;                     {Begin at the start of the list.}
  while current <> 0 do     {Continue until current moves past end of list.}
  begin
    Visit(entry[current]);      {Retrieve and process the entry at current.}
    current := nextnode[current]   {Advance to the next node on the list.}
  end
end;                                     {procedure TraverseList}
```

*insertion after a
node*

procedure InsertNodeAfter(newnode, current: cursor);
{**Pre:** current *gives the cursor for a node in a linked list, and* newnode *gives the cursor for a node that is not already in the linked list.*
 Post: *The node* newnode↑ *has been inserted after* current↑ *in the linked list.*}

```
begin                                          {procedure InsertNodeAfter}
  if (newnode = 0) or (current = 0) then
    writeln('Error: Attempt to make an incorrect insertion after a node')
  else begin
    nextnode[newnode] := nextnode[current];
                            {New node points where old node does.}
    nextnode[current] := newnode;    {Old node points to the new one.}
  end
end;                                            {procedure InsertNodeAfter}
```

Compare these two procedures with the equivalent ones for simply linked lists with pointers and dynamic memory presented in Section 8.1. You will quickly see the similarities and determine the changes that are required to translate procedures from one implementation to the other.

Linked-List Variations

Arrays with cursors are not restricted to the implementation of simply linked lists. They are equally effective with two-pointer windows, with circularly linked lists, with doubly linked lists, or with any other variation. For doubly linked lists, in fact, the ability to do arithmetic with cursors allows an implementation (which uses negative as well as positive values for the cursors) in which both forward and backward links can be included in a single cursor field. (See the Exercises.)

EXERCISES 8.4

E1. Draw arrows showing how the list entries are linked together in each of the following nextnode tables. Some tables contain more than one list.

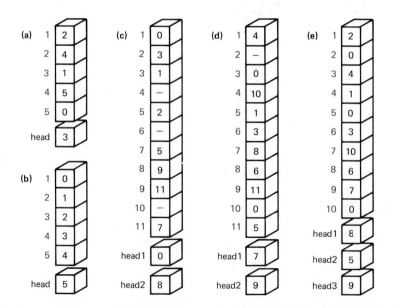

E2. Construct nextnode tables showing how each of the following lists is linked into alphabetical order. Also give the value of the variable L that starts the list.

(a)	(c)	(d)
1 array	1 the	1 London
2 stack	2 of	2 England
3 queue	3 and	3 Rome
4 list	4 to	4 Italy
5 deque	5 a	5 Madrid
6 scroll	6 in	6 Spain
	7 that	7 Oslo
(b)	8 is	8 Norway
1 push	9 I	9 Paris
2 pop	10 it	10 France
3 add	11 for	11 Warsaw
4 delete	12 as	12 Poland
5 insert		

E3. For the list of cities and countries in part (d) of the previous question construct a nextnode table that produces two linked lists, one containing all the cities in alphabetical order and the other all the countries in alphabetical order. Also give values to the two variables naming the lists.

E4. Write the following procedures and functions for simply linked lists implemented with arrays and cursors. Be sure that each conforms to the specific declarations given in Section 6.1.

    a. **procedure** CreateList(**var** L: listtype).
    b. **function** ListEmpty(L: listtype): Boolean.
    c. **function** ListFull(L: listtype): Boolean.
    d. **function** ListSize(L: listtype): integer.
    e. **function** IsFirst(w: window; L: listtype): Boolean.
    f. **function** OnList(w: window; L: listtype): Boolean.
    g. **procedure** StartList(**var** w: window; L: listtype).
    h. **procedure** FinishList(**var** w: window; L: listtype).
    i. **procedure** NextList(**var** w: window; L: listtype).
    j. **procedure** ReplaceList(w: window; x: listentry; **var** L: listtype).
    k. **procedure** RetrieveList(w: window; **var** x: listentry; **var** L: listtype).

E5. Write the procedure ClearList for the case when there is only one list (other than the available-space list) in the array nextnode. Your procedure should be very short and work very quickly.

E6. Write a procedure that will concatenate two linked lists. The procedure should have two parameters, cursors to the beginning of the lists, and the procedure should link the end of the first list to the beginning of the second.

E7. Write a procedure that will split a list in two. The procedure will use two cursors as parameters: first will point to the beginning of the list and second to the node at which it should be split. Is it easier to require that second initially point to the node that will be last in the first list after splitting or to the node that will be first in the second list?

E8. Write a procedure that will reverse a linked list within an array while traversing it only once. At the conclusion, each node should point to the node that was previously its predecessor; the header should point to the node that was formerly at the end, and the node that was formerly first should have a 0 cursor.

E9. This exercise studies the two-pointer version of linked lists implemented with arrays and cursors.

    a. Indicate the changes needed in the declarations to make a window contain two cursors indicating the current and previous nodes of the linked list.

    b. Write procedure NextList for this implementation.

    c. Write procedure InsertNodeBefore for this implementation.

    d. Write procedure DeleteList for this implementation.

E10. Consider a circularly linked list implemented in an array with cursors.

    a. Describe the required changes in the declarations.

    b. Write function IsLast for this implementation.

    c. Write procedure FinishList for this implementation.

    d. Write a procedure that will return all the nodes of a list to the stack of available space. The number of steps that your procedure performs should not increase with the length of the list.

E11. It is possible to implement a doubly linked list with a two-pointer window by using only one array nextnode. That is, we do not need to keep a separate array previousnode to find the backward links. The idea is to put into nextnode[c] not the index of the next entry on the list, but, instead, the index of the next entry *minus* the index of the entry preceding c. If w is a two-pointer window, then to find the next entry from w.current, we calculate

$$\text{nextnode}[\text{w.current}] + \text{w.previous}.$$

Similarly, to find the entry preceding w.previous we calculate

$$\text{w.current} - \text{nextnode}[\text{w.previous}].$$

An example of such a list is shown in the first part of the following diagram. Inside each box is shown the value stored in nextnode; on the right is the corresponding calculation of cursor values.

    a. For the doubly linked list shown in the second part of the following diagram, show the values that will be stored in L.head and in the occupied entries of nextnode.

    b. For the values of L.head and nextnode shown in the third part of the following diagram, draw links showing the corresponding doubly linked list.

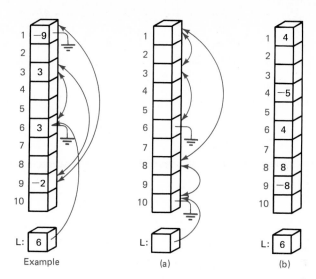

With this implementation, write the following procedures.

   c. StartList(**var** w: window; L: listtype).

   d. NextList(**var** w: window; L: listtype).

   e. PrecedingList(**var** w: window; L: listtype).

   f. DeleteList(**var** w: window; **var** L: listtype).

   g. InsertNodeAfter(**var** w: window; newnode: cursor; **var** L: listtype).

   h. InsertNodeBefore(**var** w: window; newnode: cursor; **var** L: listtype).

POINTERS AND PITFALLS

1. Before choosing implementations, be sure that all the data structures and their associated operations are fully specified on the abstract level.

2. In choosing between linked and contiguous lists, consider the necessary operations on the lists. Linked lists are more flexible in regard to insertions, deletions, and rearrangement; contiguous lists allow random access.

3. Contiguous lists usually require less computer memory, computer time, and programming effort when the entries in the list are small and the algorithms are simple. When the list holds large records, linked lists usually save space, time, and often programming effort.

4. In choosing one of the many variations of linked lists, first consider the operations that will be required, and choose the variation that does those operations more easily.

5. Dynamic memory and pointers allow a program to adapt automatically to a wide range of application sizes and provide flexibility in space allocation among different data structures. Static memory (arrays and cursors) is sometimes more efficient for applications whose size can be completely specified in advance.

6. For advice on programming with linked lists in dynamic memory, see the guidelines at the end of Section 8.2.

REVIEW QUESTIONS

8.1 1. Why, in Section 8.1, is a linked list declared as a record containing only a pointer, rather than the pointer type itself?

2. Why are there two versions of the function OnList and for what purposes is each better?

3. What is *list traversal*?

4. Why are there separate procedures for processing nodes and for processing entries in a linked list?

5. Is it easier to insert a new node before or after a specified node in a simply linked list? Why?

8.2 6. For which operation(s) do doubly linked lists save work?

7. What is the disadvantage of doubly linked lists?

8. What is the reason for introducing the *two-pointer* linked lists? For what operation(s) are they better suited than simply linked lists?

9. For which operation(s) do circularly linked lists save work?

10. Why is there little reason to use a two-pointer window with a doubly linked list (implemented with dynamic memory and pointers)?

11. Give two advantages of linked lists (in dynamic memory) over contiguous lists.

12. What is the major disadvantage of linked lists in comparison with contiguous lists?

13. If the entries in a list are integers (one word each), compare the amount of space required altogether if (a) the list is kept contiguously in an array 90 percent full, (b) the list is kept contiguously in an array 40 percent full, and (c) the list is kept as a linked list (where the pointers take one word each).

14. Repeat the comparisons of Question 13 when the entries in the list are records taking 200 words each.

15. What is an *alias* variable, and why is it dangerous?

8.3   **16.** Discuss some problems that occur in group programming projects that do not occur in individual programming projects. What advantages does a group project have over individual projects?

8.4   **17.** Give some advantages of implementing linked lists in arrays with cursors over dynamic memory with pointers.

  18. What advantage of dynamic memory and pointers is always lost when implementing linked lists with arrays and cursors?

  19. Is there likely to be a significant difference in running time or programming time between implementing linked lists in dynamic memory or in arrays? Why or why not?

  20. Why is it possible to implement a doubly linked list with only one cursor field for each node, but it is not possible to implement it in dynamic storage with only one pointer field per node?

PART III

ALGORITHMS
AND THEIR
ANALYSIS

Often in the past few chapters, we have needed to search through a list until we came to an appropriate node. In the future, we shall continue to find many applications that require searching a list to find a particular entry. In the next chapter, we shall study two simple searching methods, sequential search and binary search. We shall find that binary search is one of the best possible methods, but it requires that the list be sorted into order according to some key.

In the following chapter, we shall then examine several different sorting methods. Each one of these methods can be better than the others under appropriate conditions.

Since applications of searching and sorting are so frequent, and since there are so many different methods that can be used, we need criteria and tools to help us evaluate algorithms and select the best method for each application. Our major goal in the two chapters forming this part of the book is the development of these criteria and tools.

The first way we evaluate algorithms is to draw simple diagrams (called *comparison trees*) showing the behavior of an algorithm. Next, we develop the big Oh notation that, for algorithms applied to large problems, catches the essential count of operations while suppressing a great many details that would make the mathematics much more complicated. At the same time, we study applications of logarithms, sums, and recurrence relations to algorithm analysis.

The conditions in searching and sorting algorithms can be quite difficult to formulate correctly. We shall therefore always be careful to use preconditions and postconditions to help ensure that the algorithms are correct.

9

SEARCHING

This chapter introduces the problem of searching a list to find a particular entry. Our discussion centers on two well-known algorithms: sequential search and binary search. To help our study, we shall develop several mathematical tools. These tools will often be applied in the future both to help us demonstrate that various algorithms are correct and to enable us to calculate how much work they must do. These tools will thereby guide us in selecting the best among many possible algorithms according to the requirements of our particular application. The first of these mathematical tools is to use a condition called a *loop invariant* to ensure that we program binary search correctly. Second, we shall draw diagrams called *comparison trees* to help study algorithm behavior. Next, we study the *big Oh notation* that helps to express the important features of an algorithm's speed without unnecessary detail. Finally, we shall obtain *lower bounds* showing conditions under which any searching algorithm must do at least as much work as binary search.

SEARCHING: INTRODUCTION AND NOTATION

Information retrieval is one of the most important applications of computers. We are given a name and are asked for an associated telephone listing. We are given an account number and are asked for the transactions occurring in that account. We are given an employee name or number and are asked for the personnel records of the employee.

Keys

keys and records

In these examples and a host of others, we are given one piece of information, which we shall call a *key*, and we are asked to find a record that contains other information associated with the key. We shall allow both the possibility that there is more than one record with the same key and that there is no record at all with a given key. See Figure 9.1.

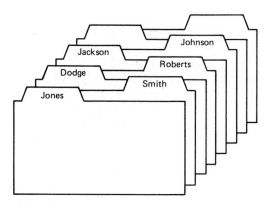

Figure 9.1. Records and their keys

Analysis

Searching for the keys that locate records is often the most time-consuming action in a program, and, therefore, the way the records are arranged and the choice of method used for searching can make a substantial difference in the program's performance. For this reason, we shall spend some time in this chapter studying how much work is done by each of the algorithms we develop. We shall find that counting the number of times that one key is compared with another gives us an excellent measure of the total amount of work that the algorithm will do and of the total amount of computer time it will require when it is run.

External and Internal Searching

The searching problem falls naturally into two cases. If there are many records, perhaps each one quite large, then it will be necessary to store the records in files on disk or tape, external to the computer memory. This case is called *external* searching. In the other case, the records to be searched are stored entirely within the computer memory. This case is called *internal* searching. In this book, we consider only internal searching. Although many of the methods we shall develop in this and later chapters are useful for external searching, a comprehensive study of methods for external searching lies beyond the scope of this book. See the References listed in Appendix C for more information.

Implementation in Pascal

To implement our programs in Pascal, we establish some conventions. We shall always be searching in a list that we generally call L. What we have called records will indeed be Pascal records, and they will be the entries in the list L. The Pascal type that these records have we shall name as listentry, as we always have for lists. One of the fields (or components) of each list entry will be denoted key and have a type called keytype. We thus assume that the program will have declarations of the form

```
type
    keytype = ...;
    listentry = record
            ...        {various components}
        key: keytype;
            ...        {more components}
    end;
```

examples   Typical declarations for the key type are

```
keytype = real;
keytype = integer;
keytype = packed array [1 .. 8] of char.
```

We begin with a *list* to be searched and use the standard declarations for a list introduced in Chapters 6 and 8. Sometimes we shall consider an arbitrary implementation of lists and write our procedures to use the general list operations specified in Section 6.1; at other times, we shall restrict our attention to one of the specific implementations given in Chapters 6 and 8 and write our procedures in ways that depend on the implementation.

target   The key for which we are searching is always called the *target* of the search, and, in programs, it is denoted target. Hence our goal is to find an entry in the list whose key is equal to the target.

Parameters

Each searching procedure we write will have two input parameters. These parameters are the target and the list being searched. It will also have two output
parameters   parameters. The first of these is the Boolean variable found, which indicates

whether or not the search was successful in finding an entry with the target key. If the search was successful, then the output parameter location will be a window to the place in the list where the target was found. If the search is unsuccessful, then the output parameter location may have an undefined value or a value that will differ from one method to another.

9.2

SEQUENTIAL SEARCH

Beyond doubt, the simplest way to do a search is to begin at one end of the list and start to traverse it, comparing the target key with each key in the list until either the desired key is found or the other end of the list is reached. This method is called *sequential search*, since it searches the keys in the list as one sequence.

General Version

Let us begin by programming sequential search for an arbitrary list, by using the general list operations from Section 6.1.

```
procedure SequentialSearch (var L: listtype; target: keytype;
                            var found: Boolean; var location: window);
{Pre:   The list L has been created.
 Post:  If an entry in L has key equal to target, then found becomes true and
        the window location gives the location of the first such entry. Other-
        wise, found becomes false and the window location is undefined.}
var
    current: listentry;      {the entry whose key is currently being checked}
begin                                           {procedure SequentialSearch}
    found := false;                                {Initialize the variables.}
    StartList (location, L);                          {Begin a traversal.}
    while (not found) and (OnList (location, L)) do
    begin
        RetrieveList (location, current, L);
        if current.key = target then
            found := true                                   {successful}
        else
            NextList (location, L)                      {not yet successful}
    end
end;                                            {procedure SequentialSearch}
```

The **while** loop in this procedure keeps moving through the list as long as the target key has not been found, but it terminates as soon as the target is found. If the search is unsuccessful, then found remains false, and, at the conclusion, location has moved to a position beyond the end of the list. (Recall that, for an unsuccessful search, the value of location may be any value; it is considered undefined.)

Contiguous Version

For the sake of improving its performance, SequentialSearch is often written in a form dependent on the implementation. Let us therefore rewrite it specifically for contiguous lists as declared in Section 6.2. Note the direct translation of most of the statements. The variable current, however, is no longer needed since we can retrieve an entry from the list in the same expression in which we check its key.

```
procedure SequentialSearch (var L: listtype; target: keytype;
                                   var found: Boolean; var location: window);
{Pre:     The contiguous list L has been created.
  Post:   If an entry in L has key equal to target, then found becomes true and
          the window location gives the location of the first such entry. Other-
          wise, found becomes false and the window location is undefined.}
begin                                                {procedure SequentialSearch}
   found := false;                                          {Initialize the variables.}
   location := 1;                                               {Begin a traversal.}
   while (not found) and (location <= L.count) do
      if L.entry [location] .key = target then
         found := true                                               {successful}
      else
         location := location + 1                           {not yet successful}
end;                                                 {procedure SequentialSearch}
```

Linked Version

Sequential search written specifically for simply linked lists as implemented in Section 8.1 is equally easy.

```
procedure SequentialSearch (var L: listtype; target: keytype;
                                   var found: Boolean; var location: window);
{Pre:     The linked list L has been created.
  Post:   If an entry in L has key equal to target, then found becomes true and
          the window location gives the location of the first such entry. Other-
          wise, found becomes false and the window location is undefined.}
begin                                                {procedure SequentialSearch}
   found := false;                                          {Initialize the variables.}
   location := L.head;                       {Begin a traversal at the head of the list.}
   while (not found) and (location <> nil) do
      if location↑.info.key = target then
         found := true                                               {successful}
      else
         location := location↑.next                         {not yet successful}
end;                                                 {procedure SequentialSearch}
```

These three procedures illustrate a common correspondence between different implementations. The best policy is usually to formulate an algorithm as generally as possible and then to code the resulting subprogram using operations that are independent of the implementation. If improvement in performance is then needed, the algorithm can be translated into a subprogram that is specific to the particular implementation being used.

Comparison of Keys Versus Running Time

Let us now estimate the amount of work that sequential search will do, so that we can make comparisons with other methods later. Suppose that sequential search was run on a long list. The statements that appear outside the main loop, since they are done only once, take insignificant computer time compared to the work done inside the loop. For each pass through the loop, one key is compared with the target key, several other statements are executed, and several expressions are checked. But all these other statements and expressions are executed in lock step with the comparison of keys: They are all done once for each iteration of the loop.

We have, moreover, three different versions of the algorithm and all three will have different running times. As you can see, however, the basic method of sequential search is exactly the same for all three versions, even though the implementation details differ. In fact, the target is compared to exactly the same keys in the entries of the list in all versions.

Although the running times of the three versions of sequential search will differ a little because of the different implementations, in all of them all the actions relate directly to the comparison of keys. If someone else, using the same method, had written the procedures, then differences in programming approach would likely make a difference in the running time. But all these cases still produce the same number of comparisons of keys. If the length of the list changes, then the work done by any implementation of the searching method will also change proportionately.

In this chapter, we shall study the way in which the number of comparisons of keys depends on the length of the list. Doing this study will give us the most useful information about the algorithm, information that can be applied equally well no matter what implementation we decide to use when we actually write the program.

importance of comparison count

Hence if we wish to estimate how much computer time sequential search is likely to require, or if we wish to compare it with some other method, then knowing the number of comparisons of keys that it makes will give us the most useful information, information actually more useful than the total running time, which is too much dependent on whether we have the contiguous or linked version, or what particular machine is being used.

No matter what algorithm for searching we develop, we can make a similar statement that we take as our fundamental premise in analyzing searching algorithms: The total work is reflected by the number of comparisons of keys that the algorithm makes.

> *To analyze the behavior of an algorithm that makes comparisons of keys, we shall use the count of these key comparisons as our measure of the work done.*

Best, Worst, and Average Behavior

How many comparisons of keys does sequential search make when it is applied to a list of n entries? Since sequential search compares the target to each key in the list in turn, the answer depends on if and where the target may be. If the procedure finds the target in the first position of the list, it does only one key comparison. If the target is second, the procedure does two key comparisons. If it is the last entry on the list, then the procedure does n key comparisons. If the search is unsuccessful, then the target will have been compared to all entries in the list, for a total of n comparisons of keys.

Our question, then, has several answers depending on if and where the target is found. If the search is unsuccessful, then the answer is n key comparisons. The best performance for a successful search is 1 comparison, and the worst is n comparisons.

We have obtained very detailed information about the performance of sequential search, information that is really too detailed for most uses, in that we generally will not know exactly where in a list a particular key may appear. *average behavior* Instead, it will generally be much more helpful if we can determine the *average* behavior of an algorithm. But what do we mean by average? One reasonable assumption, the one that we shall always make, is to take each possibility once and average the results.

provisos Note, however, that this assumption may be very far from the actual situation. Not all English words, for example, appear equally often in a typical essay. The telephone operator receives far more requests for the number of a large business than for that of an average family. The Pascal compiler encounters the keywords **if**, **begin**, and **end** far more often than the keywords **label**, **downto**, and **packed**.

There are a great many interesting, but exceedingly difficult, problems associated with analyzing algorithms where the input is chosen according to some statistical distribution. These problems, however, would take us too far afield to be considered here. We shall therefore limit our attention to the most important case, the one where all the possibilities are equally likely.

Average-Case Analysis

Under the assumption of equal likelihood, we can find the average number of *approximate* key comparisons done in a successful sequential search. Intuitively, the times *answer* when the target appears early in the search balance out the times when it appears late, and therefore, on average, we must look halfway through the list to find it, and thus the average number of key comparisons for a successful search is about $\frac{1}{2}n$.

To find the answer more precisely, we add up the numbers of comparisons in all cases and divide by the number of cases, n. Hence the answer is

$$\frac{1 + 2 + 3 + \cdots + n}{n}.$$

To evaluate this answer, we need a formula for the sum of the first n integers, and this formula is

$$1 + 2 + \cdots + n = \tfrac{1}{2}n(n + 1).$$

This formula appears so often in studying algorithms that it is worth remembering, and it has a simple and elegant proof as well. We let S equal the sum on the left side, write it down twice (once in each direction), and add vertically:

$$
\begin{array}{ccccccccccc}
1 & + & 2 & + & 3 & + & \cdots & + & n-1 & + & n & = & S \\
n & + & n-1 & + & n-2 & + & \cdots & + & 2 & + & 1 & = & S \\
\hline
n+1 & + & n+1 & + & n+1 & + & \cdots & + & n+1 & + & n+1 & = & 2S
\end{array}
$$

There are n columns on the left; hence $n(n + 1) = 2S$ and the formula follows.

The formula for the sum of the first n integers also has the proof without words shown in Figure 9.2.

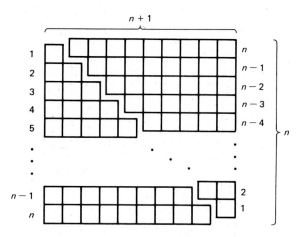

Figure 9.2. Geometrical proof for the sum of integers

To find the exact answer for the average-case analysis of sequential search, we need only take this formula for the sum of integers and divide by n. The result is:

The average number of key comparisons done by sequential search in a successful search is

$$\frac{1}{n}\left(\frac{n(n+1)}{2}\right) = \tfrac{1}{2}(n+1).$$

Notice that this exact answer differs very little from the approximate answer we found easily by intuitive reasoning.

EXERCISES 9.2

E1. One good check for any algorithm is to see what it does in extreme cases. Determine what sequential search does for the following cases:

a. There is only one entry in the list.

b. The list is empty.

c. The list is full.

E2. Trace sequential search as it searches for each of the keys present in a list containing three entries. Determine how many comparisons are made, and thereby check the formula for the average number of comparisons for a successful search.

sorted list

E3. If we can assume that the keys in the list have already been sorted into order (for example, numerical or alphabetical order), then we can terminate unsuccessful searches more quickly. Suppose that the keys have arranged with the smallest key first and then in increasing order of size, and suppose that the same key does not appear more than once in the list. We can then terminate the search as soon as a key greater than or equal to the target key has been found. If there are n different keys in the list, then there are $n+1$ ways that the search could fail: The target key could come before the first key, between any pair of keys, or after the last key. If we assume that these $n+1$ possibilities are equally likely, then what is the average number of comparisons for an unsuccessful search?

sentinel

E4. At each iteration, sequential search checks two inequalities, one a comparison of keys to see if the target has been found, and the other a comparison on the window to see if the end of the list has been reached. A good way to speed up the algorithm by eliminating the second comparison is to make sure that eventually key target will be found, by increasing the size of the list, and inserting an extra entry at the end with key target. Such an entry placed in a list to ensure that a process terminates is called a *sentinel*. Including a sentinel makes the procedure do one extra comparison of keys for each unsuccessful search, but it saves many comparisons of window locations for all searches. When the loop terminates, the search will have been successful if target was found before the last entry in the list and unsuccessful if the final sentinel entry was the one found.

a. Write a Pascal procedure that embodies the idea of a sentinel in the contiguous version of sequential search.

b. Explain why adding a sentinel to a simply linked list as declared in Section 8.1 is not a particularly helpful idea. Which variety of linked list would provide the extra information that would make it worthwhile?

■ PROJECTS 9.2

P1. Write a program to test sequential search. You should make the appropriate declarations required to set up the list and put keys into it. The entries in the list should consist of keys alone. For the sequence of n keys to put in the list, take the odd integers starting at 1 up through $2n - 1$. Then the program should search the list for each integer from 1 through $2n$. The searches for odd integers will then be successful, and the searches for even integers will be unsuccessful, and (as specified for Exercise E3) the $n + 1$ ways in which the search may fail are equally likely. Modify the sequential search procedure so that it keeps a counter of the number of key comparisons that it makes. By averaging the counts of key comparisons for each of the n successful searches and for each of the $n + 1$ unsuccessful searches, find out the average number of comparisons the program does in each case. Run your program for representative values of n, including $n = 10$, $n = 100$, and $n = 1000$. Compare your program's output with the results of the theoretical computation in this section.

a. Write the program to use the general list operations from Section 6.1, and test it with the package of contiguous list subprograms from Section 6.2 and the general version of sequential search in this section. Use Turbo Pascal units or include directives if they are available for your compiler.

b. Replace the package for contiguous lists by the package for simply linked lists from Section 8.1.

c. Use the version of sequential search written explicitly for contiguous lists.

d. Use the version of sequential search written explicitly for simply linked lists.

P2. Take the driver program written in Project P1(c) to test sequential search for contiguous lists, and insert the version of SequentialSearch that uses a sentinel (Exercise E4). Also insert instructions (system-dependent) for obtaining the CPU time used. For various values of n, determine whether the version with or without sentinel is faster. Find the cross-over point between the two versions, if there is one. That is, for what length of list is the extra CPU time needed to insert a sentinel at the end of the list the same as the time needed for the extra comparisons of indices in the version without a sentinel?

9.3

BINARY SEARCH

Sequential search is easy to write and efficient for short lists, but a disaster for long ones. Imagine trying to find the name "Amanda Thompson" in a large telephone book by reading one name at a time starting at the front of the book! To find any entry in a long list, there are far more efficient methods, provided that the keys in the list are already sorted into order. One of the best is first to compare the target key with one in the center of the list and then restrict our attention to only the first or second half of the list, depending on whether the target key comes before or after the central one. In this way, at each step, we reduce the length of the list to be searched by half. In only twenty steps, this method will locate any requested key in a list containing more than a million keys.

method

The method we are discussing is called **binary search**. This approach requires that the entries in the list be of a scalar or other type that can be regarded as having an order and that the list already be completely in order.

restrictions

What we are really doing here is introducing a new abstract data type, as follows.

An **ordered list** is a list in which each entry contains a key, such that the keys are in order. That is, if entry i comes before entry j in the list, then the key of entry i is less than the key of entry j.

The operations on an ordered list include all those for an ordinary list. For an ordered list, we have a few additional operations, such as the searching operations in this chapter and the ordered insertion of a new entry in the correct place determined by the order of the keys. We shall study this operation in the next chapter.

We shall assume that the keys in our list can be compared under the operations '$<$' and '$>$' (for example, that the keys are numbers), but the algorithms can easily be extended to care for words or other character strings as keys.

random access

Binary search is not good for linked lists, since it requires jumping back and forth from one end of the list to the middle, an action easy within an array, but slow for a linked list. Hence this section discusses only contiguous lists.

9.3.1 Algorithm Development

Simple though the idea of binary search is, it is exceedingly easy to program it incorrectly. The method dates back at least to 1946, but the first version free of errors and unnecessary restrictions seems to have appeared only in 1962. One study (see the references at the end of the book) showed that about 90 percent of professional programmers fail to code binary search correctly, even after working

dangers

on it for a full hour. Let us therefore take special care to make sure that we make no mistakes. To do this, we must state exactly what our variables designate; we must state precisely what conditions must be true before and after each iteration of the loop contained in the program; and we must make sure that the loop will terminate properly.

Our binary search algorithm will use two indices, top and bottom, to enclose the part of the list in which we are looking for the target key. At each iteration, we shall reduce the size of this part of the list by about half. To help us keep track of the progress of the algorithm, let us write down a condition that we shall require to be true before every iteration of the loop in the procedure. Such a statement is called a *loop invariant*.

> *The target key, provided it is present, will be found between the indices* bottom *and* top, *inclusive.*

We make sure that this statement is correct before the loop iterates the first time by setting bottom to 1 and top to L.count, the number of entries in the list.

Inside the loop, we first calculate the index mid halfway between bottom and top and then compare the target key against the key at position mid. If they are equal, then we are finished. Otherwise, if the target key is greater than the key at mid, we replace bottom by mid + 1, or if the target key is less than the key at mid, we replace top by mid − 1. In this way, we eliminate at least half the entries in the list at each iteration and maintain the correctness of the statement about the loop. Since at each iteration we reduce the length of the remaining list by removing at least the entry at mid (and usually much more), the problem becomes smaller at each iteration and we make progress toward termination.

loop termination
Finally, we note that the loop should continue to iterate while the target has not been found and while bottom ≤ top, that is, while the remaining part of the list is not empty. It should terminate when top < bottom, that is, when the remaining part of the list is empty, providing that we have not terminated the loop earlier by finding the target.

This outline now translates into the following procedure.

```
procedure BinarySearch(var L: listtype; target: keytype;
                          var found: Boolean; var location: window);
    {Pre:  The contiguous list L has been created, and the entries in L are or-
           dered according to increasing values of their keys.
     Post: If an entry in L has key equal to target, then found becomes true and
           the window location gives the location of such an entry. Otherwise,
           found becomes false and the window location is undefined.}
var
    top,        {The target, if present, will always be between bottom and top.}
    bottom,
    mid: integer;               {mid will be the index of target when it is found in L.}
```

```
begin                                              {procedure BinarySearch}
    top := L.count;                                  {Initialize the variables.}
    bottom := 1;
    found := false;
    while (not found) and (bottom <= top) do      {Check for termination.}
    begin
        mid := (top + bottom) div 2;
        if target = L.entry [mid] .key then       {Search terminates successfully.}
            found := true
        else if target < L.entry [mid] .key then
            top := mid − 1                        {Reduce to the bottom half of the list.}
        else
            bottom := mid + 1                     {Reduce to the top half of the list.}
    end;                    {This if statement guarantees that the invariant still holds.}
    location := mid      {This gives the location of target only if found is true.}
end;                                               {procedure BinarySearch}
```

9.3.2 Analysis of Binary Search

Tracing the Algorithm

To see how many comparisons of keys binary search will make, let us work through some of the steps of the algorithm. In the first iteration of the loop, the target key is compared to the one in the middle of the list, the one at the first value of mid. If the target key equals this one, the algorithm terminates; otherwise the search is repeated on either the left half or the right half of the list, depending on whether the target is less than or greater than the key at mid.

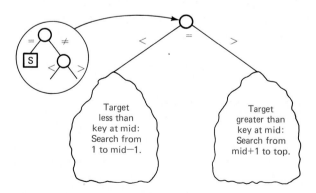

Figure 9.3. The top of a comparison tree

These steps made so far can be conveniently described by the diagram in Figure 9.3. The circle at the top of the main diagram represents the steps done so far. The line labeled '$<$' represents the outcome that the target key is less than the one at mid, and the line labeled '$>$' the outcome that the target key is greater than the one at mid. The equals sign '$=$' beneath the circle at the top indicates that no further work is done if the two keys are equal. An expanded view of the top circle appears on its left. In this expanded view, the two comparisons of keys done in the loop are shown separately. The first comparison checks for equality with the target. Its successful outcome is shown by the square labeled 'S'. Otherwise, the second comparison leads to one of the two halves shown in the main diagram.

At the next iteration of the loop, the whole process is repeated, but now working on only half of the list. We can again draw a diagram similar to the top of Figure 9.3 showing the comparisons made in this next iteration, and place this new diagram in the part of Figure 9.3 that has not yet been specified, at the end of the line labeled '$<$' or '$>$'. Continuing in this way, we can trace through all the steps of the algorithm and draw a diagram that will show all the comparisons that the algorithm will make while searching for any of the keys in a list. Such a diagram is called a *comparison tree*, and the complete comparison tree for BinarySearch for the list 1, 2, ..., 10 is shown in Figure 9.4.

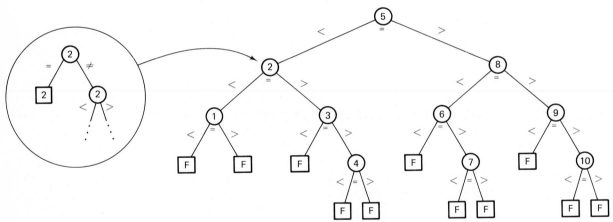

Figure 9.4. Comparison tree for BinarySearch with $n = 10$

Comparison Trees

vertex

branch

More generally, the *comparison tree* (also called *decision tree* or *search tree*) of an algorithm is obtained by tracing through the action of the algorithm, representing each comparison of keys by a *vertex* of the tree (which we draw as a circle). Inside the circle we put the index of the key against which we are comparing the target key. *Branches* (lines) drawn down from the circle represent the possible outcomes of the comparison and are labeled accordingly. When the algorithm terminates, we put either F (for failure) or the location where the target is found at the end of the appropriate branch, which we call a *leaf*, and draw as *leaf*   a square. Leaves are also sometimes called *end vertices* or *external vertices* of the tree. The remaining vertices are called the *internal vertices* of the tree.

The comparison tree for sequential search is especially simple; it is drawn in Figure 9.5.

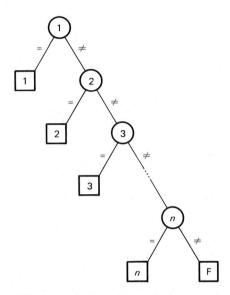

Figure 9.5. Comparison tree for sequential search

The number of comparisons done by an algorithm in a particular search is the number of internal vertices (drawn as circles) traversed in going from the top of the tree down the appropriate path to a leaf. The vertex at the top of

root   a tree is called its *root*. The number of branches on a *path* from the root to a

path, level   given vertex we shall call the *level* of the vertex. Thus the root itself has level 0, the vertices immediately below it have level 1, and so on. The largest level that occurs is called the *height* of the tree. Hence a tree with only one vertex has

height   height 0. In future chapters, we shall sometimes allow trees to be empty, that is, to consist of no vertices at all, and we adopt the convention that an empty tree has height −1.

To complete the terminology we use for trees, we shall now, as is traditional, mix our metaphors by thinking of family trees as well as botanical trees: We call

child, parent   the vertices immediately below a vertex v the *children* of v. There is only one vertex just one level above v and to which v is connected; this vertex is called the *parent* of v. The root of the tree has no parent.

Estimating Comparisons

To complete the analysis of binary search, let us draw its comparison tree for one more case; that of $n = 31$ is shown in Figure 9.6, and from this case we can

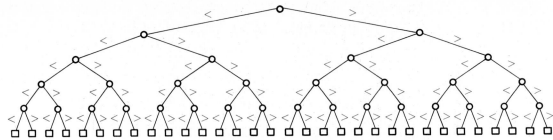

Figure 9.6. Comparison tree for BinarySearch with $n = 31$

worst-case successful and unsuccessful search

get a good idea of what happens in general. The height of the tree is 5, which means there are 5 internal vertices (drawn as circles) on a path from the root to a leaf, and these correspond to 5 iterations of the loop in binary search, giving a total of 10 comparisons of keys. From the tree, we can see that this is the answer for the worst-case successful search for $n = 31$, and also for any unsuccessful search.

To find the exact answer for the average-case successful search, we would need to add up the levels for all the internal vertices of the tree and divide by n, the number of keys in the list. Instead, let us simply observe that the answer

average case

is not going to be significantly less than that for the worst case. The reason is that more than half the vertices of the tree appear on the bottom level, more than half the remaining ones on the next level up, and so on. The number of vertices near the top of the tree is too small in comparison to the number at the bottom to make a significant difference in the result.

The same thing happens in the case for general values of n, at least when n is large enough. For general n, the leaves of the tree will not all be on the same level, but will (as shown for $n = 10$ in Figure 9.4) be on two adjacent levels. For general n, what will be the height of the tree? That is, how many times will the loop iterate in BinarySearch in the worst case?

To find the answer, let us turn the question around, and suppose that the loop iterates k times, so that the tree has height k. Then how many internal vertices can be in the tree? The answer to this question will be the corresponding number n of entries in a list that can be searched in k iterations.

We already know that when $k = 5$ then $n = 31$. For smaller values of k, the answers are even easier. The smallest tree has $k = 1$, and it has one internal vertex, so $n = 1$. The next larger case is obtained by taking each leaf of the previous tree, turning it into an internal vertex and connecting two new leaves below it. Hence, for $k = 2$, we get $n = 3$. For $k = 3$, we obtain $n = 7$. In fact, if we continue to draw comparison trees with more and more levels in this way, we see that the number n of internal vertices is $n = 2^k - 1$ when the height of the tree is k.

Another way to approximate this answer is to consider directly how binary search works. If we allow the loop in binary search to iterate one more time, then we can search at least twice as many keys, since we know that each iteration in binary search reduces the length of the list by half or more. That is, if we increase k by 1, then we at least double n. In other words, as k increases, n increases approximately like 2^k.

To answer the original question of how many iterations are needed to search an ordered list of length n, we must solve the equation $n = 2^k - 1$ for k in terms

logarithms of n. To do so, we take logarithms with base 2. We thereby obtain $k = \lg(n+1)$, where lg denotes a logarithm with base 2. For large n, the difference between $\lg(n + 1)$ and $\lg n$ is insignificant. Recall that k is the number of iterations of the loop and that BinarySearch does two comparisons of keys for each iteration. We thus arrive at the final conclusion:

> BinarySearch *makes approximately* $2\lg n$ *comparisons of keys in searching a list of n entries. There is little difference between the average and worst cases, or between successful and unsuccessful searches.*

Notation

The notation just used for logarithms with base 2 will always be our standard notation. In more general terms, let us thus summarize:

> ### Convention
>
> Unless stated otherwise, all logarithms will be taken with base 2.
> The symbol lg denotes a logarithm with base 2,
> and the symbol ln denotes a natural logarithm.
> If the base for logarithms is not specified or makes no difference,
> then the symbol log will be used.

See Appendix A or a mathematics textbook for more information on logarithms, what they mean, and how they are used.

9.3.3 Comparison with Sequential Search

That sequential search on average does far more comparisons than binary search is obvious from comparing the shape of its comparison tree shown in Figure 9.5 with those of binary search shown in the other diagrams. Sequential search has a long, narrow tree, which means many comparisons, whereas the trees for binary search are much wider and shorter.

Figure 9.7 shows the number of comparisons of keys done in the average successful case by SequentialSearch and BinarySearch. The numbers shown in the graphs are from test runs of the procedures; they are not approximations. The first graph in Figure 9.7 compares the procedures for small values of n, the number of entries in the list. In the second graph, we compare the numbers

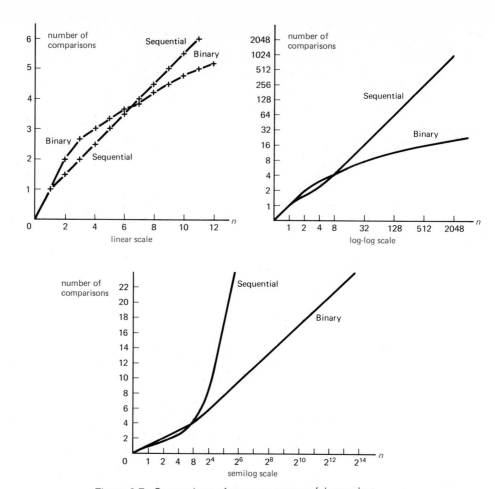

Figure 9.7. Comparison of average successful searches

logarithmic graphs   over a much larger range by employing a *log-log graph* in which each unit along an axis represents doubling the corresponding coordinate. The third graph is a *semilog graph* in which the vertical axis maintains linear units while the horizontal axis is logarithmic.

You can see from the graphs that, as the number of entries in the lists grows, the number of comparisons done by sequential search increases far more rapidly than the number done by binary search. For very small values of n, however, sequential search can actually be faster than binary search, and, since it is easier to program, sequential search is a good choice when n is small.

We should note, finally, that binary search requires that the keys be completely in order, whereas sequential search imposes no such requirement on the list. Hence in cases where we do not know that the list is ordered, we have little choice but to use sequential search.

EXERCISES 9.3

E1. Suppose that the list L contains the integers 1, 2, ..., 8. Trace through the steps of BinarySearch to determine what comparisons of keys are done in searching for each of the following targets: **(a)** 3, **(b)** 5, **(c)** 1, **(d)** 9, **(e)** 4.5.

E2. Draw the comparison trees for BinarySearch when **(a)** $n = 5$, **(b)** $n = 7$, **(c)** $n = 8$, **(d)** $n = 13$.

E3. Sequential search has less overhead than binary search, and so may run faster for small n. Find an approximate break-even point where SequentialSearch and BinarySearch make the same number of comparisons of keys, in terms of the (approximate) formulæ for the number of comparisons done in the average successful search.

E4. Suppose that you have a list of 10,000 names in alphabetical order in an array and you must frequently look for various names. It turns out that 20 percent of the names account for 80 percent of the retrievals. Instead of doing a binary search over all 10,000 names every time, consider the *high-frequency list* possibility of splitting the list into two, a high-frequency list of 2000 names, and a low-frequency list of the remaining 8000 names. To look up a name, you will first use binary search on the high-frequency list, and 80 percent of the time you will not need to go on to the second stage, where you use binary search on the low-frequency list. Is this scheme worth the effort? Justify your answer by finding the number of comparisons done for the average successful search, both in the new scheme and in a binary search of a single list of 10,000 names.

E5. If you modified binary search so that it divided the list not essentially in half at each pass, but instead into two pieces of sizes about one-third and two-thirds of the remaining list, then what would be the approximate effect on its average count of comparisons?

E6. Write a "ternary" search procedure analogous to BinarySearch that examines the key one-third of the way through the list, and if the target key x is greater, then examines the key two-thirds of the way through, and thus, in any case, at each pass the algorithm reduces the length of the list by a factor of three. Compare the count of comparisons of your algorithm with binary search.

PROJECTS 9.3

P1. Adapt the driver program outlined in Project P1(c) of Section 9.2 so that it can be used to test BinarySearch. You should check both successful and unsuccessful searches for selected values of n. If your system can provide a measure of elapsed CPU time, you should also obtain timings for average successful and unsuccessful searches for your procedure.

optimized binary search

P2. This project outlines how to program binary search so as to reduce its count of key comparisons to the minimum allowed by the lower bound. The idea is to do only one comparison of keys for each iteration of the loop, by not checking the key for equality with the target. Instead, the procedure continues reducing the size of the list being searched (whether or not it may have found the target) until one or zero entries remain. Then, after the loop, one more comparison of keys is made to determine if the search was successful or not. The way to reduce the size is, after setting mid := (top + bottom) **div** 2, to replace bottom by mid + 1 if the target is strictly greater than the key at mid, else replace top by mid.

    a. Using the fact that integer division truncates downward, show that every iteration of the loop reduces the size of the remaining list, and hence the loop will eventually terminate when we obtain top ≤ bottom.

    b. Write the procedure for binary search following this method.

    c. Test the procedure by using the driver program of Project P1 and compare its performance with the procedure BinarySearch in the text.

two-pointer binary search

P3. It is redundant to keep three pointers in binary search: bottom, mid, and top, since mid is guaranteed to be halfway between bottom and top.

    a. Modify BinarySearch so that it keeps only the index mid and the distance inc such that the target, if present, must be between mid − inc and mid + inc, inclusive.

    b. Verify the correctness of your algorithm by writing down a condition that will hold before and after every iteration of the loop and showing that it in fact holds true.

    c. Run both your version and the one in the text to see which is faster. Is the change described in this project a good idea?

P4. On most computers, addition is faster than division. Use the following idea to make a new version of binary search that does no division. First use addition to construct an auxiliary table of all powers of 2 that are less than the length of the list L.count. By adding and subtracting appropriate entries from this table, reduce the bounds of the interval being searched. Compare the computer time required by this version to the time required by BinarySearch.

P5. We have ignored the computer time needed to initialize the search procedures and to complete index calculations. For this reason, sequential search will be the better method for values of n somewhat larger than your answer to Exercise E3. Modify the test programs written for sequential search and binary search in previous sections, so that the programs will record the CPU time used, and determine the break-even point for running time on your computer.

P6. Write a program that will do a "hybrid" search, using binary search for large lists and switching to sequential search when the list is sufficiently reduced. (Because of different overhead, the best switch-over point is not necessarily the same as your answer to Exercise E3 or Project P5.)

9.4

ASYMPTOTICS

9.4.1 Introduction

The time has come to distill important generalizations from our analyses of searching algorithms. As we have progressed, we have been able to see more clearly which aspects of algorithm analysis are of great importance and which parts can safely be neglected. If a section of a program is performed only once outside any loops, for example, then the amount of time it uses is negligible compared to the amount of time used inside loops. We have found that, although binary search is more difficult to program and to analyze than sequential search, and even though it runs more slowly when applied to a very short list, for a longer list it will run far faster than sequential search.

designing algorithms for small problems
The design of efficient methods to work on small problems is an important subject to study, since a large program may need to do the same or similar small tasks many times during its execution. As we have discovered, however, for small problems, the large overhead of a sophisticated method may make it inferior to a simpler method. For a list of two or three entries, sequential search is certainly superior to binary search. To improve efficiency in the algorithm for a small problem, the programmer must necessarily devote attention to details specific to the computer system and programming language, and there are few general observations that will help with this task.

choice of method for large problems
The design of efficient algorithms for large problems is an entirely different matter. In studying binary search, we have seen that the overhead becomes relatively unimportant; it is the basic idea that will make all the difference between success and a problem too large to be attacked.

asymptotics
The word ***asymptotics*** that titles this section means the study of functions of a parameter n, as n becomes larger and larger without bound. In comparing searching algorithms, we have seen that a count of the number of comparisons of keys accurately reflects the total running time for large problems, since it has generally been true that all the other operations (such as incrementing and comparing indices) have gone in lock step with comparison of keys.

basic actions
In fact, the frequency of such basic actions is much more important than is a total count of all operations including the housekeeping. The total including housekeeping is too dependent on the choice of programming language and on the programmer's particular style, so dependent that it tends to obscure the general methods. Variations in housekeeping details or programming technique can easily triple the running time of a program, but such a change probably will not make the difference between whether the computation is feasible or not. A change in fundamental method, on the other hand, can make a vital difference. If the number of basic actions is proportional to the size n of the input, then doubling n will about double the running time, no matter how the housekeeping is done. If the number of basic actions is proportional to $\lg n$, then doubling n will

hardly change the running time. If the number of basic actions is proportional to n^2, then the running time will quadruple, and the computation may still be feasible, but may be uncomfortably long. If the number of basic operations is proportional to 2^n, then doubling n will square this number. A computation that took 1 second might involve a million (10^6) basic operations, and doubling the input might require 10^{12} basic operations, increasing the running time from 1 second to $11\frac{1}{2}$ days.

goal   Our desire in formulating general principles that will apply to the analysis of many classes of algorithms, then, is to have a notation that will accurately reflect the way in which the computation time will increase with the size, but that will ignore superfluous details with little effect on the total. We wish to concentrate on one or two basic operations within the algorithm, without too much concern for all the housekeeping operations that will accompany them. If an algorithm does $f(n)$ basic operations when the size of its input is n, then its total running time will be at most $cf(n)$, where c is a constant that depends on the algorithm, on the way it is programmed, and on the computer used, but c does not depend on the size n of the input (at least when n is past a few initial cases).

9.4.2 The Big Oh Notation

The ideas we have been discussing are embodied in the following notation:

DEFINITION

If $f(n)$ and $g(n)$ are functions defined for positive integers, then to write

$$f(n) \text{ is } O(g(n))$$

[read $f(n)$ is **big Oh** of $g(n)$] means that there exists a constant c such that $|f(n)| \leq c|g(n)|$ for all sufficiently large positive integers n.

Under these conditions we also say that "$f(n)$ has **order** at most $g(n)$" or "$f(n)$ grows no more rapidly than $g(n)$".

Examples

As a first example, consider the function $f(n) = 100n$. Then $f(n)$ is $O(n)$, since $f(n) \leq cn$ for the constant $c = 100$. Any larger constant $c > 100$ will also work just as well.

Next consider the function $f(n) = 4n + 200$. Since $f(n) \leq 4n$ is not true for large values of n, we cannot show that $f(n)$ is $O(n)$ by taking $c = 4$. But we can choose any larger value for c. If we choose $c = 5$, for example, then we will find that $f(n) \leq 5n$ whenever $n \geq 200$, and therefore $f(n)$ is again $O(n)$.

For the next example, take $f(n) = n^2$. Suppose we were to try to show that $f(n)$ is $O(n)$. Doing so would mean that we could find a *constant* such that $n^2 \leq cn$ for all sufficiently large n. When we take n to be a large positive integer and divide both sides of the inequality by n, we obtain $n \le c$ for *all* large integers and a *constant* c. This statement is obviously nonsense: We can choose the integer n to be larger than c. Hence we must conclude that n^2 is not $O(n)$.

The final example of polynomials in n that we shall choose is $f(n) = 3n^2 - 100n$. For small values of n, $f(n)$ is less than n, but for reasons similar to the last example, for any constant c, $f(n)$ will be greater than cn when n is sufficiently large. Hence $f(n)$ is not $O(n)$. On the other hand, when $c = 3$ we have $f(n) \le 3n^2$, so it is true that $f(n)$ is $O(n^2)$. Even if we were to change $f(n)$ to $3n^2 + 100n$, we would still have that $f(n)$ is $O(n^2)$. In this case, we would not be able to use $c = 3$, but any larger value for c would work.

General Observations

These examples of polynomials generalize to the first and most important rule about the big Oh notation. To obtain the order of a polynomial function, we simply need to extract the term with the highest degree, disregarding all constants and all terms with a lower degree. More formally, we have:

> *If $f(n)$ is a polynomial in n with degree r, then $f(n)$ is $O(n^r)$, but $f(n)$ is not $O(n^s)$ for any power s less than r.*

Logarithms form a second class of functions that appear frequently in studying algorithms. We have already used logarithms in the analysis of binary search, and we have seen that the logarithm of n grows much more slowly than n itself. In fact, the general observation is true:

> *Any logarithm of n grows more slowly (as n increases) than any positive power of n. Hence $\log n$ is $O(n^k)$ for any $k > 0$, but n^k is never $O(\log n)$ for any power $k > 0$.*

Common Orders

When we apply the big Oh notation, $f(n)$ will normally be the operation count or running time for some algorithm, and we wish to choose the form of $g(n)$ to be as simple as possible. We thus write $O(1)$ to mean computing time that is bounded by a constant (not dependent on n); $O(n)$ means that the time is directly proportional to n, and is called *linear time*. We call $O(n^2)$ *quadratic time*, $O(n^3)$ *cubic*, $O(2^n)$ *exponential*. These five orders, together with *logarithmic time* $O(\log n)$ and $O(n \log n)$, are the ones most commonly used in analyzing algorithms.

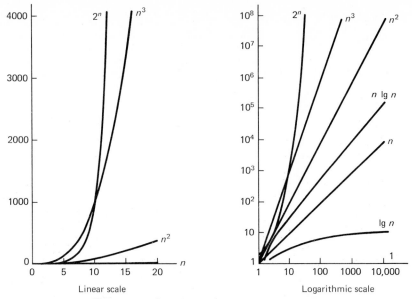

Figure 9.8. Growth rates of common functions

Figure 9.8 shows how these seven functions (with constant 1) grow with n, and the relative sizes of some of these numbers are shown in Figure 9.9. The number in the lower right corner of the table in Figure 9.9 is beyond comprehension: If every electron in the universe (10^{50} of them) were a supercomputer doing a hundred million (10^8) operations per second since the creation of the universe (perhaps 30 billion years, or about 10^{18} seconds), then a computation requiring 2^{1000} operations would have done only about 10^{76} operations, so it would have to go 10^{225} *times* as long! A computation requiring 2^n operations is feasible only for *very* small values of n.

n	1	$\lg n$	n	$n \lg n$	n^2	n^3	2^n
1	1	0.00	1	0	1	1	2
10	1	3.32	10	33	100	1000	1024
100	1	6.64	100	66	10,000	1,000,000	1.268×10^{30}
1000	1	9.97	1000	997	1,000,000	10^9	1.072×10^{301}

Figure 9.9. Relative sizes of functions

Notice especially how much slower $\lg n$ grows than n; this is essentially the reason why binary search is superior to sequential search for large lists. Notice how the functions 1 and $\lg n$ become farther and farther below all the others for large n.

Algorithm Analyses

We can now express the conclusions of our algorithm analyses very simply:

- On a list of length n, sequential search has running time $O(n)$.
- On an ordered list of length n, binary search has running time $O(\log n)$.
- The sum of the integers from 1 to n is $O(n^2)$.

9.4.3 Imprecision of the Big Oh Notation

Note that the constant c in the definition of the big Oh notation depends on which functions $f(n)$ and $g(n)$ are under discussion. Thus we can write that $17n^3 - 5$ is $O(n^3)$ (here $c = 17$ will do, as will any larger c), and also $35n^3 + 100$ is $O(n^3)$ (here $c \geq 35$).

Poor Uses

Note also that it is equally correct to write that $35n^3$ is $O(n^7)$ as that $35n^3$ is $O(n^3)$. It is correct but uninformative to write that both binary and sequential search have running time that is $O(n^5)$. If $h(n)$ is any function that grows faster than $g(n)$, then a function that is $O(g(n))$ must also be $O(h(n))$. Hence the big Oh notation can be used imprecisely, but we shall always refrain from doing so, instead using the smallest possible of the seven functions shown in Figure 9.8.

Keeping the Dominant Term

We would often like to have a more precise measure of the amount of work done by an algorithm, and we can obtain one by using the big Oh notation within an expression, as follows. We define

$$f(n) = g(n) + O(h(n))$$

to mean that $f(n) - g(n)$ is $O(h(n))$. Instead of thinking of $O(h(n))$ as the class of all functions growing no faster than $ch(n)$ for some constant c, we think of $O(h(n))$ as a single but arbitrary such function. We then use this function to represent all the terms of our calculation in which we are not interested, *search* generally all the terms except the one that grows the most quickly. The number *comparisons* of comparisons in the average successful search by one of our procedures can now be summarized as follows:

- On a list of length n, sequential search has running time $\frac{1}{2}n + O(1)$.
- On an ordered list of length n, binary search has running time $2 \lg n + O(1)$.
- The sum of the integers from 1 to n is $\frac{1}{2}n^2 + O(n)$.

In using the big Oh notation in expressions, it is necessary always to remember that $O(h(n))$ does not stand for a well-defined function, but it stands, instead, *danger*   for an arbitrary function from a large class. Hence ordinary algebra cannot be done with $O(h(n))$. For example, we might have two expressions

$$n^2 + 4n - 5 = n^2 + O(n)$$

and

$$n^2 - 9n + 7 = n^2 + O(n)$$

but $O(n)$ represents different functions in the two expressions, so we cannot equate the right sides or conclude that the left sides are equal.

9.4.4 Ordering of Common Functions

Although the seven functions graphed in Figure 9.8 are the only ones we shall usually need for algorithm analysis, a few simple rules will enable you to determine the order of many other kinds of functions.

1. *The powers of n are ordered according to the exponent: n^a is $O(n^b)$ if and only if $a \leq b$.*

2. *The order of $\log n$ is independent of the base taken for the logarithms; that is, $\log_a n$ is $O(\log_b n)$ for all $a, b > 1$.*

3. *A logarithm grows more slowly than any positive power of n: $\log n$ is $O(n^a)$ for any $a > 0$, but n^a is never $O(\log n)$ for $a > 0$.*

4. *Any power n^a is $O(b^n)$ for all a and all $b > 1$, but b^n is never $O(n^a)$ for any $b > 1$ or for any a.*

5. *If $a < b$, then a^n is $O(b^n)$, but b^n is not $O(a^n)$.*

6. *If $f(n)$ is $O(g(n))$ and $h(n)$ is an arbitrary function, then $f(n)h(n)$ is $O(g(n)h(n))$.*

7. *The above rules may be applied recursively (a chain rule) by substituting any function of n for n. For example, $\log \log n$ is $O((\log n)^{1/2})$. To verify this fact, replace n by $\log n$ in the statement "$\log n$ is $O(n^{1/2})$."*

EXERCISES 9.4

E1. For each of the following pairs of functions, find the smallest integer value of $n > 1$ for which the first becomes larger than the second.

a. n^2 and $15n + 5$.

b. 2^n and $8n^4$.

c. $0.1n$ and $10 \lg n$.

d. $0.1n^2$ and $100n \lg n$.

E2. Arrange the following functions into increasing order; that is, $f(n)$ should come before $g(n)$ in your list if and only if $f(n)$ is $O(g(n))$.

$$1000000 \qquad (\lg n)^3 \qquad 2^n$$
$$n \lg n \qquad n^3 - 100n^2 \qquad n + \lg n$$
$$\lg \lg n \qquad n^{0.1} \qquad n^2$$

E3. Let x and y be real numbers with $0 < x < y$. Prove that n^x is $O(n^y)$, but n^y is not $O(n^x)$.

E4. Show that logarithmic time does not depend on the base a chosen for the logarithms. That is, prove that

$$\log_a n \text{ is } O(\log_b n)$$

for any real numbers $a > 1$ and $b > 1$.

PROJECT 9.4

P1. Write a program to test on your computer how long it takes to do $n \lg n$, n^2, n^5, 2^n, and $n!$ additions for $n = 5, 10, 15, 20$.

9.5

A LOWER BOUND FOR SEARCHING

We know that for an ordered contiguous list, binary search is much faster than sequential search. It is only natural to ask if we can find another method that is much faster than binary search.

Polishing Programs

basic algorithms and small variations

One approach is to attempt to polish and refine our programs to make them run faster. By being clever, we may be able to reduce the work done in each iteration by a bit and thereby speed up the algorithm. Fine tuning of a program may be able to cut its running time in half, or perhaps reduce it even more, but limits will soon be reached if the underlying algorithm remains the same. The reason why binary search is so much faster than sequential search is not that there are fewer steps within its loop (there are actually more) or that the code is optimized, but that the loop is iterated fewer times, about $\lg n$ times instead of n times, and as the number n increases, the value of $\lg n$ grows much more slowly than does the value of n.

Arbitrary Searching Algorithms

Let us now ask whether it is possible for any search algorithm to exist that will, in the worst and the average cases, be able to find its target using significantly fewer comparisons of keys than binary search. We shall see that the answer is *no*, providing that we stay within the class of algorithms that rely only on comparisons of keys to determine where to look within a list.

Let us start with an arbitrary algorithm that searches a list by making comparisons of keys, and imagine drawing its comparison tree. As with all search algorithms that compare keys, the height of our tree will equal the number of comparisons that the algorithm does in its worst case. If we draw the tree in the expanded form shown for one vertex in Figure 9.3 and in Figure 9.4, then the leaves correspond to the places where the algorithm stops; that is, each possible outcome of the search corresponds to one of the leaves. Some of these outcomes are successful searches and some are unsuccessful. Searching a list of length n has at least $n + 1$ possible outcomes: finding any of the n keys or failure. For binary search (applied to an ordered list), the number of outcomes is $2n + 1$, consisting of n successful outcomes and the $n + 1$ different unsuccessful outcomes of being less than the smallest key, between any pair of keys, or greater than the largest key.

To find how many comparisons an arbitrary searching algorithm must make, we need to find a relation between the height of its comparison tree and the number of its leaves. The way to obtain the largest number of leaves in a tree with small height is to make the tree completely full, as shown for $n = 31$ in Figure 9.6. If we take such a full tree and add an additional level at the bottom, then we double the number of leaves and increase the height by 1. A tree with height 0 consists of only a single leaf, so by repeating this process we obtain:

> A comparison tree of height k contains no more than 2^k leaves.

To apply this to searching algorithms, we turn it around, taking logarithms, and deduce that a comparison tree with m leaves must have height at least $\lg m$. In the language of algorithms, this says:

> *If an algorithm that searches a list by making key comparisons has m possible outcomes, then, in its worst case, it must make at least $\lg m$ comparisons of keys.*

It is also true (for the proof see the references at the end of the book) that this kind of algorithm even in the *average* case must make at least $\lg m$ comparisons of keys.

For the class of algorithms like binary search that produce $2n + 1$ different outcomes while searching a list of length n, the lower bound on key comparisons is $\lg(2n + 1) \approx \lg n + 1$. This is about half the count of $2 \lg n$ that we obtained for our procedure BinarySearch. It turns out (see the projects at the end of the section) that, by revising the algorithm, we can optimize it to reduce its count of key comparisons to the closest integer that is at least $\lg n + 1$. Hence we conclude that

> *Binary search can be written so that it performs the smallest possible number of comparisons of keys of any algorithm that searches a sorted list by means of key comparisons.*

Other Ways to Search

Just because we have found these bounds, it does not imply that no algorithm can run faster than binary search, only those that rely only on comparisons of keys. To take a simple example, suppose that the keys are the integers from 1 to n themselves. If we know that the target key x is an integer in this range, then we would never perform a search algorithm to locate its entry; we would simply store the entries in an array indexed from 1 to n and immediately look in index x to find the desired entry.

interpolation search
This idea can be extended to give another method, called ***interpolation search***. We assume that the keys are either numerical or are information, such as words, that can be readily encoded as numbers. The method also assumes that the keys in the list are uniformly distributed, that is, that the probability of a key being in a particular range equals its probability of being in any other range of the same length. To find the target key, which we shall call target, interpolation search then estimates, according to the magnitude of the number target relative to the first and last entries of the list, about where target would be in the list and looks there. It then reduces the size of the list according as target is less than or greater than the key examined. It can be shown that on average, with uniformly distributed keys, interpolation search will take about $\lg \lg n$ comparisons of keys, which, for large n, is somewhat fewer than binary search requires. If, for example, $n = 1{,}000{,}000$, then the best version of binary search will require about $\lg 10^6 + 1 \approx 21$ comparisons, whereas interpolation search may need only about $\lg \lg 10^6 \approx 4.32$ comparisons.

Finally, we should repeat that, even for search by comparisons, our assumption that requests for all keys are equally likely may be far from correct. If one or two keys are much more likely than the others, then even sequential search, if it looks for those keys first, may be faster than any other method.

Methods for searching or, more generally, for information retrieval, form one of the most important parts of computer science. Much of data structures is devoted to its methods, and in later chapters we shall return to these problems again and again.

PROJECT 9.5

P1. Write a program to do interpolation search; verify its correctness (especially termination of its loop); and test it on the same data used for testing binary search. See the references at the end of the book for more information.

POINTERS AND PITFALLS

1. In designing algorithms, be very careful of the extreme cases, such as empty lists, lists with only one entry, or full lists.

2. Be sure that all your variables are properly initialized.

3. Double check the termination conditions for your loops, and make sure that progress toward termination always occurs.

4. In case of difficulty, formulate statements that will be correct both before and after each iteration of a loop, and verify that they hold.

5. Avoid sophistication for sophistication's sake. If a simple method is adequate for your application, use it.

6. Don't reinvent the wheel. If a ready-made procedure is adequate for your application, use it.

7. Sequential search is slow but robust. Use it for short lists or if there is any doubt that the keys in the list are properly ordered.

8. Be extremely careful if you must reprogram binary search. Verify that your algorithm is correct and test it on all the extreme cases.

9. Drawing trees is an excellent way both to trace the action of an algorithm and to analyze its behavior.

10. Rely on the Big Oh analysis of algorithms for large applications but not for small applications.

REVIEW QUESTIONS

9.1   1. Define the terms *key* and *target*.

2. What is the difference between *external* and *internal* searching?

9.2   3. In twenty words or fewer explain how sequential search works.

4. In analyzing searching methods, why is it better to count comparisons of keys than to count all the operations?

5. What do we mean by taking the *average* in analyzing a successful search?

6. What is the sum of the integers from 1 to n?

7. In the average search of a list of n entries, how many comparisons does sequential search do when successful? When unsuccessful?

8. What is a *sentinel* and why is it sometimes used?

9.3 9. In twenty words or fewer, explain how binary search works.

   10. What is an *ordered list*?

   11. What is a *loop invariant* and how is one used?

   12. What is a *comparison tree* and what does it picture?

   13. Draw the comparison tree for BinarySearch for searching a list of length **(a)** 1, **(b)** 2, **(c)** 3.

   14. Define the terms *height*, *level*, *root*, and *leaf* in a tree.

   15. In searching a list of n entries, how many comparisons does binary search do when successful? When unsuccessful?

   16. Give two reasons for using logarithms.

   17. Why is a logarithmic graph useful?

   18. What is the difference between $\lg x$ and $\ln x$?

   19. Name three conditions under which sequential search of a list is preferable to binary search.

9.4 20. Define the term *asymptotics*.

   21. What is the purpose of the big Oh notation?

   22. List, in order of increasing order according to the big Oh notation, the seven most common functions used in analyzing algorithms.

   23. For what kinds of algorithm analysis is the big Oh notation useless?

9.5 24. What is the smallest number of key comparisons that a search must make if it has as many as m different outcomes?

10

SORTING

This chapter continues the study of ordered lists begun in Chapter 9. We shall examine several methods for sorting the entries in a list into order, including insertion sort, selection sort, and Shell sort. We shall also find a lower bound on how fast it is possible to sort a list by means of comparing keys.

10.1

INTRODUCTION: ORDERED LISTS

Practical Importance

We live in a world obsessed with keeping information, and to find it, we must keep it in some sensible order. Librarians make sure that no one misplaces a book; income tax authorities trace down every dollar we earn; credit bureaus keep track of almost every detail of our actions. I once saw a cartoon in which a keen filing clerk, anxious to impress the boss, said frenetically, "Let me make sure these files are in alphabetical order before we throw them out." If we are to be the masters of this explosion instead of its victims, we had best learn how to keep track of it all!

Some years ago, it was estimated, more than half the time on many commercial computers was spent in sorting. This is perhaps no longer true, since sophisticated methods have been devised for organizing data, methods that do not require that it be kept in any special order. Eventually, nonetheless, the information does go out to people, and then it must be sorted in some way.

Because sorting is so important, a great many algorithms have been devised for doing it. In fact, so many good ideas appear in sorting methods that an entire course could easily be built around this one theme. Amongst the differing environments that require different methods, the most important is the distinction *external and internal sorting* between *external* and *internal*, that is, whether there are so many records to be sorted that they must be kept in external files on disks, tapes, or the like, or whether they can all be kept internally in high-speed memory. In this book we consider only internal sorting.

Analysis

basic operations In studying searching algorithms, it soon became clear that the total amount of work done was closely related to the number of comparisons of keys. The same observation is true about sorting algorithms, but sorting algorithms for contiguous lists must also move entries around within the list. Time spent this way is therefore also important, especially when the entries are large records containing many fields. Our analyses will therefore concentrate on these two basic actions.

As in the case of searching algorithms, both the worst-case performance and the average performance of a sorting algorithm are of interest. To find the average, we shall consider what would happen if the algorithm were run on all possible orderings of the list (with n entries, there are $n!$ such orderings altogether) and take the average of the results.

Ordered Lists

When first introducing binary search in Section 9.3, we mentioned that an **ordered list** is really a new abstract data type, which we defined as a list in which each entry contains a key, and such that the keys are in order; that is, if entry i comes before entry j in the list, then the key of entry i is less than the key of entry j. We assume that the keys can be compared under the operations '<' and '>' (for example, that they are numbers), but the algorithms can easily be extended to care for words or other character strings as keys with alphabetical ordering.

If the keys are in descending order, so that the entry with the largest key comes first, and so on, then we would also call this list an ordered list. To avoid the possibility of confusion, however, we shall only study ordered lists in which the keys are in ascending order.

Since ordered lists are lists, we can do all the same operations that we can with other lists. We can determine how many entries it contains; we can use and move windows; we can retrieve, replace, insert, and delete entries.

The preconditions that we gave for inserting a new entry into an arbitrary list are not strong enough for ordered lists. We must include additional new preconditions for insertion into an ordered list. These preconditions are that we must make sure, when a new entry is inserted into the list, that the key in the new entry comes in the correct order relative to the keys in the entries before and after it in the list.

For ordered lists, we shall often use three new operations that have no counterparts for other lists, since they use keys rather than windows to locate the entry. One operation *retrieves* an entry with a specified key from the ordered list. The second operation *inserts* a new entry into an ordered list by using the key in the new entry to determine where in the list to insert it. The third operation *sorts* a list which may not be ordered but which has keys in its entries, so that the resulting list is ordered.

Retrieval by key from an ordered list is exactly the same as searching. This problem we have already studied in the last chapter. For completeness, let us repeat the preconditions and postconditions for the searching operation in general terms:

procedure Search (**var** L: listtype; target: keytype;
                 var found: Boolean; **var** location: window):

precondition: L has been created and is an ordered list.

postcondition: If an entry in L has key equal to target, then found becomes true and the window location gives the location of such an entry. Otherwise, found becomes false and the window location is undefined.

For insertion according to order, we have the following specifications:

---

procedure InsertOrder(x: listentry; **var** L: listtype):

precondition: L has been created, is an ordered list, and is not full.

postcondition: The entry x has been inserted into L in a position such that the keys in all entries in L remain in the correct order.

The specifications for sorting are:

---

procedure Sort(**var** L: listtype):

precondition: The list L has been created. The entries of L all contain keys.

postcondition: The entries of L have been rearranged so that all the keys in the entries are sorted into nondecreasing order.

There is one case for which we must sometimes exercise special care: Two or more of the entries in an ordered list may have the same key. In this case of duplicate keys, the specifications do not indicate exactly what will happen. Searching might return any one of the entries with the target key; insertion and sorting might produce different orders of the entries with duplicate keys. If the order of entries with duplicate keys makes a difference to an application, then we must be especially careful in constructing the algorithms that manipulate ordered lists.

Implementation

Throughout this chapter, we shall use the same implementations of the abstract data type *list* and the same names for types as in previous chapters, so that *notation*   L will be a list of entries. Each entry x will have a key x.**key** by which the entries are ordered, or by which they are to be ordered if the list is not already sorted.

If we have a contiguous list L, then it will be a record containing an array entry indexed from 1 to count, where the counter count is also a field in L.

If we have a linked list, then each node will consist of a field called entry of type listentry and a field called nextnode of type listpointer. The list is specified as a record containing a single pointer to the first node in the list.

10.2

INSERTION SORT

10.2.1 Ordered Insertion

The second new operation we specified for an ordered list is the insertion of a new entry in a position that keeps the list ordered. Let us now write a procedure to perform this operation. To insert the item x into an ordered list L, we shall start traversing L until we come to a position where x.key comes before the key in the entry at that position. Since the keys in L are in nondecreasing order, the proper place to insert x is just before this position.

In terms of the general list operations, we therefore have the following procedure.

```
procedure InsertOrder(x: listentry; var L: listtype);
{Pre:   L has been created, is an ordered list, and is not full.
 Post:  The entry x has been inserted into L in a position such that the keys
        in all entries in L remain in the correct order.}
var
   current: window;                           {used to traverse L}
   currententry: listentry;             {the entry at window current}
begin                                       {procedure InsertOrder}
   if ListEmpty(L) then
      InsertBefore(current, x, L)
   else begin
      StartList(current, L);
      RetrieveList(current, currententry, L);
      if x.key < currententry.key then
         InsertBefore(current, x, L)
      else begin
         while (not IsLast(current, L)) and (currententry.key < x.key) do
         begin
            NextList(current, L);
            RetrieveList(current, currententry, L);
         end;
         if currententry.key > x.key then
            InsertBefore(current, x, L);
         else
            InsertAfter(current, x, L)
      end
   end
end;                                        {procedure InsertOrder}
```

Ordered insertion is an important operation, and it is often important that it run efficiently. It is, in fact, the key step of our first sorting method. To attain greater speed, therefore, let us rewrite ordered insertion in a way that depends on the implementation and that can take advantage of the implementation. We shall consider only contiguous lists here. The case of linked lists will appear as an exercise.

For a contiguous list, it is necessary to move items in the list to make room for the insertion. To find the place where the insertion is to be made, we must search. One method for performing ordered insertion into a contiguous list is first to do a binary search to find the correct location, then move the entries as required and insert the new entry. This method is left as an exercise. Since so much time is needed to move entries no matter how the search is done, it turns out in many cases to be just as fast to use sequential search as binary search. By doing sequential search from the *end* of the list, the search and the movement of entries can be combined in a single loop, thereby reducing the overhead required in the procedure.

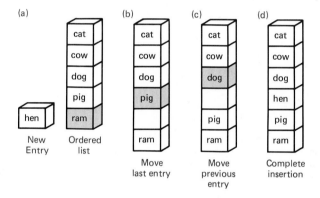

Figure 10.1. Ordered insertion

An example of ordered insertion appears in Figure 10.1. We begin with the ordered list shown in part (a) of the figure and wish to insert the new entry hen. In contrast to the implementation-independent version of InsertOrder that we have already written, we shall start comparing keys at the *end* of the list, rather than at its beginning. Hence we first compare the new key hen with the last key ram shown in the colored box in part (a). Since hen comes before ram, we move ram one position down, leaving the empty position shown in part (b). We next compare hen with the key pig shown in the colored box in part (b). Again, hen belongs earlier, so we move pig down and compare hen with the key dog shown in the colored box in part (c). Since hen comes after dog, we have found the proper location and can complete the insertion as shown in part (d).

This example generalizes to the following procedure.

```
        procedure InsertOrder(x: listentry; var L: listtype);
        {Pre:    The contiguous list L has been created, is an ordered list, and is not
                 full.
         Post:   The entry x has been inserted into L in a position such that the keys
                 in all entries in L remain in the correct order.}
        var
           current: window;                {used to traverse L, starting at the end}
           found: Boolean;                 {Has the proper place to insert x been found?}
        begin                                              {procedure InsertOrder}
          with L do
          begin
            current := count;                      {Start current at the end of the list.}
            found := false;
            repeat
              if current = 0 then
                found := true          {New entry belongs at the first of the list.}
              else if x.key >= entry[current].key then
                found := true          {New entry belongs after entry[current].}
              else begin               {Shift entry[current] one place down the list.}
                entry[current + 1] := entry[current];
                current := current - 1
              end
            until found;
            entry[current + 1] := x;
            count := count + 1
          end
        end;                                               {procedure InsertOrder}
```

10.2.2 Sorting by Insertion

Our first sorting method for a list is based on the idea of insertion into an ordered list. To sort an unordered list, we think of removing its entries one at a time and then inserting each of them into an initially empty new list, always keeping the entries in the new list in the proper order according to their keys.

example   This method is illustrated in Figure 10.2, which shows the steps needed to sort a list of six words. At each stage, the words that have not yet been inserted into the sorted list are shown in gray boxes, and the sorted part of the list is shown in white boxes. In the initial diagram, the first word hen is shown as sorted, since a list of length 1 is automatically ordered. All the remaining words are shown as unsorted at this stage. At each step of the process, the first unsorted word (shown in the uppermost gray box) is inserted into its proper place in the sorted part of the list. To make room for the insertion, some of the sorted words must be moved down the list. Each move of a word is shown as a colored arrow in Figure 10.2.

The general *insertion sort* algorithm proceeds in this way. The first part of the list, when once examined, is kept in the correct order. An initial list with

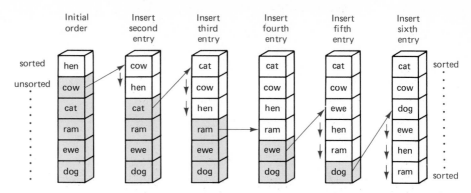

Figure 10.2. Example of insertion sort

only one entry is automatically in order. We then proceed by removing entries one at a time from the original unsorted list. When we remove each entry, we use the ordered insertion procedure to insert it into the new ordered list.

When programmed in terms of the general list operations, insertion sort takes the following form.

general insertion sort

```
procedure InsertionSort (var L: listtype);                    {general version}
{Pre:   The list L has been created. The entries of L all contain keys.
  Post:   The entries of L have been rearranged so that all the keys in the
            entries are sorted into nondecreasing order.}
var
   sortedlist: listtype;                        {the new, sorted list being built}
   current: window;                        {location of the first item not yet sorted}
   currententry: listentry;                       {the entry at window current}
begin
   if ListSize (L) > 1 then                      {Otherwise, L is already sorted.}
   begin
      CreateList (sortedlist);
      StartList (current, L);
      while OnList (current, L) do
      begin
         RetrieveList (current, currententry, L);
         InsertOrder (currententry, sortedlist);
         NextList (current, L)
      end;
      ListCopy (sortedlist, L)
   end
end;                                         {procedure InsertionSort}
```

The procedure written in this form is not very efficient. When we implement insertion sort either for contiguous lists or for linked lists, we can avoid introducing a new list and copying one list to the other. Implementation for linked lists is left as an exercise; we turn now to contiguous lists.

10.2.3 Contiguous Insertion Sort

The main step required to insert an entry denoted i into the sorted part of the list is shown in Figure 10.3. In the procedure that follows, we manipulate the variable L.count so that both the sorted list and the unsorted list occupy the same array L.entry.

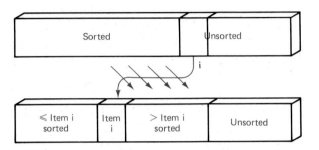

Figure 10.3. The main step of contiguous insertion sort

contiguous
insertion sort

procedure InsertionSort (**var** L: listtype) ;   {*contiguous version*}
{**Pre:**   *The contiguous list* L *has been created. The entries of* L *all contain keys.*
   Post: *The entries of* L *have been rearranged so that all the keys in the entries are sorted into nondecreasing order.*}
var
   totalsize: listcount;   {*number of entries in the list*}
   current: window;   {*location of the entry being inserted*}
begin   {*procedure InsertionSort*}
   if ListSize (L) > 1 **then**   {*Otherwise, L is already sorted.*}
      with L **do**
      begin
         totalsize := ListSize (L) ;
         count := 1;
                    {*The "official" size of L is the number of sorted entries.*}
         for current := 2 **to** totalsize **do**
            InsertOrder (entry [current] , L)
      end
end;   {*procedure InsertionSort*}

The way this procedure is written depends strongly on the way we have implemented contiguous lists. By setting count to 1, we truncate L to only its first entry, which is, by itself, automatically sorted. The remaining entries of L, however, still occupy their original positions in the array L.entry. We can therefore use a loop to take each of these entries, in turn, and insert it back into L in the proper order. Note, finally, that the proper functioning of this procedure depends on the fact that the first parameter to procedure InsertOrder is a value parameter. If it were a variable parameter, then the location entry [current] would be destroyed when InsertOrder moves an entry down the list to make room for the insertion, so the value of entry [current] would be lost before being reinserted into its proper position in the sorted list.

10.2.4 Analysis

Since the basic idea of insertion sort remains the same no matter how it is implemented, let us analyze only the performance of the contiguous version of the program. We also restrict our attention to the case when the list L is initially in random order (meaning that all possible orderings of the keys are equally likely).

Let us first observe that ordered insertion of one entry into a list of length n operates in $O(n)$ comparisons of keys and $O(n)$ movements of entries. To sort a list of length n we must insert n entries in order. Hence:

> *Insertion sort makes $O(n^2)$ comparisons of keys and $O(n^2)$ movements of entries.*

Now let us try for a somewhat more detailed analysis. The loop in contiguous InsertionSort runs from 2 to totalsize, the number of entries in L. To facilitate the mathematics, we shall write n for this number of entries, and we shall write i instead of current to denote the current iteration of the loop. The loop hence runs from $i = 2$ to $i = n$, and, at iteration i, the procedure inserts entry i into the sorted list.

To find how much work InsertOrder does to insert item i into the sorted part of the list, we assume that the original, unsorted list is in random order. Then we can expect that entry i will have to be moved halfway back into the sorted list, on average, so the loop in procedure InsertOrder iterates $\frac{1}{2}i$ times on average. Each iteration of this loop does one comparison of keys and one movement of entries. Hence the total number of comparisons (or movements) is the sum of $\frac{1}{2}i$ from $i = 2$ to $i = n$. We already know (from Section 9.2) that the sum of the integers from 1 to n is $\frac{1}{2}n^2 + O(1)$. By taking half of this result, we conclude that the number of comparisons (and of movements) in the inner loop is $\frac{1}{4}n^2 + O(1)$. Note that in this calculation we have not worried about constant terms, but we have instead absorbed them into the general term $O(1)$. Similarly, we have not considered the time needed for operations done outside the loops, since the time for these operations is absorbed by the $O(1)$.

Combining the counts for the loops in InsertionSort and in InsertOrder gives the final answer:

> *Insertion sort makes $\frac{1}{4}n^2 + O(n)$ comparisons of keys and movements of entries when sorting a list of length n in random order.*

So far we have nothing with which to compare this number, but we can note that as n becomes larger, the contribution from the term $\frac{1}{4}n^2$ becomes much larger than the remaining terms collected as $O(n)$. Hence as the size of the list grows, the time needed by insertion sort grows like the square of this size.

best and worst cases

The worst-case analysis of insertion sort will be left as an exercise. We can observe quickly that the best case for insertion sort occurs when the list is already in order, when insertion sort need do nothing except $n - 1$ comparisons of keys. We can now show that there is no sorting method that can possibly do better in its best case.

> *Verifying that a list of n entries is in the correct order requires at least $n - 1$ comparisons of keys.*

proof

Consider an arbitrary program that checks whether a list of n entries is in order or not (and perhaps sorts it if it is not). The program will first do some comparison of keys, and this comparison will involve some two entries from the list. Sometime later, at least one of these two entries must be compared with a third, or else there would be no way to decide where these two should be in the list relative to the third. Thus this second comparison involves only one new entry not previously in a comparison. Continuing in this way, we see that there must be another comparison involving some one of the first three entries and one new entry. Note that we are not necessarily selecting the comparisons in the order in which the algorithm does them. Thus, except for the first comparison, each one that we select involves only one new entry not previously compared. All n of the entries must enter some comparison, for there is no way to decide whether an entry is in the right place unless it is compared to at least one other entry. Thus to involve all n entries requires at least $n - 1$ comparisons, and the proof

end of proof

is complete.

With this result, we find one of the advantages of insertion sort: it verifies that a list is correctly sorted as quickly as can be done. Furthermore, insertion sort remains an excellent method whenever a list is nearly in the correct order and few entries are many positions removed from their correct locations.

EXERCISES 10.2

E1. By hand, trace through the steps insertion sort will use on each of the following lists. In each case, count the number of comparisons that will be made and the number of times an entry will be moved.

a. The following three words to be sorted alphabetically:

triangle   square   pentagon.

b. The three words in part (a) to be sorted according to the number of sides of the corresponding polygon, in increasing order.

c. The three words in part (a) to be sorted according to the number of sides of the corresponding polygon, in decreasing order.

d. An empty list.

e. A list with only one entry.

f. The following seven numbers to be sorted into increasing order:

$$26 \quad 33 \quad 35 \quad 29 \quad 19 \quad 12 \quad 22.$$

g. The same seven numbers in a different initial order, again to be sorted into increasing order:

$$12 \quad 19 \quad 33 \quad 26 \quad 29 \quad 35 \quad 22.$$

h. The following list of 14 names to be sorted into alphabetical order:

Tim Dot Eva Roy Tom Kim Guy Amy Jon Ann Jim Kay Ron Jan

E2. What initial order for a list of keys will produce the worst case for insertion sort in the contiguous version? In the general version?

E3. How many key comparisons and entry assignments does contiguous insertion sort make in its worst case?

PROJECTS 10.2

P1. Write a program that can be used to test and evaluate the performance of insertion sort (and, later, other methods). The following outline may be used.

a. Write the main program. It should import the list-processing package (either contiguous or linked as appropriate), and it should read keys to be placed in the list from a file (specified by the user). The keys should be real numbers.

There should be two cases that can be selected by making a simple change in the declarations written into the program. In one case, the entries in the list should be the keys alone; in the other case, each entry should consist of the key and an array capable of holding 100 integers. There is no need to initialize these arrays, but they will prove useful in evaluating the time needed to move large entries while sorting a list.

test program for sorting

The program should print out the keys in the unsorted list if the user wishes, sort the list, and print the sorted list if the user wishes. The program should also determine the amount of CPU time required in the sorting phase, and it should establish counters (which will be updated by inserting code into the sorting procedure) to keep track of the number of comparisons of keys and assignments of entries.

b. Write auxiliary programs that will produce the files of real numbers to be sorted. There should be three kinds of files: In one kind, the numbers should be in increasing order; in the second kind, in reverse order; and in the third kind (by use of a random number generator), in a random order. Suitable sizes of the files are $n = 10$, 100, and 500 numbers.

c. Run the program to test the performance of the contiguous insertion-sort procedure and contiguous InsertOrder written in this section. Use both the short files and the long ones, both small-sized entries and large ones, and keys in increasing, decreasing, and random order.

d. Make tables summarizing the results of the test runs. Compare the number of comparisons of keys and movements of entries with the theoretical calculations in this section.

P2. Replace the contiguous versions of InsertionSort and InsertOrder with the implementation-independent ones, and repeat the test runs specified in the preceding project. By changing the list package that is imported, run the tests for both **(a)** contiguous and **(b)** simply linked lists.

P3. **a.** When used with simply linked lists, the implementation-independent version of InsertOrder will prove quite inefficient. Explain why.

b. Write a version of InsertOrder specifically for simply linked lists that removes these inefficiencies.

c. Write the procedure InsertionSort specifically for simply linked lists. You may either use the procedure InsertOrder written in part (b) or you may achieve even greater efficiency by writing a self-contained procedure.

d. Run the tests specified in Project P1 for the version of InsertionSort written in part (c) and compare the results with the previous test runs.

P4. **a.** Write the contiguous version of procedure InsertOrder so that it uses binary search to locate where to insert the new entry.

b. Substitute this version of InsertOrder and run the test program for the resulting contiguous version of InsertionSort. Compare the test results with those for the original contiguous version.

c. Is it reasonable to use binary search in a version of InsertionSort written for linked lists? Why or why not?

P5. There is an even easier sorting method, which instead of using two windows to move through the list (one in InsertionSort and one in InsertOrder), uses only one. We can call it *scan sort*, and it proceeds by starting at one end and moving forward, comparing adjacent pairs of keys, until it finds a pair out of order. It then swaps this pair of entries, and starts moving the other way, continuing to swap pairs until it finds a pair in the correct order. At this point, it knows that it has moved the one entry as far back as necessary, so that the first part of the list is sorted, but, unlike insertion sort, it has forgotten how far forward has been sorted, so it simply reverses direction and sorts forward again, looking for a pair out of order. When it reaches the far end of the list, then it is finished.

scan sort

a. Write a Pascal procedure to implement scan sort for contiguous lists. Your program should use only one index variable (other than L.count), one variable of type listentry to be used in making swaps, and no other local variables.

b. Compare the test results for your procedure with those of InsertionSort.

bubble sort

P6. A well-known algorithm called ***bubble sort*** proceeds by scanning the list from left to right, and whenever a pair of adjacent keys is found to be out of order, then those entries are swapped. In this first pass, the largest key in the list will have "bubbled" to the end, but the earlier keys may still be out of order. Thus the pass scanning for pairs out of order is put in a loop that first makes the scanning pass go all the way to the end of the list, and, at each iteration, stops it one position sooner.

a. Write a Pascal procedure for bubble sort for contiguous lists.

b. Run the same testing program, and compare the results with those for contiguous insertion sort.

10.3

SELECTION SORT

Insertion sort has one major disadvantage. Even after most entries have been sorted properly into the first part of the list, the insertion of a later entry may require that many of them be moved. All the moves made by insertion sort are moves of only one position at a time. Thus to move an entry 20 positions up the list requires 20 separate moves. If the entries are small, perhaps a key alone, or if the entries are in linked storage, then the many moves may not require excessive time. But if the entries are very large, records containing hundreds of components like personnel files or student transcripts, and the records must be kept in contiguous storage, then it would be far more efficient if, when it is necessary to move an entry, it could be moved immediately to its final position. Our next sorting method accomplishes this goal.

10.3.1 The Algorithm

An example of this sorting method appears in Figure 10.4, which shows the steps needed to sort a list of six words alphabetically. At the first stage, we scan the list to find the word that comes last in alphabetical order. This word, ram, is shown in a colored box. We then interchange this word with the word in the last position, as shown in the second part of Figure 10.4. Now we repeat the process on the shorter list obtained by omitting the last entry. Again the word that comes last is shown in a colored box; it is exchanged with the last entry still under consideration; and so we continue. The words that are not yet sorted into order are shown in gray boxes at each stage, except for the one that comes last, which is shown in a colored box. When the unsorted list is reduced to length 1, the process terminates.

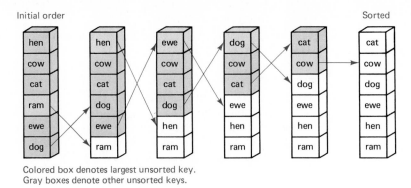

Figure 10.4. Example of selection sort

This method translates into an algorithm called *selection sort*. The general step in selection sort is illustrated in Figure 10.5. The entries with large keys will be sorted in order and placed at the end of the list. The entries with smaller keys are not yet sorted. We then look through the unsorted entries to find the one with the largest key and swap it with the last unsorted entry. In this way, at each pass through the main loop, one more entry is placed in its final position.

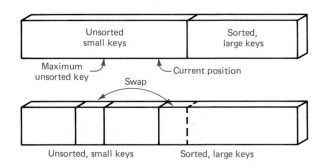

Figure 10.5. The general step in selection sort

10.3.2 Contiguous Implementation

Since selection sort minimizes data movement by putting one entry in its final position at every pass, the algorithm is primarily useful for contiguous lists with large entries for which movement of entries is expensive. If the entries are small, or if the list is linked, so that only pointers need be changed to sort the list, then insertion sort is usually faster than selection sort. We therefore give only a contiguous version of selection sort. The algorithm uses a function called MaxKey, which finds the maximum key on the part of the list L given as the parameters. The procedure Swap simply swaps the two entries with the given indices. For convenience in the discussion to follow, we write these two as separate subprograms.

contiguous
selection sort

```
procedure SelectionSort(var L: listtype);
{Pre:   The contiguous list L has been created. The entries of L all contain
        keys.
 Post:  The entries of L have been rearranged so that all the keys in the
        entries are sorted into nondecreasing order.}

var
  current,                          {index of place being correctly filled}
  maxremaining: listindex;          {index of largest remaining key}

{Declarations of the function MaxKey and the procedure Swap go here.}

begin                               {procedure SelectionSort}
  for current := L.count downto 2 do
  begin
    maxremaining := MaxKey(1, current, L);
    Swap(maxremaining, current, L)
  end
end;                                {procedure SelectionSort}
```

Note that when all entries in a list but one are in the correct place, then the remaining one must be also. Thus the **for** loop stops at 2.

largest key in a
contiguous list

```
function MaxKey(low, high: listindex; var L: listtype): listindex;
{Pre:   The contiguous list L has been created; the indices satisfy the condi-
        tion 1 ≤ low ≤ high ≤ L.count.
 Post:  The function returns the index of the entry between positions low and
        high with the largest key.}

var
  maxsofar,                         {index of the largest key found so far}
  current: listindex;               {scans the list for its largest key}

begin                               {function MaxKey}
  with L do
  begin
    maxsofar := low;
    for current := low + 1 to high do
      if entry[maxsofar].key < entry[current].key then
        maxsofar := current;
    MaxKey := maxsofar
  end
end;                                {function MaxKey}
```

interchange entries in a contiguous list

```
procedure Swap(x, y: listindex; var L: listtype);
{Pre:    The contiguous list L has been created; the indices x and y are be-
         tween 1 and L.count.
  Post:  The entries at positions x and y have been interchanged.}
var
    t: listentry;                                        {temporary storage}
begin                                                    {procedure Swap}
    with L do
    begin
        t := entry[x]; entry[x] := entry[y]; entry[y] := t
    end
end;                                                     {procedure Swap}
```

10.3.3 Analysis

À propos of algorithm analysis, the most remarkable fact about this algorithm is that both of the loops that appear are of the form **for** ... **do** ..., which means that we can calculate in advance exactly how many times they will iterate. In the number of comparisons it makes, selection sort pays no attention to the original ordering of the list. Hence for a list that is nearly correct to begin with, selection sort is likely to be much slower than insertion sort. On the other hand, selection sort does have the advantage of predictability: its worst-case time will differ little from its best.

advantage of selection sort

The primary advantage of selection sort regards data movement. If an entry is in its correct final position, then it will never be moved. Every time any pair of entries is swapped, then at least one of them moves into its final position, and therefore at most $n - 1$ swaps are done altogether in sorting a list of n entries. This is the very best that we can expect from any method that relies entirely on swaps to move its entries.

comparison count for selection sort

We can analyze the performance of procedure SelectionSort in the same way that it is programmed. The main procedure does nothing except some book-keeping and calling the subprograms. Procedure Swap is called $n - 1$ times, and each call does 3 assignments of entries, for a total count of $3(n - 1)$. The function MaxKey is called $n - 1$ times, with the length of the sublist ranging from n down to 2. If t is the number of entries on the part of the list for which it is called, then MaxKey does exactly $t - 1$ comparisons of keys to determine the maximum. Hence, altogether, there are

$$(n - 1) + (n - 2) + \cdots + 1 = \tfrac{1}{2}n(n - 1)$$

comparisons of keys, which we approximate to $\tfrac{1}{2}n^2 + O(n)$.

10.3.4 Comparisons

Let us pause for a moment to compare the counts for selection sort with those for insertion sort. The results are

	Selection	Insertion (average)
Assignments of entries	$3.0n + O(1)$	$0.25n^2 + O(n)$
Comparisons of keys	$0.5n^2 + O(n)$	$0.25n^2 + O(n)$

The relative advantages of the two methods appear in these numbers. When n becomes large, $0.25n^2$ becomes much larger than $3n$, and if moving entries is a slow process, then insertion sort will take far longer than will selection sort. But the amount of time taken for comparisons is, on average, only about half as much for insertion sort as for selection sort. Under other conditions, then, insertion sort will be better.

EXERCISES 10.3

E1. By hand, trace through the steps selection sort will use on each of the following lists. In each case, count the number of comparisons that will be made and the number of times an entry will be moved.

a. The following three words to be sorted alphabetically:

triangle   square   pentagon.

b. The three words in part (a) to be sorted according to the number of sides of the corresponding polygon, in increasing order.

c. The three words in part (a) to be sorted according to the number of sides of the corresponding polygon, in decreasing order.

d. An empty list.

e. A list with only one entry.

f. The following seven numbers to be sorted into increasing order:

26 33 35 29 19 12 22.

g. The same seven numbers in a different initial order, again to be sorted into increasing order:

12 19 33 26 29 35 22.

h. The following list of 14 names to be sorted into alphabetical order:

Tim Dot Eva Roy Tom Kim Guy Amy Jon Ann Jim Kay Ron Jan.

E2. There is a simple algorithm called *count sort* that will construct a new, sorted list from L in a new array, provided we are guaranteed that all the keys in L are different from each other. Count sort goes through L once, and, for each key L.entry [i] .key, scans L to count how many keys are less than L.entry[i].key. If c is this count, then the proper position in the sorted list for this key is $c + 1$. Determine how many comparisons of keys will be done by count sort. Is it a better algorithm than selection sort?

PROJECTS 10.3

P1. Run the test program written in Project P1 of the previous section to compare selection sort with the contiguous version of insertion sort. Use the same files of test data, and run the tests both for lists with only keys in their entries and for lists with large records in their entries.

P2. Write and test a version of selection sort written for doubly linked lists. Compare the test results with those for linked insertion sort.

P3. Write and test an implementation-independent version of selection sort (written with the general list operations of Chapter 6). Compare the test results with those for the implementation-dependent versions, both contiguous and linked.

10.4

SHELL SORT

As we have seen, in some ways insertion sort and selection sort behave in opposite ways. Selection sort moves the entries very efficiently but does many redundant comparisons. In its best case, insertion sort does the minimum number of comparisons, but is inefficient in moving entries only one place at a time. Our goal now is to derive another method avoiding as much as possible the problems with both of these. Let us start with insertion sort and ask how we can reduce the number of times it moves an entry.

diminishing increments

The reason why insertion sort can move entries only one position is that it compares only adjacent keys. If we were to modify it so that it first compares keys far apart, then it could sort the entries far apart. Afterward, the entries closer together would be sorted, and finally the increment between keys being compared would be reduced to 1, to ensure that the list is completely in order. This is the idea implemented in 1959 by D. L. SHELL in the sorting method bearing his name. This method is also sometimes called *diminishing increment sort*. Before describing the algorithm formally, let us work through a simple example of sorting names.

example

Figure 10.6 shows what will happen when we first sort all names that are at distance 5 from each other (so there will be only two or three names on each such list), then sort the names again using increment 3, and finally perform an ordinary insertion sort (increment 1).

You can see that, even though we make three passes through all the names, the early passes move the names close to their final positions, so that at the final pass (which does an ordinary insertion sort), all the entries are very close to their final positions so the sort goes rapidly.

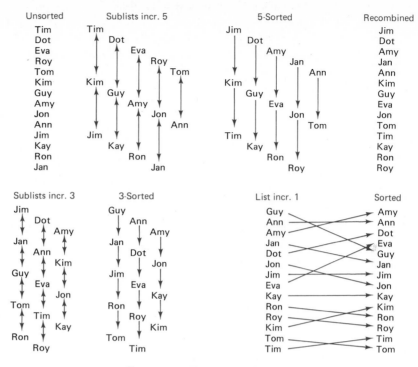

Figure 10.6. Example of Shell sort

choice of increments   There is no magic about the choice of 5, 3, and 1 as increments. Many other choices might work as well or better. It would, however, probably be wasteful to choose powers of 2, such as 8, 4, 2, and 1, since then the same keys compared on one pass would be compared again at the next, whereas by choosing numbers that are not multiples of each other, there is a better chance of obtaining new information from more of the comparisons. Although several studies have been made of Shell sort, no one has been able to prove that one choice of the increments is greatly superior to all others. Various suggestions have been made. If the increments are chosen close together, as we have done, then it will be necessary to make more passes, but each one will likely be quicker. If the increments decrease rapidly, then fewer but longer passes will occur. The only essential feature is that the final increment be 1, so that at the conclusion of the process, the list will be checked to be completely in order. For simplicity in the following algorithm, we start with increment = L.count and at each pass reduce the increment by

$$\text{increment} := \text{increment } \textbf{div } 3 + 1.$$

We can now outline the algorithm for contiguous lists.

Shell sort

```
procedure ShellSort(var L: listtype);
  {Pre:  The contiguous list L has been created. The entries of L all contain
         keys.
   Post: The entries of L have been rearranged so that all the keys in the
         entries are sorted into nondecreasing order.}
var
  increment,                                {spacing of entries in a sublist}
  start: listindex;                         {starting point of a sublist}
begin                                       {procedure ShellSort}
  increment := L.count;
  repeat
    increment := increment div 3 + 1;
    for start := 1 to increment do
      Sort(start, increment, L)
  until increment = 1
end;                                        {procedure ShellSort}
```

The procedure Sort(start, increment, L) is exactly the contiguous version of procedure InsertionSort, except that the list starts at the variable start instead of 1 and the increment between successive values is as given instead of 1. The details of modifying InsertionSort are left as an exercise.

Since the final pass through Shell sort has increment 1, Shell sort really is insertion sort optimized by the preprocessing stage of first sorting sublists using larger increments. Hence the proof that Shell sort works correctly is exactly the same as the proof that insertion sorts works correctly. And, although we have good reason to think that the preprocessing stage will speed up the sorting considerably by eliminating many moves of entries by only one position, we have not actually proved that Shell sort will ever be faster than insertion sort.

analysis   The general mathematical analysis of ShellSort, in fact, turns out to be exceedingly difficult, and to date, good estimates on the number of comparisons and moves have been obtained only under special conditions. It would be very interesting to know how these numbers depend on the choice of increments, so that the best choice might be made. But even without a complete mathematical analysis, running a few large examples on a computer will convince you that ShellSort is quite good. Very large empirical studies have been made of ShellSort, and it appears that the number of moves, when n is large, is in the range of $n^{1.25}$ to $1.6n^{1.25}$. This constitutes a substantial improvement over insertion sort.

EXERCISES 10.4

E1. By hand, sort the list of 14 names shown in Figure 10.6 using Shell sort with increments of **(a)** 8, 4, 2, 1 and **(b)** 7, 3, 1. Count the number of comparisons and moves that are made in each case.

E2. Explain why Shell sort is ill suited for use with linked lists.

■■■■■■■ **PROJECTS 10.4**

P1. Rewrite the procedure InsertionSort to serve as the procedure Sort embedded in ShellSort.

P2. Run Shell sort on the same data used to compare sorting algorithms in the previous sections, and check its performance against that of the contiguous versions of insertion sort and selection sort.

10.5

LOWER BOUNDS

The Question

Now that we have seen a method that performs much better than our first attempts, it is appropriate to ask,

> How fast is it possible to sort?

To answer, we shall limit our attention to sorting methods that rely entirely on comparisons between pairs of keys to do the sorting, and we obtain the answer only for the worst case.

Comparison Trees

Let us take an arbitrary sorting algorithm of this class and consider how it sorts a list of n entries. Imagine drawing its comparison tree. Sample comparison trees for insertion sort and selection sort applied to three numbers a, b, c are shown in Figure 10.7. As each comparison of keys is made, it corresponds to an interior vertex (drawn as a circle). The leaves (square nodes) show the order that the numbers have after sorting.

Note that the diagrams show clearly that, on average, selection sort makes more comparisons of keys than insertion sort. In fact, selection sort makes redundant comparisons, repeating comparisons that have already been made.

The comparison tree of an arbitrary sorting algorithm displays several features of the algorithm. Its height is the largest number of comparisons that will be made, and hence gives the worst-case behavior of the algorithm. To find the average number of comparisons that the algorithm will do, we can add the lengths of the paths from the root to all of the leaves, and divide by the number of leaves. The comparison tree displays all the possible sequences of comparisons that can be made as all the different paths from the root to the leaves. Since these comparisons control how the entries are rearranged during sorting, any two different orderings of the list must result in some different decisions, hence different paths through the tree, which must then end in different leaves.

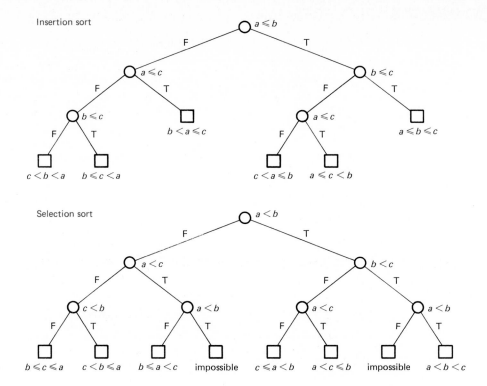

Figure 10.7. Comparison trees, insertion and selection sort, $n = 3$

Counting Leaves

The number of ways that the list containing n entries could originally have been ordered is the *factorial* of n, the mathematical function denoted

$$n! = n \times (n - 1) \times (n - 2) \times \cdots \times 2 \times 1.$$

To see why, think of taking n different objects (the n different keys) and putting them into a list. Any one of the n objects could be the first one in the list. Any of the $n - 1$ remaining objects could be the second one, and so on. Since the choices of these objects are independent of each other, the number of choices multiplies, and so we obtain the factorial.

When we draw a comparison tree, there are only two branches coming out of each vertex, and so the number of vertices on each level is at most twice the number on the level above. The shortest tree with a given number of leaves will have all the leaves on the same or adjacent levels, and since the number of vertices on each level at most doubles, if the tree has k leaves then its height must be at least $\lg k$. Our comparison tree has $n!$ leaves, so its height is at least

$\lg n!$, and the smallest number of comparisons that any sorting algorithm can make (in its worst case) is $\lg n!$.

Next, we would like to have an estimate of how large $\lg n!$ is, and for this we need a mathematical formula. This formula is based on *Stirling's Approximation*, a very accurate approximation to the size of a factorial. See Appendix A for a description of how Stirling's Approximation is derived. For our purposes, we can be content with a much rougher approximation, which is

$$\lg n! = n \lg n + O(n).$$

Applying this equation to counting comparisons, we finally obtain:

> *Any algorithm that sorts a list by comparing keys must, in its worst case on a list of length n, do at least*
>
> $$\lg n! = n \lg n + O(n)$$
>
> *comparisons of keys.*

If you compare the lower bounds derived in this section with the expected performance of insertion sort and selection sort, then you will see that there is a considerable gap. If $n = 1000$, for example, then insertion sort does about 250,000 comparisons, and selection sort does about 500,000, whereas the lower bound is about 8,500. An optimal method, therefore, should run almost 30 times faster than insertion sort when $n = 1000$. Shell sort goes a long way toward closing the gap, but it is suitable only for contiguous lists and has a performance that we do not know how to predict accurately in advance. In later chapters, we shall derive more sophisticated sorting algorithms that come even closer to providing the best performance that the lower bounds will allow.

Other Ways to Sort

Before ending this section, we should note that there are sometimes methods for sorting that do not use comparisons and can be faster. For example, if you know in advance that you have 100 entries and that their keys are exactly the integers between 1 and 100 in some order, with no duplicates, then the best way to sort them is not to do any comparisons, but simply, if a particular entry has key i, then place it in location i. With this method, we are (at least temporarily) regarding the entries to be sorted as being in an array rather than a list, and then we can use the key as an index to find the proper place in the array for each entry. Project P1 suggests an extension of this idea to an algorithm.

■■■■■■■■■ **EXERCISES 10.5**

E1. Describe how to draw the comparison trees for **(a)** insertion sort and **(b)** selection sort applied to four objects. Do not draw the entire trees; instead, show how copies of Figure 10.7 can be used to construct the comparison trees for $n = 4$.

E2. **a.** Find a sorting method for four keys that is optimal in the sense of doing the smallest possible number of key comparisons in its worst case.

b. Find how many comparisons your algorithm does in the average case (applied to four keys). Modify your algorithm to make it come as close as possible to achieving the lower bound of $\lg 4! \approx 4.585$ key comparisons. Why is it impossible to achieve this lower bound?

E3. Suppose that you have a shuffled deck of 52 cards, 13 cards in each of 4 suits, and you wish to sort the deck so that the 4 suits are in order and the 13 cards within each suit are also in order. Which of the following methods is fastest?

a. Go through the deck and remove all the clubs; then sort them separately. Proceed to do the same for the diamonds, the hearts, and the spades.

b. Deal the cards into 13 piles according to the rank of the card. Stack these 13 piles back together and deal into 4 piles according to suit. Stack these back together.

c. Make only one pass through the cards, by placing each card in its proper position relative to the previously sorted cards.

■■■■■■■■■ **PROJECTS 10.5**

P1. Construct a list of n (pseudo-)random numbers between 0 and 1. Suitable values for n are 10 (for debugging) and 500 (for comparing the program with other methods). Write a program to sort these numbers into an array via the following "interpolation sort." First, clear the array (to all 0). For *interpolation* *sort* each number from the list, multiply it by n, take the integer part, and look in that position of the array. If that position is 0, put the number there. If not, move left or right (according to the relative size of the current number and the one in its place) to find the place to insert the new number, moving the entries in the array over if necessary to make room (as in the fashion of insertion sort). Show that your algorithm will really sort the numbers correctly. Compare its running time with that of the other sorting methods applied to the same unsorted list.

P2. Write a program to perform a linked distribution sort, as follows. Take the keys to be numbers, as in the previous project; set up an array of linked *linked* *distribution sort* lists; and distribute the keys into the linked lists according to their size. The linked lists can either be kept sorted as the numbers are inserted or sorted during a second pass, during which the lists are all connected together into one sorted list. Experiment to determine the optimum number of lists to use. (It seems that it works well to have enough lists so that the average length of each list is about 3.)

POINTERS AND PITFALLS

1. Many computer systems have a general-purpose sorting utility. If you can access this utility and it proves adequate for your application, then use it rather than writing a sorting program from scratch.

2. In choosing a sorting method, take into account the ways in which the keys will usually be arranged before sorting, the size of the application, the amount of time available for programming, the need to save computer time and space, the way in which the data structures are implemented, the cost of moving data, and the cost of comparing keys.

3. Insertion sort is an excellent method for short lists or long lists that are nearly in order before sorting. Selection sort does about twice as many comparisons, on average, as insertion sort, but selection sort minimizes the movement of data and is therefore the best choice when the entries of data are large records for which movement is slow. Shell sort is an optimized version of insertion sort that can achieve excellent results, but it is suitable only for contiguous lists.

REVIEW QUESTIONS

10.1 1. What is the difference between *external* and *internal* sorting?

2. What two basic actions do we consider when comparing and analyzing sorting algorithms?

10.2 3. Explain in twenty words or less how insertion sort works.

4. How many comparisons of keys are required to verify that a list of n entries is in order?

10.3 5. Explain in twenty words or less how selection sort works.

6. On average, about how many more comparisons does selection sort do than insertion sort on a list of 20 entries?

7. What is the advantage of selection sort over all the other methods we studied?

10.4 8. What disadvantage of insertion sort does Shell sort overcome?

9. Explain how Shell sort works.

10.5   10. What is the lower bound on the number of key comparisons that any sorting method must make in its worst case to put n keys into order, if the method uses key comparisons to make its decisions?

11. What is the lower bound if the requirement of using comparisons to make decisions is dropped?

12. What is *Stirling's approximation*? State its rough form that we usually use.

PART IV

RECURSION

Recursion is the ability of a subprogram to invoke itself, or to invoke another subprogram that continues a chain of subprograms that eventually invokes the first subprogram again. Recursion is a powerful way to reduce a large problem to smaller ones than can then be solved by easier methods.

In Chapter 11, we introduce the method called "Divide and Conquer," in which a problem is divided into two problems, each similar to the original one but smaller in size. These problems are then solved by the same method used to reduce the original problem: Doing this is the essence of recursion. After some preliminary examples, we apply the method of "Divide and Conquer" to new data structures called *binary trees*. Binary trees provide us with both the speed of random access of a contiguous list and the flexibility of a linked list.

In Chapter 12, we discuss recursion in more general terms, by studying how recursive programs are implemented in computer systems in terms of the space and time that recursion requires. The chapter develops general conclusions about the usefulness of recursion and develops guidelines concerning how and when recursion should be used in algorithm design.

Chapter 13 continues with the study of two more sorting methods, *mergesort* and *quicksort*, which are among the fastest sorting methods known, and for which the recursive method of "Divide and Conquer" plays a vital role.

Chapter 14, finally, turns to other applications of recursion, illustrating a number of different ways that recursion can be used in algorithm design.

11

DIVIDE AND CONQUER: BINARY TREES

This chapter introduces one of the most powerful programming tools available, recursion. Among the important applications of recursion are problems that can be solved by dividing the original problem into pieces, each similar to the original problem but smaller in size. This technique is called "divide and conquer." We first illustrate it with a simple recreational problem, the Towers of Hanoi, and then apply it to a new data structure, the *binary tree*. Binary trees prove to be valuable data structures for a range of applications, especially for problems of information retrieval. These binary *search* trees combine the efficiency of binary search on a contiguous list with the flexibility for making changes that comes only from a linked structure.

EXAMPLES OF RECURSION

11.1.1 Factorials: A Recursive Definition

In studying algorithms, we have already met the *factorial* function of a nonnegative integer, usually defined by the formula

informal definition

$$n! = n \times (n-1) \times \cdots \times 1.$$

The ellipsis (three dots) in this formula means "continue in the same way." This notation is not precise, since there can be more than one sensible way to fill in the ellipsis. To calculate factorials, we need a precise definition, such as the following:

formal definition

$$n! = \begin{cases} 1 & \text{if } n = 0 \\ n \times (n-1)! & \text{if } n > 0. \end{cases}$$

This definition tells us exactly how to calculate a factorial, provided we follow the rules carefully and use a piece of paper to help us remember where we are.

example

Suppose that we wish to calculate 4!. Since $4 > 0$, the definition tells us that $4! = 4 \times 3!$. This may be some help, but not enough, since we do not know what 3! is. Since $3 > 0$, the definition again gives us $3! = 3 \times 2!$. Again, we do not know the value of 2!, but the definition gives us $2! = 2 \times 1!$. We still do not know 1!, but, since $1 > 0$, we have $1! = 1 \times 0!$. The definition, finally, treats the case $n = 0$ separately, so we know that $0! = 1$. We can substitute this answer into the expression for 1! and obtain $1! = 1 \times 0! = 1 \times 1 = 1$. Now comes the reason for using a piece of paper to keep track of partial results. Unless we write the computation down in an organized fashion, by the time we work our way through a definition several times we will have forgotten the early steps of the process before we reach the lowest level and begin to use the results to complete the earlier calculation. For the factorial calculation, it is of course easy to write out all the steps in an organized way:

$$\begin{aligned}
4! &= 4 \times 3! \\
&= 4 \times (3 \times 2!) \\
&= 4 \times (3 \times (2 \times 1!)) \\
&= 4 \times (3 \times (2 \times (1 \times 0!))) \\
&= 4 \times (3 \times (2 \times (1 \times 1))) \\
&= 4 \times (3 \times (2 \times 1)) \\
&= 4 \times (3 \times 2) \\
&= 4 \times 6 \\
&= 24.
\end{aligned}$$

problem | This calculation illustrates the essence of the way ***recursion*** works. To obtain
reduction | the answer to a large problem, a general method is used that reduces the large problem to one or more problems of a similar nature but a smaller size. The same general method is then used for these subproblems, and so recursion continues until the size of the subproblems is reduced to some smallest, base case, where the solution is given directly without using further recursion. In other words:

> *Every recursive process consists of two parts:*
>
> *1. A smallest, base case that is processed without recursion; and*
>
> *2. A general method that reduces a particular case to one or more smaller cases, thereby making progress toward eventually reducing the problem to the base case.*

Pascal (and most other modern computer languages) provide easy access to recursion. The factorial calculation in Pascal becomes the following function.

recursive
program

```
function Factorial(n: integer): integer;
{Pre:  n is a nonnegative integer.
  Post:  The function value is the factorial of n.}
begin
   if n = 0 then Factorial := 1
            else Factorial := n * Factorial(n − 1)
end;
```

As you can see from this example of factorials, the recursive definition and recursive solution of a problem can be both concise and elegant, but the computational details can require keeping track of many partial computations before the process is complete.

remembering | Computers are very good at keeping track of such partial computations;
partial | the human mind is not at all good for such tasks. It is exceedingly difficult to
computations | remember a long chain of partial results and then go back through it to complete the work. When we use recursion, therefore, it is necessary for us to think in somewhat different terms than with other programming methods. Programmers must look at the big picture and leave the detailed computations to the computer.

We must specify in our algorithm the precise form of the general step in reducing a large problem to smaller cases; we must determine the stopping rule (the smallest case) and how it is processed. On the other hand, except for a few simple and small examples, we should generally *not* try to understand a recursive algorithm by working the general case all the way down to the stopping rule or by tracing the action the computer will take on a good-sized case. We would quickly become so confused by all the postponed tasks that we would lose track of the complete problem and the overall method used for its solution.

There are good general methods and tools that allow us to concentrate on the general methods and key steps while at the same time analyzing the amount of work that the computer will do in carrying out all the details. We now turn to an example that illustrates some of these methods and tools.

11.1.2 The Towers of Hanoi

The Problem

the story

In the nineteenth century, a game called the ***Towers of Hanoi*** appeared in Europe, together with promotional material (undoubtedly apocryphal) explaining that the game represented a task underway in the Temple of Brahma. At the creation of the world, the priests were given a brass platform on which were 3 diamond needles. On the first needle were stacked 64 golden disks, each one slightly smaller than the one under it. (The less exotic version sold in Europe had 8 cardboard disks and 3 wooden posts.) The priests were assigned the task of moving all the golden disks from the first needle to the third, subject to the conditions that only one disk can be moved at a time, and that no disk is ever allowed to be placed on top of a smaller disk. The priests were told that when they had finished moving the 64 disks, it would signify the end of the world. See Figure 11.1.

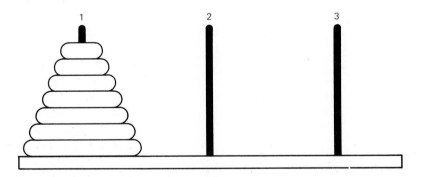

Figure 11.1. The Towers of Hanoi

Our task, of course, is to write a computer program that will type out a list of instructions for the priests. We can summarize our task by the instruction

Move(64, 1, 3, 2)

which means

Move 64 disks from needle 1 to needle 3 using needle 2 as temporary storage.

The Solution

The idea that gives a solution is to concentrate our attention not on the first step (which must be to move the top disk somewhere), but rather on the hardest step: moving the bottom disk. There is no way to reach the bottom disk until the top 63 disks have been moved, and, furthermore, they must all be on needle 2 so that we can move the bottom disk from needle 1 to needle 3. This is because only one disk can be moved at a time and the bottom (largest) one can never be on top of any other, so that when we move the bottom one, there can be no other disks on needles 1 or 3. Thus we can summarize the steps of our algorithm as

```
Move(63, 1, 2, 3);
Writeln('Move a disk from needle 1 to needle 3.');
Move(63, 2, 3, 1)
```

general reduction

We now have a small step toward the solution, only a very small one since we must still describe how to move the 63 disks two times. It is a significant step nonetheless, since there is no reason why we cannot move the 63 remaining disks in the same way. (In fact, we must do so in the same way since there is again a largest disk that must be moved last.)

This is exactly the idea of recursion. We have described how to do the key step and asserted that the rest of the problem is done in essentially the same way. This is also the idea of ***divide and conquer***: To solve a problem, we split the work into halves, each of which is easier than the original problem.

divide and conquer

Refinement

To write the algorithm formally, we shall need to know at each step which needle may be used for temporary storage, and thus we will invoke the procedure in the form

```
Move(n, start, finish, temp)
```

which will mean

> Move n disks from needle start to needle finish
> using needle temp as temporary storage.

stopping rule

Supposedly our task is to be finished in a finite number of steps (even if it does mark the end of the world!), and thus there must be some way that the recursion stops. The obvious stopping rule is that, when there are no disks to be moved, there is nothing to do. We can now write the complete program to embody these rules.

```
program Hanoi(output);
const
   ndisks = 64;
type
   disk = 0..ndisks;
   needle = 1..3;

procedure Move(n: disk; start, finish, temp: needle);
{moves n disks from start to finish using temp for temporary storage}
begin
   if n > 0 then
   begin
      Move(n − 1, start, temp, finish);
      writeln('Move a disk from needle ', start: 1, ' to needle ', finish: 1, '.');
      Move(n − 1, temp, finish, start)
   end
end;                                    {declaration of Procedure Move}

begin                                              {main program}
   Move(ndisks, 1, 3, 2)
end.
```

recursive procedure (margin note, beside procedure Move)

Recursion

With this program, we have the complete solution to the Towers of Hanoi. Recursive procedures like the one here are often the easiest and most natural way to solve a problem, but they do require careful study to understand. Recursive programming is quite different in nature from other programming methods, and most people need to take the time to work through several examples before it becomes a natural approach for them. Many people, in fact, are at first somewhat uncomfortable with recursive procedures. Recursion may perhaps appear at first to be an infinite process, but there is no more danger of writing infinite recursion than of writing an infinite iterative loop. In fact, the dangers are less, since an infinite recursion will soon run out of space and terminate the program, while infinite iteration may continue until manually terminated. Our procedure for the Towers of Hanoi continues to use recursion only while n > 0, and, at every step, n is reduced by 1. Hence, after n steps, the procedure is guaranteed to stop its recursive calls.

termination (margin note)

The importance of recursion makes it the major topic of the next several chapters. In this chapter, we shall concentrate on the study of the *divide-and-conquer* method already illustrated for the Towers of Hanoi, but now as applied to the data structures called binary trees. In the next chapter, we shall examine some details of how a recursive procedure works on most computer systems. Afterwards, we shall apply recursion to obtain two powerful sorting methods, and finally study several other applications that illustrate the range of uses for which recursion proves valuable.

further study (margin note)

Program Tracing

One useful tool in studying a recursive procedure when applied to a very small example is to construct a trace of its action. Such a trace is shown in Figure 11.2 for the Towers of Hanoi in the case when the number of disks, ndisks, is 2. Each box in the diagram shows what happens in one of the calls. The outermost call Move(2, 1, 3, 2) (the call made by the main program) results essentially in the execution of the following three statements, shown as the statements in the outer box (colored gray) of the diagram.

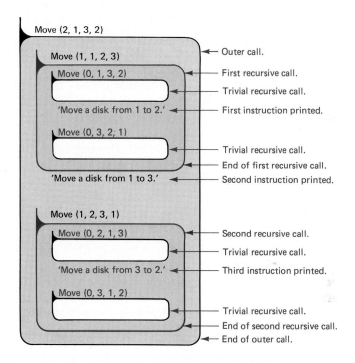

Figure 11.2. Trace of Hanoi for ndisks = 2

Move(1, 1, 2, 3);   {*Move 1 disk from needle 1 to 2 using 3.*}
writeln('Move a disk from needle 1 to needle 3.');
Move(1, 2, 3, 1)   {*Move 1 disk from needle 2 to needle 3 using needle 1.*}

Doing the first and third of these statements requires recursive calls. The statement Move(1, 1, 2, 3) means to start the procedure Move over again from the top, but now with the new parameters. Hence this statement results essentially in the execution of the following three statements, shown as the statements in the first inner box (shown in color):

Move(0, 1, 3, 2);   {*Move 0 disks.*}
writeln('Move a disk from needle 1 to needle 2.');
Move(0, 3, 2, 1);   {*Move 0 disks.*}

If you wish, you may think of these three statements as written out in place of the call Move(1, 1, 2, 3), but think of them as having a different color from the statements of the outer call, since they constitute a new and different call to the procedure. These statements are shown as colored print in the diagram.

After the box corresponding to this call comes the writeln statement and then a second box corresponding to the call Move(1, 2, 3, 1). But before these statements are reached, there are two more recursive calls coming from the first inner box. That is, we must next expand the call Move(0, 1, 3, 2). But the procedure Move does nothing when its parameter n is 0; hence this call Move(0, 1, 3, 2) executes no further procedure calls or other statements. We show it as corresponding to the first empty box in the diagram.

After this empty call comes the writeln statement shown in the first inner box, and then comes another call that does nothing. This then completes the work for the call Move(1, 1, 2, 3), so it returns to the place from which it was called. The following statement is then the writeln in the outer box, and finally the statement Move(1, 2, 3, 1) is done. This call produces the statements shown in the second inner box, which are then, in turn, expanded as the further empty boxes shown.

sorcerer's apprentice   With all the recursive calls through which we worked our way, the example we have studied may lead you to liken recursion to the fable of the Sorcerer's Apprentice, who, when he had enchanted a broom to fetch water for him, did not know how to stop it and so chopped it in two, whereupon it started duplicating itself until there were so many brooms fetching water that disaster would have ensued had the master not returned. We now turn to one more way to visualize recursive calls, a way that manages the multiplicity of calls more effectively than a program trace can.

Tree of Subprogram Calls

Drawing a tree can prove a good way to study the structure of subprogram calls, even when recursion is not involved. The main program is shown as the root of the tree, and all the calls that the main program makes directly are shown as the vertices directly below the root. Each of these subprograms may, of course, call other subprograms, which are shown as further vertices on lower levels. In this way, the tree grows into a form like the one in Figure 11.3. We shall call such a tree a **tree of subprogram calls**. We are especially interested in recursion, so that *recursion tree* often we draw only the part of the tree showing the recursive calls, and call it a **recursion tree**.

You should first notice from the diagram that there is no difference in the way a recursive call appears and the way any other subprogram call occurs. Different recursive calls appear simply as different vertices that happen to have the same name of subprogram attached. Second, note carefully that the tree *execution trace* shows the *calls* to subprograms, not the nesting of *declarations* of subprograms. Hence a subprogram called from only one place, but within a loop executed more than once, will appear several times in the tree, once for each execution of the loop. Similarly, if a subprogram is called from a conditional statement that is not executed, then the call will not appear in the tree.

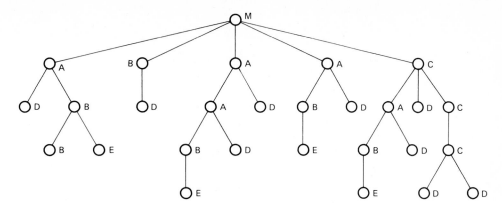

Figure 11.3. A tree of subprogram calls

The recursion tree for the Towers of Hanoi with three disks appears as Figure 11.4, and the progress of execution follows the path shown in color.

stack frames

A closely related picture of recursion is that of **stack frames**, as introduced in Chapter 4; refer for a moment to Figure 4.3. The stack frames show the nesting of recursive calls and also illustrate the storage requirements for recursion. If a procedure calls itself recursively several times, then separate copies of the variables declared in the procedure are created for each recursive call. In the usual implementation of recursion, these are kept on a stack. Note that the amount of

space requirement

space needed for this stack is proportional to the height of the recursion tree, not to the total number of nodes in the tree. That is, the amount of space needed to implement a recursive procedure depends on the *depth* of recursion, not on the *number* of times the procedure is invoked.

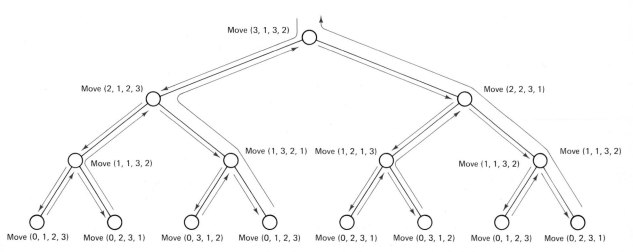

Figure 11.4. Recursion tree for 3 disks

Analysis

Note that our program for the Towers of Hanoi not only produces a complete solution to the task, but it produces the best possible solution, and, in fact, the only solution that can be found except for the possible inclusion of redundant and useless sequences of instructions such as

Move a disk from needle 1 to needle 2.

Move a disk from needle 2 to needle 3.

Move a disk from needle 3 to needle 1.

To show the uniqueness of the irreducible solution, note that, at every stage, the task to be done can be summarized as to move a certain number of disks from one needle to another. There is no way to do this task except to move all the disks except the bottom one first, then perhaps make some redundant moves, then move the bottom one, possibly make more redundant moves, and finally move the upper disks again.

Next, let us find out how many times the recursion will proceed before starting to return and back out. The first time procedure **Move** is called, it is with $n = 64$, and each recursive call reduces the value of n by 1. Thus, if we exclude the calls with $n = 0$, which do nothing, we have a total depth of recursion of 64.

depth of recursion
That is, if we were to draw the tree of recursive calls for the program, it would have 64 levels above its leaves. Except for the leaves, each vertex results in two recursive calls (as well as in writing out one instruction), and so the number of vertices on each level is exactly double that of the level above.

From thinking about its recursion tree (even if it is much too large to draw), we can easily calculate how many instructions are needed to move 64 disks. One instruction is printed for each vertex in the tree, except for the leaves (which are calls with $n = 0$). The number of non-leaves is

total number of moves

$$1 + 2 + 4 + \cdots + 2^{63} = 2^0 + 2^1 + 2^2 + \cdots + 2^{63} = 2^{64} - 1,$$

and this is the number of moves required altogether for 64 disks.

We can estimate how large this number is by using the approximation

$$10^3 = 1000 < 1024 = 2^{10}.$$

(This is an easy fact well worth remembering and well known to many people who talk about computers: The abbreviation K, as in 256K chip, means 1024.) There are about 3.2×10^7 seconds in one year. Suppose that the instructions could be carried out at the rather frenetic rate of one every second (the priests have plenty of practice). Since

$$2^{64} = 2^4 \times 2^{60} > 2^4 \times 10^{18} = 1.6 \times 10^{19},$$

the total task will then take about 5×10^{11} years. If astronomers estimate the age of the universe at about 20 billion (2×10^{10}) years, then, according to this story, the world will indeed endure a long time—25 times as long as it already has!

time and space   You should note carefully that, although no computer could ever carry out the full Towers of Hanoi, it would fail for lack of *time*, and certainly not for lack of *space*. The space needed is only that to keep track of 64 recursive calls, but the time needed is that required for 2^{64} calculations.

EXERCISES 11.1

E1. Consider the function $f(n)$ defined as follows, where n is a nonnegative integer:

$$f(n) = \begin{cases} 0 & \text{if } n = 0; \\ f(\tfrac{1}{2}n) & \text{if } n \text{ is even, } n > 0; \\ 1 + f(n-1) & \text{if } n \text{ is odd, } n > 0. \end{cases}$$

Calculate the value of $f(n)$ for the following values of n.

a. $n = 1$. c. $n = 3$. e. $n = 100$.
b. $n = 2$. d. $n = 99$. f. $n = 128$.

E2. Consider the function $f(n)$ defined as follows, where n is a nonnegative integer:

$$f(n) = \begin{cases} n & \text{if } n \leq 1; \\ n + f(\tfrac{1}{2}n) & \text{if } n \text{ is even, } n > 1; \\ f(\tfrac{1}{2}(n+1)) + f(\tfrac{1}{2}(n-1)) & \text{if } n \text{ is odd, } n > 1. \end{cases}$$

Draw the recursion tree and calculate the value of $f(n)$ for the following values of n.

a. $n = 3$. b. $n = 4$. c. $n = 5$.

E3. Let $S(n)$ be the sum of the integers from 1 to n for a nonnegative integer n. Write three different Pascal functions that will calculate $S(n)$.

a. Use the recursive formula $S(n) = n + S(n-1)$ for $n > 0$, and $S(0) = 0$.
b. Use a local variable, initialized to 0, and write a loop that calculates the sum $S(n) = 1 + 2 + \cdots + n$.
c. Use the formula derived in Chapter 9, $S(n) = \tfrac{1}{2}n(n+1)$.

Which of these is easiest to write? Which is easiest to understand for someone who knows no mathematics? Which will run the fastest for large values of n?

■■■■■■ **PROJECT 11.1**

P1. Compare the running times for the recursive factorial function written in this section with a nonrecursive function obtained by initializing a local variable to 1 and using a loop to calculate the product $n! = 1 \times 2 \times \cdots \times n$. To obtain meaningful comparisons of the CPU time required, you will probably need to write a loop in your driver program that will repeat the same calculation of a factorial several hundred times. Integer overflow will occur if you attempt to calculate the factorial of a large number. To prevent this from happening, you may declare n and the function value to have type real instead of integer.

11.2

BINARY TREES

For some time, we have been drawing trees to illustrate the behavior of algorithms. We have drawn comparison trees showing the comparisons of keys in searching and sorting algorithms; we have drawn trees of subprogram calls; and now we have started to draw recursion trees. If, for example, we consider applying binary search to the list of names in Figure 11.5, then the order in which comparisons will be made is shown in the accompanying comparison tree.

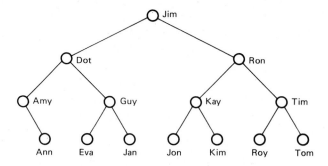

Figure 11.5. Comparison tree for binary search

11.2.1 Definitions

In binary search, when we make a comparison with a key, we then move either left or right depending on the outcome of the comparison. It is thus important to keep the relation of *left* and *right* in the structure we build. It is also possible that the part of the tree on one side or both below a given node is empty. In the example of Figure 11.5, the name Amy has an empty left subtree. For all the leaves, both subtrees are empty.

We can now give the formal definition of a new data structure.

A *binary tree* is either empty, or it consists of a node called the *root* together with two binary trees called the *left subtree* and the *right subtree* of the root.

ADT

Note that this definition is that of a mathematical structure. To specify binary trees as an abstract data type, we must state what operations can be performed on binary trees. Rather than doing so at once, we shall develop the operations as the chapter progresses.

Note also that this definition makes no reference to the way in which binary trees will be implemented in memory. As we shall presently see, a linked representation is natural and easy to use, but other methods are possible as well. Note, finally, that this definition makes no reference to keys or the way in which they are ordered. Binary trees are used for many purposes other than searching; hence we have kept the definition general.

Before we consider general properties of binary trees further, let us return to the general definition and see how its recursive nature works out in the construction of small binary trees.

small binary trees

The first case, the base case that involves no recursion, is that of an empty binary tree. For other kinds of trees, we might never think of allowing an empty one, but for binary trees it is convenient, not only in the definition, but in algorithms, to allow for an empty tree. The empty tree will usually be the base case for recursive algorithms and will determine when the algorithm stops.

The only way to construct a binary tree with one node is to make that node its root and to make both the left and right subtrees empty. Thus a single node with no branches is the one and only binary tree with one node.

With two nodes in the tree, one of them will be the root and the other will be in a subtree. Thus either the left or right subtree must be empty, and the other will contain exactly one node. Hence there are two different binary trees with two nodes.

At this point, you should note that the concept of a binary tree differs from some of the examples of trees that we have previously seen, in that left and right are important for binary trees. The two binary trees with two nodes can be drawn as

left and right

and

which are different from each other. We shall never draw any part of a binary tree to look like since there is no way to tell if the lower node is the left or the right child of its parent.

comparison trees

We should, furthermore, note that binary trees are not the same class as the comparison trees we studied in the analysis of algorithms in Chapters 9 and 10. Each node in a comparison tree has either 0 or 2 children, never 1, as can happen with a binary tree. Left and right are not fundamentally important for studying the properties of comparison trees, but they are crucial in working with binary trees.

binary trees with three nodes

For the case of a binary tree with three nodes, one of these will be the root, and the others will be partitioned between the left and right subtrees in one of the ways

$$2 + 0 \qquad 1 + 1 \qquad 0 + 2.$$

Since there are two binary trees with two nodes and only one empty tree, the first case gives two binary trees. The third case, similarly, gives two more binary trees. In the second case the left and right subtrees both have one node, and there is only one binary tree with one node, so there is one binary tree in the second case. Altogether, then, there are five binary trees with three nodes.

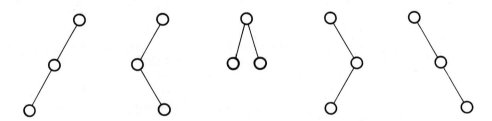

Figure 11.6. The binary trees with three nodes

These binary trees with three nodes are all shown in Figure 11.6. The steps that we went through to construct these binary trees are typical of those needed for larger cases. We begin at the root and think of the remaining nodes as partitioned between the left and right subtrees. The left and right subtrees are then smaller cases for which we know the results from earlier work.

Before proceeding, you should pause to construct all fourteen binary trees with four nodes. This exercise will further help you establish the ideas behind the definition of binary trees.

11.2.2 Traversal of Binary Trees

One of the most important operations on a binary tree is *traversal*, that is, the ability to move through all the nodes of the binary tree, visiting each one in turn.

As for traversal of lists, the action we shall take when we *visit* each node will depend on the application.

For lists, the nodes came in a natural order from first to last, and traversal followed the same order. For trees, however, there are many different orders in which we could traverse all the nodes. If there are n nodes in the binary tree, then, in fact, there are $n!$ different orders in which they could be traversed. Most of these, however, have little regularity or pattern and are of no general significance. When we write an algorithm to traverse a binary tree, we shall almost always wish to proceed so that the same rules are applied at each node, and we thereby adhere to a general pattern.

At a given node, then, there are three tasks we shall wish to do in some order: We shall visit the node itself; we shall traverse its left subtree; and we shall traverse its right subtree. The key distinction in traversal orders is to decide if we are to visit the node itself before traversing either subtree, between the subtrees, or after traversing both subtrees.

If we name the tasks of visiting a node V, traversing the left subtree L, and traversing the right subtree R, then there are six ways to arrange them:

$$V\,L\,R \qquad L\,V\,R \qquad L\,R\,V \qquad V\,R\,L \qquad R\,V\,L \qquad R\,L\,V.$$

Standard Traversal Orders

By standard convention, these six are reduced to three by permitting only the ways in which the left subtree is traversed before the right. The other three are clearly similar. These three remaining ways are given special names that we shall use from now on:

$V\,L\,R$	$L\,V\,R$	$L\,R\,V$
Preorder	*Inorder*	*Postorder*

preorder, inorder, and postorder

These three names are chosen according to the step at which the given node is visited. With **preorder traversal**, the node is visited before the subtrees; with **inorder traversal**, it is visited between them; and with **postorder traversal**, the root is visited after both of the subtrees.

Inorder traversal is also sometimes called **symmetric order**, and postorder traversal was once called **endorder**. We shall not use these terms.

Simple Examples

As a first example, consider the following binary tree:

preorder Under preorder traversal, the root, labeled 1, is visited first. Then the traversal moves to the left subtree. The left subtree contains only the node labeled 2, and it is visited second. Then preorder traversal moves to the right subtree of the root, finally visiting the node labeled 3. Thus preorder traversal visits the nodes in the order 1, 2, 3.

inorder Before the root is visited under inorder traversal, we must traverse its left subtree. Hence the node labeled 2 is visited first. This is the only node in the left subtree of the root, so the traversal moves to the root, labeled 1, next, and finally to the right subtree. Thus inorder traversal visits the nodes in the order 2, 1, 3.

postorder With postorder traversal, we must traverse both the left and right subtrees before visiting the root. We first go to the left subtree, which contains only the node labeled 1, and it is visited first. Next, we traverse the right subtree, visiting the node 3, and, finally, we visit the root, labeled 1. Thus postorder traversal visits the nodes in the order 2, 3, 1.

As a second, slightly more complicated example, let us consider the following binary tree:

preorder First, let us determine the preorder traversal. The root, labeled 1, is visited first. Next, we traverse the left subtree. But this subtree is empty, so its traversal does nothing. Finally, we must traverse the right subtree of the root. This subtree contains the vertices labeled 2, 3, 4, and 5. We must therefore traverse this subtree, again using the preorder method. Hence we next visit the root of this subtree, labeled 2, and then traverse the left subtree of 2. At a later step, we shall traverse the right subtree of 2, which is empty, so nothing will be done. But first we traverse the left subtree, which has root 3. Preorder traversal of the subtree with root 3 visits the nodes in the order 3, 4, 5. Finally, we do the empty right subtree of 2. Thus the complete preorder traversal of the tree visits the nodes in the order 1, 2, 3, 4, 5.

inorder For inorder traversal, we must begin with the left subtree of the root, which is empty. Hence the root, labeled 1, is the first node visited, and then we traverse its right subtree, which is rooted at node 2. Before we visit node 2, we must traverse its left subtree, which has root 3. The inorder traversal of this subtree visits the nodes in the order 4, 3, 5. Finally, we visit node 2 and traverse its right subtree, which does nothing since it is empty. Thus the complete inorder traversal of the tree visits the nodes in the order 1, 4, 3, 5, 2.

postorder For postorder traversal, we must traverse both the left and right subtrees of each node before visiting the node itself. Hence we first would traverse the empty left subtree of the root 1, then the right subtree. The root of a binary tree is always the last node visited by a postorder traversal. Before visiting the node 2, we traverse its left and right (empty) subtrees. The postorder traversal of the subtree rooted at 3 gives the order 4, 5, 3. Thus the complete postorder traversal of the tree visits the nodes in the order 4, 5, 3, 2, 1.

Expression Trees

The choice of the names *preorder*, *inorder*, and *postorder* for the three most important traversal methods is not accidental, but relates closely to a motivating example of considerable interest, that of expression trees.

expression tree   An **expression tree** is built up from the simple operands and operators of an (arithmetical or logical) expression by placing the simple operands as the leaves of a binary tree and the operators as the interior nodes. For each binary operator, the left subtree contains all the simple operands and operators in the left operand of the given operator, and the right subtree contains everything in the right operand.

operators   For a unary operator, one of the two subtrees will be empty. We traditionally write some unary operators to the left of their operands, such as $'-'$ (unary negation) or the standard functions like log( ), and cos( ). Other unary operators are written on the right, such as the factorial function ( )!, or the function that takes the square of a number, $(\ )^2$. Sometimes either side is permissible, such as the derivative operator, which can be written as d/dx on the left, or as ( )' on the right, or the incrementing operator ++ in the language "C" (where the actions on the left and right are different). If the operator is written on the left, then in the expression tree we take its left subtree as empty, so that the operands appear on the right side of the operator in the tree, just as they do in the expression. If the operator appears on the right, then its right subtree will be empty, and the operands will be in the left subtree of the operator.

The expression trees of a few simple expressions are shown in Figure 11.7, together with the slightly more complicated example of the quadratic formula in Figure 11.8, where we denote exponentiation by ↑.

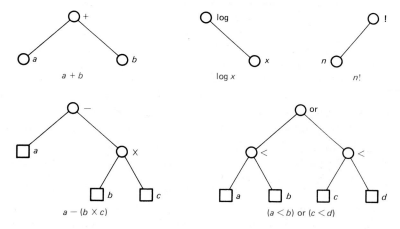

Figure 11.7. Expression trees

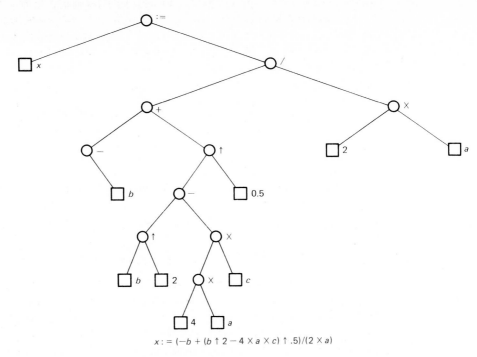

$$x := (-b + (b \uparrow 2 - 4 \times a \times c) \uparrow .5)/(2 \times a)$$

Figure 11.8. Expression tree of the quadratic formula

You should take a few moments to traverse each of these expression trees in preorder, inorder, and postorder. To help you check your work, the results of such traversals are shown in Figure 11.9. You should compare the results of the traversals with the results of translating the expressions into Polish form, as we studied in Chapter 4. You should immediately see how their names are related

Polish notation   to the Polish forms of the expressions: Traversal of an expression tree in preorder yields the **prefix form** of the expression, in which every operator is written before its operand(s); Inorder traversal gives the **infix form** (the customary way to write the expression); and postorder traversal gives the **postfix form**, in which all

Expression:	$a + b$	$\log x$	$n!$	$a - (b \times c)$	$(a < b)$ **or** $(c < d)$
Preorder :	$+\ a\ b$	$\log x$	$!\ n$	$-\ a \times b\ c$	**or** $<\ a\ b\ <\ c\ d$
Inorder :	$a + b$	$\log x$	$n\ !$	$a - b \times c$	$a\ <\ b$ **or** $c\ <\ d$
Postorder :	$a\ b\ +$	$x\ \log$	$n\ !$	$a\ b\ c \times\ -$	$a\ b\ <\ c\ d\ <\ $**or**

Figure 11.9. Traversal orders for expression trees

operators appear after their operand(s). A moment's consideration will convince you of the reason: The left and right subtrees of each node are its operands, and the relative position of an operator to its operands in the three Polish forms is the same as the relative order of visiting the components in each of the three traversal methods.

Comparison Trees

As a further example, let us take the binary tree of 14 names from Figure 11.5 (the comparison tree for binary search) and write them in the order given by each traversal method:

Preorder:

Jim Dot Amy Ann Guy Eva Jan Ron Kay Jon Kim Tim Roy Tom

Inorder:

Amy Ann Dot Eva Guy Jan Jim Jon Kay Kim Ron Roy Tim Tom

Postorder:

Ann Amy Eva Jan Guy Dot Jon Kim Kay Roy Tom Tim Ron Jim

It is no accident that inorder traversal produces the names in alphabetical order. The way that we constructed the comparison tree in Figure 11.5 was to move to the left whenever the target key preceded the key in the node under consideration, and to the right otherwise. Hence the binary tree is set up so that all the nodes in the left subtree of a given node come before it in the ordering, and all the nodes in its right subtree come after it. Hence inorder traversal produces all the nodes before a given one first, then the given one, and then all the later nodes.

In the next section, we shall study binary trees with this property. They are called *binary search trees*, since they are very useful and efficient for problems requiring searching.

11.2.3 Linked Implementation of Binary Trees

root   A binary tree has a natural implementation in linked storage. As usual for linked structures, we shall wish all the nodes to be acquired as dynamic storage, so we shall need a separate pointer variable to enable us to find the tree. Our usual name for this pointer variable will be *root*, since it will point to the root of the tree. With this pointer variable, it is easy to recognize an empty binary tree as precisely the condition

root = **nil**,

and to create a new, empty binary tree we need only assign its root pointer to **nil**.

Declarations

Each node of a binary tree (as the root of some subtree) has both a left and a right subtree, which we can reach with pointers by declaring

```
type
    treepointer = ↑treenode;
    treenode = record
        entry: treeentry;
        left,
        right: treepointer
    end
```

These declarations turn the comparison tree for the 14 names from the first tree diagram of this section, Figure 11.5, into the linked binary tree of Figure 11.10. As you can see, the only difference between the comparison tree and the linked binary tree is that we have explicitly shown the **nil** links in the latter, whereas it is customary in drawing trees to omit all empty subtrees and the branches going to them.

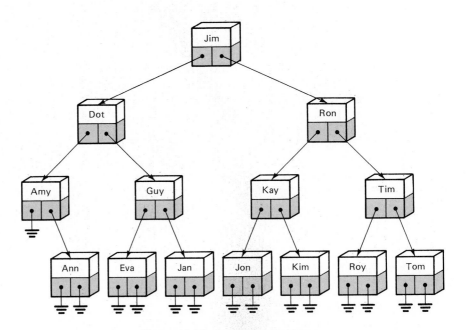

Figure 11.10. A linked binary tree

With the given declarations, we can code the first two operations for binary trees:

function TreeEmpty (root: treepointer): Boolean;
{**Pre:** *The tree to which* root *points has been created.*
  Post: *The function returns the value* true *according as the tree is empty or not.*}
begin
    TreeEmpty := (root = **nil**)
end;

```
procedure CreateTree(var root: treepointer);
{Pre:   None.
  Post: An empty binary tree has been created to which root points.}

begin
   root := nil
end;
```

Traversal

The translation from the definitions to formal procedures to traverse a linked binary tree in each of the three ways we have studied is especially easy. As usual, we take root to be a pointer to the root of the tree, and we assume the existence of another procedure Visit() that does the desired task for each node. As with the traversal procedures written for lists, we shall make Visit a parameter for the traversal procedures. For preorder traversal, we have:

visit root first

```
procedure Preorder(root: treepointer; procedure Visit(var x: treeentry));
{Pre:   The binary tree to which root points has been created.
  Post: The procedure Visit has been performed on every entry in the binary
         tree in preorder.}

begin
   if root <> nil then
   begin
      Visit(root↑.entry);
      Preorder(root↑.left, Visit);
      Preorder(root↑.right, Visit)
   end
end;
```

The procedures for inorder and postorder traversal are equally straightforward:

visit root in middle

```
procedure Inorder(root: treepointer; procedure Visit(var x: treeentry));
{Pre:   The binary tree to which root points has been created.
  Post: The procedure Visit has been performed on every entry in the binary
         tree in inorder.}

begin
   if root <> nil then
   begin
      Inorder(root↑.left, Visit);
      Visit(root↑.entry);
      Inorder(root↑.right, Visit)
   end
end;
```

visit root last

```
procedure Postorder(root: treepointer; procedure Visit(var x: treeentry));
{Pre:   The binary tree to which root points has been created.
 Post:  The procedure Visit has been performed on every entry in the binary
        tree in postorder.}
begin
   if root <> nil then
   begin
      Postorder(root↑.left, Visit);
      Postorder(root↑.right, Visit);
      Visit(root↑.entry)
   end
end;
```

EXERCISES 11.2

E1. Construct the 14 binary trees with four nodes.

E2. Determine the order in which the vertices of the following binary trees will be visited under **(1)** preorder, **(2)** inorder, and **(3)** postorder traversal.

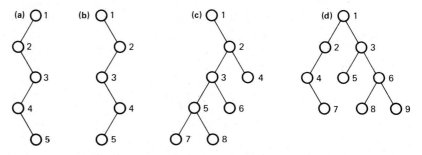

E3. Draw the expression trees for each of the following expressions, and show the order of visiting the vertices in **(1)** preorder, **(2)** inorder, and **(3)** postorder.

a. $\log n!$

b. $(a - b) - c$

c. $a - (b - c)$

d. $(a < b)$ and $(b < c)$ and $(c < d)$

TreeSize

E4. Write a Pascal function TreeSize(root: treepointer): integer that will count all the nodes of a linked binary tree.

E5. Write a Pascal function that will count the leaves (i.e., the nodes with both subtrees empty) of a linked binary tree.

TreeHeight

E6. Write a Pascal function TreeHeight(root: treepointer): integer that will find the height of a linked binary tree.

ClearTree

E7. Write a Pascal procedure ClearTree(**var** root: treepointer) that will traverse a binary tree (in whatever order you find convenient) and dispose of all its nodes.

CopyTree

E8. Write a Pascal procedure CopyTree(root: treepointer; **var** newroot: treepointer) that will make a copy of a linked binary tree. The procedure should obtain the necessary new nodes from the system and copy the information fields from the nodes of the old tree to the new one.

E9. Write a procedure to perform a ***double-order traversal*** of a binary tree, meaning that at each node of the tree, the procedure first visits the node, then traverses its left subtree (in double order), then visits the node again, and then traverses its right subtree (in double order).

double-order traversal

E10. For each of the binary trees in Exercise E2, determine the order in which the nodes will be visited in the mixed order given by invoking procedure A:

```
procedure A(root: treepointer;            procedure B(root: treepointer;
  procedure Visit(var x: treeentry));       procedure Visit(var x: treeentry));
begin                                      begin
  if root <> nil then                        if root <> nil then
  begin                                      begin
    Visit(root↑.entry);                        A(root↑.left, Visit);
    B(root↑.left, Visit);                      Visit(root↑.entry);
    B(root↑.right, Visit);                     A(root↑.right, Visit)
  end                                        end
end;                                       end;
```

E11. **a.** Write a procedure that will print the keys from a binary tree in the ***bracketed form*** (key : LT, RT) where key is the key in the root, LT denotes the left subtree of the root printed in bracketed form, and RT denotes the right subtree in bracketed form.

printing a binary tree

b. Modify the procedure so that it prints nothing instead of (:,) for an empty tree, and x instead of (x:,) for a tree consisting of only one node with key x.

E12. Write a procedure that will interchange all left and right subtrees in a linked binary tree. (See the example in Figure 11.11.)

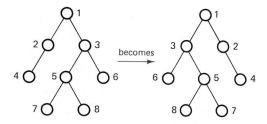

Figure 11.11. Reversal of a binary tree

E13. Write a procedure that will traverse a binary tree level by level. That is, the root is visited first, then the immediate children of the root, then the grandchildren of the root, and so on. [*Hint*: Use a queue to keep track of the children of a node until it is time to visit them.]

level-by-level traversal

width   **E14.** Write a function that will return the width of a linked binary tree, that is, the maximum number of nodes on the same level.

doubly linked   **E15.** Write a procedure that converts a binary tree into a doubly linked list, in
list   which the nodes have the order of inorder traversal of the tree. At the conclusion of the procedure, the pointer root should point to the leftmost node of the doubly linked list, and the links right and left should be used to move through the list, and be **nil** at the two ends of the list.

traversal   For the following exercises, it is assumed that the keys stored in the nodes of the
sequences   binary trees are all distinct, but it is not assumed that the trees are binary search trees. That is, there is no necessary connection between the ordering of the keys and their location in the trees. If a tree is traversed in a particular order, and each key printed when its node is visited, the resulting sequence is called the sequence corresponding to that traversal.

E16. Suppose that you are given two sequences that supposedly correspond to the preorder and inorder traversals of a binary tree. Prove that it is possible to reconstruct the binary tree uniquely.

E17. Either prove or disprove (by finding a counterexample) the analogous result for inorder and postorder traversal.

E18. Either prove or disprove the analogous result for preorder and postorder traversal.

E19. Find a pair of (short) sequences of the same keys that could not possibly correspond to the preorder and inorder traversals of the same binary tree.

11.3

BINARY SEARCH TREES

Consider the problem of searching a simply linked list for some target key. There is no way to move through the list other than one node at a time, and hence searching through the list must always reduce to a sequential search. As you know, sequential search is usually very slow in comparison with binary search. Hence, assuming we can keep the keys in order, searching becomes much faster

the dilemma   if we use a contiguous list and binary search. Suppose we also frequently need to make changes in the list, inserting new entries or deleting old entries. Then it is much slower to use a contiguous list than a linked list, because insertion or deletion in a contiguous list requires moving many of the entries every time, whereas a linked list requires only adjusting a few pointers.

The pivotal problem for this section is:

> *Can we find an implementation for ordered lists in which we can search quickly (as with binary search on a contiguous list) and in which we can make insertions and deletions quickly (as with a linked list)?*

Binary trees provide an excellent solution to this problem. By making the entries of an ordered list into the nodes of a binary tree, we shall find that we can search for a target key in $O(\log n)$ steps, just as with binary search, and we shall obtain algorithms for inserting and deleting entries also in time $O(\log n)$.

comparison trees

When we studied binary search, we drew comparison trees showing the progress of binary search by moving either left (if the target key is smaller than the one in the current node of the tree) or right (if the target key is larger). An example of such a comparison tree appears in Figure 11.5 and again in Figure 11.10, where it is shown as a linked binary tree. From these diagrams, it may already be clear that the way in which we can keep the advantages of linked storage and obtain the speed of binary search is to store the nodes as a binary tree with the structure of the comparison tree itself, with links used to describe the relations of the tree.

The essential feature of the comparison trees is that, when we move to the left subtree, we move to smaller keys, and, when we move to the right subtree, we move to larger keys. This special condition on keys in the nodes of a binary tree is is the essential part of the following important definition:

A *binary search tree* is a binary tree that is either empty or in which every node contains a key and satisfies the conditions:

1. The key in the left child of a node (if it exists) is less than or equal to the key in its parent node.

2. The key in the right child of a node (if it exists) is greater than or equal to the key in its parent node.

These two properties describe the ordering relative to the key in the root node. Note that the properties hold for all nodes in the tree; hence we can continue to use the recursive structure of the binary tree. After we examine the root of the tree, we shall move to either its left or right subtree, and this subtree is again a binary search tree. Thus we can use the same method again on this smaller tree.

The tree shown in Figure 11.5 and Figure 11.10, furthermore, is automatically a binary search tree, since the decision to move left or right at each node is based on the same comparisons of keys used in the definition of a search tree.

11.3.1 Ordered Lists and Implementations

When the time comes to start formulating Pascal procedures to manipulate binary search trees, there are at least three different points of view that we might take:

three views

- We can regard binary search trees as a new abstract data type with its own definition and its own operations.

- Since binary search trees are special kinds of binary trees, we may consider their operations as special kinds of binary tree operations.

■ Since the entries in binary search trees contain keys, and since they are applied for information retrieval in the same way as ordered lists, we may study binary search trees as a new implementation of the abstract data type *ordered list*.

In practice, programmers sometimes take each of these points of view, and so shall we. We shall find later in this section that the keys in a binary search tree can be regarded as already sorted into order, and it is therefore appropriate to think of using a binary search tree for the same applications as an ordered list. Our main tool for this is traversal, which we borrow from general binary trees. For many applications, however, it is easiest to regard binary search trees as a different abstract data type, and this we shall usually do.

Declarations

We have already introduced Pascal declarations that allow us to manipulate the nodes of a binary tree, and we can continue to use these same declarations for binary search trees. The items of information in any binary tree were declared to have a type called treeentry, the links are of a type called treepointer, and each node contains a left and right link in addition to an entry.

Recall that, for ordered lists, we used listentry as the name for the records in the list, each of which contained a key field. If we wish to make our declarations compatible with those given for ordered lists in previous chapters, we need only declare

type treeentry = listentry,

and the entries in our binary search tree become compatible with those in an ordered list.

keys　　Recall that each entry in an ordered list contains a key of a type called keytype. This condition is equally required for the entries of type treeentry in a binary search tree. We leave keytype unspecified, assuming that it is some type, such as a number or a string, for which any two keys can be compared to determine which should be first.

Since binary search trees are a special kind of binary tree, we can apply the operations already defined for general binary trees to binary search trees without difficulty. These operations include CreateTree, TreeEmpty, and the traversal procedures Preorder, Inorder, and Postorder.

11.3.2 Treesearch

The first important new operation for binary search trees is the one from which their name comes: a procedure to search through a linked binary search tree for an entry with a particular target key.

Method

To search for the target, we first compare it with the key at the root of the tree. If it is the same, then we are finished. If it is not the same, we go to the left subtree or right subtree as appropriate and repeat the search in that subtree.

Let us, for example, search for the name Kim in the binary search tree of Figure 11.5 and Figure 11.10. We first compare Kim with the key in the root, Jim. Since Kim comes after Jim in alphabetical order, we move to the right and next compare Kim with Ron. Since Kim comes before Ron, we move left and compare Kim with Kay. Now Kim comes later, so we move to the right and find the desired node.

What event will be the termination condition for the search? Clearly if we find the key, the procedure finishes successfully. If not, then we continue searching until we hit an empty subtree. By using a pointer position to move through the tree, we can use position also to send the results of the search back to the calling program. Thus we have:

specifications

---

procedure TreeSearch (root: treepointer; target: keytype;
                          var position: treepointer);

precondition: The binary search tree to which root points has been created.

postcondition: If an entry in the binary search tree has key equal to target, then position points to such a node; otherwise, position becomes **nil**.

Recursive Version

Perhaps the simplest way to write the procedure for searching is to use recursion:

recursive tree search

```
procedure TreeSearch (root: treepointer; target: keytype;
                      var position: treepointer);
begin                                        {procedure TreeSearch}
  if root = nil then
    position := nil                          {Search fails for an empty tree.}
  else if root↑.entry.key = target then
    position := root                         {Target is in the root position.}
  else if target < root↑.entry.key then
    TreeSearch (root↑.left, target, position)
  else
    TreeSearch (root↑.right, target, position)
end;                                         {procedure TreeSearch}
```

Recursion Removal

tail recursion

The only place where recursion occurs in this procedure is as the very last statement executed in the procedure. This kind of recursion is called ***tail*** recursion, and, by using a loop, it is always possible to change tail recursion into iteration. In this procedure, we write a loop in place of the nested **if** statements, and we use the variable position to move through the tree. The body of the procedure then consists essentially of the statement

```
while (position <> nil) and (target <> position↑.entry.key) do
  if target < position↑.entry.key then
    position := position↑.left
  else
    position := position↑.right;
```

With standard Pascal, however, this statement must be rewritten to avoid a runtime error when the search is unsuccessful, since it will usually attempt to look up position↑ even though position = **nil**. One way to avoid this problem is to introduce a Boolean variable, as implemented in the following procedure.

nonrecursive tree search

```
procedure TreeSearch (root: treepointer; target: keytype;
                            var position: treepointer);
var
  finished: Boolean;
begin                                          {procedure TreeSearch}
  position := root;
  repeat
    if position = nil then
      finished := true
    else if position↑.entry.key = target then
      finished := true
    else begin
      finished := false;
      if target < position↑.entry.key then
        position := position↑.left
      else
        position := position↑.right
    end
  until finished
end;                                           {procedure TreeSearch}
```

Behavior of the Algorithm

Whenever we write a procedure, it is important for us to assess how much work it must do to accomplish its task, so that we can decide whether it is a good method or not. We should therefore now determine how many comparisons of keys TreeSearch does both in its average and worst cases.

Recall that TreeSearch is based closely on binary search. If we apply binary search to an ordered list and draw its comparison tree, then we see that binary search does exactly the same comparisons as TreeSearch will do if it is applied to this same tree. We already know from Chapter 9 that binary search performs $O(\log n)$ comparisons for a list of length n. This performance is excellent in comparison to other methods, since $\log n$ grows very slowly as n increases.

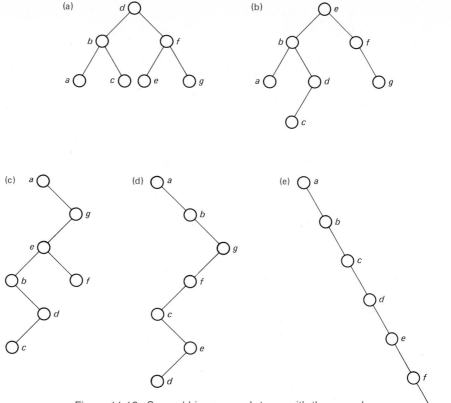

Figure 11.12. Several binary search trees with the same keys

example

Suppose, as an example, that we apply binary search to the list of seven letters *a, b, c, d, e, f,* and *g*. The resulting tree is shown in part (a) of Figure 11.12. If TreeSearch is applied to this tree, it will do the same number of comparisons as binary search.

It is quite possible, however, that the same letters may be built into a binary search tree of a quite different shape, such as any of those shown in the remaining parts of Figure 11.12.

optimal tree

The tree shown as part (a) of Figure 11.12 is the best possible for searching. It is as "bushy" as possible: It has the smallest possible height for its number of vertices. The number of vertices between the root and the target, inclusive, is the number of comparisons that must be done to find the target. The bushier the tree, therefore, the smaller the number of comparisons that will usually need to be done.

typical tree

It is not always possible to predict in advance what shape of binary search tree we will have, and the tree shown in part (b) of Figure 11.12 is more typical of what happens than is the tree in part (a). In the tree of part (b), a search for the target *c* requires four comparisons, but only three in that of part (a). The tree in part (b), however, remains fairly bushy and its performance is only a little poorer than that of part (a).

poor tree

chains

In part (c) of Figure 11.12, however, the tree has degenerated quite badly, so that a search for target *c* requires six comparisons. In parts (d) and (e), the tree reduces to a single chain. When applied to chains like these, TreeSearch can do nothing except go through the list entry by entry. In other words, TreeSearch, when applied to such a chain, degenerates to sequential search. In its worst case on a tree with n nodes, therefore, TreeSearch may require as many as n comparisons to find its target.

In practice, if the keys are built into a binary search tree in random order, then it is extremely unlikely that a binary search tree degenerates as badly as the trees shown in parts (d) and (e) of Figure 11.12. Instead, trees like those of parts (a) and (b) are much more likely. Hence TreeSort almost always performs nearly as well as binary search. In Chapter 13, in fact, we shall prove an important mathematical theorem that shows that, for random binary search trees, the performance of TreeSearch is only about 39 percent slower than the optimum of $\lg n$ comparisons, and it is therefore far superior to the n comparisons needed by sequential search.

At present, however, we can summarize our discussion with the following conclusions:

> *For random binary search trees with n nodes,* TreeSearch *can almost always search for its target in $O(\log n)$ comparisons of keys. It is possible, but extremely unlikely, that it can require as many as n comparisons.*

11.3.3 Insertion into a Binary Search Tree

The Problem

The next important operation for us to consider is the insertion of a new node into a binary search tree in such a way that the keys remain properly ordered; that is, so that the resulting tree satisfies the definition of a binary search tree. The formal specifications for this operation are:

specifications

procedure InsertTree(**var** root: treepointer; newnode: treepointer);

precondition: The binary search tree to which root points has been created. The variable newnode points to a node that has been created and contains a key in its entry.

postcondition: The node newnode↑ has been inserted into the tree in such a way that the properties of a binary search tree are preserved.

Examples

Before we turn to writing this procedure, let us study some simple examples. Figure 11.13 shows what happens when we insert the keys *e, b, d, f, a, g, c* into an initially empty tree in the order given.

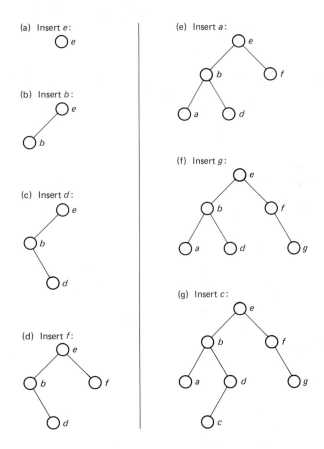

Figure 11.13. Insertions into a binary search tree

When the first entry, *e*, is inserted, it becomes the root, as shown in part (a). Since *b* comes before *e*, its insertion goes into the left subtree of *e*, as shown in part (b). Next we insert *d*, first comparing it to *e* and going left, then comparing it to *b* and going right. The next insertion, *f*, goes to the right of the root, as shown in part (d) of Figure 11.13. Since *a* is the earliest key inserted so far, it moves left from *e* and then from *b*. The key *g*, similarly, comes latest in alphabetical order, so its insertion moves as far right as possible, as shown in part (f). The insertion of *c*, finally, compares first with *e*, goes left, then right from *b* and left from *d*. Hence we obtain the binary search tree shown in the last part of Figure 11.13.

It is quite possible that a different order of insertion can produce the same binary search tree. The final tree in Figure 11.13, for example, can be obtained by inserting the keys in either of the orders

different orders, same tree

$$e, f, g, b, a, d, c \quad \text{or} \quad e, b, d, c, a, f, g,$$

as well as several other orders.

One case is of special importance. Suppose that the keys are inserted into an initially empty tree in their natural order $a, b, \ldots, g$. Then a will go into the root, b will become its right child, c will move to the right of a and b, and so on. The insertions will produce a chain for the binary search tree, as shown in the final part of Figure 11.12. Such a chain, as we have already seen, is very inefficient for searching. Hence we conclude:

natural order

> *If the keys to be inserted into an empty binary search tree are in their natural order, then procedure* InsertTree *will produce a tree that degenerates into an inefficient chain.* InsertTree *should never be used with keys that are already sorted into order.*

The same conclusion holds if the keys are in reverse order or if they are nearly but not quite sorted into order.

Method

It is only a small step from the example we have worked to the general method for inserting a new node into a binary search tree.

The first case, inserting a node into an empty tree, is easy. We need only make root point to the new node. If the tree is not empty, then we must compare the key with the one in the root. If it is less, then the new node must be inserted into the left subtree; if it is more, then it must be inserted into the right subtree. If the keys are equal, then we shall adopt the convention of inserting the duplicate key into the right subtree.

Note that we have described insertion by using recursion. After we compare the new key with the one in the root, we use exactly the same insertion method either on the left or right subtree that we previously used at the root.

Recursive Procedure

From this outline, we can now write our procedure, using the declarations from the beginning of this section.

recursive
insertion

procedure InsertTree (**var** root: treepointer; newnode: treepointer);
{**Pre:** *The binary search tree to which* root *points has been created. The*
variable newnode *points to a node that has been created and contains*
a key in its entry.
Post: *The node* newnode↑ *has been inserted into the tree in such a way*
that the properties of a binary search tree are preserved.}

```
begin                                    {procedure InsertTree}
  if root = nil then
  begin                                  {insertion into an empty tree}
    root := newnode;
    root↑.left := nil;
    root↑.right := nil
  end

  else if newnode↑.entry.key < root↑.entry.key then
    InsertTree (root↑.left, newnode)

  else
    InsertTree (root↑.right, newnode)
end;                                     {procedure InsertTree}
```

Note how this procedure handles duplicate keys: It inserts a new key that duplicates a previous key on the right side of the old entry. By doing this, when we
later traverse the tree (doing left subtrees before right subtrees), the entries with
duplicate keys will be visited in the same order in which they were inserted.
Since comparisons of keys are made in the same order as they are in TreeSearch,
the searching procedure will always find the first entry that was inserted with a
given key.

Recursion Removal

The use of recursion in procedure InsertTree is not essential, since it is used only
as the last step of the procedure. That is, InsertTree uses only tail recursion.
To replace recursion with iteration we shall write a loop. We must introduce a
local pointer variable position that will move to the left or right subtree as we
compare keys, searching for the place to insert the new node. If the new key is
not a duplicate, then this search would normally terminate with position = **nil**. To
make the insertion, however, we must stop changing position one step before it
becomes **nil**. The conditions in the following procedure therefore become slightly
more complicated, and we use a Boolean variable to indicate when the insertion
is complete.

nonrecursive insertion

```
procedure InsertTree(var root: treepointer; newnode: treepointer);
  {Pre:   The binary search tree to which root points has been created. The
          variable newnode points to a node that has been created and contains
          a key in its entry.
   Post:  The node newnode↑ has been inserted into the tree in such a way
          that the properties of a binary search tree are preserved.}
var
    position: treepointer;                      {used to move through tree}
    finished: Boolean;              {becomes true when the insertion is complete}
begin                                                     {procedure InsertTree}
    newnode↑.left := nil;                       {The new node will always be a leaf.}
    newnode↑.right := nil;
    if root = nil then                          {Care for the case of an empty tree.}
        root := newnode
    else begin                                            {case of a nonempty tree}
        finished := false;
        position := root;
        repeat           {Begin a tree search to find the place for insertion.}
            if newnode↑.entry.key < position↑.entry.key then
                if position↑.left <> nil then       {Move left and continue search.}
                    position := left
                else begin                          {Make the insertion on the left.}
                    position↑.left := newnode;
                    finished := true
                end
            else
                if position↑.right <> nil then      {Move right and continue search.}
                    position := right
                else begin                          {Make the insertion on the right.}
                    position↑.right := newnode;
                    finished := true
                end
        until finished
    end                                                   {case of a nonempty tree}
end;                                                      {procedure InsertTree}
```

Some students have difficulty understanding recursive algorithms because they try to trace through all the details instead of trusting recursion to handle a smaller case. It is always possible to change a recursive procedure into nonrecursive form, but it may require a great deal of work and the result may not be easier to understand. You should take a few moments to compare the nonrecursive version of InsertTree with the preceding, recursive version. Which of these is easier to understand?

In regard to performance, InsertTree makes the same comparisons of keys that TreeSearch would make in looking for the key being inserted. InsertTree also changes a few pointers, but does not move entries or do any other operations that

take a large amount of space or time. Therefore the performance of InsertTree
will be very much the same as that of TreeSearch:

> *Procedure* InsertTree *can almost always insert a new node into a random binary
> search tree with n nodes in* $O(\log n)$ *steps. It is possible, but extremely unlikely,
> that the tree may degenerate so that insertions require as many as n steps. If
> the keys are inserted in sorted order into an empty tree, however, this degenerate
> case will occur.*

11.3.4 Treesort

Recall from our discussion of traversing binary trees that, when we traverse a
binary search tree in inorder, then the keys will come out in sorted order. The
reason is that all the keys to the left of a given key precede it (or are equal), and
all those that come to its right follow it (or are equal). By recursion, the same
facts are applied again and again until the subtrees have only one key. Hence
inorder traversal always gives the sorted order for the keys.

The Method

treesort This observation is the basis for an interesting sorting method, called **treesort**.
We simply take the entries to be sorted, use procedure InsertTree to build them
into a binary search tree, and use inorder traversal to put them out in order.

Advantages

Treesort has the great advantage that it is easy to make changes in the list of
entries considered. Adding and deleting entries in a sorted contiguous list is
oppressively slow and painful. It requires as many as $n/2$ steps on average for
a list of length n. Searching for an entry in a sequential linked list is equally
inefficient. With a binary search tree, however, we can (almost always) do any
of these operations in only $O(\log n)$ steps. Hence binary search trees are an
excellent data structure to use for any problem that requires frequent insertions
or other changes in an ordered list, frequent searching, and sorting to keep the
entries in order.

Treesort has the considerable advantages that it is almost as easy to make
changes as in a linked list, the sort is one of the fastest ones known, and searches
can be made with the efficiency of binary search.

Analysis

We can, in fact, see easily how many comparisons treesort will usually do in
sorting a list of length n in random order. There are n items to be inserted into
an empty binary search tree, and we already know that InsertTree usually makes
$O(\log n)$ steps to insert each item, so the number of steps that treesort makes is
usually $O(n \log n)$.

Note carefully that, if the same set of entries is presented to treesort in a different order, then the binary search tree that it builds may have a different shape. When it is traversed in inorder, the keys will still be properly sorted, but the particular location of nodes within the tree depends on the way in which they were initially presented to Treesort. If the 14 names of Figure 11.5, for example, are presented in the order

Tim Dot Eva Roy Tom Kim Guy Amy Jon Ann Jim Kay Ron Jan

then the resulting binary search tree will be the one in Figure 11.14. If the names are presented sorted in their alphabetical order, then the binary search tree will degenerate into a chain.

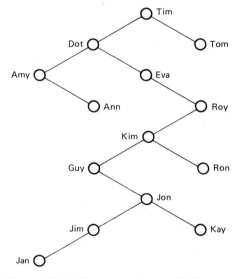

Figure 11.14. Binary search tree of 14 names

This case when the items are already in order (or nearly so), however, is a disaster for treesort: Each of the n items now requires a multiple of n steps for its insertion, so treesort's performance can deteriorate to n^2 steps.

If you recall from Section 10.5, however, the fact that any sorting algorithm must perform at least $n \lg n + O(n)$ comparisons of keys, then you will see that, in its usual case, treesort is among the best possible all all sorting algorithms, since its performance is no worse than a constant multiple of the lower bound.

In summary, we can state:

> *Treesort will almost always sort n keys in random order with $O(n \log n)$ comparisons, which makes it one of the fastest of all sorting algorithms. If the keys are already sorted, however, treesort will degenerate and require a multiple of n^2 comparisons of keys.*

In Chapter 13, we shall study further sorting methods, based on recursion, that allow many of the advantages of treesort even for contiguous or simply linked lists.

11.3.5 Deletion from a Binary Search Tree

In the discussion of treesort, we mentioned the ability to make changes in the binary search tree as an advantage. We have already obtained an algorithm that inserts a new node into the binary search tree, and it can be used to update the tree as easily as to build it from scratch. But we have not yet considered how to delete a node from the tree. If the node to be deleted is a leaf, then the process is easy: We need only replace the link to the deleted node by **nil**. The process remains easy if the deleted node has only one subtree: We adjust the link from the parent of the deleted node to point to its subtree.

When the node to be deleted has both left and right subtrees nonempty, however, the problem is more complicated. To which of the subtrees should the parent of the deleted node now point? What is to be done with the other subtree? This problem is illustrated in Figure 11.15, together with one possible solution. (An Exercise outlines another, sometimes better solution.) What we do is to attach the right subtree in place of the deleted node, and then hang the left subtree onto an appropriate node of the right subtree.

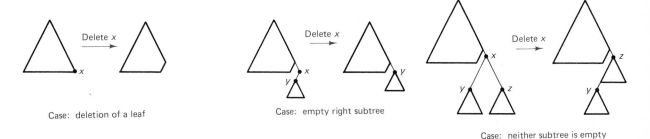

Figure 11.15. Deletion of a node from a binary search tree

To which node of the right subtree should the former left subtree be attached? Since every key in the left subtree precedes every key of the right subtree, it must be as far to the left as possible, and this point can be found by taking left branches until an empty left subtree is found.

requirements   We can now write a procedure to implement this plan. As a calling parameter, it will use a pointer position to the node to be deleted. Since the object is to update the binary search tree, we must assume that the corresponding actual parameter is one of the links of the tree, and not just a copy, or else the tree structure itself will not be changed as it should. In other words, if the node at the left of x↑ is to be deleted, the call should be

DeleteTree(x↑.left),

and, if the root is to be deleted, the call should be

$$\text{DeleteTree(root)}.$$

On the other hand, the following call will not work properly:

$$y := x\uparrow.\text{left; DeleteTree(y)}.$$

deletion

```
procedure DeleteTree(var position: treepointer);
   {Pre:   The parameter position is an actual link (not a copy) in a binary search
           tree, and position does not have the value nil.
    Post:  The node position↑ has been deleted from the binary search tree
           and the resulting smaller tree has the properties required of a binary
           search tree.}
var
   temp: treepointer;     {used to look for the place to hang the left subtree}
begin                                              {procedure DeleteTree}
   if position = nil then
      writeln('Error: Attempt to delete a nonexistent node.')
   else if position↑.right = nil then
      begin                       {Reattach the left subtree in place of position↑.}
         temp := position;
         position := position↑.left;
         dispose(temp)
      end
   else if position↑.left = nil then
      begin                       {Reattach the right subtree in place of position↑.}
         temp := position;
         position := position↑.right;
         dispose(temp)
      end
   else begin                                      {Neither subtree is empty.}
      temp := position↑.right;     {Move right, then as far left as possible.}
      while temp↑.left <> nil do
         temp := temp↑.left;
      temp↑.left := position↑.left;
      temp := position;
      position := position↑.right;
      dispose(temp)
   end
end;                                                {procedure DeleteTree}
```

one subtree empty

move subtree

You should trace through this procedure to check that all pointers are updated properly, especially in the case when neither subtree is empty. Note the steps needed to make the loop stop at a node with an empty left subtree, but not to end at the empty subtree itself.

This procedure is far from optimal, in that it can greatly increase the height of the tree. Two examples are shown in Figure 11.16. When the roots are deleted from these two trees, the one on the top reduces its height, but the one below increases its height. Thus the time required for a later search can substantially increase, even though the total size of the tree has decreased. There is, moreover, often some tendency for insertions and deletions to be made in sorted order, which will further elongate the binary search tree. Hence, to optimize the use of binary search trees, we need methods to make the left and right subtrees more nearly balanced. Consideration of such methods is an important topic in more advanced data structures.

balancing

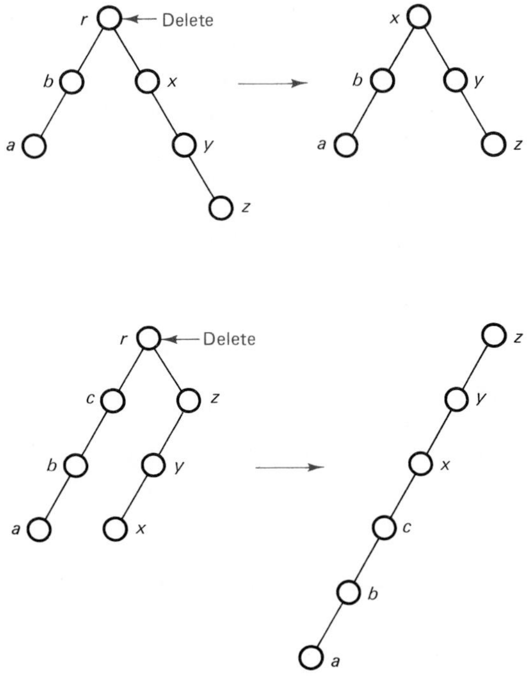

Figure 11.16. Deletions from two binary search trees

11.3.6 *Implementation of Ordered Lists*

In this section, we have treated binary search trees as a new data type with its own declarations and operations. We can equally well regard binary search trees as a way of implementing the abstract data type *ordered list* introduced in Chapters 9 and 10. By doing so, we can substitute binary search trees for the other implementations of ordered lists in an application program.

To use binary search trees as an implementation for ordered lists, we must take the standard ordered-list operations and program them using binary search trees. We shall begin with the declarations:

```
type
    listtype = record
        head: treepointer
    end;
    window = treepointer;
    treeentry = listentry;
```

We shall identify the name of a list with a pointer to the root of the binary search tree.

To convert TreeSearch to an ordered-list procedure, we embed it in the following:

searching

```
procedure Search (var L: listtype; target: keytype;
                     var found: Boolean; var location: window);
{Pre:   L has been created and is an ordered list implemented as a binary
        search tree.
 Post:  If an entry in L has key equal to target, then found becomes true and
        the window location gives the location of such an entry. Otherwise,
        found becomes false and the window location is undefined.}
begin
    TreeSearch (L.head, target, location);
    found := (location <> nil)
end;
```

Similarly, the binary search tree procedure InsertTree can easily be converted to the ordered-list procedure InsertOrder. For this procedure, we need a local pointer variable with which to create a new node.

insertion

```
procedure InsertOrder (x: listentry; var L: listtype);
{Pre:   L has been created as an ordered list implemented as a binary search
        tree.
 Post:  The entry x has been inserted into a new node in L in a position such
        that the keys in all entries in L remain in the correct order.}
var
    newnode: treepointer;
begin
    new (newnode);
    newnode.entry := x;
    InsertTree (L, newnode)
end;
```

Many of the remaining list operations are also easy to write for binary search trees. These will be left as exercises.

difficulties   A few of the operations, however, are quite difficult for binary search trees. An example is the operation NextList that moves a window one position (in order) through a list. In a binary search tree, the next node (in order of keys) may be the right child of a given node; it may be farther down in the right subtree; or it may be farther up toward the root. With all these possibilities, it becomes complicated to write a procedure to find the next node, especially if duplicate keys must be taken into account. One solution to this problem is to use *threaded* binary trees; see the References in Appendix C for more information.

In almost all applications where we have used NextList, however, it has been used to advance one step in the traversal of the list. Traversal of a binary search tree in the order of its keys is a very easy process. It is simply an inorder traversal of the binary tree and requires only the (recursive) procedure for inorder traversal already written. Hence, for most applications, the absence of the procedure NextList for binary search trees is no inconvenience at all.

EXERCISES 11.3

The first several exercises are based on the following binary search tree. Answer each part of each exercise independently, using the original tree as the basis for each part.

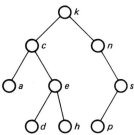

E1. Show the keys with which each of the following targets will be compared in a search of the preceding binary search tree.

a. *c*	d. *a*	g. *f*
b. *s*	e. *d*	h. *b*
c. *k*	f. *m*	i. *t*

E2. Insert each of the following keys into the preceding binary search tree. Show the comparisons of keys that will be made in each case. Do each part independently, inserting the key into the original tree.

a. *m*	c. *b*	e. *c*
b. *f*	d. *t*	f. *s*

E3. Delete each of the following keys from the preceding binary search tree, using the algorithm developed in this section to restore the properties of a binary search tree. Do each part independently, deleting the key from the original tree.

a. *a*	c. *n*	e. *e*
b. *p*	d. *s*	f. *k*

E4. Draw the binary search trees that procedure InsertTree will construct for the list of 14 names presented in each of the following orders and inserted into a previously empty binary search tree.

    a. Jan Guy Jon Ann Jim Eva Amy Tim Ron Kim Tom Roy Kay Dot
    b. Amy Tom Tim Ann Roy Dot Eva Ron Kim Kay Guy Jon Jan Jim
    c. Jan Jon Tim Ron Guy Ann Jim Tom Amy Eva Roy Kim Dot Kay
    d. Jon Roy Tom Eva Tim Kim Ann Ron Jan Amy Dot Guy Jim Kay

E5. All parts of this exercise refer to the binary search trees shown in Figure 11.12 and concern the different orders in which the keys $a, b, \ldots, g$ can be inserted into an initially empty binary search tree.

    a. Give four different orders for inserting the keys, each of which will yield the binary search tree shown in part (a).
    b. Give four different orders for inserting the keys, each of which will yield the binary search tree shown in part (b).
    c. Give four different orders for inserting the keys, each of which will yield the binary search tree shown in part (c).
    d. Explain why there is only one order for inserting the keys that will produce a binary search tree that reduces to a given chain, such as the one shown in part (d) or in part (e).

deletion **E6.** Write a procedure that will delete a node from a linked binary tree, using the following method in the case when the node to be deleted has both subtrees nonempty. First, find the immediate predecessor of the node under inorder traversal (the immediate successor would work just as well), by moving to its left child and then as far right as possible. This immediate predecessor is guaranteed to have at most one child (why?), so it can be deleted from its current position without difficulty. It can then be placed into the tree in the position formerly occupied by the node that was supposed to be deleted, and the properties of a binary search tree will still be satisfied (why?).

ordered list operations **E7.** Write procedures that perform each of the following list operations for an ordered list implemented as a binary search tree, following the declarations given in this section. Be sure that each subprogram conforms to the preconditions and postconditions specified in Chapter 6.

    a. **procedure** CreateList(**var** L: listtype)
    b. **function** ListEmpty(L: listtype): Boolean
    c. **procedure** TraverseList(**var** L: listtype; **procedure** Visit(**var** x: listentry))
    d. **function** ListSize(L: listtype): integer
    e. **function** IsFirst(w: window; L: listtype): Boolean
    f. **function** IsLast(w: window; L: listtype): Boolean
    g. **procedure** StartList(**var** w: window; L: listtype)
    h. **procedure** FinishList(**var** w: window; L: listtype)
    i. **procedure** RetrieveList(w: window; **var** x: listentry; **var** L: listtype)
    j. **procedure** ClearList(**var** L: listtype);
    k. **procedure** OnList(w: window; L: listtype);
    l. **procedure** DeleteList(w: window; L: listtype);

E8. Write the following procedures for moving a window on an ordered list. (Hint: Implement them as modified versions of an inorder traversal.).

    a. **procedure** NextList(w: window; L: listtype);

    b. **procedure** PrecedingList(w: window; L: listtype);

PROJECTS 11.3

P1. Prepare a package containing the declarations for a binary search tree and the procedures developed in this section. The package should be suitable for inclusion (either as a unit in Turbo Pascal or via the include directive if it is available for your compiler) in any application program.

P2. Produce a menu-driven demonstration program to illustrate the use of binary search trees. The entries may consist of keys alone, and the keys should be single characters. The minimum capabilities that the user should be able to demonstrate include creating (initializing) the tree, insertion and deletion of an entry, searching for a target entry, and traversal of the tree in the three standard orders. The project may be enhanced by the inclusion of additional capabilities written as exercises in this and the previous section. These include determining the size and the height of the tree, printing out all entries arranged to show the shape of the tree, traversal of the tree in various ways, and reversal of all left and right subtrees.

P3. Prepare a package containing the declarations, procedures, and functions for processing an ordered list implemented as a binary search tree. The package should include solutions to all parts of the last exercise for this section as well as the subprograms developed in the text. It should be suitable for inclusion (either as a unit in Turbo Pascal or via the include directive if it is available for your compiler) in any application program.

P4.   a. Write a program for testing treesort, as follows. Start with the files of numbers in random order used for testing the sorting programs in Chapter 10. Read all the numbers from a file into a contiguous list. Take each number from the list, in turn, and insert it into an initially empty binary search tree by using procedure InsertTree. After all numbers have been inserted, use procedure Inorder to traverse the tree, thereby obtaining the numbers in sorted order. Keep track of the CPU time used in insertion and traversal, and keep track of the number of key comparisons done in InsertTree. Compare the results with those for the sorting methods in Chapter 10.

    b. Use the same program to test procedure TreeSearch in the case of successful searches, as follows. After the binary search tree has been constructed, take each element from the contiguous (original) list and search for it in the tree, keeping track of the total number of key comparisons made in searching for each entry once. Calculate the average number of comparisons made, and compare your answer with the best possible result of $\lg n$ and with the theoretically expected answer of $1.39 \lg n$.

c. Modify the preceding test of TreeSearch so that it also keeps track of the CPU time used. Apply sequential search to find each number once in the original, unsorted list. Compare the time needed by sequential search with the time needed by treesort and treesearch (once for each number) combined.

d. Use any convenient method to sort the numbers in the original contiguous list, and then apply binary search to locate each number once. Compare the CPU time required with that for treesearch.

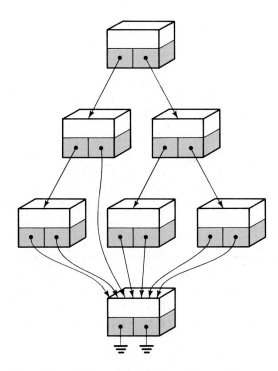

Figure 11.17. Binary search tree with sentinel

P5. Write a procedure for searching, using a binary search tree with sentinel as follows. Introduce a new sentinel node, and keep a pointer to it. See Figure 11.17. Replace all the **nil** links within the binary search tree with links to the sentinel. Then, for each search, store the target into the sentinel before starting the search. Delete the test for an unsuccessful search from TreeSearch, since it cannot now occur. Run this procedure on the test data of the preceding project to compare the performance of this version with the original procedure TreeSearch.

P6. Different authors tend to use common words with differing frequencies. Write a program that will read a text (words and sentences) from a file and split it up into individual words. You should consider that a word consists entirely of letters and terminates with the first character that is not a letter. Change the first letter of each word to upper case so there will be no distinction between words at the start of a sentence and others. Take each word as it is split from the text and insert it into an initially empty binary search tree. If it is already present, do not insert it a second time, but instead update a counter (part of the treeentry record). After the text has been finished, traverse the binary search tree and print out all the words in alphabetical order, along with the number of times each appears in the text.

POINTERS AND PITFALLS

1. Consider binary search trees as an alternative to lists (indeed, as a way of implementing the abstract data type *ordered list*). At the cost of an extra pointer field in each node, binary search trees allow random access (with $O(\log n)$ key comparisons) to all nodes while maintaining the flexibility of linked lists for insertions, deletions, and rearrangement.

2. Consider binary search trees as an alternative to arrays. At the cost of access time that is $O(\log n)$ instead of $O(1)$, binary search trees allow traversal of the data structure in the order specified by the keys while maintaining the advantage of random access provided by arrays.

3. In choosing your data structures, always consider carefully what operations will be required. Binary trees are especially appropriate when random access, traversal in a predetermined order, and flexibility in making insertions and deletions are all required.

4. While choosing data structures and algorithms, remain alert to the possibility of highly unbalanced binary trees. If the incoming data are likely to be in random order, then an ordinary binary search tree should prove entirely adequate. If the data may come in a sorted or nearly sorted order, then the algorithms should take appropriate action. If there is only a slight possibility of serious imbalance, it might be ignored. If, in a large project, there is greater likelihood of serious imbalance, then there may still be appropriate places in the software where the trees can be checked for balance and rebuilt if necessary.

5. Binary trees are defined recursively; algorithms for manipulating binary trees are usually best written recursively. In programming with binary trees, be aware of the problems generally associated with recursive algorithms. Be sure that your algorithm terminates under any condition and that it correctly treats the trivial case of an empty tree.

6. Although binary trees are usually implemented as linked structures, remain aware of the possibility of other implementations. In programming with linked binary trees, keep in mind the pitfalls attendant on all programming with linked lists.

REVIEW QUESTIONS

11.1   **1.** Define the term *divide and conquer*.

    2. What is a *recursive* procedure?

    3. Name two parts or phases that must be in every recursive process.

    4. What is a *recursion tree*?

    5. Is the reason why the Towers of Hanoi takes so long to run the huge *depth* of its recursion?

11.2   **6.** Define the term *binary tree*.

    7. What is the difference between a binary tree and an ordinary tree in which each vertex has at most two branches?

    8. Give the order of visiting the vertices of each of the following binary trees under **(1)** preorder, **(2)** inorder, and **(3)** postorder traversal.

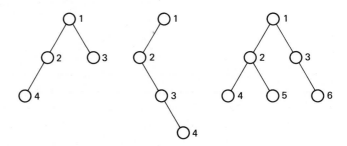

    9. Draw the expression trees for each of the following expressions, and show the result of traversing the tree in **(1)** preorder, **(2)** inorder, and **(3)** postorder.

    a. $a - b$.   **c.** $\log m!$.   **e.** $x \times y \le x + y$.

    b. $n/m!$.   **d.** $(\log x) + (\log y)$.   **f.** $a > b$ **or** $b \ge a$.

11.3   **10.** Define the term *binary search tree*.

    11. If a binary search tree with n nodes is well balanced, what is the approximate number of comparisons of keys needed to find a target? What is the number if the tree degenerates to a chain?

    12. In twenty words or less, explain how treesort works.

    13. What causes deletion from a binary search tree to be more difficult than insertion into a binary search tree?

    14. How much slower, on average, is searching a random binary search tree than is searching a completely balanced binary search tree?

12

PRINCIPLES OF RECURSION

As we have seen from studying binary trees, recursion is a powerful programming tool. This chapter discusses the basic principles of recursion, describes how it is usually implemented on a computer, and, in the process, obtains guidelines regarding good and bad uses of recursion, when it is appropriate, and when it should best be avoided.

DESIGNING RECURSIVE ALGORITHMS

Recursion is a tool to allow the programmer to concentrate on the key step of an algorithm, without having initially to worry about coupling that step with all the others. As usual with problem solving, the first approach should usually be to consider several simple examples, and as these become better understood, to attempt to formulate a method that will work more generally. In regard to using recursion, you may begin by asking yourself, "How can this problem be divided into parts?" or "How will the key step in the middle be done?" Be sure to keep your answer simple but generally applicable. Do not come up with a multitude of special cases that work only for small problems or at the beginning and end of *key step* large ones. Once you have a simple, small step toward the solution, ask whether the remainder of the problem can be done in the same or a similar way, and modify your method, if necessary, so that it will be sufficiently general.

stopping rule Once the key step is determined, find a stopping rule that will indicate that the problem or a suitable part of it is done. Build this stopping rule into your key step. You should now be able to write the main program and a recursive procedure that will describe how to carry the step through.

termination Next, and of great importance, is a verification that the recursion will always terminate. Start with a general situation and check that, in a finite number of steps, the stopping rule will be satisfied and the recursion terminate. Be sure also that your algorithm correctly handles extreme cases. When called on to do nothing, any algorithm should be able to return gracefully, but it is especially important that recursive algorithms do so, since a call to do nothing is often the stopping rule.

recursion tree The key tool for the analysis of recursive algorithms is the recursion tree. As we shall see in the next section, the height of the tree is closely related to the amount of memory that the program will require, and the total size of the tree reflects the number of times the key step will be done, and hence the total time the program will use. It is usually highly instructive to draw the recursion tree for one or two simple examples appropriate to your problem.

HOW RECURSION WORKS

design versus implementation The question of how recursion is actually done in a computer should be carefully separated in our minds from the question of using recursion in designing algorithms. In the design phase, we should use all problem-solving methods that prove to be appropriate, and recursion is one of the most flexible and powerful of these tools. In the implementation phase, we may need to ask which of several methods is the best under the circumstances. There are at least two ways to accomplish recursion in computer systems. At present, the first of these is experimental and only starting to be available in commercial systems, but with changing costs and capabilities of computer equipment, it will probably soon be regarded as quite practical. Our major point in considering two different implementations is that, although restrictions in space and time do need to be considered, they should be considered separately from the process of algorithm design, since different kinds of computer equipment in the future may lead to different capabilities and restrictions.

12.2.1 Multiple Processors: Concurrency

Perhaps the most natural way to think of implementing recursion is to think of each subprogram not as occupying a different part of the same computer, but to think of each subprogram as running on a separate machine. In that way, when one subprogram invokes another, it starts the corresponding machine going, and when the other machine completes its work, then it sends the answer back to the first machine, which can then continue its task. If a procedure makes two recursive calls to itself, then it will simply start two other processors working with the same instructions that it is using. When these processors complete their work, they will send the answers back to the processor that started them going. If they, in turn, make recursive calls, then they will simply start still more processors working.

costs At one time, the central processor was the most expensive component of a computer system, and any thought of a system including more than one processor would have been considered extravagant. The price of processing power compared to other computing costs has now dropped radically, and in all likelihood we shall, before long, see large computer systems that will include hundreds, if not thousands, of identical microprocessors among their components. When this occurs, implementation of recursion via multiple processors will become commonplace if not inevitable.

With multiple processors, programmers will no longer consider algorithms solely as a linear sequence of actions, but will instead realize that some parts of the algorithm can be done at the same time as other parts. In divide-and-conquer algorithms such as quicksort, for example, the two halves into which the problem is divided often do not depend on each other and can be worked on simultaneously by multiple processors.

concurrency Processes that take place simultaneously are called *concurrent*. The study of concurrent processes and the methods for communication between them is, at present, an active subject for research in computing science, one in which important developments will undoubtedly improve the ways in which algorithms will be described and implemented in coming years.

12.2.2 Single-Processor Implementation: Storage Areas

In order to determine how recursion can be efficiently implemented in a system with only one processor, let us first for the moment leave recursion to consider the question of what steps are needed to call a subprogram, on the primitive level of machine-language instructions in a simple computer.

The hardware of any computer has a limited range of instructions that includes (amongst other instructions) doing arithmetic on specified words of storage or on special locations within the CPU called *registers*, moving data to and from the memory and registers, and branching (jumping) to a specified address. When a calling program branches to the beginning of a subprogram, the address of the place whence the call was made must be stored in memory, or else the subprogram could not remember where to return. The addresses or values of

return address the calling parameters must also be stored where the subprogram can find them, and where the answers can in turn be found by the calling program after the subprogram returns. When the subprogram starts, it will do various calculations on its local variables and storage areas. Once the subprogram finishes,

local variables however, these local variables are lost, since they are not available outside the subprogram. The subprogram will, of course, have used the registers within the CPU for its calculations, so normally these would have different values after the subprogram finishes than before it is called. It is traditional, however, to expect that a subprogram will change nothing except its calling parameters or global variables (side effects). Thus it is customary that the subprogram will save all the registers it will use and restore their values before it returns.

In summary, when a subprogram is called, it must have a storage area

storage area (perhaps scattered as several areas); it must save the registers or whatever else it will change, using the storage area also for its return address, calling parameters, and local variables. As it returns, it will restore the registers and the other storage that it was expected to restore. After the return, it no longer needs anything in its local storage area.

In this way, we implement subprogram calls by changing storage areas, an action that takes the place of changing processors that we considered before. In these considerations, it really makes no difference whether the subprogram is called recursively or not, providing that, in the recursive case, we are careful to regard two recursive calls as being different, so that we do not mix the storage areas for one call with those of another, any more than we would mix storage areas for different subprograms, one called from within the other. For a nonrecursive subprogram, the storage area can be one fixed area, permanently reserved, since we know that one call to the subprogram will have returned before another one is made, and after the first one returns, the information stored is no longer needed. For recursive subprograms, however, the information stored must be preserved until the outer call returns, so an inner call must use a different area for its temporary storage.

Note that the common practice of reserving a permanent storage area for a nonrecursive subprogram can in fact be quite wasteful, since a considerable amount of memory may be consumed in this way, memory that might be useful for other purposes while the subprogram is not active. This is, nevertheless, the way that storage is allocated for subprograms in older languages like FORTRAN and COBOL, and this is the reason why these languages do not allow recursion.

12.2.3 Re-Entrant Programs

Essentially the same problem of multiple storage areas arises in a quite different context, that of *re-entrant* programs. In a large time-sharing system, there may be many users simultaneously using the BASIC interpreter or the text-editing system. These systems programs are quite large, and it would be very wasteful of high-speed memory to keep thirty or forty copies of exactly the same large set of instructions in memory at once, one for each user. What is generally done instead is to write large systems programs like the BASIC interpreter or the text editor with the instructions in one area, but the addresses of all variables or other data kept in a separate area. Then, in the memory of the time-sharing system, there will be only one copy of the instructions, but a separate data area for each user.

This situation is somewhat analogous to students writing a test in a room where the questions are written on the blackboard. There is then only one set of questions that all students can read, but each student separately writes answers on different pieces of paper. There is no difficulty for different students to be reading the same or different questions at the same time, and with different pieces of paper, their answers will not be mixed with each other. See Figure 12.1.

Figure 12.1. Re-entrant processes

12.2.4 Data Structures: Stacks and Trees

We have yet to specify the data structure that will keep track of all these storage areas for subprograms; to do so, let us look at the tree of subprogram calls. So that an inner subprogram can access variables declared in an outer block, and so that we can return properly to the calling program, we must, at every point in the tree, remember all vertices on the path from the given point back to the root. As we move through the tree, vertices are added to and deleted from one *stacks*

end of this path; the other end (at the root) remains fixed. Hence the vertices on the path form a stack; the storage areas for subprograms likewise are to be kept as a stack. This process is illustrated in Figure 12.2.

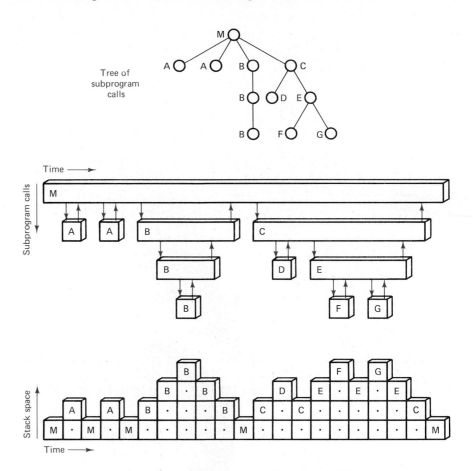

Figure 12.2. A tree of subprogram calls and the associated stack frames

time and space requirements

From Figure 12.2 and our discussion, we can immediately conclude that the amount of space needed to implement recursion (which, of course, is related to the number of storage areas in current use) is directly proportional to the height of the recursion tree. Programmers who have not carefully studied recursion sometimes think mistakenly that the space requirement relates to the total number of vertices in the tree. The *time* requirement of the program is related to the number of times subprograms are done, and therefore to the total number of vertices in the tree, but the *space* requirement is only that of the storage areas on the path from a single vertex back to the root. Thus the space requirement is reflected in the height of the tree. A well-balanced, bushy recursion tree hence signifies a recursive process that can do much work with little need for extra space.

Figure 12.2 can, in fact, be interpreted in a broader context than as the process of invoking subprograms. It thereby elucidates an easy but important observation, providing an intimate connection between arbitrary trees and stacks:

> *During the traversal of any tree, vertices are added to or deleted from the path back to the root in the fashion of a stack. Given any stack, conversely, a tree can be drawn to portray the life history of the stack, as items are added to or deleted from it.*

In most modern computers, efficient means are provided to allow the same instructions to refer to different storage areas as desired. In many large computers, for example, every instruction that refers to memory calculates the address it uses by adding some value (displacement) to the contents of a specified register called the base register. If the value in the base register is set to the beginning of one storage area, then all later instructions will refer to that area. Changing only the one value in the base register will make all the instructions refer to another storage area. Most microcomputers have built-in stack instructions. As an instruction on such a computer is done it can be made to push or pop a stack automatically as it refers to memory for its operands.

12.2.5 Conclusion

The moral of the story is that, when properly implemented, recursion is neither inefficient nor expensive, except perhaps on some machines of quite old design that are rapidly being retired. Some compilers, unfortunately, do make a mess out of recursive procedures, but, on a well-designed system, there is essentially no additional time overhead for using recursion, and no reason to avoid it when it is the natural method.

12.3

TAIL RECURSION

Suppose that the very last action of a procedure is to make a recursive call to itself. In the stack implementation of recursion, as we have seen, the local variables of the procedure will be pushed onto the stack as the recursive call *discarding stack* is initiated. When the recursive call terminates, these local variables will be *entries* popped from the stack and thereby restored to their former values. But doing so is pointless, because the recursive call was the last action of the procedure, so that the procedure now terminates and the just-restored local variables are immediately discarded.

When the very last action of a procedure is a recursive call to itself, it is thus pointless to use the stack, as we have seen, since no local variables need to be preserved. All that is needed is to set the dummy calling parameters to their new values and branch to the beginning of the procedure. We summarize this principle for future reference.

> *If the last executed statement of a procedure is a recursive call to itself, then this call can be eliminated by changing the values of the calling parameters to those specified in the recursive call, and repeating the whole procedure.*

The process of this transformation is shown in Figure 12.3. Part (a) shows the storage areas used by the calling program M and several copies of the recursive procedure P. The colored arrows show the flow of control. Since each call by P to P is its last action, there is no need to maintain the storage areas after the call, as shown in part (b). Part (c), finally, shows these calls to P as repeated in iterative fashion on the same level.

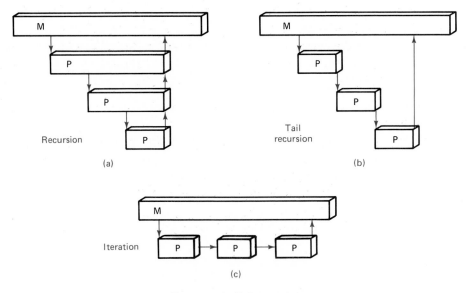

Figure 12.3. Tail recursion

tail recursion　　This special case when a recursive call is the last executed statement of the procedure is especially important because it frequently occurs. It is called **tail recursion**. You should carefully note that tail recursion means that the last executed statement is a recursive call, not necessarily that the recursive call is the last statement appearing in the procedure. Tail recursion may appear, for example, within one clause of a **case** statement or an **if** statement where other program lines appear later.

time and space　　With most modern compilers, there will be little difference in execution *time* whether tail recursion is left in a program or is removed. If *space* considerations are important, however, then tail recursion should usually be removed, whether other recursion is being removed or not. By rearranging the termination condition, if needed, it is usually possible to repeat the procedure using a **repeat** or a **while** statement.

Consider, for example, a divide-and-conquer algorithm like that devised for the Towers of Hanoi in Section 11.1. By removing tail recursion, procedure Move of the original recursive program can be expressed as

Hanoi without tail recursion

```
procedure Move(n: disk; start, finish, temp: needle);
{moves n disks from start to finish using temp for temporary storage}
var
   swap: needle;                        {temporary storage to swap needles}
begin                                                     {procedure Move}
   while n > 0 do begin
      Move(n − 1, start, temp, finish);
      writeln('Move a disk from', start: 2, 'to', finish: 2);
      n := n − 1; swap := start; start := temp; temp := swap
   end                                                    {looping down on n}
end;                                                      {procedure Move}
```

We should have been quite clever had we thought of this version of the procedure when we first looked at the problem, but now that we have discovered it via other considerations, we can give it a natural interpretation. Think of the two needles start and temp as in the same class: we wish to use them for intermediate storage as we slowly move all the disks onto finish. To move a stack of n disks onto finish, then, we must move all except the bottom to the other one of start, temp, then move the bottom one to finish, and repeat after interchanging start and temp, continuing to shuffle all except the bottom one between start and temp, and, at each pass, getting a new bottom one onto finish.

12.4

WHEN NOT TO USE RECURSION

12.4.1 Factorials

Many textbooks (including this one) present the calculation of factorials as the first example of a recursive program:

```
function Factorial(n: integer): integer;                  {recursive version}
{Pre:  n is a nonnegative integer.
  Post:  The function value is the factorial of n.}
begin                                                     {function Factorial}
   if n = 0 then Factorial := 1
            else Factorial := n * Factorial(n − 1)
end;                                                      {function Factorial}
```

Although this function is simple, there is an equally simple iterative version:

```
function Factorial(n: integer): integer;          {iterative version}
{Pre:  n is a nonnegative integer.
  Post:  The function value is the factorial of n.}
var
   count,
   product: integer;
begin                                             {function Factorial}
   product := 1;
   for count := 2 to n do
      product := product * count;
   Factorial := product
end;                                              {function Factorial}
```

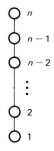

Which of these programs uses less storage space? At first glance, it might appear that the recursive one does, since it has no local variables, and the iterative program has two. But actually (see Figure 12.4), the recursive program will set up a stack and fill it with the $n - 1$ numbers

$$n, n - 1, n - 2, \ldots, 2$$

that are its calling parameters before each recursion and will then, as it works its way out of the recursion, multiply these numbers in the same order as does the second program. The progress of execution for the recursive function applied with $n = 6$ is as follows:

Figure 12.4. Recursion tree for calculating factorials

```
Factorial(6)  = 6 * Factorial(5)
              = 6 * (5 * Factorial(4))
              = 6 * (5 * (4 * Factorial(3)))
              = 6 * (5 * (4 * (3 * Factorial(2))))
              = 6 * (5 * (4 * (3 * (2 * Factorial(1)))))
              = 6 * (5 * (4 * (3 * (2 * 1))))
              = 6 * (5 * (4 * (3 * 2)))
              = 6 * (5 * (4 * 6))
              = 6 * (5 * 24)
              = 6 * 120
              = 720.
```

Thus the recursive program keeps considerably more storage, and will take more time as well, since it must store and retrieve all the numbers as well as multiply them.

12.4.2 Fibonacci Numbers

A far more wasteful example than factorials (that also appears as an apparently recommended program in some textbooks) is the computation of the *Fibonacci numbers*, which are defined by the recurrence relation

$$F_0 = 0, \quad F_1 = 1, \quad F_n = F_{n-1} + F_{n-2} \text{ for } n \geq 2.$$

The recursive program closely follows the definition:

```
function Fibonacci(n: integer): integer;            {recursive version}
{Pre:   The parameter n is a nonnegative integer.
  Post:  The function returns the nth Fibonacci number.}
begin                                               {function Fibonacci}
    if n <= 0 then        Fibonacci := 0
    else if n = 1 then    Fibonacci := 1
    else                  Fibonacci := Fibonacci(n − 1) + Fibonacci (n − 2)
end;                                                {function Fibonacci}
```

In fact, this program is quite attractive, since it is of the divide-and-conquer form: The answer is obtained by calculating two smaller cases. As we shall see, however, in this example it is not "divide and conquer," but "divide and complicate."

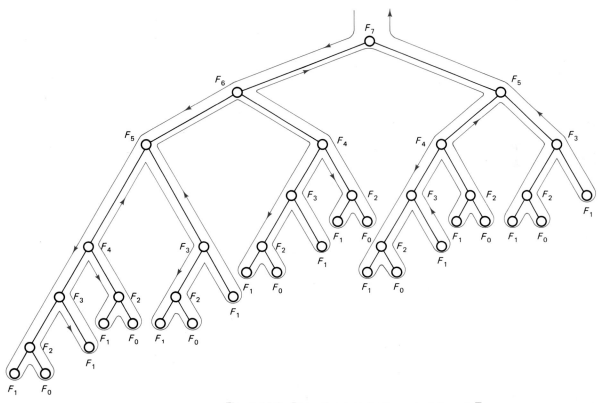

Figure 12.5. Recursion tree for the calculation of F_7

To assess this algorithm, let us consider, as an example, the calculation of F_7, whose recursion tree is shown in Figure 12.5. The procedure will first have to obtain F_6 and F_5. To get F_6 requires F_5 and F_4, and so on. But after F_5 is calculated on the way to F_6, then it will be lost and unavailable when it is later needed to get F_7. Hence, as the recursion tree shows, the recursive program needlessly repeats the same calculations over and over. Further analysis appears as an exercise. It turns out that the amount of time used by the recursive function to calculate F_n grows exponentially with n.

As with factorials, we can produce a simple iterative program by noting that we can start at 0 and keep only three variables, the current Fibonacci number and its two predecessors.

```
function Fibonacci(n: integer): integer;                    {iterative version}
{Pre:    The parameter n is a nonnegative integer.
  Post:  The function returns the nth Fibonacci number.}
var
   i,                                                {loop control variable}
   twoback,                                    {second previous number, Fi−2}
   oneback,                                        {previous number, Fi−1}
   current: integer;                                 {current number, Fi}
begin                                                   {function Fibonacci}
   if n <= 0 then
      Fibonacci := 0
   else if n = 1 then
      Fibonacci := 1
   else begin
      twoback := 0;
      oneback := 1;
      for i := 2 to n do
      begin
         current := twoback + oneback;
         twoback := oneback;
         oneback := current
      end;
      Fibonacci := current
   end
end;                                                    {function Fibonacci}
```

The iterative function obviously uses time that is $O(n)$, so that, as we saw in Section 9.4, the time difference between this function and the exponential time of the recursive function will be vast.

If you regard this nonrecursive program as too tricky, then you can write a straightforward iterative program that sets up a list of length n and calculates F_n simply by starting with F_0 and calculating and storing all the Fibonacci numbers up through F_n. Even this program will use only about n words of storage, which is less than the recursive program will use.

12.4.3 *Comparisons between Recursion and Iteration*

What is fundamentally different between these two examples and the proper uses of recursion that were illustrated in the last chapter, and more of which we shall see in future chapters? To answer this question, we shall again turn to the examination of recursion trees. It should already be clear that a study of the recursion tree will provide much useful information to help us decide when recursion should or should not be used.

chain
If a function or a procedure makes only one recursive call to itself, then its recursion tree has a very simple form: It is a chain; that is, each vertex has only one child. This child corresponds to the single recursive call that occurs. Such a simple tree is easy to comprehend. For the factorial function, it is simply the list of requests to calculate the factorials from $(n-1)!$ down to 1!. By reading the recursion tree from bottom to top instead of top to bottom, we immediately obtain the iterative program from the recursive one. When the tree does reduce to a chain, then transformation from recursion to iteration is often easy, and will likely save both space and time.

Note that a procedure's making only one recursive call to itself is not at all the same as having the recursive call made only one place in the procedure, since this place might be inside a loop. It is also possible to have two places that issue a recursive call (such as both the **then** and **else** clauses of an **if** statement) where only one call can actually occur.

duplicate tasks
The recursion tree for calculating Fibonacci numbers is not a chain, but contains a great many vertices signifying duplicate tasks. When a recursive program is run, it sets up a stack to use while traversing the tree, but if the results stored on the stack are discarded rather than kept in some other data structure for future use, then a great deal of duplication of work may occur, as in the recursive calculation of Fibonacci numbers.

change data structures
In such cases, it is preferable to substitute another data structure for the stack, one that allows references to locations other than the top. The most obvious choice is that of an ordinary list holding all information calculated so far, and this in fact works nicely for the Fibonacci numbers. The iterative program that we wrote for the Fibonacci numbers, the one that uses only three temporary variables, is in one sense tricky, even though it is easy. The reason is that nothing similar is likely to be found for the numbers defined by the following recurrence relation, one that is similar in form to that for the Fibonacci numbers, and could likely not be separated from it by general programming methods:

$$G_0 = 0, \quad G_1 = 1, \quad G_n = G_{n-1} + G_k \text{ for } n \geq 2,$$

where k is $\sqrt{n}$ increased to the next smallest integer.

symmetrical trees
After removal of tail recursion, many programs will perform only one recursive call, but often it is a call within a loop, and therefore their recursion trees will not reduce to chains. In some cases, nonetheless, it is possible to predict what the parameters of each recursive call will be, and thereby to devise an equivalent

nonrecursive program with no stacks. The References in Appendix C include some studies of such methods.

recursion removal

Finally, by setting up an explicit stack, it is possible to take any recursive program and rearrange it into nonrecursive form. The resulting program, however, is often more complicated and harder to understand than is the recursive version, and, for many applications, the saving of space and time is insignificant. On machines with hardware stack instructions, in fact, the nonrecursive form may actually require more running time than the equivalent recursive program.

12.5

GUIDELINES AND CONCLUSIONS

In making a decision, then, about whether to write a particular algorithm in recursive or nonrecursive form, a good starting point is to consider the recursion tree. If it has a simple form, the iterative version may be better. If it involves duplicate tasks, then data structures other than stacks will be appropriate, and the need for recursion may disappear. If the recursion tree appears quite bushy, with little duplication of tasks, then recursion is likely the natural method.

The stack used to resolve recursion can be regarded as a list of postponed obligations for the program. If this list can be easily constructed in advance, then iteration is probably better; if not, recursion may be. Recursion is something of

top-down design

a top-down approach to problem solving; it divides the problem into pieces or selects out one key step, postponing the rest. Iteration is more of a bottom-up approach; it begins with what is known and from this constructs the solution step by step.

It is always true that recursion can be replaced by iteration and stacks. It is

stacks or recursion

also true, conversely (see References for the proof), that any (iterative) program that manipulates a stack can be replaced by a recursive program with no stack. Thus the careful programmer should not only ask whether recursion should be removed, but should also ask, when a program involves stacks, whether the introduction of recursion might produce a more natural and understandable program that could lead to improvements in the approach and in the results.

EXERCISES 12.5

E1. In the recursive calculation of F_n, determine exactly how many times each smaller Fibonacci number will be calculated. From this, determine the order-of-magnitude time and space requirements of the recursive function. [You may find out either by setting up and solving a recurrence relation (top-down approach), or by finding the answer in simple cases and proving it more generally by mathematical induction (bottom-up approach).]

E2. The **greatest common divisor** (GCD) of two positive integers is the largest integer that divides both of them. Thus the GCD of 8 and 12 is 4, the GCD of 9 and 18 is 9, and the GCD of 16 and 25 is 1. Write a recursive function GCD(x, y: integer) that implements the **division algorithm**: If y = 0, then the GCD of x and y is x; otherwise the GCD of x and y is the same as the GCD of y and x **mod** y. Rewrite the function in iterative form.

E3. The binomial coefficients may be defined by the following recurrence relation, which is the idea of **Pascal's triangle**, the top of which is shown in Figure 12.6.

$$C(n,0) = 1 \quad \text{and} \quad C(n,n) = 1 \qquad \text{for } n \geq 0.$$
$$C(n,k) = C(n-1,k) + C(n-1,k-1) \qquad \text{for } n > k > 0.$$

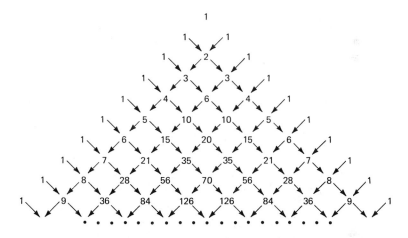

Figure 12.6. The top of Pascal's triangle of binomial coefficients

a. Write a recursive function to generate $C(n,k)$ by the foregoing formula.
b. Draw the recursion tree for calculating $C(6,4)$.
c. Use a square array, and write a nonrecursive program to generate Pascal's triangle in the lower left half of the array.
d. Write a nonrecursive program that uses neither an array nor a stack to calculate $C(n,k)$ for arbitrary $n \geq k \geq 0$.
e. Determine the asymptotic space and time requirements for each of the algorithms devised in parts (a), (c), and (d).

E4. **Ackermann's function**, defined as follows, is a standard device to determine how well recursion is implemented on a computer.

$$A(0,n) = n + 1 \qquad \text{for } n \geq 0.$$
$$A(m,0) = A(m-1,1) \qquad \text{for } m > 0.$$
$$A(m,n) = A(m-1, A(m,n-1)) \qquad \text{for } m > 0 \text{ and } n > 0.$$

  a. Write a recursive function to calculate Ackermann's Function.

  b. Calculate the following values:

$$A(0,0) \quad A(0,9) \quad A(1,8) \quad A(2,2) \quad A(2,0)$$
$$A(2,3) \quad A(3,2) \quad A(4,2) \quad A(4,3) \quad A(4,0)$$

  c. Write a nonrecursive function to calculate Ackermann's function.

POINTERS AND PITFALLS

1. Study several simple examples to see whether recursion should be used and how it will work.

2. Attempt to formulate a method that will work more generally. Ask, "How can this problem be divided into parts?" or "How will the key step in the middle be done?"

3. Ask whether the remainder of the problem can be done in the same or a similar way, and modify your method if necessary so that it will be sufficiently general.

4. Find a stopping rule that will indicate that the problem or a suitable part of it is done.

5. Verify that the recursion will always terminate.

6. Be sure that your algorithm handles extreme cases correctly.

7. The key tool for the analysis of recursive algorithms is the recursion tree. Draw the recursion tree for one or two simple examples appropriate to your problem.

8. The recursion tree should be studied to see whether the recursion is needlessly repeating work, or if the tree represents an efficient division of the work into pieces.

9. Tail recursion should be removed if space considerations are important.

10. A tree that reduces to a chain implies that recursion can be replaced by iteration.

11. If the recursion tree shows complete regularity that can be determined in advance, then sometimes this regularity can be built into the algorithm in a way that will improve efficiency and perhaps remove the recursion.

12. Recursive procedures and iterative procedures using stacks can accomplish exactly the same tasks. Consider carefully whether recursion or iteration will lead to a clearer program and give more insight into the problem.

13. Recursion can always be translated into iteration, but the general rules will often produce a result that greatly obscures the structure of the program. Such obscurity should be tolerated only when the programming language makes it unavoidable, and even then it should be well documented.

REVIEW QUESTIONS

12.1   1. What are the major phases of designing recursive algorithms?

12.2   2. What is *concurrency*?

        3. Name two different ways to implement recursion.

        4. What important kinds of information does the computer system need to keep while implementing a recursive procedure call?

        5. What is a *re-entrant* program?

        6. How does the time requirement for a recursive procedure relate to its recursion tree?

        7. How does the space requirement for a recursive procedure relate to its recursion tree?

12.3   8. What is *tail* recursion?

        9. Is the removal of tail recursion more important for saving time or for saving space?

12.4   10. Describe the relationship between the shape of the recursion tree and the efficiency of the corresponding recursive algorithm.

13

FURTHER SORTING METHODS

This chapter picks up the study of sorting methods from Chapter 10. Recursion, in particular the method of *divide and conquer*, is a powerful tool that gives us two of the most efficient sorting methods known: *mergesort* and *quicksort*. We shall also continue the study of binary trees by examining a new data structure called a *heap* that leads to an excellent sorting method called *heapsort*.

13.1

DIVIDE-AND-CONQUER SORTING

13.1.1 The Main Ideas

shorter is easier

Making a fresh start is often a good idea, and we shall do so by forgetting (temporarily) almost everything that we know about sorting. Let us try to apply only one important principle that has shown up in the methods we have previously studied and that we already know from common experience: It is much easier to sort short lists than long ones. If the number of entries to be sorted doubles, then the work more than doubles (with insertion or selection sort it quadruples, roughly). Hence if we can find a way to divide the list into two roughly equal-sized lists and sort them separately, then we will save work. If, for example, you were working in a library and were given a thousand index cards to put in alphabetical order, then a good way would be to distribute them into piles according to the first letter and sort the piles separately.

divide and conquer

Here again we have an application of the idea of dividing a problem into smaller but similar subproblems, that is, of *divide and conquer*.

First, we note that comparisons by computer are usually two-way branches, so we shall divide the entries to sort into two lists at each stage of the process.

What method, you may ask, should we use to sort the reduced lists? Since we have (temporarily) forgotten all the other methods we know, let us simply use the same method, divide and conquer, again, repeatedly subdividing the list. But we won't keep going forever: Sorting a list with only one entry doesn't take any work, even if we know no formal sorting methods.

In summary, let us informally outline divide-and-conquer sorting:

```
procedure Sort(list)
if the list has length greater than 1 then
begin
      Partition the list into lowlist, highlist;
      Sort(lowlist);
      Sort(highlist);
      Combine(lowlist, highlist)
end.
```

We still must decide how we are going to partition the list into two sublists and, after they are sorted, how we are going to combine the sublists into a single list. There are two methods, each of which works very well in different circumstances.

- *Mergesort*: In the first method, we simply chop the list into two sublists of sizes as nearly equal as possible and then sort them separately. Afterward, we carefully merge the two sorted sublists into a single sorted list. Hence this method is called ***mergesort***.

411

■ *Quicksort*: The second method does more work in the first step of partitioning the list into two sublists, and the final step of combining the sublists then becomes trivial. This method was invented and christened **quicksort** by C. A. R. HOARE. To partition the list, we first choose some key from the list for which, we hope, about half the keys will come before and half after. We shall use the name **pivot** for this selected key. We next partition the entries so that all those with keys less than the pivot come in one sublist, and all those with greater keys come in another. Finally, then, we sort the two reduced lists separately, put the sublists together, and the whole list will be in order.

pivot

13.1.2 An Example

Before we refine our methods into detailed procedures, let us work through a specific example. We take the following seven numbers to sort:

26   33   35   29   19   12   22.

Mergesort Example

The first step of mergesort is to chop the list into two. When (as in this example) the list has odd length, let us establish the convention of making the left sublist one entry larger than the right sublist. Thus we divide the list into

26   33   35   29   and   19   12   22

first half

and first consider the left sublist. It is again chopped in half as

26   33   and   35   29.

For each of these sublists, we again apply the same method, chopping each of them into sublists of one number each. Sublists of length one, of course, require no sorting. Finally, then, we can start to merge the sublists to obtain a sorted list. The sublists 26 and 33 merge to give the sorted list 26 33, and the sublists 35 and 29 merge to give 29 35. At the next step, we merge these two sorted sublists of length two to obtain a sorted sublist of length four,

26   29   33   35.

second half

Now that the left half of the original list is sorted, we do the same steps on the right half. First, we chop it into the sublists

19   12   and   22.

The first of these is divided into two sublists of length one, which are merged to give 12 19. The second sublist, 22, has length one, so it needs no sorting. It is now merged with 12 19 to give the sorted list

12   19   22.

Finally, the sorted sublists of lengths four and three are merged to produce

12   19   22   26   29   33   35.

The way that all these sublists and recursive calls are put together is shown by the recursion tree for mergesort drawn in Figure 13.1. The order in which the recursive calls is shown by the colored path. The numbers in each sublist passed to a recursive call are shown in black, and the numbers in their order after the merge is done are shown in color. The calls for which no further recursion is required (sublists of length 1) are the leaves of the tree and are drawn as squares.

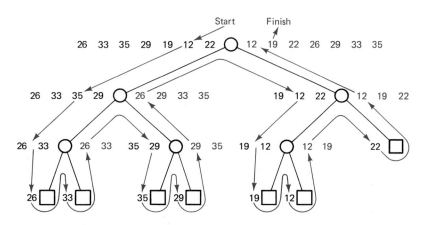

Figure 13.1. Recursion tree, mergesort of 7 numbers

Quicksort Example

Let us again work through the same example, this time applying quicksort, and keeping careful account of the execution of steps from our outline of the method. *choice of pivot* To use quicksort, we must first decide, in order to partition the list into two pieces, what key to choose as the pivot. We are free to choose any number we wish, but, for consistency, we shall adopt a definite rule. Perhaps the simplest rule is to choose the first number on a list as the pivot, and we shall do so in this example. For practical applications, however, other choices are usually better.

partition Our first pivot, then, is 26, and the list partitions into sublists

19   12   22   and   33   35   29

consisting, respectively, of the numbers less than and greater than the pivot. We have left the order of the entries in the sublists unchanged from that in the original list, but this decision also is arbitrary. Some versions of quicksort put the pivot into one of the sublists, but we choose to place the pivot into neither sublist.

We now arrive at the next line of the outline, which tells us to sort the first sublist. We thus start the algorithm over again from the top, but this time applied to the shorter list

$$19 \quad 12 \quad 22.$$

lower half   The pivot of this list is 19, which partitions its list into two sublists of one number each, 12 in the first and 22 in the second. With only one entry each, these sublists do not need sorting, so we arrive at the last line of the outline, whereupon we combine the two sublists with the pivot between them to obtain the sorted list

$$12 \quad 19 \quad 22.$$

Now the call to the sort procedure is finished for this sublist, so it returns whence it was called. It was called from within the sort procedure for the full list of seven numbers, so we now go on to the next line of that procedure.

inner and outer   We have now used the procedure twice, with the second instance occurring
procedure calls   within the first instance. Note carefully that the two instances of the procedure are working on different lists and are as different from each other as is executing the same code twice within a loop. It may help to think of the two instances as having different colors, so that the instructions in the second (inner) call could be written out in full in place of the call, but in a different color, thereby clearly distinguishing them as a separate instance of the procedure. The steps of this process are illustrated in Figure 13.2.

```
Sort (26, 33, 35, 29, 19, 12, 22)
┌─────────────────────────────────────────────────────────┐
│                                                           │
│  Partition into (19, 12, 22) and (33, 35, 29); pivot = 26 │
│  Sort (19, 12, 22)                                        │
│    ┌───────────────────────────────────────────┐         │
│    │ Partition into (12) and (22); pivot = 19    │         │
│    │ Sort (12)                                   │         │
│    │ Sort (22)                                   │         │
│    │ Combine into (12, 19, 22)                   │         │
│    └───────────────────────────────────────────┘         │
│  Sort (33, 35, 29)                                        │
│    ┌───────────────────────────────────────────┐         │
│    │ Partition into (29) and (35); pivot = 33    │         │
│    │ Sort (29)                                   │         │
│    │ Sort (35)                                   │         │
│    │ Combine into (29, 33, 35)                   │         │
│    └───────────────────────────────────────────┘         │
│  Combine into (12, 19, 22, 26, 29, 33, 35)                │
└─────────────────────────────────────────────────────────┘
```

Figure 13.2. Execution trace of quicksort

Returning to our example, we find the next line of the first instance of the procedure to be another call to sort another list, this time the three numbers

33 35 29.

upper half As in the previous (inner) call, the pivot 33 immediately partitions the list, giving sublists of length one that are then combined to produce the sorted list

29 33 35.

Finally, this call to sort returns, and we reach the last line of the (outer) instance that sorts the full list. At this point, the two sorted sublists of length three are combined with the original pivot of 26 to obtain the sorted list

12 19 22 26 29 33 35.

recombine After this step, the process is complete.

The easy way to keep track of all the calls in our quicksort example is to draw its recursion tree, as shown in Figure 13.3. The two calls to Sort at each level are shown as the children of the vertex. The sublists of size 1 or 0, which need no sorting, are drawn as the leaves. In the other vertices (to avoid cluttering the diagram), we include only the pivot that is used for the call. It is, however, not hard to read all the numbers in each sublist (but not necessarily in their original order): The numbers in the sublist at each recursive call are the number at the corresponding vertex and those at all descendents of the vertex.

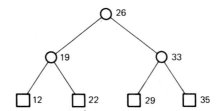

Figure 13.3. Recursion tree, quicksort of 7 numbers

example If you are still uneasy about the workings of recursion, then you will find it helpful to pause and work through sorting the list of 14 names introduced in previous sections, using both mergesort and quicksort. As a check, Figure 13.4 provides the tree of calls for quicksort in the same abbreviated form used for the previous example. This tree is given for two versions, one where the pivot is the first key in each sublist, and one where the central key (center left for even-sized lists) is the pivot.

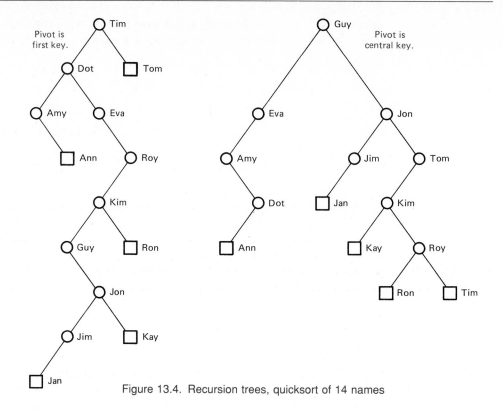

Figure 13.4. Recursion trees, quicksort of 14 names

EXERCISES 13.1

E1. Apply quicksort to the list of seven numbers considered in this section, where the pivot in each sublist is chosen to be **(a)** the last number in the sublist and **(b)** the center (or left-center) number in the sublist. In each case, draw the tree of recursive calls.

E2. Apply mergesort to the list of 14 names considered for previous sorting methods:

Tim Dot Eva Roy Tom Kim Guy Amy Jon Ann Jim Kay Ron Jan.

E3. Apply quicksort to this list of 14 names, and thereby sort them by hand into alphabetical order. Take the pivot to be **(a)** the first key in each sublist and **(b)** the center (or left-center) key in each sublist. See Figure 13.4.

E4. In both divide-and-conquer methods, we have attempted to divide the list into two sublists of approximately equal size, but the basic outline of sorting by divide-and-conquer remains valid without equal-sized halves. Consider dividing the list so that one sublist has size only 1. This leads to two methods, depending on whether the work is done in splitting one element from the list or in combining the sublists.

a. Split the list by finding the entry with the largest key and making it the sublist of size 1. After sorting the remaining entries, the sublists are combined easily by placing the entry with largest key last.

b. Split off the last entry from the list. After sorting the remaining entries, merge this entry into the list.

Show that one of these methods is exactly the same method as insertion sort and the other is the same as selection sort.

13.2

MERGESORT FOR LINKED LISTS

Let us now turn to the writing of formal procedures for each of our sorting methods. In the case of mergesort, we shall write a version for linked lists and leave the case of contiguous lists as an exercise. For quicksort, we shall do the reverse. Both of these methods, however, work well for both contiguous and linked lists.

Mergesort is also an excellent method for *external sorting*, that is, for problems in which the data are kept on disks or magnetic tapes, not in high-speed memory.

13.2.1 The Procedures

Our outline of the basic method for mergesort translates directly into the following procedure. Note that we have written this procedure in an implementation-independent form. Only the subsidiary procedures will use the specifics of a linked-list implementation.

main procedure, mergesort

```
procedure MergeSort(var L: listtype);
{Pre:    The list L has been created. The entries of L all contain keys.
 Post:   The entries of L have been rearranged so that all the keys in the
         entries are sorted into nondecreasing order.
 Uses:   Procedure Divide chops a list in half, and procedure Merge combines
         two sorted sublists.}
var secondhalf: listtype;        {holds the second half of the list after division}
begin                                               {procedure MergeSort}
  if ListSize(L) > 1 then
  begin                                     {Otherwise, there is no need to sort.}
    Divide(L, secondhalf);                         {Chop the list in half.}
    MergeSort(L);                                    {Sort the first half.}
    MergeSort(secondhalf);                          {Sort the second half.}
    Merge(L, secondhalf, L)      {Merge the two sorted sublists into one.}
  end
end;                                                {procedure MergeSort}
```

The first subsidiary procedure called by MergeSort, Divide(L, secondhalf), takes the list L, divides it in half, and returns with the first half in L and the second half in secondhalf.

chop a linked list in half

```
procedure Divide (var L, secondhalf: listtype);
{Pre:   The linked list L has been created.
 Post:  List L has been reduced to its first half, and the second half of the
        entries from L are in the linked list secondhalf.  If L has an odd number
        of entries, then its first half will be one entry larger than its second.}
var
  current,                                    {traverses the entire list L}
  midpoint: listpointer;           {moves at half speed to find the midpoint}
begin                                                    {procedure Divide}
  midpoint := L.head;                            {Start midpoint at position 1.}
  if midpoint = nil then              {If L is empty, then so is secondhalf.}
    secondhalf.head := nil
  else begin
    current := midpoint↑.nextnode;       {Start current at second position.}
    while current <> nil do
    begin                 {Move current twice for each move of midpoint.}
      current := current↑.nextnode;
      if current <> nil then
      begin
        midpoint := midpoint↑.nextnode;
        current := current↑.nextnode
      end
    end;
    secondhalf.head := midpoint↑.nextnode;        {Break after midpoint↑.}
    midpoint↑.nextnode := nil;                    {Terminate the first half.}
  end                                               {case of a nonempty list}
end;                                                     {procedure Divide}
```

The second procedure, Merge (first, second, out), merges the lists first and second, returning the merged list as its third parameter out. The action of procedure Merge is illustrated in Figure 13.5.

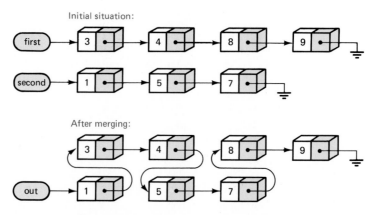

Figure 13.5. Merging two sorted linked lists

merge two sorted
linked lists

procedure Merge (first, second: listtype; **var** out: listtype) ;
{**Pre:** first *and* second *are ordered linked lists and have been created.*
    Post: out *is an ordered linked list containing all entries that were in* first *and*
        second. *The original lists* first *and* second *have been destroyed.*}
var
  p1,
  p2,   {*used to traverse first and second lists*}
  lastsorted: listpointer;   {*always points to last node of sorted list*}
begin   {*procedure Merge*}
  if first.head = **nil then**
    out := second
  else if second.head = **nil then**
    out := first
  else begin   {*First find the head of the merged list.*}
    p1 := first.head;
    p2 := second.head;
    if p1↑.entry.key <= p2↑.entry.key **then**
    begin
      out := first;
      p1 := p1↑.nextnode
    end
    else begin
      out := second;
      p2 := p2↑.nextnode
    end;
    lastsorted := out.head;   {lastsorted *gives last entry of merged list.*}
    while (p1 <> **nil**) **and** (p2 <> **nil**) **do**
      if p1↑.entry.key <= p2↑.entry.key **then**
      begin   {*Attach the node with the smaller key to the sorted list.*}
        lastsorted↑.nextnode := p1;
        lastsorted := p1;
        p1 := p1↑.next   {*Advance to the next unmerged node.*}
      end
      else begin
        lastsorted↑.nextnode := p2;
        lastsorted := p2;
        p2 := p2↑.nextnode
      end;
{*After one of the lists ends, attach the remainder of the other list.*}
    if p1 = **nil then**
      lastsorted↑.nextnode := p2
    else
      lastsorted↑.nextnode := p1
  end
end;   {*procedure Merge*}

13.2.2 Analysis of Mergesort

Now that we have a working procedure for mergesort, it is time to pause and determine its behavior, so that we can make reasonable comparisons with other sorting methods. As with other algorithms on linked lists, we need not be concerned with the time needed to move entries. We concentrate instead on the number of comparisons of keys that the procedure will do.

Counting Comparisons

merge procedure

Comparison of keys is done at only one place in the complete mergesort procedure. This place is within the main loop of the merge procedure. After each comparison, one of the two nodes is sent to the output list. Hence the number of comparisons certainly cannot exceed the number of nodes being merged. To find the total lengths of these lists, let us again consider the recursion tree of the algorithm, which for simplicity we show in Figure 13.6 for the case when $n = 2^m$ is a power of 2.

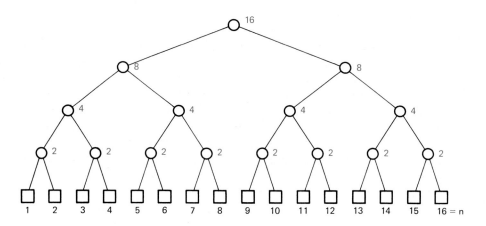

Figure 13.6. Lengths of sublist merges

It is clear from the tree of Figure 13.6 that the total lengths of the lists on each level is precisely n, the total number of entries. In other words, every entry is treated in precisely one merge on each level. Hence the total number of comparisons done on each level cannot exceed n. The number of levels, excluding the leaves (for which no merges are done), is $\lg n$ rounded up to the next smallest integer. The number of comparisons of keys done by mergesort on a list of n entries, therefore, is no more than $n \lg n$ rounded upward.

Contrast with Insertion Sort

Recall (Section 10.2.3) that insertion sort does more than $\frac{1}{4}n^2$ comparisons of keys, on average, in sorting n entries. As soon as n becomes greater than 16, $\lg n$

becomes less than $\frac{1}{4}n$, and when n is of practical size for sorting a list, $\lg n$ is far less than $\frac{1}{4}n$, and therefore the number of comparisons done by mergesort is far less than the number done by insertion sort. When $n = 1024$, for example, then $\lg n = 10$, so that the bound on comparisons for mergesort is 10,240, whereas the average number that insertion sort will do is more than 250,000. A problem requiring a half-hour of computer time using insertion sort will probably require hardly a minute using mergesort.

$n \lg n$ The appearance of the expression $n \lg n$ in the preceding calculation is by no means accidental, but relates closely to the lower bounds established in Section 10.5, where it was proved that any sorting method that uses comparisons of keys must do at least

$$\lg n! = n \lg n + O(n)$$

comparisons of keys. When n is large, the first term of this expression becomes more important than what remains. We have now found, in mergesort, an algorithm that comes within reach of this lower bound.

Conclusions

advantages of
linked mergesort

From these remarks, it may appear that mergesort is the ultimate sorting method, and, indeed, for linked lists in random order, it is difficult to surpass. We must remember, however, that considerations other than comparing keys are important. The program we have written spends significant time finding the center of the list, so that it can break it in half. The Exercises discuss one method for saving some of this time. The linked version of mergesort uses space efficiently. It needs no large auxiliary arrays or other lists, and since the depth of recursion is only $\lg n$, the amount of space needed to keep track of the recursive calls is very small.

Contiguous Mergesort

three-way
trade-off for
merging

For contiguous lists, unfortunately, mergesort is not such an unqualified success. The difficulty is in merging two contiguous lists without substantial expense in one of (1) space, (2) computer time, or (3) programming effort. The first and most straightforward way to merge two contiguous lists is to use an auxiliary array large enough to hold the combined list and copy the entries into the array as the lists are merged. This method requires extra space proportional to n. For a second method, we could put the sublists to be merged next to each other, forget the amount of order they already have, and use a method like insertion sort to put the combined list into order. This approach uses almost no extra space, but uses computer time proportional to n^2, compared to time proportional to n for a good merging algorithm. Finally (see the References in Appendix C), algorithms have been invented that will merge two contiguous lists in time proportional to n while using only a small, fixed amount of extra space. These algorithms, however, are very complicated and hard to understand.

■■■■■■ EXERCISES 13.2

E1. An article in a 1984 professional journal stated, "This recursive process [mergesort] takes time $O(n \log n)$, and so runs 64 times faster than the previous method [insertion sort] when sorting 256 numbers." Criticize this statement.

E2. The count of key comparisons in merging is usually too high, since it does not account for the fact that one list may be finished before the other. It might happen, for example, that all entries in the first list come before any in the second list, so that the number of comparisons is just the length of the first list. For this exercise, assume that all numbers in the two lists are different and that all possible arrangements of the numbers are equally likely.

a. Show that the average number of comparisons performed by our algorithm to merge two ordered lists of length 2 is $8/3$. [*Hint*: Start with the ordered list 1, 2, 3, 4. Write down the six ways of putting these numbers into two ordered lists of length 2, and show that four of these ways will use 3 comparisons, and two will use 2 comparisons.]

b. Show that the average number of comparisons done to merge two ordered lists of length 3 is 4.5.

c. Show that the average number of comparisons done to merge two ordered lists of length 4 is 6.4.

d. Use the foregoing results to obtain the improved total count of key comparisons for mergesort.

e. Show that, as m tends to infinity, the average number of comparisons done to merge two ordered lists of length m approaches $2m - 2$.

■■■■■■ PROJECTS 13.2

P1. Implement mergesort for linked lists on your computer. Use the same conventions and the same test data used for implementing and testing the linked version of insertion sort. Compare the performance of mergesort and insertion sort for short and long lists, as well as for lists nearly in correct order and in random order.

P2. Our mergesort program for linked lists spends significant time locating the center of each sublist, so that it can be broken in half. Implement the following modification that will save most of this time. First set up a record to describe a linked list that will contain not only (a) a pointer to the head of the list, but also (b) a pointer to the center of the list and (c) the length of the list. At the beginning, the original list must be traversed once to determine this information. With this information, it becomes easy to break the list in half and obtain the lengths of the sublists. The center of a sublist can be found by traversing only half the sublist. Rewrite the mergesort procedure to pass the records describing linked lists as calling parameters, and use them to simplify the subdivision of the lists.

P3. Our mergesort procedure pays little attention to whether or not the original list was partially in the correct order. In ***natural mergesort***, the list is broken into sublists at the end of an increasing sequence of keys, instead of arbitrarily at its halfway point. This project requests the implementation of two versions of natural mergesort.

natural mergesort

In the first version, the original list is traversed only once, and only two sublists are used. As long as the order of the keys is correct, the nodes are placed in the first sublist. When a key is found out of order, the first sublist is ended and the second started. When another key is found out of order, the second sublist is ended, and it is merged into the first. Then the second sublist is repeatedly built again and merged into the first. When the end of the original list is reached, the sort is finished. This first version is simple to program, but as it proceeds, the first sublist is likely to become much longer than the second, and the performance of the procedure will degenerate toward that of insertion sort.

one sorted list

The second version ensures that the lengths of sublists being merged are closer to being equal and, therefore, that the advantages of divide and conquer are fully used. This method keeps a (small) auxiliary array containing (a) the lengths and (b) pointers to the heads of the ordered sublists that are not yet merged. The entries in this array should be kept in order according to the length of the sublist. As each (naturally ordered) sublist is split from the original list, it is put into the auxiliary array. If there is another list in the array whose length is between half and twice that of the new list, then the two are merged, and the process repeated. When the original list is exhausted, any remaining sublists in the array are merged (smaller lengths first) and the sort is finished.

several sorted lists

There is nothing sacred about the ratio of 2 in the criterion for merging sublists. Its choice merely ensures that the number of entries in the auxiliary array cannot exceed $\lg n$ (prove it!). A smaller ratio (required to be greater than 1) will make the auxiliary table larger, and a larger ratio will lessen the advantages of divide and conquer. Experiment with test data to find a good ratio to use.

P4. Devise a version of mergesort for contiguous lists. The difficulty is to produce a procedure to merge two sorted lists in contiguous storage. It is necessary to use some additional space other than that needed by the two lists. The easiest solution is to use two arrays, each large enough to hold all the entries in the two original lists. The two sorted sublists occupy different parts of the same array. As they are merged, the new list is built in the second array. After the merge is complete, the new list can, if desired, be copied back into the first array. Otherwise, the roles of the two arrays can be reversed for the next stage.

13.3

QUICKSORT FOR CONTIGUOUS LISTS

We now turn to the method of quicksort, in which the list is first partitioned into lower and upper sublists for which all keys are, respectively, less than some pivot key or greater than the pivot key.

Quicksort can be developed for linked lists with little difficulty, and doing so appears as a Project. The most important applications of quicksort, however, are to contiguous lists, where it can prove to be very fast, and where it has the advantage over contiguous mergesort of not requiring a choice between using substantial extra space for an auxiliary array or investing great programming effort in implementing a complicated and difficult merge algorithm.

13.3.1 The Main Procedure

Our task in developing contiguous quicksort consists essentially in writing an algorithm for partitioning entries in a list by use of a pivot key, swapping the entries within the list so that all those with keys before the pivot come first, then the entry with the pivot key, and then the entries with larger keys. We shall let pivotlocation provide the index of the pivot in the partitioned list.

Since the partitioned sublists are kept in the same array, in the proper relative positions, the final step of combining sorted sublists is completely vacuous and thus is omitted from the procedure.

To apply the sorting procedure recursively to sublists, the bounds low and high of the sublists need to be parameters for the procedure. Our other sorting procedures, however, had the list L as the only parameter, so, for consistency with our standard use of parameters, we do the recursion in a procedure Sort that is invoked by the following procedure:

main procedure
for quicksort

```
procedure QuickSort(var L: listtype);
  {Pre:   The contiguous list L has been created. The entries of L all contain
          keys.
   Post:  The entries of L have been rearranged so that all the keys in the
          entries are sorted into nondecreasing order.
   Uses:  Procedure Sort to do the actual recursive quicksort.}
begin
  Sort(L, 1, L.count)
end;
```

The actual quicksort procedure for contiguous lists is then

recursive procedure for quicksort

procedure Sort(**var** L: listtype; low, high: integer);
{**Pre:** *The contiguous list* L *has been created, and, if* low < high, *then* L
           contains entries indexed from low *to* high, *inclusive.*
   Post: *The entries of* L *between indices* low *and* high, *inclusive, have been
           sorted into nondecreasing order according to their keys.*
   Uses: *Procedure* Partition}
var
   pivotlocation: listindex;   {*location of the pivot after partitioning*}
begin   {*procedure Sort*}
   if low < high **then**   {*If not, then no sorting is needed.*}
   begin
      Partition(L, low, high, pivotlocation);
      Sort(L, low, pivotlocation − 1);
      Sort(L, pivotlocation + 1, high)
   end
end;   {*procedure Sort*}

13.3.2 Partitioning the List

Now we must construct the procedure Partition. There are several methods that we might use (one of which is suggested as an Exercise), methods that sometimes are faster than the algorithm we develop but that are intricate and difficult to get correct. The algorithm we develop is much simpler and easier to understand, and it is certainly not slow; in fact, it does the smallest possible number of key comparisons of any partitioning algorithm.

Algorithm Development

Given a pivot value p, we must rearrange the entries of the array and compute the index pivotlocation so that the pivot is at pivotlocation, all entries to its left have keys less than p, and all entries to its right have larger keys. To allow for the possibility that more than one entry has key equal to p, we insist that the entries to the left of pivotlocation have keys strictly less than p, and the entries to its right have keys greater than or equal to p, as shown in the following diagram:

goal (postcondition)

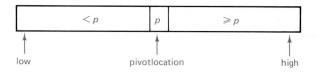

To reorder the entries this way, we must compare each key to the pivot. We shall use a **for** loop (running on a variable i) to do this. We shall use a second variable lastsmall such that all entries at or before location lastsmall have keys less than p. Suppose that the pivot p starts in the first position, and let us leave it there temporarily. Then, in the middle of the loop, the array has the following property:

loop invariant

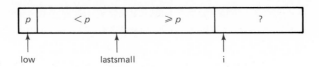

When the procedure inspects entry i, there are two cases. If the entry is greater than or equal to p, then i can be increased and the array still has the required property. If the entry is less than p, then we restore the property by increasing lastsmall and swapping that entry (the first of those at least p) with entry i, as shown in the following diagrams:

restore the invariant

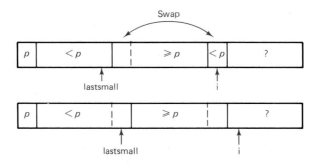

When the loop terminates, we have the situation:

final position

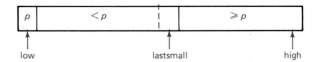

and we then need only swap the pivot from position low to position lastsmall to obtain the desired final arrangement.

Choice of Pivot

We are not bound to the choice of the first entry in the list as the pivot; we can choose any entry we wish and swap it with the first entry before beginning the loop that partitions the list. In fact, the first entry is often a poor choice for pivot, since if the list is already sorted, then the first key will have no others less than it, and so one of the sublists will be empty. Hence, let us instead choose a pivot *pivot from center* near the center of the list, in the hope that our choice will partition the keys so that about half come on each side of the pivot.

Coding

With these decisions, we obtain the following procedure, in which we use the swap procedure from Section 10.3. For convenience of reference, we also include the property that holds during iteration of the loop as an assertion (loop invariant) in the procedure.

procedure Partition(**var** L: listtype; low, high: listindex;
 var pivotlocation: listindex);
{**Pre:** *The contiguous list* L *has been created and indices* low *and* high *refer to entries of* L.

 Post: *The center (or left center) entry of* L *has been chosen as a pivot and moved to index* pivotlocation. *All entries of* L *between indices* low *and* high, *inclusive, have been rearranged so that those with keys less than the pivot come before* pivotlocation *and the remaining entries come after* pivotlocation.

 Uses: *Procedure* Swap(i, j, L), *which interchanges the entries in indices* i *and* j *of contiguous list* L.}
var
 pivot: keytype; {*will be taken from the center of the list*}
 i, {*used to scan through the list*}
 lastsmall: listindex; {*last key less than pivot*}
begin {*procedure Partition*}
 Swap(low, (low + high) **div** 2, L); {*Swap pivot into first location.*}
 pivot := L.entry[low].key;
 lastsmall := low;
 for i := low + 1 **to** high **do**
{*At the beginning of each iteration of this loop, we have the following conditions:*

 If low < j <= lastsmall *then* L.entry[j].key < pivot.
 If lastsmall < j < i *then* L.entry[j].key >= pivot.}

  if L.entry[i].key < pivot **then**
  begin
   lastsmall := lastsmall + 1;
   Swap(lastsmall, i, L)
   {*Move the large entry to the right and the small entry* i *to the left.*}
  end;
 Swap(low, lastsmall, L); {*Put the pivot into its proper position.*}
 pivotlocation := lastsmall
end; {*procedure Partition*}

13.3.3 Analysis of Quicksort

It is now time to examine the quicksort algorithm carefully. We wish to find the conditions under which it will work well and the conditions under which it will behave poorly. We shall also determine how much computation quicksort will do in sorting a list in random order.

Choice of Pivot

Our choice of a key at the center of the list to be the pivot is arbitrary. This choice may succeed in dividing the list nicely in half, or we may be unlucky and find that one sublist is much larger than the other. Some other methods for choosing the pivot are considered in the Exercises. An extreme case for our method occurs for the following list, where every one of the pivots selected turns out to be the largest key in its sublist:

$$2 \quad 4 \quad 6 \quad 7 \quad 3 \quad 1 \quad 5$$

Check it out, using the Partition procedure in the text. When quicksort is applied to this list, its label will appear to be quite a misnomer, since, at the first recursion, the nonempty sublist will have length 6, at the second, 5, and so on.

If we were to choose the pivot as the first key or the last key in each sublist, then the extreme case would occur when the keys are in their natural order or in their reverse order. These orders, of course, are more likely to happen than some random order, and therefore choosing the first or last key as pivot is likely to cause problems.

The worst-case performance of quicksort is, in fact, disastrous: It makes as many comparisons of keys as the worst case of selection sort, and making too many comparisons of keys was the weak point of selection sort (as compared with insertion sort). In its worst case, quicksort makes about three times as many movements of entries as the worst case of insertion sort, and moving too many entries was the weak point of insertion sort in comparison with selection sort. Indeed, in its worst case, quicksort is a disaster, and its name is nothing less than false advertising.

excellent average-case behavior

It must be for some other reason that quicksort was not long ago consigned to the scrap heap of programs that never worked. The reason is the *average* behavior of quicksort when applied to lists in random order, which turns out to be one of the best of any sorting methods (using key comparisons and applied to contiguous lists) yet known!

13.3.4 Average-Case Analysis of Quicksort

The average-case analysis of quicksort requires quite a bit of mathematics, but the outcome is a very interesting result that makes the effort worthwhile. And, along the way, we shall see some mathematical techniques (recurrence relations and harmonic numbers) that are important in the more advanced study of algorithms.

To do the average-case analysis, we shall assume that all possible orderings of the list are equally likely, and, for simplicity, we take the keys to be just the integers from 1 to n in some random order.

Counting Comparisons

When we select the pivot in the procedure Partition, it is equally likely to be any one of the keys. Denote by p whatever key is selected as pivot. Then, after the partition, key p is guaranteed to be in index p, since the keys $1, \ldots, p-1$ are all to its left and $p+1, \ldots, n$ are to its right.

The number of comparisons of keys that will have been made in the call to Partition is $n-1$, since every entry in the list is compared to the pivot, except for the pivot entry itself. Let us denote by $C(n)$ the average number of comparisons done by quicksort on a list of length n and by $C(n,p)$ the average number of comparisons on a list of length n where the pivot for the first partition turns out to be p. The remaining work, done in the recursive calls, consists of $C(p-1)$ comparisons for the sublist of entries less than the pivot and $C(n-p)$ comparisons for the sublist of entries greater than the pivot. We have now shown that, for $n \geq 2$,

$$C(n,p) = n - 1 + C(p-1) + C(n-p).$$

To find an expression for $C(n)$, we must now take the average of these expressions, since p is random, by adding them from $p=1$ to $p=n$ and dividing by n. We obtain the following fundamental equation for the number of comparisons done by quicksort in the average case for sorting n items.

$$C(n) = n - 1 + \frac{2}{n}(C(0) + C(1) + \cdots + C(n-1)).$$

Solving the Recurrence Relation

An equation of the form that we have just obtained is called a ***recurrence relation*** because it expresses the answer to a problem in terms of earlier, smaller cases of the same problem. We wish to solve the recurrence relation, which means that we wish to find an expression for $C(n)$ that does not involve $C(\ )$ on the other side of the equation. There are many different techniques (some quite difficult) for solving recurrence relations.

The first step toward solving the present recurrence relation is to note that, if we were sorting a list of length $n-1$, we would obtain exactly the same expression with n replaced by $n-1$, provided that $n \geq 2$:

$$C(n-1) = n - 2 + \frac{2}{n-1}(C(0) + C(1) + \cdots + C(n-2)).$$

Multiplying the first expression by n, the second by $n-1$, and subtracting, we obtain

$$nC(n) - (n-1)C(n-1) = n(n-1) - (n-1)(n-2) + 2C(n-1),$$

since all the terms in the sum on the right sides cancel except for $C(n-1)$. Next, we rearrange this equation as

$$\frac{C(n) - 2}{n + 1} = \frac{C(n - 1) - 2}{n} + \frac{2}{n + 1}.$$

The reason for choosing this mysterious form is to make the terms involving $C(n)$ and $C(n - 1)$ the same except for replacing n by $n - 1$ while, at the same time, to make what is left over particularly simple.

This relation holds for all $n \geq 2$, and, for $n = 1$, we know that no comparisons are done in sorting a list of length 1, so $C(1) = 0$. We now solve the equation by working our way down from n, each time replacing the expression by a smaller case until we reach $n = 1$:

$$\begin{aligned} \frac{C(n) - 2}{n + 1} &= \frac{C(n - 1) - 2}{n} + \frac{2}{n + 1} \\ &= \frac{C(n - 2) - 2}{n - 1} + \frac{2}{n + 1} + \frac{2}{n} \\ &= \frac{C(n - 3) - 2}{n - 2} + \frac{2}{n + 1} + \frac{2}{n} + \frac{2}{n - 1} \\ &\ \ \vdots \\ &= \frac{C(2) - 2}{3} + \frac{2}{n + 1} + \frac{2}{n} + \frac{2}{n - 1} + \cdots + \frac{2}{4} \\ &= \frac{C(1) - 2}{2} + \frac{2}{n + 1} + \frac{2}{n} + \frac{2}{n - 1} + \cdots + \frac{2}{4} + \frac{2}{3} \\ &= -1 + 2\left(\frac{1}{n + 1} + \frac{1}{n} + \frac{1}{n - 1} + \cdots + \frac{1}{4} + \frac{1}{3}\right). \end{aligned}$$

Harmonic Numbers

The next step in solving the recurrence is to evaluate the sum on the right-hand side, and this we do by first calculating

$$H(n) = 1 + \frac{1}{2} + \cdots + \frac{1}{n}.$$

This sum of the reciprocals of the integers from 1 to n is called the nth *harmonic number*.

To evaluate H_n, we use calculus, and consider the function $1/x$, together with the relationship shown in Figure 13.7. The area under the step function is clearly H_n, since the width of each step is 1, and the height of step k is $1/k$, for each integer k from 1 to n. This area is approximated by the area under the curve $1/x$ from $\frac{1}{2}$ to $n + \frac{1}{2}$. The area under the curve is

$$\int_{\frac{1}{2}}^{n + \frac{1}{2}} \frac{1}{x}\, dx = \ln(n + \tfrac{1}{2}) - \ln(\tfrac{1}{2}) \approx \ln n + 0.7.$$

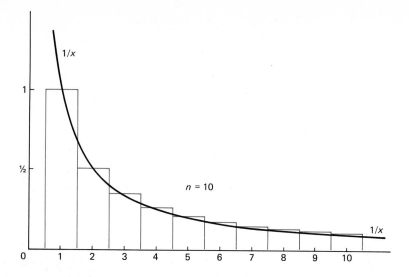

Figure 13.7. Approximation of harmonic numbers by an integral

Finally, we use the big Oh notation to replace the constant by $O(1)$, and thereby we obtain

The **harmonic numbers** *have the values*

$$H(n) = 1 + \frac{1}{2} + \cdots + \frac{1}{n} = \ln n + O(1).$$

Completing the Solution

With all of this information, we can finally complete the calculation of $C(n)$, the average number of comparisons of keys that quicksort makes in sorting a list of size n. We note that the sum in our last expression for $C(n)$ differs from the harmonic number $H(n + 1)$ only by missing the first two terms of $H(n + 1)$, which are 1 and $\frac{1}{2}$. Both of these terms are $O(1)$, as are the first term of the expression, -1, and the difference between $H(n + 1)$ and $H(n)$. We can thus combine all these terms as $O(1)$, substitute the expression for $H(n)$, and thereby obtain

$$\frac{C(n) - 2}{n + 1} = 2 \ln n + O(1).$$

The final step is to solve this equation for $C(n)$, noting that, when we multiply $O(1)$ by $n + 1$, we obtain an expression that is $O(n)$. We therefore summarize our results as:

> *In its average case, quicksort performs*
>
> $$C(n) = 2n \ln n + O(n)$$
>
> *comparisons of keys in sorting a list of n entries.*

Comparison with Mergesort

To compare this result with those for other sorting methods, we note that

$$\ln n = (\ln 2)(\lg n)$$

and $\ln 2 \approx 0.693$, so that

$$C(n) \approx 1.386 n \lg n + O(n).$$

key comparisons

This calculation shows that, on average, quicksort does about 39 percent more comparisons of keys than required by the lower bound and, therefore, also about 39 percent more than does mergesort. The reason, of course, is that mergesort is carefully designed to divide the list into halves of essentially equal size, whereas the sizes of the sublists for quicksort cannot be predicted in advance. Hence it is possible that quicksort's performance can be seriously degraded, but such an occurrence is unlikely in practice, so that averaging the times of poor performance with those of good performance yields the result just obtained.

Correspondence with Treesort

Quicksort and treesort are close relatives, even though treesort works on the dynamic structure of a binary search tree, and quicksort works on a linear list, even a contiguous list. In the first stage of quicksort, every key is compared with the first pivot key, and then put into the left or the right sublist. In treesort, as each key is inserted into the tree it is compared with the root key and then goes into either the left or right subtree. In treesort, however, as each node comes in, it goes into its final position in the linked structure, whereas in quicksort, each entry may be moved several times.

The second node becomes the root of either the left or right subtree (depending on the comparison of its key with the root key). From then on, all keys going into the same subtree are compared to this second one. Similarly, in quicksort, all keys in one sublist are compared to the second pivot, the one for that sublist. Continuing in this way, we can make the following observation.

> *Treesort makes exactly the same comparisons of keys as does quicksort when the pivot for each sublist is chosen to be the first key in the sublist.*

As we know, quicksort is usually an excellent method. On average, only merge-sort among the methods we studied makes fewer key comparisons. Hence, on average, we can expect treesort also to be an excellent sorting method in terms of key comparisons.

We can, in fact, use the correspondence between quicksort and treesort to obtain the average number of comparisons needed to search for a target in a random binary search tree. Treesort operates by searching once for each entry inserted into the tree. Hence the average number of comparisons done in a search is $1/n$ multiplied by the number of comparisons done by treesort. This number is the same as the average number of comparisons done by quicksort, and we have already proved that this number is $2n \ln n + O(n)$. We therefore obtain:

> *The average number of comparisons of keys needed to search for a target in a random binary search tree is*
>
> $$2 \ln n + O(1) \approx 1.386 \lg n + O(1).$$

Comparison of Quicksort and Treesort

advantages of treesort

Quicksort needs to have access to all the entries to be sorted throughout the process. With treesort, the nodes need not all be available at the start of the process, but are built into the tree one by one as they become available. Hence treesort is preferable for applications where the nodes are received one at a time. The major advantage of treesort is that its search tree remains available for later insertions and deletions, and that the tree can subsequently be searched in logarithmic time, whereas all our previous sorting methods either required contiguous lists, for which insertions and deletions are difficult, or produced simply linked lists, for which only sequential search is available.

drawbacks of treesort

The major drawback of treesort is already implicit in its correspondence with quicksort. Quicksort has a very poor performance in its worst case, and, although a careful choice of pivots makes this case extremely unlikely, the choice of pivot to be the first key in each sublist produces the worst case whenever the keys are already sorted. If the keys are presented to treesort already sorted, then treesort too will be a disaster—the search tree it builds will reduce to a chain. Treesort should never be used if the keys are already sorted, or are nearly so. There are few other reservations about treesort that are not equally applicable to all linked structures. For small problems with small entries, contiguous storage is usually the better choice, but for large problems and bulky records, linked storage comes into its own.

■■■■■■ **EXERCISES 13.3**

E1. How will the quicksort procedure (as presented in the text) function if all the keys in the list are equal?

E2. [Due to KNUTH] Describe an algorithm that will arrange a contiguous list whose keys are real numbers so that all the entries with negative keys will come first, then those with nonnegative keys. The final list need not be completely sorted. Make your algorithm do as few movements of entries and as few comparisons as possible. Do not use an auxiliary array.

E3. [Due to HOARE] Suppose that, instead of sorting, we wish only to find the mth smallest key in a given list of size n. Show how quicksort can be adapted to this problem, doing much less work than a complete sort.

E4. Given a list of integers, develop a procedure, similar to the partition procedure, that will rearrange the integers so that either all the integers in even-numbered positions will be even or all the integers in odd-numbered positions will be odd. (Your procedure will provide a proof that one or the other of these goals can always be attained, although it may not be possible to establish both at once.)

E5. A different method for choosing the pivot in quicksort is to take the median of the first, last, and central keys of the list. Describe the modifications needed to the procedure QuickSort (contiguous version) to implement this choice. How much extra computation will be done? For $n = 7$, find an ordering of the keys

$$1, 2, \ldots, 7$$

that will force the algorithm into its worst case. How much better is this worst case than that of the original algorithm?

E6. Suppose that the keys in a list are numbers. A different approach to the selection of pivot is to take the mean (average) of all the keys in the list as the pivot. The resulting algorithm is called *meansort*.

meansort

 a. Write a procedure to implement meansort. The partition procedure must be modified, since the mean of the keys is not necessarily one of the keys in the list. On the first pass, the pivot can be chosen any way you wish. As the keys are then partitioned, running sums and counts are kept for the two sublists, and thereby the means (which will be the new pivots) of the sublists can be calculated without making any extra passes through the list.

 b. In meansort, the relative *sizes* of the keys determine how nearly equal the sublists will be after partitioning; the initial *order* of the keys is of no importance, except for counting the number of swaps that will take place. How bad can the worst case for comparisons of keys by meansort be in terms of the relative sizes of the two sublists? Find a set of n integers that will produce the worst case for meansort.

E7. [Requires elementary probability theory] A good way to choose the pivot is to use a random-number generator to choose the index for the next pivot at each call to Sort. Using the fact that these choices are independent, find the probability that quicksort will happen upon its worst case.

    a. Do the problem for $n = 7$.

    b. Do the problem for general n.

optimize Partition

E8. At the cost of a few more comparisons of keys, the partition procedure can be rewritten so that the number of swaps is reduced by a factor of about 3, from $n/2$ to $n/6$ on average. The idea is to use two indices moving from the ends of the lists toward the center and to perform a swap only when a large key is found by the low index and a small key by the high index. This exercise outlines the development of such a procedure.

    a. Establish two indices i and j, and maintain the invariant property that all keys before position i are less than the pivot and all keys after position j are greater than or equal to the pivot. For simplicity, swap the pivot into the first position, and start the partition with the second element. Write a loop that will increase the index i as long as the invariant holds and another loop that will decrease j as long as the invariant holds. Your loops must also ensure that the indices do not go out of range, perhaps by checking that i ≤ j. When a pair of entries, each on the wrong side, is found, then they should be swapped and the loops repeated. What is the termination condition of this outer loop? At the end, the pivot can be swapped into its proper place.

    b. Using the invariant property, verify that your procedure works properly.

    c. Show that each swap performed within the loop puts two entries into their final position. From this, show that the procedure does at most $\frac{1}{2}n + O(1)$ swaps in its worst case for a list of length n.

    d. If, after partitioning, the pivot belongs in position p, then the number of swaps that the procedure does is approximately the number of entries originally in one of the p positions at or before the pivot, but whose keys are greater than or equal to the pivot. If the keys are randomly distributed, then the probability that a particular key is greater than or equal to the pivot is $(n - p - 1)/n$. Show that the average number of such keys, and hence the average number of swaps, is approximately $p(n - p)/n$. By taking the average of these numbers from $p = 1$ to $p = n$, show that the number of swaps is approximately $n/6 + O(1)$.

    e. The need to check to make sure that the indices i and j in the partition procedure stay in bounds can be eliminated by using the pivot key as a sentinel to stop the loops. Implement this method in your procedure. Be sure to verify that your procedure works correctly in all cases.

f. [Due to WIRTH] Consider the following simple and "obvious" way to write the loops using the pivot as a sentinel:

```
repeat
    repeat i := i + 1 until L.entry [i] .key >= pivot;
    repeat j := j − 1 until L.entry [j] .key <= pivot;
    Swap (i, j, L)
until i >= j;
```

Find a list of keys for which this version fails.

PROJECTS 13.3

P1. Implement quicksort (for contiguous lists) on your computer, and test it with the same data used with previous sorting algorithms. Compare the number of comparisons of keys, assignments of entries, and total time required for sorting.

linked quicksort

P2. Write a version of quicksort for linked lists, and run it on your computer for the same test data used for previous methods. The simplest choice for pivot is the first key in the list being sorted. You should find the partition procedure conceptually easier and more straightforward than the contiguous version, since entries need not be swapped, but only links changed. You will, however, require a short additional procedure to recombine the sorted sublists into a single linked list. To facilitate this step, you may wish to keep pointers both to the first and last entries of each list.

P3. Because it may involve more overhead, quicksort may be inferior to simpler methods for short lists. Find experimentally a value where, on average, quicksort becomes more efficient than insertion sort. Write a hybrid sorting procedure that starts with quicksort and, when the sublists are sufficiently short, switches to insertion sort. Determine if it is better to do the switchover within the recursive procedure or to terminate the recursive calls when the sublists are sufficiently short to change methods and then at the very end of the process run through insertion sort once on the whole list.

13.4

HEAPS AND HEAPSORT: CONTIGUOUS IMPLEMENTATION OF BINARY TREES

Quicksort and treesort have the disadvantage that, even though their usual performance is excellent, some kinds of input can make them misbehave badly. In this section we study another sorting method that overcomes this problem. This algorithm, called *heapsort,* sorts a contiguous list of length n with $O(n \log n)$ comparisons and movements of entries, even in its worst case. Hence it achieves worst-case bounds better than those of quicksort, and for contiguous lists is better than mergesort, since it needs only a small and constant amount of space apart from the list being sorted.

Heapsort is based on binary trees, but binary trees in an implementation quite different from the one we studied in Chapter 11, and with the keys arranged in the tree in a way entirely different from binary search trees.

13.4.1 Binary Trees in Contiguous Storage

Let us begin with a complete binary tree, such as the one shown in Figure 13.8, and number the vertices, beginning with the root, from left to right on each level.

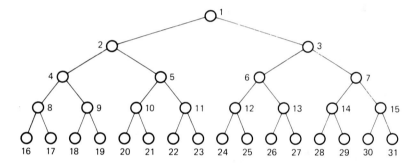

Figure 13.8. Complete binary tree with 31 vertices

We can now put the binary tree into a contiguous array by storing each node in the position shown by its label. We conclude that

> *The left and right children of the node with index k are in positions $2k$ and $2k + 1$, respectively. If these positions are beyond the bounds of the array, then these children do not exist.*

This contiguous implementation can, in fact, be extended to arbitrary binary trees, provided that we can flag locations in the array to show that the corresponding nodes do not exist. The results for several binary trees are shown in Figure 13.9.

It is clear from the diagram that, if a binary tree is far from a complete tree, then the contiguous representation wastes a great deal of space. Under other conditions, however, no space at all is wasted. It is this case that we shall now apply.

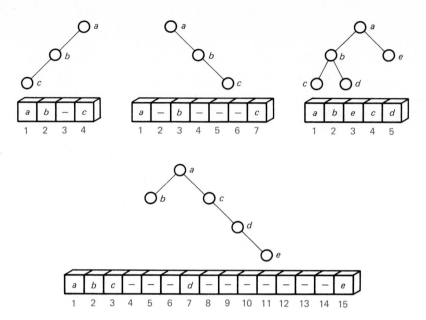

Figure 13.9. Binary trees in contiguous implementation

13.4.2 Heaps and Heapsort

Definition

> A *heap* is defined to be a binary tree with a key in each node, such that
>
> 1. All the leaves of the tree are on two adjacent levels.
>
> 2. All levels of the tree, except possibly the lowest, are completely filled; that is, each node except the leaves has two children. All nodes on the lowest level of the tree occur as far to the left side of the tree as possible.
>
> 3. The key in the root is at least as large as the keys in its children (if any), and the left and right subtrees (if they exist) are again heaps.

The first two conditions ensure that the contiguous representation of the tree will be space efficient. The third condition determines the ordering. Note that a heap is definitely *not* a binary search tree. The root, in fact, must have the largest key in the heap, whereas all keys in the right subtree of a binary search tree have larger keys than the root.

not search trees

Figure 13.10 shows four trees, the first of which is a heap, with the others violating one of the three properties.

examples

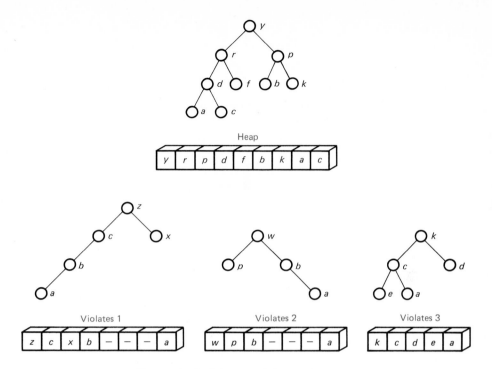

Figure 13.10. A heap and three other trees

> Some manuals on Pascal compilers refer to the storage space used for dynamic memory as the "heap." This use of the word "heap" has no connection and nothing in common with the present definition.

Outline of Heapsort

two-phase procedure

Heapsort proceeds in two phases. The entries in the list being sorted are interpreted as a binary tree in contiguous implementation. The first two properties of a heap are automatically satisfied, but the keys will not generally satisfy the third property. Hence the first phase of heapsort is to convert the tree into a heap. This we shall accomplish in a procedure called BuildHeap.

For the second phase, we recall that the root (which is the first entry of the list as well as the top of the heap) has the largest key in the list. This key belongs at the end of the list. We therefore move the first entry to the last unsorted position, replacing an entry that we call current. We then decrease a counter lastunsorted that keeps track of the size of the first, unsorted part of the list, thereby excluding the largest entry from further sorting. The entry current that has been moved from the last position, however, may not belong on the top of the heap, and therefore we must insert current into the proper position to restore the heap property before continuing to loop in the same way, reducing the size of the unsorted list by 1 at each iteration.

Let us summarize this outline by rewriting it in Pascal. We use the same notation and conventions used for all the contiguous sorting algorithms of Chapters 10 and 13.

main procedure

```
procedure HeapSort(var L: listtype);
    {Pre:    The contiguous list L has been created. The entries of L all contain
             keys.
     Post:   The entries of L have been rearranged so that all the keys in the
             entries are sorted into nondecreasing order.
     Uses:   Procedures BuildHeap and InsertHeap.}
var
    current: listentry;                     {temporary storage for moving entries}
    lastunsorted: listindex;        {Entries past lastunsorted have been sorted.}
begin                                                        {procedure HeapSort}
    BuildHeap(L);                                                   {first phase}
    for lastunsorted := L.count downto 2 do
    begin
        current := L.entry[lastunsorted];       {Extract last element from list.}
        L.entry[lastunsorted] := L.entry[1];       {Move top of heap to end.}
        InsertHeap(current, 1, lastunsorted − 1, L)
                                                     {Restore heap properties.}
    end
end;                                                         {procedure HeapSort}
```

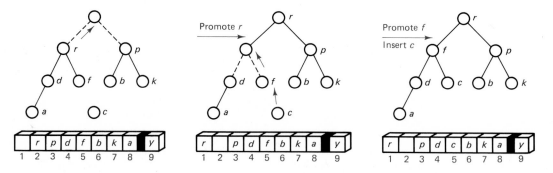

Figure 13.11. First stage of HeapSort

An Example

Before we begin work on the two procedures BuildHeap and InsertHeap, let us see what happens in the first few stages of sorting the heap shown as the first diagram in Figure 13.10. These stages are shown in Figure 13.11. In the first step, the largest key, *y*, is moved from the first to the last entry of the list. The first diagram shows the resulting tree, with *y* removed from further consideration, and the entry that was formerly last, *c*, put aside as the temporary variable current. To find how to rearrange the heap and insert *c*, we look at the two children of the root. Each of these is guaranteed to have a larger key than any other entry in its subtree, and hence the larger of these two entries belongs in the root. We therefore promote *r* to the top of the heap, and repeat the process on the subtree whose root has just been removed. Hence the larger of *d* and *f* is now inserted where *r* was formerly. At the next step, we would compare current = *c* with the two children of *f*, but these do not exist, so the promotion of entries through the tree ceases, and current = *c* is inserted in the empty position formerly occupied by *f*.

At this point, we are ready to repeat the algorithm, again moving the top of the heap to the end of the list and restoring the heap property. The sequence of actions that occurs in the complete sort of the list is shown in Figure 13.12.

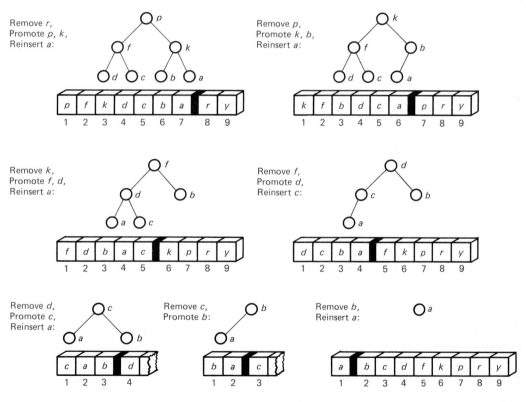

Figure 13.12. Trace of HeapSort

The Procedure InsertHeap

It is only a short step from this example to a formal procedure for inserting the entry current into the heap.

heap insertion

```
procedure InsertHeap (current: listentry; low, high: listindex; var L: listtype);
  {Pre:   The entries of contiguous list L between indices low + 1 and high,
          inclusive, form a heap. The entry in index low will be discarded.
   Post:  The entry current has·been inserted into L and the entries rearranged
          so that the entries between indices low and high, inclusive, form a
          heap.}
  var large: integer;              {index of child of L.entry [low] with larger key}
  begin                                                      {procedure InsertHeap}
    large := 2 * low;                            {large is now the left child of low.}
    while large <= high do
    begin
      if large < high then
        if L.entry [large].key < L.entry [large + 1].key then
          large := large + 1;        {large is the child of low with larger key.}
      if current.key >= L.entry [large].key then    {current belongs in low.}
        large := high + 1          {Set large as a flag to terminate the loop.}
      else begin              {Promote L.entry [large] and move down the tree.}
        L.entry [low] := L.entry [large];
        low := large;
        large := 2 * low
      end
    end;
    L.entry [low] := current
  end;                                                       {procedure InsertHeap}
```

Building the Initial Heap

initialization

The remaining task that we must specify is to build the initial heap from a list in arbitrary order. To do so, we first note that a binary tree with only one node automatically satisfies the properties of a heap, and therefore we need not worry about any of the leaves of the tree, that is, about any of the entries in the second half of the list. If we begin at the midpoint of the list and work our way back toward the start, we can use the procedure InsertHeap to insert each entry into the partial heap consisting of all later entries, and thereby build the complete heap. The desired procedure is therefore simply

```
procedure BuildHeap (var L: listtype);
  {Pre:   The contiguous list L has been created. The entries of L all contain
          keys.
   Post:  The entries of L have been rearranged so that L becomes a heap.}
  var
    low: listindex;              {All entries beyond index low form a partial heap.}
  begin
    for low := (L.count div 2) downto 1 do
      InsertHeap (L.entry [low], low, L.count)
  end;
```

13.4.3 Analysis of Heapsort

From the example we have worked, it is not at all clear that heapsort is an efficient sorting method. In fact, heapsort is not a good choice for short lists. It seems quite strange that we can sort by moving large keys slowly toward the beginning of the list before finally putting them away at the end. When n becomes large, however, such small quirks become unimportant, and heapsort proves its worth as one of very few sorting algorithms for contiguous lists that is guaranteed to sort a list of length n in time $O(n \log n)$ with minimal space requirements.

worst-case
insertion
First, let us determine how much work InsertHeap does in its worst case. At each pass through the loop, the index low is (at least) doubled; hence the number of passes cannot exceed lg(high **div** low); this is also the height of the subtree rooted at L.entry [low]. Each pass through the loop does two comparisons of keys (usually) and one assignment of entries. Therefore, the number of comparisons done in InsertHeap is at most 2 lg(high **div** low) and the number of assignments lg(high **div** low).

first phase
Let m be the greatest integer that does not exceed $\frac{1}{2}n$. In BuildHeap, we make m calls to InsertHeap, for values of k = low ranging from m down to 1. Hence the total number of comparisons is about

$$2\sum_{k=1}^{m} \lg(n/k) = 2(m \lg n - \lg m!) \approx 5m \approx 2.5n.$$

Here we have applied Stirling's Approximation from Appendix A. Also, since $\lg m \approx \lg n - 1$, we have

$$\lg m! \approx m \lg m - 1.5m \approx m \lg n - 2.5m.$$

second phase
Similarly, in the sorting and insertion phase, we have about

$$2\sum_{k=2}^{n} \lg k = 2 \lg n! \approx 2n \lg n - 3n$$

comparisons. This term dominates that of the initial phase, and hence we con-
total worst-case clude that the number of comparisons is $2n \lg n + O(n)$.
counts
One assignment of entries is done in InsertHeap for each two comparisons (approximately). Therefore the total number of assignments is $n \lg n + O(n)$.

In summary, we can state:

In its worst case for sorting a list of length n, heapsort performs $2n \lg n + O(n)$ comparisons of keys and $n \lg n + O(n)$ assignments of entries.

---

comparison with quicksort

From Section 13.3.4 we can see that the corresponding numbers for quicksort in the *average* case are $1.39n \lg n + O(n)$ comparisons and $0.69n \lg n + O(n)$ swaps, which can be reduced to $0.23n \lg n + O(n)$ swaps. Hence the *worst* case for heapsort is somewhat poorer than is the *average* case for quicksort. Quicksort's worst case is $O(n^2)$, however; far worse than the worst case of heapsort for large n. An average-case analysis of heapsort appears to be very complicated, but empirical studies show that (as for selection sort) there is relatively little difference between the average and worst cases, and heapsort usually takes about twice as long as quicksort.

Heapsort, therefore, should be regarded as something of an insurance policy: On average, heapsort costs about twice as much as quicksort, but heapsort avoids the slight possibility of a catastrophic degradation of performance.

13.4.4 Priority Queues

To conclude this section, we briefly mention another application of heaps.

> A *priority queue* consists of entries, each of which contains a key called the *priority* of the entry. A priority queue has only two operations other than the usual creation, size, full, and empty operations:
>
> **1.** Insert an entry.
> **2.** Retrieve and remove the entry having the highest priority.
>
> If entries have equal priorities, then the first entry inserted is removed first.

applications

In a time-sharing computer system, for example, a large number of tasks may be waiting for the CPU. Some of these tasks have higher priority than others. Hence the set of tasks waiting for the CPU forms a priority queue. Other applications of priority queues include simulations of time-dependent events (like the airport simulation in Chapter 5) and solution of sparse systems of linear equations by row reduction.

implementations

We could represent a priority queue as a sorted contiguous list, in which case removal of an entry is immediate, but insertion would take time proportional to n, the number of entries in the queue. Or we could represent it as an unsorted list, in which case insertion is rapid but removal is slow. If we used an ordinary binary search tree (sorted by the size of the key), then, on average, insertion and removal could both be done in time $O(\log n)$, but the tree could degenerate and require time $O(n)$. Extra time and space may be needed, as well, to accommodate the linked representation of the binary search tree.

Now consider the properties of a heap. The entry with largest key is on the top and can be removed immediately. It will, however, take time $O(\log n)$ to restore the heap property for the remaining keys. If, however, another entry is to be inserted immediately, then some of this time may be combined with the

$O(\log n)$ time needed to insert the new entry. Thus the implementation of a priority queue as a heap proves advantageous for large n, since it is represented efficiently in contiguous storage and is guaranteed to require only logarithmic time for both insertions and deletions.

EXERCISES 13.4

E1. Determine the contiguous representation of each of the following binary trees. Which of these trees are heaps? For those that are not, state which rule(s) is (are) violated at which node(s).

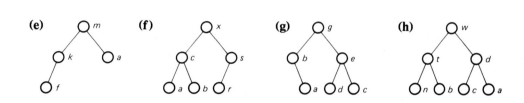

E2. By hand, trace the action of HeapSort on each of the following lists. Draw the initial tree to which the list corresponds, show how it is converted into a heap, and show the resulting heap as each entry is removed from the top and the new entry inserted.

  a. The following three words to be sorted alphabetically:

     triangle   square   pentagon.

  b. The three words in part (a) to be sorted according to the number of sides of the corresponding polygon, in increasing order.

  c. The three words in part (a) to be sorted according to the number of sides of the corresponding polygon, in decreasing order.

  d. The following seven numbers to be sorted into increasing order:

     26   33   35   29   19   12   22.

  e. The same seven numbers in a different initial order, again to be sorted into increasing order:

     12   19   33   26   29   35   22.

f. The following list of 14 names to be sorted into alphabetical order:

Tim Dot Eva Roy Tom Kim Guy Amy Jon Ann Jim Kay Ron Jan

E3. a. Design a procedure that will insert a new entry into a heap, obtaining a new heap. (The procedure InsertHeap in the text requires that the root be unoccupied, whereas, for this exercise, the root will already contain the entry with largest key, which must remain in the heap. Your procedure will increase the count of entries in the list.)

b. Analyze the time and space requirements of your procedure.

E4. a. Design a procedure that will delete the entry with the largest key (the root) from the top of the heap and restore the heap properties of the resulting, smaller list.

b. Analyze the time and space requirements of your procedure.

E5. a. Design a procedure that will delete the entry with index i from a heap and restore the heap properties of the resulting, smaller list.

b. Analyze the time and space requirements of your procedure.

E6. Consider a heap of n keys, with x_k being the key in position k (in the contiguous representation) for $1 \le k \le n$. Prove that the height of the subtree rooted at x_k is the greatest integer not exceeding $\lg(n/k)$, for all k satisfying $1 \le k \le n$. [*Hint*: Use "backward" induction on k, starting with the leaves and working back toward the root, which is x_1.]

E7. Define the notion of a *ternary heap*, analogous to an ordinary heap except that each node of the tree except the leaves has three children. Devise a sorting method based on ternary heaps, and analyze the properties of the sorting method.

PROJECT 13.4

P1. Implement heapsort (for contiguous lists) on your computer, and test it with the same data used with previous sorting algorithms. Compare the number of comparisons of keys, assignments of entries, and total time required for sorting with the equivalent results for quicksort.

13.5

REVIEW: COMPARISON OF METHODS

In the past several chapters, we have studied and carefully analyzed quite a large variety of sorting methods. Perhaps the best way to summarize this work is to emphasize in turn each of the three important efficiency criteria:

- Use of storage space;
- Use of computer time;
- Programming effort.

Use of Space

In regard to space, most of the algorithms we have discussed use little space other than that occupied by the original list, which is rearranged in its original place to be in order. The exceptions are quicksort, treesort, and mergesort, where the recursion does require a small amount of extra storage to keep track of the sublists that have not yet been sorted. But, in a well-written procedure, the amount of extra space used for recursion is $O(\log n)$ (the length of the list is n) and will be trivial in comparison with that needed for other purposes.

The binary search tree built by treesort, of course, requires space for $2n$ links as well as the entries from the original list, but the main application of treesort is to problems where the tree will continue to be used for later searches, insertions, and deletions.

Finally, we should recall that a major drawback of mergesort for contiguous lists is that the straightforward version requires extra space equal to that occupied by the original list.

In many applications, the list to be sorted is much too large to be kept in high-speed memory, and when this is the case, other methods become necessary. A frequent approach is to divide the list into sublists that can be sorted internally *external sorting* within high-speed memory and then merge the sorted sublists externally. Hence *and merging* much work has been invested in developing merging algorithms, primarily when it is necessary to merge many sublists at once. Several references given at the end of the book discuss external sorting at length.

Computer Time

The second efficiency criterion is use of computer time, which we have already carefully analyzed for each of the methods we have developed. In summary, the simple methods insertion sort and selection sort have time that increases like n^2 as the length n of the list increases; Shell sort is much faster; and the remaining methods are usually the fastest, with time that is $O(n \log n)$. Quicksort and treesort, however, have a worst-case time that increases like n^2. Heapsort is something of an insurance policy. It usually is more costly than quicksort, but avoids the slight possibility of a serious degradation in performance.

Programming Effort

The third efficiency criterion is often the most important of all: this criterion is the efficient and fruitful use of the programmer's time.

If a list is small, the sophisticated sorting techniques designed to minimize computer time requirements are usually worse or only marginally better in achieving their goal than are the simpler methods. If a program is to be run only once or twice and there is enough machine time, then it would be foolish for a programmer to spend days or weeks investigating many sophisticated algorithms that might, in the end, only save a few seconds of computer time.

When programming in languages like FORTRAN, COBOL, or most versions of BASIC that do not support recursion, implementation of mergesort and quicksort becomes considerably more complicated, although it can be done by using stacks to hold the values of variables, as we observed in Chapter 12.

Shell sort comes not far behind mergesort and quicksort in performance, does not require recursion, and is easy to program. One should therefore never sell Shell sort short.

The saving of programming time is an excellent reason for choosing a simple algorithm, even if it is inefficient, but two words of caution should always be remembered. First, saving programming time is never an excuse for writing an incorrect program, one that may usually work but can sometimes misbehave. Murphy's law will then inevitably come true. Second, simple programs, designed to be run only a few times and then discarded, often instead find their way into applications not imagined when they were first written. Lack of care in the early stages will then prove exceedingly costly later.

For many applications, insertion sort can prove to be the best choice. It is easy to write and maintain, and it runs efficiently for short lists. Even for long lists, if they are nearly in the correct order, insertion sort will be very efficient. If the list is completely in order, then insertion sort verifies this condition as quickly as can be done.

Statistical Analysis

The final choice of algorithm will depend not only on the length of list, the size of records, and their representation in storage, but very strongly on the way in which the records can be expected to be ordered before sorting. The analysis of algorithms from the standpoint of probability and statistics is of great importance. For most algorithms, we have been able to obtain results on the mean *mean* (average) performance, but the experience of quicksort shows that the amount by which this performance changes from one possible ordering to another is also an important factor to consider.

standard deviation The **standard deviation** is a statistical measure of this variability. Quicksort has an excellent mean performance, and the standard deviation is small, which signifies that the performance is likely to differ little from the mean. For algorithms like selection sort, heapsort, and mergesort, the best-case and worst-case performances differ little, which means that the standard deviation is almost 0. Other algorithms, like insertion sort, will have a much larger standard deviation in their performance. The particular distribution of the orderings of the incoming lists is therefore an important consideration in choosing a sorting method. To enable intelligent decisions, the professional computer scientist needs to be knowledgeable about important aspects of mathematical statistics as they apply to algorithm analysis.

Empirical Testing

Finally, in all these decisions, we must be careful to temper the theoretical analysis of algorithms with empirical testing. Different computers and compilers will produce different results. It is most instructive, therefore, to see by experiment how the different algorithms behave in different circumstances.

EXERCISES 13.5

E1. Classify the sorting methods we have studied into one of the following categories: (a) the method does not require access to the entries at one end of the list until the entries at the other end have been sorted; (b) the method does not require access to the entries that have already been sorted; (c) the method requires access to all entries in the list throughout the process.

E2. Some of the sorting methods we have studied are not suited for use with linked lists. Which ones, and why not?

E3. Rank the sorting methods we have studied (both for linked and contiguous lists) according to the amount of extra storage space that they require for indices or pointers, for recursion, and for copies of the entries being sorted.

E4. Which of the methods we studied would be a good choice in each of the following applications? Why? If the representation of the list in contiguous or linked storage makes a difference in your choice, state how.

a. You wish to write a general-purpose sorting program that will be used by many people in a variety of applications.

b. You wish to sort 1000 numbers once. After you finish, you will not keep the program.

c. You wish to sort 50 numbers once. After you finish, you will not keep the program.

d. You need to sort 5 entries in the middle of a long program. Your sort will be called hundreds of times by the long program.

e. You have a list of 1000 keys to sort in high-speed memory, and key comparisons can be made quickly, but each time a key is moved, a corresponding 500 block file on disk must also be moved, and doing so is a slow process.

f. There is a twelve foot long shelf full of computer science books all catalogued by number. A few of these have been put back in the wrong places by readers, but rarely are they more than one foot from where they belong.

g. You have a stack of 500 library index cards in random order to sort alphabetically.

h. You are told that a list of 5000 words is already in order, but you wish to check it to make sure, and sort any words found out of order.

E5. Discuss the advantages and disadvantages of designing a general sorting procedure as a hybrid between quicksort and Shell sort. What criteria would you use to switch from one to the other? Which would be the better choice for what kinds of lists?

E6. Summarize the results of the test runs of the sorting methods of this chapter for your computer. Also include any variations of the methods that you have written as exercises. Make charts comparing the following:

    a. the number of key comparisons,

    b. the number of assignments of entries,

    c. the total running time,

    d. the working storage requirements of the program,

    e. the length of the program,

    f. the amount of programming time required to write and debug the program.

E7. Write a one-page guide to help a user of your computer system select one of our sorting algorithms according to his needs.

stable sorting methods

E8. A sorting procedure is called ***stable*** if, whenever two entries have equal keys, then on completion of the sorting procedure, the two entries will be in the same order in the list as before sorting. Stability is important if a list has already been sorted by one key and is now being sorted by another key, and it is desired to keep as much of the original ordering as the new one allows. Determine which of the sorting methods of this chapter are stable and which are not. For those that are not, produce a list (as short as possible) containing some entries with equal keys whose orders are not preserved. In addition, see if you can discover simple modifications to the algorithm that will make it stable.

POINTERS AND PITFALLS

1. Divide and conquer is one of the most widely applicable and most powerful methods for designing algorithms. When faced with a programming problem, see if its solution can be obtained by first solving the problem for two (or more) problems of the same general form but of a smaller size. If so, you may be able to formulate an algorithm that uses the divide-and-conquer method and program it using recursion.

2. Mergesort, quicksort, and heapsort are powerful sorting methods, more difficult to program than the simple methods of Chapter 10, but much more efficient when applied to large lists. Consider the application carefully to determine whether the extra effort needed to implement one of these sophisticated algorithms will be justified.

3. For general advice on the use, programming, and comparison of sorting algorithms, see the Pointers and Pitfalls at the end of Chapter 10.

4. Priority queues are important for many applications, and heaps provide an excellent implementation of priority queues.

5. Heapsort is like an insurance policy: It is usually slower than quicksort, but it guarantees that sorting will be completed in $O(n \log n)$ comparisons of keys, as quicksort cannot always do.

REVIEW QUESTIONS

13.1   1. Explain in twenty words or less how mergesort works.

2. Explain in twenty words or less how quicksort works.

13.2   3. Explain why mergesort is better for linked lists than for contiguous lists.

4. Compare the approximate numbers of comparisons of keys made by merge-sort and by insertion sort on lists of lengths 4, 16, 64, and 2048.

13.3   5. Which part of the quicksort procedure requires special care to formulate correctly?

6. In quicksort, why did we choose the pivot from the center of the list rather than from one of the ends?

7. On average, about how many more comparisons of keys does quicksort make than the optimum? About how many comparisons does it make in the worst case?

8. What are the *harmonic numbers* H_n, and what is the approximate value of H_n?

9. What is a *recurrence relation*?

13.4   10. What is a *heap*?

11. How does heapsort work?

12. Compare the worst-case performance of heapsort with the worst-case performance of quicksort, and compare it also with the average-case performance of quicksort.

13. What is a *priority queue*?

14. Give three possible implementations of priority queues, and give the approximate number of key comparisons needed, on average, for insertion and deletion in each implementation.

13.5   15. Name three important efficiency criteria for a program.

16. Under what conditions are simple sorting algorithms better than sophisticated ones?

14

FURTHER APPLICATIONS OF RECURSION

Up to now, all the applications of recursion that we have studied have been of the form *divide and conquer*. This chapter presents several applications of recursion that illustrate other ways in which it can be applied to algorithm design. Some of these applications are simple; others are quite sophisticated.

BACKTRACKING: POSTPONING THE WORK

Let us consider the puzzle of how to place eight queens on a chessboard so that no queen can take another. Recall that in the rules for chess a queen can take another piece that lies on the same row, the same column, or the same diagonal (either direction) as the queen. The chessboard has eight rows and eight columns.

It is by no means obvious how to solve this puzzle, and its complete solution defied even the great C. F. GAUSS, who attempted it in 1850. It is typical of puzzles that do not seem suitable for analytic solutions, but require either luck coupled with trial and error, or else much exhaustive (and exhausting) computation. To convince you that solutions to this problem really do exist, two of them are shown in Figure 14.1.

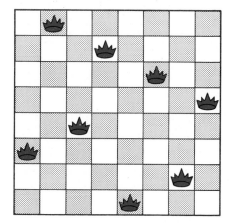 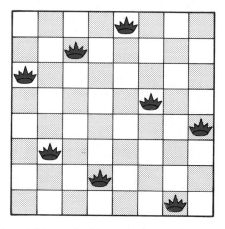

Figure 14.1. Two configurations showing eight nonattacking queens

14.1.1 Solving the Eight-Queens Puzzle

A person attempting to solve the Eight-Queens problem will usually soon abandon attempts to find all (or even one) of the solutions by being clever and will start to put queens on the board, perhaps randomly or perhaps in some logical order, but always making sure that no queen placed can take another already on the board. If the person is lucky enough to place eight queens on the board by proceeding in this way, then he has found a solution; if not, then one or more of the queens must be removed and placed elsewhere to continue the search for a solution. To start formulating a program, let us sketch this method in algorithmic form. We denote the number of queens on the board by n; initially, $n = 0$. The key step is described as follows.

outline

```
procedure AddQueen;
    for every unguarded position p on the board do
    begin
        Place a queen in position p;
        n : = n + 1;
        if n = 8 then
            print the configuration
        else
            AddQueen;
        Remove the queen from position p;
        n : = n − 1
    end.
```

This sketch illustrates the use of recursion to mean "Continue to the next stage and repeat the task." Placing a queen in position p is only tentative; we leave it there only if we can continue adding queens until we have eight. Whether we reach eight or not, the procedure will return when it finds that it has finished or there are no further possibilities to investigate. After the inner call has returned, then, it is time to remove the queen from position p, because all possibilities with it there have been investigated.

14.1.2 Example: Four Queens

Let us see how this algorithm works for a much simpler problem, that of placing four queens on a 4 × 4 board, as illustrated in Figure 14.2.

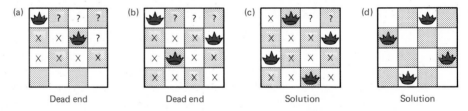

Figure 14.2. Solution to the Four-Queens problem

We shall need to put one queen in each row of the board. Let us first try to place the queen as far to the left in the row as we can. Such a choice is shown in the first row of part (a) of Figure 14.2. The question marks indicate other legitimate choices that we have not yet tried. Before we investigate these choices, we move on to the second row and try to insert a queen. The first two columns are guarded by the queen in row 1, as shown by the crossed-off squares. Columns 3 and 4 are free, so we first place the queen in column 3 and mark column 4 with a question mark. Next we move on to row 3, but we find that all four squares are guarded by one of the queens in the first two rows. We have now reached a dead end.

When we reach a dead end, we must *backtrack* by going back to the most recent choice we have made and trying another possibility. This situation is shown in part (b) of Figure 14.2, which shows the queen in row 1 unchanged, but the queen in row 2 moved to the second possible position (and the previously occupied position crossed off as no longer possible). Now we find that column 2 is the only possible position for a queen in row 3, but all four positions in row 4 are guarded. Hence we have again reached a dead end and must backtrack.

At this point, we no longer have another choice for row 2, so we must move all the way back to row 1 and move the queen to the next possible position, column 2. This situation is shown in part (c) of Figure 14.2. Now we find that, in row 2, only column 4 is unguarded, so a queen must go there. In row 3, then, column 1 is the only possibility, and, in row 4, only column 3 is possible. This placement of queens, however, leads to a solution to the problem.

If we wish to find *all* the solutions, we can continue in the same way, backtracking to the last choice we made and changing it to the next possibility. In part (c) we had no choice in rows 4, 3, or 2, so we now back up to row 1 and move the queen to column 3. This choice leads to the unique solution shown in part (d).

Finally, we should investigate the possibilities with a queen in column 4 of row 1, but, as in part (a), there will be no solution in this case. In fact, the configurations with a queen in either column 3 or column 4 of row 1 are just the mirror images of those with a queen in column 2 or column 1. If you do a left-right reflection of the board shown in part (c), you will obtain the board shown in (d), and the boards with a queen in column 4, row 1, are just the reflections of those shown in parts (a) and (b).

14.1.3 Backtracking

This procedure is typical of a broad class called *backtracking algorithms*, which attempt to complete a search for a solution to a problem by constructing partial solutions, always ensuring that the partial solutions remain consistent with the requirements of the problem. The algorithm then attempts to extend a partial solution toward completion, but when an inconsistency with the requirements of the problem occurs, the algorithm backs up (*backtracks*) by removing the most recently constructed part of the solution and trying another possibility.

Backtracking proves useful in situations where many possibilities may first appear, but few survive further tests. In scheduling problems, for example, it will likely be easy to assign the first few matches, but as further matches are made, the constraints drastically reduce the number of possibilities. Or consider the problem of designing a compiler. In some languages (but not Pascal), it is impossible to determine the meaning of a statement until almost all of it has been read. Consider, for example, the pair of FORTRAN statements

DO 17 K = 1, 6
DO 17 K = 1. 6

parsing

Both of these are legal: The first starts a loop, and the second assigns the number 1.6 to the variable DO17K. In such cases where the meaning cannot be deduced immediately, backtracking is a useful method in *parsing* (that is, splitting apart to decipher) the text of a program.

14.1.4 Refinement: Choosing the Data Structures

To fill in the details of our algorithm for the Eight-Queens problem, we must first decide how we will determine which positions are unguarded at each stage and how we will loop through the unguarded positions. This amounts to reaching some decisions about the representation of data in the program.

square Boolean array

A person working on the Eight-Queens puzzle with an actual chessboard will probably proceed to put queens into the squares one at a time. We can do the same in a computer by introducing an 8×8 array with Boolean entries and by defining an entry to be true if a queen is there and false if not. To determine if a position is guarded, the person would scan the board to see if a queen is guarding the position, and we could do the same, but doing so would involve considerable searching.

A person working the puzzle on paper or on a blackboard often observes that when a queen is put on the board, time will be saved in the next stage if all the squares that the new queen guards are marked off, so that it is only necessary to look for an unmarked square to find an unguarded position for the next queen. Again, we could do the same by defining each entry of our array to be true if it is free and false if it is guarded.

square integer array

A problem now arises, however, when we wish to remove a queen. We should not necessarily change a position that she has guarded from false to true, since it may well be that some other queen still guards that position. We can solve this problem by making the entries of our array integers rather than Boolean, each entry denoting the number of queens guarding the position. Thus, to add a queen, we increase the count by 1 for each position on the same row, column, or diagonal as the queen, and, to remove a queen, we reduce the appropriate counts by 1. A position is unguarded if and only if it has a count of 0.

In spite of its obvious advantages over the previous attempt, this method still involves some searching to find unguarded positions and some calculation to change all the counts at each stage. The algorithm will be adding and removing queens a great many times, so that this calculation and searching may prove expensive. A person working on this puzzle soon makes another observation that saves even more work.

pigeonhole principle

Once a queen has been put in the first row, no person would waste time searching to find a place to put another queen in the same row, since the row is fully guarded by the first queen. There can never be more than one queen in each row. But our goal is to put eight queens on the board, and there are only eight rows. It follows that there must be a queen, exactly one queen, in every one of the rows. (This is called the **pigeonhole principle**: If you have n pigeons and n pigeonholes, and no more than one pigeon ever goes in the same hole, then there must be a pigeon in every hole.)

Thus, we can proceed by placing the queens on the board one row at a time, starting with the first row, and we can keep track of where they are with a single

array of locations array

var col: **array** [1 .. 8] **of** 1 .. 8

guards where col[i] gives the column containing the queen in row i. To make sure that no two queens are on the same column or the same diagonal, we need not keep and search through an 8 × 8 array, but we need only keep track of whether each column is free or guarded, and whether each diagonal is likewise. We can do this with three Boolean arrays: colfree, upfree, and downfree, where diagonals from the lower left to the upper right are considered upward and those from the upper left to lower right are considered downward.

How do we identify the positions along a single diagonal? Along the main (downward) diagonal, the entries are

[1,1], [2,2], ..., [8,8].

These have the property that the row and column indices are equal; that, is, their *difference* is 0. It turns out that, along any downward diagonal, the row and column indices will have a constant difference. This difference is 0 for the main diagonal, and ranges from $1-8 = -7$ for the downward diagonal of length 1 in the upper right corner, to $8 - 1 = 7$ for the one in the lower left corner. Similarly, along upward diagonals, the *sum* of the row and column indices is constant, ranging from $1 + 1 = 2$ to $8 + 8 = 16$.

After making all these decisions, we can now define all our data structures formally, and, at the same time, we can write the main program.

main program

```
program Queen (output);
{Pre:   None.
 Post:  All solutions to the Eight-Queens problem are printed.
 Uses:  Procedure AddQueen performs the recursive backtracking.}
var
   col: array [1 .. 8] of 1 .. 8;                {column with the queen}
   colfree: array [1 .. 8] of Boolean;           {Is the column free?}
   upfree: array [2 .. 16] of Boolean;       {Is the upward diagonal free?}
   downfree: array [-7 .. 7] of Boolean;     {Is downward diagonal free?}
   row: 0 .. 8;                          {row whose queen is currently placed}
   position: integer;                        {index to initialize arrays}
{declaration of procedure AddQueen to be inserted here}

begin                                                 {program Queen}
   row := 0;
   for position := 1 to 8 do colfree [position] := true;
   for position := 2 to 16 do upfree [position] := true;
   for position := -7 to 7 do downfree [position] := true;
   AddQueen
end.                                                  {program Queen}
```

Translation of the sketch of the procedure AddQueen into a program is straightforward, given the use of the arrays that have now been defined.

<table>
<tr><td>recursive
procedure</td><td>

procedure AddQueen;
{**Pre:**   *Queens have been properly placed in rows 1 through* row *(provided* row > 0*) and the information recorded in the above arrays.*
    Post: *All solutions beginning with this configuration have been printed, and the variable* row *and values in all arrays have been returned to their original values.*
    Uses: *Global variable* row, *global arrays* col, colfree, upfree, *and* downfree, *and procedure* WriteBoard.}
</td></tr>
</table>

var
   column: 1 .. 8;   {*column being tried for the queen*}
begin   {*procedure AddQueen*}
row := row + 1;
for column := 1 **to** 8 **do**
   if colfree [column] **and** upfree [row + column]
              and downfree [row − column] **then**
   begin   {*Put a queen in position* [row, column] .}
     col [row] := column;
     colfree [column] := false;
     upfree [row + column] := false;
     downfree [row − column] := false;
     if row = 8 **then**   {*termination condition*}
       WriteBoard
     else
       AddQueen;   {*Proceed recursively.*}
   {*Now backtrack by removing the queen.*}
     colfree [column] := true;
     upfree [row + column] := true;
     downfree [row − column] := true;
   end;   {*processing queen at* column}
row := row − 1
end;   {*procedure AddQueen*}

Local and Global Variables

Note that, in the program Queen, almost all the variables and arrays are declared in the main program, whereas, in the program Hanoi of Chapter 11, the variables were declared in the recursive procedure. If variables are declared within a procedure, then they are local to the procedure and not available outside it. In particular, variables declared in a recursive procedure are local to a single occurrence of the procedure, so that if the procedure is called again recursively, the variables are new and different, and the original variables will be remembered after the procedure returns. The copies of variables set up in an outer call are not available to the procedure during an inner recursive call. In the program Queen, we want the same information about guarded rows, columns, and diagonals to be available to all the recursive occurrences of the procedure, and to do this, the appropriate arrays are declared not in the procedure but in the main program.

The only reason for the array col[ ] is to communicate the positions of the queens to the procedure WriteBoard. The information in this array is also preserved in the eight local copies of the variable column set up during the recursive calls, but only one of these local copies is available to the program at a given time.

14.1.5 Analysis of Backtracking

Finally, let us estimate the amount of work that our program will do. If we had taken the naïve approach by writing a program that first placed all eight queens on the board and then rejected the illegal configurations, we would be investigating as many configurations as choosing eight places out of sixty-four, which is

$$\binom{64}{8} = 4{,}426{,}165{,}368.$$

The observation that there can be only one queen in each row immediately cuts this number to

$$8^8 = 16{,}777{,}216.$$

This number is still large, but our program will not investigate nearly this many positions. Instead, it rejects positions whose column or diagonals are guarded. The requirement that there be only one queen in each column reduces the number to

reduced count

$$8! = 40{,}320$$

which is quite manageable by computer, and the actual number of cases the program considers will be much less than this (see the Projects), since positions with guarded diagonals in the early rows will be rejected immediately, with no need to make the fruitless attempt to fill the later rows.

effectiveness of backtracking

This behavior summarizes the effectiveness of backtracking: positions that are early discovered to be impossible prevent the later investigation of many fruitless paths.

Another way to express this behavior of backtracking is to consider the tree of recursive calls to procedure AddQueen, part of which is shown in Figure 14.4. The two solutions shown in this tree are the same as the solutions shown in Figure 14.1. It appears formally that each node in the tree might have up to eight children corresponding to the recursive calls to AddQueen for the eight possible values of column. Even at levels near the root, however, most of these branches are found to be impossible, and the removal of one node on an upper level removes a multitude of its descendents. Backtracking is a most effective tool to prune a recursion tree to manageable size.

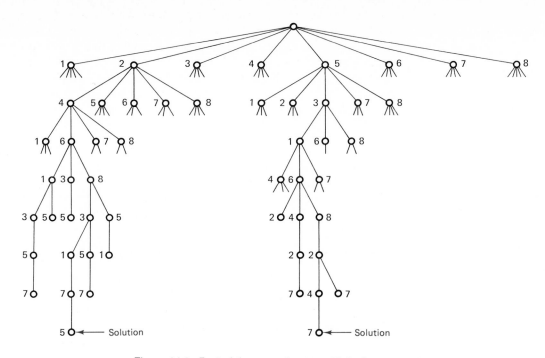

Figure 14.3. Part of the recursion tree, Eight-Queens problem

■ EXERCISES 14.1

E1. What is the maximum depth of recursion in program Queen?

E2. Starting with the following partial configuration of five queens on the board, construct the recursion tree of all situations that program Queen will consider in trying to add the remaining three queens. Stop drawing the tree at the point where the program will backtrack and remove one of the original five queens.

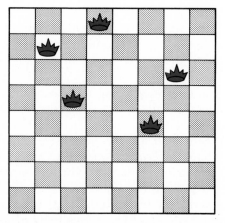

E3. By performing backtracking by hand, find all solutions to the problem of placing five queens on a 5×5 board. You may use the left-right symmetry of the first row by considering only the possibilities when the queen in row 1 is in one of columns 1, 2, or 3.

■ PROJECTS 14.1

P1. Run program Queen on your computer. You will need to write procedure WriteBoard to do the output. In addition, find out exactly how many positions are investigated by including a counter that is incremented every time procedure AddQueen is started. [Note that a method that placed all eight queens before checking for guarded squares would be equivalent to eight calls to AddQueen.]

P2. Describe a rectangular maze by indicating its paths and walls within an array. Write a backtracking program to find a way through the maze.

P3. Another chessboard puzzle (this one reputedly solved by GAUSS at the age of four) is to find a sequence of moves by a knight that will visit every square of the board exactly once. Recall that a knight's move is to jump two positions either vertically or horizontally and, at the same time, one position in the perpendicular direction. Such a move can be accomplished by setting x to either 1 or 2, setting y to $3 - x$, and then changing the first coordinate by $\pm x$ and the second by $\pm y$ (providing the resulting position is still on the board). Write a backtracking program that will input an initial position and search for a knight's tour starting at the given position and going to every square once and no square more than once. If you find that the program runs too slowly, a good method to help the knight find its way is to order the list of squares to which it can move from a given position so that it will first try to go to the squares with the least accessibility, that is, to the squares from which there are the fewest knight's moves to squares not yet visited.

14.2

TREE-STRUCTURED PROGRAMS: LOOK-AHEAD IN GAMES

In games of mental skill, the person who can anticipate what will happen several moves in advance has a substantial advantage over a competitor who looks only for immediate gain. In this section, we develop a computer algorithm to play games by looking at possible moves several steps in advance. This algorithm can be described most naturally in terms of a tree; afterward, we show how recursion can be used to program this tree structure.

14.2.1 Game Trees

We can picture the sequences of possible moves by means of a *game tree*, in which the root denotes the initial situation, and the branches from the root denote the legal moves that the first player could make. At the next level down, the branches correspond to the legal moves by the second player in each situation, and so on, with branches from vertices at even levels denoting moves by the first player, and from vertices at odd levels denoting moves by the second player.

"Eight" The complete game tree for the trivial game of *Eight* is shown in Figure 14.4. In this game, the first player chooses one of the numbers 1, 2, or 3. At each later turn the appropriate player chooses one of 1, 2, or 3, but the number previously chosen is not allowed. A running sum of the numbers chosen is kept, and if a player brings this sum to exactly eight, then the player wins. If the player takes the sum over eight, then the other player wins. No draws are possible. In the diagram, F denotes a win by the first player, and S a win by the second player.

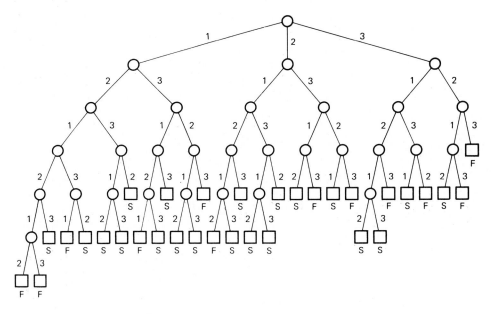

Figure 14.4. Tree for the game of Eight

Even a trivial game like Eight produces a good-sized tree. Games of real interest like Chess or Go have trees so huge that there is no hope of investigating all the branches, and a program that runs in reasonable time can examine only a few levels below the current vertex in the tree. People playing such games are also unable to see every possibility to the end of the game, but they can make intelligent choices, because, with experience, a person comes to recognize that some situations in a game are much better than others, even if they do not guarantee a win.

For any interesting game that we propose to play by computer, therefore, we shall need some kind of *evaluation function* that will examine the current situation and return a number assessing its benefits. To be definite, we shall assume that large numbers reflect favorable situations for the first player, and therefore small (or more negative) numbers show an advantage for the second player.

14.2.2 The Minimax Method

Part of the tree for a fictitious game appears in Figure 14.5. Since we are looking ahead, we need the evaluation function only at the leaves of the tree (that is, the positions from which we shall not look further ahead in the game), and, from this information, we wish to select a move. We shall draw the leaves of the game tree as squares and the remaining nodes as circles. Hence Figure 14.5 provides values only for the nodes drawn as squares.

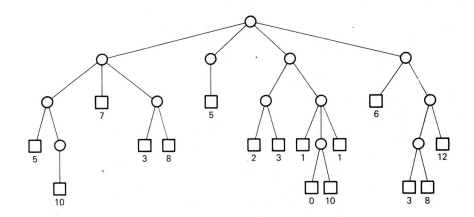

Figure 14.5. A game tree with values assigned at the leaves

The move we eventually select is one of the branches coming directly from the root, at the top level of the tree. We take the evaluation function from the perspective of this player, which means that this player selects the maximum value possible. At the next level down, the other player will select the smallest value possible, and so on.

By working up from the bottom of the tree, we can assign values to all the *tracing the tree* vertices. Let us trace this process part of the way through Figure 14.5, starting at the lower left side of the tree. The first unlabeled node is the circle above the square labeled 10. Since there is no choice for the move made at this node, it must also have the value 10. Its parent node has two children now labeled 5 and 10. This parent node is on the third level of the tree. That is, it represents a move by the first player, who wishes to maximize the value. Hence, this player will choose the move with value 10, and so the value for the parent node is also 10.

Next let us move up one level in the tree to the node with three children. We now know that the leftmost child has value 10, and the second child has value 7. The value for the rightmost child will be the maximum of the values of its two children, 3 and 8. Hence its value is 8. The node with three children is on the second level; that is, it represents a move by the player who wishes to minimize the value. Thus this player will choose the center move of the three possibilities, and the value at this node is therefore 7.

And thus the process continues. You should take a moment to complete the evaluation of all the nodes in Figure 14.5. The result is shown in Figure 14.6. The value of the current situation turns out to be 7, and the current (first) player will choose the leftmost branch as the best move.

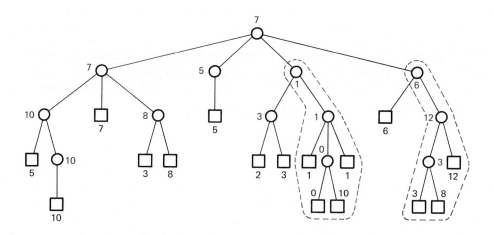

Figure 14.6. Minimax evaluation of a game tree

The dotted lines shown in color will be explained later, in one of the Projects. It turns out, by keeping track of the minimum and maximum found so far, that it is not necessary to evaluate every node in a game tree, and, in Figure 14.6, the nodes enclosed in the dotted lines need not be evaluated.

minimax   Since in evaluating a game tree we alternately take minima and maxima, this process is called a *minimax* procedure.

14.2.3 Algorithm Development

Next let us see how the minimax method can be embodied in a formal algorithm for looking ahead in a game-playing program. We wish to write a general-purpose algorithm that can be used with any two-player game; we shall therefore leave various types and data structures unspecified, since their choice will depend on the particular game being played. First, we shall need to use a procedure that we call

procedure Recommend(P: player; **var** L: listtype; **var** v: value)

recommended moves that will return a list L of recommended moves for the player P, as well as a value v that depends on the current situation in the game (but not yet on which of the recommended moves is eventually made). For the player, we use the enumerated type declaration

type player = (first, second)

and always take the first player as the one who wishes to maximize the value, whereas the second player wishes to minimize the value. The value will normally be a number. Whether it is an integer or a real number depends on the game.

list implementation How the list of recommended moves is to be implemented depends on the game. In some games, the moves can be described concisely, and only a few different kinds of moves are appropriate; for such games a contiguous list may be best. In other games, the number of recommended moves can change greatly from one turn to another, and a linked list may prove better. Hence, we leave listtype unspecified, and use the standard procedures for processing lists. The entries in the list are moves. Thus, we have

type listentry = move.

Again, the declaration of the type move depends on the game.

termination Before writing the procedure that looks ahead to evaluate the tree, we should decide when the algorithm is to stop looking further. For a game of reasonable complexity, we must establish a number of levels maxdepth beyond which the search will not go. But there are at least two other conditions under which exploring the tree is unnecessary. The first occurs when the procedure Recommend returns a list with only one recommended move, and the other occurs when the outcome of the game is already completely determined (it is a certain win, loss, or tie). We coalesce these two conditions by requiring the procedure Recommend to return only one move when the outcome of the game is certain. Thus, even if the procedure Recommend finds several winning moves, it must return only one of them.

The basic task of looking ahead in the tree can now be described with the following recursive algorithm.

outline
procedure LookAhead(depth: integer; P: player;
 var recmove: move; **var** recvalue: value);
{**Pre:** *The game is in a legitimate position; it is the turn of player P, and at least one move is possible.*
Post: *After looking ahead* depth *levels through the game tree (except in the case of forced moves), the procedure returns the recommended move* recmove, *which has a calculated value of* recvalue.}
begin   {*Procedure LookAhead*}
 Recommend(P, L, recvalue);
 if the list L contains only one recommended move **then**
  Return the one move and associated value
 else begin
  for each recommended move **do**
   Tentatively make the move and recursively LookAhead for the best move for the other player;
  Select the best value for P among the values returned in the loop;
  Return the corresponding move and value as the result
 end
end;   {*procedure LookAhead*}

14.2.4 Refinement

To specify the details of this algorithm, we must, finally, employ two more procedures that depend on the game:

MakeMove(P: player; m: move)   and   UndoMove(P: player; m: move).

These procedures make and undo tentative moves as indicated. In the formal procedure, we also rearrange some of the steps from the outline.

procedure LookAhead(depth: integer; P: player;
 var recmove: move; **var** recvalue: value);
{**Pre:** *The game is in a legitimate position; it is the turn of player P, and at least one move is possible.*
Post: *After looking ahead* depth *levels through the game tree (except in the case of forced moves), the procedure returns the recommended move* recmove, *which has a calculated value of* recvalue.
Uses: *Procedures* Recommend, Forfeit, MakeMove, UndoMove, *package of list procedures, constant* infinity *(larger than value of any move).*}
var
 opponent: player;   {*opponent of P*}
 oppmove: move;   {*recommended move for opponent*}
 oppvalue: value;   {*value returned for opponent's move*}
 L: listtype;   {*list of recommended moves for P*}
 tentmove: move;   {*tentative move being tried in tree*}
 w: window;   {*used to traverse list* L; tentmove *is at* w}

```
begin                                          {procedure LookAhead}
   Recommend(P, L, recvalue);
   if ListEmpty(L) then
      Forfeit                                  {cannot make any move}
   else if (ListSize(L) = 1) or (depth = 0) then
      RetrieveList(1, recmove, L)    {Return the one move as the answer.}

                              {The value recvalue has been set by Recommend.}
   else begin
      if P = first then
      begin                                {Prepare to maximize recvalue.}
         opponent := second;
         recvalue := − infinity     {Set to a value less than any that occurs.}
      end
      else begin                           {Prepare to minimize recvalue.}
         opponent := first;
         recvalue := infinity    {Set to a value greater than any that occurs.}
      end;
      StartList(w, L);
      repeat
         RetrieveList(w, tentmove, L);
         MakeMove(P, tentmove);
         LookAhead(depth − 1, opponent, oppmove, oppvalue);
         UndoMove(P, tentmove);
         if ((P = first)     and (oppvalue > recvalue)) or
            ((P = second) and (oppvalue < recvalue)) then
         begin
            recvalue := oppvalue;
            recmove := tentmove
         end;
         NextList(w, L)
      until not OnList(w, L)
   end
end;                                            {procedure LookAhead}
```

EXERCISES 14.2

E1. Assign values of +1 for a win by the first player and −1 for a win by the second player in the game of Eight, and apply the minimax procedure to its tree, as shown in Figure 14.4.

E2. A variation of the game of *Nim* begins with a pile of sticks, from which a player can remove 1, 2, or 3 sticks at each turn. The player must remove at least 1 (but no more than remain on the pile). The player who takes the last stick loses. Draw the complete game tree that begins with **(a)** 5 and **(b)** 6 sticks. Assign appropriate values for the leaves of the tree, and evaluate the other nodes by the minimax method.

E3. Draw the top three levels (showing the first two moves) of the game tree for the game of tic-tac-toe (Noughts and Crosses), and calculate the number of vertices that will appear on the fourth level. You may reduce the size of the tree by taking advantage of symmetries: At the first move, for example, show only three possibilities (the center square, a corner, or a side square) rather than all nine. Further symmetries near the root will reduce the size of the game tree.

■■■■■■■ **PROJECTS 14.2**

P1. Write a main program and the other procedures needed to play Eight against a human opponent. The procedure Recommend can return all legal moves at each turn.

P2. [*Major project*]   Write a look-ahead program for playing tic-tac-toe. In the simplest version, the procedure Recommend returns all empty positions as recommended moves. Approximately how many possibilities will then be investigated in a complete search of the game tree? Implement this simple method. Second, modify the procedure Recommend so that it searches for two marks in a row with the third empty, and thereby recommends moves more intelligently. Compare the running times of the two versions.

P3. [*Major project*]   Consider the following game played on an $n \times n$ board. Each player alternately puts a 1 or a 0 into an empty square (either player can use either number), and the game continues until the board is completely filled. The numbers along each row, column, and the two main diagonals are then added. If there are more odd sums than there are even sums, then the first player wins. If the number of even sums is greater, then the second player wins. Otherwise, the game is a tie. Write a look-ahead program to play this game against a human opponent who chooses the value of n.

P4. [*Major project*]   Write a look-ahead program that plays three-dimensional tic-tac-toe. This game is played on a $4 \times 4 \times 4$ cube, with the usual rules. There are 76 possibly winning lines (rows, columns, stacks, and diagonals) with four in a row.

three-dimensional tic-tac-toe

P5. If you have worked your way through the tree in Figure 14.5 in enough detail, you may have noticed that it is not necessary to obtain the values for all the vertices while doing the minimax process, for there are some parts of the tree in which the best move certainly cannot appear. Let us suppose that we work our way through the tree starting at the lower left, and filling in the value for a parent vertex as soon as we have the values for all its children. After we have done all the vertices in the two main branches on the left, we find values of 7 and 5, and therefore the maximum value will be at least 7. When we go to the next vertex on level 1 and its left child, we find that the value of this child is 3. At this stage, we are taking minima, so the value to be assigned to the parent on level 1 cannot possibly be more than 3 (it is actually 1). Since 3 is less than 7, the first player will take the leftmost branch instead, and we can exclude the other branch. The vertices that, in this way, need never be evaluated, are shown within dotted lines in color in Figure 14.6.

alpha-beta pruning

The process of eliminating vertices in this way is called ***alpha-beta pruning***. The Greek letters α (alpha) and β (beta) are generally used to denote the cutoff points found.

Modify the procedure LookAhead so that it uses alpha-beta pruning to reduce the number of branches investigated. Compare the performance of the two versions in playing several games.

14.3

COMPILATION BY RECURSIVE DESCENT

Consider the problem of designing a compiler that translates a program written in Pascal into machine language. As the compiler reads through the source program written in Pascal, it must understand the syntax and translate each line into the equivalent instructions in machine language.

The first part of a Pascal program (or subprogram) contains declarations of labels, constants, types, and variables. The compiler will use this information to allocate space for variables, and to determine what kinds of operations can be done with the variables. At the same time, the compiler must remember the

identifiers

identifiers that have been declared as names of types, variables, and the like, so that these identifiers can be interpreted correctly when they appear later in the program. Hence the compiler sets up a ***symbol table*** to keep track of the identifiers. Some compilers use a binary tree to contain the symbol table; others use a hash table; still other compilers use some combination or some other data structure. Although many interesting ideas appear in the design and use of symbol tables, our goal here is only to obtain an overview of how a compiler can use recursion, so we shall not study symbol tables further.

subprograms

The next part of a Pascal program contains declarations of procedures and functions, and the final part consists of the action (statements) of the program. The declarations of procedures and functions provide a good application of recursion. Pascal syntax is designed so that the overall form of a subprogram is the same as that of the main program. Hence there is no need to write another complete section of the compiler to translate the declarations and statements within a subprogram. Instead, the compiler can in essence call itself recursively to compile each subprogram, and after the recursive call returns, it will go on to compile the next subprogram. After all the subprograms are compiled, it will translate the statements in the main program. The main program itself, in fact, can be regarded as a subprogram within a mythical outer block in which all the standard identifiers (such as the constant maxint, the types Boolean and text, the procedures writeln and dispose) have already been declared. In this way, the main program can be treated almost completely symmetrically with subprograms.

14.3.1 The Main Program

In this section, we shall use the term *module* to refer to any one of a procedure, function, or program being compiled. The overall task of the compiler is described as follows:

outline

```
program PascalCompiler;
begin
    Set up symbol table and declarations for all standard identifiers;
    Check that first word of the input is ' program';
    DoModule;
    Check that the last symbol is a period '.'
end.
```

The procedure DoModule translates a program, procedure, or function.

tokens

Note that the compiler must continually check what is the next word or symbol in the program. Depending on what this word or symbol is, various actions will be taken. Such a word or symbol is called a *token*, and, for our purposes, we take a token to be any one of a Pascal reserved word, identifier, literal constant, operator, or punctuation mark. Note, furthermore, that the only way to tell that many constructions in Pascal have terminated is when a token is found that is *not* part of the construction. A statement, for example, terminates when the next token is a semicolon or one of the words **end**, **else**, or **until**. Hence whenever we start to process part of the program, the variable nexttoken will be the token that initiates that part, and when the processing is complete, then nexttoken will be the first token not in the part just processed. The procedure GetToken will split out the next token.

With this understanding, we can expand the procedure DoModule. The first step it will do is to obtain the next token, so that it will effectively skip over the word **program**, **procedure**, or **function**, and it is almost irrelevant which of these is being processed.

outline

```
procedure DoModule;
begin
    Initialize the symbol table for the symbols in this module;
    GetToken(nexttoken);
    if nexttoken = '(' then DoParameters;        {returns after matching ')'}
    if this module is a function then DoFunctionValue;
    if nexttoken = ' label' then DoLabelSection;
    if nexttoken = ' const' then DoConstantSection;
    if nexttoken = ' type' then DoTypeSection;
    if nexttoken = ' var' then DoVariableSection;
    while (nexttoken = ' function') or (nexttoken = ' procedure') do
        DoModule;
    if nexttoken = ' begin' then DoCompoundStatement else Error
end;
```

14.3.2 Type Declarations

In order to see a further application of recursion, let us take a slightly more detailed look at the declaration of types. In Pascal, arrays may contain arrays; records may contain records. A well-designed compiler will use a separate procedure to process each of the standard categories of types. Thus there will be a procedure DoType that will, as required, invoke procedures that we call DoArray, DoRecord, DoSet, and DoScalarType (amongst others).

The way in which these procedures work is closely related to their syntax diagrams. In particular, DoArray will invoke DoScalarType to determine the type by which the array is indexed, and DoType to determine the type of the entries. DoRecord will invoke a procedure called DoVariable for each of the fields within the record. DoVariable will, in turn, invoke DoType to find out the type of the variable. These recursive calls thus eventually work their way down to the simple types, and the meaning of the entire construction is then determined.

top-down parsing

The process of splitting a text or expression into pieces to determine its syntax is called **parsing**. Parsing can proceed either by first examining the atomic (indivisible) building blocks and how they are put together (called **bottom-up parsing**) or by splitting the text or expression into simpler components (called **top-down parsing**). Hence comes the motivation for the term **recursive descent**: the compiler parses large constructions by splitting them into smaller pieces and recursively parses each of the pieces. It thereby descends to simpler and smaller constructions, which are finally split apart into their atomic components, which can be evaluated directly.

recursive descent

example

As an example, consider the following declaration, which results in the tree of procedure calls shown in Figure 14.7. The scalar type index is assumed to be previously defined in the program:

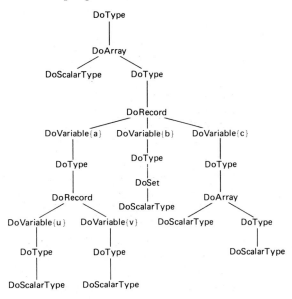

Figure 14.7. Parse tree for a type declaration by recursive descent

```
type
  item = array [index] of
    record
      a: record u: integer; v: index end;
      b: set of index;
      c: array [index] of real;
    end;
```

14.3.3 Parsing Statements

Now let us turn to the statements in a program, the part that performs the program's action. We shall also use recursive descent to parse the statements in the program. The action part of a program is one compound statement (going from **begin** to **end**) and is parsed by the procedure DoCompoundStatement. A compound statement is made up of zero or more statements, each of which will be parsed by DoStatement, which, in turn, invokes a different procedure for each possible kind of statement.

As an example, let us see how an **if** statement might be parsed and translated into an assembler language (that is, into a language that corresponds directly with machine-level instructions, but still allows symbolic names and statement labels). From its syntax diagram, we know that an **if** statement consists of the token **if** followed by a Boolean expression, followed by the token **then** and a statement, and, finally, optionally followed by the token **else** and another statement. See Figure 14.8.

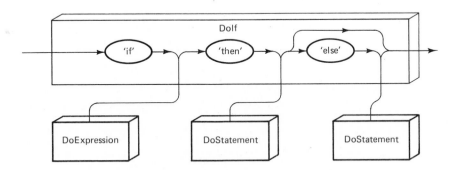

Figure 14.8. Parse tree for an **if** statement

The assembler-language equivalent of the **if** statement will first evaluate the expression, and then use conditional jumps (**goto** statements) to branch around the assembler code corresponding to the statements in the **then** or **else** clauses, as appropriate. The syntax diagram therefore translates into the following procedure.

As we found when parsing declarations, each part of a statement is usually recognized only when a token is encountered that does not belong. Hence we shall again use a procedure GetToken and always keep the variable nexttoken one step ahead of what has been processed.

outline

```
procedure DoIf;
begin                                              {procedure DoIf}
    GetToken(nexttoken);
    DoExpression;          {Write code to evaluate the Boolean expression.}
    if nexttoken <> ' then' then
        Error
    else begin
        Generate a new assembler-language label x;
        Write assembler code that will cause a conditional jump
            to label x when the Boolean expression is false;
        GetToken(nexttoken);
        DoStatement;       {Write code for the statement in the then clause.}
    end;
    if nexttoken = ' else' then
    begin
        Generate a new assembler-language label y;
        Write an assembler unconditional jump to label y;
        Write the label x at this point in the assembler code;
        GetToken(nexttoken);
        DoStatement;          {Write code for statement in the else clause.}
        Write the label y at this point in the assembler code
    end
    else                                       {case with no else clause}
        Write the label x at this point in the assembler code
end;                                               {procedure DoIf}
```

exercise Finally, as an exercise, you should apply this algorithm to the statement

if a > 0 **then** b := 1 **else** **if** a = 0 **then** b := 2 **else** b := 3;

Since this line is made up of two **if** statements, the parsing procedure will call itself recursively and generate a total of four labels. The parse tree for this statement is shown in Figure 14.9.

In practice, an actual compiler may rearrange some of the jumps and thereby produce an answer superficially different from yours. The output of one such *sample output* compiler applied to the preceding statement is given in Figure 14.10, where the only changes made from the actual output of the compiler are to replace some numeric displacements calculated by the compiler by their symbolic forms. This particular compiler generates extra statement labels because, for technical reasons, it must follow the wasteful practice of generating branch instructions to do

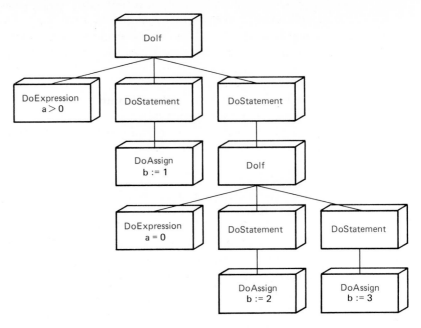

Figure 14.9. Parse tree for a nested **if** statement

nothing but branch around other jump instructions. In the resulting assembler language, the instruction TST tests the sign of an integer; BEQ branches if the integer is equal to 0, and BGT branches if it is greater than 0. JMP is an unconditional jump. MOV moves the first number given to the second location specified.

```
        TST     A           ; if a > 0 then
        BGT     L0
        JMP     L1
L0:     MOV     #1, B       ; b := 1
        JMP     L2          ; else if a = 0 then
L1:     TST     A
        BEQ     L3
        JMP     L4
L3:     MOV     #2, B       ; b := 2
        JMP     L5          ; else
L4:     MOV     #3, B       ; b := 3
L5:
L2:
```

Figure 14.10. Output from a Pascal compiler

compilers As you can see from all this, the construction of a compiler is quite a complicated process. A typical Pascal compiler (when written in Pascal) may be five to ten thousand lines of code. The present discussion has attempted only to give a broad overview of the way in which recursion proves useful in writing a compiler. If you take a more detailed view, you will find that we have not only omitted programming steps, but that it is necessary to address many problems that we have not considered at all (for example, error processing). Many interesting ideas arise in the consideration of these problems, so that compiler design and construction constitute a major subject within computer science, one worthy of extensive study in its own right.

EXERCISES 14.3

E1. For each of the following declarations, draw a tree similar to Figure 14.7 showing the subprogram calls that will occur in parsing the declaration.

    a. **type** complex = **record** x: real; y: real **end;**
    b. **type** listtype = **record** count: index; L: **array** [index] **of** item **end;**
    c. **var** X: listtype;
    d. **var** A: **array** [index] **of set of** index;

E2. For each of the following statements, draw a tree similar to Figure 14.9 showing the subprogram calls that will occur in parsing the statement. You may assume the existence of subprograms such as DoCase, DoWhile, and the like.

    a. **while** x > 0 **do if** x > 10 **then** x := −x **else** x := y − x;
    b. **if** a > b **then if** c > d **then** x := 1 **else if** e > f **then** x := 3;
    c. **begin end;**

E3. Draw parse trees and write outlines of procedures for parsing the following kinds of statements.

    a. **while** expression **do** statement.
    b. Compound statement: **begin** statement(s) **end.**
    c. **case** ... **end.**
    d. **for** variable := expression **to** (or **downto**) expression **do** statement.

E4. Write a Pascal procedure GetToken that will read through an input text and return each token (as defined in this section) one at a time as the procedure is invoked.

POINTERS AND PITFALLS

    1. Recursion should be used freely in the initial design of algorithms. It is especially appropriate where the main step toward solution consists of reducing a problem to one or more smaller cases.

2. Be very careful that your algorithm always terminates and handles trivial cases correctly.

3. Study your problem to see if it fits one of the standard paradigms for recursive algorithms, such as divide and conquer, backtracking, tree structure, or recursive descent. Let the use of recursion fit the structure of the problem.

REVIEW QUESTIONS

14.1   1. Describe *backtracking* as a problem-solving method.

2. State the pigeonhole principle.

3. What effect does backtracking have on the recursion tree compared to investigating all possibilities?

14.2   4. Explain the *minimax* method for finding the value of a game.

14.3   5. What is *parsing*?

6. What is *recursive descent*?

7. Draw a parse tree for the type declaration

list = **record** e: **array** [1 .. max] **of** item; n: 0 .. max **end**;

8. Draw a parse tree for the statement

for i := 1 **to** 10 **do if** odd(i) **then** Process(i) **else** Redo(i);

PART V

FURTHER STRUCTURES AND ALGORITHMS

This final part of the book develops several important structures useful both for storing data and for problem solving, as well as algorithms for their processing. In Chapter 15, we consider tables as a generalization of arrays. Tables are accessed not by the *position* of the data, as in lists, but by the value of a key. These ideas are further refined and developed in the study of *hash tables* in Chapter 16. Chapter 17 then turns to *graphs*, which we can regard as problem-solving structures that generalize trees. Chapter 18, finally, introduces the subject of *software engineering* by developing a large program that uses several of the methods that we have studied in earlier chapters.

15

TABLES

This chapter continues the study of information retrieval begun in previous chapters, but now concentrating on tables instead of lists or trees. We begin with a deeper consideration of ordinary rectangular arrays, then we turn to other kinds of arrays. Next we discuss tables as a new abstract data type, and conclude by applying the ideas to develop yet another sorting method.

15.1

INTRODUCTION: BREAKING THE lg n BARRIER

In Chapter 9, we showed that, by use of key comparisons alone, it is impossible to complete a search of n items in fewer than $\lg n$ comparisons, on average. But this result speaks only of searching by key comparisons such as we do by applying binary search to a list or by using a binary search tree. If we can use some other method, then we may be able to arrange our data so that we can locate a given item even more quickly.

table lookup

In fact, we commonly do so. If we have 500 different records, with an index between 1 and 500 assigned to each, then we would never think of using sequential or binary search to locate a record. We would simply store the records in an array of size 500 and use the index n to locate the record of item n by ordinary table lookup.

functions for information retrieval

Both table lookup and searching share the same essential purpose, that of *information retrieval*. We begin with a key (which may be complicated or simply an index) and wish to find the location of the item (if any) with that key. In other words, both table lookup and our searching algorithms provide *functions* from the set of keys to locations in a list or array. The functions are in fact one-to-one from the set of keys that actually occur to the set of locations that actually occur, since we assume that each item has only one key, and there is only one item with a given key.

tables

In this chapter, we study ways to implement and access arrays in contiguous storage, beginning with ordinary rectangular arrays, and then considering tables with restricted location of nonzero entries, such as triangular tables. We turn afterward to more general problems, with the purpose of introducing and motivating the use first of access tables and then hash tables for information retrieval.

We shall see that, depending on the shape of the table, several steps may be needed to retrieve an entry, but, even so, the time required remains $O(1)$—that is, it is bounded by a constant that does not depend on the size of the table—and thus table lookup can be more efficient than any searching method.

15.2

RECTANGULAR ARRAYS

Because of the importance of rectangular arrays, almost all high-level languages provide convenient and efficient means to store and access them, so that generally the programmer need not worry about the implementation details. Nonetheless, computer storage is fundamentally arranged in a contiguous sequence (that is, in a straight line with each entry next to another), so for every access to a rectangular array, the machine must do some work to convert the location within a rectangle to a position along a line. Let us take a slightly closer look at this process.

Row- and Column-Major Ordering

Perhaps the most natural way to read a rectangular array is to read the entries of the first row from left to right, then the entries of the second row, and so on until the last row has been read. This is also the order in which most compilers store a rectangular array, and is called *row-major ordering*. For example, if the rows of an array are numbered from 1 to 2 and the columns are numbered from 1 to 3, then the order of indices with which the entries are stored in row-major ordering is

$$[1, 1] \qquad [1, 2] \qquad [1, 3] \qquad [2, 1] \qquad [2, 2] \qquad [2, 3].$$

FORTRAN   Standard FORTRAN instead uses *column-major ordering*, in which the entries of the first column come first, and so on. This example in column-major ordering is

$$[1, 1] \qquad [2, 1] \qquad [1, 2] \qquad [2, 2] \qquad [1, 3] \qquad [2, 3].$$

Figure 15.1 further illustrates row- and column-major orderings for an array with three rows and four columns.

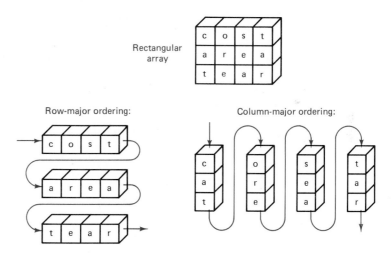

Figure 15.1. Sequential representation of a rectangular array

Indexing Rectangular Arrays

In the general problem, the compiler must be able to start with an index $[i, j]$ and calculate where the corresponding entry of the array will be stored. We shall derive a formula for this calculation. For simplicity, we shall use only row-major ordering and suppose that the rows are numbered from 0 to $m - 1$ and the columns from 0 to $n - 1$. The general case is treated as an Exercise. Altogether, the array will have mn entries, as must its sequential implementation. We number the entries in the array from 0 to $mn - 1$. To obtain the formula calculating the position where $[i, j]$ goes, we first consider some special cases. Clearly $[0, 0]$ goes to position 0, and, in fact, the entire first row is easy: $[0, j]$ goes to position j. The first entry of the second row, $[1, 0]$, comes after $[0, n - 1]$, and thus goes into position n. Continuing, we see that $[1, j]$ goes to position $n + j$. Entries of the next row will have two full rows, that is, $2n$ entries, preceding them. Hence entry $[2, j]$ goes to position $2n + j$. In general, the entries of row i are preceded by ni earlier entries, so the desired formula is

$$\text{Entry } [i, j] \text{ goes to position } ni + j.$$

A formula of this kind, which gives the sequential location of an array entry, is called an **index function**.

Variation: An Access Table

The index function for rectangular arrays is certainly not difficult to calculate, and the compilers of most high-level languages will simply write into the machine-language program the necessary steps for its calculation every time a reference is made to a rectangular array. On small machines, however, multiplication can be quite slow, so a slightly different method can be used to eliminate the multiplications.

access table, rectangular array

This method is to keep an auxiliary array, a part of the multiplication table for n. The array will contain the values

$$0, \quad n, \quad 2n, \quad 3n, \quad \ldots, \quad (m - 1)n.$$

Note that this array is much smaller (usually) than the rectangular array, so that it can be kept permanently in memory without losing too much space. Its entries then need be calculated only once (and note that they can be calculated using only addition). For all later references to the rectangular array, the compiler can find the position for $[i, j]$ by taking the entry in position i of the auxiliary table, adding j, and going to the resulting position.

This auxiliary table provides our first example of an **access table** (see Figure 15.1). In general, an access table is an auxiliary array used to find data stored elsewhere. The terms **access vector** and **dope vector** (the latter especially when additional information is included) are also used.

■ EXERCISES 15.2

E1. What is the index function for a two-dimensional rectangular array with bounds

$$\textbf{array}\,[0\,..\,m - 1, 0\,..\,n - 1]$$

under column-major ordering?

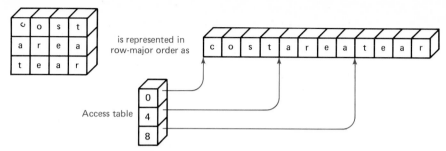

Figure 15.2. Access table for a rectangular array

E2. Give the index function, with row-major ordering, for a two-dimensional array with arbitrary bounds

$$\textbf{array}\,[\,\textsf{r}\,..\,\textsf{s},\,\textsf{t}\,..\,\textsf{u}\,].$$

E3. Find the index function, with the generalization of row-major ordering, for an array with d dimensions and arbitrary bounds for each dimension.

15.3

TABLES OF VARIOUS SHAPES

matrix

Information that is usually stored in a rectangular array may not require every position in the rectangle for its representation. If we define a ***matrix*** to be an array of numbers, then often some of the positions within the matrix will be required to be 0. Several such examples are shown in Figure 15.3. Even when the entries in a table are not numbers, the positions actually used may not be all of those in a rectangle, and there may be better implementations than using a rectangular array and leaving some positions vacant. In this section, we examine ways to implement tables of various shapes, ways that will not require setting aside unused space in a rectangular array.

15.3.1 Triangular Tables

Let us consider the representation of a lower triangular table shown in Figure 15.3. Such a table can be defined formally as a table in which all indices $[i, j]$ are required to satisfy $i \geq j$. We can implement a triangular table in a sequential array by sliding each row out after the one above it, as shown in Figure 15.4.

To construct the index function that describes this mapping, we again make the slight simplification of assuming that the rows and the columns are numbered starting with 0. To find the position where $[i, j]$ goes, we now need to find where row number i starts, and then to locate column j we need only add j to the

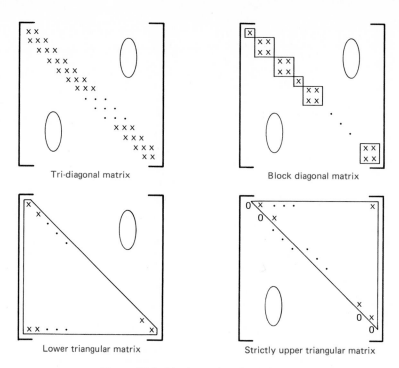

Tri-diagonal matrix

Block diagonal matrix

Lower triangular matrix

Strictly upper triangular matrix

Figure 15.3. Matrices of various shapes

starting point of row i. If the entries of the contiguous array are also numbered starting with 0, then the index of the starting point will be the same as the number of entries that precede row i. Clearly there are 0 entries before row 0, and only the one entry of row 0 precedes row 1. For row 2, there are $1 + 2 = 3$ preceding entries, and, in general, we see that preceding row i there are exactly

$$1 + 2 + \cdots + i = \tfrac{1}{2}i(i+1)$$

entries. Hence the desired function is that entry $[i, j]$ of the triangular table

index function, rectangular table

corresponds to entry

$$\tfrac{1}{2}i(i+1) + j$$

of the contiguous array.

access table, triangular table

As we did for rectangular arrays, we can again avoid all multiplications and divisions by setting up an access table whose entries correspond to the row indices of the triangular table. Position i of the access table will permanently contain the value $\tfrac{1}{2}i(i+1)$. The access table will be calculated only once at the start of the program, and then used repeatedly at each reference to the triangular table. Note that even the initial calculation of this access table requires no multiplication or division, but only addition to calculate its entries in the order

$$0, \quad 1, \quad 1 + 2, \quad (1 + 2) + 3, \quad \ldots .$$

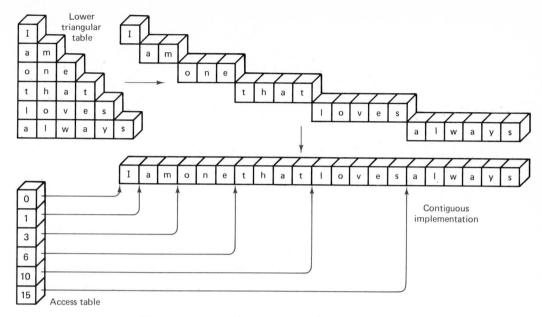

Figure 15.4. Contiguous implementation of a triangular table

15.3.2 Jagged Tables

In both of the foregoing examples, we have considered a rectangular table as made up from its rows. In ordinary rectangular arrays, all the rows have the same length; in triangular tables, the length of each row can be found from a simple formula. We now consider the case of jagged tables, such as the one in Figure 15.5, where there is no predictable relation between the position of a row and its length.

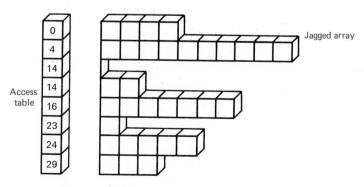

Figure 15.5. Access table for a jagged table

It is clear from the diagram that, even though we are not able to give an *a priori* function to map the jagged table into contiguous storage, the use of an access table remains as easy as in the previous examples, and elements of the jagged table can be referenced just as quickly. To set up the access table, we must construct the jagged table in its natural order, beginning with its first row. Entry 0 of the access table is, as before, the start of the contiguous array. After each row of the jagged table has been constructed, the index of the first unused position of the contiguous storage should then be entered as the next entry in the access table and used to start constructing the next row of the jagged table.

15.3.3 Inverted Tables

Next let us consider an example illustrating multiple access tables, by which we can refer to a single table of records by several different keys at once.

Consider the problem faced by the telephone company in accessing the records of its customers. To publish the telephone book, the records must be sorted alphabetically by the name of the subscriber. But to process long-distance charges, the accounts must be sorted by telephone number. To do routine mainte-nance, the company also needs to have its subscribers sorted by their address, so *multiple records* that a repairman may be able to work on several lines with one trip. Conceivably, the telephone company could keep three (or more) sets of its records, one sorted by name, one by number, and one by address. This way, however, would not only be very wasteful of storage space, but would introduce endless headaches if one set of records were updated but another was not, and erroneous and unpredictable information might be used.

By using access tables, we can avoid the multiple sets of records, and we can still find the records by any of the three keys almost as quickly as if the records *multiple access* were fully sorted by that key. For the names, we set up one access table. The first *tables* entry in this table is the position where the records of the subscriber whose name is first in alphabetical order are stored, the second entry gives the location of the second (in alphabetical order) subscriber's records, and so on. In a second access table, the first entry is the location of the subscriber's records whose telephone number happens to be smallest in numerical order. In yet a third access table, the entries give the locations of the records sorted lexicographically by address. Notice that in this method all the fields that are treated as keys are processed in the same way.

There is no particular reason why the records themselves need to be sorted according to one key rather than another, or, in fact, why they need to be sorted at all. The records themselves can be kept in an arbitrary order—say, in the order in which they were first entered into the system. It also makes no difference *unordered* whether the records are in an array, with entries in the access tables being indices *records for* of the array, or whether the records are in dynamic storage, with the access tables *ordered access* holding pointers to individual records. In any case, it is the access tables that *tables* are used for information retrieval, and, as ordinary contiguous arrays, they may be used for table lookup, or binary search, or any other purpose for which a contiguous implementation is appropriate.

An example of this scheme for a small number of accounts is shown in Figure 15.6.

Index	Name	Address	Phone
1	Hill, Thomas M.	High Towers #317	2829478
2	Baker, John S.	17 King Street	2884285
3	Roberts, L. B.	53 Ash Street	4372296
4	King, Barbara	High Towers #802	2863386
5	Hill, Thomas M.	39 King Street	2495723
6	Byers, Carolyn	118 Maple Street	4394231
7	Moody, C. L.	High Towers #210	2822214

Access Tables

Name	Address	Phone
2	3	5
6	7	7
1	1	1
5	4	4
4	2	2
7	5	3
3	6	6

Figure 15.6. Multikey access tables: an inverted table

EXERCISES 15.3

E1. The *main diagonal* of a square matrix consists of the entries for which the row and column indices are equal. A *diagonal matrix* is a square matrix in which all entries not on the main diagonal are 0. Describe a way to store a diagonal matrix without using space for entries that are necessarily 0, and give the corresponding index function.

E2. A *tri-diagonal matrix* is a square matrix in which all entries are 0 except possibly those on the main diagonal and on the diagonals immediately above and below it. That is, T is a tri-diagonal matrix means that $T[i, j] = 0$ unless $|i - j| \leq 1$.

    a. Devise a space-efficient storage scheme for tri-diagonal matrices, and give the corresponding index function.

    b. The *transpose* of a matrix is the matrix obtained by interchanging its rows with the corresponding columns. That is, matrix B is the transpose of matrix A means that $B[j, i] = A[i, j]$ for all indices i and j corresponding to positions in the matrix. Write a procedure that transposes a tri-diagonal matrix using the storage scheme devised in part (a).

E3. An *upper triangular matrix* is a square array in which all entries below the main diagonal are 0.

   a. Describe the modifications necessary to use the access-table method to store an upper triangular matrix.

   b. The transpose of a lower triangular matrix will be an upper triangular matrix. Write a procedure that will transpose a lower triangular matrix, using access tables to refer to both matrices.

E4. Consider a table of the triangular shape shown in Figure 15.7, where the columns are indexed from $-n$ to n and the rows from 0 to n.

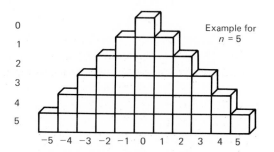

Figure 15.7. A table symmetrically triangular around 0

   a. Devise an index function that maps a table of this shape into a sequential array.

   b. Write a procedure that will generate an access table for finding the first entry of each row of a table of this shape within the contiguous array.

   c. Write a procedure that will reflect the table from left to right. The entries in column 0 (the central column) remain unchanged, those in columns -1 and 1 are swapped, and so on.

PROJECTS 15.3

Implement the method described in the text that uses an access table to store a lower triangular table, as applied in the following projects.

P1. Write a procedure that will read the entries of a lower triangular table from the terminal.

P2. Write a procedure that will print a lower triangular table at the terminal.

P3. Suppose that a lower triangular table is a table of distances between cities, as often appears on a road map. Write a procedure that will check the triangle rule: The distance from city A to city C is never more than the distance from A to city B, plus the distance from B to C.

15.4

TABLES: A NEW ABSTRACT DATA TYPE

At the beginning of this chapter, we studied several *index functions* used to locate entries in tables, and then we turned to *access tables*, which were arrays used for the same purpose as index functions. The analogy between functions and table lookup is indeed very close: With a function, we start with an argument and calculate a corresponding value; with a table, we start with an index and look up a corresponding value. Let us now use this analogy to produce a formal definition of the term *table*, a definition that will, in turn, motivate new ideas that come to fruition in the following section.

Functions

domain, codomain, and range

In mathematics, a ***function*** is defined in terms of two sets and a correspondence from elements of the first set to elements of the second. If f is a function from a set A to a set B, then f assigns to each element of A a unique element of B. The set A is called the ***domain*** of f, and the set B is called the ***codomain*** of f. The subset of B containing just those elements that occur as values of f is called the ***range*** of f. This definition is illustrated in Figure 15.8.

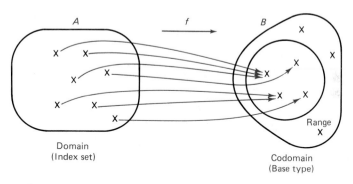

Figure 15.8. The domain, codomain, and range of a function

index set, value type

Table access begins with an index and uses the table to look up a corresponding value. Hence, for a table, we call the domain the ***index set***, and we call the codomain the ***base type*** or ***value type***. (Recall that, in Section 7.6.2, a *type* was defined as a set of values.) If, for example, we have the array declaration

array [m .. n] **of** real

then the index set is the set of integers between m and n, and the base type is the set of all real numbers. As a second example, consider a triangular table with m rows whose entries have type item. The base type is then simply type item and the index type is the set of ordered pairs of integers

$$\{(i,j) \mid 1 \leq j \leq i \leq \mathsf{m}\}.$$

An Abstract Data Type

We are now well on the way toward defining *table* as a new abstract data type, but to complete the definition, we must, of course, also specify the operations that can be performed. Before doing so, let us summarize what we know.

A *table* with index set I and base type T is a function from I into T together with the following operations.

1. *Table access*: Evaluate the function at any index in I.

2. *Table assignment*: Modify the function by changing its value at a specified index in I to the new value specified in the assignment.

These two operations are all that are provided by Pascal and some other languages, but that is no reason why we cannot allow the possibility of further operations. If we compare the definition of a list, we find that we allowed insertion and deletion as well as access and assignment. We can do the same with tables.

---

3. *Insertion*: Adjoin a new element x to the index set I and define a corresponding value of the function at x.

4. *Deletion*: Delete an element x from the index set I and restrict the function to the resulting smaller domain.

Even though these last two operations are not available directly in Pascal, they remain very useful for many applications, and we shall study them further in the next section. In some other languages, such as APL and SNOBOL, tables that change size while the program is running are an important feature. In any case, we should always be careful to program *into* a language and never allow our thinking to be limited by the restrictions of a particular language.

Implementation

index functions and access tables

The definition just given is that of an abstract data type and in itself says nothing about implementation, nor does it speak of the index functions or access tables studied earlier. Index functions and access tables are, in fact, implementation methods for more general tables. An index function or access table starts with a general index set of some specified form and produces as its result an index in some subscript range, such as a subrange of the integers. This range can then be used directly as subscripts for arrays provided by the programming language. In this way, the implementation of a table is divided into two smaller problems: finding an access table or index function, and programming an array. You should note that both of these are special cases of tables, and hence we have an example *divide and* of solving a problem by dividing it into two smaller problems of the same nature. *conquer* This process is illustrated in Figure 15.9.

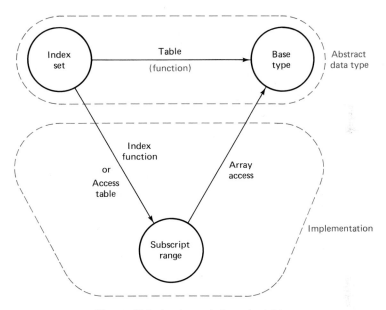

Figure 15.9. Implementation of a table

Comparisons

Let us compare the abstract data types *list* and *table*. The underlying mathematical construction for a list is the sequence, and for a table, it is the set and the *lists and tables* function. Sequences have an implicit order: a first element, a second, and so on; but sets and functions have no such order. (If the index set has some natural order, then sometimes this order is reflected in the table, but this is not a necessary aspect of using tables.) Hence information retrieval from a list naturally involves a search like the ones studied in the previous chapter, but information *retrieval* retrieval from a table requires different methods, access methods that go directly to the desired entry. The time required for searching a list generally depends on the number n of items in the list and is at least $\lg n$. The time for accessing a table, however, does not usually depend on the number of items in the table; that is, it is usually $O(1)$. For this reason, in many applications, table access is significantly faster than list searching.

traversal On the other hand, traversal is a natural operation for a list but not for a table. It is generally easy to move through a list, performing some operation with every item in the list. In general, it may not be nearly so easy to perform an operation on every item in a table, particularly if some special order for the items is specified in advance.

tables and arrays Finally, we should clarify the distinction between the terms *table* and *array*. In general, we shall use *table* as we have defined it in this section and restrict the term *array* to mean the programming feature available in Pascal and most high-level languages and used for implementing both tables and contiguous lists.

15.5

APPLICATION: RADIX SORT

A formal sorting algorithm predating computers was first devised for use with punched cards, but can be developed into a very efficient sorting method for linked lists.

15.5.1 The Idea

The idea is to consider the key one character at a time and to divide the items, not into two sublists, but into as many sublists as there are possibilities for the given character from the key. If our keys, for example, are words or other alphabetic strings, then we divide the list into 26 sublists at each stage. That is, we set up a *table* of 26 lists and distribute the items into the lists according to one of the characters in the key.

Old fashioned punched cards have 12 rows; hence mechanical card sorters were designed to work on only one column at a time and divide the cards into 12 piles.

method A person sorting words by this method might first distribute the words into 26 lists according to the initial letter, then divide each of these sublists into further sublists according to the second letter, and so on. The following idea eliminates this multiplicity of sublists: Partition the items into the table of sublists first by the least significant position, not the most significant. After this first partition, the sublists from the table are put back together as a single list, in the order given by the character in the least significant position. The list is then partitioned into the table according to the second least significant position and recombined as one list. When, after repetition of these steps, the list has been partitioned by the most significant place and recombined, it will be completely sorted.

This process is illustrated by sorting the list of nine three-letter words in Figure 15.10. The words are in the initial order shown in the left column. They are first divided into three lists according to their third letter, as shown in the second column, where the colored boxes indicate the resulting sublists. The order of the words in each sublist remains the same as it was before the partition. Next, the sublists are put back together as shown in the second column of the diagram, and they are now distributed into two sublists according to the second letter. The result is shown in the colored boxes of the third column. Finally, these sublists are recombined and distributed into four sublists according to the first letter. When these sublists are recombined, the whole list is sorted.

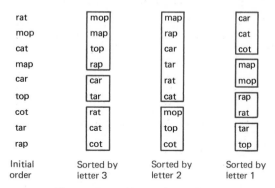

rat	mop	map	car
mop	map	rap	cat
cat	top	car	cot
map	rap	tar	map
car	car	rat	mop
top	tar	cat	rap
cot	rat	mop	rat
tar	cat	top	tar
rap	cot	cot	top
Initial order	Sorted by letter 3	Sorted by letter 2	Sorted by letter 1

Figure 15.10. Trace of a radix sort

15.5.2 Implementation

We shall implement this method in Pascal for linked lists, where the keys are strings of characters of fixed length. After each time the items have been partitioned into sublists in a table, the sublists must be recombined into a single list so that the items can be redistributed according to the next most significant position in the key. We shall treat the sublists as linked queues to facilitate this work. As items are being distributed onto the sublists, they will be added to the rears of the queues. To recombine the sublists, we need only connect the rear of each queue to the front of the next queue. This process is illustrated in Figure 15.11 for the same list of nine words used previously. At each stage, the links shown in black are those within one of the queues, and the links shown in color are those added to recombine the queues into a single list.

We shall set up an array of 27 linked queues, indexed by the letters and by another character. We shall treat any character other than a letter as this final character. Within a loop running from the least to most significant positions of the key, we shall traverse the linked list and add each item to the end of the appropriate queue. After the list has been thus partitioned, we recombine the queues into one list by linking the rear of each queue to the front of the next. At the end of the major loop on positions in the key, the list will be completely sorted.

With regard to declarations and notation, finally, let us use the standard declarations and operations for a simply linked list (from Chapter 8) and for a linked queue (from Chapter 7). We assume the declaration

$$\text{keytype} = \textbf{array}\,[1\mathrel{.\,.}\text{keysize}]\ \textbf{of}\ \text{char},$$

where the constant keysize is declared appropriately.

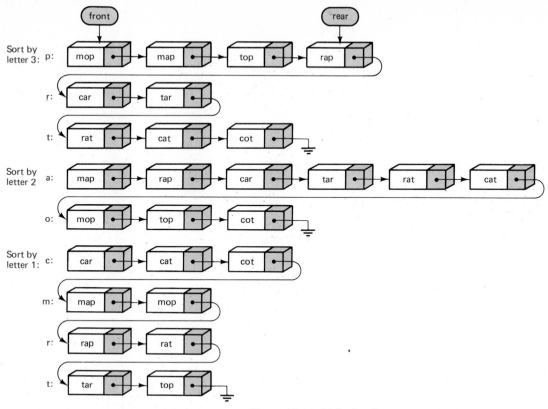

Figure 15.11. Linked radix sort

The Main Procedure

The sorting procedure then takes the following form:

procedure RadixSort(**var** L: listtype);
{**Pre:** *The linked list* L *has been created. The entries of* L *all contain keys that are arrays of letters of size* keysize *(a constant).*
Post: *The entries of* L *have been rearranged so that all the keys in the entries are sorted into alphabetical order.*
Uses: *Package for processing linked queues, subprograms* Position *and* Rethread.}
type
    keyposition = 1 .. keysize;
    arrayindex = 1 .. 27;
    queuearray = **array** [arrayindex] **of** queuetype;
var
    i: keyposition;   {*loop control variable for selecting position in a key*}
    j: arrayindex;   {*loop control variable for initializing array of queues*}
    p: listpointer;   {*used to traverse the linked list*}
    Q: queuearray;   {*the array of 27 linked queues*}

```
begin                                          {procedure RadixSort}
  for j := 1 to 27 do
    CreateQueue(Q[j]);
  if L.head <> nil then                        {Do not sort an empty list.}
    for i := keysize downto 1 do               {Do least to most significant place.}
    begin
      p := L.head;                             {Commence the traversal of the list.}
      while p <> nil do                        {Insert each key into the proper queue.}
      begin
        L.head := p↑.nextnode;
        p↑.nextnode := nil;                    {Safeguard: Remove item from the list.}
        AppendNode(p, Q[Position(p↑.entry.key[i])]);
        p := L.head                            {Continue the traversal.}
      end;
      Rethread(L, Q)                           {Reassemble the list.}
    end
end;                                           {procedure RadixSort}
```

This procedure uses two subsidiary procedures: Position determines into which queue a particular key should go, and Rethread connects the queues back together as a single list.

Selecting a Position

The function Position checks whether the character is in the alphabet and assigns it to the appropriate position and assigns all non-alphabetical characters to position 27. It is also adjusted to make no distinction between upper and lower case. As with most procedures manipulating characters, Position is system dependent; it will work with the ASCII encoding, but may require modification for other systems.

```
function Position(x: char): arrayindex;
{Pre:  None.
 Post: If x is a letter of the alphabet (either upper or lower case) then the
       function returns the position of x within the alphabet (from 1 for 'a' or
       'A' to 26 for 'z' or 'Z'). Otherwise, the function returns the value 27.
 Uses: System requirement that the letters have adjacent codes (true for
       ASCII, not true for EBCDIC)}
begin                                          {function Position}
  if x in ['A'..'Z'] then
    Position := ord(x) − ord('A') + 1          {system dependent}
  else if x in ['a'..'z'] then
    Position := ord(x) − ord('a') + 1          {system dependent}
  else
    Position := 27
end;                                           {function Position}
```

Connecting the Queues

The procedure Rethread connects the 27 linked queues together as a single list. It is made slightly more complicated by the fact that some of the queues may be empty and should therefore not be linked into the list. Since procedure RadixSort checks for an empty list, we can safely assume that at least one of the queues is not empty.

```
procedure Rethread(var L: listtype; var Q: queuearray);
{Pre:    All 27 linked queues in array Queuearray have been created. At least
         one of these queues must be nonempty.
 Post:   All the queues are linked together to form one linked list L; leaves all
         the queues empty
 Uses:   Implementation-dependent features of linked queues and linked lists.}
var
    current,                                  {index of a nonempty queue}
    next: arrayindex;                         {index of the next queue to process}

begin                                                    {procedure Rethread}
    current := 1;
    while Q[current].front = nil do           {Find the first nonempty queue.}
        current := current + 1;
    L.head := Q[current].front;                          {Start the new list.}
    Q[current].front := nil;              {Initialize the queue for the next pass.}
    while current < 27 do                     {Find all the other nonempty queues.}
    begin
        next := current + 1;
        while (next < 27) and (Q[next].front = nil) do
            next := next + 1;
        if Q[next].front <> nil then      {Another nonempty queue was found.}
        begin
            Q[current].rear↑.nextnode := Q[next].front;
                                                      {Link the lists together.}
            Q[current].rear := nil;                   {Empty the previous list.}
            Q[next].front := nil
        end;
        current := next
    end;
    if current <= 27 then
    begin
        Q[current].rear↑.nextnode := nil;      {Set the end of the list to nil.}
        Q[current].rear := nil
    end
end;                                                     {procedure Rethread}
```

15.5.3 Analysis

Note that the time used by radix sort is proportional to nk, where n is the number of items being sorted and k is the number of characters in a key. The time for all our other sorting methods depends on n but not directly on the length of a key. The best time was that of mergesort, which was $n \lg n + O(n)$. The relative performance of the methods will therefore relate in some ways to the relative sizes of nk and $n \lg n$. If the keys are long but there are relatively few of them, then k is large and n relatively small, and other methods (such as mergesort) will outperform radix sort; but if k is small and there are a large number of keys, then radix sort will be faster than any other method we have studied.

EXERCISES 15.5

E1. Trace the action of radix sort on the list of 14 names studied for other methods:

Tim Dot Eva Roy Tom Kim Guy Amy Jon Ann Jim Kay Ron Jan.

E2. Trace the action of radix sort on the following list of seven numbers considered as two-digit integers:

26   33   35   29   19   12   22.

E3. Trace the action of radix sort on the preceding list of seven numbers considered as six-digit binary integers.

PROJECT 15.5

P1. Design, program, and test a version of radix sort for contiguous lists with alphabetic keys.

POINTERS AND PITFALLS

1. Use top-down design for your data structures, just as you do for your algorithms. First determine the logical structure of the data, then slowly specify more detail, and delay implementation decisions as long as possible.

2. Before considering detailed structures, decide what operations on the data will be required, and use this information to decide whether the data belong in a *list*, a binary tree, or a *table*. Traversal of the data structure or access to

all the data in a prespecified order generally implies choosing a list or tree. Access to any item in time $O(1)$ generally implies choosing a table.

3. Use the logical structure of the data to decide what kind of table to use: an ordinary array, a table of some special shape, a system of inverted tables, or (see the next chapter) a hash table. Choose the simplest structure that allows the required operations and that meets the space requirements of the problem. Don't write complicated procedures to save space that will then remain unused.

4. A binary search tree can not only be regarded as a way to implement ordered lists but also as a way to implement tables, but with logarithmic, not constant, time needed for access. If your problem requires sorting or traversal as well as fast access, binary trees may be better than tables.

5. Let the structure of the data help you decide whether an index function or an access table is better for accessing a table of data. Use the features built into your programming language whenever possible.

REVIEW QUESTIONS

15.1 1. In terms of the big Oh notation, compare the difference in time required for table lookup and for list searching.

15.2 2. What are *row-* and *column-major ordering*?

3. What is an *index function*?

4. What is an *access table*?

15.3 5. Why do jagged tables require access tables instead of index functions?

6. For what purpose are inverted tables used?

7. What is the difference in purpose, if any, between an index function and an access table?

15.4 8. What operations are available for an abstract table?

9. What operations are usually easier for a list than for a table?

10. Indicate the difference between the terms *table* and *array*.

15.5 11. In 20 words or less, describe how *radix sort* works.

12. In radix sort, why are the keys usually partitioned first by the least significant position, not the most significant?

16

HASH TABLES

In the last chapter, we studied tables both as an abstract data type and as implemented in arrays. For many important applications, however, the possible number of different keys is too large to implement the table directly as an array, and it is for these applications that the methods of hash tables that we study in this chapter prove valuable.

SPARSE TABLES

In the last chapter we studied tables indexed in various ways. Radix sort, for example, used a table indexed by the letters of the alphabet. We could also easily set up a table indexed by pairs of letters or even by strings of three letters. But suppose that we have a thousand words, each a string of eight or fewer letters, and we wish to use these thousand words to index a table. The difficulty arises in that the number of possible keys now greatly exceeds the amount of space available for our table. The number of strings of eight letters is $26^8 \approx 2 \times 10^{11}$, a number much greater than the number of positions that will be available in high-speed memory. In practice, however, only a small fraction of these keys will actually occur. That is, the table that we wish to construct is *sparse*. Conceptually, we can regard it as indexed by a very large set, but with relatively few positions actually occupied. In Pascal, for example, we might think in terms of conceptual declarations such as

type ... = **sparse table** [keytype] **of** item.

Even though it may not be possible to implement a declaration such as this directly, it is often helpful in problem solving to begin with such a picture, and only slowly tie down the details of how it is put into practice.

Index Functions

We can continue to exploit table lookup even in situations where the key is no longer an index that can be used directly as in array indexing. What we can do is to set up a one-to-one correspondence between the keys by which we wish to retrieve information and indices that we can use to access an array. The index function that we produce will be somewhat more complicated than those of previous sections, since it may need to convert the key from, say, alphabetic information to an integer, but in principle it can still be done.

Hash Tables

index function
not one to one

The idea of a *hash table* (such as the one shown in Figure 16.1) is to allow many of the different possible keys that might occur to be mapped to the same location in an array under the action of the index function. Then there will be a possibility that two records will want to be in the same place, but if the number of records that actually occur is small relative to the size of the array, then this possibility will cause little loss of time. Even when most entries in the array are occupied, hash methods can be an effective means of information retrieval.

hash function

We begin with a *hash function* that takes a key and maps it to some index in the array. This function will generally map several different keys to the same index. If the desired record is in the location given by the index, then our problem is solved; otherwise, we must use some method to resolve the *collision* that may

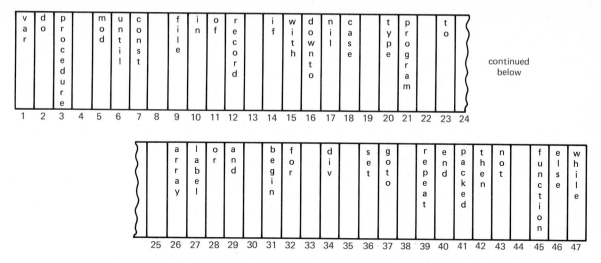

Figure 16.1. A hash table

collision have occurred between two records wanting to go to the same location. There are thus two questions we must answer to use hashing. First, we must find good hash functions, and, second, we must determine how to resolve collisions.

Before approaching these questions, let us pause to outline informally the steps needed to implement hashing.

Algorithm Outlines

First, an array must be declared that will hold the hash table. With ordinary arrays, the keys used to locate entries are usually the indices, so there is no need to keep them within the array itself. For a hash table, however, several possible
keys in table keys will correspond to the same index, so one field within each record in the array must be reserved for the key itself.
initialization Next, the hash table must be created by initializing all locations in the array to show that they are empty. How this is done depends on the application; often it is accomplished by setting the key fields to some value that is guaranteed never to occur as an actual key. With alphanumeric keys, for example, a key consisting of all blanks might represent an empty position.
insertion To insert a record into the hash table, the hash function for the key is first calculated. If the corresponding location is empty, then the record can be inserted, or else if the keys are equal, then insertion of the new record would not be allowed, and in the remaining case (a record with a different key is in the location), it becomes necessary to resolve the collision.
retrieval To retrieve the record with a given key is entirely similar. First, the hash function for the key is computed. If the desired record is in the corresponding location, then the retrieval has succeeded; otherwise, while the location is nonempty and not all locations have been examined, follow the same steps used

for collision resolution. If an empty position is found, or all locations have been considered, then no record with the given key is in the table, and the search is unsuccessful.

16.2

CHOOSING A HASH FUNCTION

The two principal criteria in selecting a hash function are that it should be easy and quick to compute and that it should achieve an even distribution of the keys that actually occur across the range of indices. If we know in advance exactly what keys will occur, then it is possible to construct hash functions that will be very efficient, but generally we do not know in advance what keys will occur.

method   Therefore, the usual way is for the hash function to take the key, chop it up, mix the pieces together in various ways, and thereby obtain an index that (like the pseudorandom numbers generated by computer) will be uniformly distributed over the range of indices.

It is from this process that the word *hash* comes, since the process converts the key into something that bears little resemblance. At the same time, it is hoped that any patterns or regularities that may occur in the keys will be destroyed, so that the results will be randomly distributed. If the keys are likely to be put anywhere in the table, then, as the number of keys increases, all the space in the table is likely to be used more efficiently.

Even though the term *hash* is very descriptive, in some books the more technical terms **scatter-storage** or **key-transformation** are used in its place.

We shall consider three methods that can be put together in various ways to build a hash function. What particular method is used, of course, depends on how the particular keys are constructed. Sometimes we use keys that are numbers, and sometimes we use keys that are words or other strings of characters. Let us first look at some of the methods that are useful for numbers, and then develop a hash function for strings of characters.

Truncation

Ignore part of the key, and use the remaining part directly as the index (considering non-numeric fields as their numerical codes). If the keys, for example, are eight-digit integers and the hash table has 1000 locations, then the first, second, and fifth digits from the right might make the hash function, so that 62538194 maps to 394. Truncation is a very fast method, but it often fails to distribute the keys evenly through the table.

Folding

Partition the key into several parts and combine the parts in a convenient way (often using addition or multiplication) to obtain the index. For example, an eight-digit integer can be divided into groups of three, three, and two digits, the groups added together, and truncated if necessary to be in the proper range of indices. Hence 62538194 maps to $625 + 381 + 94 = 1100$, which is then truncated to 100. In this case, we truncated by taking the rightmost digits, but we could have chosen the leftmost digits instead. Since all information in the key can affect the value of the function, folding often achieves a better spread of indices than does truncation by itself.

Modular Arithmetic

prime modulus

Convert the key to an integer (using the preceding devices as desired), divide by the size of the index range, and take the remainder as the result. This amounts to using the Pascal operator **mod**. The spread achieved by taking a remainder depends very much on the modulus (in this case, the size of the hash array). If the modulus is a power of a small integer like 2 or 10, then many keys tend to map to the same index, while other indices remain unused. The best choice for modulus is a prime number, which usually has the effect of spreading the keys quite uniformly. (We shall see later that a prime modulus also improves an important method for collision resolution.) Hence, rather than choosing a hash table size of 1000, it is better to choose either 997 or 1009; on the other hand, $1024 = 2^{10}$ would usually be a poor choice. If we start with the number 62538194 and modulus 997, we obtain a result of 372 by first dividing the number by the modulus and then taking the remainder. If the modulus is 1001, then result is the remainder 719.

Taking the remainder is usually the best way to conclude calculating the hash function, since it can achieve a good spread at the same time that it ensures that the result is in the proper range. About the only reservation is that, on a tiny machine with no hardware division, the calculation can be slow, so other methods should be considered.

Pascal Example

As a first example, let us write a hash function in Pascal for transforming a key consisting of eight alphanumeric characters into an integer in the range

$$0..\text{hashsize} - 1.$$

That is, we shall begin with the declarations

```
const
    hashmax = hashsize − 1;
type
    hashaddress = 0..hashmax;
    keytype = array[1..8] of char;
```

(The expression hashsize − 1 in the declaration of a constant is not standard Pascal, but it is allowed by many compilers and is easy to convert to standard Pascal in any case.) We can then write a simple hash function as follows:

simple hash function

```
function Hash(x: keytype): hashaddress;
{Pre:  x is a string of eight characters.
   Post:  The function returns an integer between 0 and hashmax as a function
          of x.}
var
   position: 1 .. 8;
   result: integer;
begin
   result := 0;
   for position := 1 to 8 do
      result := result + ord(x[position]);
   Hash := result mod hashsize
end;
```

We have simply added the integer codes corresponding to each of the eight characters. There is no reason to believe that this method will be better (or worse), however, than any number of others. We could, for example, subtract some of the codes, multiply them in pairs, or ignore every other character. Sometimes an application will suggest that one hash function is better than another; sometimes it requires experimentation to settle on a good one.

16.3

COLLISION RESOLUTION WITH OPEN ADDRESSING

Linear Probing

The simplest method to resolve a collision is to start with the hash address (the location where the collision occurred) and do a sequential search for the desired key or an empty location. Hence this method searches in a straight line, and it is therefore called *linear probing*. The array should be considered circular, so that when the last location is reached, the search proceeds to the first location of the array.

Clustering

The major drawback of linear probing is that, as the table becomes about half full, there is a tendency toward *clustering*; that is, records start to appear in long strings of adjacent positions with gaps between the strings. Thus the sequential searches needed to find an empty position become longer and longer.

example of clustering

Consider the example in Figure 16.3, where the occupied positions are shown in color. Suppose that there are n locations in the array and that the hash function chooses any of them with equal probability $1/n$. Begin with a fairly uniform spread, as shown in the top diagram. If a new insertion hashes to location b, then it will go there, but if it hashes to location a (which is full), then it will also go into b. Thus the probability that b will be filled has doubled to $2/n$. If an

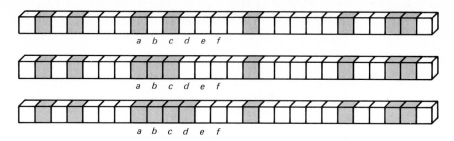

Figure 16.2. Clustering in a hash table

attempt is now made to insert a new entry into any one of the locations *a, b, c,* or *d*, it will end up in *d*. The probability of filling *d* is therefore now $4/n$. After this, *e* has probability $5/n$ of being filled.

The conclusion is that, as additional insertions are made, the most likely effect is to make the string of full positions beginning at location *a* longer and longer, and hence the performance of the hash table starts to degenerate toward that of sequential search. This is the problem of *clustering*.

instability   The problem of clustering is essentially one of instability; if a few keys happen randomly to be near each other, then it becomes more and more likely that other keys will join them, and the distribution will become progressively more unbalanced.

Increment Functions

If we are to avoid the problem of clustering, then we must use some more sophisticated way to select the sequence of locations to check when a collision *rehashing* occurs. There are many ways to do so. One, called **rehashing**, uses a second hash function to obtain the second position to consider. If this position is filled, then some other method is needed to get the third position, and so on. But if we have a fairly good spread from the first hash function, then little is to be gained by an independent second hash function. We will do just as well to find a more sophisticated way of determining the distance to move from the first hash position and apply this method, whatever the first hash location is. Hence we wish to design an increment function that can depend on the key or on the number of probes already made and that will avoid clustering.

Quadratic Probing

If there is a collision at hash address h, the method called **quadratic probing** looks in the table at locations $h + 1$, $h + 4$, $h + 9$, ..., that is, at locations $h + i^2$ (mod hashsize) for $i = 1, 2, \ldots$. In other words, the increment function for quadratic probing is i^2.

Quadratic probing substantially reduces clustering, but it is not obvious that it will probe all locations in the table, and in fact it does not. For some values of hashsize, for example powers of 2, the function will probe relatively few positions in the array. When hashsize is a prime number (one that cannot be divided by any positive integer other than itself and 1), however, quadratic probing reaches half the locations in the array.

proof To prove this observation, suppose that hashsize is a prime number. Also suppose that we reach the same location at probe i and at some later probe that we can take as $i + j$ for some integer $j > 0$. Suppose that j is the smallest such integer. Then the values calculated by the function at i and at $i + j$ differ by a multiple of hashsize. In other words,

$$h + i^2 \equiv h + (i + j)^2 \ (\text{mod hashsize}).$$

When this expression is simplified, we obtain

$$j^2 + 2ij = j(j + 2i) \equiv 0 \ (\text{mod hashsize}).$$

This last expression means that hashsize divides (with no remainder) the product $j(j+2i)$. The only way that a prime number can divide a product is to divide one of its factors. Hence hashsize either divides j or it divides $j + 2i$. If the first case occurred, then we would have made hashsize probes before duplicating probe i. (Recall that j is the smallest positive integer such that probe $i + j$ duplicates probe i.) The second case, however, will occur sooner, when $j = \text{hashsize} - 2i$, or, if this expression is negative, at this expression increased by hashsize. Hence the total number of distinct positions that will be probed is exactly

$$(\text{hashsize} + 1) \ \textbf{div} \ 2.$$

It is customary to regard the table as full when this number of positions has been probed, and the results are quite satisfactory.

calculation Note that quadratic probing can be accomplished without doing multiplications in the program: After the first probe at position x, the increment is set to 1. At each successive probe, the increment is increased by 2 after it has been added to the previous location. Since

$$1 + 3 + 5 + \cdots + (2i - 1) = i^2$$

for all $i \geq 1$ (you can prove this fact by mathematical induction), probe i will look in position

$$x + 1 + 3 + \cdots + (2i - 1) = x + i^2,$$

as desired. Quadratic probing is therefore not only easy to program, but it runs efficiently.

Key-Dependent Increments

Rather than having the increment depend on the number of probes already made, we can let it be some simple function of the key itself. For example, we could truncate the key to a single character and use its code as the increment. In Pascal, we might write increment := ord(k[1]).

A good approach, when the remainder after division is taken as the hash function, is to let the increment depend on the quotient of the same division. An optimizing compiler should specify the division only once, so the calculation will be fast and the results generally satisfactory.

In this method, the increment, once determined, remains constant. If hashsize is a prime, it follows that the probes will step through all the entries of the array before any repetitions. Hence overflow will not be indicated until the array is completely full.

Random Probing

A final method is to use a pseudorandom number generator to obtain the increment. The generator used should be one that always generates the same sequence provided it starts with the same seed. The seed, then, can be specified as some function of the key. This method is excellent in avoiding clustering, but is likely to be slower than the others.

Pascal Algorithms

To conclude the discussion of open addressing, we continue to study the Pascal example already introduced, which used alphanumeric keys of the type

type keytype = **array** [1 .. 8] **of** char.

We set up the hash table with the declarations

declarations

```
const
   hashsize = 997;              {a prime number of appropriate size}
   hashmax = 996;               {should be 1 less than hashsize}
type
   hashaddress = 0 .. hashmax;
   hashtable = array [hashaddress] of tableentry;
var
   H: hashtable;
```

initialization The hash table must be created by defining a special key called blankword that consists of eight blanks and setting the key field of each item in H to blankword. This is the task of the procedure CreateTable, whose specifications are:

---

procedure CreateTable(**var** H: hashtable):

precondition: None.

postcondition: The hash table H has been created and initialized to be empty.

There should also be a procedure ClearTable that returns a table that already has been created to an empty state. Its declarations follow, but its code (for the case of hash tables with open addressing) will be identical to that of CreateTable.

---

procedure ClearTable(**var** H: hashtable):

precondition: The hash table H has been created.

postcondition: H is empty.

To show how the code for additional procedures will be written, we shall follow the example of the hash function already written in Section 16.2, together with quadratic probing for collision resolution. We have shown that the maximum number of probes that can be made this way is (hashsize + 1) **div** 2, and we keep a counter probecount to check this upper bound.

With these conventions, let us write a procedure to insert a new entry newentry into the hash table H.

insertion
```
procedure InsertTable(var H: hashtable; newentry: tableentry);
{Pre:   The hash table H has been created and is not full. H has no current
          entry with key equal to that of newentry.
  Post:  The item newentry is inserted into H.}
var
    probecount,                              {counter to be sure that table is not full}
    increment: integer;                      {increment used for quadratic probing}
    probe: hashaddress;                      {position currently probed in H}
begin                                        {procedure InsertTable}
    probe := Hash(newentry.key);
    probecount := 0;
    increment := 1;
    while (H[probe].key <> blankword)        {Is the location empty?}
      and (H[probe].key <> newentry.key)     {Duplicate key present?}
      and (probecount <= hashsize div 2) do  {Has overflow occurred?}
    begin
        probecount := probecount + 1;
        probe := (probe + increment) mod hashsize;
        increment := increment + 2         {Prepare increment for next iteration.}
    end;
    if H[probe].key = blankword then
        H[probe] := newentry                 {Insert the new entry.}
    else if H[probe].key = newentry.key then
        writeln('Error: The same key cannot appear twice in a hash table.')
    else
        writeln('Error: Hash table is full; insertion cannot be made.')
    end;                                     {procedure InsertTable}
```
quadratic probing

A procedure to retrieve the record (if any) with a given key will have a similar form and is left as an Exercise. The retrieval procedure should return the full entry associated with a target key. Its specifications are:

---

procedure RetrieveTable(**var** H: hashtable; target: keytype;
　　　　　　　　　　　　　　var found: Boolean; **var** targetentry: tableentry):

precondition:　The hash table H has been created.

postcondition:　If an entry in H has key equal to target, then found becomes true and the parameter targetentry takes on the value of such an entry. Otherwise, found becomes false and targetentry is undefined.

Deletions

Up to now, we have said nothing about deleting items from a hash table. At first glance, it may appear to be an easy task, requiring only marking the deleted location with the special key indicating that it is empty. This method will not work. The reason is that an empty location is used as the signal to stop the search for a target key. Suppose that, before the deletion, there had been a collision or two and that some item whose hash address is the now-deleted position is actually stored elsewhere in the table. If we now try to retrieve that item, then the now-empty position will stop the search, and it is impossible to find the item, even though it is still in the table.

special key　　　One method to remedy this difficulty is to invent another special key, to be placed in any deleted position. This special key would indicate that this position is free to receive an insertion when desired but that it should not be used to terminate the search for some other item in the table. Using this second special key will, however, make the algorithms somewhat more complicated and a bit slower. With the methods we have so far studied for hash tables, deletions are indeed awkward and should be avoided as much as possible.

EXERCISES 16.3

E1. Write a Pascal procedure to insert an item into a hash table with open addressing and linear probing.

E2. Write a Pascal procedure to retrieve an item from a hash table with open addressing and **(a)** linear probing; **(b)** quadratic probing.

E3. In a student project for which the keys were integers, one student thought that he could mix the keys well by using a trigonometric function, which had to be converted to an integer index, so he defined his hash function as

$$\text{trunc}(\sin(n)).$$

What was wrong with this choice? He then decided to replace the function sin(n) by exp(n). Criticize this choice.

E4. Devise a simple, easy to calculate hash function for mapping three-letter words to integers between 0 and $n - 1$, inclusive. Find the values of your function on the words

PAL LAP PAM MAP PAT PET SET SAT TAT BAT

for $n = 11, 13, 17, 19$. Try for as few collisions as possible.

E5. Suppose that a hash table contains hashsize = 13 entries indexed from 0 through 12 and that the following keys are to be mapped into the table:

10 100 32 45 58 126 3 29 200 400 0

   a. Determine the hash addresses and find how many collisions occur when these keys are reduced **mod** hashsize.
   b. Determine the hash addresses and find how many collisions occur when these keys are first folded by adding their digits together (in ordinary decimal representation) and then reducing **mod** hashsize.
   c. Find a hash function that will produce no collisions for these keys. (A hash function that has no collisions for a fixed set of keys is called *perfect*.)
   d. Repeat parts (a) to (c) for hashsize = 11. (A hash function that produces no collision for a fixed set of keys that completely fill the hash table is called *minimal perfect*.)

E6. Another method for resolving collisions with open addressing is to keep a separate array called the *overflow table*, into which all items that collide with an occupied location are put. They can either be inserted with another hash function or simply inserted in order, with sequential search used for retrieval. Discuss the advantages and disadvantages of this method.

E7. Write a deletion procedure for a hash table with open addressing, using a second special key to indicate a deleted item (see the last part of Section 16.3). Change the retrieval and insertion algorithms accordingly.

E8. With linear probing, it is possible to delete an item without using a second special key, as follows. Mark the deleted entry empty. Search until another empty position is found. If the search finds a key whose hash address is at or before the first empty position, then move it back there, make its previous position empty, and continue from the new empty position. Write an algorithm to implement this method. Do the retrieval and insertion algorithms need modification?

■ PROJECT 16.3

P1. Consider the 35 Pascal reserved words listed in Appendix B.2.1. Consider these words as strings of nine characters, where words less than nine letters long are filled with blanks on the right.

a. Devise an integer-valued function that will produce different values when applied to all 35 reserved words. [You may find it helpful to write a short program to assist. Your program could read the words from a file, apply the function you devise, and determine what collisions occur.]

b. Find the smallest integer hashsize such that, when the values of your function are reduced **mod** hashsize, all 35 values remain distinct.

c. Modify your function as necessary until you are able to achieve hashsize = 35 in part (b). (You will then have discovered a *minimal perfect* hash function for the 35 Pascal reserved words.)

16.4

COLLISION RESOLUTION BY CHAINING

So far in this chapter, we have implicitly assumed that we are using only contiguous storage while working with hash tables. Contiguous storage for the hash table itself is, in fact, the natural choice, since we wish to be able to refer quickly

linked storage   to random positions in the table, and linked storage is not suited to random access. There is, however, no reason why linked storage should not be used for the records themselves. We can take the hash table itself as an array of pointers to the records, that is, as an array of list headers. An example appears in Figure 16.3.

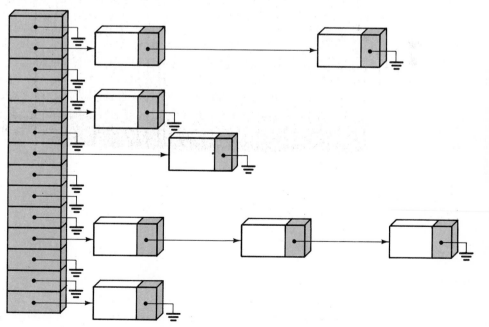

Figure 16.3. A chained hash table

It is traditional to refer to the linked lists from the hash table as *chains* and call this method collision resolution by *chaining*.

Advantages of Linked Storage

space saving

There are several advantages to this point of view. The first, and the most important when the records themselves are quite large, is that considerable space may be saved. Since the hash table is a contiguous array, enough space must be set aside at compilation time to avoid overflow. If the records themselves are in the hash table, then if there are many empty positions (as is desirable to help avoid the cost of collisions), these will consume considerable space that might be needed elsewhere. If, on the other hand, the hash table contains only pointers to the records, pointers that require only one word each, then the size of the hash table may be reduced by a large factor (essentially by a factor equal to the size of the records), and will become small relative to the space available for the records, or for other uses.

collision resolution

The second major advantage of keeping only pointers in the hash table is that it allows simple and efficient collision handling. We need only add a link field to each record and organize all the records with a single hash address as a linked list. With a good hash function, few keys will give the same hash address, so the linked lists will be short and can be searched quickly. Clustering is no problem at all, because keys with distinct hash addresses always go to distinct lists.

overflow

A third advantage is that it is no longer necessary that the size of the hash table exceed the number of records. If there are more records than entries in the table, it means only that some of the linked lists are now sure to contain more than one record. Even if there are several times more records than the size of the table, the average length of the linked lists will remain small and sequential search on the appropriate list will remain efficient.

deletion

Finally, deletion becomes a quick and easy task in a chained hash table. Deletion proceeds in exactly the same way as deletion from a simple linked list.

Disadvantage of Linked Storage

use of space

These advantages of chained hash tables are indeed powerful. Lest you believe that chaining is always superior to open addressing, however, let us note one important disadvantage: All the links require space. If the records are large, then this space is negligible in comparison with that needed for the records themselves; but if the records are small, then it is not.

small records

Suppose, for example, that the links take one word each and that the items themselves take only one word (which is the key alone). Such applications are quite common, where we use the hash table only to answer some yes-no question about the key. Suppose that we use chaining and make the hash table itself quite small, with the same number n of entries as the number of items. Then we shall use $3n$ words of storage altogether: n for the hash table, n for the keys, and n for the links to find the next node (if any) on each chain. Since the hash table will be nearly full, there will be many collisions, and some of the chains will have several items. Hence searching will be a bit slow. Suppose, on the other hand, that we use open addressing. The same $3n$ words of storage put entirely into the hash table will mean that it will be only one third full, and therefore there will be relatively few collisions and the search for any given item will be faster.

Pascal Algorithms

A chained hash table in Pascal takes the simple declaration

type hashtable = **array** [0 .. hashmax] **of** listtype,

where listtype refers to the simply linked implementation of lists studied in Chapter 8. For consistency with the previous procedures for hash tables, we shall also make the type declaration listentry = tableentry.

initialization   The code needed to create the hash table is

for i := 0 **to** hashmax **do** CreateList(H[i]);

To clear a chained hash table that has previously been created is a different task, in contrast to open addressing, where it was the same as creating the table. To clear the table, we must clear the linked list in each of the table positions. This task can be done by using the linked-list procedure ClearList.

We can even use procedures from the list package to access the hash table. The hash function itself is no different from that used with open addressing; for data retrieval, we can simply use a linked version of procedure SequentialSearch, as follows:

retrieval
```
procedure RetrieveNodeTable(var H: hashtable; target: keytype;
                            var found: Boolean; var location: window);
{Pre:  H has been created.
 Post: If an entry in H has key equal to target, then found becomes true
       and the (linked list) window location gives the location of such an
       entry. Otherwise, found becomes false and the window location is
       undefined.}
begin
   SequentialSearch(H[Hash(target)], target, found, location)
end;
```

The details of converting this procedure into one that retrieves a table *entry* instead of a *node* are left as an Exercise.

Our procedure for inserting a new node into the appropriate chain in the table will assume that the key does not appear already; otherwise, only the most recent insertion with a given key will be retrievable.

insertion

```
procedure InsertNodeTable (var H: hashtable; newnode: window);
  {Pre:   The chained hash table H has been created.
   Post:  The node newnode↑ has been inserted into H.}
var
   location: hashaddress;
begin                                    {procedure InsertNodeTable}
   location := Hash (newnode↑.entry.key);      {Find the hash address.}
   InsertNodeBefore (H [location].head, newnode, H [location])
   {The previous instruction inserts the new node at the head of the linked list
    selected by the hash function.}
end;                                     {procedure InsertNodeTable}
```

Again, an Exercise requests the conversion of this procedure into one that inserts a new *entry* into the table.

As you can see, both insertion and retrieval are simpler than the versions for open addressing, since collision resolution is not a problem and we can make use of the previous work done for linked lists.

deletion

Deletion from a chained hash table is also much simpler than it is from a table with open addressing. To delete the entry with a given key, we need only find the node where it is and then delete the node from its linked list.

```
procedure DeleteTable (var H: hashtable; target: keytype);
  {Pre:   The chained hash table H has been created and contains an entry
          with key equal to target.
   Post:  The entry with key equal to target has been deleted from H.}
var
   found: Boolean;                          {Is target present in H?}
   location: window;                        {Where is target?}
   chain: hashaddress;            {index of chain containing target}
begin                                       {procedure DeleteTable}
   chain := Hash (target);
   SequentialSearch (H [chain], target, found, location)
   if not found then
      writeln ('Error: Attempt to delete an entry not in the hash table.')
   else
      DeleteList (location, H [chain])
end;                                        {procedure DeleteTable}
```

EXERCISES 16.4

E1. Convert the procedure for inserting a new *node* into a chained hash table into one that inserts a new *entry*.

E2. Convert the procedure for retrieving a *node* from a chained hash table into one that retrieves an *entry*.

16.5

ANALYSIS OF HASHING

The Birthday Surprise

The likelihood of collisions in hashing relates to a well-known mathematical diversion: How many randomly chosen people need to be in a room before it becomes likely that two people will have the same birthday (month and day)? Since (apart from leap years) there are 365 possible birthdays, most people guess that the answer will be in the hundreds, but in fact, the answer is only 24 people.

We can determine the probabilities for this question by answering its opposite: With m randomly chosen people in a room, what is the probability that no two have the same birthday? Start with any person, and check his or her birthday off on a calendar. The probability that a second person has a different birthday is $364/365$. Check it off. The probability that a third person has a different birthday is now $363/365$. Continuing this way, we see that if the first $m - 1$ people have different birthdays, then the probability that person m has a different birthday is $(365 - m + 1)/365$. Since the birthdays of different people are independent, the probabilities multiply, and we obtain that the probability that m people all have different birthdays is

probability
$$\frac{364}{365} \times \frac{363}{365} \times \frac{362}{365} \times \cdots \times \frac{365 - m + 1}{365}.$$

This expression becomes less than 0.5 whenever $m \geq 24$.

collisions likely
In regard to hashing, the birthday surprise tells us that with any problem of reasonable size, we are almost certain to have some collisions. Our approach, therefore, should not be only to try to minimize the number of collisions, but also to handle those that occur as expeditiously as possible.

Counting Probes

As with other methods of information retrieval, we would like to know how many comparisons of keys occur on average during both successful and unsuccessful attempts to locate a given target key. We shall use the word *probe* for looking at one item and comparing its key with the target.

load factor
The number of probes we need clearly depends on how full the table is. Therefore (as for searching methods), we let n be the number of items in the table, and we let t (which is the same as hashsize) be the number of positions in the array. The **load factor** of the table is $\lambda = n/t$. Thus $\lambda = 0$ signifies an empty table; $\lambda = 0.5$ a table that is half full. For open addressing, λ can never exceed 1, but, for chaining, there is no limit on the size of λ. We consider chaining and open addressing separately.

Analysis of Chaining

With a chained hash table, we go directly to one of the linked lists before doing any probes. Suppose that the chain that will contain the target (if it is present) has k items.

unsuccessful retrieval If the search is unsuccessful, then the target will be compared with all k of the corresponding keys. Since the items are distributed uniformly over all t lists (equal probability of appearing on any list), the expected number of items on the one being searched is $\lambda = n/t$. Hence the average number of probes for an unsuccessful search is λ.

successful retrieval Now suppose that the search is successful. From the analysis of sequential search, we know that the average number of comparisons is $\frac{1}{2}(k+1)$, where k is the length of the chain containing the target. But the expected length of this chain is no longer λ, since we know in advance that it must contain at least one node (the target). The $n-1$ nodes other than the target are distributed uniformly over all t chains; hence the expected number on the chain with the target is $1 + (n-1)/t$. Except for tables of trivially small size, we may approximate $(n-1)/t$ by $n/t = \lambda$. Hence the average number of probes for a successful search is very nearly

$$\tfrac{1}{2}(k+1) \approx \tfrac{1}{2}(1 + \lambda + 1) = 1 + \tfrac{1}{2}\lambda.$$

Analysis of Open Addressing

For our analysis of the number of probes done in open addressing, let us first ignore the problem of clustering, by assuming that not only are the first probes random, but after a collision, the next probe will be random over all remaining *random probes* positions of the table. In fact, let us assume that the table is so large that all the probes can be regarded as independent events.

unsuccessful retrieval Let us first study an unsuccessful search. The probability that the first probe hits an occupied cell is λ, the load factor. The probability that a probe hits an empty cell is $1 - \lambda$. The probability that the unsuccessful search terminates in exactly two probes is therefore $\lambda(1 - \lambda)$, and, similarly, the probability that exactly k probes are made in an unsuccessful search is $\lambda^{k-1}(1-\lambda)$. The expected number $U(\lambda)$ of probes in an unsuccessful search is therefore

$$U(\lambda) = \sum_{k=1}^{\infty} k\lambda^{k-1}(1 - \lambda).$$

To evaluate this sum, we start with the following identity, which, for any value of $x \neq 1$, can be verified simply by multiplying both sides by $x - 1$:

$$1 + x + x^2 + \cdots + x^m = \frac{x^{m+1} - 1}{x - 1}$$

for any $x \neq 1$. Next, we differentiate both sides of this equation with respect to x:

$$1 + 2x + 3x^2 + \cdots + mx^{m-1} = \frac{(x-1)(m+1)x^m - (x^{m+1} - 1)}{(x-1)^2}$$

for any $x \neq 1$.

Now suppose that $|x| < 1$ in this formula. As m becomes large, it follows that x^m becomes closer and closer to 0, that is,

$$\lim_{m \to \infty} x^m = 0.$$

Taking the limit as $m \to \infty$ in the preceding equation means turning the left side into an infinite sum and replacing x^m by 0 in the right side. The result is

$$\sum_{k=1}^{\infty} kx^{k-1} = \frac{1}{(1-x)^2}.$$

Let us now, finally, replace x by λ and multiply the equation by $1 - \lambda$. The result is that the infinite sum on the left becomes the same as the one we previously obtained for $U(\lambda)$. We therefore conclude that

$$U(\lambda) = \frac{1}{(1-\lambda)^2}(1-\lambda) = \frac{1}{1-\lambda}.$$

To count the probes needed for a successful search, we note that the number needed will be exactly one more than the number of probes in the unsuccessful search made before inserting the item. Now let us consider the table as beginning empty, with each item inserted one at a time. As these items are inserted, the load factor grows slowly from 0 to its final value, λ. It is reasonable for us to approximate this step-by-step growth by continuous growth and replace a sum with an integral. We conclude that the average number of probes in a successful search is approximately

successful
retrieval

$$S(\lambda) = \frac{1}{\lambda} \int_0^{\lambda} U(\mu)d\mu = \frac{1}{\lambda} \ln \frac{1}{1-\lambda}.$$

linear probing

Similar calculations may be done for open addressing with linear probing, where it is no longer reasonable to assume that successive probes are independent. The details, however, are rather more complicated, so we present only the results. For the complete derivation, consult the References in Appendix C. For linear probing, the average number of probes for an unsuccessful search increases to

$$\frac{1}{2}\left(1 + \frac{1}{(1-\lambda)^2}\right)$$

and, for a successful search, the number becomes

$$\frac{1}{2}\left(1 + \frac{1}{1 - \lambda}\right).$$

Theoretical Comparisons

Figure 16.4 gives the values of the preceding expressions for different values of the load factor.

Load factor	0.10	0.50	0.80	0.90	0.99	2.00
Successful search, expected number of probes:						
Chaining	1.05	1.25	1.40	1.45	1.50	2.00
Open, Random probes	1.05	1.4	2.0	2.6	4.6	—
Open, Linear probes	1.06	1.5	3.0	5.5	50.5	—
Unsuccessful search, expected number of probes:						
Chaining	0.10	0.50	0.80	0.90	0.99	2.00
Open, Random probes	1.1	2.0	5.0	10.0	100.	—
Open, Linear probes	1.12	2.5	13.	50.	5000.	—

Figure 16.4. Theoretical comparison of hashing methods

We can draw several conclusions from this table. First, it is clear that chaining consistently requires fewer probes than does open addressing. On the other hand, traversal of the linked lists is usually slower than array access, which can reduce the advantage, especially if key comparisons can be done quickly. Chaining comes into its own when the records are large, and comparison of keys takes significant time.

Chaining is also especially advantageous when unsuccessful searches are common, since with chaining, an empty list or very short list may be found, so that often no key comparisons at all need be done to show that a search is unsuccessful.

With open addressing and successful searches, the simpler method of linear probing is not significantly slower than more sophisticated methods, at least until the table is almost completely full. For unsuccessful searches, however, clustering quickly causes linear probing to degenerate into a long sequential search. We might conclude, therefore, that if searches are quite likely to be successful, and the load factor is moderate, then linear probing is quite satisfactory, but, in other circumstances, another method should be used.

Empirical Comparisons

It is important to remember that the computations that produce the numbers in Figure 16.4 are only approximate. In practice, nothing is completely random, so we can always expect some differences between the theoretical results and actual computations. For sake of comparison, therefore, Figure 16.5 gives the results of one empirical study, using 900 keys that are pseudorandom numbers between 0 and 1.

Load factor	0.1	0.5	0.8	0.9	0.99	2.0
Successful search, average number of probes:						
Chaining	1.04	1.2	1.4	1.4	1.5	2.0
Open, Quadratic probes	1.04	1.5	2.1	2.7	5.2	—
Open, Linear probes	1.05	1.6	3.4	6.2	21.3	—
Unsuccessful search, average number of probes:						
Chaining	0.10	0.50	0.80	0.90	0.99	2.00
Open, Quadratic probes	1.13	2.2	5.2	11.9	126.	—
Open, Linear probes	1.13	2.7	15.4	59.8	430.	—

Figure 16.5. Empirical comparison of hashing methods

conclusions In comparison with other methods of information retrieval, the important thing to note about all these numbers is that they depend only on the load factor, not on the absolute number of items in the table. Retrieval from a hash table with 20,000 items in 40,000 possible positions is no slower, on average, than is retrieval from a table with 20 items in 40 possible positions. With sequential search, a list 1000 times the size will take 1000 times as long to search. With binary search, this ratio is reduced to 10 (more precisely, to lg 1000), but still the time needed increases with the size, which it does not with hashing.

Finally, we should emphasize the importance of devising a good hash function, one that executes quickly and maximizes the spread of keys. If the hash function is poor, the performance of hashing can degenerate to that of sequential search.

EXERCISES 16.5

E1. Suppose that each item (record) in a hash table occupies s words of storage (exclusive of the pointer field needed if chaining is used), and suppose that there are n items in the hash table.

a. If the load factor is λ and open addressing is used, determine how many words of storage will be required for the hash table.

b. If chaining is used, then each node will require $s + 1$ words, including the pointer field. How many words will be used altogether for the n nodes?

c. If the load factor is λ and chaining is used, how many words will be used for the hash table itself? (Recall that, with chaining, the hash table itself contains only pointers requiring one word each.)

d. Add your answers to the two previous parts to find the total storage requirement for load factor λ and chaining.

e. If s is small, then open addressing requires less total memory for a given λ, but for large s, chaining requires less space altogether. Show that the break-even value for s, at which both methods use the same total storage, is

$$ s = \frac{1 + \lambda}{1 - \lambda}. $$

E2. One reason why the answer to the birthday problem is surprising is that it differs from the answers to apparently related questions. For the following, suppose that there are n people in the room, and disregard leap years.

a. What is the probability that someone in the room will have a birthday on a random date drawn from a hat?

b. What is the probability that at least two people in the room will have that same random birthday?

c. If we choose one person and find his birthday, what is the probability that someone else in the room will share the birthday?

ordered hash table **E3.** In a chained hash table, suppose that it makes sense to speak of an order for the keys, and suppose that the nodes in each chain are kept in order by key. Then a search can be terminated as soon as it passes the place where the key should be, if present. How many fewer probes will be done, on average, in an unsuccessful search? In a successful search? How many probes are needed, on average, to insert a new node in the right place? Compare your answers with the corresponding numbers derived in the text for the case of unordered chains.

E4. In our discussion of chaining, the hash table itself contained only pointers, list headers for each of the chains. One variant method is to place the first actual item of each chain in the hash table itself. (An empty position is indicated by an impossible key, as with open addressing.) With a given load factor, calculate the effect on space of this method, as a function of the number of words (except links) in each item. (A link takes one word.)

■■■■■■■■ **PROJECT 16.5**

P1. Produce a table like Figure 16.5 for your computer, by writing and running test programs to implement the various kinds of hash tables and load factors.

16.6

CONCLUSIONS: COMPARISON OF METHODS

In this book, we have explored five quite different methods of information retrieval:

- Sequential search,

- Binary search,

- Binary search trees,

- Table lookup, and

- Hashing.

Which of these methods is the best choice for a particular application depends on several criteria.

If we are concerned exclusively with information retrieval, then fastest execution times will be given by ordinary tables (if the set of keys can be used directly as indices) or by hash tables (if the set of keys is sparse). The time for table retrieval does not depend directly on the number of entries in the table; it is $O(1)$.

If other operations need to be done, however, tables may not be the best choice. If insertions and deletions are frequent, then binary trees may prove superior. The time required for insertion, deletion, or retrieval is normally $O(\log n)$ but can degenerate to become proportional to n, the number of items in the tree.

Sequential search is certainly the most flexible of our methods, but it is also the slowest, requiring time proportional to n for almost any operation on a list of size n. The data may be stored in any order, with either contiguous or linked representation.

Binary search is much more demanding. The keys must be in order, and the data must be in random-access representation (contiguous storage). Insertions and deletions, therefore, are slow, but retrieval is fast, guaranteed to be done in time $O(\log n)$.

Hashing requires even more, a peculiar ordering of the keys well suited to retrieval from the hash table, but generally useless for any other purpose. If the data are to be available immediately for human inspection, then some kind of order is essential, and a hash table is inappropriate.

near miss Finally, there is the question of the unsuccessful search. Sequential search, table lookup, and hashing, by themselves, say nothing except that the search was unsuccessful. Binary search and binary search trees can determine which data have keys closest to the target, and perhaps thereby can provide useful information.

POINTERS AND PITFALLS

1. In using a hash table, let the nature of the data and the required operations help you decide between chaining and open addressing. Chaining is generally preferable if deletions are required, if the records are relatively large, or if overflow might be a problem. Open addressing is usually preferable when the individual records are small and there is no danger of overflowing the hash table.

2. Hash functions must usually be custom designed for the kind of keys used for accessing the hash table. In designing a hash function, keep the computations as simple and as few as possible while maintaining a relatively even spread of the keys over the hash table. There is no obligation to use every part of the key in the calculation. For important applications, experiment by computer with several variations of your hash function, and look for rapid calculation and even distribution of the keys.

3. Recall from the analysis of hashing that some collisions will almost inevitably occur, so don't worry about the existence of collisions if the keys are spread nearly uniformly through the table.

4. For open addressing, clustering is unlikely to be a problem until the hash table is more than half full. If the table can be made several times larger than the space required for the records, then linear probing should be adequate; otherwise, more sophisticated collision resolution may be required. On the other hand, if the table is many times larger than needed, then initialization of all the unused space may require inordinate time.

REVIEW QUESTIONS

16.1 1. What is the difference in purpose, if any, between an *index function* and a *hash function*?

2. What is a *collision*?

16.2   3. What objectives should be sought in the design of a hash function?

4. Name three techniques often built into hash functions.

16.3   5. What is *clustering* in a hash table?

6. What is *linear probing*?

7. Describe two methods for minimizing clustering.

16.4   8. Name four advantages of a chained hash table over open addressing.

9. Name one advantage of open addressing over chaining.

16.5   10. If a hash function assigns 30 keys to random positions in a hash table of size 300, about how likely is it that there will be no collisions?

17

GRAPHS

This chapter introduces important mathematical structures called graphs that have applications in subjects as diverse as sociology, chemistry, geography, and electrical engineering. We shall study methods to represent graphs in the data structures available to us and shall construct several important algorithms for processing graphs. Finally, we look at the possibility of using graphs themselves as data structures.

17.1

MATHEMATICAL BACKGROUND

17.1.1 Definitions and Examples

graphs and directed graphs

drawings

A **graph** G consists of a set V, whose members are called the **vertices** of G, together with a set E of pairs of distinct vertices from V. These pairs are called the **edges** of G. If $e = (v, w)$ is an edge with vertices v and w, then v and w are said to *lie on e*, and e is said to be **incident** with v and w. If the pairs are unordered, then G is called an **undirected graph**; if the pairs are ordered, then G is called a **directed graph**. The term *directed graph* is often shortened to **digraph**, and the unqualified term *graph* usually means *undirected graph*.

The natural way to picture a graph is to represent vertices as points or circles and edges as line segments or arcs connecting the vertices. If the graph is directed, then the line segments or arcs have arrowheads indicating the direction. Figure 17.1 shows several examples of graphs.

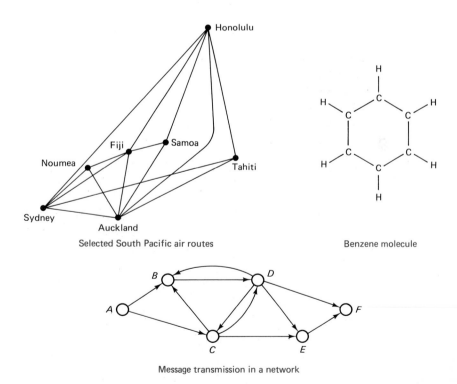

Selected South Pacific air routes

Benzene molecule

Message transmission in a network

Figure 17.1. Examples of graphs

The cities in the first part of Figure 17.1 are the vertices of the graph, and the air routes connecting them are the edges. In the second part, the hydrogen and carbon atoms (denoted H and C) are the vertices, and the chemical bonds are the edges. The third part of Figure 17.1 shows a directed graph, where the nodes of the network (A, B, ..., F) are the vertices and the edges from one to another have the directions shown by the arrows.

applications   Graphs find their importance as models for many kinds of processes or structures. Cities and the highways connecting them form a graph, as do the components on a circuit board with the connections among them. An organic chemical compound can be considered a graph with the atoms as the vertices and the bonds between them as edges. The people living in a city can be regarded as the vertices of a graph with the relationship *is acquainted with* describing the edges. People working in a corporation form a directed graph with the relation "supervises" describing the edges. The same people could also be considered as an undirected graph, with different edges describing the relationship "works with."

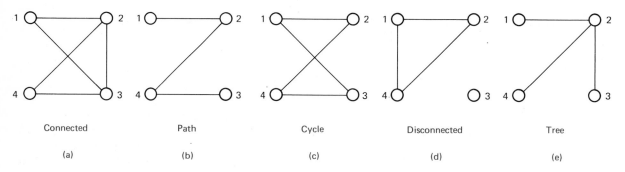

Connected	Path	Cycle	Disconnected	Tree
(a)	(b)	(c)	(d)	(e)

Figure 17.2. Various kinds of undirected graphs

17.1.2 Undirected Graphs

Several kinds of undirected graphs are shown in Figure 17.2. Two vertices in an undirected graph are called **adjacent** if there is an edge from the first to the second. Hence, in the undirected graph of part (a), vertices 1 and 2 are adjacent, as are 3 and 4, but 1 and 4 are not adjacent. A **path** is a sequence of distinct

paths, cycles, vertices, each adjacent to the next. Panel (b) shows a path. A **cycle** is a path
connected   containing at least three vertices such that the last vertex on the path is adjacent to the first. Panel (c) shows a cycle. A graph is called **connected** if there is a path from any vertex to any other vertex; parts (a), (b), and (c) show connected graphs, and part (d) shows a disconnected graph.

Panel (e) of Figure 17.2 shows a connected graph with no cycles. You will notice that this graph is, in fact, a tree, and we take this property as the definition:
free tree   A **free tree** is defined as a connected undirected graph with no cycles.

17.1.3 Directed Graphs

For directed graphs, we can make similar definitions. We require all edges in a path or a cycle to have the same direction, so that following a path or a cycle

directed paths and cycles

means always moving in the direction indicated by the arrows. Such a path (cycle) is called a ***directed*** path (cycle). A directed graph is called ***strongly connected*** if there is a directed path from any vertex to any other vertex. If we suppress the direction of the edges and the resulting undirected graph is connected, we call the directed graph ***weakly connected***. Figure 17.3 illustrates directed cycles, strongly connected directed graphs, and weakly connected directed graphs.

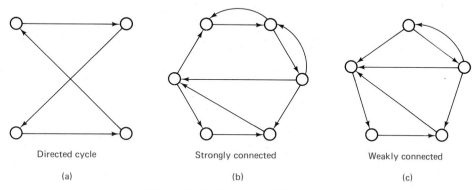

Directed cycle

(a)

Strongly connected

(b)

Weakly connected

(c)

Figure 17.3. Examples of directed graphs.

multiple edges

self-loops

The directed graphs in parts (b) and (c) of Figure 17.3 show pairs of vertices with directed edges going both ways between them. Since directed edges are ordered pairs and the ordered pairs (v, w) and (w, v) are distinct if $v \neq w$, such pairs of edges are permissible in directed graphs. Since the corresponding unordered pairs are not distinct, however, in an undirected graph there can be at most one edge connecting a pair of vertices. Similarly, since the vertices on an edge are required to be distinct, there can be no edge from a vertex to itself. We should remark, however, that (although we shall not do so) sometimes these requirements are relaxed to allow multiple edges connecting a pair of vertices and self-loops connecting a vertex to itself.

17.2

COMPUTER REPRESENTATION

If we are to write programs for solving problems concerning graphs, then we must first find ways to represent the mathematical structure of a graph as some kind of data structure. There are several methods in common use, which differ fundamentally in the choice of abstract data type used to represent graphs, and there are several variations depending on the implementation of the abstract data type. In other words, we begin with one mathematical system (a *graph*), then we study how it can be described in terms of abstract data types (*sets*, *tables*, and *lists* can all be used, as it turns out), and finally we choose implementations for the abstract data type that we select.

The Set Representation

Graphs are defined in terms of sets, and it is natural to look first to sets to determine their representation as data. First, we have a set of vertices, and, second, we have the edges as a set of pairs of vertices. Rather than attempting to represent this set of pairs directly, we divide it into pieces by considering the set of edges attached to each vertex separately. In other words, we can keep track of all the edges in the graph by keeping, for all vertices v in the graph, the set E_v of edges containing v, or, equivalently, the set A_v of all vertices adjacent to v. In fact, we can use this idea to produce a new, equivalent definition of a graph:

> A *graph* G consists of a set V, called the *vertices* of G, and, for all $v \in V$, a subset A_v of V, called the set of vertices *adjacent* to v.

From the subsets A_v we can reconstruct the edges as ordered pairs by the rule: The pair (v, w) is an edge if and only if $w \in A_v$. It is easier, however, to work with sets of vertices than with pairs. This new definition, moreover, works for both directed and undirected graphs; the graph is undirected means that it satisfies the following symmetry property: $w \in A_v$ implies $v \in A_w$ for all v, $w \in V$. This property can be restated in less formal terms: It means that an undirected edge between v and w can be regarded as made up of two directed edges, one from v to w and the other from w to v.

Implementation of Sets

There are two general ways for us to implement sets of vertices in data structures and algorithms. One way is to represent the set as a *list* of its elements; this method we shall study presently. The other implementation, often called a *bit string*, keeps a Boolean value (hence a single bit) for each possible member of the set to indicate whether or not it is in the set. This latter method is used in the Pascal type constructor **set**, which we consider first. To employ Pascal sets, we must begin with an ordinal type whose values correspond to the possible vertices. For simplicity, we shall consider that these vertices are indexed with the integers from 1 to n, where n denotes the number of vertices. Since we shall wish n to be variable, we shall also introduce a constant max bounding the number of vertices, with which we can fully specify the first representation of a graph:

sets as bit strings

first implementation: sets

```
type
  vertex = 1 .. max;                {Identify vertices with their indices.}
  adjacencyset = set of vertex;
  graph = record
    n: 0 .. max;                    {number of vertices in the graph}
    A: array [vertex] of adjacencyset
  end;
```

In this implementation, the array entry A[v] is the set of all vertices adjacent to the vertex v.

Adjacency Tables

restrictions

There is one practical problem with the foregoing implementation: The type constructor **set** is not available in all programming languages, and, when it is, there are often impractically small limits on the maximum size of a set. We can overcome this difficulty, however, and at the same time obtain a better representation of graphs.

sets as arrays

We have already seen that the Pascal type **set of** vertex is essentially implemented as **array** [vertex] **of** Boolean, where each array entry indicates whether or not the corresponding vertex is a member of the set. If we substitute this array for the adjacency set, we find that the array A in the declaration of type graph can be changed to an array of arrays, that is, to a two-dimensional array, as follows:

second implementation: adjacency table

```
type
    vertex = 1 .. max;                    {Identify vertices with their indices.}
    adjacencytable = array [vertex, vertex] of Boolean;
    graph = record
        n: 0 .. max;                      {number of vertices in the graph}
        A: adjacencytable
    end;
```

meaning

The adjacency table A has a natural interpretation: A[v, w] is true if and only if vertex v is adjacent to vertex w. If the graph is directed, we interpret A[v, w] as indicating whether or not the edge from v to w is in the graph. If the graph is undirected, then the adjacency table is symmetric, that is, A[v, w] = A[w, v] for all v and w. The representation of a graph by adjacency sets and by an adjacency table is illustrated in Figure 17.4.

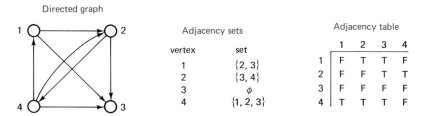

Figure 17.4. Adjacency set and an adjacency table

Adjacency Lists

Another way to represent a set is as a *list* of its elements. For representing a graph, we shall then have both a list of vertices and, for each vertex, a list of adjacent vertices. We shall consider implementation of graphs by using both contiguous lists and simply linked lists. For more advanced applications, however, it is often useful to employ more sophisticated implementations of lists as binary or multiway search trees or as heaps.

Note that, by identifying vertices with their indices in the previous representations, we have *ipso facto* implemented the vertex set as a contiguous list, but now we should make a deliberate choice concerning the use of contiguous or linked lists.

Linked Implementation

Greatest flexibility is obtained by using linked lists for both the vertices and the adjacency lists. This implementation is illustrated in part (a) of Figure 17.5 and results in a declaration such as the following:

third implementation: linked lists

```
type
   pointvertex = ↑vertex;
   pointedge = ↑edge;
   vertex = record
      firstedge: pointedge;              {start of the adjacency list}
      nextvertex: pointvertex            {next vertex on the linked list}
   end;
   edge = record
      endpoint: pointvertex;             {vertex to which the edge points}
      nextedge: pointedge;               {next edge on the adjacency list}
   end;
   graph = pointvertex;                  {header for the list of vertices}
```

Contiguous implementation

Although this linked implementation is very flexible, it is sometimes awkward to navigate through the linked lists, and many algorithms require random access to vertices. Therefore the following contiguous implementation is often better. For a contiguous adjacency list, we must keep a counter, and for this we use standard notation from graph theory: The *valence* of a vertex is the number of edges on which it lies, and hence it is also the number of vertices adjacent to it. This contiguous implementation is illustrated in part (b) of Figure 17.5.

fourth implementation: contiguous lists

```
type
   vertex = 1 .. max;
   counter = 0 .. max;
   adjacencylist = array [vertex] of vertex;
   graph = record
      n: counter;                        {number of vertices in the graph}
      valence: array [vertex] of counter;
      A: array [vertex] of adjacencylist
   end;
```

Mixed Implementation

The final implementation uses a contiguous list for the vertices and linked storage for the adjacency lists. This mixed implementation is illustrated in part (c) of Figure 17.5.

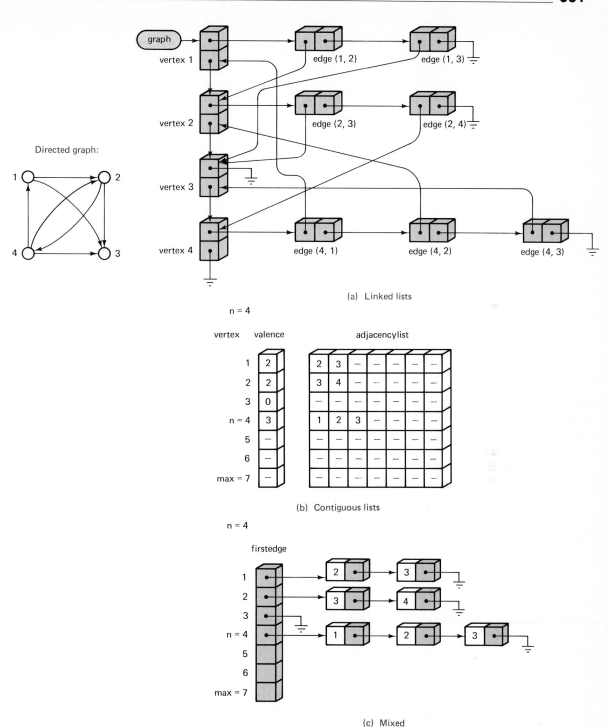

Directed graph:

(a) Linked lists

(b) Contiguous lists

(c) Mixed

Figure 17.5. Implementations of a graph with lists

fifth
implementation:
mixed lists

```
type
    vertex = 1 .. max;
    pointedge = ↑edge;
    edge = record
        endpoint: vertex;
        next: pointedge
    end;
    graph = record
        n: 0 .. max;                                    {number of vertices in graph}
        firstedge: array [vertex] of pointedge
    end;
```

Information Fields

Many applications of graphs require not only the adjacency information specified in the various representations but also further information specific to each vertex or each edge. In the linked representations, this information can be included as additional fields within appropriate records, and, in the contiguous representations, it can be included by making array entries into records.

networks,
weights

An especially important case is that of a ***network***, which is defined as a graph in which a numerical ***weight*** is attached to each edge. For many algorithms on networks, the best representation is an adjacency table, where the entries are the weights rather than Boolean values. We shall return to this topic later in the chapter.

17.3
GRAPH TRAVERSAL

17.3.1 Methods

In many problems, we wish to investigate all the vertices in a graph in some systematic order, just as with binary trees, where we developed several systematic traversal methods. In tree traversal, we had a root vertex with which we generally started; in graphs, we often do not have any one vertex singled out as special, and therefore the traversal may start at an arbitrary vertex. Although there are many possible orders for visiting the vertices of the graph, two methods are of particular importance.

depth-first

Depth-first traversal of a graph is roughly analogous to preorder traversal of an ordered tree. Suppose that the traversal has just visited a vertex v, and let $w_1, w_2, \ldots, w_k$ be the vertices adjacent to v. Then we shall next visit w_1 and keep $w_2, \ldots, w_k$ waiting. After visiting w_1, we traverse all the vertices to which it is adjacent before returning to traverse $w_2, \ldots, w_k$.

breadth-first   **Breadth-first traversal** of a graph is roughly analogous to level-by-level traversal of an ordered tree. If the traversal has just visited a vertex v, then it next visits *all* the vertices adjacent to v, putting the vertices adjacent to these in a waiting list to be traversed after all vertices adjacent to v have been visited. Figure 17.6 shows the order of visiting the vertices of one graph under both depth-first and breadth-first traversals.

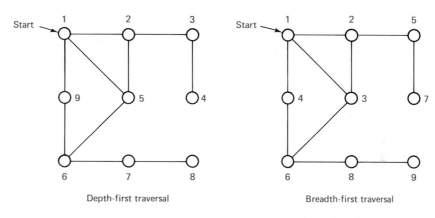

Note: The vertices adjacent to a given one are considered as arranged in clockwise order.

Figure 17.6. Graph traversal

17.3.2 Depth-First Algorithm

Depth-first traversal is naturally formulated as a recursive algorithm. Its action, when it reaches a vertex v, is

> Visit(v);
> **for** all vertices w adjacent **to** v **do**
> Traverse(w);

complications   In graph traversal, however, two difficulties arise that cannot appear for tree traversal. First, the graph may contain cycles, so our traversal algorithm may reach the same vertex a second time. To prevent infinite recursion, we therefore introduce a Boolean-valued array visited, set visited[v] to true before starting the recursion, and check the value of visited[w] before processing w. Second, the graph may not be connected, so the traversal algorithm may fail to reach all vertices from a single starting point. Hence we enclose the action in a loop that runs through all vertices.

With these refinements, we obtain the following outline of depth-first traversal. Further details depend on the choice of implementation of graphs, and we postpone them to application programs.

main procedure

```
procedure DepthFirst(var G: graph; procedure Visit(var v: vertex));
{Pre:    The graph G has been created.
  Post:  The procedure Visit has been performed at each vertex of G in depth-
         first order.
  Uses:  Procedure Traverse produces the recursive depth-first order.}

var
  visited: array [vertex] of Boolean;
  v: vertex;

begin                                          {procedure DepthFirst}
  for all v in G do
    visited [v] := false;
  for all v in G do
    if not visited [v] then
      Traverse (v)
end;                                           {procedure DepthFirst}
```

The recursion is performed in the following procedure, to be declared within the previous one.

recursive
traversal

```
procedure Traverse(var v: vertex; procedure Visit(var v: vertex));
{Pre:    v is a vertex of the graph G.
  Post:  The depth-first traversal, using procedure Visit, has been completed
         for v and for all vertices adjacent to v.}

var
  w: vertex;

begin                                          {recursive depth-first traversal}
  visited [v] := true;
  Visit (v);
  for all w adjacent to v do
    if not visited [w] then
      Traverse (w)
end;                                           {recursive depth-first traversal}
```

17.3.3 Breadth-First Algorithm

stacks and
queues

Since using recursion and programming with stacks are essentially equivalent, we could formulate depth-first traversal with a stack, pushing all unvisited vertices adjacent to the one being visited onto the stack and popping the stack to find the next vertex to visit. The algorithm for breadth-first traversal is quite similar to the resulting algorithm for depth-first traversal, except that a queue is needed instead of a stack. Its outline follows.

breadth-first traversal

procedure BreadthFirst(**var** G: graph; **procedure** Visit(**var** v: vertex));
{**Pre:** *The graph G has been created.*
   Post: *The procedure* Visit *has been performed at each vertex of* G, *where the vertices are chosen in breadth-first order.*
   Uses: *Package of queue operations.*}
type
   queueentry = vertex;
var
   Q: queuetype;
   visited: **array** [vertex] **of** Boolean;
   v, w: vertex;
   begin   {*procedure BreadthFirst*}
      for all v **in** G **do**
         visited [v] := false;
      CreateQueue(Q);
      for all v **in** G **do**
         if not visited [v] **then**
         begin
            Append(v, Q);
            repeat
               Serve(v, Q);
               visited [v] := true;
               Visit(v);
               for all w adjacent **to** v **do**
                  if not visited [w] **then**
                     Append(w, Q)
            until QueueEmpty(Q)
         end
   end;   {*procedure BreadthFirst*}

17.4

TOPOLOGICAL SORTING

17.4.1 The Problem

topological order

If G is a directed graph with no directed cycles, then a *topological order* for G is a sequential listing of all the vertices in G such that, for all vertices $v, w \in G$, if there is an edge from v to w, then v precedes w in the sequential listing. Throughout this section, we shall consider only directed graphs that have no directed cycles. The term *acyclic* is often used to mean that a graph has no cycles.

applications

Such graphs arise in many problems. As a first application of topological order, consider the courses available at a university as the vertices of a directed graph, where there is an edge from one course to another if the first is a prerequisite for the second. A topological order is then a listing of all the courses such that all prerequisites for a course appear before it does. A second example is a glossary of technical terms that is ordered so that no term is used in a definition before it is itself defined. Similarly, the author of a textbook uses a topological order for the topics in the book. Two different topological orders of a directed graph are shown in Figure 17.7.

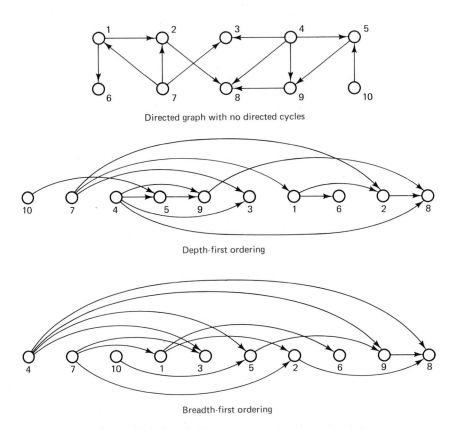

Directed graph with no directed cycles

Depth-first ordering

Breadth-first ordering

Figure 17.7. Topological orderings of a directed graph

As an example of algorithms for graph traversal, we shall develop procedures that produce a topological ordering of the vertices of a directed graph that has no cycles. We shall develop two procedures: first, for depth-first traversal, and, then, for breadth-first traversal. Both procedures will operate on a graph G given in the mixed implementation (with a contiguous list of vertices *graph* and linked adjacency lists), and both procedures will produce an array of type *representation*

toporder = **array** [vertex] **of** vertex;

that will specify the order in which the vertices should be listed to obtain a topological order.

17.4.2 Depth-First Algorithm

method

In a topological order, each vertex must appear before all the vertices that are its successors in the directed graph. For a depth-first topological ordering, we therefore start by finding a vertex that has no successors and place it last in the order. After we have, by recursion, placed all the successors of a vertex into the topological order, then we can place the vertex itself in a position before any of its successors. The variable place indicates the position in the topological order where the next vertex to be ordered will be placed. Since we first order the last vertices, we begin with place equal to the number of vertices in the graph. The main procedure is a direct implementation of the general algorithm developed in the last section.

depth-first topological sorting

```
procedure TopSort(var G: graph; var T: toporder);
{Pre:    G is a directed graph with no cycles implemented with a contiguous
         list of vertices and linked adjacency lists.
 Post:   The procedure makes a depth-first traversal of G and generates the
         resulting topological order in the array T.
 Uses:   Procedure Sort performs the recursive depth-first traversal.}
var
    visited: array [vertex] of Boolean;    {checks that G contains no cycles}
    v: vertex;                             {next vertex whose successors are to be ordered}
    place: 0 .. max;                       {next position in the topological order to be filled}
begin                                                          {procedure TopSort}
    for v := 1 to G.n do
        visited [v] := false;
    place := G.n;
    for v := 1 to G.n do
        if not visited [v] then
            Sort(v, place, T);
end;                                                           {procedure TopSort}
```

The procedure Sort that performs the recursion, based on the outline for the general procedure Traverse, first places all the successors of v into their positions in the topological order and then places v into the order.

recursive traversal

```
procedure Sort(v: vertex; var place: integer; var T: toporder);
{Pre:    v is a vertex of the graph G and place is the next location in the
         topological order T to be determined (starting from the end of the final
         ordered list).
 Post:   The procedure puts all the successors of v and finally v itself into the
         topological order T in depth-first order.
 Uses:   Global array visited and global graph G.}
```

```
    var
      w: vertex;                        {one of the vertices that immediately succeed v}
      p: pointedge;                    {traverses the adjacency list of vertices succeeding v}
    begin                                               {recursive procedure Sort}
      visited [v] := true;
      p := G.firstedge [v];                    {Find the first vertex succeeding v.}
      while p <> nil do
      begin
        w := p↑.endpoint;                      {w is an immediate successor of v.}
        if not visited [w] then
            Sort (w, place, T);        {Order all the successors of w and w itself.}
        p := p↑.next                   {Go on to the next immediate successor of v.}
      end;
      T [place] := v;                          {Put v itself into the topological order.}
      place := place − 1
    end;                                              {recursive procedure Sort}
```

Since this algorithm visits each node of the graph exactly once and follows each edge once, doing no searching, its running time is $O(n + e)$, where n is the number of nodes and e is the number of edges in the graph.

performance

17.4.3 Breadth-First Algorithm

method
In a breadth-first topological ordering of a directed graph with no cycles, we start by finding the vertices that should be first in the topological order and then apply the fact that every vertex must come before its successors in the topological order. The vertices that come first are those that are not successors of any other vertex. To find these, we set up an array predecessorcount whose entry at index v is the number of immediate predecessors of vertex v. The vertices that are not successors are those with no predecessors. We therefore initialize the breadth-first traversal by placing these vertices into the queue of vertices to be visited. As each vertex is visited, it is removed from the queue, assigned the next available position in the topological order (starting at the beginning of the order), and then removed from further consideration by reducing the predecessor count for each of its immediate successors by one. When one of these counts reaches zero, all predecessors of the corresponding vertex have been visited, and the vertex itself is then ready to be processed, so it is added to the queue. We therefore obtain the following procedure.

breadth-first topological order

```
procedure TopSort (var G: graph; var T: toporder);
  {Pre:  G is a directed graph with no cycles implemented with a contiguous
         list of vertices and linked adjacency lists.
   Post: The procedure makes a breadth-first traversal of G and generates the
         resulting topological order in T.
   Uses: Package for processing queues.}
```

```
var
    predecessorcount: array [vertex] of integer;
                            {number of immediate predecessors of each vertex}
    Q: queuetype;                      {vertices ready to be placed into the order}
    v,                                          {vertex currently being visited}
    w: vertex;                      {one of the immediate successors of v}
    p: pointedge;                      {traverses the adjacency list of v}
    place: integer;                      {next position in topological order}

begin                                            {procedure TopSort}
    for v := 1 to G.n do              {Initialize all predecessor counts to 0.}
        predecessorcount [v] := 0;
    for v := 1 to G.n do
    begin      {Increase predecessor count for vertices that are successors.}
        p := G.firstedge [v];
        while p <> nil do
        begin
            predecessorcount [p↑.endpoint] :=
                predecessorcount [p↑.endpoint] + 1;
            p := p↑.next
        end
    end;

    CreateQueue (Q);
    for v := 1 to G.n do        {Put vertices with no predecessors into queue.}
        if predecessorcount [v] = 0 then
            Append (v, Q);
    place := 0;                              {Start the breadth-first traversal.}
    while not QueueEmpty (Q) do
    begin
        Serve (v, Q);            {Visit v by placing it into the topological order.}
        place := place + 1;
        T [place] := v;
        p := G.firstedge [v];
                            {Traverse the list of the immediate successors of v.}
        while p <> nil do
        begin      {Reduce predecessor count for each immediate successor.}
            w := p↑.endpoint;
            predecessorcount [w] := predecessorcount [w] − 1;
            if predecessorcount [w] = 0 then
                    {w has no further predecessors, so it is ready to process.}
                Append (w, Q);
            p := p↑.next
        end
    end
end;                                            {procedure TopSort}
```

set predecessor counts

find vertices going first

process a vertex

This algorithm requires one of the packages for processing queues. The entries in the queue are to be vertices, and the queue can be implemented in any of the ways described in Chapters 5 and 7.

performance   As with depth-first traversal, the time required by the breadth-first procedure is $O(n + e)$, where n is the number of vertices and e is the number of edges in the directed graph.

17.5

A GREEDY ALGORITHM: SHORTEST PATHS

The Problem

As a final application of graphs, one requiring somewhat more sophisticated reasoning, we consider the following problem. We are given a directed graph G in which every edge has a nonnegative *weight* attached, and our problem is to find a path from one vertex v to another w such that the sum of the weights on *shortest path*   the path is as small as possible. We call such a path a ***shortest path***, even though the weights may represent costs, time, or some quantity other than distance.

We can think of G as a map of airline routes, for example, with each vertex representing a city and the weight on each edge the cost of flying from one city to the second. Our problem is then to find a routing from city v to city w such that the total cost is a minimum. Consider the directed graph shown in Figure 17.8. The shortest path from vertex 1 to vertex 2 goes via vertex 3 and has a total cost of 4, compared to the cost of 5 for the edge directly from 1 to 2 and the cost of 8 for the path via vertex 5.

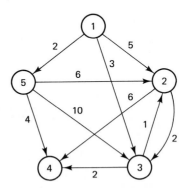

Figure 17.8. A directed graph with weights

source   It turns out that it is just as easy to solve the more general problem of starting at one vertex, called the ***source***, and finding the shortest path to every other vertex, instead of to just one destination vertex. For simplicity, we take the source to be vertex 1, and our problem then consists of finding the shortest path from vertex 1 to every vertex in the graph. We require that the weights are all nonnegative.

Method

The algorithm operates by keeping a set S of those vertices whose shortest distance from 1 is known. Initially, 1 is the only vertex in S. At each step, we add to S a remaining vertex for which the shortest path from 1 has been determined. The problem is to determine which vertex to add to S at each step. Let us think of the vertices already in S as having been labeled with some color, and think of the edges making up the shortest paths from the source 1 to these vertices as also colored.

distance table
We shall maintain a table D that gives, for each vertex v, the distance from 1 to v along a path all of whose edges are colored, except possibly the last one. That is, if v is in S, then $D[v]$ gives the shortest distance to v and all edges along the corresponding path are colored. If v is not in S, then $D[v]$ gives the length of the path from 1 to some vertex w in S plus the weight of the edge from w to v, and all the edges of this path except the last one are colored. The table D is initialized by setting $D[v]$ to the weight of the edge from 1 to v if it exists and to ∞ if not.

greedy algorithm
To determine what vertex to add to S at each step, we apply the *greedy* criterion of choosing the vertex v with the smallest distance recorded in the table D, such that v is not already in S.

verification
We must prove that, for this vertex v, the distance recorded in D really is the length of the shortest path from 1 to v. For suppose that there were a shorter path from 1 to v, such as shown in Figure 17.9. This path first leaves S to go to some vertex x, then goes on to v (possibly even reentering S along the way). But if this path is shorter than the colored path to v, then its initial segment from 1 to x is also shorter, so that the greedy criterion would have chosen x rather *end of proof* than v as the next vertex to add to S, since we would have had $D[x] < D[v]$.

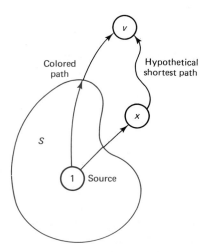

Figure 17.9. Finding a shortest path

When we add v to S, we think of v as now colored and also color the shortest path from 1 to v (every edge of which except the last was actually already colored). Next, we must update the entries of D by checking, for each vertex w not in S, whether a path through v and then directly to w is shorter than the previously recorded distance to w. That is, we replace $D[w]$ by $D[v]$ plus the weight of the edge from v to w if the latter quantity is smaller.

Example

Before writing a formal procedure incorporating this method, let us work through the example shown in Figure 17.10. For the directed graph shown in part (a), the initial situation is shown in part (b): The set S (colored vertices) consists of 1 alone, and the entries of the distance table D are shown as numbers in color beside the other vertices. The distance to vertex 5 is shortest, so 5 is added to S in part (c), and the distance $D[4]$ is updated to the value 6. Since the distances to vertices 2 and 3 via vertex 5 are greater than those already recorded in T, their entries remain unchanged. The next closest vertex to 1 is vertex 3, and it is added in part (d), which also shows the effect of updating the distances to vertices 2 and 4, whose paths via vertex 3 are shorter than those previously recorded. The final two steps, shown in parts (e) and (f), add vertices 2 and 4 to S and yield the paths and distances shown in the final diagram.

Implementation

For the sake of writing a procedure to embody this algorithm for finding shortest distances, we must choose an implementation of the directed graph. Use of the adjacency-table implementation facilitates random access to all the vertices of the graph, as we need for this problem. Moreover, by storing the weights in the table, we can use the table to give weights as well as adjacencies. We shall place a special large value ∞ in any position of the table for which the corresponding edge does not exist. These decisions are incorporated in the following Pascal declarations to be included in the calling program.

```
const
    max = {to be provided; maximum number of vertices in the graph}
    infinity = maxint;
type
    weight = integer;
    count = 0 .. max;
    vertex = 1 .. max;
    adjacencytable = array [vertex, vertex] of weight;
    distancetable = array [vertex] of weight;
var
    n: count;                        {number of vertices in the graph}
    cost: adjacencytable;                   {describes the graph}
    D: distancetable;           {shortest distances from vertex 1}
```

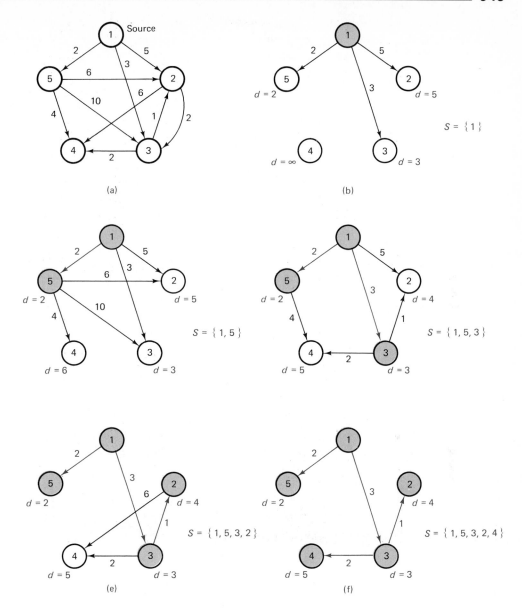

Figure 17.10. Example of shortest paths

The procedure that we write will accept the adjacency table and the count of vertices in the graph as its input parameters and will produce the table of closest distances as its output parameter.

shortest distance procedure

```
procedure Distance (n: count; var cost: adjacencytable;
                    var D: distancetable);
```

{**Pre:** *A directed graph with n vertices is given by the weights in the table cost.*

Post: *The procedure calculates the cost of the shortest path from vertex 1 to all the other vertices of the graph and returns the result in the array D.*}

```
var
  final: array [vertex] of Boolean;
```
{*Has the final distance from 1 to v been found? final [v] is true if and only if v is in the set S.*}
```
  i,                                  {repetition count for the main loop}
```
{*One distance is finalized on each pass through the loop.*}
```
  w,                                  {a vertex not yet added to the set S}
  v: vertex;                {vertex with minimum tentative distance in D [ ]}
  min: weight;                        {distance of v, equals D [v]}

begin                                              {procedure Distance}
  final [1] := true;             {Initialize with vertex 1 alone in the set S.}
  D [1] := 0;
  for v := 2 to n do
  begin
    final [v] := false;
    D [v] := cost [1, v]
  end;
  for i := 2 to n do
  begin          {Start the main loop; add one vertex v to S on each pass.}
    min := infinity;                       {Find the closest vertex v to vertex 1.}
    for w := 2 to n do
      if not final [w] then
        if D [w] < min then
        begin
          v := w;
          min := D [w]
        end;
    final [v] := true;                                    {Add v to the set S.}
    for w := 2 to n do                 {Update the remaining distances in D.}
      if not final [w] then
        if min + cost [v, w] < D [w] then
          D [w] := min + cost [v, w];
  end
end;                                                      {procedure Distance}
```

performance   To estimate the running time of this procedure, we note that the main loop is executed $n - 1$ times, and within it are two other loops, each executed $n - 1$ times, so these loops contribute a multiple of $(n - 1)^2$ operations. Statements done outside the loops contribute only $O(n)$, so the running time of the algorithm is $O(n^2)$.

17.6

GRAPHS AS DATA STRUCTURES

In this chapter, we have studied a few applications of graphs, but we have hardly begun to scratch the surface of the broad and deep subject of graph algorithms. In many of these algorithms, graphs appear, as they have in this chapter, as mathematical structures capturing the essential description of a problem rather than as computational tools for its solution.

mathematical structures and data structures

Note that in this chapter we have spoken of graphs as mathematical structures, and not as data structures, for we have used graphs to formulate mathematical problems, and, to write algorithms, we have then implemented the graphs within data structures like tables and lists. Graphs, however, can certainly be regarded as data structures themselves, data structures that embody relationships among the data more complicated than those describing a list or a tree.

flexibility and power

Because of their generality and flexibility, graphs are powerful data structures that prove valuable in more advanced applications such as the design of data-base management systems. Such powerful tools are meant to be used, of course, whenever necessary, but they must always be used with care so that their power is not turned to confusion. Perhaps the best safeguard in the use of powerful tools is to insist on regularity, that is, to use the powerful tools only in carefully defined and well-understood ways. Because of the generality of graphs, it is not always easy to impose this discipline on their use.

irregularity

In this world, nonetheless, irregularities will always creep in, no matter how hard we try to avoid them. It is the bane of the systems analyst and programmer to accommodate these irregularities while trying to maintain the integrity of the underlying system design. Irregularity even occurs in the very systems that we use as models for the data structures we devise, models such as the family trees whose terminology we have always used. An excellent illustration of what can happen is the following classic story, quoted by N. WIRTH[1] from a Zurich newspaper of July 1922.

> I married a widow who had a grown-up daughter. My father, who visited us quite often, fell in love with my step-daughter and married her. Hence, my father became my son-in-law, and my step-daughter became my mother. Some months later, my wife gave birth to a son, who became the brother-in-law of my father as well as my uncle. The wife of my father, that is my step-daughter, also had a son. Thereby, I got a brother and at the same time a grandson. My wife is my grandmother, since she is my mother's mother. Hence, I am my wife's husband and at the same time her step-grandson; in other words, I am my own grandfather.

---

[1] *Algorithms + Data Structures = Programs*, Prentice Hall, Englewood Cliffs, N. J., 1976, page 170.

EXERCISES 17.6

E1. **(a)** Find all the cycles in each of the following graphs. **(b)** Which of these graphs are connected? **(c)** Which of these graphs are free trees?

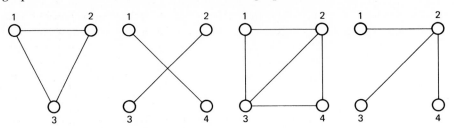

E2. For each of the graphs shown in Exercise E1, give the implementation of the graph as **(a)** an adjacency table, **(b)** a linked vertex list with linked adjacency lists, **(c)** a contiguous vertex list of contiguous adjacency lists.

E3. A graph is *regular* if every vertex has the same valence (that is, if it is adjacent to the same number of other vertices). For a regular graph, a good implementation is to keep the vertices in a linked list and the adjacency lists contiguous. The length of all the adjacency lists is called the *degree* of the graph. Write Pascal declarations for this implementation of regular graphs.

E4. The topological sorting procedures as presented in the text are deficient in error checking. Modify the **(a)** depth-first and **(b)** breadth-first procedures so that they will detect any (directed) cycles in the graph and indicate what vertices cannot be placed in any topological order because they lie on a cycle.

PROJECTS 17.6

P1. Write Pascal procedures called ReadGraph that will read from the terminal the number of vertices in an undirected graph and lists of adjacent vertices. Be sure to include error checking. The graph is to be implemented as

    a. an adjacency table,
    b. a linked vertex list with linked adjacency lists,
    c. a contiguous vertex list of linked adjacency lists.

P2. Write Pascal procedures called WriteGraph that will write pertinent information specifying a graph to the terminal. The graph is to be implemented as

    a. an adjacency table,
    b. a linked vertex list with linked adjacency lists,
    c. a contiguous vertex list of linked adjacency lists.

P3. Use the procedures ReadGraph and WriteGraph to implement and test the topological sorting procedures developed in this section for **(a)** depth-first order and **(b)** breadth-first order.

P4. Implement and test the procedure for determining shortest distances in directed graphs with weights.

POINTERS AND PITFALLS

1. Graphs provide an excellent way to describe the essential features of many applications, thereby facilitating specification of the underlying problems and formulation of algorithms for their solution. Graphs sometimes appear as data structures but more often as mathematical abstractions useful for problem solving.

2. Graphs may be implemented in many ways by the use of different kinds of data structures. Postpone implementation decisions until the applications of graphs in the problem-solving and algorithm-development phases are well understood.

3. Many applications require graph traversal. Let the application determine the traversal method: depth first, breadth first, or some other order. Depth-first traversal is naturally recursive (or can use a stack). Breadth-first traversal normally uses a queue.

4. Greedy algorithms represent only a sample of the many paradigms useful in developing graph algorithms. For further methods and examples, consult the references given in Appendix C.

REVIEW QUESTIONS

17.1 1. In the sense of this chapter, what is a *graph*? What are *edges* and *vertices*?

2. What is the difference between an *undirected* and a *directed* graph?

3. Define the terms *adjacent*, *path*, *cycle*, and *connected*.

4. What does it mean for a directed graph to be strongly connected? Weakly connected?

17.2 5. Describe three ways to implement graphs in computer memory.

17.3 6. Explain the difference between *depth-first* and *breadth-first* traversal of a graph.

7. What data structures are needed to keep track of the waiting vertices during **(a)** depth-first and **(b)** breadth-first traversal?

17.4 8. For what kind of graphs is *topological sorting* defined?

9. What is a *topological order* for such a graph?

17.5 10. Why is the algorithm for finding shortest distances called *greedy*?

18

INTRODUCTION TO SOFTWARE ENGINEERING

Software engineering is the discipline within computer science concerned with techniques for the production and maintenance of large software systems. These techniques include problem specification, algorithm development, verification, and analysis, as well as program testing and maintenance. In this chapter, we discuss some of these techniques and illustrate their application to a project that simulates the game called Life.

THE SOFTWARE LIFE CYCLE

Software engineering is the study and practice of methods helpful for the construction and maintenance of large software systems. Software engineering begins with the realization that it is a very long process to obtain good software. It begins before any programs are coded and continues maintenance for years after the programs are put into use. This continuing process is known as the *life cycle* of software. This life cycle can be divided into phases as follows:

phases of the life cycle

- *Analyze* the problem precisely and completely. Be sure to *specify* all necessary user interface with care.

- *Build* a prototype and *experiment* with it until all specifications can be finalized.

- *Design* the algorithm, using the tools of data structures and of other algorithms whose function is already known.

- *Verify* that the algorithm is correct, or make it so simple that its correctness is self-evident.

- *Analyze* the algorithm to determine its requirements and make sure that it meets the specifications.

- *Code* the algorithm into the appropriate programming language.

- *Test* and *evaluate* the program on carefully chosen test data.

- *Refine* and *repeat* the foregoing steps as needed for additional subprograms until the software is complete and fully functional.

- *Optimize* the code to improve performance, but only if necessary.

- *Maintain* the program so that it will meet the changing needs of its users.

Most of these topics have been discussed and illustrated in various sections of this book, but a few further remarks on some of the phases are in order.

Problem Analysis

Analysis of the problem is often the most difficult phase of the software life cycle. This is not because practical problems are conceptually more difficult than are computing science exercises—the reverse is often the case—but because users and programmers tend to speak different languages. Here are some questions on which the analyst and user must reach an understanding:

specifications

1. What form will the input and output data take? How much data will there be?

2. Are there any special requirements for the processing? What special occurrences will require separate treatment?

3. Will these requirements change? How? How fast will the demands on the system grow?

4. What parts of the system are the most important? Which must run most efficiently?

5. How should erroneous data be treated? What other error processing is needed?

6. What kinds of people will use the software? What kind of training will they have? What kind of user interface will be best?

7. How portable must the software be, so that it can be moved to new kinds of equipment? With what other software and hardware systems must the project be compatible?

8. What extensions or other maintenance are anticipated? What is the history of previous changes to software and hardware?

Requirements Specification

The problem analysis and experimentation for a large project finally lead to a formal statement of the requirements for the project. This statement becomes the primary way in which the user and the software engineer attempt to understand each other and establishes the standard by which the final project will be judged. Among the contents of this specification will be the following:

1. *Functional requirements* for the system: what it will do and what commands will be available to the user.

2. *Assumptions* and *limitations* on the system: what hardware will be used for the system, what form the input must take, the maximum size of input, the largest number of users, and so on.

3. *Maintenance requirements*: anticipated extensions or growth of the system, changes in hardware, changes in user interface.

4. *Documentation requirements*: what kind of explanatory material is required for what kinds of users.

The requirements specifications state *what* the software will do, not *how* it will be done. These specifications should be understandable both to the user and to the programmer. If carefully prepared, they will form the basis for the subsequent phases of design, coding, testing, and maintenance.

Prototyping

No matter how much work has been invested in problem analysis and specification of design requirements, it is usually not possible to make all decisions wisely until users have the opportunity to work with the software, reassess their needs, and suggest possible improvements.

An excellent way to avoid having to rewrite a large project from scratch in order to build in proposed improvements is instead to plan from the beginning to write two versions of the software. Before a program is running, it is often impossible to know what parts of the design will cause difficulty or what features need to be changed to meet the needs of the users. Engineers have known for many years that it is not possible to build a large project directly from the drawing board. For large projects engineers always build **prototypes**, that is, scaled-down models that can be studied, tested, and sometimes even used for limited purposes. Models of bridges are built and tested in wind tunnels; pilot plants are constructed before attempting to use new technology on the assembly line.

software prototypes

Building prototypes is especially helpful for computer software, since it eases communication between users and designers early in the project, thereby reducing misunderstandings and helping to settle the design to everyone's satisfaction. In building a software prototype, the designer can use programs that are already written for input-output, for sorting, or for other common requirements. The building blocks can be assembled with as little new programming as possible to make a working model that can do some of the intended tasks. Even though the prototype may not function efficiently or do everything that the final system will, it provides an excellent laboratory for the user and designer to experiment with alternative ideas for the final design.

Programming Precept

Always plan to build a prototype and throw it away.
You'll do so whether you plan to or not.

That is, even if you produce what seems to be a final version the first time, there are sure to be so many further changes that need to be made that you will end up rewriting all the software from scratch a second time.

There are computer languages like LISP and Smalltalk that can sometimes make prototyping easier.

Verification

Verification of algorithms, that is, *proving* the correctness of algorithms, is a subject requiring careful attention and considerable work. We shall return to this question later in the chapter. C. A. R. HOARE, who invented the quicksort algorithm of Chapter 11, wrote, "There are two ways of constructing a software design: One way is to make it so simple that there are obviously no deficiencies, and the other way is to make it so complicated that there are no obvious deficiencies. The first method is far more difficult."[1]

Analysis

A major goal of this book is to evaluate algorithms and data structures that purport to solve a problem. Some of this analysis is the mathematical computation of the time required by various algorithms, but there are other, nonmathematical

---

[1] "The Emperor's Old Clothes," *Communications of the ACM* 24 (1981), 75–83.

criteria by which we can judge a program, and which are equally important. Some of these are:

1. Does it solve the problem that is requested, according to the given specifications?

2. Does it work correctly under all conditions?

3. Does it include clear and sufficient information for its user, in the form of instructions and documentation?

4. Is it logically and clearly written, with short modules and subprograms as appropriate to do logical tasks?

5. Does it make efficient use of time and of space?

Maintenance

Small programs written as exercises or demonstrations are usually run a few times and then discarded, but the disposition of large practical programs is quite different. A program of practical value will be run many times, usually by many different people, and its writing and debugging mark only the beginning of its use. They also mark only the beginning of the work required to make and keep the program useful. It is necessary to *review* the program continually to ensure that it still meets the requirements specified for it, *adapt* it to changing environments, and *modify* it to make it better meet the needs of its users.

Sometimes the required modifications to a program are so extensive that it is more efficient to write a completely new version than to patch the old one. A good rule of thumb is that, if more than ten percent of a program must be modified, then it is time to rewrite the program completely. With repeated patches to a large program, the number of bugs tends to remain constant. That is, the patches become so complicated that each new patch tends to introduce as many new errors as it corrects.

Programming Precept

Starting afresh is usually easier than patching an old program.

18.2

THE GAME OF LIFE

case study

If I may take the liberty to abuse an old proverb, "One concrete problem is worth a thousand unapplied abstractions." Throughout this chapter we shall concentrate on one case study that, while very small by realistic standards for software engineering, illustrates many of its methods. Sometimes the example motivates general principles; sometimes the general discussion comes first; always it is with the view of discovering general methods that will prove their value in a range of practical applications.

The example we shall use is the game called *Life*, which was introduced by the British mathematician J. H. Conway in 1970.

18.2.1 Rules for the Game of Life

definitions

Life is really a simulation, not a game with players. It takes place on an unbounded rectangular grid in which each cell can either be occupied by an organism or not. Occupied cells are called *alive*; unoccupied cells are called *dead*. Which cells are alive changes from generation to generation according to the number of neighboring cells that are alive, as follows:

transition rules

1. The neighbors of a given cell are the eight cells that touch it vertically, horizontally, or diagonally.

2. If a cell is alive but either has no neighboring cells alive or only one alive, then in the next generation the cell dies of loneliness.

3. If a cell is alive and has four or more neighboring cells also alive, then in the next generation the cell dies of overcrowding.

4. A living cell with either two or three living neighbors remains alive in the next generation.

5. If a cell is dead, then in the next generation it will become alive if it has exactly three neighboring cells, no more or fewer, that are already alive. All other dead cells remain dead in the next generation.

6. All births and deaths take place at exactly the same time, so that dying cells can help to give birth to another, but cannot prevent the death of others by reducing overcrowding, nor can cells being born either preserve or kill cells living in the previous generation.

18.2.2 Examples

As a first example, consider the community

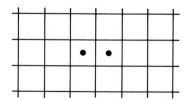

Although this diagram shows only three rows and six columns, recall that the grid is really unbounded, extending infinitely far in all directions. The counts of living neighbors for the cells are as follows:

0	0	0	0	0	0
0	1	2	2	1	0
0	1	•1	•1	1	0
0	1	2	2	1	0
0	0	0	0	0	0

moribund example By rule 2 both the living cells will die in the coming generation, and rule 5 shows that no cells will become alive, so the community dies out.

On the other hand, the community

0	0	0	0	0	0
0	1	2	2	1	0
0	2	•3	•3	2	0
0	2	•3	•3	2	0
0	1	2	2	1	0
0	0	0	0	0	0

stability has the neighbor counts as shown. Each of the living cells has a neighbor count of three, and hence remains alive, but the dead cells all have neighbor counts of two or less, and hence none of them becomes alive.

The two communities

0	0	0	0	0
1	2	3	2	1
1	•1	•2	•1	1
1	2	3	2	1
0	0	0	0	0

and

0	1	1	1	0
0	2	•1	2	0
0	3	•2	3	0
0	2	•1	2	0
0	1	1	1	0

alternation continue to alternate from generation to generation, as indicated by the neighbor counts shown.

It is a surprising fact that, from very simple initial configurations, quite complicated progressions of Life communities can develop, lasting many generations, and it is usually not obvious what changes will happen as generations progress.

variety Some very small initial configurations will grow into large communities; others will slowly die out; many will reach a state where they do not change, or where they go through a repeating pattern every few generations.

popularity Not long after its invention, MARTIN GARDNER discussed the Life game in his column in *Scientific American*, and, from that time on, it has fascinated many people, so that for several years there was even a quarterly newsletter devoted to related topics. It makes an ideal display for home microcomputers.

Our goal, of course, is to write a program that will show how an initial community will change from generation to generation. The more specific problem specifications are that the program should first read an initial configuration of living and dead cells and should calculate how this configuration will change in the next generation under the given rules for the game of Life. After printing the new configuration, the program should pause until the user gives an input to continue to calculate and print the next generation.

18.2.3 The First Solution

The first solution to the Life problem is quite simple and will serve as an excellent prototype to help us learn more both about the way the game proceeds and about desirable features in the program.

method We shall set up a large rectangular array whose entries correspond to the Life cells and will be marked with the status of the cell, either alive or dead. To determine what happens from one generation to the next, we shall count the number of living neighbors of each cell and apply the rules. Since, however, we shall be using loops to go through the array, we must be careful not to violate rule 6 by allowing changes made earlier to affect the count of neighbors for cells studied later. The easiest way to avoid this pitfall is to set up a second array that will represent the community at the next generation and, after it has been completely calculated, then make the generation change by copying it to the original array.

Next let us rewrite this method as the steps of an informal algorithm.

algorithm Initialize a table called map to contain the initial configuration of living cells.

Repeat the following steps for as long as desired:
> For each cell in the array do the following:
>> Count the number of living neighbors of the cell. If the count is 0, 1, 4, 5, 6, 7, or 8, then set the corresponding cell in another array called newmap to be dead; if the count is 3, then set the corresponding cell to be alive; and if the count is 2, then set the corresponding cell to be the same as the cell in array map (since the status of a cell with count 2 does not change).
>
> Copy the array newmap into the array map.
> Print the array map for the user.

18.2.4 Life: The First Main Program

The preceding outline of an algorithm for the game of Life translates into the following Pascal program.

main program

```pascal
program ProtoLife(input, output);
{Pre:  The user must supply an initial configuration of living cells.
 Post: The program prints a sequence of maps showing the changes in the
       configuration of living cells according to the rules for the game of Life.}
{simulation of Conway's game of Life on a bounded grid, first version}
const
    maxrow = 50;                        {maximum number of rows allowed}
    maxcol = 80;                        {maximum number of columns allowed}
type
    rowrange = 1 .. maxrow;
    colrange = 1 .. maxcol;
    state = (dead, alive);
    grid = array [rowrange, colrange] of state;
var
    map,                               {description of the current generation}
    newmap: grid;                      {description of the next generation}
    row: rowrange;
    col: colrange;

    {The declarations of the procedures and functions will go here.}
```

initialization

calculate changes

advance the generation

```pascal
begin                                  {main program ProtoLife}
    Initialize(map);                   {Obtain the initial configuration for map.}
    WriteMap(map);                     {Write out the initial configuration as a check.}
    repeat                             {Begin the main loop on generations.}
        for row := 1 to maxrow do      {Loop through the entire array.}
            for col := 1 to maxcol do
                case NeighborCount(row, col) of
                    0, 1: newmap[row, col] := dead;        {dies of loneliness}
                    2: newmap[row, col] := map[row, col];  {stays the same}
                    3: newmap[row, col] := alive;          {becomes alive}
                    4, 5, 6, 7, 8: newmap[row, col] := dead  {overcrowded}
                end;
        map := newmap;
        WriteMap(map);
        write('Continue ')             {Determine if the user wishes to continue.}
    until not UserSaysYes
end.                                   {main program ProtoLife}
```

subprograms

In this program, we still must write the procedures Initialize and WriteMap that will do the input and output and the function NeighborCount(row, col) that will count the number of cells neighboring the one in (row, col) that are occupied in the array map. We shall take the procedure UserSaysYes from Section 2.2.3.

18.2.5 Subprograms for Life

Counting Neighbors

function
NeighborCount

The function that counts neighbors of the cell in (row, col) requires that we look in the eight adjoining positions. We shall use a pair of **for** loops to do this, one running usually from row − 1 to row + 1 and the other usually from col − 1 to col + 1. We need only be careful, when (row, col) is on a boundary of the grid, that we look only at legitimate positions in the grid. To do so, we introduce four variables for the lower and upper limits of the loops, and make sure that they remain within range. Since the loops will incorrectly consider that the cell in position (row, col) is a neighbor of itself, we must make a correction after completing the loops.

```
function NeighborCount(row: rowrange; col: colrange): integer;
{Pre:   The pair (row, col) gives a cell in a Life configuration.
 Post:  The function returns the number of living neighbors of the given cell.
 Uses:  Array map that contains the Life configuration.}
var
   x,                                        {loop index for row}
   xlow, xhigh: rowrange;                    {limits for row loop}
   y,                                        {loop index for column}
   ylow, yhigh: colrange;                    {limits for column loop}
   count: integer;                           {counter of occupied neighbors}
begin                                        {function NeighborCount}
   if row = 1                                {First determine the boundaries.}
      then xlow := 1
      else xlow := row − 1;
   if row = maxrow
      then xhigh := row
      else xhigh := row + 1;
   if col = 1
      then ylow := 1
      else ylow := col − 1;
   if col = maxcol
      then yhigh := col
      else yhigh := col + 1;
   count := 0;
   for x := xlow to xhigh do
      for y := ylow to yhigh do             {Use nested loops to count neighbors.}
         if map[x, y] = alive then
            count := count + 1;
   if map[row, col] = alive then            {(row, col) is not its own neighbor.}
      count := count − 1;
   NeighborCount := count
end;                                         {function NeighborCount}
```

Initialization

input method

The task that procedure Initialize must accomplish is to set the map to its initial configuration. To initialize the map, we could consider each possible coordinate pair separately and request the user to indicate whether the cell is to be occupied or not. This method would require the user to type in

$$\text{maxrow} \times \text{maxcol} = 50 \times 80 = 4000$$

entries, which is prohibitive. Hence, instead, we input only those coordinate pairs corresponding to initially occupied cells.

initialization

```
procedure Initialize(var map: grid);
{Pre:   None.
  Post:  The array map is set to the initial configuration of living cells.}
var
  row,                                        {coordinates of a cell}
  col: integer;    {Use integer rather than a subrange to catch user errors.}
begin                                           {procedure Initialize}
  writeln('This program is a simulation of the game of Life.');
  for row := 1 to maxrow do
    for col := 1 to maxcol do
      map[row, col] := dead;
  writeln('On each line give a pair of coordinates for a living cell.');
  writeln('Terminate the list with the special pair   0  0');
  readln(row, col);
  while (row <> 0) or (col <> 0) do        {Check termination condition.}
  begin                                       {Check input for legality.}
    if (row >= 1) and (row <= maxrow) and
      (col >= 1) and (col <= maxcol)
      then map[row, col] := alive
      else writeln('Values are not within range.');
    readln(row, col);
  end                                     {loop processing pair row,col}
end;                                            {procedure Initialize}
```

output

The output procedure WriteMap simply writes the array at each generation, with occupied cells denoted by * and empty cells by blanks.

```
procedure WriteMap(map: grid);
{Pre:    The grid map contains the current Life configuration.
  Post:  The current Life configuration is written for the user.}
const
  full = '*';
  empty = '  ';
var
  row: rowrange;
  col: colrange;
```

```
begin                                                {procedure WriteMap}
  writeln('The map is below:');
  for row := 1 to maxrow do
  begin
    for col := 1 to maxcol do
      if map[row, col] = alive then
        write(full)
      else
        write(empty);
    writeln
  end                                                {processing row}
end;                                                 {procedure WriteMap}
```

At this point, we have all subprograms for the Life simulation. It is time to pause and check how it works.

◼ EXERCISES 18.2

Determine by hand calculation what will happen to each of the communities shown in Figure 18.1 over the course of five generations.   [*Suggestion*: Set up the Life configuration on a checkerboard. Use one color of checkers for living cells in the current generation and a second color to mark those that will be born or die in the next generation.]

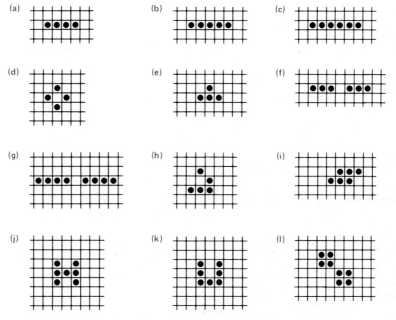

Figure 18.1. Life configurations

PROJECTS 18.2

P1. Test the procedures Initialize and WriteMap by writing and running a driver program consisting essentially of the statement

begin Initialize(map); WriteMap(map) **end.**

P2. The results of the function NeighborCount are not shown directly to the user, so it is important that it be tested separately to be sure that it is correct. Write a driver program for NeighborCount and run it with test data that will check that NeighborCount treats every case correctly.

P3. Enter the complete ProtoLife program of this section on your computer and make sure that it works correctly.

P4. Test the program with the examples shown in Figure 18.1.

P5. Run the Life program with the initial configurations shown in Figure 18.2.

18.3

PROGRAM REVIEW AND PROBLEM SOLVING

problems

If you have run the prototype Life program on a small computer or on a busy time-sharing system, then you will likely have found two major problems. First, the method for input of the initial configuration is poor. It is unnatural for a person to calculate and type in the numerical coordinates of each living cell. The form of input should instead reflect the same visual imagery as the way the map is printed. Second, you may have found the program's speed somewhat disappointing. There can be a noticeable pause between printing one generation and starting to print the next.

Our goal is to improve the program so that it will run really efficiently on a microcomputer. The problem of improving the form of input is addressed as an exercise; the text discusses the problem of improving the speed.

Analysis of the Life Program

operation counts

We must first find out where the program is spending most of its computation time. If we examine the program, we can first note that the trouble cannot be in the procedure Initialize, since this is done only once, before the main loop is started. Within the loop that counts generations, we have a pair of nested loops that, together, will iterate

$$\mathsf{maxrow} \times \mathsf{maxcol} = 50 \times 80 = 4000$$

times. Hence program statements within these loops will contribute substantially to the time used.

nested loops

The loops begin by invoking the function NeighborCount(row, col). The function itself includes a pair of nested loops (note that we are now nested to a total

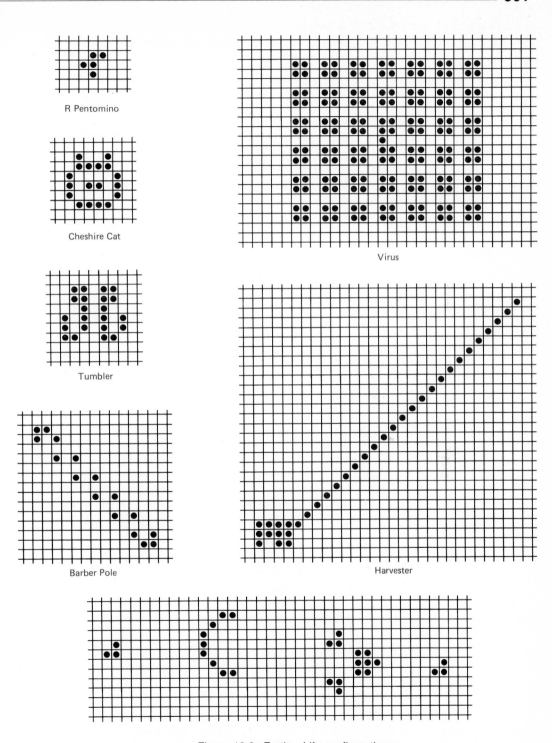

Figure 18.2. Further Life configurations

depth of 5), which usually do their inner statement 9 times. The function also does 7 statements outside the loops, for a total (usually) of 16.

Within the nested loops of the main program there are, along with the call to the function, only the comparison to find which case to do and the appropriate assignment statement, that is, there are only 2 statements additional to the 16 in the function. Outside of the nested loops there is the assignment of arrays map := newmap, which, in copying 4000 entries, is about equivalent to 1 more statement within the loops. There is also a call to the procedure WriteMap, some variation of which is needed in any case so that the user can see what the program is doing. Our primary concern is with the computation, however, so let us not worry about the time that WriteMap may need. We thus see that for each generation, the computation involves about

$$4000 \times 19 = 76{,}000$$

statements, of which about $4000 \times 16 = 64{,}000$ are done in the function.

On a small microcomputer or a tiny share of a busy time-sharing system, each statement can easily require 100 to 500 microseconds for execution, so the time to calculate a generation may easily range as high as 40 seconds, a delay that most users will find unacceptable.

Since by far the greatest amount of time is used in the function calculating the number of occupied neighbors of a cell, we should concentrate our attention on doing this job more efficiently. Before starting to develop some ideas, however, let us pause momentarily to note:

Programming Precept

Most programs spend 90 percent of their time
doing 10 percent of their instructions.
Find this 10 percent, and concentrate your efforts for efficiency there.

It takes much practice and experience to decide what is important and what may be neglected in analyzing algorithms for efficiency, but it is a skill that you should carefully develop to enable you to choose alternative methods or to concentrate your programming efforts where they will do the most good.

Problem-Solving Alternatives

Once we know where a program is doing most of its work, we can begin to consider alternative methods in the hope of improving its efficiency. In the case of the Life game, let us ask ourselves how we can reduce the amount of work needed to keep track of the number of occupied neighbors of each Life cell. Is it necessary for us to calculate the number of neighbors of every cell at every *use of table* generation? Clearly not, if we use some way (such as a table) to remember the number of neighbors, and if this number does not change from one generation to the next. If you have spent some time experimenting with the Life program, then you will certainly have noticed that in many interesting configurations, the number of occupied cells at any time is far below the total number of positions available. Out of 4000 positions, typically fewer than 100 are occupied. Our program is spending much of its time laboriously calculating the obvious facts that cells isolated from the living cells indeed have no occupied neighbors and will not become occupied. If we can prevent or substantially reduce such useless calculation, we shall obtain a much better program.

As a first approach, let us consider trying to limit the calculations to cells in a limited area around those that are occupied. If this occupied area (which we would have to define precisely) is roughly rectangular, then we can implement this scheme easily by replacing the limits in the loops by other variables that would bound the occupied area. But this scheme would be very inefficient if the occupied area were shaped like a large ring, or, indeed, if there were only two small occupied areas in opposite corners of a very large rectangle. To try to carry out this plan for occupied areas not at all rectangular in shape would probably require us to do so many comparisons, as well as the loops, as to take away any saving of time.

A Fresh Start and a New Method

Let us back up for a moment. If we can now decide to keep a table to remember the number of occupied neighbors of each cell, then the only counts in the table that will change from generation to generation will be those that correspond to immediate neighbors of cells that die or are born. We can substantially improve the running time of our program if we convert the function NeighborCount into a table and add appropriate statements to update the table while we are doing the changes from one generation to the next.

tables and functions

This method still requires scanning once through the full array map at every generation to find out which cells will become alive or dead, and this likely means much useless work. By being slightly more careful, we can avoid the need ever to look at unoccupied areas.

algorithm development

As a cell is born or dies, it changes the neighbor counts for each of its immediate neighbors. While making these changes, we can note when we find a cell whose count becomes such that it will be born or die in the next generation. Thus we should set up two *lists* that will contain the cells that, so to speak, are moribund or are expecting in the coming generation. In this way, once we have finished making the changes of the current generation and printing the map, we will have waiting for us complete lists of all the births and deaths to occur in the coming generation. It should now be clear that we really need two lists for births and two for deaths, one each for the changes being made now (which lists are depleted as we proceed) and one list each (which are being added to) containing the changes for the next generation. When the changes on the current lists are complete, we print the map, move the coming lists to the current ones, and go on to the next generation. The changes made during one generation for a simple configuration are illustrated in Figure 18.3.

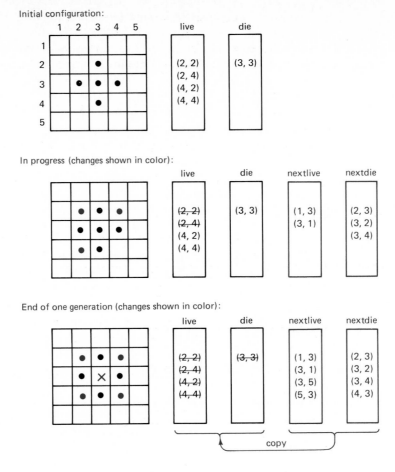

Figure 18.3. Life using lists

Algorithm Outline

Let us now summarize our decisions by writing down an informal outline of the program we shall develop.

Declare a *table* to hold the neighbor counts of all cells and four *lists* to remember the cells becoming alive or dead in the current generation and in the next generation.

initialization   Get the initial configuration of living cells and use it to calculate the table holding the neighbor counts of all cells. Construct the lists of the cells that will become alive and that will become dead in the first generation;

main loop   Repeat the following steps as long as desired:
For each cell on the list of cells to become alive do

Make the cell alive;
Update the neighbor counts for each neighbor of the cell;
If a neighbor count reaches the appropriate value, then add the cell to the list of cells to be made alive or dead in the next generation;

For each cell on the list of cells to become dead do
> Make the cell dead;
> Update the neighbor counts for each neighbor of the cell;
> If a neighbor count reaches the appropriate value, then add the cell to
> > the list of cells to be made alive or dead in the next generation;

prepare for the next generation

Write out the map for the user;
Move the lists of cells to be changed in the next generation to the lists for
> the current generation.

Clearly a great many details remain to be specified in this outline, but it does provide the basic ideas that we can refine into a complete algorithm.

EXERCISES 18.3

E1. Sometimes the user might wish to run the Life game (prototype version) on a grid smaller than 50×80. Determine how it is possible to make maxrow and maxcol into variables that the user can set when the program is run. Try to make as few changes in the program as possible.

E2. One idea for changing the first program to save some of the **if** statements in the function NeighborCount is to add two extra rows and columns to the arrays map and newmap, by changing their dimensions to

$$[0 .. maxrow + 1, 0 .. maxcol + 1].$$

Entries in the extra rows and columns would always be dead, so that the loops in NeighborCount could always run their full range from $i - 1$ to $i + 1$ and $j - 1$ to $j + 1$. How would this change affect the count of statements executed in NeighborCount?

PROJECT 18.3

P1. Rewrite the procedure Initialize so that it accepts the occupied positions in some symbolic form, such as a sequence of blanks and X's in appropriate rows, rather than requiring the occupied positions to be entered as numerical coordinate pairs.

18.4

ALGORITHM DEVELOPMENT: A SECOND VERSION OF LIFE

After deciding on the basic method and the overall outline of the data structures needed for solving a problem, it is time to commence the process of algorithm development, beginning with an overall outline and slowly introducing refinements until all the details are specified and a program is formulated in a computer language.

The Main Program

The main program will bring in declarations for the table and lists. At this time, we can assign names to these data structures. Let us call the table map, as we did in the prototype program, but now we shall think of the entries of map as containing neighbor counts as well as the status (living or dead) of each cell. Let us call the four lists live, die, nextlive, and nextdie. Let us, however, postpone the implementation decisions for these data types until we have more information on how they will be used.

Life, main program

```
program Life (input, output);          {Simulation of Conway's game of Life}
{Pre:  The user must supply an initial configuration of living cells.
 Post: The program prints a sequence of maps showing the changes in the
       configuration of living cells according to the rules for the game of Life.
 Uses: Packages for processing a table and for processing lists of cells.}
var
    map: table;
    live,
    die,
    nextlive,
    nextdie: listtype;
```

initialization

```
begin                                              {main program, Life}
    Initialize (live, die, nextlive, nextdie, map);
    repeat
```

main loop

```
        Vivify (live);
        Kill (die);
        WriteMap (live, die, map);
        AddNeighbors (live, nextlive, nextdie, map);
        SubtractNeighbors (die, nextlive, nextdie, map);
        MoveList (nextlive, live);
        MoveList (nextdie, die);
        write ('Continue ')
    until not UserSaysYes
end.                                               {main program, Life}
```

description

Most of the action of the program is postponed to various procedures. After initializing the lists and table, the program begins its main loop. At each generation we first go through the cells waiting in lists live and die in order to update the table map, which, as in the prototype version of Life, keeps track of which cells are alive. This work is done in the procedures Vivify (which means *make alive*) and Kill. After writing the revised configuration, we update the count of neighbors for each cell that has been born or has died, using the procedures AddNeighbors and SubtractNeighbors and the table map. As part of the same procedures, when the neighbor count reaches an appropriate value, a cell is added to the list nextlive or nextdie to indicate that it will be born or die in the coming generation. Finally, we must move the lists for the coming generation into the current ones.

Refinement: Development of the Subprograms

After the solution to a problem has been outlined, it is time to turn to the various parts of the outline, to include more details and thereby specify the solution exactly. While making these refinements, however, the programmer often discovers that the task of each subprogram was not specified as carefully as necessary, *specifications* that the interface between different subprograms must be reworked and spelled *and problem* out in more detail, so that the different subprograms accomplish all necessary *solving* tasks, and so that they do so without duplication or contradictory requirements. In a real sense, therefore, the process of refinement requires going back to the problem-solving phase to find the best way to split the required tasks among the various subprograms. Ideally, this process of refinement and specification should be completed before any coding is done.

Let us illustrate this activity by working through the requirements for the various subprograms for the Life game.

The Task for AddNeighbors

Much of the work of our program will be done in the procedures AddNeighbors and SubtractNeighbors. We shall develop the first of these, leaving the second as an exercise. The procedure AddNeighbors will go through the list live, and, for each entry, will find its immediate neighbors (as done in the original function NeighborCount), will increase the neighbor count in map for each of these, and must put some of these on the lists nextlive and nextdie. To determine which, let us denote by n the updated count for one of the neighbors and consider cases.

cases for 1. It is impossible that $n = 0$, since we have just increased n by 1.
AddNeighbors

2. If $n = 1$ or $n = 2$, then the cell is already dead and it should remain dead in the next generation. We need do nothing.

3. If $n = 3$, then a previously live cell still lives; a previously dead cell must be added to the list nextlive.

4. If $n = 4$, then a previously live cell dies; add it to nextdie. If the cell is dead, it remains so.

5. If $n > 4$, then the cell is already dead (or is already on list nextdie) and stays there.

Problems

One subtle problem arises with this procedure. When the neighbor count for a dead cell reaches 3, we add it to the list nextlive, but it may well be that later *spurious entries* in procedure AddNeighbors, its neighbor count will again be increased (beyond 3) so that it should not be vivified in the next generation after all. Similarly, when the neighbor count for a live cell reaches 4, we add it to nextdie, but the procedure SubtractNeighbors may well reduce its neighbor count below 4, so that it should be removed from nextdie. Thus the final determination of lists nextlive and nextdie cannot be made until the table map has been fully updated, but yet, as we proceed, we must tentatively add entries to the lists.

postpone difficulty

It turns out that, if we postpone solution of this problem, it becomes much easier. In the procedures AddNeighbors and SubtractNeighbors, let us add cells to nextlive and nextdie without worrying whether they will later be removed. Then, when we move nextlive and nextdie to lists live and die, we can check that the neighbor counts are correct (in live, for example, only dead cells with a neighbor count of exactly 3 should appear) and delete the erroneous entries with no difficulty.

duplicate entries

After doing this, however, an even more subtle error remains. It is possible that the same cell may appear in list nextlive (or nextdie) more than once. A dead cell, for example, may initially have a count of 2, which, when increased, adds the cell to nextlive. Its count may then be increased further, and in SubtractNeighbors decreased one or more times, perhaps ending at 3, so that SubtractNeighbors again adds it to nextlive. Then, when neighbor counts are updated in the next generation, this birth will incorrectly contribute 2 rather than 1 to the neighbor counts. We could solve this problem by searching the lists for duplicates before moving them, but to do so would be slow, and we can again solve the problem more easily by postponing it. When, in the next generation, we wish to vivify a cell, we shall first check whether it is already alive. If so, then we know that its entry is a duplicate of one earlier on list live. While we are postponing work, we might as well also postpone checking the neighbor counts, so that the moving procedure will now do nothing but move lists, and all the checking is done in Vivify and Kill. Figure 18.4 shows the trace of Life for one small configuration and exhibits the appearance and deletion of spurious and duplicate entries in the various lists.

Programming Precept

Sometimes postponing problems simplifies their solution.

Summary: Specifications for the Subprograms

With the decisions we have made, we can finally specify exactly what each subprogram is to do.

- Vivify takes the list live, which may contain duplicate and spurious entries, checks each entry to see if it satisfies the rules to become alive (it must be dead with a neighbor count of exactly 3), sets it to be alive if so, and removes it from the list live if not. At the conclusion of the procedure, the list live contains exactly those cells that were vivified, with no duplicates.

- Kill takes the list die, which may contain duplicate and spurious entries, checks each entry to see if it satisfies the rules to become dead (it must be alive with a neighbor count not 2 or 3), sets it to be dead if so, and removes it from the list die if not. At the conclusion of the procedure, the list die contains exactly those cells that were killed, with no duplicates.

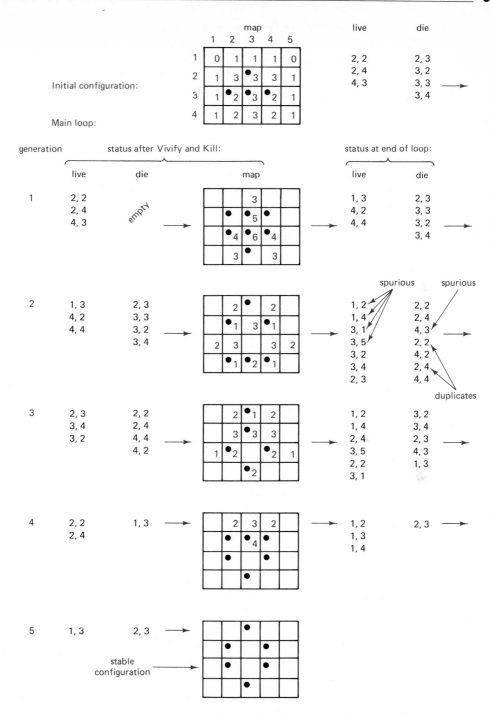

Figure 18.4. A trace of program Life

- AddNeighbors takes the list live, which must contain exactly the cells just vivified with no duplicates, increases the neighbor counts for each neighbor of one of these cells, and puts a neighboring cell onto one of the lists nextlive or nextdie whenever its neighbor count reaches the correct value.

- SubtractNeighbors takes the list die, which must contain exactly the cells just killed with no duplicates, decreases the neighbor counts for each neighbor of one of these cells, and puts a neighboring cell onto one of the lists nextlive or nextdie whenever its neighbor count reaches the correct value.

- MoveList takes the list given as its first parameter and moves it to become the list given as the second parameter. The first list is left empty.

18.5

VERIFICATION OF ALGORITHMS

purpose

Another important aspect of the design of large programs is algorithm verification, that is, a *proof* that the algorithm accomplishes its task. This kind of proof is usually formulated by looking at the specifications for the subprograms and then arguing that these specifications combine properly to accomplish the task of the whole algorithm. While constructing such a proof, we may find that the specifications must be changed to enable us to infer the correctness of the algorithm, and, in doing so, the proof itself helps us formulate the specifications for each subprogram with greater precision. Hence algorithm verification and algorithm design can go hand-in-hand, and sometimes the verification can even lead the way. In any case, algorithm verification should precede coding.

18.5.1 Proving the Program

Let us again illustrate these concepts by turning to the Life program, first, to be sure that its algorithm is correct and, second, to assist us in designing the remaining procedure, Initialize.

caution

Indeed, the fact that there were subtle errors in our initial attempts to organize the work done in procedures Vivify, Kill, AddNeighbors, SubtractNeighbors, and MoveList should alert us to the possible presence of further errors, or at least to the necessity of exercising considerably more care to be sure that our algorithms are correct.

Possible Problems

By postponing the checking of neighbor counts, we were able to avoid difficulties both with the problems of duplicate and of erroneous entries. But, for example, how can we be sure that it is not still possible that the same cell might erroneously be included in both lists nextlive and nextdie? If so, then it might first be vivified and then killed immediately in the following generation (clearly an illegal happening). The answer to this particular question is *no*, since the main program calls both procedures Vivify and Kill before either procedure AddNeighbors or SubtractNeighbors. Thus the cell keeps the same status (alive or dead) from the end of procedure Kill until the next generation, and the procedures AddNeighbors and SubtractNeighbors check that only dead cells are added to nextlive and only living cells to nextdie.

How can we be sure that there are not more subtle questions of this sort, some of which might not be so easy to answer? The only way we can really be confident is to *prove* that our program does the right action in each case.

The Main Loop

The difficulty with our program is that what happens in one generation might affect the next generation in some unexpected way. Therefore we focus our attention on the large loop in the main program. At the beginning of the loop, it is the contents of lists live and die that determine everything that happens later. Let us therefore summarize what we know about these lists from our previous study.

> *At the beginning of the main loop, list* live *contains only dead cells, and list* die *contains only living cells, but the lists may contain duplicate entries, or spurious entries whose neighbor counts are wrong. The lists* nextlive *and* nextdie *are empty.*

At the very start of the program, it is one task of procedure Initialize to ensure that the lists live and die are set up properly, so that the preceding statements are correct at the start of the first generation. What we must prove, then, is that if the statements are true at the start of any one generation, then after the eight procedure calls within the loop, they will again be true for the next generation.

Proof by Mathematical Induction

At this point, you should note that what we are really doing is using the method of **mathematical induction** to establish that the program is correct. In this method of proof, we begin by establishing the result for an initial case. Next we prove the result for a later case, say case n, by using the result for earlier cases (those between the initial case and case $n - 1$).

initial case

For our program, verification of the initial case amounts to a verification that Initialize works properly. For the second part of the proof, let us examine the actions in the main loop, assuming that the statements are correct at its beginning. Procedure Vivify uses only list live and carefully checks each entry before it vivifies a cell, removing erroneous and duplicate entries from list live as it goes. Hence at the conclusion of Vivify, list live contains only those cells that were properly vivified, and no duplicates. Procedure Kill similarly cleans up list die. Since the two lists originally had no cells in common, and none has been added to either

induction step

list, no cells have been improperly both vivified and killed. Next, procedure WriteMap is called, but does not change the lists. Procedure AddNeighbors works only from list live and puts only dead cells on list nextlive, and only living ones on list nextdie. Similarly, procedure SubtractNeighbors keeps the dead and living cells properly separated. These two procedures together add all the cells whose status should change in the next generation to the lists, but may add duplicate or spurious entries. Finally, procedure MoveList sets up lists live and die and empties lists nextlive and nextdie, as required to show that all conditions in our statements are again true at the beginning of the next generation. The logic of our program is therefore correct.

end of proof

18.5.2 Invariants and Assertions

Statements such as the one we established in the preceding proof are called *loop invariants*. In general, a loop invariant is a statement that is true at the beginning of every iteration of the loop. The statements we made about the status of various lists at different points of the loop are called *assertions*. Among the most important assertions are the ones with which we are already the most familiar, the *preconditions* and *postconditions* that hold at the beginning and end of each procedure.

Let us summarize our decisions required to prove the correctness of our algorithm by writing down preconditions and postconditions for the procedures we have studied:

---

procedure Vivify (**var** live: listtype):

precondition: List live contains only dead cells and contains all cells ready to be vivified.

postcondition: Table map has been updated with vivified cells, and list live contains only those cells that were vivified, with no duplicates or spurious entries.

---

procedure AddNeighbors (**var** live, nextlive, nextdie: listtype; **var** map: table):

precondition: List live contains all vivified cells whose neighbor counts have not yet been updated.

postcondition: Table map has increased neighbor counts for all of the cells neighboring cells in list live. If the increased neighbor count makes the cell a candidate to be vivified [*resp*. killed] then the cell has been added to list nextlive [*resp*. nextdie].

procedure Initialize(**var** live, die, nextlive, nextdie: listtype; **var** map: table):

precondition: None.

postcondition: Table map contains the initial configuration of living and dead cells and the associated neighbor counts for all cells. List live contains only dead cells and includes all candidates that may be vivified in the first generation. List die contains only living cells and contains all candidates that may die in the first generation.

The purpose of loop invariants and assertions is to capture the essence of the dynamic process. It is not always easy to find loop invariants and assertions that will lead to a proof that a program is correct, but it is a very useful exercise.

simplification   Attempting to find invariants and assertions sometimes leads to simplifications in design of the algorithm, which make its correctness more obvious. Our goal should always be to make our algorithms so straightforward and clear that their logic is obviously correct, and the use of loop invariants can help in this process.

Algorithm verification is a subject under active research, in which many important questions remain to be answered. Correctness proofs have not yet been supplied for a large number of important algorithms that are in constant use. Sometimes exceptional cases appear that cause an algorithm to misbehave; correctness proofs would provide a consistent means to delineate these exceptions and provide for their processing.

18.5.3 Initialization

As we turn, finally, to the specifications for the procedure Initialize, let us use the postconditions for the procedure to help in its composition. The first postcondition states that the table map is to be initialized with the starting configuration of living and dead cells. We shall do this in two stages. First, we use a procedure InitializeTable(map) to initialize the table to contain all dead cells with neighbor counts all 0. Second, we use a procedure ReadMap(map) that will obtain from the user the cells that should be alive and will set them to be alive, but will not *design of* Initialize   calculate the neighbor counts. We shall also need the list of initially living cells for calculating the neighbor counts, so we shall also require ReadMap to put this list into list live. As one of its postconditions ReadMap will be required to make sure that there are no duplicates in this list. (This can be achieved easily if the reading is done properly.)

The second task is to initialize the neighbor counts in the table map. But we have required ReadMap to set up list live so that it contains exactly the information needed for procedure AddNeighbors to set the neighbor counts properly for all neighbors of living cells, since we have already initialized all neighbor counts in map to 0. As well as initializing the neighbor counts, procedure AddNeighbors will locate all dead cells that will become alive in the following generation and add them to list nextlive. Hence, by setting nextlive to be empty before calling AddNeighbors and moving nextlive to live afterward, we accomplish another of the postconditions of Initialize.

The final postcondition is that list die contain all living cells that should die in the next generation. Some, but perhaps not all, of these may be found by AddNeighbors (in the main loop, the remainder would be found by Subtract-Neighbors, which we have no way to use in Initialize). We can accomplish the postcondition more easily, however, by simply putting *all* the living cells into list die: Recall that procedure Kill allows spurious entries on its input list.

By using these postconditions to help in writing the procedure, we now have a complete outline of Initialize, which we summarize as follows.

initialization

procedure Initialize (**var** live, die, nextlive, nextdie: listtype; **var** map: table);
  {**Pre:** *None.*
    Post: *Table* map *contains the initial configuration of living and dead cells and the associated neighbor counts for all cells. List* live *contains only dead cells and includes all candidates that may be vivified in the first generation. List* die *contains only living cells and contains all candidates that may die in the first generation.*}
begin   {*procedure Initialize*}
  CreateTable (map);   {*Set all cells in* map *dead with 0 neighbor counts.*}
  CreateList (Die);
  ReadMap (live, map);   {*Read all living cells into* map *and* live.}
  WriteMap (live, die);
  CreateList (nextlive);   {*Create the lists used by* AddNeighbors.}
  CreateList (nextdie);
  AddNeighbors (live, nextlive, nextdie, map);
  MoveList (live, die);
  {*Some of the cells just read in should die in the first generation.* Kill *will catch them but will do nothing to the cells that should not die.*}
  MoveList (nextlive, live);
                {*Put output from* AddNeighbors *where it is needed.*}
  ClearList (nextdie)
end;   {*procedure Initialize*}

This outline, as you see, is very close to final code, if not completely ready for insertion into the program. As of now, we have made no decisions whatever concerning the implementation of the data types, but, by using the generic procedure CreateList, we can specify the necessary operations without needing to know how the lists will eventually be implemented.

EXERCISES 18.5

Write down preconditions and postconditions for each of the following procedures.

E1. MoveList (**var** A, B: listtype).

E2. Kill (**var** die: listtype).

E3. SubtractNeighbors (**var** die, nextlive, nextdie: listtype; **var** map: table).

E4. WriteMap (live, die: listtype; **var** map: table).

E5. ReadMap (**var** live: listtype; **var** map: table).

18.6

IMPLEMENTATION AND CODING

Now that we have spelled out completely and precisely the requirements for each procedure, it is time to code them into our programming language. In a large software project, it is necessary to do the coding at the right time, and certainly not too soon. Most programmers err seriously by starting to code too soon. If *specifications* coding is begun before the requirements are made precise, then unwarranted *complete* assumptions about the specifications will inevitably be made while coding, and these assumptions may render different subprograms incompatible with each other or make the programming task much more difficult than it need be.

For very large projects, on the other hand, it may sometimes be possible to *top-down coding* delay coding too long. Just as we design from the top down, we should code from the top down. Once the specifications at the top levels are complete and precise, we may code the subprograms at these levels and test them by including appropriate stubs. If we then find that our design is flawed, we can modify it without paying a high price in low-level procedures that have been rendered useless.

18.6.1 Implementation of Data Types

Now that the specifications for the Life subprograms are complete, let us embody our decisions into procedures coded in Pascal. To do this, we shall need declarations of the data types used in the program.

Implementation of the Table

In the prototype version of the Life program we used a 50×80 array to hold the map. We chose these bounds arbitrarily; the rules for the game of Life do not specify any bounds on the grid or mention what happens when a configuration comes up against a boundary. Indeed, there are not supposed to be any boundaries on the map. In other words, we would really like to have the Pascal declaration

type grid = **array** [integer, integer] **of** cell;

which is, of course, illegal. Since only a limited number of these cells will actually *sparse table* be occupied at any one time, we should really regard the grid for the Life game as a sparse table, and, therefore, a hash table proves an attractive way to represent the grid.

use of space

Next we need to decide between open addressing and chaining. For each cell, we must keep the status of the cell (alive or dead), the number of living neighbors, and (since the key itself must be explicitly kept when using a hash table) the row and column of the cell. With these four entries in each record, there are few space considerations to advise our decision. With chaining, the size of each record will increase 25 percent to accommodate the necessary pointer, but the hash table itself will be smaller and can take a higher load factor than with open addressing. With open addressing, the records will be smaller, but more room must be left vacant in the hash table to avoid long searches and possible overflow.

flexibility

After space considerations, the second question we should ask concerns flexibility. Do we need to make deletions, and, if so, when? We could keep track of all cells until the memory is full, and then delete those that are not needed. But this would require rehashing the full table, which would be slow and painful. With chaining we can easily dispose of cells as soon as they are not needed, and thereby reduce the number of cells in the hash table as much as possible. For this reason, let us choose a chained hash table for the implementation of the table map.

decision

We can now summarize these decisions with the following declarations.

declarations, table implementation

```
const
  hashsize = 997;                {Choose a convenient prime.}
  hashmax = 996;                           {= hashsize −1}
type
  state = (dead, alive);                    {the state of a cell}
  count = 0 .. 9;            {number of living neighbors of a cell}
  cellpointer = ↑cell;      {used to make chains from the hash table}
  cell = record
    row,                               {the row number of the cell}
    col: integer;                   {the column number of the cell}
    status: state;                       {Is the cell alive or dead?}
    neighborcount: count;
                       {How many living neighbors does the cell have?}
    nextonchain: cellpointer
                    {pointer to the next cell on the chain from the table}
  end;
  hashaddress = 0 .. hashmax;
  table = array [hashaddress] of cellpointer;    {for the hash table map}
var
  map: table;              {the hash table implementing the Life grid}
```

Implementation of Lists

access

Next, let us review the requirements for accessing the cells. As we work with a given cell, we need to locate its eight neighbors, and we can use the hash table map to do so. Some of these neighbors may be inserted into the four lists live, die, nextlive, and nextdie. One method is to put only the row and column of the cell into the list, and then, when we later retrieve a cell from one of these lists, to use the hash table again to find the other information about it, but doing so would be repeating work.

A second method is to make a copy of the entire record for the cell and put the copy into the list. This method, however, is very dangerous. When a program keeps multiple copies of the same information, then it is very easy to update one copy but not the other, and then use information that is now erroneous from the other copy. In the Life game, it is quite possible that the same cell can be on more than one of the lists at once. With multiple copies, it would be quite difficult to ensure that all copies were kept updated together. Hence it would be a mistake to put cells into the lists as well as into the chained hash table.

Yet another method is to put only pointers to the cells into the lists, and this method has several advantages. First, there is only one record corresponding to each cell, even though there may be several pointers to it. Second, there is no need to consult the hash table again to find the information about a cell, since we need only follow a pointer to find it. Third, the size of the entries in the lists is the smallest of any of the three proposed implementations. Let us therefore choose this method.

Next, we must decide between contiguous and linked implementations for the lists. The lists are not sufficiently large that space considerations are likely to be important. Let us consider how the lists are used. They are traversed, insertions are made at one end only, deletions are made anywhere in the list, and one list must frequently be moved to another, with the first left empty. The deletions and movements of one list to another will be much faster with linked lists; there will be no significant difference in the time needed for traversal or insertion. Let us therefore choose a linked implementation. We have no need to move both directions through the lists; using doubly linked or circularly linked lists is unnecessary. We do need frequent deletions, however, and this operation is greatly expedited if we use the implementation (mentioned in Section 8.2.3) that keeps two pointers to adjacent positions in the list. Let us therefore settle *indirect linked* on this two-pointer implementation. The result is illustrated in Figure 18.5. Each *list* node of the list thus contains two pointers: one to a cell and one to the next node of the list.

These decisions are implemented by declaring the type listentry = cellpointer for compatibility with the standard list declarations and including a package of declarations and operations for linked lists with a trailing pointer.

18.6.2 High-Level Procedures

Procedure Vivify

These declarations are all that we need to write procedure Vivify in accordance with its specifications.

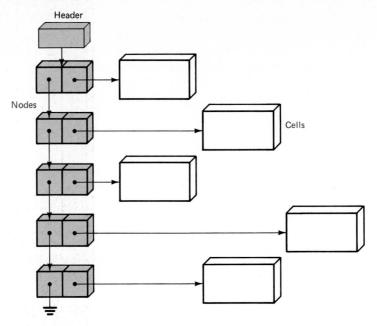

Figure 18.5. An indirect linked list

procedure Vivify (**var** live: listtype);
{**Pre:** *List* live *contains only dead cells and contains all cells ready to be vivified.*

   Post: *Table* map *has been updated with vivified cells, and list* live *contains only those cells that were vivified, with no duplicates or spurious entries.*}
var
   w: window;   {*used to traverse list* live}
   current: cellpointer;   {*pointer to the cell currently at the window*}
begin
   StartList (w, live);   {*Prepare to begin traversal.*}
   while OnList (w, live) **do**
   begin
      RetrieveList (w, current, live);
      with current↑**do**
         if (status = dead) **and** (neighborcount = 3) **then**
         begin
            status := alive;   {*Vivify the cell.*}
            NextList (w, live)   {*Continue the traversal.*}
         end
         else   {*This cell is either erroneous or a duplicate already vivified.*}
            DeleteList (w, live)   {*The window moves to the next entry.*}
   end
end;

Procedure AddNeighbors

At the conclusion of procedure Vivify, the duplicate and spurious entries have all been removed from list live, and what remains are the cells that were actually vivified. The task of **AddNeighbors** is to increase the neighbor count by 1 for each neighbor of all the cells that remain on list live and to add cells to lists nextlive and nextdie when appropriate. Most of this work is postponed to the procedure

$$\text{IncreaseNeighborCounts(row, col: integer)}$$

that finds and processes all the neighbors of the cell with the given coordinates; the outer procedure performs only the list processing.

```
procedure AddNeighbors(var live, nextlive, nextdie: listtype; var map: table);
{Pre:    List live contains all vivified cells whose neighbor counts have not yet
         been updated.
 Post:   Table map has increased neighbor counts for all of the cells neigh-
         boring cells in list live. If the increased neighbor count makes the cell
         a candidate to be vivified [resp. killed] then the cell has been added
         to list nextlive [resp. nextdie].
 Uses:   Procedure IncreaseNeighborCounts handles all the neighbors of one
         cell.}
var
   w: window;                              {used to traverse list live}
   current: cellpointer;                   {points to a cell from list live}
begin                                      {procedure AddNeighbors}
   StartList(w, live);
   while OnList(w, live) do
   begin
      RetrieveList(w, current, live);
      with current↑do
         IncreaseNeighborCounts(row, col, nextlive, nextdie, map);
      NextList(w, live)
   end                                     {processing list node}
end;                                       {procedure AddNeighbors}
```

continue traversal

Processing the Neighbors

Finding the neighbors of a given cell will require using the hash table; we shall postpone this task by referring to

$$\text{procedure GetCell(row, col: integer; var p: cellpointer; var map: table);}$$

hash table retrieval

which will return a pointer to the cell being sought, creating the cell if it was not previously in the hash table.

```
procedure IncreaseNeighborCounts(row, col: integer;
                        var nextlive, nextdie: listtype; var map: table);
{Pre:    The pair (row, col) is a vivified cell.
 Post:   The count (in map) of living neighbors has been increased for each
         neighbor of (row, col). If the count reaches an appropriate value,
         then the neighbor is inserted into nextlive or nextdie.}
var
    neighbor: cellpointer;                      {points to a neighboring cell}
    rowneighbor,
    colneighbor: integer;                    {row and column of a neighbor}
begin
    for rowneighbor := row − 1 to row + 1 do
        for colneighbor := col − 1 to col + 1 do
            if (rowneighbor <> row) or (colneighbor <> col) then
            begin                         {Exclude the position row, col itself.}
                GetCell(rowneighbor, colneighbor, neighbor, map);
                with neighbor↑do begin
                    neighborcount := neighborcount + 1;
                    case neighborcount of
                        0: writeln('Impossible case in AddNeighbors.');
                        1, 2: ;                          {no action needed}
                        3: if state = dead then InsertList(neighbor, nextlive);
                        4: if state = alive then InsertList(neighbor, nextdie);
                        5, 6, 7, 8: ;                    {no action needed}
                    end                                  {case statement}
                end                   {with statement processing one neighbor}
            end                               {looping through neighbors}
end;                                      {procedure IncreaseNeighborCounts}
```

The annotations in the left margin of the code: *find a neighbor*, *get the neighbor*, *update count and lists*.

The procedure InsertList is not part of the standard list package. The order of the entries in the lists does not matter; hence InsertList can insert the new entry in any convenient location. With linked lists, it may be easiest to insert the new entry at the head of the list. The details are left as an exercise.

Procedure MoveList

The task of procedure MoveList is only to move one list to another and leave the first empty. Since we are using linked lists, we can easily write the following implementation-dependent version.

move one list

```
procedure MoveList(var A, B: listtype);
{Pre:    The linked list A has been created.
 Post:   List B contains all nodes formerly in A, and list A is empty.}
begin                                             {procedure MoveList}
    ClearList(B);
    B := A;                  {Connect the header for list B to first node of A.}
    A.head := nil                            {Set the first list to be empty.}
end;                                              {procedure MoveList}
```

18.6.3 Processing the Hash Table

Finding a Cell

The first procedure that explicitly references the hash table is

GetCell(row, col: integer; **var** p: cellpointer; **var** map: table).

task Its task is first to look in the hash table for the cell with the given coordinates. If the search is successful, then the procedure returns a pointer to the cell. Otherwise, it must create a new cell, assign it the given coordinates, and initialize its other fields to their default values. Finally, it must put this new cell into the hash table as well as return a pointer to it.

This outline translates into the following Pascal procedure.

```
procedure GetCell(row, col: integer; var p: cellpointer; var map: table);
{Pre:    The hash table map has been initialized.
  Post:  The procedure returns a pointer p to the cell (row, col) from the hash
         table map if it is present; otherwise, the procedure creates the cell,
         initializes its fields, puts it into H, and returns a pointer to it.}
var
   location: hashaddress;          {location returned by the hash function}
   found: Boolean;                 {Is the cell already in the hash table?}
begin                                          {procedure GetCell}
   found := false;
   location := Hash(row, col);
   p := map[location];          {p starts chain containing cell at (row, col).}
   while (not found) and (p <> nil) do   {Search chain for desired cell.}
      if (p↑.row = row) and (p↑.col = col) then
         found := true
      else
         p := p↑.nextcell;
{If the cell was found in table, then we are finished; otherwise, we must create
 a new cell, initialize it, and insert it into the hash table.}
   if not found then
   begin
      new(p);
      p↑.row := row;
      p↑.col := col;
      p↑.status := dead;
      p↑.neighborcount := 0;
      nextcell := map[location];    {Push onto the chain in the hash table.}
      map[location] := p
   end                                            {creating the new cell}
end;                                              {procedure GetCell}
```

look in hash table (margin note)

make a new cell (margin note)

The Hash Function

Our hash function will differ slightly from those in the last chapter, in that its argument already comes in two parts (row and column), so that some kind of folding can be done easily. Before deciding how, let us for a moment consider the special case of a small array, where the function is one-to-one and is exactly the index function. When there are exactly maxrow entries in each row, the index (row, col) maps to

$$i + \text{maxrow} * j$$

to place the rectangular array into contiguous storage, one row after the next.

It should prove effective to use a similar mapping for our hash function, where we replace maxrow by some convenient number (like a prime) that will maximize the spread and reduce collisions. Hence we obtain

```
function Hash(row, col: integer): hashaddress;
{Pre:    The pair (row, col) gives a cell.
  Post:  The function returns the address of the chain in map corresponding
          to the given cell.}
const
   factor = 101;                              {Choose a convenient prime.}
begin
   Hash := abs(row + factor * col) mod hashsize
end;
```

18.6.4 Other Subprograms

The procedures Kill and SubtractNeighbors are similar in form to Vivify and Add-Neighbors; they will be left as exercises, as will ReadMap. The procedure WriteMap can be used with few changes from the first version, but a much more efficient version is possible that makes use of the lists live and die to update the screen rather than rewriting it at each generation.

PROJECTS 18.6

P1. Write the procedure Kill(**var** die: listtype).

P2. Write the procedure SubtractNeighbors. When a cell is dead and has a neighbor count of 0 it should be removed from the hash table. However, since there may easily be more than one pointer to this cell (nextlive and nextdie are allowed to contain redundant entries) a simple dispose will not work. For now, write the procedure so that it does nothing in this case and later we will look at a way to solve the problem.

P3. Write the procedure InsertList.

P4. Write driver programs for the procedures **(a)** Kill and **(b)** SubtractNeighbors, and devise appropriate test data to check the performance of these procedures.

18.7

PROGRAM ANALYSIS AND COMPARISON

In designing algorithms, we need methods to separate bad algorithms from good ones, to help us decide, when we have several possible ways in which proceed, which way will prove the most effective for our problem. For this reason, the analysis of algorithms and the comparison of alternative methods constitute an important part of software engineering.

Statement Counts

Let us now see about how much more quickly the program Life should run than the prototype version. As we did for the first version, let us ignore the time needed for input and output in the main program, and look only at the statements inside the principal loop counting generations. Since all the work of Life is done within procedures, we must analyze each in turn. Each of the procedures does most of its work within a loop that runs through the entries of one of the lists live, die, nextlive, or nextdie.

Thus the key improvement of Life over the original program is that the amount of computation is no longer proportional to the size of the grid, but to the number of changes being made. For a typical configuration, there might be about 100 occupied cells, with likely no more than 50 dying or being born in a single generation. With these assumptions, we see that each statement within the inner loops will be executed about 50 times. In Vivify, there are 3 statements within the loop, in MoveList only 1. Within the loop of AddNeighbors, there are first 4 **if** statements, then 2 statements each done 9 times, and the **case** statement done 8 times, for a total count of 30. The counts for Kill and SubtractNeighbors

count for Life are similar; thus we obtain for each generation about

$$50 \times (3 + 1 + 30 + 3 + 1 + 30) = 3400$$

statements. The number of statements executed outside the loops is insignificant (it is less than 10), so 3400 is a reasonable estimate of the statement count for each generation.

count for ProtoLife Our first version of the Life program had a count of 76,000 statements per generation. Thus our revised program should run as much as 20 times faster. This constitutes a substantial improvement, particularly in view of the fact that when program Life slows down, it is because many changes are being made, not because it is repeating the same predictable calculations.

Comparisons

programming effort From other points of view, however, our second program is not as good as the first. The first of these is the point of view of programming effort. The first program was short and easy to write, simple to understand, and easy to debug. The second program is longer, entailed subtle problems, and required sophisticated reasoning to establish its correctness. Whether this additional work is worthwhile depends on the application and the number of times the program will be used. If a simple method works well enough, then we should not go out of our way to find a more sophisticated approach. Only when simple methods fail do we need to try further devices.

Programming Precept

Keep your algorithms as simple as you can.
When in doubt, choose the simple way.

Programming Precept

Don't overdesign.
Use the simplest data structures that meet the requirements of your problem.

---

space requirements The second point of view is that of storage requirements. Our first program used very little memory (apart from that for the instructions) except for the two tables map and newmap. These tables have entries that, in assuming only the two values alive and dead, can be packed so that each entry takes only a single bit. In a typical computer with word size of 32 or 16 bits, the two tables need then occupy no more than 250 or 500 words, respectively. On the other hand, program Life requires, along with the space for its instructions, five words for each cell in the table map and two words for each entry in a list. With the assumption of about 100 living cells, there may be about 300 entries in the table, and with about 50 entries on each of four lists, we find that program Life may require about 1900 words of storage.

Time and Space Trade-Offs

This project gives us a good example illustrating the substantial trade-offs that can occur between time and space in computer algorithms. Which to choose depends on available equipment. If the storage space is available and otherwise unused, it is obviously preferable to use the algorithm requiring more space and less time. If not, then time may have to be sacrificed. Finally, for an important problem, by far the best approach may be to sit back and rethink the whole problem: you will have learned much from your first efforts and may very well be able to find another approach that will save both time and space.

Programming Precept

Consider time and space trade-offs in deciding on your algorithm.

EXERCISES 18.7

E1. We could save the space needed for the field status in each record for a cell by making a slight modification in how we keep information in each record. We could use positive entries in the field neighborcount to denote living cells and negative entries to denote dead cells. However, we could then not tell whether an entry of 0 meant a dead cell or a living cell with no living neighbors. We could easily overcome that problem by changing the definition of neighbor so that a cell is considered its own neighbor (so the neighbor count for a dead cell would range from 0 to 8, stored in the neighborcount field as 0 to −8, and that for a living cell from 1 to 9).

   a. With this change of definition, write down the revised rules for the game of Life.

   b. Do you think that implementing these changes to save space is worth the effort? Why or why not?

   c. If you answered the last question positively, describe what changes are needed in the program.

E2. Note that there is some inefficiency in the program Life in having procedures AddNeighbors and SubtractNeighbors called once from the main program, since these procedures must loop through the lists live and die just as Vivify and Kill already do. It would be faster if these procedures were written to update the neighbors of only one cell and were called from Vivify and Kill whenever a cell was vivified or killed.

   a. Will the program work correctly if these changes are made?

   b. If not, what further changes will make it work?

   c. With your revised program, find the proper loop invariants and verify that your algorithm is correct.

PROJECTS 18.7

P1. If you use a video terminal with direct cursor addressing, write a version of the procedure WriteMap that takes advantage of the lists live and die to update the map rather than completely rewriting it at each generation.

P2. Run the complete program Life and compare timings with those of ProtoLife.

P3. Recall from Section 18.6, Project P2, the problem of trying to dispose of an entry in the hash table. Instead of doing nothing in this case and letting the unused memory build up, keep a stack of available space. Implement Life so that when an entry must be disposed, it is placed in a stack whose entries are cell pointers. When a new node must be created, first check to see if the stack is empty. If it is empty, create a new node. Otherwise, pop a node from the stack.

P4. A simpler algorithm for the Life game comes from eliminating the table and using only lists to keep all the necessary information. In this algorithm, we keep a main list living of all the living cells and update the list at each generation. To obtain the count of living neighbors of a cell, we look in living for each of the eight possible neighbors of the cell and count the number that we find. At each generation, we calculate the neighbor counts of all the living cells and of all their (dead) neighbors. When one of these counts has the appropriate value, we add the cell to one of two lists nextlive and nextdie. After calculating all the neighbor counts, we use these two lists to update the master list living and go on to the next generation.

This method produces a lot of duplicate work. Each dead cell, for example, that will be vivified in the next generation is the neighbor of three living cells and will therefore appear three times in nextlive. To eliminate this duplication, we introduce a fourth list, checked, which will contain the dead cells (that are neighbors of living cells) whose neighbor counts have already been checked. This list is cleared at the start of each generation, and each dead cell is added to it as soon as its neighbor count is calculated. By first checking whether a cell is on this list, it is possible to save the time needed to recalculate its neighbor count.

To choose an implementation for the lists, note that the list living requires many retrievals, frequent insertions, and frequent deletions. A binary search tree therefore proves attractive. Similarly, the list checked is searched frequently. It is unimportant how lists nextlive and nextdie are implemented.

   a. Implement this algorithm for the Life game.
   b. Compare performance and operation counts with the programs ProtoLife and Life developed in the text.
   c. If you find the performance of the program disappointing, then determine where it is spending most of its time and suggest improvements.

P5. *One-dimensional Life* takes place on a straight line instead of a rectangular grid. Each cell has four neighboring positions: those at distance 1 or 2 from it on each side. The rules are similar to those of two-dimensional Life except (1) a dead cell with either two or three living neighbors will become alive in the next generation, and (2) a living cell dies if it has zero, one, or three living neighbors. (Hence a dead cell with zero, one, or four living neighbors stays dead; a living cell with two or four living neighbors stays alive.) The progress of sample communities is shown in Figure 18.6. Design, write, and test a program for one-dimensional Life.

POINTERS AND PITFALLS

1. To improve your program, review the logic. Don't optimize code based on a poor algorithm.

2. Never optimize a program until it is correct and working.

3. Don't optimize code unless it is absolutely necessary.

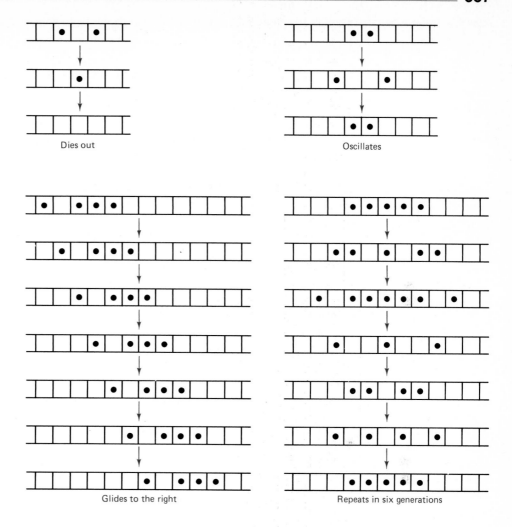

Figure 18.6. One-dimensional Life configurations

4. Determine where your program is spending most of its time, and optimize only those parts.

5. Keep your procedures short; rarely should any procedure be more than a page long.

6. Be sure your algorithm is correct before starting to code.

7. Verify the intricate parts of your algorithm.

8. Keep your logic simple.

9. Review the Programming Precepts!

REVIEW QUESTIONS

18.1   **1.** Name at least six phases of the *software life cycle* and state what each is.

   2. What are some of the important parts of the *problem* and *requirements specifications?*

   3. What is *prototyping* and why is it important?

   4. Name some aspects of program analysis.

   5. What is program *maintenance?*

18.5   **6.** What is a *loop invariant?*

   7. What is *mathematical induction?*

   8. Why is it important to give *preconditions* and *postconditions* for each subprogram?

18.7   **9.** What is a time-space trade-off?

APPENDIX **A**

LOGARITHMS AND FACTORIALS

Logarithms provide an important mathematical tool for the study of many algorithms. Let us therefore review some of their basic properties. If you wish further examples or exercises, consult a mathematics textbook.

The primary reason for using logarithms is to turn multiplication and division into addition and subtraction, and exponentiation into multiplication. Before the advent of pocket calculators, logarithms were an indispensable tool for hand calculation: witness the large tables of logarithms and the once ubiquitous slide rule. Even though we now have other methods for numerical calculation, the fundamental properties of logarithms give them importance that extends far beyond their use as computational tools.

A.1

APPLICATIONS

physical measurements

The behavior of many phenomena, first of all, reflects an intrinsically logarithmic structure; that is, by using logarithms, we find important relationships that are not otherwise obvious. Measuring the loudness of sound, for example, is logarithmic: if one sound is 10 dB (decibels) louder than another, then the actual acoustic energy is 10 times as much. If the sound level in one room is 40 dB and it is 60 dB in another, then the human perception may be that the second room is half again as noisy as the first, but there is actually 100 times more sound energy in the second room. This phenomenon is why a single violin soloist can be heard above a full orchestra (when playing a different line), and yet the orchestra requires so many violins to maintain a proper balance of sound.

589

■ LOGARITHMS AND FACTORIALS

large numbers   Logarithms, secondly, provide a convenient way to handle very large numbers. The scientific notation, where a number is written as a small real number (often in the range from 1 to 10) times a power of 10, is really based on logarithms, since the power of 10 is essentially the logarithm of the number. Scientists who need to use very large numbers (like astronomers, nuclear physicists, and geologists) frequently speak of orders of magnitude, and thereby concentrate on the logarithm of the number.

graphs   A logarithmic graph, thirdly, is a very useful device for displaying the properties of a function over a much broader range than a linear graph. With a logarithmic graph, we can arrange to display detailed information on the function for small values of the argument and at the same time give an overall view for much larger values. Logarithmic graphs are especially appropriate when we wish to show percentage changes in a function.

A.2

DEFINITION AND PROPERTIES

base   Logarithms are defined in terms of a real number $a > 1$, which is called the **base** of the logarithms. (It is also possible to define logarithms with base a in the range $0 < a < 1$, but doing so would introduce needless complications into our discussion.) For any number $x > 0$, we define $\log_a x = y$, where y is the real number such that $a^y = x$. The logarithm of a negative number, and the logarithm of 0, are not defined.

Simple Properties

From the definition and from the properties of exponents we obtain

$$\log_a 1 = 0,$$
$$\log_a a = 1,$$
$$\log_a x < 0 \quad \text{for all } x \text{ such that } 0 < x < 1.$$
$$0 < \log_a x < 1 \quad \text{for all } x \text{ such that } 1 < x < a.$$
$$\log_a x > 1 \quad \text{for all } x \text{ such that } a < x.$$

The logarithm function has a graph like the one in Figure A.1. We also obtain the identities

$$\log_a(xy) = (\log_a x) + (\log_a y)$$
$$\log_a(x/y) = (\log_a x) - (\log_a y)$$
$$\log_a x^z = z \log_a x$$
$$\log_a a^z = z$$
$$a^{\log_a x} = x$$

that hold for any positive real numbers x and y, and for any real number z.

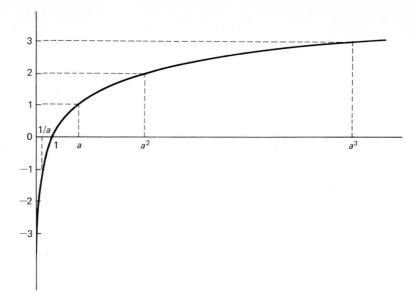

Figure A.1. Graph of the logarithm function

From the graph in Figure A.1, you will observe that the logarithm grows more and more slowly as x increases. The graphs of positive powers of x less than 1, such as the square root of x or the cube root of x, also grow progressively more slowly, but never become as flat as the graph of the logarithm. In fact,

> *As x grows large, $\log x$ grows more slowly than x^c, for any $c > 0$.*

Logarithmic Graphs

In a logarithmic scale, the numbers are arranged as on an old-fashioned slide rule, with larger numbers closer together than smaller numbers. In this way, equal distances along the scale represent equal *ratios* rather than the equal *differences* represented on an ordinary linear scale. A logarithmic scale should be used when percentage change is important to measure, or when perception is logarithmic. Human perception of time, for example, would seem to be nearly linear in the short term—what happened two days ago is twice as distant as what happened yesterday—but perhaps may be more nearly logarithmic in the long term: We draw less distinction between one million years ago and two million years ago than we do between ten years ago and one hundred years ago.

log-log graphs   Graphs in which both the vertical and horizontal scales are logarithmic are called ***log-log graphs***. In addition to phenomena where the perception is naturally logarithmic in both scales, log-log graphs are useful to display the behavior of a function over a very wide range. For small values, the graph records a detailed view of the function, and, for large values, a broad view of the function appears on the same graph. For searching and sorting algorithms, we wish to compare methods both for small problems and large problems; hence log-log graphs are appropriate.

One observation is worth noting: Any power of x graphs as a straight line with a log-log scale. To prove this, we start with an arbitrary power function $y = x^n$ and take logarithms on both sides, obtaining

$$\log y = n \log x.$$

A log-log graph in x and y becomes a linear graph in $u = \log x$ and $v = \log y$, and the equation becomes $v = nu$ in terms of u and v, which indeed graphs as a straight line.

A.3

CHOICE OF BASE

common logarithms Any real number $a > 1$ can be chosen as the base of logarithms, but certain special choices appear much more frequently than others. For computation and for graphing, the base $a = 10$ is often used, and logarithms with base 10 are called *common* logarithms. In studying computer algorithms, however, base 10 appears infrequently, and we do not often use common logarithms. Instead, logarithms with base 2 appear the most frequently, and we therefore reserve the special symbol

$$\lg x$$

to denote a logarithm with base 2.

Natural Logarithms

In studying mathematical properties of logarithms, and in many problems where logarithms appear as part of the answer, the number that appears as the base is

$$e = 2.718281828459\ldots.$$

Logarithms with base e are called *natural* logarithms. In this book we always denote the natural logarithm of x by

$$\ln x.$$

In many mathematics books, however, other bases than e are rarely used, in which case the unqualified symbol $\log x$ usually denotes a natural logarithm. Figure A.2 shows the graph of logarithms with respect to the three bases 2, e, and 10.

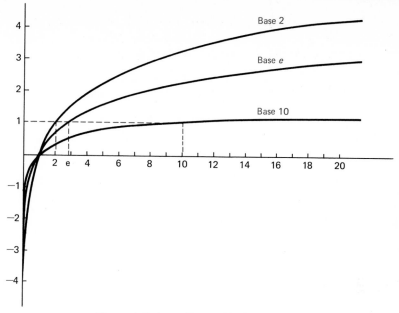

Figure A.2. Logarithms with three bases

Notation

The notation just used for logarithms with different bases will be our standard. We thus summarize:

Convention

Unless stated otherwise, all logarithms will be taken with base 2.
The symbol lg denotes a logarithm with base 2,
and the symbol ln denotes a natural logarithm.
If the base for logarithms is not specified or makes no difference,
then the symbol log will be used.

Change of Base

Logarithms with respect to one base are closely related to logarithms with respect to any other base. To find this relation, we start with the following relation, which is essentially the definition:

$$x = a^{\log_a x}$$

for any $x > 0$. Then

$$\log_b x = \log_b a^{\log_a x} = (\log_a x)(\log_b a).$$

The factor $\log_b a$ does not depend on x, but only on the two bases. Therefore:

> *To convert logarithms from one base to another, multiply by a constant factor, the logarithm of the first base with respect to the second.*

conversion factors The most useful numbers for us in this connection are

$$\lg e \approx 1.442695041,$$
$$\ln 2 \approx 0.693147181,$$
$$\ln 10 \approx 2.302585093.$$

A.4

STIRLING'S APPROXIMATION

Logarithms can be used to help determine the approximate value of the *factorial* of a nonnegative integer,

$$n! = n \times (n - 1) \times \cdots \times 1.$$

This excellent approximation to $n!$ was obtained by JAMES STIRLING in the eighteenth century:

$$n! = \sqrt{2\pi n} \left(\frac{n}{e}\right)^n \left[1 + \frac{1}{12n} + O\left(\frac{1}{n^2}\right)\right].$$

This approximation is very close indeed, much closer than we ever need for studying algorithms. If we take the natural logarithm of the approximation, we obtain

$$\ln n! = \left(n + \tfrac{1}{2}\right) \ln n - n + \tfrac{1}{2} \ln(2\pi) + \frac{1}{12n} + O\left(\frac{1}{n^2}\right).$$

Instead of this, we can be content with the much rougher approximation

$$\ln n! = n \ln n + O(n).$$

The complete proof of Stirling's Approximation requires techniques from advanced calculus that would take us too far afield here. We can, however, use a bit of elementary calculus to illustrate the first step of the approximation.

First, we take the natural logarithm of a factorial, noting that the logarithm of a product is the sum of the logarithms:

$$\ln n! = \ln(n \times (n-1) \times \cdots \times 1)$$
$$= \ln n + \ln(n-1) + \cdots + \ln 1$$
$$= \sum_{x=1}^{n} \ln x.$$

Next, we approximate the sum by an integral, as shown in Figure A.3.

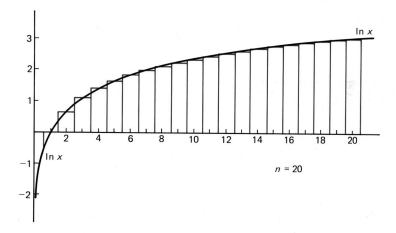

Figure A.3. Approximation of $\ln n!$ by an integral

It is clear from the diagram that the area under the step function, which is exactly $\ln n!$, is approximately the same as the area under the curve, which is

$$\int_{\frac{1}{2}}^{n+\frac{1}{2}} \ln x \, dx = (x \ln x - x) \Big|_{\frac{1}{2}}^{n+\frac{1}{2}}$$
$$= (n + \tfrac{1}{2}) \ln(n + \tfrac{1}{2}) - n + \tfrac{1}{2} \ln 2.$$

For large values of n, the difference between $\ln n$ and $\ln(n + \tfrac{1}{2})$ is insignificant, and hence this approximation differs from Stirling's only by the constant difference between $\frac{1}{2} \ln 2$ (about 0.35) and $\frac{1}{2} \ln(2\pi)$ (about 0.919).

B

PASCAL NOTES

B.1

SYNTAX DIAGRAMS

explanation

The syntax of Pascal is determined by tracing through the diagrams in the direction shown by arrows. Symbols or words within circles or ovals must be included exactly as given. These Pascal keywords are shown in all capital letters. Rectangular boxes refer to other syntax diagrams. All the classes such as function identifier, variable identifier, or type identifier have the same syntax as identifier: the qualifying words in braces are only intended to clarify the meanings of the diagrams.

These diagrams are based on the ISO international standard DIS 7185 for Pascal and include some features, such as conformant array schemata, that may not be available on all compilers. These features are marked with asterisks (*) in the diagrams.

program

program

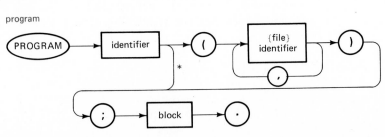

block

declarations

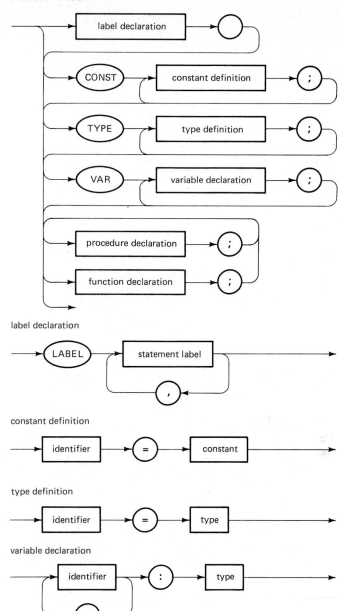

declaration section

label declaration

constant definition

type definition

variable declaration

subprograms

procedure declaration

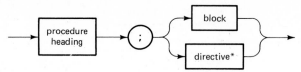

function declaration

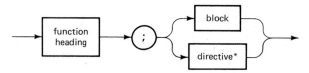

procedure heading

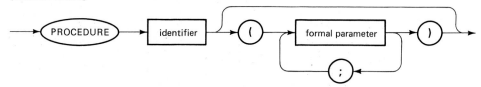

function heading

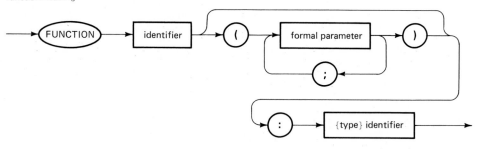

formal parameter

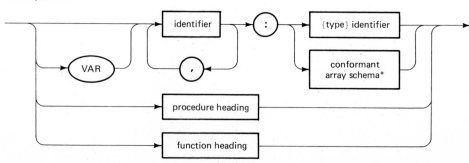

(not always implemented)

conformant array schema*

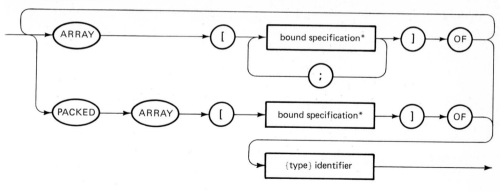

bound specification*

statement label

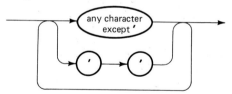

string

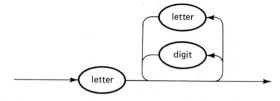

identifier, directive*

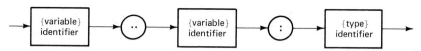

numbers   constant

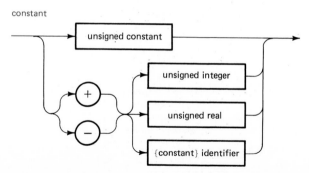

types

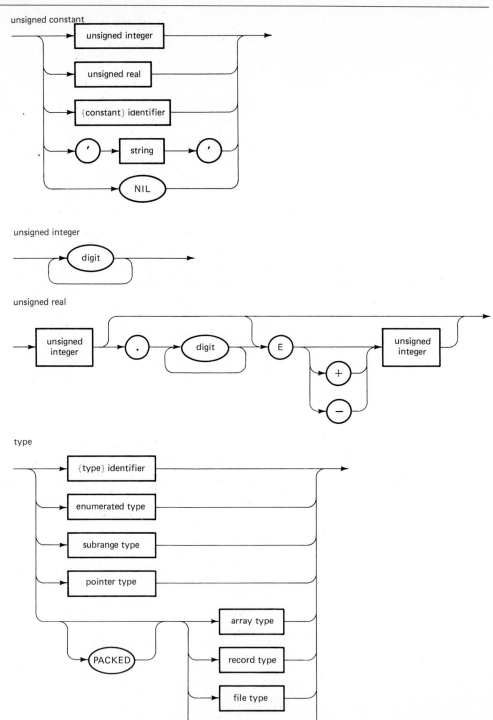

enumerated type

subrange type

pointer type

array type

record type

field list

variant

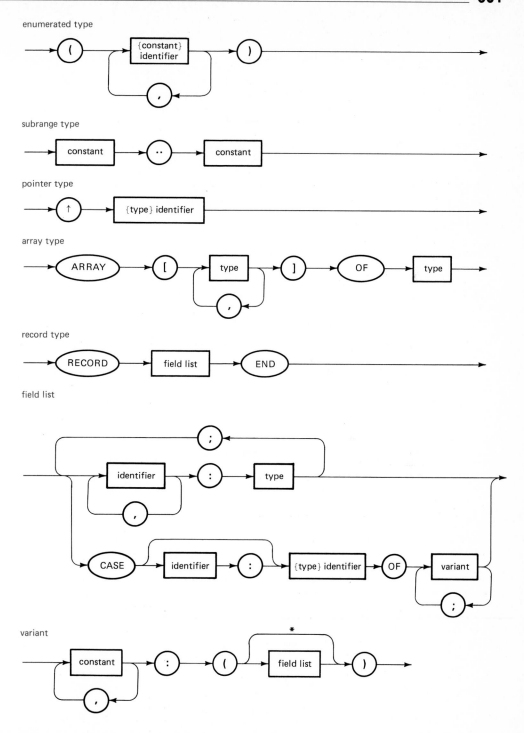

file type

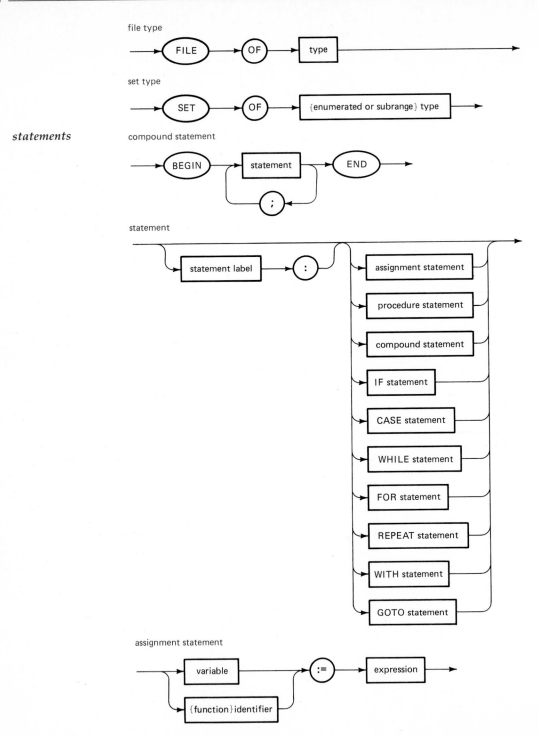

set type

statements

compound statement

statement

assignment statement

procedure statement

selection statements

IF statement

CASE statement

iteration statements

WHILE statement

FOR statement

REPEAT statement

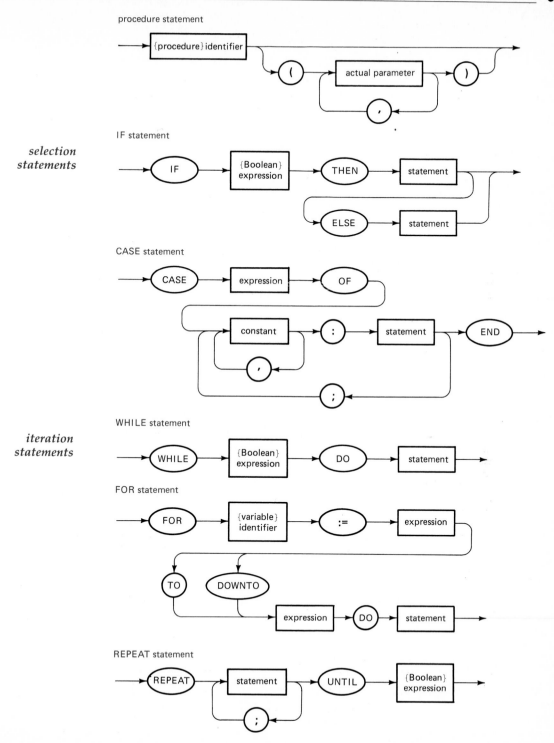

WITH statement

GOTO statement

actual parameter

expression

expressions

simple expression

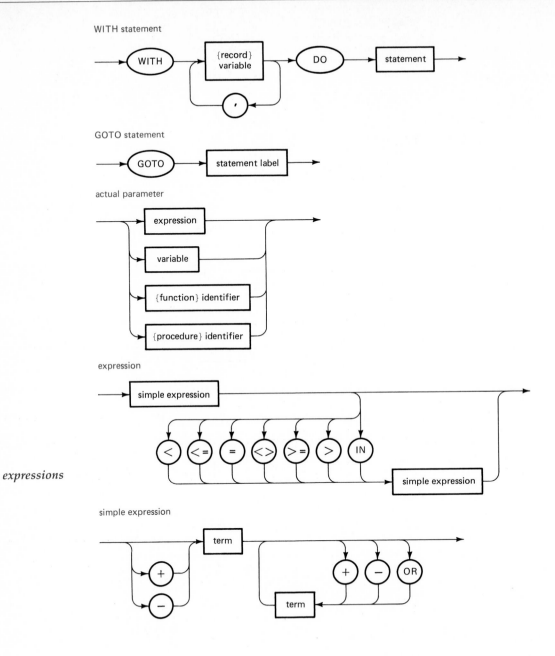

term

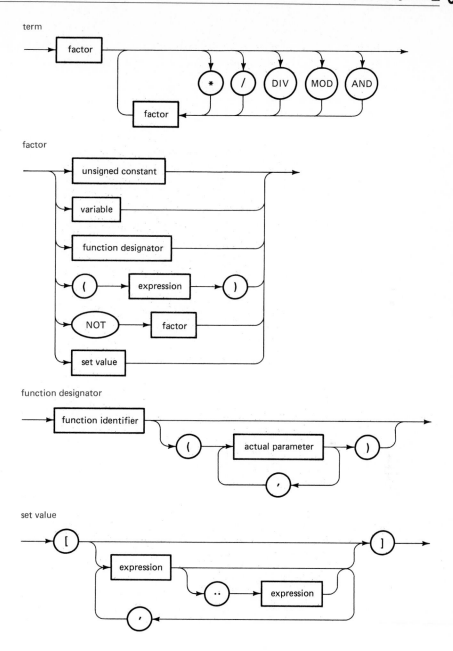

factor

function designator

set value

variable

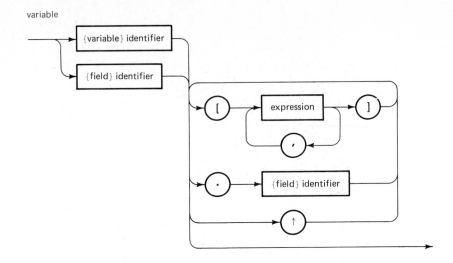

B.2

GENERAL RULES

B.2.1 Identifiers

An identifier can be as long as desired, subject to the following rules.

1. No blanks (spaces) can be inside an identifier.
2. An identifier cannot be divided between two lines. (Thus its maximum length is the length of a line, usually 80 characters.)
3. Standard Pascal requires that, to be regarded as different, identifiers must differ somewhere in the first eight characters. (Many Pascal compilers relax this rule to recognize differences in any position.)
4. Small letters and capital letters can be used as desired (if both are available). Most, but not all, compilers treat small and capital letters as the same. For the sake of portability, however, the same identifier should always be written in exactly the same way.
5. The following ***reserved words*** may not be used as identifiers, or for any purpose other than the uses specified for them in appropriate syntax diagrams:

reserved words

and	downto	if	or	then
array	else	in	packed	to
begin	end	label	procedure	type
case	file	mod	program	until
const	for	nil	record	var
div	function	not	repeat	while
do	goto	of	set	with

underscore 6. Although it is not standard Pascal, some compilers allow the underscore character '_' within identifiers. How this symbol is treated depends on the compiler: it may be ignored, treated like a letter, or treated like a numeral.

7. The following ***standard identifiers*** are predefined as part of the Pascal language. It is legal for the programmer to use these identifiers for purposes other than the usual ones, but it is generally unwise to do so, since by declaring a different use, the original use is lost. You can, for example, declare the word write to be a variable if you so desire, but if you do so, you will *standard* be unable to use the standard procedure that writes to a file or the terminal. *identifiers* The complete list of standard identifiers follows.

abs	eoln	new	read	sqrt
arctan	exp	odd	readln	succ
Boolean	false	ord	real	text
char	get	output	reset	true
chr	input	pack	rewrite	trunc
cos	integer	page	round	unpack
dispose	ln	pred	sin	write
eof	maxint	put	sqr	writeln

8. See Section 1.9 for guidelines on choosing identifiers.

B.2.2 Rules for Spaces

1. Spaces are never allowed inside identifiers, reserved words, numbers or the special symbols made up of more than one character. (for example, `<=` , `<>` , `>=` , `:=`).

2. At least one space must be included when needed to prevent one identifier, reserved word, or number from running into another. (For example,

ForX := AtoBdo

would be a syntactically correct assignment statement in Pascal if the variables were declared, not the beginning of a **for** loop.)

3. Inside of apostrophes `'...'` (i.e., in a string constant) spaces are treated like any other character.

4. Except in the preceding cases, all spaces are ignored and may be inserted where desired.

5. The end of a line is treated in exactly the same way as a space, and, therefore, a statement can be continued from one line to the next at any place where a space is allowed.

6. A comment is treated in exactly the same way as a space: It can be inserted wherever a space is allowed, and it can be continued from one line to the next.

B.2.3 Guidelines Used for Program Format

The following guidelines for indenting are used in most, but not all, programs in this book.

1. The words **const, type, var,** and **record** appear alone on a line, unless the complete declaration easily fits on one line.

2. Only one item is declared per line, except when several logically related items share exactly the same declaration.

3. The lines containing items being declared are each indented slightly.

4. The word **begin** appears on a line by itself, except in the phrase **else begin**, which usually appears on one line.

5. The word **end** appears on a line by itself, and is lined up with the corresponding word or phrase **begin, else begin, case,** or **record.**

6. Statements or declarations between one of these words or phrases and its corresponding **end** are indented slightly.

7. A single statement immediately following one of the words **then, do, repeat,** or **else** is indented slightly, but the word **begin** is not indented after any of these words.

8. Normally only one assignment statement appears per line.

9. Each alternative of a **case** statement appears on a new line, indented slightly beyond the word **case.**

10. Blank lines are inserted in longer programs wherever needed to separate logical sections of the program.

11. In the text, the declarations of functions and procedures are generally separated from that of the main program. When the declarations are inserted in their proper place, however, they are surrounded by enough blank space to show clearly where one subprogram stops and the next starts.

B.2.4 Punctuation

The syntax diagrams provide precise rules for the punctuation of a Pascal program, and when difficulties arise, you should check the syntax diagrams to locate the errors. Even so, there remain several errors common for programmers new to Pascal, for which some guidelines and hints may help.

commas and semicolons

1. Items that Pascal is to treat in the same way are generally separated by commas, and items that may be treated differently, by semicolons. Thus variables with exactly the same declaration are separated by commas, as are the indices in a (multidimensional) array, the actual parameters for a subprogram, and the alternatives sharing the same action in a **case** statement. On the other hand, semicolons separate declarations of variables of

(possibly) different types, separate different statements, separate formal parameters (which may be declared differently) of subprograms, and different alternatives in a **case** statement.

2. Semicolons are used to separate items or statements, not to terminate statements.

3. The illegal inclusion or omission of a semicolon will usually not produce an error diagnostic for the line on which the error occurs, but will usually produce a strange and irrelevant diagnostic for the line *after* the error.

4. A semicolon is always illegal immediately before (or at the end of the line immediately preceding) one of the words

and	downto	mod	or	set
array	else	nil	packed	then
div	file	not	program	to
do	in	of	record	

Of all these reserved words, the only one likely to cause trouble is **else**.

5. A semicolon is almost never needed immediately after **begin** or immediately before **end** or **until**, but its redundant inclusion is not an error.

B.2.5 Alternative Symbols

On systems where certain standard symbols are not available, the following substitutions are made:

For ↑ or ∧, substitute @.
For { and }, substitute (* and *).
For [and], substitute (. and .).

B.3

STANDARD DECLARATIONS

B.3.1 Constants

The predefined constants are false, true, and maxint.

Common Values for maxint

For most 8 and 16 bit machines: maxint = 32,767
For most 32 bit machines: maxint = 2,147,483,647
For most 60 bit machines: maxint = 281,474,976,710,655

ASCII codes for Characters, with Ordinals

0 NUL	16 DLE	32 SP	48 0	64 @	80 P	96 `	112 p
1 SOH	17 DC1	33 !	49 1	65 A	81 Q	97 a	113 q
2 STX	18 DC2	34 "	50 2	66 B	82 R	98 b	114 r
3 ETX	19 DC3	35 #	51 3	67 C	83 S	99 c	115 s
4 EOT	20 DC4	36 $	52 4	68 D	84 T	100 d	116 t
5 ENQ	21 NAK	37 %	53 5	69 E	85 U	101 e	117 u
6 ACK	22 SYN	38 &	54 6	70 F	86 V	102 f	118 v
7 BEL	23 ETB	39 '	55 7	71 G	87 W	103 g	119 w
8 BS	24 CAN	40 (	56 8	72 H	88 X	104 h	120 x
9 HT	25 EM	41)	57 9	73 I	89 Y	105 i	121 y
10 LF	26 SUB	42 *	58 :	74 J	90 Z	106 j	122 z
11 VT	27 ESC	43 +	59 ;	75 K	91 [	107 k	123 {
12 FF	28 FS	44 ,	60 <	76 L	92 \	108 l	124	
13 CR	29 GS	45 −	61 =	77 M	93]	109 m	125 }
14 SO	30 RS	46 .	62 >	78 N	94 ^	110 n	126 ~
15 SI	31 US	47 /	63 ?	79 O	95 _	111 o	127 DEL

Alternative symbols are:

Code 94 may print as $\wedge$ or as ↑.

Code 126 may print as ¬.

EBCDIC Codes for Characters, with Ordinals

0 NUL	21 NL	43 CU2	79		124 @	150 o	195 C	227 T
1 SOH	22 BS	45 ENQ	80 &	125 '	151 p	196 D	228 U
2 STX	23 IL	46 ACK	90 !	126 =	152 q	197 E	229 V
3 ETX	24 CAN	47 BEL	91 $	127 "	153 r	198 F	230 W
4 PF	25 EM	50 SYN	92 *	129 a	155 }	199 G	231 X
5 HT	26 CC	52 PN	93)	130 b	161 ~	200 H	232 Y
6 LC	27 CU1	53 RS	94 ;	131 c	162 s	201 I	233 Z
7 DEL	28 IFS	54 UC	95 ¬	132 d	163 t	208 }	240 0
10 SMM	29 IGS	55 EOT	96 −	133 e	164 u	209 J	241 1
11 VT	30 IRS	59 CU3	97 /	134 f	165 v	210 K	242 2
12 FF	31 IUS	60 DC4	106 ¦	135 g	166 w	211 L	243 3
13 CR	32 DS	61 NAK	107 ,	136 h	167 x	212 M	244 4
14 SO	33 SOS	63 SUB	108 %	137 i	168 y	213 N	245 5
15 SI	34 FS	64 SP	109 _	139 {	169 z	214 O	246 6
16 DLE	36 BYP	74 ¢	110 >	145 j	173 [	215 P	247 7
17 DC1	37 LF	75 .	111 ?	146 k	189]	216 Q	248 8
18 DC2	38 ETB	76 <	121 '	147 l	192 {	217 R	249 9
19 DC3	39 ESC	77 (	122 :	148 m	193 A	224 \	250	
20 RES	42 SM	78 +	123 #	149 n	194 B	226 S	

Meanings of Common Control Codes

The *control codes* are the characters with ASCII ordinals of 32 or less, together with 127, or the EBCDIC characters with ordinals of 64 or less. These characters do not produce a visible printed output, but may produce special effects. The meanings of some of the common control codes follow.

NUL	null (ignored)	HT	horizontal tab	CR	carriage return
ETX	end of text	LF	line feed	ESC	escape
BEL	rings a bell	VT	vertical tab	SP	space (blank)
BS	back space	FF	form feed	DEL	delete

B.3.2 Types

The predeclared types are

```
integer;
real;
Boolean = (false, true);
char;
text = packed file of char;
```

The terms used to display various categories of types are shown in Figure B.1.

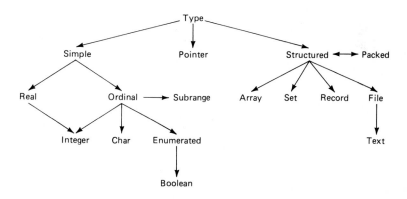

Figure B.1. Categories of types

B.3.3 Variables

The only predeclared variables are the files, with type text,

```
input     output.
```

B.3.4 Procedures

The predeclared procedures are:

For input and output:

reset, rewrite, get, put, read, write, readln, writeln, page.

For pointer types:

new, dispose.

For packed data:

pack, unpack.

B.3.5 Functions

Name	Argument	Result	Action
Arithmetic functions:			
abs	integer, real	*same as argument*	*Absolute value*
sqr	integer, real	*same as argument*	*Square of argument*
sqrt	integer, real	*real*	*Square root of argument*
exp	integer, real	*real*	*Exponential*
ln	integer, real	*real*	*Natural logarithm*
sin	integer, real	*real*	*Sine*
cos	integer, real	*real*	*Cosine*
arctan	integer, real	*real*	*Angle with given tangent*
Type conversion:			
chr	integer	char	*Character with given code*
ord	*ordinal type*	integer	*Ordinal code of argument*
round	real	integer	*Rounds to closest integer*
trunc	real	integer	*Truncates to integer part*
File processing:			
eof	*file type*	Boolean	*Checks end of file*
eoln	text	Boolean	*Checks end of line*
Miscellaneous:			
odd	integer	Boolean	*Is integer odd?*
succ	*ordinal type*	*same type*	*Next value in order*
pred	*ordinal type*	*same type*	*Preceding value in order*

B.4

OPERATORS

Operator	Operand Type(s)	Result Type	Action
Assignment:			
:=	*any type but file*	*same type*	*copies right operand to left*
Arithmetic:			
+	integer, real	*same type*	*addition or unary positive*
−	integer, real	*same type*	*subtraction or unary negative*
*	integer, real	*same type*	*multiplication*
div	integer	integer	*division with truncation*
mod	integer	integer	*remainder after* **div**
/	integer, real	real	*division*
Comparison:			
=	*any type but file*	Boolean	*equality*
<>	*any type but file*	Boolean	*not equals*
<	*any simple type*	Boolean	*less than, precedes*
>	*any simple type*	Boolean	*greater than, follows*
<=	*any simple type*	Boolean	*less than or equal to*
>=	*any simple type*	Boolean	*greater than or equal to*
Logical:			
not	Boolean	Boolean	*logical negation*
and	Boolean	Boolean	*conjunction*
or	Boolean	Boolean	*disjunction*
Set operations:			
+	*any set type*	*same type*	*set union*
*	*any set type*	*same type*	*set intersection*
−	*any set type*	*same type*	*set difference*
<=	*any set type*	Boolean	*set inclusion*
>=	*any set type*	Boolean	*set containment*
in	*left: ordinal type*	Boolean	*set membership*
	right: set of type of left operand		
[ ]	*ordinal type*	*set of type*	*constructs set of operand(s)*

Priorities of operators:

Highest:	1.	*	/	**div**	**mod**	**and**		
	2.	+	−	**or**				
	3.	=	<	<=	>	>=	<>	**in**
Lowest:	4.	:=						

APPENDIX **C**

REFERENCES FOR FURTHER STUDY

PART I. PROGRAMMING PRINCIPLES

Problem Solving

The first step in computer programming is problem solving and formulation of the solution as an algorithm. Some books that contain many ideas and suggestions to help with this process are:

> GEORGE PÓLYA, *How to Solve It*, second edition, Doubleday, Garden City, N.Y., 1957, 253 pages.

> WAYNE A. WICKELGREN, *How to Solve Problems*, W. H. Freeman, San Francisco, 1974, 262 pages.

> GREGORY F. WETZEL and WILLIAM G. BULGREN, *The Algorithmic Process: An Introduction to Problem Solving*, Science Research Associates, Chicago, 1985, 292 pages.

> PETER GROGONO and SHARON H. NELSON, *Problem Solving and Computer Programming*, Addison–Wesley, Reading, Mass., 1982, 284 pages.

Program Design and Style

Three books that contain many helpful hints on programming style and correctness, as well as examples of good and bad practices, are

BRIAN KERNIGHAN and P. J. PLAUGER, *The Elements of Programming Style*, second edition, McGraw–Hill, New York, 1978, 168 pages.

HENRY F. LEDGARD, PAUL A. NAGIN, and JOHN F. HUERAS, *Pascal with Style: Programming Proverbs*, Hayden Book Company, Hasbrouck Heights, N.J., 1979, 210 pages.

DENNIE VAN TASSEL, *Program Style, Design, Efficiency, Debugging, and Testing*, second edition, Prentice Hall, Englewood Cliffs, N.J., 1978, 323 pages.

EDSGER W. DIJKSTRA pioneered the movement known as structured programming, which insists on taking a carefully organized top-down approach to the design and writing of programs, when, in March 1968, he caused some consternation by publishing a letter entitled "Go To Statement Considered Harmful" in the *Communications of the ACM* (vol. 11, pages 147–148). DIJKSTRA has since published several papers and books that are most instructive in programming method. One book of special interest is

E. W. DIJKSTRA, *A Discipline of Programming*, Prentice Hall, Englewood Cliffs, N.J., 1976, 217 pages.

Pascal

The programming language Pascal was devised by NIKLAUS WIRTH, who first published its description in 1971. For older versions of the language, the standard reference manual was

K. JENSEN and N. WIRTH, *PASCAL User Manual and Report*, second edition, Springer–Verlag, Berlin, Heidelberg, New York, 1974, 167 pages.

More recently, the International Standards Organization (ISO) has specified a standard version of Pascal to which most newer compilers adhere. This standard Pascal is succinctly but clearly described in the following book, to which you may refer with subtle problems in Pascal behavior:

DOUG COOPER, *Standard Pascal User Reference Manual*, W. W. Norton, New York, 1983, 176 pages.

Many good textbooks provide a more leisurely description of Pascal, too many books to list here. These textbooks also provide many examples and applications. Some books designed for introductory courses, however, omit important "advanced" features of Pascal that will be used often in this book. Be sure that any textbook you select covers the full syntax of standard Pascal.

The Calendar Project

The following article presents the history and functioning of the Julian and Gregorian calendars:

GORDON MOYER, "The Gregorian Calendar," *Scientific American* 246, no. 5 (May, 1982), 144–152.

Many variations on the calendar problem and further projects appear on pages 65–67, 101–103, 120–154, 166–182 of

EDWARD M. REINGOLD and RUTH N. REINGOLD, *PascAlgorithms: An Introduction to Programming*, Scott, Foresman, and Company, Glenview, Illinois, 1988, 650 pages.

See also pages 51–67 of

DERICK WOOD, *Paradigms and Programming with Pascal*, Computer Science Press, Rockville, Maryland, 1982, 425 pages.

PART II. LINEAR DATA STRUCTURES

Data Abstraction

The separation of properties of data structures and their operations from the implementation of the data structures in memory and procedures is called *data abstraction.* The following books take this point of view consistently and develop further properties of lists:

JIM WELSH, JOHN ELDER, and DAVID BUSTARD, *Sequential Program Structures*, Prentice–Hall International, London, 1984, 385 pages.

DANIEL F. STUBBS and NEIL W. WEBRE, *Data Structures with Abstract Data Types and Pascal*, Brooks/Cole Publishing Company, Monterey, Calif., 1985, 459 pages.

Comprehensive Reference

For many topics concerning data structures, the best source for additional information, historical notes, and mathematical analysis is the following series of books, which can be regarded almost like an encyclopædia for the aspects of computing science that they discuss:

encyclopædic reference: KNUTH

DONALD E. KNUTH, *The Art of Computer Programming*, published by Addison–Wesley, Reading, Mass.

Three volumes have appeared to date:

1. *Fundamental Algorithms*, second edition, 1973, 634 pages.
2. *Seminumerical Algorithms*, second edition, 1980, 700 pages.
3. *Sorting and Searching*, 1973, 722 pages.

From now on, we shall often give references to this series of books. For convenience, we shall do so by specifying only the name KNUTH together with the volume and page numbers. In particular, stacks, queues, and deques are studied in KNUTH, Volume 1, pages 234–251, with the inclusion of many interesting extensions and exercises. Linked lists are studied in depth in KNUTH, Volume 1, pages 251–272, and an algorithm for polynomial addition appears in pages 272–276. The algorithms are written both informally and in an assembler language, where KNUTH calculates detailed counts of operations to compare various algorithms.

Polish Notation

The Polish notation is so natural and useful that one might expect its discovery to be hundreds of years ago. It may be surprising to note that it is a discovery of this century:

JAN ŁUKASIEWICZ, *Elementy Logiki Matematyczny*, Warsaw, 1929; English translation: *Elements of Mathematical Logic*, Pergamon Press, London, 1963.

The development of algorithms to form and evaluate Polish expressions (usually postfix form) can be found in several data structures books, as well as more advanced books on compiler theory. The algorithm for translating an expression from infix to postfix form appears to be due independently to E. W. DIJKSTRA and to C. L. HAMBLIN, and appears in

E. W. DIJKSTRA, "Making a Translator for ALGOL 60," *Automatic Programming Information* number 7 (May 1961); reprinted in *Annual Revue of Automatic Programming* 3 (1963), 347–356.

C. L. HAMBLIN, "Translation to and from Polish notation," *Computer Journal* 5 (1962), 210–213.

Simulation

In Volume 2, pages 1–177, KNUTH studies the construction and testing of pseudo-random number generators in depth.

An elementary survey of computer simulations appears in *Byte* 10 (October 1985), pp, 149–251. A simulation of the National Airport in Washington, D.C., appears on pages 186–190.

String Searching

The algorithm given in Section 6.3 that searches one string for a second, target string is simple but inefficient. Two superior algorithms are the KNUTH–MORRIS–PRATT and the BOYER–MOORE algorithms. Straightforward expositions and examples for these algorithms appear on pages 211–222 of

GILLES BRASSARD and PAUL BRATLEY, *Algorithmics: Theory and Practice*, Prentice Hall, Englewood Cliffs, N. J., 1988, 361 pages.

This book also contains clear expositions of many of the topics appearing in Parts III, IV, and V.

PART III. ALGORITHMS AND THEIR ANALYSIS

The primary reference for this part of the book is KNUTH, Volume 3. (The bibliographic details were given previously.) Sequential search occupies pages 389–405; binary search covers pages 406–414; then comes Fibonacci search, and a section on history. Insertion sort appears on pages 80–84, selection sort on pages 139–142, and Shell sort on pages 84–95. The book provides an extensive study of external searching and sorting methods. KNUTH studies every method we have touched and many others besides. He does algorithm analysis in a great deal of detail, writing his algorithms in a pseudo-assembly language.

Binary Search

Proving the correctness of the binary search algorithm is the topic of

JON BENTLEY, "Programming pearls: Writing correct programs," *Communications of the ACM* 26 (1983), 1040–1045.

In this column, BENTLEY shows how to formulate a binary search algorithm from its requirements, points out that about ninety percent of professional programmers whom he has taught were unable to write the program correctly in one hour, and gives a formal verification of correctness.

"Programming Pearls" is a regular column that contains many elegant algorithms and helpful suggestions for programming. These columns have been collected in the following two books:

JON BENTLEY, *Programming Pearls*, Addison–Wesley, Reading, Mass., 1986, 195 pages.

JON BENTLEY, *More Programming Pearls: Confessions of a Coder*, Addison–Wesley, Reading, Mass., 1988, 224 pages.

Lower Bounds

For a complete proof for the lower bounds on key comparisons required for searching and for sorting, see the following book, which covers all the material of the current book in a much more comprehensive way.

ROBERT L. KRUSE, *Data Structures and Program Design*, second edition, Prentice Hall, Englewood Cliffs, N. J., 1987, 586 pages.

PART IV. RECURSION

General Expositions

Among the general references for recursion are the following books, each of which contains many examples of recursive algorithms and a discussion of the principles of recursion.

ERIC S. ROBERTS, *Thinking Recursively*, John Wiley & Sons, New York, 1986, 179 pages.

J. S. ROHL, *Recursion via Pascal*, Cambridge University Press, Cambridge, 1984, 192 pages.

E. HOROWITZ and S. SAHNI, *Fundamentals of Computer Algorithms*, Computer Science Press, Rockville, Md., 1978, 626 pages.

ROBERT SEDGEWICK, *Algorithms*, second edition, Addison–Wesley, Reading, Mass., 1988, 640 pages.

Towers of Hanoi

The Towers of Hanoi is commonly used to introduce recursion and appears in many textbooks. A survey of related papers is found in

D. WOOD, "The Towers of Brahma and Hanoi revisited," *Journal of Recreational Mathematics* 14 (1981–82), 17–24.

Further papers on the Towers of Hanoi have appeared sporadically in the *SIGPLAN Notices* published by the Association for Computing Machinery (ACM).

Binary Trees

The most comprehensive source of information on binary trees is the series of books by KNUTH. The properties of binary trees, other classes of trees, algorithms, mathematical analysis, and history altogether occupy pages 305–405 of Volume 1 and pages 422–505 of Volume 3.

There are many generalizations of binary trees that are useful both as data structures and for information retrieval. The most important of these are discussed in pages 336–398 and pages 536–547 of the following book:

> ROBERT L. KRUSE, *Data Structures and Program Design*, second edition, Prentice Hall, Englewood Cliffs, N.J., 1987, 586 pages.

This book also gives further references for the study of binary trees and related topics.

Sorting

Expository surveys of various sorting methods are

> W. A. MARTIN, "Sorting," *Computing Surveys* 3 (1971), 148–174.

> H. LORIN, *Sorting and Sort Systems*, Addison–Wesley, Reading, Mass., 1975, 456 pages.

Divide-and-Conquer Sorting

The unified derivation of mergesort and quicksort, which can also be used to produce insertion sort and selection sort, is based on the work

> JOHN DARLINGTON, "A synthesis of several sorting algorithms," *Acta Informatica* 11 (1978), 1–30.

A relatively simple contiguous merge algorithm that operates in linear time with a small, constant amount of additional space appears in

> BING-CHAO HUANG and MICHAEL A. LANGSTON, "Practical in-place merging," *Communications of the ACM* 31 (1988), 348–352.

The original reference for quicksort is

> C. A. R. HOARE, "Quicksort," *Computer Journal* 5 (1962), 10–15.

The algorithm presented in this book for partitioning the list in quicksort was discovered by NICO LOMUTO and was published in

> JON L. BENTLEY, "Programming pearls: How to sort," *Communications of the ACM* 27 (1984), 287–291.

An extensive analysis of the quicksort algorithm is given in

> ROBERT SEDGEWICK, "The analysis of quicksort programs," *Acta Informatica* 7 (1976/77), 327–355.

The exercise on meansort (taking the mean of the keys as pivot) comes from

> DALIA MOTZKIN, "MEANSORT," *Communications of the ACM* 26 (1983), 250–251; 27 (1984), 719–722.

Heapsort

Heapsort is discussed in pages 145–149 of Volume 3 of KNUTH. Heapsort was discovered and so named by

J. W. J. WILLIAMS, *Communications of the ACM* 7 (1964), 347–348.

A simple development of algorithms for heaps and priority queues appears in

JON BENTLEY, "Programming pearls: Thanks, heaps," *Communications of the ACM* 28 (1985), 245–250.

Backtracking

Our treatment of the Eight-Queens problem especially follows that given in

N. WIRTH, *Algorithms + Data Structures = Programs*, Prentice Hall, Englewood Cliffs, N.J., 1976, pages 143–147.

This book by WIRTH also contains solutions of the Knight's Tour problem (pages 137–142), as well as a chapter (pages 280–349) on compiling and parsing.

Look-Ahead in Games

The book by HOROWITZ and SAHNI at the beginning of this section contains (pages 290–302) a discussion and analysis of game trees and look-ahead programs. An outline of a programming project for the game of Kalah appears in

CHARLES WETHERELL, *Etudes for Programmers*, Prentice Hall, Englewood Cliffs, N. J., 1978.

Compilation by Recursive Descent

Compilation by recursive descent is a standard topic in compiler design, a topic treated in detail in most newer textbooks in compiler design. Consult, for example,

ALFRED V. AHO and JEFFREY D. ULLMAN, *Principles of Compiler Design*, Addison-Wesley, Reading, Mass., 1977.

Stacks and Recursion

A proof that stacks may be eliminated by introducing recursion appears in

S. BROWN, D. GRIES, and T. SZYMANSKI, "Program schemes with pushdown stores," *SIAM Journal on Computing*, 1 (1972), 242–268.

PART V. FURTHER STRUCTURES AND ALGORITHMS

Tables

The following book (pages 156–185) considers arrays of various kinds, index functions, and access tables in considerable detail:

C. C. GOTLIEB and L. R. GOTLIEB, *Data Types and Structures*, Prentice Hall, Englewood Cliffs, N.J., 1978.

KNUTH, Volume 3, pages 506–549 studies hash tables and associated algorithms in detail, touching on many additional methods and deriving careful algorithm analyses.

Extensions of the birthday surprise are considered in

> M. S. KLAMKIN and D. J. NEWMAN, *Journal of Combinatorial Theory* 3 (1967), 279–282.

Graphs

The study of graphs and algorithms for their processing is a large subject and one that involves both mathematics and computing science. Four books, each of which contains many interesting algorithms, are

> R. E. TARJAN, *Data Structures and Network Algorithms*, Society for Industrial and Applied Mathematics, Philadelphia, 1983, 131 pages.

> SHIMON EVEN, *Graph Algorithms*, Computer Science Press, Rockville, Md., 1979, 249 pages.

> E. M. REINGOLD, J. NIEVERGELT, N. DEO, *Combinatorial Algorithms: Theory and Practice*, Prentice Hall, Englewood Cliffs, N. J., 1977, 433 pages.

> GILLES BRASSARD and PAUL BRATLEY, *Algorithmics: Theory and Practice*, Prentice Hall, Englewood Cliffs, N. J., 1988, 361 pages.

The original reference for the greedy algorithm determining the shortest paths in a graph is

> E. W. DIJKSTRA, "A note on two problems in connexion with graphs," *Numerische Mathematik* 1 (1959), 269–271.

Software Engineering

A thorough discussion of many aspects of structured programming is:

> EDWARD YOURDON, *Techniques of Program Structure and Design*, Prentice Hall, Englewood Cliffs, N. J., 1975, 364 pages.

A perceptive discussion (in a book that is also enjoyable reading) of the many problems that arise in the construction of large software systems is:

> FREDERICK P. BROOKS, JR., *The Mythical Man–Month: Essays on Software Engineering*, Addison–Wesley, Reading, Mass., 1975, 195 pages.

A good textbook on software engineering is:

> IAN SOMMERVILLE, *Software Engineering*, second edition, Addison–Wesley, Wokingham, England, 1985, 345 pages.

Algorithm Verification

A good place to learn how to prove the correctness of programs and how to use assertions and invariants to develop algorithms is

> DAVID GRIES, *The Science of Programming*, Springer–Verlag, New York, 1981, 366 pages.

The Game of Life

The prominent British mathematician J. H. CONWAY has made many original contributions to subjects as diverse as the theory of finite simple groups, logic, and combinatorics. He devised the game of Life by starting with previous technical studies of cellular automata and devising reproduction rules that would make it difficult for a configuration to grow without bound, but for which many configurations would go through interesting progressions. CONWAY, however, did not publish his observations, but communicated them to MARTIN GARDNER. The popularity of the game skyrocketed when it was discussed in

> MARTIN GARDNER, "Mathematical Games" (regular column), *Scientific American* 223, no. 4 (October 1970), 120–123; 224, no. 2 (February 1971), 112–117.

The examples in Chapter 18 are taken from these columns. These columns have been reprinted with further results in

> MARTIN GARDNER, *Wheels, Life and Other Mathematical Amusements*, W. H. Freeman, New York, 1983, pages 214–257.

This book also contains a bibliography of articles on Life. A quarterly newsletter, entitled *Lifeline*, was even published for several years to keep the real devotees up to date on current developments in Life and related topics.

The programming project on one-dimensional life is taken from

> JONATHAN K. MILLER, "One-dimensional Life", *Byte* 3 (December, 1978), 68–74.

LOGARITHMS AND OTHER MATHEMATICAL METHODS

An excellent discussion of the importance of logarithms and of the subtle art of approximate calculation is given in

> N. DAVID MERMIN, "Logarithms!", *American Mathematical Monthly* 87 (1980), 1–7.

Several interesting examples of estimating large numbers and thinking of them logarithmically are discussed in

> DOUGLAS R. HOFSTADTER, "Metamagical themas," *Scientific American* 246, no. 5 (May 1982), 20–34.

Several surprising and amusing applications of harmonic numbers (as used to analyze quicksort in Chapter 13) are given in the nontechnical article

> RALPH BOAS, "Snowfalls and elephants, pop bottles and π," *Two–Year College Math. Journal* 11 (1980), 82–89.

The detailed estimates for both harmonic numbers and factorials (Stirling's Approximation) are quoted from KNUTH, Volume 1, pages 108–111, where detailed proofs may be found. KNUTH, Volume 1, is also an excellent source for further information regarding permutations, combinations, and related topics. The original reference for Stirling's Approximation is

> JAMES STIRLING, *Methodus Differentialis*, 1730, page 137.

INDEX